Cases on Transnational Learning and Technologically Enabled Environments

Siran Mukerji
IGNOU, India

Purnendu Tripathi
IGNOU, India

Information Science REFERENCE

INFORMATION SCIENCE REFERENCE
Hershey · New York

Director of Editorial Content:	Kristin Klinger
Director of Book Publications:	Julia Mosemann
Acquisitions Editor:	Lindsay Johnston
Development Editor:	Beth Ardner
Publishing Assistant:	Keith Glazewski
Typesetter:	Michael Brehm
Production Editor:	Jamie Snavely
Cover Design:	Lisa Tosheff
Printed at:	Yurchak Printing Inc.

Published in the United States of America by
Information Science Reference (an imprint of IGI Global)
701 E. Chocolate Avenue
Hershey PA 17033
Tel: 717-533-8845
Fax: 717-533-8661
E-mail: cust@igi-global.com
Web site: http://www.igi-global.com/reference

Library of Congress Cataloging-in-Publication Data

Cases on transnational learning and technologically enabled environments / Siran Mukerji and Purnendu Tripathi, editors.
p. cm. Includes bibliographical references and index. Summary: "This book offers case studies on divergent themes addressing the core perspecitve of technological adaptability and transnational learning"-- Provided by publisher.
ISBN 978-1-61520-749-7 (hardcover) -- ISBN 978-1-61520-750-3 (ebook) 1. Transnational education. 2. Educational technology. 3. Internet in education. I. Mukerji, Siran. II. Tripathi, Purnendu, 1975-
LC1095.C37 2010
371.33'44678--dc22

2009039678

British Cataloguing in Publication Data
A Cataloguing in Publication record for this book is available from the British Library.

Table of Contents

Detailed Table of Contents

The case aims to explore and discuss the challenges of introducing technology-enhanced learning in geographically dispersed learners wherein majority of them are in rural areas and who are post-diploma nursing learners with minimal computer literacy. Despite a varied range of challenges facing them, they end up being motivated to learn computers so that they can access learning material and also use them for lifelong learning. The authors point towards the value of simple and economical technologies like an interactive CD-ROM in initiating students to e-learning and in overcoming their bandwidth problems.

This study presented by Omiunota Ukpokodu documents one of the teacher educator's successful adaptations of traditional pedagogies in online teaching. Using data from a graduate online course, it examines the general concern and beliefs that online teaching is an inadequate and inappropriate substitute for the traditional face-to-face instruction in a teacher education course aimed at transformative learning but both quantitative and qualitative data revealed that online teaching evidenced successful student quality learning and adaptability of traditional pedagogies.

This case on authentic assessment contribution to competence based education by Luis, Alda and Isolina explores a tool (the Learning Contract) to facilitate assessment authenticity as a way to promote student learning. It evaluates the use of the Learning Contract to increase student's responsibility and commitment for their own learning, while at the same time facilitates its alignment with their professional practice, and contributes to the development of their life-long learning competencies.

This chapter by Merrilee and Ruth underscores the importance of linked courses that serve as an excellent example of what can happen when two educators in diverse disciplines work together to blend, syncretize, and synergize the learning experience. The authors present this as a model for global research and demonstrate how in a regionally accredited urban university, high risk students enrolled in a freshman English course are simultaneously enrolled in a freshman level computer information systems class where project learning is taking place.

Foreword

The importance of transnational learning is evident both within institutions and in relation to partnership programs. Increasingly, institutions are seeking student applicants from other countries and expecting that globalization of the curriculum will occur. Similarly, despite the rise of the Internet and the globalization of culture, the differences embedded in home programs are not always immediately evident but can have a major impact on the success or failure of partnership programs. The use of e-learning technologies adds another layer of complexity.

The editors, Drs. Mukerji and Tripathi make a sincere attempt to provide an international platform through this book for sharing innovations in technology for the development of interactive and collaborative learning environments. It is creditable to have contributions on transnational learning from Rwanda, Austria with its partnership projects in Nepal, India, China, Kyrgyzstan, Azerbaijan, Slovakia, Slovenia, Armenia, and Georgia, the Netherlands, and USA. The book also aggregates experiences of technology enabled environments such as ORIENT, self paced learning, personalized t-learning, and spatial ability training.

In this book, cases cluster into two major foci. Those with a focus on technology applications cover a variety of topics from tools for assessment and collaboration to professional development strategics to engender change. Some raise questions about assessment practices from doing marking on line versus on paper to the utility of self-assessment questions and the combination of online assessments and face-to-face examinations in Turkish universities. Others focus on online instruction for K-12 teachers or teacher education candidates. Immediacy and virtual presence is explored with language learners and through interactive television while the visual ability of the learner and the learner's preference for collaboration versus personal learning are examined in two other papers. The result is a rich amalgam of viewpoints and ideas, valuable both to the newcomer to the area as well as to those already experienced in online learning.

The second cluster more directly foregrounds aspects of transnational education. The papers describe programs in different countries. Some focus on cross-cultural issues such as learners' level of understanding and ability to speak the language of instruction or the particular rules for group work or teacher–student relations. Others examine the broader context and explore issues around the importance of policies, lack of training, and the impact of the digital divide on the use of ICT in transnational education.

The cases in this book raise several important questions for the reader. Many writers are in countries that are still examining ways to use the online environment for education. What have we learned? What can we share? For those of us with ready acceptance of online learning, what should we reconsider in light of the issues raised by those just beginning to explore these issues? In terms, of transnational education, how do we do more than just make space for the non-resident in the learning environment but recognize and include the knowledge and cultural understandings these newcomers bring to a program? In a partnership, how can the design of a program include not only the requirements of the offering institution but also the cultural context and social and economic requirements of the partnership institution?

A good book is one that helps raise at least as many questions as it answers; I hope you find yourself with many questions—and answers.

Margaret Haughey
Vice President, Academic,
Athabasca University, Athabasca, Canada.

Margaret Haughey, *presently the Vice President, Academic in Athabasca University, Canada, has a background in education administration and policy. She has rich and varied experience in distance education and online learning, having served as an instructor, instructional designer, course producer, administrator and researcher in various aspects of distance education and online learning. She has been a regular conference presenter and invited speaker and has published a number of books on aspects of distance education. Being the President of the Canadian Association for Distance Education and editor of its journal, JDE (1998-2006), she was closely associated with a network of practitioners and researchers in the world-wide distance education community and with provincial and federal government agencies for the growth and development of distance education. She has worked at a number of universities in Canada including as a Professor of Educational Policy Studies and as an Associate Dean, Faculty of Graduate Studies and Research in University of Alberta.*

Preface

In the present era, development and technology are becoming synonymous whether by synergy or by synthesis in every domain be it social, cultural, educational, agricultural, industrial, or medical at national or at international level, and alliance is its catalyst. Twese Hamwe project, Schools on Ice, UniGIS, UniNet, Global Studies, ESD and Twinning are real world instances of such transnational interventions signifying greater role of sharing, collaborating, exchanging, and integrating. Albeit the nomenclature here differs but the spirit remains the same, i.e. spirit of interacting, spirit of joining hands, spirit of pooling resources, spirit of strengthening, cooperating, partnering, and so on for educational development. This book is an endeavour to demonstrate this through its collection of cases on transnational learning and technologically enabled environments and it presents numerous evidences of digital dividends mitigating the once upon a time divide through collaborative technologically enhanced interactive environments.

The case studies here speak volumes on the national and international initiatives undertaken worldwide for adapting the advancements in information and communication technology for successfully facing the challenges posed by various social and economic forces. They represent both instances of institutions, that are in transition and contrarily those that are readily using technology in education. As there are cases on interactive Digital Television (iDTV) for personalised t-learning, classroom management through synchronous online learning, and open source Dokeos / Claroline system based e-learning system "Minerva" as applied in Belgium and China that demonstrate the wide ranging application of technology in education, so are also its other purposeful uses in cases namely ORIENT (overcoming refugee integration with empathetic novel technology) for inter-cultural learning to improve social integration of youths with migration background in European countries, self paced learning (SPL) for healthcare providers in Ghana, spatial ability training in virtual environment for engineering drawing and collaborative knowledge construction in interactive online learning environment.

Being transnational in letter and spirit, the book has an assortment of case chapters on exemplary academic pursuits representing many nations. These include Rwanda, Ghana, Nigeria, South Africa, the Netherlands, Germany, Belgium, Italy, Spain, UK, Portugal, Turkey, Israel, Iran, Saudi Arabia, USA, China, Malaysia, and finally Austria and its transcontinental educational ventures in Nepal, India, China, Kyrgyzstan, and Azerbaijan and also in European nations of Slovakia, Slovenia, Armenia, and Georgia.

The first chapter by Gilbert Ahamer and Thomas Jekel of the Institute for Geographic Information Science at the Austrian Academy of Sciences begins with a conceptual background of how spaces are constructed from the perspectives of societal learning and formation of social spaces. The authors accentuate the importance of design of structures in time, space and in the space of opinions and suggest that these facilitate multi-perspectivist and multidisciplinary understanding of involved stakeholders. This belief is aptly supported by projects of cooperative learning through dialogue.

Moving on to the second chapter where Paul Breen explores the case of *International Collaboration for Technology Enhanced Education in Rwanda.* The case study is an interesting account of the collaborative project of teacher training depicting true partnership between western institutions and their counterparts in the developing world addressing the social, technological, economic, and political factors of this African nation.

In the next chapter, the challenges of national culture in delivering MBA programs in emerging markets through transnational learning and collaboration have been examined by Stephanie Jones. The author takes into account number crucial cultural dimensions in this study that have notable implication on the delivery of the program.

In the fourth chapter of the book *ORIENT – The Intercultural Empathy through Virtual Role-play*, authors elucidate ORIENT (Overcoming Refugee Integration with Empathic Novel Technology) towards developing inter-cultural empathy for 12-14 year olds. The paper endeavors to discuss games and role playing exercises for fostering social and emotional learning, besides illustrating ORIENT in the psychological and pedagogical domains. It also highlights role of novel interaction modalities as active engagement in collaborative learning environment.

Karina Clemmons, Amanda Nolen, Andrew Hunt, Cheryl Grable, Shirley Pickle in the fifth chapter attempt to address the critical issue of educating teacher candidates for managing synchronous online secondary classes. While exploring important questions like "how is classroom management addressed in an online learning environment?" and "what are the necessary components of an effective online learning environment?", the authors examine various issues that affect the classroom management in the online environment.

Self Paced learning (SPL) intervention together with paired learning teams, clinical practice with feedback, and supervision for health care workers in Ghana are core issues examined in the sixth chapter by Nancy Kiplinger and Hannum Wallace. The authors while evaluating this approach opine that this approach being cost effective produces greater learning gains as compared to traditional face to face approaches and suggest strategies for technology mediated effective learning design.

The seventh chapter of this case book is on the use of interactive digital television (iDTV) for personalised t-learning given the wide spread use of this medium. The technological framework presented in the study by the authors is divided into two main parts: the production side, where the course is created and the client side, where it is presented on interactive digital television (iDTV) through an interactive learning environment. For this purpose, experimental television learning (t-learning) courses were created which served as an important test and evaluation parameter for the framework.

In the next chapter, Chang Zhu, Martin Valcke and Tammy Schellens explore the comparative e-learning environments which are based on Dokeos/Claroline system in the overall perspective of student, teacher and context. While comparing the learning environment in Belgium and China, authors were of the view that not only the Chinese and Flemish students differ in their perception and satisfaction towards technology enabled learning environments but also their teachers are in different stages of familiarising and adopting the technology for education. This case makes a sincere attempt to establish a linkage between cultural dimension and the specific contexts of institutions and culture in order to overcome the disparities identified in the paper.

The research by Ahmad Rafi and Khairul Anuar B. Samsuddin on Impact of Spatial Ability Training in Desktop Virtual Environment shows that spatial visualization was significant in predicting performance in basic engineering drawing task. In the ninth chapter, authors investigate the extent of Spatial Visualization (SV) and Mental Rotation (MR) training improvement, differential impact attributed to gender and training method, and training transfer to engineering drawing task. The outcome of the study shows that while transfer of training to performance in solving engineering drawing task with groups of differential performances, the group with higher spatial ability managed to perform the task better than the group with lower spatial ability post spatial training.

Rikki Rimor and Yigal Rosen in the case of Collaborative Knowledge Construction in Online Learning Environment attempt to find the answer of the question: Do learners through the process of knowledge construction with a collaborative learning orientation differ from learners with an individual learning orientation? The results of the study in this chapter demonstrate that learners with collaborative learning orientation succeeded more in the collective criteria of knowledge construction, compared to those in the less collaborative ones. Rikki and Yogel advocate that findings in this study can have lasting implications on planning, coordinating and evaluating collaborative learning environment.

The authors in the eleventh chapter make an effort to link the Faculty Professional Development project (FPD) with the demands for student competence and teaching accountability. The authors believe since FPD aims at developing and implementing online courses for training faculty members, it facilitates in understanding how effective faculty is critical to understanding the success or failure of the FPD innovation. The arguments in this chapter response to the needs of potential impact of e-development on faculty and agency staff members' learning and electronic training for quality assurance specifications.

Ruth Reynard in the next chapter *Real Time Internet-Based English as a Foreign Language Learning* makes an effort to explore the potential for using simple online technology to connect native language speakers of English in the USA and foreign language learners of English in China. The auhor investigates upon the factors that lead to the successes in language and cultural exchange within a real time technology-mediated class and also identifies the challenges thereupon.

The following chapter in this collection of cases is yet another unique case of applying technology-enhanced learning methods for skill enhancement however this is pertaining to geographically dispersed post-diploma nursing learners who are located in remote rural places of South Africa and are with minimal computer literacy. The authors Mirriam Tlhapane and Sibongile Simelane identify the issues and challenges in using technology enabled teaching and learning methods to such segment of learners and determine viable means of providing easily accessible modes of education and training.

In the fourteenth chapter of the book, Omiunota N. Ukpokodu documents the teacher educator's successful adaptations of traditional pedagogies in online teaching. In this case, he tries to find the answer to the question "whether online teaching is an inadequate and inappropriate substitute for the traditional face-to-face instruction in a teacher education?" The outcome of the case suggests that online teaching paves the way for successful student quality learning and adaptability of traditional pedagogies. Besides, it also discusses the promises and challenges in designing and implementing an online teacher education course.

Alda Maria Pereira, Luis Tinoca and Isolina Oliveira in the chapter, *Authentic assessment contribution to competence based education: questions and challenges* look at the Learning Contract to facilitate assessment authenticity for enhancing student learning. The authors' viewpoint is that use of the Learning Contract can increase student's responsibility and commitment in their learning and it also facilitates learners towards contributing to the development of their life-long learning competencies.

The Linked Course, Project Learning, and Ramifications for Global Research, the next in the sequence of chapters, authored by Merrilee Cunningham and Ruth Robbins, underscores the importance of linked courses that serve as an excellent example of what can happen when two educators in diverse disciplines work together to blend, syncretize, and synergize the learning experience. The authors present this study as a model for global research and demonstrate how in a regionally accredited urban university, high risk students enrolled in a freshman English course are simultaneously enrolled in a freshman level computer information systems class where project learning is taking place.

Mohammed Saleh Al Balawi of King Fahad Naval Academy, Saudi Arabia analyses the preparedness of conventional universities in Saudi Arabia for implementing Web-Based Instruction (WBI) methods. In the sixteenth chapter of the book, he attempts to find incentives for faculty to use WBI in their instructional strategies, the institutional and personal barriers to implementation of WBI as well as investigates the attitudes of the faculty members at Saudi universities toward WBI.

Assessment methods used in an educational program go a long way in determining the quality of teaching and learning. The chapter by Erman Yukselturk and Orhan Curaoglu analyzes eleven online educational programs of different universities in Turkey with regard to the use of a blend of assessment methods based on various parameters. They identify the most commonly used online assessment techniques, the issues involved in using these techniques and the most effective methods for assessing the performance of the students.

Abbas Bazargan and Amin Mousavi consider blended approach as more promising in the teaching-learning process in developing research competencies. In this chapter, they outline an experimental approach in designing and developing an e-course, factors affecting its design and development and share the experiences gained through building the community of inquiry together with lessons learned.

The next case study authored by Luis Palacios and Chris Evans is on the use of interactive self-assessment questions (ISAQs) for helping undergraduate students learn in an e-learning environment. The study tries to determine the relationship between different levels of interactivity and memory and understanding of the students.

Finally this case study makes an attempt to identify the problems and perspectives of integrating innovative methods of technology enhanced instructional system with the traditional system in the higher education setup in Nigeria, focusing specifically on teaching and learning in the Obafemi Awolowo University, (OAU).

It is hoped that this book will be beneficial for educational technologists since it showcases varied applications of technology enabled environments in teaching, learning and research. This collection of analytical and evaluative cases on how institutions of learning across the globe are adapting to technology enabled environments for promoting transnational learning will be certainly a good resource book for all in education, its management and development.

We are greatly indebted to all the authors who have contributed interesting and remarkable case studies for this volume and have helped us in making this project successful. We have thoroughly enjoyed working with each one of the authors and we also hope it is the same for all of you and we are glad to have this book which is finally another model of excellent team work, collaboration and partnership. Our sincerest gratitude to the IGI-Global team members for their kind assistance and cooperation, and the incredible support rendered to us since the very outset of the project.

Siran Mukerji
Purnendu Tripathi
Editors

Chapter 1
Make a Change by Exchanging Views

Gilbert Ahamer
Austrian Academy of Sciences, Austria

Thomas Jekel
Austrian Academy of Sciences, Austria

ABSTRACT

Initially, this case presents a theoretical description highlighting how spaces are constructed. Perspectives onto reality are the elemental units of our world. They are changed through learning processes. Societal learning can enlarge and approximate spaces of understanding. Social spaces are a type of "social capital". Design of learning procedures refers to the design of structures in time, space and in the space of opinions that facilitates multi-perspectivist and multidisciplinary understanding of involved stakeholders. The following section of this case dwells on several cases of cooperative learning through dialogue: the project Schools on Ice, the UniGIS online curriculum, the UniNet network in Kyrgyzstan and Nepal, Global Studies, the ESD forum, the Environmental Systems Analysis Curriculum USW, and the European Union Twinning tool applied in Slovakia, Slovenia, Armenia, Georgia and Azerbaijan.

BACKGROUND

The *organisations* involved in the following cases include secondary schools, universities, university clusters, transnational university partnerships, international environmental NGOs, and the European Union's external policy. These organisations range from public to private and from idealistic to pragmatic. All of them plan to "change the world" and for that target they undertake to *exchange views and perspectives* among the stakeholders concerned. This paper approaches to find answers to the specific set of questions through cases of international collaborative educational projects.

QUESTIONS AND ANSWERS

1. What is the inner meaning of learning?
2. Which role plays learning in global civilisatoric evolution?

DOI: 10.4018/978-1-61520-749-7.ch001

3. How to overcome individualistic and sectoral views that hinder intercultural understanding?
4. Is it helpful to use recent concepts such as network society, social capital or structural capital?
5. Was "dialogic learning" and "exchanging views on reality" applied in more than a dozen cases of individual and societal learning and to what extent was this successful?

SETTING THE STAGE

Learning is Dialogue

As a starting point, we look at the core element of any social progress, namely at "dialogue". Dialogue leads to reflection and reflection, in turn, leads to awareness.

The final target of evolution (encompassing amongst others the evolution of mankind) is to *build consciousness* (Ahamer & Strobl, 2009). Consciousness governs procedures in the material world.

Dialogue is a suitable means to approximate divergent views – which is one of the main issues of learning – and to ultimately facilitate changes in consciousness.

Regarding learning, we may distinguish between *individual* learning and *societal* learning. Regarding the multiplicity of learning objects and learners, we distinguish the following types of learning:

- Individual learning
  - traditional learning (1:1)
  - interdisciplinary learning (1:n)
  - intercultural learning (n:m)
- Societal learning, e.g.
  - responding to climate change
  - political integration (globally, Europe-wide).

We are traditionally used to approach learning objects from one perspective (1:1) and consider it a progress to view objects from several, interdisciplinary perspectives (1:n). A still more advanced learning procedure would take into account the *multitude of learning subjects* (m) in addition to the *multiplicity of learning objects* (n), we will refer to it as *intercultural learning* (m:n) in this text because subjects are considered to be rooted and coached in their respective cultures inducing the subject to see and view reality as they decide to.

Useful training situations are spatial planning exercises and other space-related procedures that are open to GIS applications (Jekel, 2007, 2008ab, Strobl, 2007, 2008), or political, technological, civil engineering, cultural or peace negotiations in the classroom (Ahamer, 2004).

Learning Means Converging Divergent World Views

For very complex, interdisciplinary and intercultural learning issues a purely cognitive approach (an individual learner cognises a well-defined object of learning) appears too simple and the approach of "converging individual perspectives" (Ahamer et al., 2009) seems more appropriate.

Here, the object of learning is not regarded as something unchangeable (such as facts in natural sciences), but rather as the result of a constructivist procedure.

In such a procedure, individual perceptions (e.g. of international conflicts such as the complex Nagorny Karabakh conflict between two Caucasian states) are reshaped and reframed, which constitutes the core of "learning" on a societal level.

An early historic example for such *dialogic reframing* might be Galileo Galilei's (1632) strategy of making a discourse out of life's irreconcilable problems: "Dialogue of the two most important systems of the world" that were at odds at his time. As another example, the "greatest American philosopher" according to his students, John Dewey, sees *dialogue as the basis of education* – and art as the most effective communication that exists (Dennis, 1970: 3).

Learning Means Evolution of Spaces of Understanding

Also practical-minded disciplines take a similar stance: Taylor (2009: 198) stems from spatial planning. He says that *spaces are constructed*: "The most influential recent writer on the social construction of space is Manuel Castells who argues that, in an emerging network society, 'a new spatial logic', 'spaces of flows', is superseding the former logic, 'spaces of places' (Castells, 1996: 378). Both of these spatial forms are created through material practices. In his social theory, 'space is the material support of time-sharing practices'. That is to say, social spaces are created to bring together practices requiring simultaneous attention."

Castells is reported to condense this view to the statement "Our societies are increasingly structured around the bipolar opposition of the *Net* and the *Self*". The Net means the new, networked forms of organisation which are replacing vertically integrated hierarchies as the dominant form of social organization. The Self, on the other hand, relates to the multiple practices through which people try to reaffirm identity and meaning in a landscape of rapid change. Castells also coined the term 4th World for the poorest nations. Castells is defining space as the physical support of the way we live in time. The space and time we are used to, "real world time", is referred to by him as a space of places.

Manuel Castells (2001: 4f) himself says: "So what we have, for instance, in the case of Europe, is a complex system of institutional relations, which I call the *network state*, because, in fact, it's a network of interactions of shared sovereignty". "In a world of global flows of wealth, power, and images, the search for identity - collective or individual, ascribed or constructed - becomes the fundamental source of social meaning." Such views come close to Horx's (200x) emerging "*society of sense*", Renard's "mental structures" and the evolution towards a societal structure autopoietically optimizing towards values such as sense and human well-being (Ahamer & Strobl, 2009: Fig. 4). On this basis we can say: *the ultimate civilisatoric aim is to create meaning*, be it called "sense of life", "quality of life" or other immaterial values.

Castells writes in his famous trilogy (1996-1998) what is comparable to the above-mentioned evolutionist views:

- "Social movements in the Information Age are essentially mobilized around *cultural values*. The struggle to change the *codes of meaning* in the institutions and practice of the society is the essential struggle in the process of social change in the new historical context, movements to seize the power of the minds, not state power."
- "The networks are not programmed by technology; technological tools are programmed by minds. So the *human consciousness is the source*, because everything now depends on our ability to generate knowledge and process information in every domain and activity. Knowledge and information are cognitive qualities from the human mind."
- "Now, therefore, in a world in which signals, processed by our minds, are constantly shaping and reshaping what we do, the ability to influence, to change the categories through which we think our world (here, what I call the code of our culture) -- this becomes the essential battle. If you win the battle of minds, you win the battle of politics, the battle of the economy, because people will decide what they want to buy or what they don't want to buy, for instance."

- "So it's a *battle*, but ideas and talents are, ultimately, the source of productivity and competitiveness. The same thing is true in terms of the overall social organization, how people *change their minds* determines how they change their behavior. And the change of behavior would, ultimately, translate into changes in the overall social organization."

Castells says according to Stalder (2000): "New social formations emerge around primary identities. These identities are often seen as biologically or socially unchangeable. In the *interplay of the Net and the Self* the conditions of human life and experience around the world are deeply reconfigured."

The first assumption structures Castells' account of the rise of the Net: the dialectical interaction of social relations and technological innovation, or, in Castells' terminology, modes of production and modes of development. The second assumption underlines the importance of the Self: the way social groups define their identity shapes the institutions of society. As Castells (1997: 6-8) notes "each type of identity-building process leads to a different outcome in constituting society". - "Identity-building itself is a dynamic motor in forming society. *Identity* is defined as the *process of construction of meaning* on the basis of a cultural attribute, or a related set of cultural attributes that are given priority over other sources of meaning". – Remember here that the final result of the GCDB analyses (Ahamer & Strobl, 2009) was "to accelerate (social as compared to physical) time" in order to allow for more sustainability in society building.

Learning is Facilitated by a "Geography of Opinions and Perspectives"

Geography is the branch of science offering *perspectives onto reality*. Let us use such an unusual definition for the following deliberations.

Consequently, *geography creates spaces* (of understanding) that may be converging in the best case. The main tool for converging spaces of understanding is the dialogue. The circle of argumentation is closed.

Fundamentally, spaces are "spaces of (common) understanding", i.e. clusters of the same or similar "explanatory software" for the perceptions of the world. In our century, fortunately the path of intercultural understanding is followed more at the expense of thinking in terms of "cultural clashes".

An audacious statement can be made: *Our world is the entirety of perceptions*. (Our world is not the entirety of facts.) In this train of thought, it makes sense to envisage a (spatial) documentation of "perspectives onto realities" that would complement classical mapping by the additional aspect of the individual's opinion (Ahamer et al., 2009) (See Figure 1).

Actually, the approach of "attributing a place to each perspective onto reality" is not as theoretic as it might seem at first glance. Any democracy lives on "mapping all perspectives" into the seats of a parliament – this is state-of-the-art. Not only stable states but also transnational procedures are designed this way: one of the vastest self-responsible and peaceful political restructuring processes is an example, namely the recent European integration process and the ongoing European Neighbourhood Policy with the EU's new neighbour states.

European Integration as Prime Case for a Discursive Building of Structures

As a response to the new geopolitical situation following the events of 1989, the European Union (EU) has seen a round of enlargement in May 2004 based on dialogic procedures, and consequently adopted a new framework for relations with its neighbours, the *European Neighbourhood*

Figure 1. Our world as the entirety of perceptions of reality. Above far left: one human perception of reality; above left: many perceptions, in disorder; above right: the dimensions represent possible perspectives, e.g. scientific disciplines, values, cultures or religions. Below far left and left: many perceptions, each aligned by the identities of two scientific cultures; below right: the entirety of all viewers' perception, taking all possible standpoints. Far right: to become aware of all possible perspectives onto realities will facilitate the dialogue among viewers

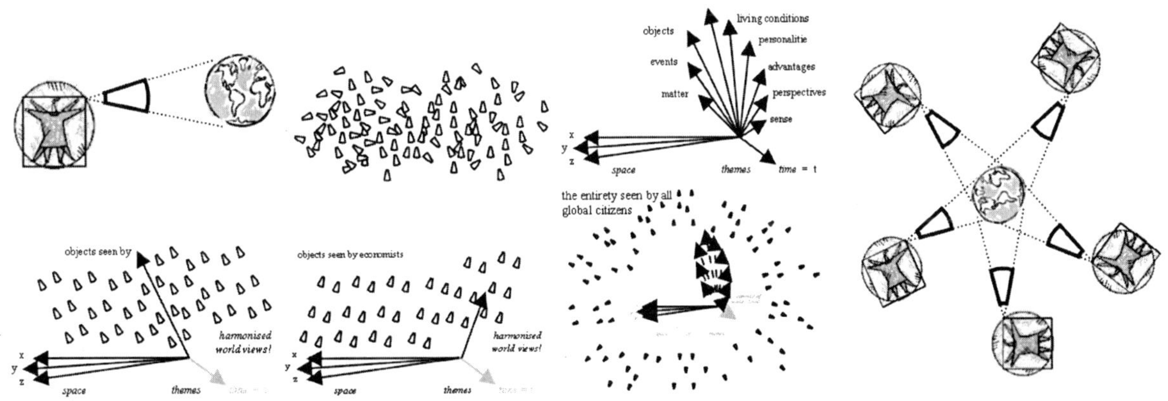

Policy (ENP, 2009). The ENP offers neighbouring countries the prospect of an increasingly closer relationship with the EU with the overall goal of fostering the political and economic reform processes including democratization (Berman, 1997), promoting closer economic integration as well as legal and technical approximation and sustainable development. In ENP, the cluster of ex-communist "transition economies" is comprised as ENP-East (Taylor et al., 2009, Derudder et al., 2007).

The central element of the ENP is a bilateral Action Plan (AP) which clearly sets out policy targets and benchmarks through which progress with an individual neighbouring country can be assessed over several years. The ENP Action Plan defines a considerable number of priority areas among which environment, aviation and education, which are at the core of the five cases reported in this article. Such deeper integration is based on – if not common – at least approximating human and societal values and constitutes a case of "identity building", as mentioned by Castells above.

European political genesis, its enlargement and subsequent neighbourhood policy represent "societal learning" in the deeper sense of the word.

In a theoretical approach, Eder (2007: 33) discerns two steps in the process of (European or any large-scale political) integration:

- Transcending the utilitarian needs and
- Closing the gaps by discourse.

Eder's (2007) paper develops a sociological perspective on the process of social integration that has been initiated in the course of the evolution of European political institutions. An abstract notion of social integration is presented as providing an analytical framework for understanding and explaining the process of socially integrating a culturally heterogeneous Europe. The key concept is that of a *transnational space of communication and its discursive closure* (compare Bourdieu, 1997). The central theoretical idea is to use communicative density (compare Ahamer, 2009) as the criterion of the emergence of a communicative space in which two different types of experience make possible its discursive closure:

1. the experience of being *treated in a fair way by the others* inhabiting this space (the *cognitive* capital of a community) and
2. the *construction of a common memory frame* resulting from the confrontation of differing national (and subnational) memories in this space (the *narrative* capital of a community).

Thus two mechanisms can be identified which explain discursive closure. This model leaves open whether this will happen, but it offers a strategy for identifying the extent and the causes of such processes without recourse to normatively motivated wishful thinking.

The main dimensions of such a creation of a society are increasing density of interaction (or density of communication) in a European social space and its discursive closure by cognitive and narrative construction of mutuality, common ground and common interest (Eder, 2007: 37).

The two factors listed above are seen as forms of accumulation of *symbolic capital* while the two mentioned appearances of symbolic capital are relevant: cognitive capital and narrative capital (p. 39). In Bourdieu's concept of symbolic capital memory and remembrance become a constitutive part of the structure of collective social practice. Cultures of remembrance are a form of symbolic capital that attributes a certain value (or lack of value) to the constituents of the "common" (Eder, 2007: 40, Bourdieu, 1991).

On the practical level of countries, a well-targeted strategy for the creation and further development of such communality is a series of so-called Twinning projects that have been developed by the European commission for the mutual help of administrations in the member states and the candidate countries. Twinning means "Institution Building" (compare Berman, 1997). A suitable definition of the "*Twinning principles*" applicable to European neighbourhood countries (from Belarus across Azerbaijan to Morocco) can be found on the Twinning web page (EU, 2009):

- "In addition to meeting requirements laid down in the EU's agreements with third countries, Twinning must also aim at developing *structural* reforms.
- At the end of a project, any new or adapted system must be *self-sufficient* and function under the auspices of the beneficiary country.
- Projects must also include some elements relating to the adoption of EU *legislation*. An approximation to the acquis communautaire is called for, rather than full integration of EU legislation as was demanded of the candidate countries.
- The local partner in a Twinning should be represented by a *public body* that is capable of working with a Member State organisation which has a similar structure and function.
- The beneficiary country partner must be able to adapt and take on board *change*: the Twinning project is not about the EU providing one-way technical assistance."

Several cases for Twinnings will be presented in the practical part of this contribution.

Social Spaces and Social Capital

At the end of the above *theoretical section* "setting the stage" we refresh some of the proposed approaches: Apart from the well-known notion of "human capital" also other vocabulary has entered scientific reasoning while denoting *structural stocks of a community* of varying degree of novelty to the reader – such as "*social capital*" (Adler & Kwon, 2000, Bourdieu, 1997). There is evidence for the connection between social networks and social capital (Mohan & Mohan, 2002: 196, Burt, 2000). Entrepreneurship (Chung & Gibbons, 1997), civil society (Hyden, 1997) and civic engagement (Kenworthy, 1997, Larsen et al., 2004, Brownlow, 2005, Purcell, 2001, Kirby, 2007) have been linked to social capital in several studies. Attempts have been made to map social structures (Zheng & Niu, 2007) or to explain their topology by biological arguments (Lemke, 2000). Anyhow, e-learning can be seen as the reconstruction of space along other lines.

Information technologies such as the internet (Arnold, 2003), social network sites (Hargittai, 2008) and other "public electronic spaces" (Crang, 2000) were identified to enhance the making of *social spaces* – a diagnosis that can be corroborated by the authors to the extent that appropriate application of ICT is cared for, best in a stepwise and rhythmised manner.

Before the start of the following *practical chapter* containing the "case descriptions" we link both chapters by stating that all cases implement the above main guideing ideas of dialogue and discourse for societal learning. The network society is implemented by mapping controversial perspective into one interdisciplinary and intercultural synthetic view. New common spaces of understanding are stretched out and new and common identities are synthesised as structural capital.

CASE DESCRIPTIONS

The following cases narrated in the practical part of this contribution will illustrate (individual and societal) collaborative initiatives of providing learning opportunities that may be supported by suitable information technologies:

- Geographic Information based learning in Schools on Ice;
- E-learning based studies UniGIS;
- Austro-Asian university network UniNet, with local cases in:
    - Kyrgyzstan
    - Nepal;
- Developmental curricula in Austria called Global Studies;
- European Association for the Promotion of Sustainable Development ESD;
- Interdisciplinary Environmental Systems Analysis curriculum USW; and
- European Union enlargement Twinning tool with cases in:
    - Slovakia
    - Slovenia
    - Armenia
    - Georgia
    - Azerbaijan.

The following five short sub-paragraphs will introduce some key features of the volume (Mukerji & Tripathi, 2009) linked to some of the presented cases.

Technological Adaptability

Technological adaptability is of key interest because (1) not the same IT tools are suitable for the wide range of the 14 above-mentioned cases. Generally it was found that modest application of technological support was suitable and that strong interpersonal communication is indispensable for overall success of the learning settings. (2) Self-adaptive learning designs would certainly be the optimum – this has been achieved by "Surfing Global Change" (SGC).

Resulting Changes in Organisations

University structures have been changed or kept changing in an evolutionary sense:

- The themes of "Global Change" and "Global Studies" are essentially connecting different schools and university faculties by the inauguration of "curricula commissions" and can be a general vehicle to improve university structures across disciplines ac-

cording to authentic interdisciplinarity of real-world problems
- Institutional change is a result of a saturation phase in the view of a GCDB evolutionary cycle (Ahamer & Strobl, 2009: Figures 1 & 4). In this view, institutions are the timeless effect of an evolutionary society (just as a snail produces its house)
- Institutions are the vessels for the intersubjectively agreed and trans-subjectively applied values that a society has generated.

What exactly is a "Developing" Nation?

Especially after administrative experiences as experts in countries which are usually referred to as "developing", a strong feeling of structural similarity arises that similar impediments govern the bottlenecks towards a sustainable evolution: lack of assuming responsibilities, unclear division of tasks, an innovation-unfriendly system of payment in the public sector, premature obedience and submissivity. In this sense, everybody should be developing (= intrinsically living); any nation is on a path, but somewhere else in the complex pattern of factors.

Transnational Learning

This type of social learning is enhanced by a programme called "Cross-Boundary Cooperations" (CBC) linking countries inside and outside the EU.

On EU level and also during Twinnings, societal learning occurs along the following steps:

- Agree by consensus on a "EU Directive" (level of governments)
- Elaborate "best practice guidelines" (level of task forces)
- Manuals for practical work (level of administrations).

Changes in Organisations

For universities, the Bologna system in the EU (which means to render "quality" comparable) has created a rule-based system, which coincides with the "Atlantic ethics", as opposed to a personality-based system, more prevalent in Central European or other attitudes. Applications may be web-based socializing or person-centred socializing, as analysed in (MacGregor, 2002).

Case Schools on Ice

Invented and organized by one of the authors, this series of *pedagogic projects* (Jekel, 2008a) includes scientific and adventurous components for the students of several Salzburg-based secondary schools: they hike across the glacier of the 2995m high "Hoher Dachstein", which is a mountain of key interest to tourists at the triangle of the Austrian provinces of Salzburg, Upper Austria and Styria, and take note of the precipitous melting of the glacier ice. The focus lies on the GIS methodologies they apply after preparation during their regular lessons in geography. Intense collaboration is enhanced both by the project's adventurous component and the interdisciplinary character, spanning measurement technology, statistics, geology, glaciology, climate change and raising of public awareness.

Along a given path across the glacier, students measure the depth by sonar echo as well as the extension of the glacier (Figure 2, Figure 3, Figure 4). By comparison with old maps they derive the areas and volumes that have disappeared due to global warming.

In these interdisciplinary analyses, Geographic Information Systems (GIS) play a crucial role to support students' analyses (Figure 5) and they arrive at the following conclusions:

- Skiing on this glacier will be nearly impracticable in summer

Figure 2. Results and processes in the "Schools on Ice" project: Measuring points and glacier extension

Figure 3. Measuring method by echo

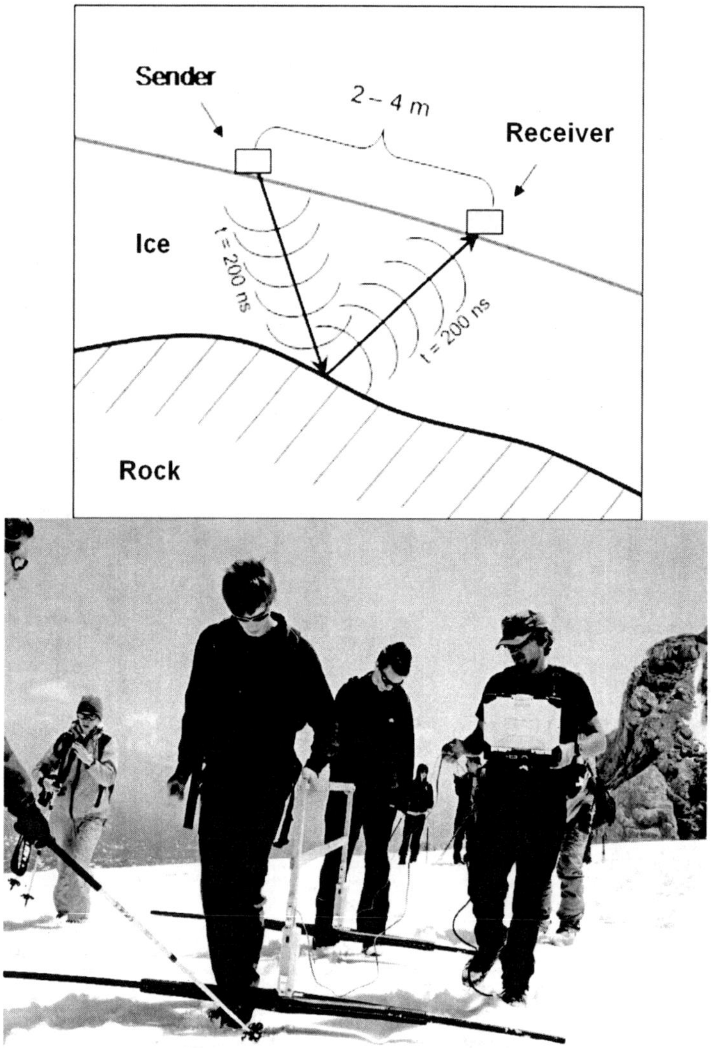

- Touristic areas based on glacier skiing should develop new economic strategies
- Glacier areas will receive a new chance in the winter season because regions under 1000m altitude will face snow problems
- If speed of decrease is maintained, the entire glacier will have disappeared in about 18 years.

Figure 6 shows the learner-based concept of this concrete project (at left) and its embedding in the overall concept of developing civic responsibilities using spatially oriented IT systems (at right). In all the projects, GIS is not the central aim of the learning process, but is rather embedded in real world problems (Jekel, 2008a). This is considerably different from recent attempts to 'learn GIS at school', i.e. a type of hardware and software training. Geoinformation here is used to a thematic end. First, Geographic Information (GI) is used as part of actively researching and analysing data, as in the project analyzing the development of housing and commercial building at the outskirts of Osnabrück. The second

Figure 4. Result showing lost ice volume since 1967

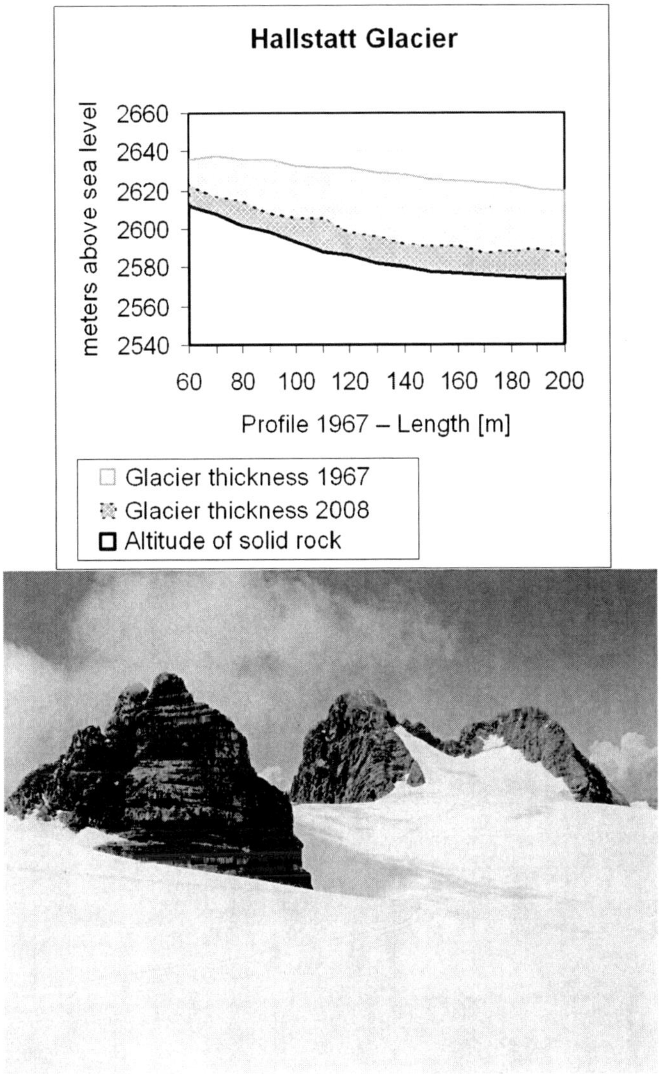

possibility is to use digital globes as a tool to integrate and communicate pupils' research into various themes, as in the Schools on Ice project. Third, GI can be put to use as a graphic backdrop stimulating and structuring pupils' discussions in local decision-making processes on change. In all three approaches collaborative and participative mapping comes to the fore. All approaches however put a high emphasis on visualization rather than analysis. The technical knowledge needed to use Geoinformation this way is minimal and compatible with the teachers' expertise, which is one of the main question marks regarding the use of Geoinformatics in school. As an added bonus, the techniques used in the learning process are compatible with learning theory and pedagogic thinking on learning processes.

To arrive at this point, Jekel (2008b) proposes just a few guidelines that provide a mix of learning theory and geography:

- a minimal technological focus should do (in general, any web-based GIS, in many cases digital globes will be sufficient). This

Figure 5. Geographic information systems in the classroom (Foto: Koller 2008)

Figure 6. Left: General concept of learner-based learning within "Schools on Ice" project (Jekel, 2008a). Right: Citizens, Analysts & GI Systems Experts (Strobl, 2008, Jekel, 2008b)

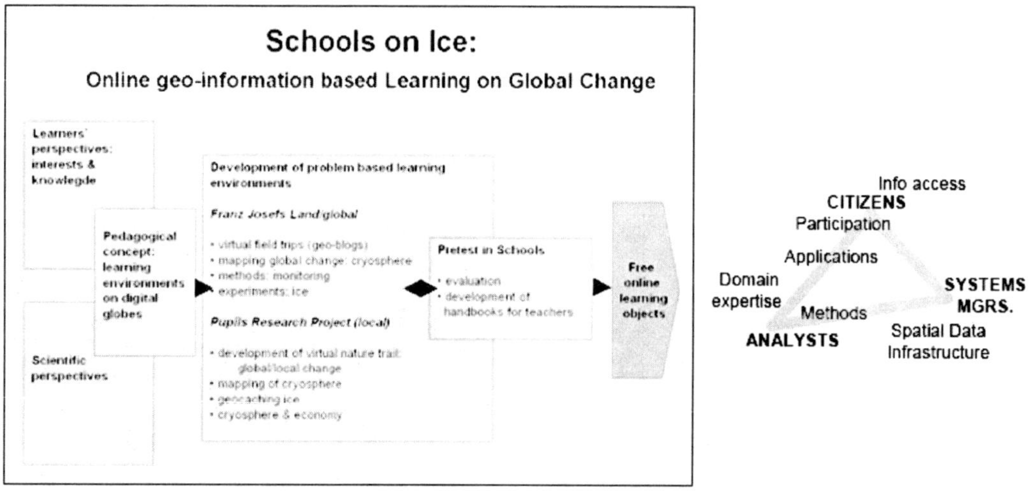

is also in respect to hardware and software costs.

- learning environments should be set as real world problems, allowing for identification with the problem. Planning one's environment or the city's traffic, tracking migration with data of the class, or planning one's holiday are examples where subjectivities and identities are included -

this should make for reasonable learning environments
- collaboration and collaborative construction of meaning should be offered - this can be done in cooperation with any learning system in the market, many of which are available free of charge.
- To test results, new methodologies have to be used, that do not look for right or wrong, but for good arguments, creativity, and participation in a social process.

All these achievements are possible on the basis of digital globes (such as Google Earth or Virtual Earth). Recent empirical research has shown that with simple GI-based learning environments both interest of learners as well as actual learning processes can be fostered. Therefore, simply let children map their own (future) worlds!

For learning purposes Jekel (2007) has classified conceptions of space drawing on Vielhaber and Habermas (see Table 1).

Case UNIGIS

University studies of "Geographic Information Sciences" (GIS) can very well be conducted via internet, making use of e-learning experiences of its founder (Strobl, 2004). *The* global success story is the UNIGIS network that has developed out of the Salz burg based GIS cluster presently encompassing a university institute, an applied near-industry research institute and an institute of the Academy of Sciences.

Necessary ingredients for this world-leading consortium of universities and curricula in *Geographic Information Sciences* are:

- technologies (= the web platform Blackboard)
- clear rules (what is necessary to reach at the MSc)
- driving spirit (the person of the initiator).

The classical curriculum of technology-supported learning is the internationally successful master course in geographic information science. It comprises a well-defined content that can neither be altered by individual views nor be changed as a function of discussions, but constitutes a clear target of cognitive learning. Every single learner faces his precisely defined content. Dialogue and discussion is only a means to enhance the learning process, not to alter or adapt the content.

A group of several dozen students per year go through a bimonthly cascade of twelve courses (one building upon the other). After two months, the results of a difficult exam are transmitted by email to the instructor. Several electives, a master thesis and a collaborative project round out this curriculum (www.unigis.net). Students meet for attendance units during a three-day introductory meeting in Salzburg and during a second seminar after one year. Online collaboration is enhanced by informal learning groups that are set up as a function of geographic vicinity of the individual learners across the German-speaking countries. Over one thousand students have successfully

Table 1. Human interests, knowledge and space (from Jekel, 2007)

Human Interest	Knowledge	Research Methods	Concepts of Space
Technical	Instrumental	Positivistic Sciences (empirical-analytic)	Absolute space
Practical	Practical (understanding)	Interpretative research (hermeneutic methods)	+ Perceived space
Emancipatory	Emancipation (reflection)	Critical Social Sciences (critical theory)	+ Relational space

completed this postgraduate course in the last few years. Inter-university comparability is guaranteed by an overarching organisation convening experts from all participating universities (www.unigis.net).

Technology plays an important role in this learning setting: it is the target of any action (mastering GIS software), technology facilitates communication among learners, and is the method of delivery for well-defined results.

The created space of understanding consists in the enlargement of individual understanding of geographic information science, systems and technologies.

Typical difficulties encountered are lack of cognitive achievement or deficits in establishing collaborative structures for individual students. In this case, the dialogue is not yet creating content, but just facilitating its acceptance.

Case UNINET

The *Eurasia-Pacific Uninet* established between Austrian and Asian universities is the largest of its kind in the world and reunites a total of 113 member institutions. This university network promotes multilateral scientific cooperation, joint research projects, conferences as well as faculty and student exchange. Contacts stemming from the Salzburg-based GIS cluster (Strobl, 2004, Strobl et al., 2008) led to international institution building among others in India, Central Asia (ACA*GIS in Bishkek/Kyrgyz Republic), South East Asia, China and other countries.

A small office of five has developed out of the China Center of Salzburg University and has managed to establish the largest existing Europe-Asia-university network. Funded by the Austrian ministry of science, annually almost hundred study visits, conferences, workshops, scholarships, preparatory missions, are attended by members of Austrian and Asian universities, who have gradually succeeded in building a network structure and even distinctly institutionalised branches of research and teaching.

Dialogue is occurring during the typically week-long visits and study tours. The foundation of collaboration is created by such structured discourse, whereas the content only acts as intermediary means for building such structures. The target of Uninet is not to hold conferences as a target in itself, but to create structures that might be institutionalised using personal contacts in such conferences. Hence Uninet might be the most constructivist of all case studies mentioned here. Difficulties encountered might be political instability or a subcritical mass of too few involved persons on either side of the network.

Case Kyrgyzstan

The Austrian-Central Asian Centre for Geographic Information Science (ACA*GIS) was founded in 2008 in Bishkek (Kyrgyzstan) as an offspring of both Unigis and Uninet activities. Starting from this Kyrgyz cooperation, the workshop openSolar'09 (www.aca-giscience.org/opensolar) is organized in August 2009 together with the annual Central Asian GIS conference GISCA'09. Again, its target is to create sufficient personal links between stakeholders in order to promote institutionalising of solar-oriented collaboration: construction and deployment of thermal and photovoltaic solar cells, cooperation in research and in legal matters. For this target, high-ranking officials from administration are expected to enhance solar implementation in Kyrgyzstan.

Regarding solar energy applications, the necessity to bridge standpoints occurs (1) between Central Asian and European views to consider for example to what extent the Kyrgyz economy should master the modernisation of the energy system by its own force and (2) among Central Asian standpoints themselves, for example regarding the question of the water management of the Syr-Darya river, if water from the Toktogul reservoir should be released during summer for the needs of the Uzbek cotton plantations or during winter for the needs of the Kyrgyz electricity generation. As another example, the tariff for electricity in Kyrgyztan is presently still so low, that it does not at all cover the cost of electricity generation, which holds back the engagement of foreign investors to exploit the huge hydroelectricity potential of Kyrgyztan. Additionally, an escape from the deadlock of the Kyrgyz electricity market cannot be imagined without external help: the Kyrgyz viewpoint might be too restricted, so that raising electricity tariffs is only seen as socially negative, whereas the World Bank report identifying weak financial sustainability and corruption as prime obstacle might be seen as capitalistically inspired.

Foreign experts are useful in such a situation not only for delivering know-how but also because they are not part of the pattern of interest of the respective country. Therefore, they can play the role of a social catalyst. The very essence of such consultancy work is to bring the social procedures beyond the point of a deadlock when opposing national interests bring national planning efforts to a standstill. The mere fulfilment of World Bank advice does not always seem a possible strategy for everyday politics, especially because the so-called "Tulip-Revolution" in 2003 was initiated among others by a rise in electricity tariffs.

Dialogue and discourse in this case may construct a real-world escape from an unsatisfying situation after the collapse of the Soviet Empire.

The technological substrate of this type of collaboration is a web site containing the lectures of Austrian authors and also a web space containing the contributions of the workshop attendants who have computed the solar energy potential of their respective Central Asian home country, such as Kyrgyztan, Uzbekistan, Kazakhstan, Tajikistan, and Turkmenistan. Continued interlacing of social webs in Austria and Central Asia will be performed during a discussion session on the last day of the workshop, where professors from both sides take part and also industrial actors and development helpers in order to prepare concrete implementation of solar energy in Kyrgyztan.

Case Nepal

Both Austria and the Himalayan countries have special experience with problems in high mountain ranges: natural disasters, earth slides, climate change. Therefore, a long cooperation between Austrians and members of a centre of mountain research has been developed and led to the joint organisation of an annual conference. Additionally, Himalayan countries might encounter political difficulties when cooperating among themselves; they reach from Afghanistan to Myanmar. Therefore, it is important to have a joint platform for discussing scientific and environmental issues without disturbances due to different political systems. Such a platform allows to adopt different viewpoints and to go beyond limited national views. Additionally, the presence of Austrian experts has enlarged the scope of existing perspectives. This annual conference is also organized through Uninet, in this case the scientific output and the technological support were comparable to a conventional conference.

Case Global Studies

Over the last decade, initiatives for "Global Studies" have emerged in the Austrian cities of Vienna, Graz, Salzburg and Innsbruck. The idea is to found a sound scientific curriculum that is inspired by developmental ethics. The first of these developmental studies has been established at the University of Vienna and has recently reached an annual throughput of some two hundred students per year.

Formally, this initiative has been led by the Department for African Studies in Vienna, but is still identified as a "project" and is carried out mainly by a group of half a dozen university lecturers. Despite the growing importance of developmental studies on an international level and their longer traditions in the Anglo-Saxon countries, the institution building process at the University of Vienna has been very slow.

At Graz University, a "bundle of electives" has been offered since 2003 (www.uni-graz.at/globalstudies) and is currently merged into a regular curriculum for the master course "Global Study". Whereas the Viennese initiative is mostly rooted in political sciences and sociology, the Graz initiative always maintained a very broad scope encompassing all faculties of this university: economics, political science, international law, languages, theology, global change, and sociological methods. The Graz curriculum is composed of 6 components and ensures a broad understanding. The Graz initiative was founded by a long-standing expert in peace research, Dr. Karl Kumpfmüller, and was implemented by a peer group of active members of Graz University, the so-called "Steering Committee Global Studies", who have been meeting bimonthly for the last 6 years. This bundle of electives amounts to 24 hours per semester or 36 ECTS, of which the only mandatory lecture is one introductory lecture to Global Studies held by the founder and one of the authors. A strength of the master curriculum is the mandatory three-month practical that might consist in developmental work abroad.

The Salzburg initiative is organised by initiative of the Institute for Geography and has accumulated a budget of eight hours per semester for a just starting curriculum also called "Global Studies". The Innsbruck initiative gained momentum after the biannual Austrian developmental conference 2008 in Innsbruck.

Case ESD

The conviction that only radical reforms of our present economic system can heal the environmental and economic crisis to a sufficient extent, has led to the foundation of the European panel on the promotion of sustainable development ESD. This is a loose but clearly organized group of idealists, who have formed as a vivid and constructive discussion round with illustrious authors of critical books in Austria. In an iterative process of mutual review, a book was authored that immediately after its publication reached the second highest rank of the evaluated books in future science. This structured discussion process is maintained and will soon lead to a second reworked edition of the book "The turn of the Titanic". ESD has its own website (www.esd-eu.org) but is mainly relying on personal contacts and face-to-face debates and structured discussion. In no other case is the orientation to "discursive society" so clearly implemented as in ESD. The special chance and the special risk at the same time of this idealistic corporation might be the strong individualism and the deep ethical motivation that cared for a small but very dedicated group of activists, who managed to disseminate their thoughts in numerous public discussions and debates, especially with high ranking stakeholders from industry, banking and administration.

Case Environmental Systems Analysis (USW)

A worldwide unique curriculum is "Environmental Systems Analysis" (Umweltsystemwissenschaften, USW) at Graz University, which comprises 5 specialties: economics, business administration, geography, chemistry and physics. Students of USW have to select one of these 5 specialties and additionally complete one quarter of their studies in the field of systems analysis, including a so-called "interdisciplinary practical" (IP). The special identity of USW is to train interdisciplinary dialogue already during the course of studies as a constitutive element. More than a dozen of such IPs have been conducted by one of the authors.

Problems related to Environmental Systems Analysis are the increasing character of this curriculum as a mass course of study. The number of students has reached 200 per year, which is a considerable change compared to the initial years of a dozen students who had to apply for their own curricula to be accepted by the university authorities as "studium irregulare". Initially swept away by a very positive public response, the percentage of highly motivated students has decreased to a normal level. An institution that might have been the hope for a generation may even lose its inner drive after having become part of "the system".

A *web-supported negotiation game "Surfing Global Change"* (SGC) was used as a dramatic foundation for these interdisciplinary practicals. SGC is a discussion-oriented negotiation game that trains consensus building.

Its structure along time is symbolically depicted in Figure 7 that leads through the five levels of SGC. Rhythmisation of social procedures is the key didactic element of this web-supported negotiation game.

A brief outline of the social processes and the game activities that are used for the design of consensus building can be taken from Figure 8.

The entire set of rules can be retrieved in journals (Ahamer, 2004). Experience has shown that SGC can be applied effectively to "distributed learning processes", especially to intercultural learning processes, because the focus is on viewing others' standpoints and dealing with them.

Lessons learned from the invention of SGC are: how can the rhythmized interplay of different communicative phases (real ⇔ virtual; conflict ⇔ cooperation; etc.) be applied to other learning settings? Two dozens of SGC games have been implemented to date at two Austrian universities and received positive feedback from students. SGC represents the idea of "*learning as gaming*".

Case Twinning as a Tool

The historic processes of the break-up of the former Eastern-European Bloc in the year 1989 and the subsequent independence of these nation

Figure 7. Symbolic depiction of the communicative setting (left) and the consecutive social processes (right) in which the five phases of Surfing Global Change (SGC) are developing: the evolution from dwelling upon single technical details towards a coherent view

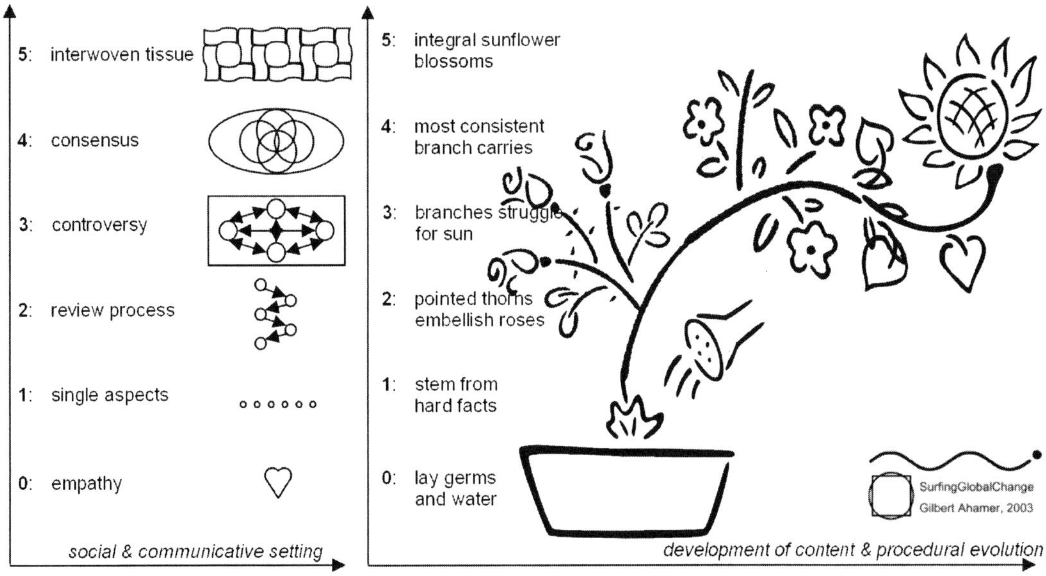

Figure 8. A folder displays the successive levels of gaming in SGC (© G. Ahamer)

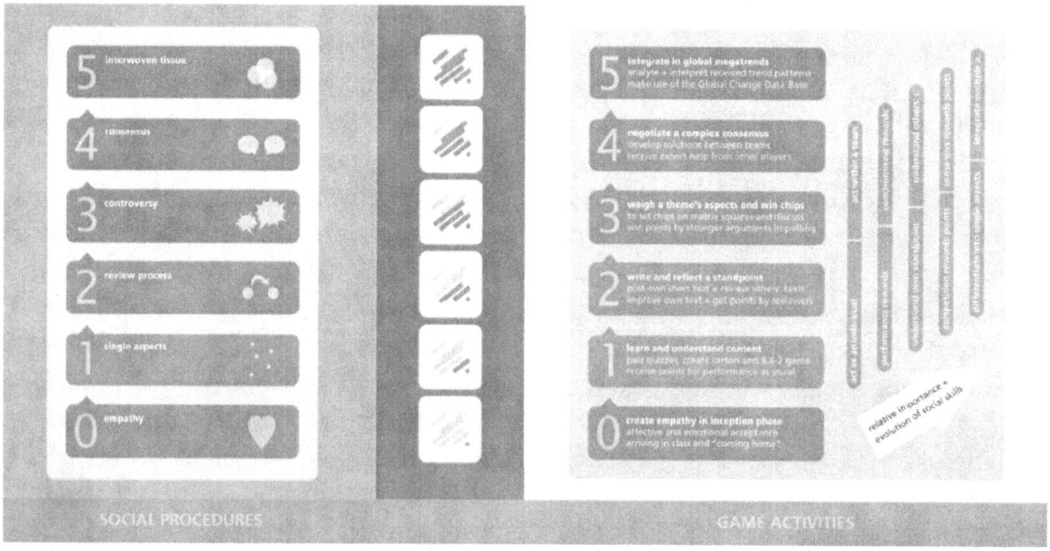

states has led them to pursue,, membership in the European Union. Consequently, a political and administrative tool on a continental scale had to be developed, that would be useful in defining a clear process of these new states towards restructuring into a democratic society. Such societal procedures can only occur on a voluntary basis; or else they would not be successful because of a lack of perceived ownership in the respective administrations. In 1998, the European Commission started the first "Twinning projects" that where designed to train administrative staff in the candidate countries for their future duties as member state administrations.

The main idea of these Twinning projects is to *jointly solve issues* posed by membership. Both physically and symbolically, civil servants of the candidate country and of a new member state sit next to one another and together face their issues and problems of daily work. Training is done on the job, in partnership, on the same height of eyes (symbolically and literally) and in a non-confrontational manner. The experts of the new member states are not standing "in front" of the experts of the candidate countries and giving them "good advice", but the "common enemy" is the task to be mastered. Therefore, the stakeholders are trained for their future roles as colleagues on EU level. Additionally, the spirit of work and the democratic culture of self-responsible fulfilment of work duties are implemented in real live, not only theoretically taught. The side effects of gradually adapting to a different work attitude after decades of communism where rules and regulations might have been perceived as unnecessary attack on the individual might have constituted the most important achievement in many cases. Hence, Twinning offered a double achievement: learning new matters and new procedures. Anyhow, learning procedures always necessitates "matters" as a substrate of learning.

According to the philosophy of Twinning, concrete projects had to be formulated and applied for by people in the candidate country's administration. Often the most dedicated individuals have taken the effort to define a Twinning project and thus have contributed to the advancement of their specialties and maybe sometimes also to their personal careers. However, an almost invisible "cultural change" in EU financing took place, namely the shift from "demand driven" to "accession driven" projects. Whereas the first type of projects often meant: "candidate country demands, EU pays", towards "if you fulfil your own tasks in approaching the EU system, we will help you with that".

Every year, one hundred Twinning projects have been carried out since 1998 all over Europe in such areas as environment, justice and home affairs, and other key areas that have been enlarged to practically all issues of the so-called 33 "chapters" of the European Union accession mechanism. Twinning philosophy is deeply rooted in dialogue and discourse and was documented by the so-called Twinning Handbook (EU, 2009) and has been subject to iterative improvements on the basis of annual reviews assessing the success of the individual projects and the Twinning tool as such.

The last Twinnings for the enlargement round of the Central European countries have been performed in 2006. Due to the overall success of this type of programming the tool of Twinning has been subsequently applied also to the countries of the so-called "European Neighbourhood Policy" (ENP). This is a set of countries reaching from Belarus to Azerbaijan in the East and to Morocco in the West; however, these projects do not lead to accession, only to approximation of states.

The core of any Twinning is the voluntary act of absorbing the so-called "acquis communautaire" which means the entire set of EU legislation.

Many Twinning projects have a typical budget of one million Euros. Regarding the project structure, key roles are the "Resident Twinning Advisor" (RTA), who resides in the beneficiary country for one to two years and acts as a link between the European Union member states (MS) and the candidate countries or beneficiary countries (BC). RTAs report to the project leaders, one from the BC and one from the MS. Apart from the long-term expert RTA, typically five to forty short-term experts (STE) come to missions in the beneficiary country for typically one or two weeks. They should cooperate on a daily basis with their local homologues, who are civil servants on the beneficiary side. Twinning experts must come from an administration and are typically civil servants; STEs are not consultants in the usual sense of the word. This leads to the main characteristic of Twinning: *Twinning is institution building*, not technical consultancy. Twinning means "*strengthening of institutions*"; after a Twinning the beneficiary country should be able to perform its administrative tasks relying on its own strengths, its own motivation and its own financial and organisational means.

Twinning is certainly not a theoretical exercise limited to science only. It means changed realities in such concrete fields as taxation, border control, anti-corruption within the police, waste management, vocational education, or aviation safety. In this sense Twinning is institutional learning and societal learning in the sense as described in the first chapters. Twinnings may be seen as *one of the most effective methods for societal learning* as such.

Often considerable obstacles may arise in intercultural understanding. Also very often, the understanding prevails that the "western consultants" come, do the work and leave and thus spare the local consultants from this workload. Such an attitude would not comply with the requested ownership leading to empowerment of the beneficiary.

An overall analysis of the Twinning tool will arrive at seeing as a highly effective program enabling smooth transition processes of a large group of countries towards a democratic system. The latest enlargement of the European Union might even be seen as a third world war without one single victim. It represents possibly the first example in human history of an area one thousand kilometres wide encompassing an entire continent that has deliberately and voluntarily changed its political system, ultimately backed by the will of the majority of the population.

The core of the success of a Twinning lies in its potential to provide new perspectives on the same reality by incorporating the Twinning partner's view. When jointly sitting over a task, the expert colleagues exchange their views in an undramatic manner as part of their daily lives in an atmosphere that does not encourage competition but constitutes a win-win situation where the personal success of each one is the highest when having attained consensus with the partner. However, also cases of less harmonious Twinnings have been experienced where the long-term expert was replaced on the basis of dissatisfaction in the beneficiary country.

Case Twinning in Slovakia

An example for an early Twinning project during the early phase of accession is one of the first hundred Twinnings: "Strengthening of Institutions in the Air Quality Sector" in Slovakia in 2000-2001 led by the Austrian Federal Environment Agency.

Initially planned as a technical investment project to provide 40 PCs for the Slovak air monitoring system, this project became a full-fledged Twinning and was later inofficially named "the best Twinning in Slovakia". It produced over twelve concise reports on air quality measurement methodologies that were very positively received by the European Court of Auditors. However, some of the possible shortcomings of Twinnings played a considerable role here: during the planning process, all three involved actors (Slovakia, Austria, and European Commission) contributed to delays during the preparative phase of preparing the Twinning contract (Twinning Covenant). During these early years the Twinning tool was not yet fully developed, the rules were subject to change, and all involved actors lacked experience. The resulting delay of more than one year prompted the beneficiary country to assume that it would no longer need a Twinning at all.

However, the ongoing legal analysis of the "Act on Air" text of the Slovak Republic revealed that there were still considerable shortcomings of the transposition of the EU legal texts (the EU Framework Directive on Air Quality and their related daughter directives). As a consequence, during long periods of this Twinning, the Slovak partners showed considerable reluctance to sufficiently collaborate with the Austrian partners because the beneficiary thought it had sufficiently accomplished transposition. Nonetheless, more gaps emerged in the field of implementation, and even more in enforcement – these three steps are the main phases of any Twinning procedure.

Ultimately, this single Twinning reflected very well the subjective perceptions of the civil society on both sides of the former "Iron Curtain", namely that each one thought the processes on their own side to be much more mature than perceived by the other side. Slovaks considered themselves over-matured to approach the EU, whereas Austrians felt alleged backwardness of any Central or Eastern European country. This fundamental bias of perception of the role of one's own country with respect to the role of the partner country led to a decrease in factual collaboration during the Twinning process. In contradiction to the mutually agreed plans, the Twinning reports were authored by Austrian experts to 95%, whereas Slovak experts restricted themselves to delivering data in cases they have been asked for expressly. As a result, the Twinning targets, that actually are understood as "guaranteed results" were watered down and fulfilled either too late or only formally or not at all. Such severe assessment comes from a long-term expert who is one of the authors. The Slovak administration repeatedly declared that it was willing to achieve only the minimum performance in transposition of the acquis into Slovak legislation.

During the same time period, another Twinning on water quality in Slovakia was very successful due to the high level of dedication of the Slovak project leader and his team. A third Twinning on waste suffered from distributed responsibilities among several Slovak ministries. In general, Slovak administration was severely understaffed (that was partly triggered by EU advice to cut down costly administrative staff in ministries) and severely underpaid which resulted in a brain drain towards private economy. Ten years after the Velvet Revolution, a change of working atmosphere, the degree of taking responsibilities and self-guidedness of civil servants had not yet reached a sufficient level. This is only one of the conclusions after having spent a year in another working culture. Another conclusion was that after returning home many aspects of administrative life in the home country resembled considerably the unsatisfactory impressions in the beneficiary country. Consequently, the returning long-term expert perceived his own country as a "developing country" - only at a different stage of development. Any country that is reluctant to develop further its social structures and institutions is in danger of creating bottlenecks for fruitful societal evolution.

What were the lasting benefits of such a project? Firstly, training on the technical level of how to fulfil the reporting duties for air quality matters, secondly, personal knowledge of the environmental administration in the partner country and thirdly, and foremostly, the ability to step out of the perspective of one's own country and to adopt the perspective of a member of the other country. This latter *ability of "switching roles and switching perspectives"* is the *core of social learning* in such *intercultural* interdisciplinary projects.

Case Twinning in Slovenia

A different country with a different history and a different phase in the overall accession process has led to very different experiences, self-conceptions and resulting interpersonal relationships. One year after the accession of Slovakia to the EU had already taken place, the Twinning on "Pricing of Water According to the EU Water Framework Directive" has been performed by a mixed German-Austrian team from 2005 to 2006. For half a year of the Twinning period, Slovenia itself adopted the role of EU presidency and fulfilled its duties in a highly respected manner.

A rather complex issue was selected, namely the question of how market mechanisms could control the amount of water consumption as a function of the water price. The aim of the project was to use different levels of water pricing to determine the levels of water consumption in different geographic areas of Slovakia with its only two million inhabitants. The task of the Twinning experts was to develop an algorithm of computing water prices that would sufficiently take into account the ecological ("external") costs linked to the supply of fresh water and subsequent management of waste water.

The selection procedures by the Slovenian administration revealed later on that existing personal contacts had led to the decisions which partner to select.

During the entire Twinning a friendly interpersonal atmosphere prevailed among the experts. However, the collaboration among the RTAs and project leaders was not always without problems. Lack of knowledge of the subject itself might have led to a visibly formalistic attitude on one side of the Twinning partnership.

The fulfilment of the "guaranteed results" in this Twinning was endangered by the interdisciplinary complicatedness of the field and the audacious underlying assumption of controlling water demand by the price level. A very positive aspect was that Slovenia's very young staff in administration saw an active collaboration in this international project as a chance to advance their own careers and showed ongoing consistent activity that was only hampered by the generally very high workload imposed on the exhausted staff of this small EU member country. Different working attitudes were no problem at all, given the folkloristic designation of Slovenes as "the Prussians of the Balkan" based on the century-long common history with its northern neighbours. There were no frictions between the EU member state senior partner (Germany) and junior partner (Austria) due to the friendly overall attitude of the resident Twinning advisor (RTA). His fair and empathic attitude might have added to a low level of clarity and resistance against the formalistic behaviour exhibited by the other partner. As in all such cases of international projects, final reports reflect mainly the harmonious side of completed projects. The role as EU presidency has prohibited Slovenia to succumb to a role of the recipient of "good advice". Patterns of interaction within the senior member state partner were overshadowed by relationships to the original workplace in the home country, which brought about an inclination to solve strategic issues around a small table "behind closed doors". Also here, social interactions during this exercise of social learning were not ideal, but they did not hamper the overall project success at all.

Case Twinning for Armenia

When the tool of Twinning had been transferred to the countries of the "European Neighbourhood Policy" (ENP), an additional item was introduced: authoring of the so-called "Twinning Fiche" (the tendering document clearly defining the targets and contents of the Twinning project) was also transferred to a team of two or three consultants from the European Union member states, because administrations in the ENP did not usually dispose of sufficient knowledge of EU procedures and institutions to draft this text on their own.

One of the first three Twinning fiches drafted for the Ex-Soviet Republic of Armenia was on aviation safety. For this target, two missions of two weeks and one week respectively took place and comprised mainly visits to Armenian officials in the responsible ministries in descending order of hierarchy. This process ensured the active involvement of the local government and enhanced the spirit of ownership of the institution demanding assistance before the target of meeting the criteria of the international aviation association. The main phase of this preparatory project consisted in long-hour conversations with the national experts on aviation that revealed and precisely defined the real needs of the beneficiary country for EU assistance. The findings of these conversations were moulded into a clear work plan containing clearly defined tasks for the future Twinning project.

During the month between the first and second mission the Armenian experts had the chance to review in detail the draft fiche that has also been translated into Armenian language by the translator who was part of the consultant's team. Additionally, the relative amount of manpower flowing into each expert's area of responsibility has also been clarified during a hearing convening all Armenian experts. In such a way the philosophy of partnership and peer activity was guaranteed.

In a subsequent procedure, the line DGs in Brussels expressed their review comments on the draft fiche. After these last comments had been taken into account by the team of experts, the fiche was published and the bidding procedure was able to start.

Given the highly difficult traffic situation of Armenia it is understandable that one of the first Twinnings related to aviation in order to secure the country's accessibility.

Generally, the level of intercultural understanding between European and Armenian experts was very high and no severe mismatches in working attitudes occurred.

Case Twinning for Georgia

Half a year later, a Twinning fiche preparation project on the same subject matter of aviation safety was held in Georgia. The same geopolitical circumstances were prevailing, namely the wish of a country to have access to European Union traffic schemes. Additionally, in Georgia the wish to adhere to the European Union's system of values, democratic principles and political organisations was very developed, as could be seen during numerous encounters with the local population. In a similar procedure of two missions a first draft fiche was prepared, and then reviewed by the Georgian partners and finally completed by adding a very concrete work plan that defined targets and volume of numerous short-term missions.

In both these Caucasian aviation Twinnings, the task of creating a precise and adequate list of "guaranteed results" was relatively simple, because the targets of the European aviation requirements are precise, independent of the country's characteristics and well-documented. Neither the existence of the working targets nor their concrete definition is questioned – and could not have been questioned, because they lie out of the reach of both actors. Rather, working targets are defined by an international institution that is responsible for civil aviation safety. Consequently, the task of defining the workload boiled down to attributing numbers of weekly missions to each one of the subdivisions of aviation safety requirements.

Also in this case there occurred no cultural inconsistencies between the partners as a function of different working attitudes, despite the large geographic distance. It was visible both from the numbers of European flags on public buildings and from the behaviour of "people on the street" that Georgian self-understanding was truly European. However, considerable weakening of Georgian integrity was perceived to have occurred by recent military and political issues in two northern territories of Georgia. Not even the presence of three different international bodies of observers seemed to have been able to help out of this impasse.

Case Twinning for Azerbaijan

A third project preparing a Twinning fiche took place recently in the third and largest Caucasian republic of Azerbaijan. The theme of Twinning in this case was "Vocational Education in the Field of Agriculture". At a first glance, almost all the parameters guaranteeing project success seemed to have been lower in this case: possibly a lower level of involvement on part of the beneficiary, possibly a less clear division of responsibilities among the ministries, possibly lower clarity in communication with the Twinning team and in general, and possibly a lower degree of experience with clear, objective, personality-independent ways of working.

Such first impressions have been corroborated by personal experiences with the police on the street, who took money out of our wallets during the course of a passport inspection and during other incidents with street police, who halted taxis on the highway without visible reason but only in order to bluntly ask for money from the taxi driver. An elevated level of informal economic behaviour and corruption is reported by outside perspectives, but not always by spectators from inside the country. Azerbaijan is highly ranked in the international corruption index. In almost any office of mid-level civil servants, a dozen of devotional objects such as photos, portraits, books and videos of political leaders were present in a very self-understood manner.

In parallel to this internal situation, a frozen military and political conflict with the neighbour country was perceived by citizens in an astonishing manner, taking into account only one's own national lines of argumentation and not seeing or perceiving arguments brought forth by the conflict partner.

During the first week of the mission, the impression arose among the European experts that Azerbaijani counterparts were not particularly interested in the project at all. However, with time and as a result of a repeated attempt to communicate by telephone rather than by email (typically officials have no administrative email addresses but only public domain addresses like Gmail and Yahoo) the success of communication increased substantially. Therefore, the assumption became more convincing that not a substantial lack of interest but maybe just general self-constraint and caution were the reason for unsuccessful communication in the first place.

In total, the communicative procedures in Azerbaijan were far more difficult than in the case of the other two Caucasian republics. However, final results will be achieved also there and the prospects are promising that during the three weeks of the project dedication of the actors can be generated and enhanced, even if it might not be present right from the outset.

CONCLUSION

This text has provided an overview of "dialogic learning". For complex interdisciplinary and intercultural issues, "learning" is seen as converging different and divergent world views into a common synthetic perspective on reality. Manuel Castells concept of the "network society" combines easily with such concept.

One motto of this entire volume is: how have organizations adapted to the advancement of learning options? Therefore this contribution illustrates the genesis and evolutive growth of "structural capital and social capital" which consists in common institutions, common procedures and common values of diverse individuals, communities and societies.

The target of this contribution is transcultural learning. Cultures may be delimited spatially, politically, or also mentally such as different scientific disciplines.

Consequently, the described 14 cases in this contribution

- extending on both individual and societal learning
- comprising aspects of interdisciplinary and intercultural learning settings

all attempt to illustrate that a suitable way to "make a change" in our world is to exchange and adapt our world views.

REFERENCES

Adler, P.S. & Kwon. (2002). Social Capital: Prospects for a New Concept. *Academy of Management Review*, *27*(1), 17–40. doi:10.2307/4134367

Ahamer, G. (2004). Negotiate your Future: Web Based Role Play. *Campus-Wide Information Systems*, *21*(1), 35–58. doi:10.1108/10650740410512329

Ahamer, G. (2009). A geo-referenced method to project trends into the long future. In *Proceedings of the Third Central Asia GIS Conference - GISCA'09, Austria-Central Asia Centre for GIScience ACA*GIScience*, Bishkek, Kyrgyzstan, (pp. 85-90).

Ahamer, G., Car, A., Marschallinger, R., Wallentin, G., & Zobl, F. (2009). How to map perspectives: Moving GISc to IISc. In *Proceedings of the ICIT'09 conference in* Amman, Jordan.

Ahamer, G., & Strobl, J. (2009). Learning across Social Spaces. In S. Mukerji & P. Tripathi, (Eds.), Cases on Transnational Learning and Technologically Enabled Environments. Hershey, PA: IGI Global.

Arnold, M. (2003). Intranets, community, and social capital: The case of Williams Bay. *Bulletin of Science, Technology & Society*, *23*(2), 78–87. doi:10.1177/0270467603251297

Berman, S. (1997). Civil society and political institutionalization. *The American Behavioral Scientist*, 40(*5*), 562–574. doi:10.1177/0002764297040005003

Bourdieu, P. (1997). The Forms of Capital. Education: Culture, Economy, and Society, (pp. 46-58). A. H. Halsey, H. Lauder, P. Brown, & A. S. Wells (Eds.). Oxford, UK: Oxford University Press.

Brownlow, A. (2005). A Geography of Men's Fear. *Geoforum*, *36*, 581–592. doi:10.1016/j.geoforum.2004.11.005

Burt, R. S. (2000). The network structure of social capital. *Research in Organizational Behavior*, 22, 345–423. doi:10.1016/S0191-3085(00)22009-1

Castells, M. (1996-8). *The Information Age: Economy, Society and Culture*. Cambridge, MA: Blackwell.

Chung, L. H., & Gibbons, P. T. (1997). Corporate Entrepreneurship: The roles of ideology and social capital. *Group & Organization Management*, *22*(1), 10–30. doi:10.1177/1059601197221004

Crang, M. (2000). Public Space, Urban Space and Electronic Space: Would the Real City Please Stand Up? *Urban Studies (Edinburgh, Scotland)*, *37*(2), 301–317. doi:10.1080/0042098002203

Dennis, L. (1970). Dewey's Brief for the Fine Arts. *Studies in Art Education, 11*(3), 3-8. Retrieved from http://www.jstor.org/stable/1319771

Derudder, B., Devriendt, L., & Witlox, F. (2007). An Empirical Analysis of Former Soviet Cities in Transnational Airline Networks. *Eurasian Geography and Economics*, *48*(1), 95–110. doi:10.2747/1538-7216.48.1.95

Eder, K. (2007). Europe as a particular space of communication. On the question of the social integration of a culturally heterogeneous community. *Berliner Journal fur Soziologie, 17*(1), 33-50+140.

ENP. (2009). *European Neighbourhood Policy.* See http://ec.europa.eu/world/enp/

EU. (2009). *Boosting Co-operation through Twinning*. European Commission, EuropeAid, Retrieved from http://ec.europa.eu/europeaid/where/neighbourhood/overview/Twinning_en.htm

Galileo, G. (1632). Dialogo dei due massimi sistemi del mondo, tolemaico e copernicano. Firenze.

Hargittai, E. (2008). Whose Space? Differences Among Users and Non-Users of Social Network Sites. *Journal of Computer-Mediated Communication, 13*(1), 276–297. doi:10.1111/j.1083-6101.2007.00396.x

Hyden, G. (1997). Civil society, social capital, and development: Dissection of a complex discourse. *Studies in Comparative International Development, 32*(1), 3–30. doi:10.1007/BF02696304

Jekel, T. (2007). What you all want is GIS 2.0. Collaborative GI based learning environments: spatial planning and education. In Car, A. et al. (Eds.), GI-Crossroads @ GI-Forum. Heidelberg, Germany: Wichmann.

Jekel, T. (2008a). Children Mapping Global Change. Participatory GI-Based Learning. In *Proceedings, Map India*, Noida. Retrieved from http://www.gisdevelopment.net/application/miscellaneous/mi08_227.htm

Jekel, T. (2008b), Developing spatial concepts: GI based learning in secondary education. In *Proceedings GISCA '08, KSUCTA News*, Bishkek, Kyrgyzstan.

Kenworthy, L. (1997). Civic engagement, social capital, and economic cooperation. *The American Behavioral Scientist*, 40(*5*), 645–656. doi:10.1177/0002764297040005010

Kirby, A. (2007). The production of private space and its implications for urban social relations. *Political Geography*, *27*, 74–95. doi:10.1016/j.polgeo.2007.06.010

Larsen, L., Harlan, S. L., Bolin, B., Hackett, E. J., Hope, D., & Kirby, A. (2004). Bonding and Bridging. Understanding the Relationship between Social Capital and Civic Action. *Journal of Planning Education and Research, 24*(1), 64–77. doi:10.1177/0739456X04267181

Lemke, J. L. (2000). Across the scales of time: Artifacts, activities, and meanings in ecosocial systems. *Mind, Culture, and Activity*, *7*(4), 273–290. doi:10.1207/S15327884MCA0704_03

MacGregor, S. (2002). New Perspectives for Distributed Design Support. *Journal of Desert Research*, *2*(2).

Mohan, G., & Mohan, J. (2002). Placing social capital. *Progress in Human Geography*, *26*(2), 191–210. doi:10.1191/0309132502ph364ra

Mukerji, S., & Tripathi, P. (2009). *Editorial: Cases on Technological Adaptability and Transnational Learning: Issues & Challenges, Riyadh.* Retrieved from http://www.igi-global.com/requests/details.asp?ID=588

Purcell, M. (2001). Neighborhood Activism among Homeowners as a Politics of Space. *The Professional Geographer*, *53*(2), 178–194. doi:10.1111/0033-0124.00278

Stalder, F. (2000). The Network Paradigm: Social Formations in the Age of Information. *The Information Society, 14*(1). Retrieved from http://www.indiana.edu:80/~tisj/readers/full-text/14-4%20 Stalder.html

Strobl, J. (2004). GIScience Education for Professionals – the UNIGIS Distance Learning Model. *Geospatial Today*, 6/2004.

Strobl, J. (2007). *Regional Models for Renewable Energy Potentials. Conference on "Eco-Energies for Future Generations*. Northwest Agricultural and Forestry University, Yangling, China.

Strobl, J. (2008). Digital Earth Brainware. A Framework for Education and Qualification Requirements. In J. Schiewe, & U. Michel (Eds.), Geoinformatics paves the Highway to Digital Earth. gi-reports@igf, Universität Osnabrück, S. 134-138.

Taylor, P. J., Derudder, B., García, C. G., & Witlox, F. (2009). From North-South to 'Global' South An investigation of a changing 'South' using airline flows between cities, 1970-2005. *Geography Compass*, *3*(2), 836–855. doi:10.1111/j.1749-8198.2009.00216.x

Zheng, J., & Niu, J. (2007). Computer and Computational SciencesUnified Mapping of Social Networks into 3D Space. In IMSCCS 2007, Second International Multi-Symposiums on Computer and Computational Sciences, 13.-15.8.2007, Iowa City.

ADDITIONAL READING

Acemoglu, D., Johnson, S., & Robinson, J. A. (2002). Reversal of Fortune: Geography and Institutions in the Making of the Modern World Income Distribution. *The Quarterly Journal of Economics, 117*(4), 1231–1294. doi:10.1162/003355302320935025

Acemoglu, D., & Ventura, J. (2002). The World Income Distribution. *The Quarterly Journal of Economics*, *117*(2), 659–694. doi:10.1162/003355302753650355

Adely, F. (2004). Learning and Teaching about Participatory Development: The Practical & Theoretical Challenges. *Current Issues in Comparative Education, 6*(2).

Ades, A., & Glaeser, E. L. (1999). Evidence on Growth, Increasing returns, and the Extent of the Market. *The Quarterly Journal of Economics, 114*(3), 1025–1045. doi:10.1162/003355399556205

Ahamer, G. (2001). Documentation of existing air quality measurement sites in the Slovak Republic. Report 9 in the framework of the Twinning Project SR98/IB/EN/03 on Air Quality, Bratislava, ISBN 80-88907-20-9, 250 pages, as Slovak translation: Dokumentácia existujúcich monitorovacích staníc kvality ovzdušia na Slovensku.

Ahamer, G. (2002). Twinning on air quality: comparison of results regarding the Slovak accession process. *Meteorological Journal* (Meteorologický Časopis), Bratislava, ISSN 1335-339X, *5*(1), 3-19.

Ahamer, G. (2005). Imposing A Dialogue Helps to Minimize a Potential "Clash of Cultures". In: The Challenge of the EU Enlargement, ed. by Tschandl, M., Leykam Graz, 2005, pp. 35-63.

Ahamer, G. (2005). How Accession to the EU Could Change the Atmosphere in a New Member State. In: The Challenge of the EU Enlargement, ed. M. Tschandl, Leykam, Graz, 2005, pp. 91-108.

Ahamer, G. (2005). Mutual review processes facilitate comprehension of opposed standpoints. International Conference on Interactive Computer Aided Learning (ICL05) in Villach 2005, 14 pages, see http://www.icl-conference.org/archive.htm and http://www.cti.ac.at/online-lab/ICL_Archive/2005/presentations/index.htm.

Ahamer, G. (2008). Virtual Structures for mutual review promote understanding of opposed standpoints. The Turkish Online Journal of Distance Education (TOJDE), *9*(1), 17-43, January 2008, ISSN 1302-6488, http://tojde.anadolu.edu.tr/.

Ahamer, G. (2008). Geo-strategic similarities facilitate intercultural discursive strategies. [Bishkek, Kyrgyzstan.]. *KSUCTA News*, *4*(22), 67–71.

Ahamer, G., & Wahliß, W. (2008). Guidelines for establishing a baseline scenario. Twinning Project SI06/IB/EN/01 on development of financial instruments according to the Water Framework Directive, Twinning Component 1 & 2, Ljubljana.

Baldwin, R. E., Francois, J. F., & Portes, R. (1997). The costs and benefits of eastern enlargement: the impact on the EU and central Europe. *Economic Policy*, *12*(24), 125–176. doi:10.1111/1468-0327.00018

Barro, R.J. (1999). Determinants of Democracy. *Journal of Political Economy, 107*(6)2, S158-S183.

Baumol, W. J. (1990). Entrepreneurship: Productive, Unproductive and Destructive. *The Journal of Political Economy*, *98*(5), 893–921. doi:10.1086/261712

Berding, J. W. A. (2000). John Dewey's participatory philosophy of education - Education, experience and curriculum. The History of Education and Childhood, Nijmegen University, http://www.socsci.kun.nl/ped/whp/histeduc/misc/dewey01.html.

Binder, D., Jekel, T., Mitterbauer, U., Hausmann, H., Behm, M., Wallentin, G., & Brückl, E. (2008). Schools on Ice - Bringing the IPY to the classroom. Proceedings EGU.

Collier, P., & Gunning, J. W. (1999). Why has Africa Grown Slowly? *The Journal of Economic Perspectives*, *13*(3), 3–22.

Cooper, C., Johansen, M. (2003). An evaluation of completed Twinning projects, A report presented to the National Contact Points' meeting in Brussels on 30th/31st January 2003.

Corbeil, P. (1999). Learning from Children. *Simulation & Gaming*, *30*(2), 163–180. doi:10.1177/104687819903000206

Dillard, D. (1990). Review of "Evolutionary Economics: Applications of Schumpeter's Ideas", ed. by Hanusch, H. Cambridge University Press, in: Journal of Economic Literature, 28(2), 662-664.

Frey, R. S., & Al-Roumi, A. (1999). Political Democracy and the Physical Quality of Life: the Cross-National Evidence. *Social Indicators Research*, *47*, 73–97. doi:10.1023/A:1006967124534

Grübler, A., & Nakicenovic, N. (1991). Long Waves, Technology Diffusion, and Substitution. Review 14/2 1991, 313-342, also available as RR-91-17, International Institute for Applied Systems Analysis IIASA, Laxenburg, http://www.iiasa.ac.at.

Haack, S. (2004). Pragmatism, Old and New. *Contemporary Pragmatism, 1*(1), 3–41.

Hall, R., & Jones, C. I. (1999). Why do Some Countries Produce so Much More Output per Worker than Others? *The Quarterly Journal of Economics, 114*(1), 83–116. doi:10.1162/003355399555954

Hanley, P. (2005). "Holistic yet tangible": Embracing the Challenge of Complexity for Education for Sustainable Development. *Current Issues in Comparative Education, 7*(2).

Hölbling, D., Pernkopf, M.-L., Jekel, T., & Albrecht, F. (2008). An exploratory Comparison of Metrics for Line Error. In: Car, A. et al (Eds), Geospatial Crossroads @ GI-Forum, pp. 134-139.

Jekel, T. (2008). Children Mapping Global Change. Participatory GI-Based Learning. - In: Proceedings, Map India, Noida (CD-ROM bzw. http://www.gisdevelopment.net/application/miscellaneous/mi08_227.htm).

Jekel, T. (2008). Developing spatial concepts: GI based learning in secondary education. - In: Proceedings GIS-CA, Bishkek.

Jekel, T. (2008). Plädoyer für relationale Raumkonzepte in einer Bildung für nachhaltige Entwicklung. - In: Geographie und ihre Didaktik 2/2008, p. 65-84.

Jekel, T., & Dobler, K. (2008). Kinder sind unschlagbar. Christian Vielhaber im Interview. In: Dobler, K., Jekel, T. & Pichler, H. (Hrsg), kind: macht: raum. Heidelberg: Wichmann, S. 168 – 171.

Jekel, T., Pernkopf, M.-L., & Hölbling, D. (2008), Rethinking Spatial Thinking: an empirical case study and some implications for GI-based learning. In: Donert, K. et al., Future Prospects in Geography. Liverpool.

Kok, W. (2003). Enlarging the European Union, Achievements and Challenges. Report to the European Commission, European University Institute, Robert Schuman Center for Advanced Studies, San Domenico di Fiesole, Italy.

Mitterbauer, U., & Jekel, T. (2008). Schools on Ice – Classroom Experiments on Global Change of the Cryosphere. Proceedings EGU.

Murell, P. (1996). How Far Has the Transition Progressed? *The Journal of Economic Perspectives, 10*(2), 25–44.

Naidu, S., Ip, A., & Linser, R. (2003). Dynamic Goal-Based Role-Play Simulation on the Web: A Case Study. Univ. of Melbourne, Australia, see http://www.roleplaysim.org.

Ofer, G. (1987). Soviet Economic Growth 1928-1985. *Journal of Economic Literature, 25*, 1767–1833.

OMAS Consortium. (2001). Assessment of the European Union Phare Programmes – Ad Hoc Report on the Twinning Instrument. Multi-Country Report No. S/ZZ/EUR/01006, see EU Twinning website.

Pritchett, L. (1999). Divergence – Big Time. *The Journal of Economic Perspectives, 11*(3).

Rauch, H., & Strigl, A. (2006). Die Wende der Titanic [The Turn of the Titanic], oekom, Vienna.

Richmond, B. (2001). An Introduction to Systems Thinking – Stella Software, High Performance Systems Inc., The Systems Thinking Company, compare also website at http://www.hps-inc.com.

Ristinen, R. A., & Kraushaar, J. J. (1998). Energy and the Environment, New York, 1998.

Rivera-Batiz, L. A., & Romer, P. M. (1991). Economic Integration and Endogenous *Growth. The Quarterly Journal of Economics, 106*(2), 1051–1054. doi:10.2307/2937946

Rodrik, D. (1999). Democracies Pay Higher Wages. *The Quarterly Journal of Economics, 114*(3), 707–738. doi:10.1162/003355399556115

KEY TERMS AND DEFINITIONS

Organisations: Institutionalised aggregates of inter-individual communicative structures that are strengthened by discursive processes along evolution in the long run.

Spaces of Understanding: Overlapping mindsets of individuals consisting of similar perceptions of reality.

Civilisatoric Aim: The target of long-term evolutionary development of mankind. When having the conviction that "care for the common good" pays off, and when believing that global society is a self-regulating, autoadaptive organism, it becomes clear that the target where civilisations *will* develop and where societies *should* develop are ultimately identical.

Create Meaning: If "meaning" is a non-material value in the mindset of a human that is able to trigger efforts and activities, then the creation of meaning is a profoundly human act of defining directions of future societal evolution. Optimally, "meanings" should sufficiently overlap among individuals to allow for successful intercultural evolution and development.

Geography of Perspectives: Based on the "bird's eye view" in classical cartography that perceives all possible geometric locations of an actor on the Earth's surface, a hypothetical view encompassing all possible "perspectives on complex intercultural issues" can be thought of. Such (mental or suitably documented) "map of all standpoints" can facilitate concrete intercultural work.

Social capital: Based on authors such as Bourdieu, this term was coined as an enlargement of the concepts (originally stemming from pure economics) of material stocks (capital) and human capital (educated labour force in a society). Inventing and using such term implies that social structures in a society have to be cared for during many years, have to be cultivated and represent a true value that can be invested into the further development of this society. Such structures transcend the plain material value (of any object or society); and suitable structures increase their potential for problem solving. Rendering structures suitable (i.e. social capital) is a highly energy consuming and time consuming process. Such process can also be named "institution building".

Twinning Project: Means "institution building". In order to make societal structures suitable for successfully resolving their tasks, societal learning is a suitable approach. Twinning projects (as designed and implemented by the European Commission during the last decade) are typically 1-2 year projects bringing one or more dozens of administrative experts on both EU member countries and EU candidate (or neighbouring) countries together in a well-defined process of dialogic interaction. Twinnings reshape the legislative and administrative structure of a country if it decides by own responsibility to do so.

Global Studies: A newly emerging tradition of university curricula trying to promote intercultural understanding and trying to professionalise intercultural action for any of our present-day complex interdisciplinary issues.

Environmental Systems Analysis: A unique interdisciplinary curriculum at Graz University in Austria that trains systems analytic understanding and includes professional formation in one of the five specialties economics, business administration, geography, chemistry or physics.

Surfing Global Change: A web-supported five level negotiation game suitable for university courses or real-world projects that trains consensus building for complex interdisciplinary and intercultural issues. Its rules are published in literature by one of the authors.

Chapter 2
International Collaboration for Technology Enhanced Education in Rwanda

Paul Breen
University of East Anglia, UK

ABSTRACT

This case is a case study of a collaborative project in the field of international education, within the specific discipline of teacher training. The author had an advisory role in this project which serves as a positive example of how STEP (social, technological, economic, and political) factors can be dealt with in the context of true partnership between western institutions and their counterparts in the developing world.

INTRODUCTION

Within both the academic and business worlds, and indeed further beyond into media and popular culture, there is a belief that one of the most pressing issues that must be addressed is a resolution to the growing problem of a technological gap between the developed and developing worlds, and between the rich and poor within developed societies themselves. This belief that technology can serve as the key factor in providing opportunities for learning, growth, and development can be traced back to the turn of the century, and found in references, not just in academia but also contemporary politics.

DOI: 10.4018/978-1-61520-749-7.ch002

Such instances include a speech by former United Nations Secretary General Kofi Annan to the Millennium Assembly in 1999 when he spoke of “a yawning digital divide” between developed countries, such as Japan and the US, and their less developed counterparts in Africa. He exemplified this by pointing out that at this time there were “more computers in the USA than in the rest of the world combined and more telephones in Tokyo alone than in the whole of Africa” (1999); the perception being that enhanced access would be the best means of bridging the developmental gap.

Others such as Brenda Gourley (2004), speaking about the particular context of Africa, argued that there is “no simple solution (technology) to a complex problem.” Mark Warschauer (2003), in earlier writings about technology and social inclusion, had argued that the very notion of a digital divide is somewhat oversimplified, and that knowledge is an equally important component in the battle to bridge not just the digital divide but also concurrent and interlinked divides in such areas as income, opportunity, and information.

As a means of highlighting this from a global perspective he uses case studies from across the world, similar to those found in the work of Keniston (2001), and the aforementioned Gourley (2004). The latter author offers an excellent example from the work of Lumbreras & Sanchez (1998) where new technologies, if exploited effectively, can offer light in the darkness to those who may have previously been marginalised from society. This scenario, described by Gourley, was of teachers working in Chile on a project called *Hyperstories* which "exposes blind children to a learning methodology that uses 3D sound interactive software to help them construct cognitive structures that represents their surrounding space" and aims to move the participants from darkness to what they describe as "aural vision" (2004).

Through this example, described by its creators Lumbreras & Sanchez (1998) as one that "opens a path for disadvantaged blind children to enjoy the benefits made possible by the new technologies", it is easier to readily envision how, if the affordances of technology can be exploited to overcome blindness, the same tools can be used to close the lips of Annan's (1999) "yawning" divide. Yet this project did not work with such effectiveness on the merits of technology alone, but rather found its success in allowing participants to engage with it in a meaningful and beneficial manner, as envisioned by Warschauer (2003). Common sense should dictate that there is no point in facilitating ease of access to technology, which could be defined as *process*, if there is no tangible *product* at the end of that facilitation. For that reason this paper argues strongly for pragmatic solutions as exemplified by the case study described herein.

SETTING THE STAGE

The approaches used in this paper have been heavily shaped by the writings of Brown & Rodgers (2002) research framework, and White's (2003) work in the evaluation and research of Language Learning in Distance Education. White herself draws heavily on the influence of Inglis (2001) in the selection and management of the educational domains used in distance education, Salmon's (2000) work on e-moderating and platforms for designing online courses, and Richards' (2001) studies in the fields of curriculum design and methodology used in the area of language teaching as a whole.

With regard to the abundant supply of contemporary literature on teacher education, influence has been drawn from authors who stress the importance of professionalism, personal experience and reflective practice, going as far back as Strevens (1974) and O'Brien (1981) to the more modern works of Ellis (1986), Woodward (1988), Pennington (1990), Richards & Nunan (1990), Wallace (1991), Parrott (1993), McGrath (1995), and Richards & Renandya (2002). Aside from this mainstream literature which has shaped my personal attitude to teacher education there is now a growing body of literature related to local contexts in Africa and Asia.

Brown & Rodgers (2002), in describing the process of embarking on research, argue that the main goal is "to report your findings to the world and hopefully to help reshape that world in some small measure as a result of your study" (p. 32). This is a view echoed by Silverman (2005) who suggests that case studies should be "exploratory" rather than "definitive", so that they leave enough scope for further analytical opportunities. These studies should also feature "thick" descriptions of the context and the evolution of the particular project (Lincoln and Guba, 1985). It is around this framework of a concisely described Case Study that this chapter has been formulated. The goal is not to promote the project on its own merits but rather to share its description with others in the field so that they can learn from it and apply its lessons to their own settings/context.

This case study features a teacher training project delivered to Rwandan students, through the medium of the English language and new technologies, and it serves as a positive example of how a tertiary institution in a developing country has made use of international collaboration and new technology to successfully face the demands posed by Social, Technological, Economical and Political (STEP) factors.

As an example of a society in desperate need of progress from a colonial and dismembered past to a harmonious future, thankfully there are few places in the world that can contemporarily compare with Rwanda. Prior to European colonization, Rwanda had one of Africa's most organised and unified monarchies, before being stripped of its own identity and eroded into what it is today, a heavily indebted poor country with ninety per cent of its population engaged in mainly subsistence farming, with a huge social, economic and educational disparity between urban and rural areas.

In order to rectify this situation, 22% of all public expenditure was invested in schools and educational scholarships in mainly disadvantaged areas such as Kibungo where there has been a staggering 500% growth in the demand for educational instruction since the opening of a new university of Agriculture, Technology, and Education in February 2003. Fittingly, in the context of the argument in this paper, the present government there believes that the best means of progress is through the utilisation of new technologies to empower its people with knowledge, because it was the manipulation of ignorance through propaganda that fuelled the internecine conflict of the middle nineties as explained in de Swaan's (1997) essay on the social construction of hatred.

Unfortunately, the infrastructure was unsatisfactory at the outset and the teacher supply insufficient, which is why the agricultural university wanted to foster international cooperation on an institutional level and to create a certified training course for the native teachers to set up the necessary conditions for the autonomous replication of this course in the future. On the basis of this desire to engage with new technologies and new ideas, an Italian university set out to build an online bridge of equal partnership between Rome and Rwanda, whereby a teacher training programme was designed and delivered to a group of African students. The pre-stated objective was that this course would then be replicated by the latter in the future, without the need for any further intervention from the westerners. This cross continent initiative bore the name *Twese Hamwe*, which translates as 'all together', a clever play on words that were used as a source of division during the civil war. It took as its motto the words of the Taoist philosopher Lao Tzu *(to give a man a fish, you feed him for a day, but if you teach a man to fish, you feed him for a lifetime)*, and adopted the latter part to "give someone the Net, you feed them..."

The net that connected Rome and Rwanda in the Twese Hamwe project was the World Wide Web which incorporated the use of contemporary online cooperative learning methodology and materials to deliver a training course for teacher trainers. These trainees, who were being prepared for the autonomous replication of this same course in the future, were fifteen Rwandan students, both male and female, ranging in age from middle twenties to late thirties; all of whom had lived through the civil strife. Basically the project was taught partly in real time, by Rwandan lecturers based in their home university, and Italian tutors delivering tutorial-style instruction through the medium of a Virtual Learning Environment, which in this case was MOODLE. Two factors made this delivery easier, firstly the fact that the tutors were working voluntarily and secondly that all of the trainees had prior experience of using computers and thus were able to "participate equally and fully in the learning experience" (Davis, 2006).

Although it was a small scale independent project, administered by students and staff of the Italian university, it serves as an example of what can be achieved through the medium of new technologies and how the lessons learned from such projects can be beneficial if they engender a foundation for collaboration and replication rather than being an end result in themselves, a condition which Davis (2006) defines as being "doomed to succeed." This often comes from a false sense of accomplishment in having "re-invented the online learning wheel" (ibid), as echoed by Keniston's (2001) analysis of the Indian context where pilot projects are plentiful, in the field of new technology, but rarely form part of any larger, interconnected plan with a longer term vision.

Conflicting Voices in the African Context

The absence of a long term vision has also been criticised by other voices in the African context such as Asmal (2004) who spoke of Africa being used as a laboratory "for educational experiments for external agencies" in a speech at the All-Africa Ministers' Conference on Open Learning and Distance Education. Africa's history, down from the Islamic north to the sub-Saharan south, has left the continent sceptical of the intentions of outsiders and this is a feeling that pervades much of the literature.

For example, in Cedric Taylor's seminal (1995) paper on education in South Africa, there is a description of events before and after the colonisation of the sub-Saharan region and the author details the colonial influence upon African education. He argues that the great age-old African tradition of cooperative learning *(which is now ironically very much in fashion throughout the western world)* was almost irreparably destroyed by the influence of missionary and colonial education. He asserts that this is why a noticeable discrepancy exists "between African culture, which may be seen as defining some form of cooperative learning, and the present school culture" (1995, 240).

The evidence he uses to support his argument is cited in the examples of Rwanda's close neighbours Kenya and Tanzania with the latter context also described in the much earlier work of Nyerere (1968) who bemoans the fact that "the educational system introduced into Tanzania by the colonialists was modelled on the British system." He elaborates that "inevitably too, it was based on the assumption of a colonialist and capitalist mankind instead of on his (*the native Tanzanian race*) cooperative instincts."

Returning to Asmal's (2004) speech in the light of this literature there clearly exists, within the African psyche, a lingering and justified fear of being manipulated. Yet these voices, despite their cynicism, are not necessarily saying that a combination of technology and western initiatives has no place in the contemporary world of African education. Rather, they are making two points that should be listened to carefully. Firstly, in the words of Asmal (2004), "technology is not a panacea for the challenges that confront education and training on the African continent" and secondly Africans must guard against the "uncritical introduction and adoption of distance education and the associated new technologies", in a view which has also been stated by western thinkers such as Thorpe (2002) who says that projects are not "necessarily collaborative or constructivist purely on the basis of using new technologies" (p.107).

From Asmal's speech (2004), it is apparent that he is demanding realism and informed research rather than dismissing the benefits of technology out of hand. Without a careful approach, history is possibly going to repeat itself and problems may occur, as in the example that he offers of a failed education system propounded by the World Bank in the nineteen sixties which emphasised the provision of basic education above all else, thereby cutting domestic and international funding for tertiary education and subsequently leading to "the demise of many great universities". However, it is important to note that this is the very same World Bank which is praised by other voices in the literature such as Dzvimbo's (2004) references to the Virtual Colombo Plan.

Through this, one can see that there are a range of conflicting voices in Africa at the present time and this argument extends into the fields of economics and accreditation. Perraton (2000), one of the leading voices in the literature on distance education for teacher training, may well remind his readers that "good education demands good teachers" but he also admits that today in the developed world there sometimes appears to be more concern with profit than pedagogy, as earlier stipulated by Butcher (2004) who makes the additional point that in the African context ideology often takes second place to economic arguments when it comes to the issue of distance learning.

Yet ultimately it is important to remember that Distance Learning, defined by Murray (2000) as "the traditional stepchild of most educational systems" (p.414), has been a feature of African education for decades. A significant statistic, uncovered in Yates (2004) reveals that teacher training courses account for three quarters and a half of all distance learning education courses in Francophone and Anglophone Africa respectively. This is the tradition into which the Twese Hamwe project fits, amongst other contemporary educational initiatives that have taken place across the breadth of the African continent.

CASE DESCRIPTION

Importance of Course Design

Davis (2006) writes that "building the infrastructure for online learning requires that many factors be considered, so it is difficult to provide a straightforward checklist or recipe to follow." He goes on to quote Lu (2002), writing about gases, who says that "scientists often classify systems as 'ideal' versus 'non-ideal', (more commonly understood as 'real') and "if we apply this concept we can define the ideal and then look at the deviations from ideality that manifest themselves in the real."

Others such as Keniston (2001) argue that this very obsession with the search for an 'ideal' is what hinders many of these projects from reaching their full potential, by being inhibited in their approach to 'real' analysis. Breen (2008) echoes this view by claiming that too many of these online experiments are kept as "trophies on the mantelpiece" rather than being held under the microscope for public scrutiny. In order to fully understand what a course or a case study can offer to the wider community; a goal suggested by Silverman (2005, p. 39); there has to be a clear framework for analysis and the analysis, in this instance, will begin by looking at how the course was designed.

The course was designed to run for thirty five weeks, for a total of approximately two hundred and ten hours. This was broken down into three hours per week of formal academic training in the classroom, provided by lecturers from the Rwandan university, and then one hundred and five hours of more flexible, self-paced online training managed from a distance by the tutors from the Italian university. The lecturers who provided the course from the Rwandan end were receptive to the exchange of ideas which is important because other experiences of mine, in the Korean context, suggest that sometimes there can be hostility to new ideas within the local educational territory (Breen, 2006). Unless the 'local' teachers are brought on board and made to feel as if they too are shaping the direction of the course, things can very easily break down at the interface.

In the formal classroom based lessons the Rwandan lecturers would explain theoretical and methodological aspects of the course whilst online activities, supported by the project's learning platform, would provide deeper insight into those theories explained during formal class work and provide for interaction and collaboration amongst

Figure 1. Adaptation of Salmon's framework of development. (In Salmon's work the five stages of development are sometimes illustrated in the form of a pyramid but they are detailed in tabular form below. Adapted from White's (2003:57) summary of Salmon's (2000) framework.)

Stage	Features
(1) Access and Motivation	Getting used to the computer interface and becoming familiar with the technology and courseware. Individual access and ability to use CMC is essential for participation.
(2) Online Socialisation	Participants establish their online identities and find others with whom to interact, namely the other teacher trainers in the Twese Hamwe project.
(3) Information Exchange	Participants contribute course-related information with tutors acting as guides and catalysts for discussion.
(4) Knowledge construction	Course related group discussions occur and the interaction becomes collaborative – participants move towards a stage of working amongst themselves rather than relying on the tutors for guidance.
(5) Development	Participants look to more benefits from the system to help them achieve their personal goals, explore how to integrate CMC into other forms of learning and reflect on the learning process.

participants. This again is something that has to be managed effectively because, for the project to be successful, both parts need to have equal appeal to the students. Often, there are students who do not engage fully with online materials and environments. To make them do so there had to be active encouragement from the classroom-based teachers.

The creators and tutors wanted a flexible platform which allowed teachers to put a wide range of materials online, including lesson notes, PowerPoint presentations, discussion forums, and bulletin boards. In this way it could serve as a forum for interactivity for both students and teachers and allow students to work at the course in their own time and pace. The 'ideal' format which the programme followed was a generic framework shaped around the basic principles of Salmon's (2000) five step pyramid for developing online educational courses through the medium of Computer Mediated Communication.

The framework in Figure 1 was then adapted to fit the principles of a social-constructivist model of learning, which basically holds the belief that knowledge is best constructed through social activities, with those activities in this case being conducted through the interactive platform of a Virtual Learning Environment. Many voices in the literature stress the importance of collaboration in online learning projects and constructivists argue that "learners should construct their own knowledge rather than accepting that given by the instructor" (Murphy & Cifuentes, 2001).

This, of course, is completely at odds with the way that Rwandan students have traditionally been taught across all age levels. Even though there have been many educational initiatives in Africa that employ the use of new technologies, Rwanda's slow emergence from civil war has left its developments lingering behind others such as the creation of the African Virtual University in 1997 and the implementation of the Virtual Colombo Plan which targets poverty alleviation through the increased access to and use of ICTs in education and other sectors critical to socio economic development.

Furthermore, in terms of new technologies being used to assist language learning by distance education, an excellent precedent has been created by The University of South Africa (UNISA) which has been offering a distance course in Mandarin Chinese since 1993, as described in White (2003, pp.219-220). This course has evolved and modified around the changing "generations of distance education" (ibid) particularly with the rapid advancements of the nineties through the advent of asynchronous computer based education and interactive multimedia facilities.

On top of these advances, the former President Mbeki of South Africa has advocated a network of distance learning centres scattered out across the continent, networked with each other, with universities and with government departments, which would facilitate the delivery of a range of development oriented educational programmes. Another important initiative in the African context is the University of Botswana's blended learning and online programmes detailed by Giannini-Gachago & Seleka (2005).

Research Conducted During of the Course

As the course progressed, there was ease of outside access to both student and tutor records of its progress which made it easier to conduct qualitative and quantitative research of its results. This fitted in with Davis's (2006) assertion that "ideally, the development of an e-learning system should include a plan for the independent evaluation of all aspects of the system and especially of the degree to which it enables or enhances the achievement of the stated learning outcomes". However it is important to stress that in the nature of these one-off projects, as spoken of by Keniston (2001), my own subjective perception is that there is a general reluctance amongst participants to say anything that is too critical. Therefore my research was based primarily on the subjects' thoughts and feelings rather than an analysis of the project's successes and failures.

This evaluation was carried out by means of a survey which asked three straightforward questions to the Rwandan participants on the teacher education course:

1. What do you like about the online learning platform?
2. What do you dislike about the online learning platform?
3. What do you find difficult about the platform?

Although answers were not compulsory and only nine out of fifteen trainees responded, the responses provided a valuable insight into areas of consideration for designers of courses and materials in this field. It is clearly vital to create a sense of belonging to a community of learners, in order to establish a space in which students can deliver their skills in the areas of critical thinking and expression of their own opinions. Responses also show that it is essential to have ease of access, for students, and to avoid information overload. It is similarly essential that good content is not drowned out in a sludge of inaccessibility, poor graphics, and useless information. It is also particularly important that the voice of students is listened to, that there is an open forum for discussion and partnership, and that the tutors are not just critics but also facilitators of new ideas, perhaps even incorporating student participation, which can be easily monitored in Virtual Learning Environments, into more traditional modes of assessment.

Contribution of Tutors' Thoughts to the Research

Having looked at the attitude of students to this online learning project, the next step was to examine the opinions of those at the wheel of the learning platform, as such, namely the Italians who were tutoring the Rwandans from a distance. Therefore, a set of Likert survey statements was formulated, adapted from the standard model of measuring attitudes to one that allowed for more detailed statements. The questions that were posed to the tutors concentrated on issues related to the teaching of the course, its level of interactivity, the access, the pacing, and the cost effectiveness.

1. You have enjoyed the experience of teaching on this course and as a result this course has been good for your own professional development.
2. At the beginning the tutors and students in the developing country (Rwanda) were as comfortable with the technology and the methodology used as the tutors in the developed country (Italy).
3. Students have learnt as much from this course as in a traditional classroom based teacher training course.
4. Students have participated actively in the interactive (information exchange) parts of the course i.e. bulletin boards, forum, online café, etc.
5. Students have been able to understand the different stages of the course and this has allowed it to progress at an appropriate speed.
6. More time could have been spent on the introductory phase of online socialisation.
7. Students have been comfortable with the use of Moodle as a learning platform.
8. The online socialisation phase is crucial to determining the eventual progress and development of the course.
9. At the end of this course the trainees will be able to transfer the training model to other courses inside and outside the Rwandan university with minimal guidance from the tutors in Rome.
10. Projects such as Twese Hamwe are a cost effective means of providing teacher education in developing countries.

Through these questions, I sought to find answers to how collaboration, in practical terms, was helping to cope with the demands posed by Social, Technological, Economical and Political (STEP) factors (See Figure 2).

The responses show that there were three particular points within this survey which met with very strong agreement in the eyes of most tutors. The first two were related to the areas of enjoying teaching on the course; and an acceptance that online socialisation *(building an online community)* is crucial to determining the eventual progress and development of the course. This echoed the views of students and such thinkers as Salmon (2000), Collis & Moonen (2001), and White (2003), but a very interesting slant on this issue came from one of the tutors who spoke about socialisation being a three stage process composed of student socialisation with the platform, student interaction with other students, and simultaneously student interaction with the tutors. This shows how collaboration was not restricted to discussions between the western tutors and the African

Figure 2. Responses to the Likert Survey Statements (Key: 5 = Strong Agreement 4= Agreement 3= In the Middle 2= Disagreement 1= Strong disagreement)

Name of Respondent.	Q.1	Q.2	Q.3	Q.4	Q.5	Q.6	Q.7	Q.8	Q.9	Q.10
Tutor A.	5	1	1*	3	3	1	3	5	5	5
Tutor B.	4	3	2	2	2	2	3	5	4	5
Tutor C.	4	2	3	3	3	3	3	4	4	4
Tutor D.	5	3	4	4	4	2	4	5	4	5
Tutor E.	4	2	2	3	2	3	3	5	3	4
TOTAL.	22	11	12	15	14	13	16	24	20	23
MEAN FIGURE.	4.4	2.2	2.4	3	2.8	2.6	3.2	4.8	4	4.6

N.B. Tutor A, in response to question three, felt the need to add the following comment as a footnote: *"They have learnt more, how to collaborate, how to share knowledge and how to experiment with new ways of attending lessons and studying."*

students. There was also discussion between the African students themselves.

The first of the three components is most interesting in terms of the discussion about access because it really encapsulates that idea of the online platform as an interactive force, almost a living, breathing, heaving sea, in which students play around with Lao Zhu's metaphorical net. Another fact that clearly emerged from the Twese Hamwe experience is that there must be a monitoring system built into the VLE so that the efforts of students are recorded and the material is online for practical rather than cosmetic purposes. Only in this manner can the net capture the imagination of the students.

Perhaps most crucially, in the light of winning the economic argument for collaborative education in the digital age, the third area of agreement was that projects such as Twese Hamwe are a cost effective means of providing teacher education in developing countries. Basically the largest outlay of funds in a project such as this comes at the outset when there is a need to facilitate access, accreditation, and course design. Once this has been achieved, if procedures are put in place for replication of the course, with the usage of the same materials, then long-term costs can be substantially reduced.

As stated in Butcher (2004), the case for using new technologies and digital education to cross the divide between developed countries and their less developed counterparts will only be convincing for such sceptics as Asmal (2004) when the economic benefits are proven and visible for all to see. This further supports Keniston's (2001) recommendation that these projects should be transparent and the lessons learned from them shared freely amongst others in the field. It is important to balance the costs of access with the cost of providing a quality learning experience, but few organisations or institutions are ever fully transparent or forthcoming with budgets.

In terms of policy, it is also vital that these projects are driven by pedagogic rather than economic concerns. Some sceptics often ask whether or not online courses actually work as a means of meeting the standard dictionary definition of what education is supposed to do. Indeed, this is a question that has been posed throughout much of the literature, with the underlying assumption being that the classroom based educational experience provides the yardstick to which its online mirror image should aspire.

However, with specific reference to one of the statements in the Likert survey, one of the tutors did not agree that students had learnt as much from this blended learning course as in a traditional classroom based teacher training course. Upon clarifying this response with an interview, *(which perhaps highlights the weakness of Likert surveys as a stand alone research tool)* it transpired that the respondent actually believed students can learn more in an online or blended learning domain because, in keeping with constructivist theories, there is greater demand on them to engage in their own learning process.

How Blended Learning Facilitates Collaboration?

The use of blended learning approaches provides a means of overcoming the constraints of social, technological, economic and political factors that might normally inhibit collaboration across continents and contexts. It allows overseas agencies to work in partnership and share ideas, at the stage of conception and then throughout the life of a project, and offers a relatively low-cost means of communication for educational providers in developing countries. Naturally it is not cost free, and may not even be said to be value-free, but it is a cheap solution in which benefits outweigh disadvantages. That does not mean it is either perfect or that it can serve as the aforementioned panacea but it does have a vital role to play in education in the twenty first century.

Basically, blended learning is the combination of multiple approaches to pedagogy or teaching.

Usually, as in the case of Twese Hamwe, it involves classroom-based instruction complemented by an online educational platform. Often the classroom based aspect is ignored when these projects are analysed and this is largely because there is such a wealth of literature on traditional teaching methods. It is sometimes felt that traditional classroom teaching needs no explanation or justification, but some may argue that we have entered a phase where it actually does need to defend and promote itself in order to avoid becoming the junior partner in these blended learning approaches.

As many voices in the literature, including Bersin (2004), point out, there will always be a need for teachers or experts in a particular subject area to have a physical presence in the classroom. That need should not be underestimated and in the case of this project the need was filled by Rwandan teachers from the university of Agriculture, Technology, and Education. This was not an ideal scenario in light of Rwanda itself having already identified a need to change its traditional teaching practices, but the goal was to train participants in the first course to then replicate the successive courses with themselves becoming the providers of the classroom-based aspect. It is therefore for reasons of brevity, rather than pedagogic supremacy, that this work has chosen to focus more on the online instead of the traditional classroom domain.

Online learning itself can be difficult to define in a single sentence but a range of suggestions are offered in the literature of Inglis (1999), Salmon (1998/2000), Barajas & Owen (2000), Franklin & Peat (2001), Collis & Moonen (2001), and the more recent Ally (2006) with a growing range of new ideas coming to the fore in regard to related concepts such as blended learning, in the work of Valiathan (2002) and Gonzalez (2004). Terms which are commonly listed under the umbrella heading of online learning include electronic learning *(sometimes written as e-learning)*, Internet learning, distributed learning, networked learning, tele-learning, virtual learning, computer assisted learning, Web-based learning and Distance learning. However, in the context of this report, the most suitable definition is Khan's (1997) description of online learning as "an innovative approach for delivering instruction to a remote audience, using the web as the medium."

The online platform in this instance was MOODLE, which is an acronym for Modular Object Oriented Dynamic Learning Environment, detailed on the website http://moodle.org. One advantage of Moodle is its strength in the area of presentation and pacing of lessons. Furthermore it allows tutors to build up an inexhaustible range of complementary technologies around the core technology of the VLE as advocated in Collis & Moonen (2001) and allows students themselves to build up an online library of resources over time, which was one of the project's key aims; stated as the desire to set up a shared virtual library to smooth and reduce barriers (economic, geographical and technological) to knowledge access for students and lecturers of both universities. Here, geography is seen as a barrier on the same level as social, technological, economic, and political obstacles because of the difficulties of physical access to post-war Rwanda.

The importance of self access has long been voiced in educational contexts and the equally pressing need for it in Distance Education is stressed by White (2003, p.26) who states that "self Access has occupied an important position in language learning for some two decades" and that online libraries and resource centres represent much "more than a collection of materials." Having good self access facilities empowers the learners and this empowerment of learners was another vital component of this project and one that should be sought in all ventures that feature this type of cross-world collaboration.

In the early stages of development of blended learning strategies Garrison (1997) classified it as a "balanced approach between teacher- centred relationships found in face to face education and to a lesser extent traditional distance education and the tendency to stress learner centred relationships in the emerging electronic environment."

This means that equal emphasis should be placed on both the classroom and the online domain and that a western educational style should not necessarily prevail in the pedagogic approach taken to design and delivery of the curriculum. In a case such as collaboration between Rwanda and the west this can at first seem difficult but common areas need to be unearthed in order to fully enrich the partnership ideal.

Constructivist Approach Towards Finding Common Ground

Many critics within the African context, including Annan (1999), Asmal (2004), and Gourley (2004) see a common western hegemony in the design of learning materials as being demotivational for non western students. Taylor (1995, pp.240-241) has also touched on this by giving examples of how African children have traditionally been taught through a combination of storytelling, elicitation and *ujamaa* (1995, p.243) which is a sense of familyhood or togetherness in keeping with the collaborative tradition of Africa's forgotten past. This is at variance with the way that westerners have tried to teach them throughout colonisation. Ironically, too, projects such as Twese Hamwe are now trying to get back what the colonists destroyed, answering the call of Taylor (p. 244) who says that "the time may have come for the rediscovery of the idea of cooperation in education, and for its incorporation in the ways and means by which Africa teaches its young."

He describes a particular game called "*Qash, Qash*" which translates as "Guess, Guess" and was a popular technique amongst the Xhosa people of sub-Saharan Africa "by which children shared knowledge about an idea, object phenomenon, or theme." The way in which this game was played has much in common with today's teaching methods in the fields of both language teacher education and second language education, based on strong principles of elicitation and the construction of knowledge, not that dissimilar from Woodward's (1988) theory of "loop input". The gist of this is that for hundreds of years African children have been participating in a game that is now being re-enacted in other scenarios in the classrooms of the western world that once tried to eradicate the constructive mindset in the education system of a supposedly backward continent that has still not shaken off the effects of using the outdated behaviouristic Acquisition model of teaching and learning imposed upon the continent by its European colonisers.

In following the theories espoused by Taylor (1995) and the Xhosa people *(for centuries)* the Twese Hamwe course designers needed material, images and ideas from which the Rwandan students could elicit information and ideas in order to construct knowledge for themselves. Gourley (2004) has said that it is difficult to make African students "hunger to use technological resources in the absence of local software and content." In order to make the course effective, the Rwandan students had to be able to recognise the images and artefacts they saw on screen and able to relate to what Gourley (2004) calls "the discourse or assumptions built into the text or what they hear."

The tutors of Twese Hamwe firstly asked students to reconstruct and paraphrase folk tales, from their own language into English, exchanging and comparing ideas from western folk tales with a similar theme. In the past, within a behaviouristic mindset, such a lesson would undoubtedly have been taught in the didactic manner of providing details of western fairy tales and then asking students to give a pre-judged set of responses to the morals within the stories. However the constructivist approach demanded much more than that. Students were required to think for themselves and to collaborate with their tutors so that they could then use these techniques to construct tales of their own with regard to study and experience in the context of their actual teacher education course.

Ultimately then, a balanced approach in terms of design, teaching, and provision can help sate the critical voices that exist in the literature, going as far back as Clark (1983) who famously said that "educational technologies in themselves are mere vehicles that deliver instruction but do not influence student behaviour any more than the truck that delivers groceries causes changes in our nutrition." This demand for the substantial over the superficial is echoed by Turvey (2005) who has written about the dangers connected to the fast tracking of knowledge in online courses. Moreover, Butcher (1998) has highlighted the lack of proper accreditation in some instances, especially in education for profit scenarios; and Keniston (2001), as mentioned previously, has criticised the lack of comparative studies and collaboration in the field of online learning.

Skill-Driven Approach to Blended Learning

Now that the electronic environment, referred to in Garrison (1997), has well and truly emerged, a more technical definition is provided by Valiathan (2002) who says that the term is "used to describe a solution that combines several different delivery methods" and can also be used to describe learning that "mixes various event based activities, including face to face classrooms, live e-learning and self paced learning." This latter part of the definition, which can be described as skill-driven learning, best describes the Twese Hamwe project. The reason that Twese Hamwe meets the description of a skill-driven blended learning project, when evaluated in terms of Valiathan's criteria, is that it "creates a group learning plan that's self paced but bound to a tight schedule", provides email support, designs long-term projects and demonstrates "procedures and processes through synchronous online learning labs or a traditional classroom setting" (2002).

The author then goes on to say that "this type of approach is analogous to a chemical reaction, in which interaction with the instructor or facilitator acts as a catalyst to achieve the desired reaction" which is learning and that "combining self-paced learning with facilitator support keeps the learner from feeling isolated which assists in the successful completion of the self-paced modules" (2002). This catalytic reaction is what Twese Hamwe tried to achieve. It certainly did achieve this in terms of course delivery although there was an under estimation of the amount of time that it would take Rwandan students to reverse decades, centuries even, of being taught in a behaviouristic fashion.

Using a skill driven approach can contribute to overcoming social, technological, economic, and political factors that inhibit development, especially the ability to replicate courses. In the past westerners have gone into Africa on the pretext of offering something wonderful and revolutionary but then stayed there to act as takers rather than givers. Developing countries should not serve as laboratories for the interests of their wealthier counterparts but they should not be wholly sceptical of intentions either. In this case the Rwandans, having been convinced of the worth of this project, wanted the collaboration to continue after the initial project was finished, well into the replication stage. This shows what can be achieved when partnership rather than dictatorship is utilised.

There are a great many skills that people in the western world take for granted in modern times, one of which is the ability to utilise all the affordances of new technology. This overlooks the fact that many people have never had the training to become computer literate and are further handicapped by the evident language bias of internet content, since the vast majority of material is delivered and posted through the medium of English.

CONCLUSION

In essence, Africa is a continent weary of one form of revolution and in the midst of another, "the digital revolution" as referred to in Gourley (2004). Yet there is nothing revolutionary in providing a teacher training course to African students by distance mode. The revolution comes in providing a course that is designed to allow the trainees themselves to disseminate that course to others in the future, contradicting the traditional image that Africans might have of western intentions to use their nations as laboratories.

Today's rapid developments in technology may not be the panacea for all problems in developing countries where there are a range of equally pressing social needs such as health, crime, housing and welfare, but they offer these societies self-management that has often been denied to them in the past and it is this self-management that can help them. It is also possible to use a project such as this to look beyond continental boundaries and consider other developing nations that might benefit from this type of project, such as Bangladesh described in an article by Islam and Selim (2006), where the tone is one of slight dejection that online learning is "still a dream for the less developed countries because of poor ICT infrastructure and other socioeconomic reasons."

This seems to be the case in many other developing nations, where governments still have to be convinced of the benefits of sustained investment in ICT and education in the face of many other problems. Yet, in the literature, there are sound economic and social arguments for governments supporting initiatives that make education accessible to a greater number of their citizens and projects such as Twese Hamwe make a valuable contribution to the field by providing practical examples of the theory in action.

Hopefully this one small-scale example of continents 'coming together' can add to the body of support for educational initiatives in developing countries because, to quote Olakulein and Ojo (2006), in citing Azikwe (1992) and Ocholi (1999), "studies over time have revealed that education is the most potent instrument for the emancipation of any group of people" and surely developing countries deserve emancipation from poverty and the current lack of equal educational and technological opportunity.

On the surface, one small project may not seem to offer much to a huge debate, where more expansive answers are currently being sought, but this is possibly the mistake that has been made in the search for a solution to the problem of the digital divide. The age of grand crusades to impart knowledge from the top down should have died a long time ago, and given way to a more simple approach where small scale projects and the voices of marginalised communities are brought together on a flatter plain of partnership than was offered by the hierarchical models of the past. It is also a time when more concentration should be placed on the smaller details of these courses, such as focusing on the attitudes of tutors at the interface as has been done in the research described herein.

This paper is not laying claim to the uncritical success of this project in Rwanda and nor is it elevating it to the status of a trophy on the mantelpiece, or a reinvention of the online learning wheel (Davis, 2006). It has simply shown an example of what can be implemented and achieved with new technologies, and how the knowledge gained from such small scale projects can be put to broader use in the field of online learning, if people pool their knowledge, learn from their mistakes, and create clear blueprints for the future, dictated by pedagogic rather than purely economic principles. It has also proven that some interesting lessons can be shaped from the most basic of sources *(in this case folk stories)* when there is a combination of motivation, creativity, and technology.

Of course giving people access to technology is not enough on its own. That alone shall not empower those who are currently alienated, marginalised, disaffected, computer-illiterate, or under-utilising the power of new technology to educate themselves or in the case of teachers, to educate their students in a more engaging and interactive manner. Users, and not just creators of digital education resources, also need access to a form of partnership that in all cases does not have to be or indeed cannot be a partnership of equals, but rather a partnership that means having the right to have their voices heard.

Access is the key to opening doors to an era where social, technological, economic, and political problems can be overcome, remembering that access to machines alone will not make the world a better place in the twenty first century. Rather, as suggested by Warschauer (2003), there must be equilibrium of access to knowledge, education, opportunity, creation, and employment. Only then can there be a true achievement of the task of giving people a net to feed from the seas of knowledge for a lifetime.

We are all learners in this new age, from the students we teach, and the societies we assist, to teachers themselves who, in the words of Yates (2004) are "gatekeepers of culture and guardians of democracy" in this era when individual identities often seem to get lost in the great rush towards globalisation.

Being a learner in this age, though, is different to the past. This is an age where both learners and tutors, recipients and creators, need to work in the kind of partnership that made the Twese Hamwe project successful in building a foundation for the future.

Through this, social, technological, economical, and political obstacles can be overcome for the betterment of all. Twese Hamwe offers evidence that it is possible for western agencies to establish projects that are initially based on partnership and collaboration and can eventually be passed into a state of total ownership for those developing countries that choose to utilise the benefits of this evolving medium. It is vitally important though that one should not underestimate the barriers that can be presented by STEP factors, particularly with regard to political and economic issues.

There are serious challenges that still need to be addressed in the coming century, regardless of the technological advances of the one that has come before, but so long as there is international collaboration across continents, contexts, and institutions there will be substantial progress made in overcoming these often tenacious obstacles.

REFERENCES

Ally, M. (2006). Foundations of Educational Theory for Online Learning. In Theory and Practice of Online Learning. Athabasca, Canada: Athabasca University Publications, Athabasca University.

Annan, K. (1999). Speech given to the Millennium Assembly. In Gourley, B. (2004). *'The Digital Divide: Solution or Problem.'* Paper Presented at the All Africa Ministers Conference on Distance Education.

Asmal, K. (2004). *Prospects, Possibilities and Perils: Distance education's response to Africa's development needs.* Paper Presented at the *2004 All Africa Ministers Conference on Distance Education*, Cape Town, South Africa. Retrieved November 8, 2007 from http://www.polity.org.za/article.php?a_id=46293

Barajas, M., & Owen, M. (2000). Implementing virtual learning environments: looking for a holistic approach. *Educational Technology and Society*, *3*(3), 39–53.

Bersin, J. (2004). The Blended Learning Book: Best Practices, Proven Methodologies, and Lessons Learned. San Francisco, CA: Jossey-Bass.

Breen, P. (2006). The Education of Language Teachers in East Asia. *Asian EFL Journal, 13*(1). Retrieved from http://www.asian-efl-journal.com/pta_july_06_pb.php

Breen, P. (2008). Maritime Lessons for the Digital Age. *Research Paper on how online learning can make a positive contribution to British universities - submitted to Association of Learning Technology Conference 2008.*

Brown, J. D., & Rodgers, T. S. (2002). Doing Second Language Research. New York: Oxford University Press.

Butcher, N. (2004). *Financing Distance Education Programmes in African Education: A Guide for Sound Investment.* Paper presented at the All-Africa Minister's Conference on Open Learning and Distance Education.

Clark, R. E. (1983). In Taylor, J. (1995), Distance Education Technologies: the fourth generation. *Australian Journal of Educational Technology, 11*(2), 1–7.

Collis, B., & Moonen, J. (2001). Flexible Learning in the Digital Age. London: Kogan Page.

Davis, A. (2006). Developing an infrastructure for online learning. In T. Anderson & F. Elloumi (Eds.), *Theory and Practice of Online Learning.* Athabasca, Canada: AUPress. Retrieved April 7, 2007 from, http://cde.athabascau.ca/online_book/ch4.html

Dornyei, Z. (2001). Teaching and Researching - Motivation. Upper Saddle River, NJ: Pearson Education Limited.

Dzvimbo, K. B. (2004). *The Challenges and Potential of Distance Teaching and Open Learning in Africa: Experiences from the African Virtual University.* Paper presented at the All-Africa Minister's Conference on Open Learning and Distance Education.

Ellis, R. (1986). Activities and procedures for teacher training. *ELT Journal, 40*(2), 91–99. doi:10.1093/elt/40.2.91

Franklin, S., & Peat, M. (2001). Managing change: The use of mixed delivery modes to increase learning opportunities. *Australian Journal of Educational Technology, 17*(1), 37–49.

Garrison, D. R. (1997). Computer conferencing: the post industrial age of distance education. *Open Learning, 12*(2), 3–11. doi:10.1080/0268051970120202

Giannini-Gachago, D., & Seleka, G. (2005). Experiences with international online discussions. Participation patterns of Botswana and American students in an Adult Education and Development course at the University of Botswana. *International Journal of Education and Development using ICT, 1*(2).

Gonzalez, C. (2004). The Role of Blended Learning in the World of Technology. In G. Siemens, (2005). *Connectivism: A Learning Theory for the Digital Age.*' Retrieved July 13, 2006 from: http://www.itdl.org/Journal/Jan-05/article01.htm

Gourley, B. (2004). *The Digital Divide: Solution or Problem.* Paper presented at the All-Africa Minister's Conference on Open Learning and Distance Education.

Inglis, A. (2001). Selecting an integrated electronic learning environment. In F. Lockwood & A. Gooley (eds.), Innovation in Open and Distance Learning: Successful development of online and web based learning. London: Kogan Page.

Islam, M.T., & Selim, Abu Sadeque Md. (2006). Current Status and Prospects for E-Learning in the Promotion of Distance Education in Bangladesh. *Turkish Online Journal of Distance Education – TOJDE, 7*(1), Article 11.

Keniston, K. (2001, December). *IT for the Common Man: Lessons from India, MN Srinivas Memorial Lecture.* Bangalore: National Institute of Advanced Studies, India Institute of Science. [MIT published as a working paper in 2002].

Khan, B. (1997). Web Based Instruction - What is it and why is it? In B.H. Khan, (ed.) Web based instruction (pp. 5-18). Englewood Cliffs, NJ: Educational Technology Publications.

Lincoln, Y., & Guba, E. (2000). Paradigmatic controversies contradictions and emerging influences. In N. Denzin & Y. Lincoln (Eds.), Handbook of Qualitative Research, (pp.162-88) (2nd ed.). Thousand Oaks, CA: SAGE.

Lu, M. (2002). Spark Notes Study Guide on ideal gases. In A. Davis, (2006), Developing an Infrastructure for Online Learning. Theory and Practice of Online Learning.

Lumbreras, M., & Sanchez, J. (1998). 3D aural interactive hyperstories for blind children. In *Proceedings of the 2nd European Conference on Disability, Virtual Reality and Associated Technologies*, Skovde, Sweden, 1998.

Mcgrath, I. (1995). Feeding, Leading, showing, throwing: Process Choices in Teacher training and Trainer Training, in Learning to Train: Perspectives on the Development of Language Teacher Trainers. (pp. 162-172). Upper Saddle River, NJ: Prentice Hall Europe in association with the British Council.

Meyer, K.A. (2003). Face to face versus threaded discussions: the role of time and higher order thinking. *JALN, 7* (3).

Motteram, G. (2001). The role of synchronous communication in fully distance education. *Australian Journal of Educational Technology, 17*(2), 131–149.

Murphy, K. L., & Cifuentes, L. (2001). Using Web Tools, collaborating and learning online. *Distance Education, 22*(2), 285–305. doi:10.1080/0158791010220207

Nyerere, J. K. (1968). Freedom and Socialism. Dar es Salaam, Tanzania: Oxford University Press.

Olakulein, F. K., & Olugbenga, D. (2006). Distance Education as a Women Empowerment Strategy in Africa. Turkish Online Journal of Distance Education – TOJDE January 2006, 7(1), Article 14.

Parrott, M. (1993). Tasks for Language Teachers. Cambridge, UK: CUP.

Pennington, M. C. (1990). A professional development focus for the language teaching practicum. In Richards & Nunan (Eds.), pp.132 – 151.

Perraton, H. (2000). Open and Distance Learning in the Developing World. London: Routledge.

Richards, J., & Nunan, D. (Eds.). (1990). Second Language Teacher Education. Cambridge, UK: Cambridge University Press.

Richards, J. C. (2001). Curriculum Development in Language Teaching. Cambridge, UK: Cambridge University Press.

Richards, J. C., & Renandya, W. (2000). (Eds.). Methodology in Language Teaching: An Anthology of Current Practice. Cambridge: Cambridge University Press.

Salmon, G. (1998). Developing learning through effective online moderation. *Active Learning, 9.*

Salmon, G. (2000). E-moderating: The key to teaching and learning online. London: Kogan Page.

Silverman, D. (2005) Doing Qualitative Research. London: SAGE.

Strevens, P. (1974). Some basic principles of teacher training. *ELT Journal, 29*(1), 19–27.

dSwaan, e, A. (1997). Widening Circles of Disidentification. On the Psycho- and Sociogenesis of the Hatred of Distant Strangers. Reflections on Rwanda. *Theory, Culture & Society, 14*(2), 105–122. doi:10.1177/026327697014002010

Taylor, C. (1995). *Cooperative Learning in an African Context.* Accessed via www.selu.edu/Academics/Faculty/ dshwalb/files/Cooperative_Learning.pdf

Taylor, J. (1995). Distance Education Technologies: the fourth generation. *Australian Journal of Educational Technology, 11*(2), 1–7.

Thorpe, M. (2002). Rethinking Learner Support: the Challenge of On-line Learning. *Open Learning, 17*(2), 105–120.

Turvey, K. (2005). Elearning, efacilitation, ecommunities, epedagogies: a professional standpoint based on evidence. *Reflecting Education, 1*(1-2), 24–40.

Valiathan, P. (2002). *Blended Learning Models.* Retrieved July 13, 2006 from http://www.learningcircuits.org/2002/aug2002/valiathan.html

Wallace, M. (1991). Training Foreign Language Teachers: A Reflective Approach. Cambridge, UK: Cambridge University Press.

Warschauer, M. (2003). Technology and social inclusion: Rethinking the digital divide. Cambridge, MA: MIT Press.

White, C. (2003). Language learning in distance education. Cambridge, UK: Cambridge University Press.

Woodward, T. (1988). Loop Input. Exeter, CT: Pilgrim Publications.

Yates, C. (2004). *Teacher Education at a Distance: Lessons and Experience from Sub Saharan Africa.* Paper presented at the All-Africa Minister's Conference on Open Learning and Distance Education, 2004. http://moodle.org (n.d.). Retrieved 10th May 2009.

ADDITIONAL READING

Anderson, N., & Henderson, M. (2004). e-PD: blended models of sustaining teacher professional development in digital literacies. *E-Learning, 1*, 383–394. doi:10.2304/elea.2004.1.3.4

Conole, G., & Dyke, M. (2004). What are the affordances of information and communication technologies? *ALT-J, 12*, 113–124. doi:10.1080/0968776042000216183

Delfino, M., & Persico, D. (2007). Online or face-to-face? Experimenting with different techniques in teacher training. *Journal of Computer Assisted Learning, 23*, 351–365. doi:10.1111/j.1365-2729.2007.00220.x

Garrison, R., & Anderson, T. (2003). E-Learning in the 21st Century: AFramework for Research and Practice. New York: Taylor and Francis.

Garrison, R., Anderson, T., & Archer, W. (2000). Critical Inquiry in a Text-Based Environment: Computer Conferencing in Higher Education. *The Internet andHigher Education, 2*, 87-105.

Ginns, P., & Ellis, R. (2007). Quality in blended learning: Exploring the relationships between on-line and face-to-face teaching and learning. *The Internet and Higher Education, 10*, 53–64. doi:10.1016/j.iheduc.2006.10.003

Gulati, S. (2004). Constructivism and emerging online learning pedagogy: a discussion for formal to acknowledge and promote the informal. *Annual Conference of the Universities Association for Continuing Education - Regional Futures: Formal and Informal Learning Perspectives*, Centre for Lifelong Learning, University of Glamorgan, April 2004.

Hawkridge, D. (2003). The Human in the Machine: Reflections on Mentoring at the British Open University. *Mentoring & Tutoring*, 11.

Hughes, G. (2007). Using blended learning to increase learner support and improve retention. *Teaching in Higher Education*, *12*, 349–363. doi:10.1080/13562510701278690

Kelly, P., Gale, K., Wheeler, S., & Tucker, V. (2007). Taking a stance: promoting deliberate action through online postgraduate professional development. *Technology, Pedagogy and Education*, *16*(2), 153–176. doi:10.1080/14759390701406760

Laurillard, D. (2007). Technology, pedagogy and education: concluding comments. *Technology, Pedagogy and Education*, *16*, 357–360. doi:10.1080/14759390701614496

Motteram, G. (2006). 'Blended' education and the transformation of teachers: a long-term case study in postgraduate UK Higher Education. *British Journal of Educational Technology*, *37*, 17–30. doi:10.1111/j.1467-8535.2005.00511.x

Olapiriyakul, K., & Scher, J. (2006). A guide to establishing hybrid learning courses: Employing information technology to create a new learning experience, and a case study. *The Internet and Higher Education*, *9*, 287–301. doi:10.1016/j.iheduc.2006.08.001

Paulus, T., Woodside, M., & Ziegler, M. (2006). Creating a Climate of Engagement in a Blended Learning Environment. *Journal of Interactive Learning Research*, 17.

Puntambekar, S. (2006). Analyzing collaborative interactions: divergence, shared understanding and construction of knowledge. *Computers & Education*, *47*, 332–351. doi:10.1016/j.compedu.2004.10.012

Roberts, T. (2004). Online Collaborative Learning: Theory and Practice, Hershey, PA: Idea Group Publishing.

Rovai, A., & Jordan, H. (2004). Blended Learning and Sense of Community: A comparative analysis with traditional and fully online graduate courses. *International Review of Research in Open and Distance Learning*, *5*, 1–13.

Salaberry, M. (2001). The Use of Technology for Language Learning and Teaching: A Retrospective. *Modern Language Journal*, *85*, 39–56. doi:10.1111/0026-7902.00096

Salmon, G. (2002). E-tivities: The Key to Active Online Learning. London: Kogan Page.

Sehrt, M. (2003). Digital Divide into Digital Opportunities: E-Learning in the Developing Countries. *UN Chronicle*, 40.

Singh, H. (2003). Building Effective Blended Learning Programs. *Educational Technology*, *43*, 51–61s.

Warschauer, M. (2003a). Demystifying the Digital Divide. *Scientific American*, *289*, 42. doi:10.1038/scientificamerican0803-42

Warschauer, M. (2003b). Technology and Social Inclusion: Rethinking the Digital Divide. Cambridge, Massachusetts: MIT Press.

Wettasinghe, M., & Hazan, M. (2006). Motivating learners in an online collaborative environment using a blended model for enhanced learning. FORMATEX 2006.

KEY TERMS AND DEFINITIONS

Blended Learning: An educational approach that espouses a combination of traditional classroom teaching and online delivery of learning materials.

Case Study: Research performed in detail on a single case in order to give an insight into characteristics of the broader population of similar or diverse cases.

Construct/Construction: The process of building something over a period of time, which in the context of education usually refers to skills and knowledge.

Constructivism: This is a learning theory which advocates the view that learners construct theories and models of the world around them by actively engaging with their social surroundings.

Digital Divide: The assumed disparity in access to new technologies for the developing world in comparison with the developed world.

Hyperstories: A conceptual model for developing interactive stories delivered in a hypermedia format using educational software and the notion of virtual worlds. Users build up their own narrative whilst navigating a path through the virtual world. These virtual worlds can assume any format from everyday life to Dungeons and Dragons type fantasy situations.

Online Courses: Courses that are delivered either partially or exclusively by means of computer, usually through the medium of a Virtual Learning Environment or similar multimedia platform.

Trophies on the Mantelpiece: Phrase coined by myself to describe the tendency for self congratulation and use of projects for purposes of display rather than serious analysis.

Virtual Learning Environment or Online Learning Platform: A Virtual Learning Environment is a software system designed for educational purposes which uses the medium of the Internet to facilitate delivery of online courses and learning materials.

Chapter 3
Transnational Learning and Collaboration in Delivering MBA Programs in Emerging Markets:
The Challenge of National Culture

Stephanie Jones
Maastricht School of Management, The Netherlands

ABSTRACT

This case focuses on the challenges of delivering Western-style MBA programs in emerging markets, looking at the experience of the Researcher in teaching and assessing courses within management programs (especially in Organizational Behavior and Human Resource Management) and in thesis and dissertation research and writing. The case considers: cultural differences, learning style differences, language differences, economic backgrounds of students, classroom behavior and etiquette, involvement in the learning process, teaching methods, the teacher and the students, group work, examining and evaluating, assignments, projects and reports, theses and major pieces of research-based work, life in the classroom, inter-student behavior, and life out of the classroom. The case focuses on MBA course delivery in China, the Arab World, Africa, Iran, Malaysia and Indonesia, Vietnam, Eastern Europe, former Russian states such as Kazakhstan, and South America, such as Peru and Suriname. Examples of specific MBA teaching and assessment are provided to give in-depth insights into the issues involved.

ORGANIZATION BACKGROUND

The organization under reference in this case is one of the leading Schools of Management in the Netherlands. The school has more than 20 transnational learning collaborations across the developing world. Some of these collaborations have been in operation for over ten years and have produced as many as 1,000 MBA graduates per single academic partnership. Overall, nearly 1,000 graduates emerge from all the collaborations annually.

DOI: 10.4018/978-1-61520-749-7.ch003

SETTING THE STAGE

MBA programs from "the West" are now increasingly being delivered in emerging markets, such as in Asia, Africa and Middle East. An MBA from a reputable and accredited international business school or university enables students in these countries to join international companies, become expatriates, earn significantly more money, and gain elite status in society. For the MBA providers, this expansion possibility internationally – together with online and distance courses – can facilitate these business schools and universities to increase revenues and remain competitive. This can be both outbound – the providers go to them – and inbound – they come to the providers. Here, the focus is on the former scenario – transnational learning provided by the School of Management considered here through collaboration with partners (mostly other universities or business schools) in China and the countries of Africa, The Middle East, South-East Asia, South America, Eastern Europe, etc.

CASE DESCRIPTION

The following case study has been based on the experience of the Researcher in four and a half years of teaching around the world, following four years of delivering "Western" style MBAs whilst based in one of the countries of the Middle East.

MBA program delivery outbound to emerging markets can present completely new challenges, especially for faculty. The students behave in completely unexpected ways, and demand unheard of – and sometimes quite unacceptable – new arrangements. These can include issues of academic integrity and other matters relating to academic standards. The students ask for special treatment with more time to finish assignments and examinations, want to attend less than the full hours of study, expect compromising insights into the assessment items, resist individual accountability, refuse to accept rules about plagiarism, and admire those who can hoodwink or otherwise undermine authority. These issues can be seen as reflecting cultural norms: high power distance, uncertainty avoidance, ascribed leadership, collectivism, synchronism and diffuseness, particularistic behaviors and other national cultural concepts identified in by theorists in the literature.

This case study has aimed to identify the cultural barriers to successful MBA delivery in emerging market contexts and to recommend strategies for maintaining product quality and integrity, through evidence-based research to help decision-making for hands-on faculty members and the initiators of international partnerships, who should take these operational, delivery issues into account when preparing their strategies. This can be seen as a perspective for technology-related issues, which must take the socio-cultural-economic aspects of transnational learning initiatives into account.

In summary, the rationale for this case study stems from the fact that more and more MBA courses are being launched in emerging markets, despite the overall worldwide recession; that this represents an ongoing challenge for teachers of these courses, sometimes ill-prepared for these environments, given the lack of orientation provided to them; and the existence of considerable cross-cultural issues, which are rarely explored in detail. Teachers of executive courses, language teachers, aid workers and all visiting expatriate teachers and consultants focused on emerging market participants will also probably face these and similar issues. How can MBA faculty in particular gain insights to overcome cross-cultural barriers, keep up standards of the course and product, and manage multicultural training groups in the best way they can? Technology can be both an enabler and a barrier here. The standardization of course materials, the ability to electronically send materials in advance, the use of technology in the classroom when delivering the program – all these have benefits and drawbacks. These issues are discussed in detail in the following case.

CURRENT CHALLENGES FACING THE ORGANIZATION

The faculty members of the School of Management considered here spend much of their time teaching MBA (and doctoral-level, DBA) courses to emerging market students in their own locations, at the premises of the partner institution. Through trial and error and some sharing of experiences, the faculty members encounter (and try to cope with) many challenges. In some countries, these challenges include technology-related issues based on intermittent electricity supply, lack of internet connectivity, supply of outdated hardware and software and lack of funds to purchase laptop computers, etc. Other countries have advanced technology but significant language barriers (all the courses are taught in English). Some countries experience students using technology to circumvent accurate assessment (i.e. cheating such as plagiarism). But this mostly tacit knowledge of these challenges and how to deal with them is rarely shared outside the organization – hence this case study.

Most of the research on the challenges of teaching MBA students seems to be focused on the USA and Europe, without much attention to emerging market MBA students, despite impressive statistics, and upward trends in emerging-market student MBA enrollments.

However, there are significant cultural barriers to successfully delivering MBAs to emerging-market students. There are issues in terms of creating sustainable programs which build local capacity, of both faculty and students, including developing the necessary technology. There can be pressure to compromise on academic standards. Many students are unable to successfully complete the programs. Some of these programs are failing and closing, and even this school – which enjoys a strong track record of partnerships – has to pull out of a program occasionally. More practical insights are needed into many aspects of these programs, including the critical issue of cultural challenges in program delivery. The faculty members involved in this delivery process, often finding themselves the bastions of the academic standards of the MBA provider, are trying to prevent "the debasing of the coinage" – yet most MBA deliverers in emerging markets are "reinventing the wheel". They do not often learn from their predecessors (many of whom are unknown to them, are competitors, and as mentioned above, the most vital knowledge is of a tacit nature). There is a particular concern among many faculty with cultural differences and attitudes which can compromise the quality of the product which the provider has developed and on which its reputation depends.

TRANSNATIONAL LEARNING AND COLLABORATION ISSUES

Cultural Differences

In coping with these issues, there is a need to basically understand the theoretical framework to national cultures: power distance, uncertainty avoiding behaviors, individualism and collectivism, sequential and synchronistic behaviors and other dimensions, derived from theorists such as Hofstede (1984, 1991, 1993) and Trompenaars (1997). This basic understanding of cross-cultural management theory can help, but it won't guarantee success – cultural stereotypes can be misleading and all students are different – especially would-be MBAs, always the elite of the local society. It is clearly important for teachers to be culturally sensitive, as there is a heightened risk of exposure of cultural prejudices, which might be tolerated at the home campus. The relevance of the historical, social, political and religious context of each country must be appreciated, as these can impact on students. Technology tends to straddle different cultures, and possession of the latest technological aids is a source of status to consumer-conscious and social-climbing MBA students in emerging markets. They expect teachers coming from the West to understand and use the latest teaching technology. They criticize local teachers for old-fashioned 'chalk-and-talk' methods, and look to visiting foreign professors to use web-based materials, interactive technology, video-clips and other multimedia teaching aids. This is particularly challenging when the teaching environment provided by the local partner lacks a reliable electricity supply and internet connection. The visiting faculty member is then the butt of complaints, most of which are completely outside his or her domain.

Learning Style and Content Differences

This former issue of learning style can have a relationship with culture, in terms of preferences for visual, aural, oral, and written information and learning materials. The ways in which students learn in emerging market environments and the ability to concentrate, and the length of concentration span, often have a cultural dimension. In the latter issue of content differences, for many faculty members, the challenge of arousing interest and creating curiosity in presenting completely new material, which may be unrelated to the experience of the students, is always there. Taking ideas imported from the West, including concepts of employee empowerment and autonomy, and presenting these in command-and-control leadership environments, is often received with incomprehension, doubt or hostility – or all three emotions. The use of technology here can help visually-oriented students and can be used to present course content in a way which can be more attractive and acceptable than in a plain written/printed format. However, there can be a danger of over-simplification of material, the use of distracting transitions and animations obscuring real information, and more interest in the delivery vehicle than the content.

Language Differences

The implications of teaching courses in English when many of the students are not fully conversant in the language; the use of group-based and practical study techniques to allow participants and students to operate in their own language; the challenges of teaching through a translator/interpreter; the assessment of the work of these participants and students, alone and in partnership with local teachers; the teacher's need to understand the classroom discussions, when these need to be translated back; these are all important transnational learning issues. Sometimes the pronunciation of English by some students is more challenging to visiting professors than the students' vocabulary or grammar. Some students, especially from wealthier backgrounds, have been toying with the use of speech-recognition technology to save their time in transcribing interviews, etc. When inadequately edited by the students, this creates challenging reading for the faculty members.

Economic Backgrounds

The socio-economic level of the students and participants, in terms of being hard-working achievers or wealthy aristocrats, is a further issue. Study time can involve a sacrifice of much-needed potential income for some students; others expect to buy qualifications without studying, like buying a new car. There is a further challenge in teaching and assessing members of the country's royal family, who own the university, for example. All of these issues can compromise the fair and meritocratic treatment of students in the teaching process. The more wealthy students have access to a higher level of technology, so it can be seen as important for teachers to create a level playing field for all participants in the program.

Classroom Behavior and Etiquette

This issue includes attendance, punctuality, mobile phone usage; emailing and sending text messages during class-time; side-talking; the constant in-and-out of the classroom behavior of students making and receiving phone calls, and smoking and chatting outside the classroom regardless of official breaks. The tolerance of lax classroom discipline can lead to tolerance of non-completion of assessment items, late submissions and a feeling by students and participants that they can get their MBA Certificate and still get away with whatever they like. Many students in emerging markets are trying to demonstrate their perceived higher status in society, or are showing their attitude of 'buying' their qualifications, and thus disregarding the authority of their teachers. Other cultures show an immediate respect for their teachers, which can be sustained throughout the course or can be lost when the teacher is perceived to be indulgent and easy-going. The use of individual communications technology in the classroom – which many faculty members did not experience when they were students themselves – puts more pressure on teachers to either 'act the policeman' and ban these items – or try to make the class sufficiently interesting to hold the students' attention.

Involvement in the Learning Process

Related to the above points, this issue considers classroom behavior during instruction, including the students making notes or just sitting at the desk; and the presence or absence of learning accessories, such as pen and paper, or just mobile phone and car keys. What is the attitude of students to their classroom experience in terms of expectation of entertainment value, or of the need to work and study? Is there a preference for "interesting" classes, or desire to maximize potential learning by attending all classes, whatever the subject might be? How do the students feel about the sharing of ideas, or do they prefer to keep quiet and wait for others? Do they expect the teacher to provide all of the learning opportunities, and show scant regard for the contributions of other students, such as side-talking whilst other students are speaking in class? Do the students tend to actively participate in the class or do they think that being an empty vessel into which information should be poured is OK? All these issues can result in variations in student performance which does not necessarily reflect an accurate summary of their academic abilities, and can also be reflected in faculty evaluations. There is always the problem that many students think that if they possess the content materials – without actually reading them – then the information will magically be transmitted into their brains without any effort on their part. The same thinking applies to hard copy books and print-outs as it does to soft copy documents. When asked if they read an article sent by email, some students explain (and perhaps believe) that they downloaded it and saved it to their hard drive, which is 'doing the work' and as much as they are prepared to do!

Teaching Methods

Continuing from the point above, this issue considers the role of lectures and the degree of participation in these, in terms of asking and answering questions; the extent and nature of reading assignments; the use of handouts and textbooks and the requirement to read these; presentations with PowerPoint slides and their effectiveness; the value of cases, examples, guest speakers, videos and films, current events and newspaper clippings, and the overall need for variety in the use of teaching methods and materials. Teachers used to a high level of participation can find it difficult to vary their teaching methods to get more results, and may not give accurate marks because students are unused to their approach (as above). There is a problem with video clips that students watch them in a mindless way and switch off mentally, whereas they might be forced to concentrate with a more conventional presentation. Business case examples – especially those presented in a visual and practical way – can be attractive to students, but many regard them as entirely academic and not relevant to their own experience. Many excellent guest speakers – with many years of experience behind them – can be interesting to students – but in some cases they are also subjected to the 'technology-test'. If their PowerPoint slides lack sophistication, if their presentation lacks any multimedia content, they can be seen as 'old-fashioned'. This is less of a problem with more mature students, who see through presentation issues and are more interested in content – but these are not necessarily the kind of students encountered in some emerging markets.

The Teacher and the Students

The impact of the personal experiences of the teacher on the learning experience, and that of the students, can be a further issue. The differing appeal of the teacher and the subject can influence the teaching outcome, and this is more the case in some cultures than in others. Some students are most influenced by the teacher, regardless of the subject. The level of dependence of the students on their teacher also varies: can they study independently or do they require a high level of direction? Students from cultures expecting a high level of 'spoon-feeding' who do not receive this can be highly critical of visiting faculty, and the latter may feel that this requirement is beyond their obligations. This can be seen in cultures where students pay their money and expect a high level of service, such as staying in a five star hotel; in other cultures the level of dependence is the same, but stems from huge respect for the teacher and reluctance to challenge his or her views. Such students are anxious to please and, being of a strong uncertainty-avoiding culture, are afraid of 'making mistakes' and 'doing the wrong thing'. Teachers from cultures which accept a high level of ambiguity can become frustrated and irritated by students insisting on a huge level of detail in every instruction, such as font size, margins and headers in an essay and exact pages of the textbook to be read for revision.

Group Work

The issue of the learning value in the interaction between group members is culturally-loaded, and teachers assuming that group work can lead to positive learning outcomes are not always on the right track. Some students show perceptions of superiority and inferiority in relationships with others, and the mixing of genders in groups can be problematic in some cultures. In Saudi Arabia, for example, there can be a screen in the classroom between male and female students, or even separate classes. Even in some of the more modern cities of the Middle East, seen as open and Western, some students refuse to sit in a mixed gender group for discussion. Experience with group projects and the perception of their value is therefore varied. Equality of contribution between group members can be an issue. There can be differing attitudes towards group-based games and simulations, in terms of taking them seriously. The attitudes towards practical activities, compared with the expectation of chalk-and-talk lecturing, can mean that although students enjoy them – particularly the visually-oriented multimedia-based exercises – they see them as entertaining rather than academically useful. There is clearly a need for careful facilitation and interpretation here. The value of group outings to companies, factories etc. can be questioned. Members of some cultures refuse to board a bus with other students, insist on coming in their own cars, and arrive late or cannot find the destination. Some cultures are much less individualistic than others, and depend on group work to get through the programs; it can be important to offset this with some individual assessments, otherwise the results may not be accurate. Some expatriate students attending classes in the countries of emerging and rich markets find themselves doing 'all the work' for their group-mates. What you said is completely true but for publication, it can be moderated to avoid any confrontation at the later stage.

Examination and Evaluation

As this is an academic course, there will be a need for written examinations at the end of each MBA program, and this can be a challenging cultural issue. Should these assessments be held in examination conditions or as take-home exams? When operating with open-book exams, even in exam conditions, there can be issues of marking-up the textbook and bringing-in crib-sheets. Cheating and copying others during the exams can be seen as culturally acceptable, and can even be considered as admired behavior in some cultures. MBAs generally are increasingly seen as having a tendency to cheat (Reeves & Knell, 2009). The use of model exam answers is often demanded by students, who want to do everything 'exactly right'. Faculty members from different cultures are concerned with the impact on creativity and originality, especially in more 'soft skill' courses. The announcing of exam performance and the giving and receiving of feedback needs to be handled in culturally-sensitive ways, with some cultures suffering 'loss of face' with public exhibitions of their performance. This can be a very difficult issue when one student is in a more senior job and can be the manager of some of the others (see below in the country-specific cases,). Social and cultural pressure on faculty members to mark over-generously is a very difficult issue in several target countries for the MBA program. The formality of examination conditions can vary considerably and this can impact on attempts to maintain academic standards. One of the problems here can result from the attitude of partner institutions, where a business school from the West partners with a local university, and the staff of the local university collaborate with the local students to undermine the authority of the business school from the West. In some cultures, where local administrators support local students against foreign education providers, evidence of leniency in examination and evaluation of performance is common. These clearly cannot be compared with students who are very strictly monitored. This reflects the on-going problem of a lack of supervision and control from a distance.

Assignments, Projects and Reports

Attitudes by students vary here – are assignments better or worse than exams in terms of the effort involved? Are these written projects carried out in their own time easier or harder? The teaching of research and writing skills in different cultural environments can be problematic. Integrity in research and writing are culturally loaded, with varying attitudes to copyright and intellectual property ownership. The challenge of teaching referencing and the avoidance of plagiarism have been compounded by advances in technology. 'Cutting and pasting' from the internet is all too easy for students, but so is the use of plagiarism detection software by teachers. However, some 'talented' students have found a way around it, by saving an old version of their work on the internet in a website, which is then found by the search engine which then searches no further. Also, the saving of whole theses and dissertations as a .jpg file can mean that, as a picture, they cannot be searched! Many faculty members lament that such ingenuity is used for purposes of deception rather than for the pursuit of academic excellence. Attitudes to the acceptability of these practices by students can clearly impact on academic standards.

For students with comparatively weak written English, there are further issues. Problems can arise with the use of Microsoft tools such as 'SpellCheck' and 'GrammarCheck'. The students see underlining in green and red and then lack judgment about correct usage. Many incorrect words are not underlined, because although incorrect in spelling and usage, they are proper words and are thus not detected. Many students have become lazy, expecting these tools to do their work for them. Also, the use of personal reflections, diaries and log entries is quite strange to some cultures, and can be seen as an invasion of privacy. They sometimes fear compromising organizational secrecy by discussing issues experienced by their companies. Even in an assignment read by only the foreign teacher, who knows none of the background of the company being described, they present a 'whitewashed' view, refusing to tackle contentious issues for fear of reprisals.

Theses and Major Pieces of Research-Based Work

The approach of students to long-term, lengthy and research-based projects can present even greater challenges for faculty to avoid plagiarism and copying. The task of sustaining students over two- and three- month projects, when they find it hard to concentrate for an hour at a time, can be problematic. There is a strong tendency for students to 'sub-contract' such large tasks to fellow students and 'professional' thesis and dissertation-writers. These 'providers' sometimes coach their 'customers' so successfully that it can be very difficult for the examiners to differentiate between authentic students doing their own work and those sub-contracting. In a recent series of thesis defenses in one of the country where the MBA program is running with local collaboration, there were instances of plagiarism and, indeed, were competent pieces of work. But they were not researched and written by the student with his or her name on the cover!

Behaviour in the Classroom

The use of jokes is clearly culturally difficult, and can be pointless and time-wasting if students do not understand them. The jokes told by the students are similarly often incomprehensible to the teachers. Laughing at individual students can be OK for other students, but not always for the teacher. Much humor is cruel and hurtful, with different cultures taking different attitudes to picking on each other. Acceptable subjects of conversation, during periods of small-talk during break times, can be limited; as in other situations, the weather and tourism are always safe, if boring. Religion and politics are probably to be avoided, unless the students initiate the subjects after a long period of getting to know the teacher. The challenge of remembering the names of students, especially in a big class, can be extreme. It depends on the personal experience of the teacher – some find Arabic names easy; Chinese names less so; and Vietnamese names impossible. However, the effectiveness of this technique, once mastered, can improve the ability of the teacher to manage the class effectively. Dealing with gender issues – of the faculty member and the students – can be more of a problem in some cultures than others. Women faculty can be seen as more sympathetic towards personal issues, and may be taken less seriously in some cultures. The task of failing a student can be more difficult for female teachers in the Middle East. The male student being failed can find his humiliation compounded by the gender of the teacher. The role of life in the classroom is more important to some cultures than others; some cultures find distance-learning programs requiring a level of self-starting ability and discipline beyond their inclination. They need the classroom experience to keep going.

Inter-Student Behavior

They are our friends; or they are the enemy – there can be a "them-and-us" situation between groups of students. Co-operation and competition between students can go different ways. There can be too much collaboration – when sharing the load goes too far and some students do too much work on a project, and others too little. The importance of relationship-driven cultures in inter-student behavior is culturally-loaded, and there is therefore a need for faculty to appreciate differences here.

Life out of the Classroom

When faculty members hold private meetings with students – how much is acceptable and what is beyond the call of duty? Meetings in the classroom or faculty office can be safer for many reasons. Hospitality is offered in many cultures and a decline to accept can offend. As in the case of corporate ethics, dinner invitations and small gifts are more acceptable for faculty members after the event. This can be at the end of a course or after marking exam papers and assignments. In many cultures, offering bribes is common practice, and most business schools lack clear guidelines on how faculty should deal with these. Relationships outside the classroom with students are universally regarded as probably ill-advised by most academic institutions, but students from some cultures (such as Chinese) use these as a vehicle for self-advancement.

NATIONAL CONTEXTS FOR TRANSNATIONAL LEARNING AND COLLABORATION

The researcher has used her personal teaching experience while delivering the MBA program of this particular School of Management in the different countries of emerging markets. These include: China, Jordan, Kuwait, Dubai, Saudi Arabia, Africa, including Egypt, Cyprus, Iran, Malaysia, Indonesia, Vietnam, Bangladesh, Hungary, Romania, Russia, Kazakhstan, Argentina, Peru, and Suriname.

(In this study, the Researcher has not included USA, Canada, UK, Europe, Australasia, and India as teaching delivery locations – as these countries do not necessarily attract overseas teachers, have enough domestic teaching talent of their own; or are developed markets for education delivery; similarly, Hong Kong, Singapore and Taiwan are probably not seen as "emerging" any more.)

SPECIFIC COUNTRY-BASED OBSERVATIONS IN TRANSNATIONAL LEARNING AND COLLABORATION

This series of detailed observations, illustrating key points of teaching delivery, experienced by the Researcher as a teacher in the field, have been selected to express concerns, reveal insights, and suggest a discussion of how important issues in MBA teaching have been handled.

Should You Know about Their History and Politics?

I was teaching in one of the countries of Arabian Peninsula, on a Human Resource module in the MBA course, and I wanted to illustrate the varied tasks faced by an HR manager. In particular I wanted to talk about how HR managers help employees to cope in times of crisis and emergency in a company. I found a very good Harvard Business Review case, which I had used successfully before in another country of this area, on the role of HR in a company which lost over a hundred staff in the September 11th incident. Bad idea! The class erupted into a huge anti-American outpouring. Several of their comments were irrational and over-emotional, and did not make sense, but this was no time for argument, I decided. My heart missed a beat as I could suddenly see myself arrested, deported, etc. etc. So I announced that this case was clearly not appropriate, they got the message anyway, let's move on, it's time for a break from class. They all rushed out of the class as students do anyway, and I followed them and spoke to a couple of them I knew well. I apologized for being 'culturally-insensitive'. I went back to the classroom and collected as many copies of the handout as I could and stuffed them in my bag and later threw them out in the hotel waste bin. Meanwhile the students were distracted by the release of marks from the previous class, which took place in the break, so they forgot all about this offending article. A lucky escape!

Implications

This does mean that it can be impossible to use uniform handouts and materials in teaching in different locations, so there will be more work for faculty preparing extra cases and examples, etc. It also shows a level of diffuse thinking, that political and nationalistic views cannot be easily kept outside of the classroom – the students don't see their different interests and activities as separate, but all mixed up together. This can have implications for maintaining academic standards as the students can accuse foreign teachers of cultural insensitivity and can thereby avoid studying certain topics, take extra time off for religious observances and other ways around the system. Foreign teachers can be intimidated into agreeing to student demands because of a fear of cultural offence – and legal implications, even deportation.

How Can We Arouse their Interest and Create Curiosity?

I was in east-central Africa, in Rwanda, again presenting a module in HRM. All the students were public-sector managers. They were very quiet when I first arrived, for several reasons. I was a stranger, their country is quite isolated, as a nation they are still recovering from a bloody Genocide, they are typically high power-distant, and their English language skills are variable, from weak to hesitant at best. Rwanda was a Belgian colony and French is widely spoken, although many of those escaping the Genocide went to nearby Uganda and Kenya and their English is quite good. But in the first few hours, they weren't saying much. So I asked them about their jobs – which I found very difficult to understand. I could work out what the Tourism, Utilities, Transport and Education Ministries might be doing, but what about the Genocide Reconciliation Ministry? Then I asked them what they had studied before – theoretical HRM. What were their ambitions? To get promoted, change jobs – but how? Through trial and error I discovered that they wanted to hear about new things no-one knew about in Rwanda, to challenge existing practice, and learn new skills. I reworked the syllabus and every day we learned about new HR practices, policies and initiatives; we discussed what was wrong in their ministries and how it might be fixed; and tried out new HR tools. We practiced basic forms of job evaluation, psychometrics, competency-based interviews, manpower-planning and all manner of exercises, mostly quite new to them. Even though some of these tools were probably impossible to implement in the near future (if at all) the participants were excited, empowered and were curious about what was going to happen next.

Implications

Again, not only do faculty flying in need a range of materials to suit different interests, but also different teaching approaches, such as more group-based work, to accommodate students with language difficulties. There is also the issue here of a high power-distant culture hesitating to discuss problems with this remote figure, the foreign teacher! This can mean that participants will sit in classes hour after hour, day after day, without understanding much of what is going on. Then it can be a big shock for the students when they receive failing grades, especially if they are used to high ones from their own local institutions. There is often a co-existence of high uncertainty avoiding behaviors at the same time in this environment, with students demanding a high level of detail about assessment items, to a much greater extent than they might in the home campus. This can create a discrepancy in standards.

Dealing with Members of the Royal Family

I was teaching at a university in one of the Middle East countries, and one of our students was a son of the then Crown Prince. He was tall, good-looking, popular with the other students but lazy, unpunctual and infrequent in attendance, and expected the others to do the work, which they gladly did. One of the assessment items on the course was a group project. His group made a video of themselves acting out a management problem – 'How to Deal with Difficult People'. It was really good, and funny, and the Royal played a prominent role. They got 19/20 for this, but the remaining 80% of the marks were based on essays and exams. The Royal never appeared again. I called his mobile phone several times, but he never took my calls. I went to see the Dean, who gave me a lecture on the cost and sacrifices involved in doing business in emerging markets. He didn't want to come up with any kind of policy statement or make a decision about my problem. I posted the marks, and the Royal got 19%. Nothing happened, although I was worried at the time. But I'm glad I did this now.

Implications

In many hierarchical societies, there are different rules for different levels of people, and attempts by faculty members to create a meritocratic classroom can be fraught with problems. In particularistic cultures, where relationships can be more important than rules, there's an understanding that rules exist for most people but not for some special people. The foreign teacher can 'pretend' that he or she didn't know these exceptions to rules, and that all students have to be treated the same. The problem is that exceptions can become norms and students with special status can gain more and more favors, undermining the standards which foreign education providers are trying to maintain.

Active Participation or Empty Vessels?

I was teaching in mainland China for the first time, having spent time in Hong Kong, and I started off my topic by asking the students questions. What are some of the greatest management concerns you face in your companies? How is the level of productivity of your staff? What is your organization culture? Is it positive or negative? What is the staff turnover level? They looked at me blankly. Some fidgeted. Some whispered to their neighbors. But no-one answered. So I carried on anyway, presenting my material. In the break one of the students, an elected group representative, came up to me and explained that it is my job to give a lecture, not to ask questions. And their job is to listen. So I carried on with my lectures, and it took a while to get them to participate, as they had to feel comfortable with me first, and I must have put them off a bit at first, by being so demanding and provocative and confrontational.

Implications

This highly neutral, power-distant behavior, where the students are expecting to be recipients of received wisdom rather than being critical, challenging and argumentative, is a difficult one for foreign faculty. It can also potentially compromise learning outcomes where critical reasoning, the balancing of different points of view and creation of arguments is rewarded behavior, as is often the case, especially in MBA programs. It is impossible to change mindsets formed over centuries overnight, but there will be a need for a much fuller explanation of expected learning outcomes of the courses, with many examples for clarity. The larger and more progressive cities in China – such as Shanghai and Beijing – may pose fewer problems than the more remote cities.

Cheating and Copying

One of my colleagues was teaching his last class in the series of an MBA in one of the countries in the Middle East region and the administrative staff member came around with the teaching evaluation forms. As is required, the faculty member left the room. Then one of the students quietly crept up to the computer and stuck in his memory stick. Then he downloaded all the files off the teacher's memory stick onto his own. He was in the middle of doing this (and looking for the exam questions amongst the teacher's files) when the teacher came back. Despite being caught red-handed he denied everything and lied about his intentions. Then he made out that others had put him up to it and it as their fault, really. The incident became huge. But the college administration was reluctant to investigate the students, who were regarded as customers. In the end they all got off the hook. The lesson is, don't make it easy for them. Make it more or less impossible for them to steal any valuable information. OK, they can hack into your computer, but there's not much you can do about this. But you can make sure you always have your memory stick with you – that's why they have a string to hang around your neck!

Implications

Levels of honesty and tolerance of telling untruths clearly varies a great deal between different societies, and the concept of students being 'customers' rather than 'candidates' is also a contrasting feature. We can buy anything we like – we have the money. For people wealthy enough to watch the movie *Casino Royale* and then buy a 50% stake in the Aston Martin car company because they liked the car – 'buying' an MBA seems logical. Taking any other short cuts, such as buying exam questions obtained by others, also follows. This can be highly compromising and means that examination and assessment committees can receive disproportionate numbers of queries (especially challenges to grades) from these countries. Only by standing firm can the standards be maintained.

Further Short Observations

I was teaching an MBA module wearing Islamic-style clothes and having to fit in with their culture. This is essential to avoid problems with the academic authorities, and to win the students' trust and respect. Then they open-up and share some very personal insights, although there is always a strict **Islamic Republic** *supporter in the class keeping an eye on the foreign teacher and everyone else ...*

Implications

It takes time to break down the barriers, lots of political censorship going on, could be cultural insensitivity on the part of foreign faculty, fear and anxiety from the students in case of unacceptable material being presented and how to deal with this

I was teaching an HR module, in one of the major cities in the **Middle East**, *in interviewing skills, and the participants were asked to conduct role plays. Students who regarded themselves as superior in rank to others refused to be "interviewed" by those whom they saw as junior and inferior...,*

Implications

Hierarchical societies, high power distance, classroom management issues, group work problems – when part of an assessment, can be difficult

I was teaching a group exercise in **a** *much more cosmopolitan city in the* **Middle East**, *in a classroom of around 50, and many of the men would only work in a group with other men, and would not accept female group members. Many of the students arrive late, but must be accommodated,* *in a group of their choice. If attempts are made to strictly enforce punctuality, it can alienate these students, who will resort to complaining to the university president....*

Implications

Students as 'customers' rather than 'candidates', strong role of status and power

I was running a class of **Kazakhstan** *students, of very wealthy individuals (mostly females) who were more interested in shopping, fashion, surfing the internet and going to night clubs. It was very challenging to encourage them to focus on the class...*

Implications

Ascribed rather than achieved status issues – they have a position in society because of their wealth, so they can do whatever they want

I was teaching an MBA module in **China** *and warned the students against the consequences of plagiarism. I spent hours explaining the concept, with examples. Nevertheless, when I came to mark their exam papers and assignments, the incidences of plagiarism were almost universal. And several students reused material in their exams and in their assignments, and could not understand why this might not be acceptable, and argued in emails for weeks later...*

Implications

Different moral perspectives – 'stealing' of intellectual property, feeling of superiority of own rules

In a class in **Kuwait***, we had several people from one organization, including their boss. Unfortunately this student was weaker than all the others, but this fact (known to all the teachers) could not be exposed, as then all the students would withdraw from the program en masse, forcing it to close. This was a very delicate situation, reflecting the tendency towards high power distance in this environment...*

Implications

Ascribed rather than achieved leadership roles, power distance

In **Yemen***, I was expected to train two local teachers to teach the course for the next intake after I left. One was quite extravert and a good laugh and we got on well but when he had the class to himself he would not focus on the subject, but talk about anything, as he never did any preparation. The other was very old, traditional, very strict and religious, gained his PhD about 50 years ago, spoke no English, and didn't have a clue about any research in his subject in the last 50 years. He tried hard but I think it was probably too much for him to cope with...*

Implications

Different mindsets, different ways of thinking, lack of exposure, need to save face of local teachers but face up to the challenges of the course

I had a mixed group of students on a course in the Netherlands, some **Europeans** *(Belgians, Dutch) who were very outspoken, lively, and talkative and had very good English – and a group of* **Chinese** *who remained a mystery. The latter didn't join in much, and were anxious to not be put on the spot, so it was hard to know if they were following the course or not, and if they were getting anything out of it...*

Implications

Cultural differences in behaviors within a group, dealing with noisy and quiet participants, need to work with all, even those less attention-seeking.

SOLUTIONS AND RECOMMENDATIONS

This case, based on the personal experiences of the Researcher, primarily from insights gained whilst working among the Outreach Programs of the School, considers a wide range of cross-cultural issues in MBA teaching delivery. These issues are important, as they can compromise not just effective delivery and the teaching and assessment of the program, but can threaten the academic standards and reputation of the mother campus. Yet most practitioners of MBA delivery of offshore courses work in isolation and rarely share ideas and experiences. Faculty members newly-exposed to working in the field cannot easily access the insights of their more experienced colleagues. Hence this case, which seeks to consider these challenges, especially in the light of new advances in educational technology. A number of solutions and recommendations are suggested in the discussion of issues and the specific observations, but it is impossible for the current case to a) offer hard-and-fast rules or b) try to replace individual judgment in specific cases. Faculty members develop their own approaches to these issues; this case can only raise awareness of some of the dangers and threats to academic integrity which can be faced by individuals and institutions.

This study focuses on the teaching delivery aspects of transnational collaboration in advanced-level management education; it does not look at the development of collaborations between education providers, and all the technical, administrative and financial aspects involved.

REFERENCES

Hofstede, G. (1984). Culture's Consequences: International Differences in Work-Related Values. Beverley Hills, CA: Sage.

Hofstede, G. (1991). Cultures and Organizations: Software of the Mind. London: McGraw-Hill.

Hofstede, G. (1993). Cultural Constraints in Management Theories. *The Academy of Management Executive*, *7*(1), 81–94.

Reeves, R., & Knell, J. (2009). The 80 Minute MBA. London: Headline.

Trompenaars, F., & Hampden-Turner, C. (1997). Riding the waves of culture: understanding cultural diversity in business. London: Nicholas Brealey.

ADDITIONAL READING

De Bono, S., Jones S. & Van der Heijden. (2008). *Managing Cultural Diversity.* Maidenhead: Meyer & Meyer.

Jones, S. (1997). Managing in China: an executive survival guide. Singapore: Butterworth Heinemann.

Jones, S. (2008). Conducting Business in Malta: a guide for international managers. *Global Business and Organisational Excellence*, *27*(6), 58–77. doi:10.1002/joe.20231

Jones, S. (2008). The Impact of Socio-Political Context on Preferred Conflict Mode Styles of Business Trainees: a UAE Case Study. *Employee Relations*, *30*(1), 48–62. doi:10.1108/01425450810835419

Jones, S. (2009). (Forthcoming). Implementing Software for Managing Organizational Training and Development: cultural and political barriers. Experiences of consulting to a large public sector organization in the State of Kuwait. *International Journal of Commerce and Management*, (September): 2009.

Jones, S. et. al. (2004). The Impact of Socio-Political Context on the Efficacy of Customer Service Training: a UAE Case Study. *The Australasian Journal for Business and Social Inquiry, 2*(3).

More Torres, D. A., & Jones, S. (2010). (Forthcoming). A Changing Scene: Comparing Business Cultures in Peru and the Netherlands. *Global Business and Organisational Excellence*, (May/June): 2010.

KEY TERMS AND DEFINITIONS

Cross-Cultural Management: The study of cultural differences between nations in management terms, especially relevant for multinational businesses and their executives operating cross-culturally; can also be an issue in trade between nations.

Cultural Barriers: Can be experienced when cultures between two countries or persons are radically different and can prevent effective communications, teaching, doing business, etc.

Cultural Norms: Seen as typical behaviors by persons of specific countries.

Emerging Markets: Defined in various ways but in this study especially China and South East Asia, the Middle East, Africa, Eastern Europe and the former Soviet bloc, and South America. India, Hong Kong, Singapore and Taiwan are not included, as educationally these are no longer viewed as 'emerging'.

Faculty Members: Usually PhD qualified teachers working more-or-less full-time for a university or business school in the West, in this case then travelling to emerging markets to teach, which might comprise all or part of their workloads.

MBA Programs: A series of courses, each with separate modules, which as a whole comprise a master's level qualification. Can be full-time or (usually, in emerging markets) part-time – taught in evening classes and/or over weekends. Different programs can have a broad or specific focus, with concentration courses at the end. Can include a thesis or dissertation.

Plagiarism: The representation of the work of other authors as one's own work, strictly not allowed by most business schools and universities in the West, but culturally-acceptable in some emerging markets. Enabled by internet technology, which can also be used for detection.

Tacit Knowledge: Knowledge accumulated from experience but often not codified or recorded, and may be only informally passed-on, or retained in the consciousness of the person who has gained the knowledge.

Chapter 4
ORIENT: The Intercultural Empathy Through Virtual Role-Play

Sibylle Enz
Otto-Friedrich-Universitaet Bamberg, Germany

Carsten Zoll
Otto-Friedrich-Universitaet Bamberg, Germany

Natalie Vannini
Julius-Maximilians Universität, Germany

Mei Yii Lim
Heriot-Watt University, UK

Wolfgang Schneider
Julius-Maximilians Universität, Germany

Lynne Hall
University of Sunderland, UK

Ana Paiva
INESC-ID, Portugal

Ruth Aylett
Heriot-Watt University, UK

ABSTRACT

In a globalised world, cultural diversity is a challenge for everyone. Even for those staying "at home" cultural diversity enters their daily lives by people migrating from other regions of the world, sharing their social world. While intercultural encounters pose a great enrichment to one's experiences and perspectives, they also represent an immense challenge, confronting us with different languages, attitudes, habits, and social norms. The work presented in this chapter takes up this challenge by developing and evaluating a believable agent-based educational application ("ORIENT") designed to develop intercultural empathy for 12-14 year olds. The following chapter: (1) discusses the approach to use the appealing character of games in order to foster social and emotional learning in the age group while drawing on effective pedagogical interventions like role-play that have previously been successfully used to trigger social and emotional learning in a variety of real-world contexts; (2) introduces the development of ORIENT as an affective agent architecture modeling culturally-specific agent behavior, drawing on the psychological and pedagogical theories outlined; (3) considers the role of novel interaction modalities in supporting an empathic engagement with culturally-specific characters as well as active engagement in collaborative learning within a group of learners; and (4) presents and discusses results of preliminary evaluation studies based on an early prototype.

DOI: 10.4018/978-1-61520-749-7.ch004

BACKGROUND

eCIRCUS (Education through Characters with emotional Intelligence and Role-playing Capabilities that Understand Social interaction)has developed a new approach in the use of ICT to support social and emotional learning within Personal and Social Education (PSE). This was achieved through virtual role-play with synthetic characters that establish credible and empathic relations with learners. eCIRCUS investigated educational role-play using autonomous synthetic characters and involving the child through affective engagement, including the use of standard and highly innovative interaction mechanisms. This has developed novel conceptual models based on theories of narrative and role-play from psychology and implemented them in affectively driven autonomous graphically embodied agents – actors with attitude. It has delivered early prototype showcases through a VLE for emotional and social learning, one on anti-bullying education and one on intercultural empathy.

SETTING THE STAGE

ORIENT (Overcoming Refugee Integration with Empathic Novel Technology) focuses on the domain of intercultural learning, aiming at the home community with the ultimate goal of improving the social integration of youths with migration background in European countries. ORIENT is a showcase developed for Personal and Social Education by the EU-funded project eCIRCUS, funded within its Framework VI program. It offers a virtual learning environment for a group of three learners who are interacting with autonomous artificial characters representing another species (the "Sprytes") on an alien planet called ORIENT, a distant planet under threat of destruction by a large meteor. Interacting with the ORIENT application, a small group of adolescent learners equipped with innovative interaction technology are asked to solve – as foreigners on the alien planet of ORIENT – story-based problems and learn by interacting with the software how to get into contact, communicate, and cooperate with others who are fundamentally different from themselves.

The virtual world of the Sprytes is represented on a large screen of the real-world interaction space of the three learners, allowing for interaction between the learners in the real-world context as well as for interaction between the learners and the virtual world of the Sprytes; interaction devices used include RFID tagged real-world objects and RFID reading mobile phones, a game mat for navigation in the virtual world, and a WiiMote controller. First participants are told about their role as applicants for an internship in Space Command who will travel to an alien planet called ORIENT to find out about the inhabitants, the so-called Sprytes, of whom only very little is known so far. Their mission goal is to find out about Spryte habits and ways, to allow Space Command to judge whether it would be safe to establish further contact with the Sprytes. Then they are allocated the three roles:

- Navigation officer, who navigates on ORIENT using the game mat and handles the ORA-CLE;
- Communication officer, who communicates with the Sprytes by using expert knowledge about Spryte gestures, using the WiiMote;
- Intelligence officer, who can exchange objects with the Sprytes and attract the Sprytes attention, using the mobile phone.

The team then "teleport" to ORIENT, which is displayed via projector on a wall of the room after the participants have moved to their respective places.

In the course of the role-play, the group of learners and the Sprytes gradually learn from each other and the learners share the engaging experience of cooperatively handling novel interaction technology, implemented to enable communication with the Sprytes. ORIENT as a semi-immersive graphical environment depicting an imaginary foreign culture thus couples social learning in a group with intercultural learning. Its development was guided by pedagogical and psychological theories to develop an existing affective agent architecture (Dias & Paiva, 2005; Paiva et al., 2005) into one that also models cultural behavior in its full range.

As far as the intercultural learning challenge is concerned, ORIENT first and foremost draws on contact theory (Allport, 1954), the idea that inter-group prejudice can be reduced through contact between different cultural groups under specific conditions, such as equal status between the groups in the situation, common goals, intergroup cooperation, and the support of authorities, law, or custom. Carefully trying to design a learning experience that takes up at least some of these situational characteristics, ORIENT provides the adolescent user with the experience of role-play within an unfamiliar culture in which problems have to be solved. By experiencing for themselves the stresses of dealing with an unfamiliar culture, we hope to trigger transfer in learners, ultimately empathizing with those in their own peer group going through the same process. Dangers that lie in using real cultures for this type of role-play e.g. relate to misrepresentation of the depth of a depicted human culture, or to specific prejudices that may be present in the host group. For these reasons it was decided ORIENT would take place on a distant planet populated by non-human aliens, carefully balancing these risks and dangers with the heightened challenge to secure transfer to real-world settings. What cultural theory can help in designing such an environment? Here the project drew on the cultural dimensions derived by Hofstede (1991, 2001) from empirical work with employees of IBM in a variety of countries.

CASE DESCRIPTION

ORIENT: A Novel Learning Application

In recent years, a diverse range of applications designed for education, training, therapy or entertainment purposes have been developed that rely more and more on technology to augment user experiences. For instance, believable autonomous synthetic characters (Core et al., 2006; Kenny et al., 2007; Paiva et al., 2005; Rossen et al., 2008; Rowe et al., 2007) that have been previously shown to enrich interaction with human users (Cassell et al., 2000) draw on the engagement of human-human interaction, trying to reproduce it. Particularly in areas where changes in attitude and behavior change are in the focus (i.e. in social and emotional learning) rather than pure acquisition of knowledge, autonomous synthetic characters may have good potential as a pedagogical instrument to change cognition, emotion, and behavior. Based on these considerations, synthetic characters may be designed to specifically trigger affective engagement through the creation of an empathic relationship between user and character, for instance based on psychological theories and models of cognitive appraisal (Ortony et al., 1988) and coping behavior (Lazarus, 1991).

The aim in the work presented in this case study is to develop characters with social and emotional capabilities for the application area of intercultural learning, with capabilities such as emotionally driven behavior including emotional expressivity, determined by emotional variables in their action-selection mechanisms. As a result different patterns of character behavior emerge which support e.g. the users ascribing personality to the characters when they interact with them.

Such characters seem particularly suitable for applications in which emotionally expressive behavior is required (Allbeck & Badler, 2004;

Isbister, 2004; Koda et al., 2008; Rehm et al., 2007). In the application area of intercultural learning however, other factors than emotional expressivity come into focus. Being faced with the challenges of intercultural encounters, highly routinized behavioral reactions such as the unconscious application of stereotypes are rather common and persistent (as well as highly psychologically plausible), calling for a learning application that tackles cognitive as well as affective bases of behavior.

Another novelty of the approach presented in this chapter is to develop synthetic characters that are not only psychologically plausible due to their believable behavior and underlying action selection mechanism, but also act according to their cultural characteristics, thus specifically linking behavior to cultural standards and norms: not only their expressive behavior (including language and clothing, see e.g. Hall et al., 2006) is modified according to their cultural background, but they are considered as social actors within their respective cultural context. In ORIENT, characters' verbal and non-verbal behaviors are culturally mediated from a model-based perspective. While it is highly reasonable to assume that cultural ways and assumptions always play their role in the design of virtual worlds and believable characters inhabiting them (e.g. Rosis et al., 2004), ORIENT tries to create a new culture with which the learners are confronted, triggering reflection about similarities and differences and ultimately reinforcing the overcoming of prejudices and fears by learning more about each other as well as learning to cooperate. For these sensitive learning mechanisms, the virtual learning application offers a safe and secure as well as engaging environment to carefully open up for intercultural experiences.

The theoretical work behind ORIENT informs three different areas of development: (1) the change in attitude, emotion, and behavior in intercultural encounters; (2) the cultural specification of ORIENT and the implementation of a model that allows for representation of the cultural parameters impacting action-selection of the Sprytes; and (3) the modeling of the impact of the user interaction on the Sprytes behavior. Hence, the following chapter outlines the design process of ORIENT and the implementation of the underpinning theories on social and emotional learning (e.g. educational role-play) and on culture and intercultural learning which are then introduced in detail in subsequent section of the paper.

The ORIENT Application: Emotion, Personality, Culture

Designing the Spryte Culture along the Dimensions of Cultural Variability

Hofstede (1991, 2001) posited five dimensions to describe different cultures. These dimensions were used to design the artificial culture for the inhabitants of ORIENT. The following chapter first provides some basic information about the concept of culture, before the links with the modeling of culture in ORIENT, in particularly in the mind of the artificial agents that inhabit ORIENT is explained in more detail.

Culture has an effect on human cognition, affect and behavior. To define cultural differences in agents, variables which describe the cultural personality of an agent have to be defined. There are systematic similarities and differences across cultures that can be explained and predicted theoretically using dimensions of cultural variability (e.g. individualism-collectivism). Classifications of culture and dimensions of cultural variability have for example been provided by Hall (2001) or Hofstede (1991), who created a five factor cultural model. Hofstede (2001) defines culture as "the collective programming of the human mind that distinguishes the members of one human group from those of another. Culture in this sense is a system of collectively held values" (p. 9). Enculturation takes place during socialization, the time when children adopt orientation of a specific culture without further reflection. Based on work by Inkeles and Levinson (1969), Hofstede's empirical work carried out with IBM employees in a number of different cultures yielded five cultural dimensions that have since been widely used to describe a wide range of different cultures, with one of the characteristics within each dimension tending to predominate.

Individualism-Collectivism is the major dimension of cultural variability used to explain similarities and differences in communication across cultures. "Individualism pertains to societies in which the ties between individuals are loose: everyone is expected to look after himself or herself and his or her immediate family. Collectivism as its opposite pertains to societies in which people from birth onwards are integrated into strong cohesive in-groups, which throughout people's lifetime continue to protect them in exchange for unquestioning loyalty" (Hofstede, 1991, p. 51). One tendency tends to predominate in each culture, e.g. individualism in the United States, Canada, Australia, New Zealand, and northern Europe and collectivism in African, Arab, Latin, and southern European cultures (Gudykunst & Mody, 2002). As humans seek for autonomy and community, moderate or hybrid forms of individualism and collectivism have to be assumed. Individual-level characteristics, such as personality, individual values and self construals mediate the influence of cultural individualism-collectivism on individuals' communication and might explain variability in communication within cultures (Gudykunst & Mody, 2002). The individual's psychological needs, e.g. the need for affiliation, are influenced by parameters like community, collaboration, shared interests, harmony, traditions and public good being emphasized in collectivistic cultures and personal rights, responsibilities, privacy, freedom and self-expression in individualistic cultures. This provides a link from the general cultural stereotype to the intentions and behaviors of the individual agent (Kriegel et al., 2008).

The dimension of uncertainty avoidance describes the degree, to which members of a culture try to avoid uncertainty. In high uncertainty avoidance cultures (e.g. Japan, Mexico, France, Chile, Egypt), members have a lower tolerance for uncertainty and ambiguity, "which expresses itself in higher levels of anxiety and energy release, greater need for formal rules and absolute truth, and less tolerance for people or groups with deviant ideas or behavior" (Hofstede, 1979, p. 395) than members of low uncertainty avoidance cultures (e.g. Canada, Denmark, India, United States) which are more comfortable with ambiguous situations and unfamiliar risks.

Powers distance "is the extent to which the less powerful members of institutions and organizations accept that power is distributed unequally" (Hofstede & Bond, 1984, p. 419). Members of high power distance cultures tend to see and accept power as a part of society and make use of referent power (e.g. Egypt, Ethiopia, Nigeria, Venezuela), whereas members of low power distance cultures assume that power should only be used when legitimate and accordingly use more reward, legitimate, and expert power (e.g. Australia, Canada, Germany, United States).

Masculinity-Femininity: Masculine and feminine cultures are particularly differentiated through gender role distribution. In traditional-gender-oriented masculine cultures, distinct social gender roles (e.g. men are assertive and focused on material success, women are modest and concerned with the quality of life) can be identified. Individuals belonging to masculine cultures tend to organize information on the basis of their genders and to follow cultural definitions of appropriate behavior (Bem, 1993). In contrast, gender roles overlap in feminine cultures (e.g. both men and women might be modest, tender and concerned with the quality of life) (Hofstede, 1991).

Long term / short term orientation: While long-term oriented cultures value thrift and perseverance, short-term oriented cultures value respect for tradition, fulfilling social obligations, and "saving face".

These dimensions are linked with manifestations that have been described (Hofstede, 1991) as values (internal manifestations) on the individual level, and rituals, heroes, and symbols (external manifestations) on the societal level. A subset of the Hofstede dimensions discussed above served as guidelines for the design of an artificial culture for the people on ORIENT, with its tribal and hierarchical culture, the Sprytes. Hierarchy (power distance) values respect and age; the Sprytes are a militarily active culture who believe in using force and power to influence others and to protect their habitat. They are a collectivistic culture (individualism-collectivism), being largely compassionate with each other, and living in groups where usually the majority holds power. Sprytes are highly traditional in their ways and view uncertainty as a threat (uncertainty avoidance). The hierarchy in Spryte culture has three layers: The top layer is represented by the Elder, followed by the members of its council (tribal elders, military generals and the like) and Spryte population. Gender is absent in the Spryte culture (masculinity-femininity), and their graphical representation, as seen for one character in Figure 1, is intentionally ambiguous.

In order to reinforce the believability of the characters and the sets, a large screen projection is used so that characters are close to life-size. The importance of close-to-life-size characters and world is that the users are put on a more equal footing, with their movements and actions in the real world serving as interaction modes with the virtual world. The learners' own bodies thus are in the focus of interaction. For this reason, keyboard interaction is replaced by other more novel interaction modalities designed to promote cooperation between the three users as well as more direct interaction with the characters. These are discussed below.

Baseline Architecture

The ORIENT agent architecture started from FAtiMA (Dias & Paiva, 2005; see Figure 2), an agent architecture used for synthetic agents in which emotions and personality take a central role in influencing behavior and thus achieving more believable agents. In FAtiMA emotions are based on the OCC cognitive theory of emotions (Ortony et al., 1988), which views the emotional process as based on appraisal, with the quality of emotions resulting from the appraisals of events.

In FAtiMA there are two main layers for the appraisal and coping processes: the Reactive Layer, which is responsible for the character's emotional reactions and reactive behavior, and the Deliberative Layer, responsible for the character's goal-oriented behavior. To appraise an event in the world, agents use their memories and knowledge

Figure 1. Spryte character

Figure 2. Agent architecture

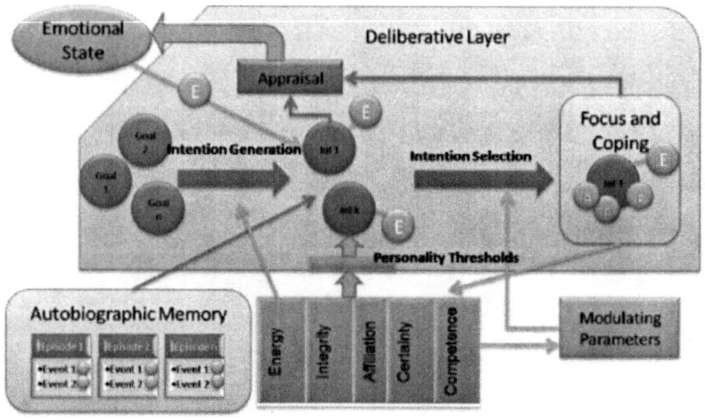

about the world, stored in a knowledge base and in an autobiographic memory. The knowledge base is responsible for storing semantic knowledge, such as properties about the world and their relations, while the autobiographic memory contains information concerning past events in the character's personal experience. Every time the sensors of the agent perceive an event, that event is appraised, generating a set of emotions forming an emotional state.

Once the emotional state has been updated by the appraisal process, it is used by the reactive level to trigger action tendencies, generating the agent's emotional reactive behavior. In parallel the deliberative level (which includes a continuous planner; Aylett et al., 2006) selects the most appropriate goal and the most adequate coping strategies. Note that the event perceived will also be used to update existing plans triggering the goal activation process. Finally, after an action is selected for execution, it is performed in the virtual world through the agent's effectors.

While FAtiMA has been very successfully applied in the FearNot! application (Dias & Paiva, 2005) it is subject to certain disadvantages common to symbolically-represented cognitive appraisal architectures. The OCC taxonomy is extensive but still fails to capture significant outcomes of empathic processes, especially in relation to social behavior. FAtiMA in its original form also requires a substantial authoring effort in which goals, emotional reactions, actions and effects are all authored. For this reason, the architecture was extended for ORIENT by incorporating aspects of a needs driven architecture, PSI (Dörner et al., 2003).

This is a comprehensive psychologically-grounded model of human-action regulation encompassing perception, motivation, cognition, memory, learning and emotions. It is based on a set of drives, such as existence-preserving, species-preserving, certainty, competence and affiliation (see also Figure 2). This seemed a good way of extending FAtiMA with a motivational structure that could allow goals to be dynamically managed rather than pre-set. The drives set was modified slightly and the five drives Energy, Integrity, Certainty, Competence and Affiliation were implemented (Lim et al, 2009). The strength of a drive ranges from 0 (complete deprivation) to 10 (complete satisfaction) and goals and actions are tagged with their expected contribution to Energy, Integrity and Affiliation, allowing their update. Competence is related to success in the environment and thus to goal achievement, so that goal outcomes change its value. Certainty is also related to goal success but less directly, since it represents the extent to which current knowledge about the outcomes of goals and actions are accurate. It is represented as an error prediction based on past successes and failures and thus as an exponential moving average. The need for certainty is not about avoiding those goals with high uncertainty but rather trying to reduce estimation errors; this may mean selecting uncertain goals in order to examine their outcome and reduce their uncertainty via trial-and-error.

This links naturally into the Autobiographic Memory component of the architecture which holds information about past successes and failures and thus acts as a mechanism for learning about the outcome of goals and actions.

The incorporation of aspects of the PSI architecture provides a flexible and context-sensitive goal-management system. A goal may satisfy one or more needs, and a need may be satisfied by different goals.

Symbols, Rituals and Culture

FAtiMA was also extended beyond the individual affective settings to allow for cultural adaptation of the agents via cultural dimension values for the culture of the character, cultural specific symbols, culturally specific goals and needs, and the rituals of the culture (Mascarenhas et al., 2009).

As outlined above, agents perceive the world based on their sensors. However, once an event is perceived, it is passed to a symbol translation process that captures specificities of communication in the culture of that agent. Thus, different cultures perceive events differently according to their symbols, so that the symbol translation process logically precedes the cognitive appraisal process relating events to individual goals. The architecture captures this by allowing for a specific culture parameterization of the symbols in a culture. Once the event has been identified by the agent, the appraisal process is triggered. The appraisal structure contains three variables associated with the OCC model. They are: desirability for the agent, desirability for others and praiseworthiness. The desirability for the agent is calculated based on the motivational system and thus depends on the agents' needs and drives. If an event is positive for the agent's needs, the desirability of the event is high, and vice versa.

The second variable in the appraisal structure is related to how good the event is for other agents, a social judgment, and so some of the aspects of the culture are taken into account in this appraisal using the Hofstede cultural dimension values. For example, in collectivist culture events that are good for others are appraised more positively than in an individualist culture.

Finally, the praiseworthiness of the event is considered as a cultural appraisal in that it captures the social norms of the culture that the agent is part of. For example, an event that shows that the agent is not following the steps of a ritual is appraised as negative. The appraisal component will then activate an emotion producing an update of the memory of the agent and starting the deliberation process. Once an action is chosen, symbol translation is invoked again, and the agent translates the action taking into account relevant symbols, before the action is performed by its actuators.

One other component included in the architecture is rituals capturing in an explicit way some specific rituals of that culture. A ritual is defined as a set of actions with symbolic value, the performance of which is prescribed by the culture.

Interaction in ORIENT

With culture being a social process it is vital to the success of the role-play in ORIENT that user interaction modalities reinforce the story-world and bring it into the real world.

For this reason, user interaction is based on real, physical and tangible objects surrounding them. In the real world the user can see, touch and manipulate objects whose material and shape may support intuitive use and represent real issues. These are always visible and ubiquitous, encouraging a pragmatic approach to problem-solving. Finally, movement in physical space supports social behavior (gestures, speech, movements) and full body interaction that are particularly important in supporting the social nature of culturally-specific interaction.

Appropriate interaction devices for ORIENT were based on a controlled study with 18 children exploring different multi-user settings for pervasive games (Leichtenstern et al., 2007). This study revealed that an appropriate distribution of interaction devices may have a positive effect on collaboration in role play. There was clear evidence that a setting where each user was assigned a role via an interaction device with a dedicated function helps organize interactions within a group, balances the level of interactivity and avoids dominant users. This setting promoted collaboration among users in a better way than a setting where just one interaction device was given to the whole group or a setting where each group member was equipped with an identical device. Based on this study, the assignment of roles in ORIENT is supported by the use of three different interaction devices: a game mat, a mobile phone and a WiiMote. Each interaction device has a different function and attached role, but all of them are necessary to accomplish the overall goal of the game.

Navigation within the ORIENT world is via walking on the spot using a game mat. The Sprytes speak a 'gibberish' generated on the fly related to

Figure 3. Interaction devices

the language output by the character minds, and this is represented in English (or German) text on the screen with the story-world explanation of a high-tech translator device embedded in a mobile phone carried by a second user. This phone also allows the user to speak 'magic words' that act as symbols within the culture and for SMS communication with the characters. It can recognize RFID tags attached to real world objects that also have an existence in the virtual world.

The third user carries a WiiMote, and this is used to replicate important gestures in order to successfully enter into greetings rituals for example. Figure 3 above shows the devices used. The intention in using novel interaction devices was to incite the adolescents' curiosity and increase their motivation to learn more about the Spryte culture. In this vein, the adolescents are not only taken through the different stages of intercultural sensitivity (Bennett, 1986) by the story line, they may actively experience these stages by engaging in interactions with the characters. Addressing explicitly experiential learning approaches (Kolb, 1984), we make use of interaction devices that require bodily activity, such as the game mat and the WiiMote. By employing interaction devices that are intuitive to use and support collaboration among the adolescents, we also hope to encourage intergroup collaboration which is one of the conditions of Contact Theory (Allport, 1954).

Furthermore, the ORA-CLE (Onboard Resource Agent for Cultural and Liaison Engagements), an embodied computer character, aims at enhancing learning in the game. It stimulates the learners' reflection on the events and outcomes of ORIENT by asking suitable questions, by encouraging the recording of both personal and collective diaries, and by commenting on the learners' actions. It also helps the transfer of learning to real-world situations, by carrying out a "debriefing" session with learners when they report back to the ORA-CLE with material collected during the mission. The ORA-CLE also fosters learner motivation and keeps them engaged by not disrupting the game flow, stimulating group collaboration (by suggesting participants to use cooperative actions when the team is in a deadlock), keeping players' focus on the task (by reminding them that time is passing by and the meteorite is arriving), and providing help during the mission. It has its own emotional status, which changes during the game according to the team's progress.

Learning in ORIENT: Theories and Outcomes

Social and Emotional Learning

Social and emotional learning (SEL) is defined by Elias et al. (1997) as a process through which learners "enhance their ability to integrate thinking, feeling, and behaving to achieve important life tasks" and embraces such competencies as recognition and management of emotions, establishing healthy relationships, setting of positive goals, meeting personal and social needs, and making responsible and ethical decisions. This can be achieved through different learning processes such as learning through the building of associations between experiences and emotional reactions (associative learning), e.g. due to appropriate reinforcement (e.g. Rotter, 1954; Seligman, 1972), as well as on learning through observation of models and their behavior (e.g. Bandura, 1973; Bandura & Adams, 1977).

One example of a successful didactical tool to foster SEL is role-play. Role-play can be used as training method for empathy in social interactions, experimenting with different reactions to a given situation and exploring experiences of self and other. Role-play thus supports experiential learning in which learners acquire and apply knowledge, skills and feelings in a specific setting, emphasizing the importance of a direct encounter with the subject of study "rather than merely thinking about the encounter [with the subject], or only considering the possibility of doing something about it" (Borzak, 1981). Role-play supports the creation of knowledge and meaning from concrete – though imagined – experiences and uses perspective-taking and empathy as mechanisms for a learner-centered constructivist approach. It is therefore an effective way of addressing intercultural learning as it will be outlined in the course of this chapter. The educational impact of virtual as well as real-life role-play draws on the willingness of participants to commit to the roles they have decided to play. In virtual role-play, believable characters are seen as fundamental both to producing the required social immersion in the story world and also to creating a specific social pressure to stay in role. Implementing role-play in virtual reality thus offers the possibility to combine a successful didactical tool to challenge cognition, emotion, and behavior in school as well as in therapeutic contexts and a virtual, and thus safe and secure learning environment that is fun to explore and to interact with. It helps learners to take over the perspective of the member of another culture, and to understand the similarities and differences in ways of feeling and thinking between their own and the other culture, which – on the one hand – leads to a reflection of their own cultural traditions and boundaries, and on the other hand helps them to alter their own behavior and attitudes in order to better match the challenges of complex (multicultural) social encounters.

Theories of social learning (e.g. Bandura, 1973; Bandura & Adams, 1977) and experiential learning (e.g. Kolb, 1984) suggest that a number of different aspects must be addressed in an application of this nature and help to establish generic requirements. Firstly, it is important that users can identify and acquire knowledge about "adequate" behavior options, and for this reason a cooperative task has been selected in which success depends on overcoming cultural differences. Secondly, scenarios should feature characters that are similar to and stories that are attractive to the target group. This is seen as both facilitating the learning process and representing the learner's own experience. Thirdly, the system should not only provide the learner with scenarios, but also allow them to act and interact with the characters, so that behavior options are not only witnessed but also carried out, producing role commitment.

In sum, the learning process prompted by ORIENT is social and emotional, since attitudes, emotions and behavioral reactions are prompted through the interaction members of the other culture that are reflected upon and discussed in a team of learners that collaboratively try to meet a common goal through understanding and empathizing with members of the other culture.

Collaborative Learning

ORIENT as a group-based learning application focuses on collaborative learning among a group of three adolescent learners. Collaborative learning in a group serves the enhancement of school achievement and the improvement of intergroup relations (Auernheimer, 2003). It is a specific form of small-group education, which emphasizes and structures the social processes during learning. While learners keep independent subtasks and merge them to an overall result of "cooperative learning", the collective development of a solution is in the focus of "collaborative learning"1 (e.g. Slavin, 1995; Roschelle & Teasley, 1995). Being characterized by the sharing of work as well as by the dependence between single tasks, collaborative learning ensures that learners work together during the whole learning process. Usually, a group for collaborative learning is composed heterogeneously concerning abilities, individual characteristics, gender, cultural background, social competence, native language, and learning styles (Weidner, 2006). Basic elements of collaborative learning (Johnson, Johnson & Holubec, 1993) are

- positive mutual dependence: all members of the team feel involved based on the working for a shared aim. The team is only successful, if everyone makes a contribution to it.
- individual accountability: every team-member feels responsible for the own and for the group learning processes and contributes to their achievement. The team-members consider it important to maximize the learning outcome of one another.
- face-to-face interaction: to optimize communication and interaction processes, the members of a group sit close together and must additionally learn to think and act relating to one another. A consensus is gathered through discussion, negotiation, and balance of the arguments.
- social and team-competence (social skills, such as to encourage, listen to, help, compliment one another better communication, trustfulness, negotiation ability, decision making, and appropriate conflict resolution strategies).
- evaluation of group processes: the group members reflect and appraise their common efforts, to constantly ameliorate their cooperative competencies and working strategies.

By comparison, Slavin (1995) differentiates three principles, which control the setting: team rewards, individual accountability, and equal opportunity for success. Every advancement counts for the team, so that the individuals are stimulated to cooperate and mutually help each other, which means that from a motivational perspective, cooperative goal structures create a situation in which group members can only attain their personal goals if the group is successful. Each team-member brings in certain competencies or perceptions and is important to achieve the shared goal.

ORIENT aims at intercultural learning through collaboration. Considering the theories and models outlined above, the following principles are reflected in the design and development of ORIENT (Slavin, 1995):

- interacting with ORIENT provides the learner with the possibility to get into con tact with members of other cultures (virtual and/or real);
- the collaborative task allows for equal status roles for learners;
- it specifies different tasks for different learners and makes sure that each team-member brings in certain competencies or perceptions and is important to achieve the shared goal;
- the collaborative task also emphasizes a collective development of a solution.

Learning Outcomes of Social and Emotional Learning and Collaborative Learning

As described above, the personal developmental process comprises changes on the cognitive, affective and behavioral level (Grosch & Leenen, 1998) and needs to connect learning experiences on all three levels. On the cognitive level, the learning individual for example takes over other perspectives of interpretation, which are partly oppositional and conflictive to earlier beliefs. This perspective-taking leads to a better understanding of the thoughts and feelings of members of other cultures, in general as well as in specific situations. Particularly in cross-cultural encounters, where uncertainty (as far as the differences between self and other are concerned) and the resulting fears and anxieties represent cognitive and affective challenges to the "appropriate" behavioral choices, social and emotional learning is a suitable approach, because of its explicit aim of developing people's skills "to recognize and manage their emotions, appreciate the perspective of others, establish positive goals, make responsible decisions, and handle interpersonal situations effectively" (Greenberg et al., 2003, p. 468).

One outcome of collaborative learning is group cohesion (e.g. Carron et al., 1985) which can be defined as degree of commitment of group members concerning common standards and aims and additionally as degree of mutual positive feelings (Forgas, 1994). Those mutual positive feelings act as a reinforcement of learning in a group and are positively related to the group's performance, in particular in small groups and when the collaborative task is attractive and engaging (e.g. Mullen & Copper, 1994). However, the danger that comes with high group cohesion is a high conformity among the members of the group, resulting in the fact that divergent and creative ideas are not verbalized ("group think", Janis, 1982). While ORIENT focuses on other group interaction characteristics such as active engagement and collaboration among a team of learners, group cohesion is a phenomenon that might become more important when established groups of learners who know each other well continue to interact with the software over a longer period of time. For assessing the quality of group interaction within ORIENT teams, dimensions like those suggested by Bales (1976) seem more appropriate, which categorizes communication according to its perceived interpersonal goal, such as expressing social information and emotions (positive / negative socio-emotional dimensions), or inquiring about the task or procedure at hand (task-oriented questions dimension and a task-oriented answers/solutions dimension).

Behavior-related categories that are relevant for collaboration in groups are – among others – helping one another, sharing resources, valuing others and treating them respectfully. Moreover, communicative competence (e.g. to be a good listener, a good speaker, to interpret gestures and facial expression adequately, to give constructive feedback), conflict behavior (e.g. to accept differences, to handle and solve a conflict), and emotional competence (e.g. to identify, express and control one's own feelings, to show compassion, to empathize) are crucial (Weidner, 2006). These variables will be drawn on when it comes to developing novel methodologies for evaluating the ORIENT learning outcomes.

Intercultural Learning

As was outlined earlier, ORIENT draws on contact theory (Allport, 1954), the idea that inter-group prejudice can be reduced through contact between the groups under specific conditions, such as equal status between the groups in the situation, common goals, intergroup cooperation, and the support of authorities, law, or custom. Contact theory is controversial and some work argues against it, but a recent survey of existing studies (Pettigrew & Tropp, 2006) gives support to it and it has been applied with some success to the integration of child refugees (Cameron et al., 2006).

But mere contact to other cultures does not allow for an understanding of the learning process behind intercultural learning. According to Gudykunst et al. (1977), taking over a third-culture-perspective fosters cultural awareness as precondition for intercultural competence, and allows analyzing differences and similarities. Beside (cognitive) uncertainty, anxiety is assumed to be crucial in the cultural learning and adaptation process (Gudykunst et al., 1977). Due to the latter approach of anxiety/uncertainty management

Table 1. Bennett's development model of intercultural sensitivity

Ethno-centric Stages			Ethno-relative stages		
Denial	Defense	Minimization	Acceptance	Adaptation	Integration
There is no reason to know something about foreign cultures	My own culture is superior to foreign cultures in many respects	All human beings are similar despite some superficial differences	Differences among people are not a problem, they are of interest for me	I use different standards for the evaluation of situations in foreign cultural contexts	I almost feel as comfortable in another culture as I do in my own culture

(AUM) theory, individuals should learn about the impact of anxiety and uncertainty on the development of intercultural empathy and how to cope with anxiety and uncertainty in a different culture. But how can such intercultural empathy develop? Based on empathy models (Davis, 1996) and Bennett's (1993) model of intercultural sensitivity which are both described below, we suggest that intercultural empathy is the ability to understand and share the thoughts and feelings of members of other cultures.

As far as empathy is concerned, Davis (1996) distinguishes in his organizational model between several processes within the mind of an empathic observer which can be organized according to the cognitive effort they consume. As outcomes of these empathic processes, affective and non-affective outcomes are identified. Affective outcomes are emotions that emerge in the observer, which can be parallel to the emotions detected in the target (emotional contagion, e.g. resulting from motor mimicry or conditioning), or reactive to them (empathic concern or personal distress).

As far as intercultural learning in cross-cultural contexts is concerned, Bennett (1986, 1993) conceptualizes it as a process of personal development, with changing attitudes, feelings and reactions towards own and foreign culture. His Developmental Model of Intercultural Sensitivity (Table 1) as a dynamic approach reflects "how individuals construe their world in terms of dealing with cultural differences between themselves and others as members of distinct groups" (Hesse & Goebel, 2003, p. 2). Because of a missing empirical foundation, this model must be understood as phenomenological and thus as an idealized description of personality development. Bennett (1993) assumes a continuum of intercultural sensitivity. Six stages of development represent different ways of experiencing difference and every stage indicates a particular cognitive structure that is expressed in certain kinds of attitudes and behavior related to cultural difference. The development leads from a more ethno-centrist view, especially considering the own culture, towards ethno-relativism, being characterized by tolerant and respectful openness towards other cultures.

In ORIENT, Bennett's developmental model of intercultural sensitivity was used to describe the stages that guide learners through the interaction with ORIENT as a result from a careful design of the application. Along Bennett's continuum they pass the stages of denial, defense, minimization, acceptance, adaptation, and integration (see Table 1).

Denial of cultural differences may occur, when "physical or social isolation precludes any contact at all with significant cultural differences" (Bennett, 1986, p. 182). Another more common form of denial is parochialism, emerging from a lower degree of contact with other cultures. In extreme cases, cultural differences may be attributed to subhuman status. An individual at this level of sensitivity either doesn't perceive difference at all, or uses wide categories in perceiving difference (e.g. "us"/"them").

Defense as second stage is characterized by strategies such as denigrating differences ("negative stereotyping") or assuming cultural superiority. Cultural differences are identified, but they appear to threaten the centrality of one's world view.

Minimization means that cultural differences are recognized, but considered insignificant or trivial. Instead, commonness is underlined, so that the own world view doesn't need to be questioned. "Minimization may serve the function of preserving for these people a kind of "enlightened ethnocentrism" that sounds interculturally sensitive while allowing them to avoid the sense of incompetence which might arise from confronting cultural unknowns" (Bennett, 1986, p. 190).

A major shift from an ethnocentric to an ethnorelative approach can be seen in the subjective re-construal of difference as a "thing" to difference as a "process", which means that people don't "have" patterns, but rather "behave". Learners change their attitudes, towards more openness and tolerance, and intercultural behavioral competence develops.

Acceptance leads over to ethno-relativism. Instead of appraising cultural differences as positive or negative, they are simply acknowledged in a value-free way. Bennett (1993) differentiates two major levels of acceptance: The acceptance of behavioral difference (language, communication style, and nonverbal patterns) and the acceptance of underlying cultural value differences. Individuals at this stage of intercultural sensitivity enjoy recognizing and exploring difference.

Adaptation to difference as the "heart of intercultural communication" (Bennett, 1986, p. 185) relates to the ability to act ethno-relatively and so the ability to act outside of the own native world view. New skills appropriate to a different world view are acquired in an additive process. Adaptation allows for consciously shifting the frame of reference, because two or more cultural orientation systems have been internalized.

Integration of difference means to apply ethno-relativism to one's own identity. According to Bennett (1986), an individual operating at an integrative level can construe differences as processes, can adapt to these differences, and can construe him or herself in various cultural ways. Phenomena are evaluated as relative to the cultural context and cultural difference is considered as an essential and joyful aspect of life. The achievement of this level normally implies long and intense contacts to different cultures.

The development of ORIENT is based on Bennett's model in that it serves as a reliable guide to the stages the participants pass through on their way to intercultural sensitivity. The "tasks" (based on the interaction with the characters) that the users are confronted with progress according to the different stages of the model, e.g. the first level of ORIENT focuses on the promotion of users' awareness that it is important to learn about a given different cultural background in order to interact successfully in an intercultural context. However, not all of the stages are addressed: The focus lies on the exploration of another (virtual) culture and on the reflection of similarities and differences between the own and the foreign culture (stages of acceptance and adaptation). ORIENT thus is designed to lead the learner to understand how to explore a culture and to understand that thoughts and feelings are culturally driven (see Table 2). A danger attached to such a limitation can be seen in the assumption that the learner has already internalized the earlier stages, i.e. that they are motivated to, curious about and open towards interacting with another culture.

Table 2. Intercultural learning in ORIENT

ORIENT	Stage
Reflection of the meaning of culture and the own culture previous to the role-play.	Acceptance
Role-play as in-world activities.	Acceptance, Adaptation
Reflection (during and after the role play) to enhance learning outcome through learning from each other's experiences: what happened (cognition), how do the characters feel (affect), how would you react (behavior)?	Adaptation

Learning Outcomes of Intercultural Learning

Intercultural competence as a learning outcome is the basis for efficient and successful behavior in cross-cultural encounters (Barmeyer, 2003). According to Hesse and Goebel (2003), intercultural competence is not simply about acquisition of knowledge about another culture or the ability to behave appropriately in that culture – it is about understanding and internalizing appropriate behavior which should emerge naturally in the respective cultural context. Hence, culture-general components (e.g. coping with stress; suspension of overhasty appraisals; consciousness of the culture dependence of cognition, interpretation and action; familiarity with mechanisms of intercultural communication and with principles of acculturation) as well as culture-specific components and abilities provide the basis for intercultural competence; the latter are abilities such as to achieve competences in a target culture, to gain mastery in ethnographic knowledge, and to get to know the world view and behavior in a specific culture. Moreover, Grosch, Groß and Leenen (2002) describe interculturally relevant general personality characteristics, such as resilience, uncertainty- and ambiguity tolerance, cognitive flexibility, emotional resilience, and personal autonomy. These skills that are closely linked to social and emotional learning outcomes lead to the next learning outcome – intercultural empathy – as a concept combining social and emotional learning with the challenges of cross-cultural encounters.

Intercultural Empathy is the core learning outcome of ORIENT; it builds on the general ability to empathize (Davis, 1996) that constitute empathy in the mind of an empathic observer, but it poses more challenges in that it focuses on targets that are less similar than members of the home culture: Building empathy to those who are dissimilar to us not only personality-wise but culture-wise thus should represent a greater challenge than empathizing with members of our own group or culture (Similarity Principle, e.g. Byrne, 1971). The components included in intercultural empathy are outlined in the following:

Firstly, intercultural empathy builds on self-reflection and mental flexibility: being aware of one's own cultural identity as well as being able to temporarily suppress it in order to understand the impact of culture on others (cognitive aspect: resilience, cognitive flexibility, and personal autonomy).

Secondly, they involve stress and ambiguity tolerance: not being afraid of others that seem to be different (affective aspect: uncertainty- and ambiguity tolerance, and emotional resilience). Finally, they involve communicative skills: being able to feed the shared experiences back to others.

ORIENT addresses adolescents being confronted with peers and classmates that are dissimilar to them, but with whom they have to get along and effectively cooperate, for instance in the classroom context. Because it is easier to empathize with those you we perceive as similar to us (e.g. Davis, 1996; Byrne, 1971), ORIENT has to carefully balance the challenge inherent in the experience of dissimilarity between self and other in intercultural contexts with positive reactions to ORIENT that could be provided by perceived similarity between own experiences and the content presented in the software.

HOW EFFECTIVE ARE VIRTUAL LEARNING APPLICATIONS?

General Considerations

Virtual worlds which provide opportunities for exploration, practice, experiments, and construction, have an enriching function to traditional learning tools. They allow for experiential learning (Kolb, 1984) in safe and secure learning environments, in particular for social and emotional learning in complex social situations, without the social risks (e.g. stigmatization, doing harm or being harmed) that the learner faces in real social situations. ORIENT represents a possibility for learners to experience encounters and relations with members of another culture. Moreover, the depicted virtual cultures that struggle with their own intercultural conflicts can act as coping model to the users.

Nevertheless, there is not much empirical evidence yet concerning the relation of learning in virtual worlds and the effectiveness and efficiency of knowledge acquisition (Schwan & Buder, 2002). Moreno et al. (2001) deduce from Vygotskys (1978) assumption of the learning process being routed in social processes in which communication plays an essential role, that an agent can represent the necessary characteristics of a social agent in the learning process. Once a positive relationship is established between agent and learner, it enhances motivation and interest and hence constructive learning. Motivation is critical, because it fosters a more intense occupation with the material as well as transfer activities: "More motivated students try harder to make sense of the presented material than do less motivated students. They are also more likely to form a coherent mental model that enables them to apply what they learned to challenging new problem solving situations." (Moreno et al., 2001, p. 193). The social relationship between learner and agent is the key mechanism to foster interaction and promote learning within a computer-based learning system (Baylor & Ryu, 2003). Baylor (2001) summarizes the main factors which influence the learner's development of confidence in agents: agent believability, motivational attachment to the agent(s), agent competence, and agent trustworthiness. Moreover, to assure quality and quantity of knowledge acquisition, a specific pedagogical arrangement is necessary, such as to choose appropriate tasks, to structure the learning process, to ensure meaningful operation alternatives, and to support the learner through feedback and reflection challenges. Especially in explorative learning environments, specific goals facilitate an integrative and elaborative data processing. Structuring the learning experience in single, clear steps can be realized through an adequate choice of tasks on the one hand (different, temporally short learning episodes for cognitive release, higher motivation, and flexible knowledge representation), as well as through an adequate creation of the virtual reality on the other hand. The former is realized in ORIENT through single scenarios, in which the users need to solve different tasks and conflicts with the Sprytes. However, to ensure the learning outcomes, the process of interacting with a virtual world should be embedded in sessions that serve to prepare and reflect upon the experiences in the virtual learning environment. Therefore, reflection circles before and after the role play are highly recommended to complement the ORIENT learning experience. A facilitator can support the learners by stimulating the discussions when needed, e.g. through helpful questions. Additionally, support is integrated in the virtual world via the ORA-CLE, which provides further information and help for the user. Apart from the carefully designed structure of the application and the inclusion of reflection cycles, the virtual learning environment offers innovative reinforcement for getting into contact with members of other cultures: exciting and highly activating interaction devices such as the WiiMote controller, a game mat or RFID technology will be used by the user to interact with the virtual world.

Results of Evaluating an Early ORIENT Prototype

ORIENT poses a number of different issues for evaluation: the user perspective focuses on a successful outcome in saving the planet while from the design team perspective, success involves both a resulting change in intercultural awareness and behavior (the pedagogical and psychological impact) as well as a high degree of user immersion, engagement and suspension of disbelief (interaction and technical impact). As has been discussed in the context of pervasive games (Vavoula et al., 2006), the use of the real world as part of the application and of novel interaction technology make some traditional forms of evaluation, especially of usability in its narrow sense, somewhat problematic. In the wider sense, the presence of a large number of interacting factors make it hard to evaluate which part of the overall design is responsible for which specific effects.

Evaluation of ORIENT itself is necessarily group-based and focused on qualitative rather than quantitative responses. The instruments used are incorporated into the role-play as Space Command debriefing and as support for the users' "mission" to gain greater awareness of the Spryte culture rather than being presented as an explicit evaluation. For instance, to show they are "qualified" for the internship in general and this mission in particular, participants fill in an applicant's form (demographic data) and the Cultural Intelligence Scale. This approach seeks to capture relevant data in an interesting and engaging way for users and to extend their sense of their role in the ORIENT scenarios.

ORIENT was evaluated in Germany and the UK with four groups in the first and three in the second, each interacting with ORIENT for around two hours. The German groups were all girls aged 13-14, while the UK groups included 6 boys and 3 girls and were somewhat younger, aged 12-13. A set of questionnaires were used, listed in Table 1, which were customized to fit in with the story-world being used as Space Command briefings and debriefings. Interaction behavior within the group of learners was observed in real-time: The technical evaluation team sat behind the team with two laptops and the projector, while the psychological evaluation team members sat in left and right corners of the room filling in the ORAT (Orient Rating process for the Assessment of the Team) and taking notes. The interaction was also videotaped by two cameras and attached microphones, placed in the remaining two corners of the room, directed towards the participants.

ORAT was used to assess whether ORIENT fosters cooperation, with team members coordinating their actions in order to reach their common goal of learning more about the Sprytes. On the whole teams were rated by independent observers as showing a high degree of solution orientation in their activities (UK and German groups), also a high degree of communication related to the content of the application, interaction, and cooperation (UK groups more than German groups). In post-interaction discussions learners reported quite positive feedback about how they felt they had done. The post-interaction questionnaires showed differences between the UK and German groups in their knowledge of and attitude towards the Sprytes. The German girls found Sprytes friendlier, less advanced, younger, and more 'together' compared to their own culture, whereas the UK teenagers saw Sprytes as less friendly, more advanced, older though also more 'together' than their own culture. The UK groups felt significantly more negative (e.g. more threatened, more nervous, more alert, etc.) when interacting with the Sprytes than the German teenagers did. Finally, one significant difference from the Orient Evaluation Questionnaire was that the UK groups thought Sprytes considered them enemies whereas the German teenagers thought Sprytes considered them friends. This may of course have been related to gender rather than culture as only the UK groups contained boys. Despite the large similarities between the learners and the virtual culture of the Sprytes, all groups managed to see some similarities as well as differences between themselves and the Sprytes, suggesting the basis for empathy exists. The conclusion of this evaluation was that ORIENT lays the basis for the development of intercultural empathy. Far more story content needs to be developed however and the personalities of individual Sprytes need to be clearly established, as well as conflicts between them in which teenagers can intervene. The interaction technologies used were both a plus and a minus: they did indeed engage, but required far too much concentration on interaction mechanics, distracting from the Sprytes and their story. More intuitive and less cognitively demanding interaction is a priority in the further development of ORIENT.

CONCLUSIONS

The ORIENT application is an innovative character-based educational role-play aimed at developing inter-cultural empathy in participating users. A culture-specific character architecture has been developed based solidly on theories of cultural dimensioning and intergroup interaction. Initial evaluation shows that this architecture can meet the demands of the social process and story-world of ORIENT and that, combined with the novel interaction modalities discussed above, it offers a new approach to an increasingly important area of Personal and Social Education in which beliefs, attitudes and behaviors are necessarily the pedagogical focus. Evaluation has raised the interesting question of the relationship between personality and culture in synthetic character models and interaction, and further work will be carried out investigating this.

ACKNOWLEDGMENT

This work was partially supported by European Community (EC) and is currently funded by the eCIRCUS project IST-4-027656-STP with university partners Heriot-Watt, Hertfordshire, Sunderland, Warwick, Bamberg, Augsburg, Wuerzburg plus INESC-ID and Interagens. The authors are solely responsible for the content of this publication. It does not represent the opinion of the EC, and the EC is not responsible for any use that might be made of data appearing therein.

REFERENCES

Allbeck, J. M., & Badler, N. I. (2004). Creating Embodied Agents With Cultural Context. In S. Payr, & R. Trappl (eds.), Agent Culture: Human-Agent Interaction in a Multicultural World, (pp. 107—126). London: Lawrence Erlbaum Associates.

Allport, G. W. (1954). The nature of prejudice. Reading, MA: Addison-Wesley.

Andersen, P. A. (2000). Explaining intercultural differences in nonverbal communication. In L. A. Samovar, & R. E. Porter (eds.), Intercultural communication: A reader. Belmont, CA: Wadsworth.

Auernheimer, G. (2003). Einführung in die interkulturelle Pädagogik [Introduction to Intercultural Pedagogy]. Darmstadt, Germany: Wiss. Buchges.

Aylett, R. S., Dias, J., & Paiva, A. (2006). An affectively-driven planner for synthetic characters. In [Cumbria, UK: AAAI Press.]. *Proceedings of ICAPS, 2006*, 2–10.

Bailenson, J. N., Blascovich, J., & Guadagno, R. E. (2008). Self representations in immersive virtual environments. *Journal of Applied Social Psychology*, *38*(11), 2673–2690. doi:10.1111/j.1559-1816.2008.00409.x

Bales, R. F. (1976). Interaction process analysis: A method for the study of small groups. Chicago: University Press.

Bandura, A. (1973). Aggression: a social learning analysis. Englewood Cliffs, NJ: Prentice-Hall.

Bandura, A., & Adams, N. E. (1977). Analysis of self-efficacy theory of behavioral change. *Cognitive Therapy and Research*, *1*(4), 287–310. doi:10.1007/BF01663995

Barmeyer, C. (2003). Interkulturelles Coaching [Intercultural Coaching]. In C. Rauen (ed.), Handbuch Coaching (pp. 241 – 272). Göttingen: Hogrefe.

Baylor, A. L. (2001). Permutations of control: Cognitive considerations for agent-based learning environments. *Journal of Interactive Learning Research*, *12*(4), 403–425.

Baylor, A. L., & Ryu, J. (2003). Evidence that multiple agents facilitate greater learning. International Artificial Intelligence in Education (AI-ED), Sydney, Australia.

Bem, S. (1993). The lenses of gender. New Haven, CT: Yale University Press.

Bennett, M. (1986). A developmental approach to training for Intercultural Sensitivity. *International Journal of Intercultural Relations*, *10*(2), 179–195. doi:10.1016/0147-1767(86)90005-2

Bennett, M. (1998). Intercultural communication: a current perspective. In M. Bennett (ed.), Basic Concepts of Intercultural Communication. Yarmouth, MA: Intercultural Press.

Bennett, M. J. (1993). Towards enthnorelativism: A developmental model of intercultural sensitivity. In M. Paige (ed.), Education for the intercultural experience. Yarmouth, MA: Intercultural Press.

Borde, D. (2007). Psychosoziale Potentiale und Belastungen der Migranten – globale, institutionelle und individuelle Perspektiven [Psycho-social potentials and burdens of migrants – global, instituational and individual perspectives]. In D. Borde, & M. David (ed.), Migration und psychische Gesundheit. Frankfurt am Main, Germany: Mabuse.

Borzak, L. (1981) (ed.). Field study: A source book for experiential learning. Beverly Hills, CA: Sage Publications.

Byrne, D. (1971). The attraction paradigm. New York: Academic Press.

Cameron, L., Rutland, A., Brown, R., & Douch, R. (2006). Changing children's intergroup attitudes toward refugees: Testing different models of extended contact. *Child Development*, *77*(5), 1208–1219. doi:10.1111/j.1467-8624.2006.00929.x

Carron, A. V., Widmeyer, W. N., & Brawley, L. R. (1985). The development of an instrument to assess cohesion in sport teams: The Group Environment Questionnaire. *Journal of Sport Psychology*, *7*, 244–266.

Cassell, J., Sullivan, J., Prevost, S., & Churchill, E. (2000). Embodied Conversational Agents. Cambridge, MA: MIT Press.

Core, M., Traum, D., Lane, H. C., Swartout, W., Gratch, J., van Lent, M., & Marsella, S. (2006). Teaching negotiation skills through practice and reflection with vVirtual humans. *Simulation*, *82*(11), 685–701. doi:10.1177/0037549706075542

Davis, M. H. (1996). Empathy – a social psychological approach. Madison, WI: Brown & Benchmark Publishers.

de Rosis, F., Pelachaud, C., & Poggi, I. (2004). Transcultural Believability in Embodied Agents: A Matter of Consistent Adaptation. In S. Payr, & R. Trappl (eds.), Agent Culture: Human-Agent Interaction in a Multicultural World (pp. 75-106). London: Lawrence Erlbaum Associates.

Dias, J., & Paiva, A. (2005). Feeling and reasoning: a computational model. In *Proceedings of the 12th Portuguese Conference on Artificial Intelligence*, EPIA 2005 (pp. 127-140). Berlin: Springer.

Dörner, D. (2003). The mathematics of emotions. In F. Detje, D.Dörner, & H. Schaub (Eds.), *Proceedings of the Fifth International Conference on Cognitive Modeling* (pp. 75–79). Bamberg, Germany: Universitäts-Verlag.

Elias, M. J., Zins, J. E., Weissberg, R. P., Frey, K. S., Greenberg, M. T., Haynes, N. M., et al. (1997). Promoting social and emotional learning: Guidelines for educators. Alexandria, VA: Association for Supervision and Curriculum Development.

Forgas, J. (1994). Soziale Interaktion und Kommunikation, [Social interaction and communication]. Weinheim, Germany: Beltz.

Gratch, J., & Marsella, S. (2005). Evaluating a computational model of emotion. *Autonomous Agents and Multi-Agent Systems, 11*(1), 23–43. doi:10.1007/s10458-005-1081-1

Greenberg, M. T., Weissberg, R. P., O'Brien, M. U., Zins, J. E., Fredericks, L., Resnik, H., & Elias, M. J. (2003). Enhancing School-Based Prevention and Youth Development Through Coordinated Social, Emotional and Academic Learning. *The American Psychologist, 58*, 466–474. doi:10.1037/0003-066X.58.6-7.466

Grosch, H., Groß, A., & Leenen, W. R. (2002). Interkulturelle Kompetenz in der sozialen Arbeit [Intercultural competence in social work]. In G. Auernheimer (ed.), Interkulturelle Kompetenz und pädagogische Professionalität. Opladen, Germany: Leske + Budrich.

Grosch, H., & Leenen, W. R. (1998). Bausteine zur Grundlegung interkulturellen Lernens [Modules for intercultural learning]. In Interkulturelles Lernen. Arbeitshilfen für politische Bildung. Bonn, Germany: Bundeszentrale für politische Bildung.

Gudykunst, W. B., Hammer, M. R., & Wiseman, R. (1977). An analysis of an integrated approach to cross-cultural training. *International Journal of Intercultural Relations, 1*, 99–109. doi:10.1016/0147-1767(77)90045-1

Gudykunst, W. B., & Mody, B. (2002). Handbook of international and intercultural communication. Thousand Oaks, CA: Sage Publications.

Hall, E. T. (1990). The silent language. New York: Anchor Press.

Hall, E. T. (2001). Understanding cultural differences. Yarmouth, MA: Intercultural Press.

Hall, L., Vala, M., Hall, M., Webster, M., Woods, S., Gordon, A., & Aylett, R. (2006). FearNot's appearance: Reflecting children's expectations and perspectives. In J. Gratch, M. Young, R. Aylett, D. Ballin, & P. Olivier (eds.), *6th International Conference, IVA 2006* (pp. 407-419). Berlin: Springer.

Herskovits, M. (1955). Cultural anthropology. New York: Knopf.

Hesse, H.-G., & Göbel, K. (2003). *Evaluation and quantitative methods in global learning: A contribution from the field of intercultural sensitivity.* Paper presented at the Global Education Network Europe Seminar: Starting practice and theory in global education. Improving quality and raising standards through evaluation. University of Erlangen-Nürnberg, 29.03.2003.

Hinsch, R., & Pfingsten, U. (2002). Gruppentraining Sozialer Kompetenzen (GSK) [Group Training of Social Competencies]. Weinheim, Germany: BeltzPVU.

Hofstede, G. (1979). Value systems in forty countries. In L. Eckensberger, W. Lonner, & Y. Poortinga (eds.), Cross-cultural contributions to psychology. Amsterdam: Swets and Zeitlinger.

Hofstede, G. (1991). Cultures and Organizations. Thousand Oaks, CA: Sage Publications.

Hofstede, G. (2001). Culture's consequences: Comparing values, behaviors, institution, and organizations across nations. Thousand Oaks, CA: Sage Publications.

Hofstede, G., & Bond, M. (1984). Hofstede's culture dimensions. *Journal of Cross-Cultural Psychology, 15*, 417–433. doi:10.1177/0022002184015004003

Huntington, S. P. (2000). Cultures count (Foreword). In L. E. Harrison, & S. Huntington (Eds.), Culture Matters. How Values Shape Human Progress. New York: Basic Books.

Inkeles, A., & Levinson, J. (1969). National character: The study of modal personality and sociocultural systems. In G. Lindzey, & E. Aronson (Eds.), Handbook of social psychology, (Vol. 4, pp. 418-506.). Reading, MA: Addison-Wesley

Isbister, K. (2004). Building bridges through the unspoken: Embodied agents to facilitate intercultural communication. In S. Payr, & R. Trappl (Eds.), Agent Culture: Human-Agent Interaction in a Multicultural World. London: Lawrence Erlbaum Associates.

Janis, I. (1982). Groupthink, (2nd ed.). Boston: Houghton-Mifflin.

Johnson, D. W., Johnson, R. T., & Holubec, E. J. (1993). Cooperation in the classroom. Edina, MN: Interaction Book Company.

Kanther, M. (2001). Interkulturelles Lernen [Intercultural learning]. Stuttgart, Germany: ibidem-Verlag.

Keesing, R. (1974). Theories of culture. *Annual Review of Anthropology, 3*, 73–97. doi:10.1146/annurev.an.03.100174.000445

Kenny, P., Parsons, T., Gratch, J., Leuski, A., & Rizzo, A. (2007) Virtual patients for clinical therapist skills training. In *Proceedings of the 7th International Conference on Intelligent Virtual Agents* (pp. 197-210). Berlin: Springer.

Kluckhohn, C. (1962). Culture and Behavior. New York: The Free Press of Glencoe.

Koda, T., Rehm, M., & André, E. (2008). Cross-cultural evaluations of avatar facial expressions designed by Western Designers. In *Intelligent Virtual Agents.* [Berlin: Springer.]. *Proceedings of IVA, 2008*, 245–252.

Kolb, D. A. (1984). Experiential learning: Experience as the source of learning and development. Englewood Cliffs, NJ: Prentice Hall.

Kriegel, M., Lim, M. L., Nazir, A., Aylett, R., Cawsey, A., Enz, S., & Zoll, C. (2008). Culture-personality based affective model. Enculturating conversational interfaces by socio-cultural aspects of communication. In *Workshop on IUI 2008*, Canary Islands, Jan 13, 2008.

Kroeber, A., & Kluckhohn, C. (1952). Culture. New York: Meridian Books.

Lazarus, R. (1991). Emotion and adaptation. New York: Oxford University Press.

Leichtenstern, K., André, E., & Vogt, T. (2007). Role assignment via physical mobile interaction techniques in mobile multi-user applications for children. In *Ambient Intelligence.* [Berlin: Springer.]. *Proceedings of the AmI, 2007*, 38–54.

Lim, M. Y., Dias, J., Aylett, R., & Paiva, A. (2009) Intelligent NPCs for Educational Role Play Game. In Proceedings of Agents for Games and Simulation Workshop, AAMAS 09, Budapest, Hungary, May 10-15, 2009.

Lohaus, A., Jerusalem, M., & Klein-Heßling, J. (2006). Gesundheitsförderung im Kindes- und Jugendalter [Health promotion in education of children and adolescents]. Göttingen, Germany: Hogrefe.

Mascarenhas, S., Dias, J., Afonso, N., Enz, S., & Paiva, A. (2009) Using Rituals to Express Cultural Differences in Synthetic Characters. In *Proceedings of AAMAS 2009*, Budapest, May 10-15, 2009.

Moreno, R., Mayer, R. E., Spires, H., & Lester, J. (2001). The case for social agency in computer-based teaching: Do students learn more deeply when they interact with animated pedagogical agents? *Cognition and Instruction, 19*, 177–213. doi:10.1207/S1532690XCI1902_02

Mullen, B., & Copper, C. (1994). The Relation between Group Cohesiveness and Performance: An Integration. *Psychological Bulletin, 115*, 210–227. doi:10.1037/0033-2909.115.2.210

Ortony, A., Clore, G., & Collins, A. (1988). The cognitive structure of emotions. Cambridge: Cambridge University Press.

Paiva, A., Dias, J., Aylett, R., Woods, S., Hall, L., & Zoll, C. (2005). Learning by feeling: Evoking empathy with synthetic characters. *Applied Artificial Intelligence, 19*, 235–266. doi:10.1080/08839510590910165

Pettigrew, T. F., & Tropp, L. R. (2006). A meta-analytic test of intergroup contact theory. *Journal of Personality and Social Psychology, 90*, 751–783. doi:10.1037/0022-3514.90.5.751

Rehm, M., André, E., Bee, N., Endrass, B., Wissner, M., Nakano, Y., et al. (2007). The CUBE-G approach – Coaching culture-specific nonverbal behavior by virtual agents. In I. Mayer, & H. Mastik (eds.), *Organizing and Learning through Gaming and Simulation. Proceedings of ISAGA 2007,* (pp. 313-321). Delft: Eburon.

Roschelle, J., & Teasley, S. D. (1995). The construction of shared knowledge in collaborative problem solving. In C. E. O'Malley (Ed.), Computer-supported Collaborative Learning (pp. 69-197). Berlin: Springer.

Rossen, B., Lok, B., Johnsen, K., Lind, S., & Deladisma, A. (2008). Virtual Humans Elicit Skin-Tone Bias Consistent with Real-World Skin-Tone Biases. In *Intelligent Virtual Agents.* [Berlin: Springer.]. *Proceedings of IVA, 2008*, 237–244.

Rotter, J. B. (1954). Social learning and clinical psychology. New York: Prentice-Hall.

Rowe, J., McQuiggan, S., & Lester, J. (2007). Narrative Presence in Intelligent Learning Environments. In *Working Notes of the 2007 AAAI Fall Symposium on Intelligent Narrative Technologies* (pp. 126–133). Arlington, VA.

Schulz von Thun, F. (1001). *Miteinander reden 1: Störungen und Klärungen* [Talking to each other 1: interferences and clarifications]. Reinbek, Germany: Rowohlt.

Schwan, S., & Buder, J. (2002). Lernen als Wissenserwerb in virtuellen Realitäten [Learning as knowledge acquisition in virtual realities]. In G. Bente, N. Krämer, A. Petersen (eds.), Virtuelle Realitäten (pp. 109-129). Göttingen, Germany: Hogrefe.

Seligman, M. E. P. (1972). Learned helplessness. *Annual Review of Medicine, 23*, 407–412. doi:10.1146/annurev.me.23.020172.002203

Slavin, R. E. (1995). Cooperative Learning: theory, research and practice. Boston: Allyn and Bacon.

Triandis, H. C. (1989). The self and social behavior in differing cultural contexts. *Psychological Review, 96*(3), 506–520. doi:10.1037/0033-295X.96.3.506

Tuckman, B. (1965). Developmental sequence in small groups. *Psychological Bulletin, 63*, 384–399. doi:10.1037/h0022100

Turner, J. C. (1987). Rediscovering the social group. Oxford, UK: Blackwell.

Vavoula, G., Meek, J., Sharples, M., Lonsdale, P., & Rudman, P. (2006). A lifecycle approach to evaluating MyArtSpace. In S. Hsi, Kinshuk, T. Chan, & D. Sampson (Eds.), *Proceedings of the 4th IEEE International Workshop on Wireless and Mobile Technologies in Education (WMUTE 2006)* (pp. 18-22). Athens, Greece: IEEE Computer Society.

Vygotsky, L. S. (1978). Mind in society: The development of higher psychological processes. Cambridge, MA: Harvard University Press.

Weidner, M. (2006). Kooperatives Lernen im Unterricht [Cooperative learning in school]. Seelze, Germany: Erhard Friedrich Verlag.

ADDITIONAL READING

Aylett, R., Paiva, A., Woods, S., Hall, L., & Zoll, C. (2005). Expressive Characters in Anti-Bullying Education. In L. Canamero, & R. Aylett (Eds.), Animating Expressive Characters for Social Interaction. (pp. 161-176). Amsterdam: John Benjamins.

Aylett, R. S., & Louchart, S. (2003). Towards a narrative theory of VR. [Special Edition on Storytelling in Virtual Environments]. *Virtual Reality Journal*, *7*(1), 2–9. doi:10.1007/s10055-003-0114-9

Brna, P., Martins, A., & Cooper, B. (1999). My first story: Support for learning to Write Stories. In G. Cumming, T. Okamoto, & L. Gomez (Eds.) Advanced Research in Computers and Communications in Education (Vol. 1, pp. 335-341). Amsterdam: IOS.

Dautenhahn, K. (1996). Embodiment in animals and artifacts. In AAAI FS Embodied Cognition and Action (pp. 27–32). AAAI Press.

de Vries, G. (1997). Involvement of School-aged Children in the Design Process. *Interaction*, *4*(2), 41–42.

Enz, S., & Brosch, S. (2008). Autonomous Agents with Personality. *International Journal of Psychology*, *43*(3/4).

Enz, S., Zoll, C., Vannini, N., Schneider, W., Hall, L., Paiva, A., & Aylett, R. (2007). E – Motional Learning in Primary Schools: FearNot! An Anti-bullying Intervention Based on Virtual Role-play with Intelligent Synthetic Characters. *Electronic Journal e-Learning, 6(2), 111 – 118.*

Hall, L., Woods, S., Dautenhahn, K., & Wolke, D. (2007). Implications of gender differences for the development of animated characters for the study of bullying behavior. *Computers in Human Behavior*, *23*(1), 770–786. doi:10.1016/j.chb.2004.11.018

Ho, W. C., & Watson, S. (2006). Autobiographic knowledge for believable virtual characters. In Intelligent Virtual Agents 2006 (pp. 383 – 394). Springer.

Louchart, S., & Aylett, R. (2004). Narrative theory and emergent interactive narrative. *International Journal of Continuing Engineering Education and Lifelong Learning*, *14*(6), 506–518. doi:10.1504/IJCEELL.2004.006017

Lyons, E., & Chryssochoou, X. (2000). Cross-cultural research methods. In G. M. Breakwell, & S. e. a. Hammond (Eds.) Research methods in psychology (2nd ed., pp. 134-146). London, England: Sage Publishers Ltd.

KEY TERMS AND DEFINITIONS

ORIENT: A software prototype developed by the EU FP6 project eCIRCUS to help teenagers to overcome integration problems.

WiiMote: An interaction device to interact with virtual environments and computer games.

ORA-CLE: A device to help the players of ORIENT to structure their experience in the virtual world.

FAtiMA: An architecture for the building of agents minds.

Social & Emotional Learning: Elias et al. (1997): "process through which children enhance their ability to integrate thinking, feeling, and behaving to achieve important life tasks"

Collaborative Learning: A specific form of small human group-education, which emphasizes and structures the social processes while learning.

Anxiety/Uncertainty Management: Strategies to cope with uncertainty and anxiety when being faced with highly ambiguous situations, e.g. cross-cultural situations.

Ethno-Relative: Learners change their attitudes, towards more openness and tolerance, and intercultural behavioral competence develops.

Ethno-Centric: Learners are centered in their own cultural ways and habits.

Role-Play: A technique to acquire or perform behavior that is currently not available, either because it was not yet learned, or – if it has been learned – is for some reason not executed. It thus aims at the acquisition and rehearsal of new behavior as well as at the actualization of already acquired behavior.

ORAT: An assessment tool for behavioral observation of group interaction, developed by the project team.

ENDNOTE

1 In fact, both terms are often used interchangeably.

Chapter 5
Classroom Management in Synchronous Online Secondary Classrooms

Karina Clemmons
University of Arkansas at Little Rock, USA

Amanda Nolen
University of Arkansas at Little Rock, USA

Andrew Hunt
University of Arkansas at Little Rock, USA

Cheryl Grable
University of Arkansas at Little Rock, USA

Shirley Pickle
Arkansas Department of Education Distance Learning Center, USA

ABSTRACT

Virtual schooling in the United States has continued to grow since the first virtual schools were established over ten years ago. A review of literature related to online education has largely centered on the experience of students in online classes (Barbour & Reeves, 2009), with little emphasis on the experiences of teachers who teach online classes (Robinson, 2008). The current study fills a critical gap in knowledge for teacher educators faced with the complex questions of how best to educate teacher candidates for the modern challenges of online teaching (Zeichner, 2008). Specifically, this study explores the following questions: How is classroom management addressed in an online learning environment? What are the necessary components of an effective online learning environment? The issues examined parallel Domain B of the Pathwise Assessment (Educational Testing Service, 2006): creating a climate of fairness, establishing rapport with students, communicating challenging learning expectations, establishing

DOI: 10.4018/978-1-61520-749-7.ch005

and maintaining consistent standards for classroom behavior, and making the classroom environment conducive to learning. A mixed-methods approach yields quantitative and qualitative data for analysis. The results indicate that the skills teachers acquire managing classroom behavior in traditional classroom settings do not transfer to online environments. Additional results suggest that the role of the facilitator, the students' schools, and technology that allows equitable access is critical to the success of teachers creating an effective online learning environment. A discussion and implications for future research are also included.

ORGANIZATIONAL BACKGROUND

Arkansas Department of Education Distance Learning Center

Davis & Roblyer (2005) suggest that a need to provide equal access to rural, under-served, and at-risk populations precipitated the first virtual schools. Online classrooms can be broadly categorized by two different delivery methods, asynchronous and synchronous. Asynchronous delivery methods are more common in online schools and are characterized by interactions that allow students and teachers to work independently at their own pace, whereas synchronous delivery methods utilize real-time technologies such as chat, video conferencing, instant messages, and real-time audio conferencing (Barbour & Reeves, 2009). In the synchronous classroom, educators become facilitators of the content, technology becomes the catalyst in launching students on their path of discovery, and students are engaged in expanding and satisfying their intellectual needs.

Arkansas is a state in the southern region of the United States with over 37% of students in rural school districts (National Center for Education Statistics, 2009). In an effort to better serve its rural student population, the Arkansas Department of Education established a Distance Learning Center (DLC) to provide online learning instruction in all content areas to school districts across the state. The DLC provides synchronous, interactive teaching/learning experiences in real time through Compressed Interactive Video (CIV), internet, and document camera images displayed on computer monitors (Arkansas Department of Education Distance Learning Center, 2009).

The primary focus of the DLC is to assist secondary schools (grades 9 through 12) that cannot find teachers qualified in specific subject areas and to provide flexibility in class scheduling for students. During the initial year of operation in 2001, the DLC employed five Spanish teachers, one mathematics teacher, and one language arts/journalism teacher. Currently, at the completion of the eighth academic year of operation, the DLC employs 25 teachers who provide elementary and secondary content to schools throughout Arkansas. All of the teachers are located at the main DLC facility in Maumelle, Arkansas. The DLC provides all of the state-required units of instruction except music and physical education.

During the 2008-2009 academic year, the DLC instructed close to 3,000 secondary students representing the majority of school districts across the state. In one class period, a teacher may have students from as many as four different locations across the state of Arkansas. While students and teachers are geographically separated, the lack of physical proximity does not prevent the teachers and students from developing personal connections. In addition to synchronous online classroom interaction, teachers also meet students at venues around the state for enrichment activities, and students sometimes visit the DLC to meet their teachers.

The DLC content is designed to meet the Arkansas Curriculum Frameworks and National Standards, with major assessments that measure what the students have been taught over the course of a semester. Students' academic success in a technology-rich environment is reflected in the fact that 95 percent of students achieve a passing grade in DLC classes.

The DLC teachers conduct their classes from self-contained offices. Each office is equipped with a Compressed Interactive Video (CIV) system, document camera, computer, VCR, DVD player, and CD player. Each teacher is provided with technology specific to his/her instructional needs. All of the mathematics and science teachers have TI-85 calculators that are connected directly to the CIV systems and software specific to the content areas. The journalism, creative writing, and art teachers have digital cameras, scanners, and the Adobe Creative Suite of software products to use when teaching the students and to facilitate grading of student work. The guiding principle concerning the use of technology at the DLC is to ensure that the teachers have the resources to provide quality instruction to students and make the process as efficient as possible. The DLC has integrated real-time features of CIV technologies that result in a highly interactive and technology-rich educational experience for the students.

The DLC has been instrumental in moving Arkansas secondary schools that receive content from the DLC to 1:1 computing, meaning that schools that receive content from the DLC must provide a networked computer for each student during the class period. With the realization of 1:1 computing, the DLC has been able to implement online testing that provides students with immediate feedback. Additionally, 1:1 computing helps engage students during instructional time. For example, in the math classes, the teachers use the whiteboard feature of the synchronous computer conferencing program and have up to six students work the identical problem at the same time and monitor the work of each student. Every student in the class period is able to view the work of the students and listen to the teacher simultaneously. This is something that cannot be accomplished in the traditional classroom.

Classroom Management at the DLC

Effective classroom management, a teacher's ability to maintain cooperative and pro-social student behavior that is conducive to learning, clearly presents challenges for a teacher of a virtual class who may be hundreds of miles away from the students he or she is teaching. Each classroom where the students are located for their online class has a facilitator, an adult supervisor who has been trained to work with the DLC teachers and aid in classroom management, test monitoring, and other duties required to maintain the classroom. Although the facilitator is in the classroom throughout the entire class session, classroom management of student behavior remains the responsibility of the DLC teacher.

The DLC has a defined discipline policy which is discussed and signed by each student and his/her parent/guardian before being allowed to attend the class, but the policy primarily addresses consequences of infractions. Infractions may include but are not limited to, cheating, disturbing class, plagiarism, cyber bullying, and improper internet use. One of the primary consequences for disregarding the DLC discipline policy is the origination of a discipline report that is signed by the teacher, facilitator, DLC director, and student, and then given to the parent/guardian and school site administrator as documentation of the infraction. If a student receives two discipline reports, the DLC director calls the school site principal and requests a conference with the parent/guardian of the student via phone or CIV to inform the parent/guardian that if a third discipline report is originated, the student will receive a failing grade for the semester in which he/she is dropped from the class.

While the DLC's discipline policy clearly addresses punitive responses to undesired student behavior, what is missing is a clear understanding of what special skills are required for a teacher of a synchronous online class to effectively maintain positive, cooperative, and pro-social student behavior that is conducive to learning. What is the skill set necessary for teachers in online classrooms to manage student behavior? Is that skill set similar to that of a traditional classroom? New technology has offered new media of learning, yet teacher education programs have neglected to prepare teachers for online environments; perhaps assuming that the same skills transfer from the traditional classroom to the online classroom.

SETTING THE STAGE

Background and Objectives

Online education continues to grow throughout the developed and developing world, motivated in large part by increased accessibility and equitable education for rural, underserved, and at-risk students (Davis & Roblyer, 2005). Classroom management has long been recognized as a foundation of effective instruction, as indicated by its prominent weight on teacher evaluations such as Pathwise Assessment (Educational Testing Service, 2006) used by the State of Arkansas, yet current research offers little examination of contemporary issues and challenges in classroom management faced by P-12 educators teaching online.

This case study of teachers in a synchronous online secondary classroom seeks to answer the following questions: How is classroom management addressed in an online learning environment? What are the necessary components of an effective online learning environment? The results offer critical insight into contemporary issues in online classrooms, touching on several of the social, technological, economical, and political factors facing the global education community, and are of vital importance to educators, administrators, and institutions of higher learning involved in teacher preparation. Specific areas examined parallel Domain B of the Pathwise Assessment (Educational Testing Service, 2006): creating a climate of fairness, establishing rapport with students, communicating challenging learning expectations, establishing and maintaining consistent standards for classroom behavior, and making the classroom environment conducive to learning.

Though the number of students enrolled in online classes continues to increase, the educational community cannot simply assume that classroom management, or any other aspect of teaching, is the same in an online classroom as in a face-to-face (F2F) classroom. A new research agenda with methodologies tailored to the online teaching experience is required to learn more about how to best prepare teachers to teach online classes (Dede, Ketelhut, Whitehouse, Breit, & McClosky, 2009; Schlager, Farooq, Fusco, Schank, & Dwyer, 2009).

Previous Research

Teacher preparation programs must continually reinvent degree programs to effectively train teacher education candidates for the challenges of education in the 21st century. One of the most pressing contemporary challenges is how to train teacher candidates to effectively integrate technology into the classroom, and how to prepare for the growing need to teach virtual classes. "If schools are to foster meaningful learning, then the ways that we use technologies in schools must change from technology-as-teacher to technology-as-partner in the learning process" (Jonassen, Howland, Marra, & Crismond, 2008, p. 7).

Since the turn of the 21st Century, greater emphasis has been placed on anytime, anywhere learning environments in teacher preparation. The Web-Based Education Commission (WBEC) was established as part of the re-authorization of the Higher Education Act in 1998. The charter for this commission was to report research findings and policy recommendations regarding online education to the President of the United States and the U.S. Congress. Reporting to the U.S. Congress in 2000, the WBEC challenged teacher preparation programs to offer relevant professional development for educators and administrators in integrating technology in the classroom. The report stated that, "not enough is being done to assure that today's educators have the skills and knowledge needed for effective web-based teaching." Further, the report issued a call to action suggesting that if we do not "address this issue at once, we will soon have lost the opportunity to enhance the performance of a whole generation of new teachers, and the students they teach" (p. iv). The Commission recommended that the educational community develop common standards for high quality online courses that are comparable to the standards required for onsite programs (WBEC, 2000).

Another dilemma for initial teacher preparation programs is how to manage distant field placements. The challenge for remote field placements and supervision is the actual distance which becomes costly in travel as well as in time for the supervisor. Simpson (2006) states, "It may be impossible to release the lecturer from other teaching duties to visit the students who are on field experience. Cost is a consideration. Travel is expensive" (p. 244). Online field supervision provides flexibility of time by eliminating transportation and distance.

Davis & Roblyer (2005) suggest that even though the first virtual schools were created to provide equal access to high quality education, today's virtual school student is just as likely to be one who prefers the self-pacing and flexibility of virtual learning as one who lacks local access to courses needed for graduation" (p. 400). Furthermore,"...the provision of guided observations and effective mentoring to develop the candidates' practice in live K-12 virtual classroom(s) needs to be creatively developed, so that some beginning teachers join the profession with an ability to assist other teachers in VS [virtual schools] or have teaching experience in VS" (p. 402).

Skylar, Higgins, Boone, & Jones (2005) compared the academic performance of distance learners via online learning environment to that of students in a traditional setting. The study indicated that there is no significant difference in the achievement and satisfaction of students participating in these environments. Grable, Hunt, & Unrue (2008) also found little difference in the performance of pre-service teachers in traditional and distance learning field experiences, but their research unearthed a critical issue: educators teaching online have begun to notice differences in classroom management skills needed in an online classroom versus a traditional classroom, but have received little preparation in how to deal with these challenges. The merging of traditional instruction and modern technology through elearning presents unique issues that are vital to understand in order to prepare teachers worldwide to adapt to the rapidly changing nature of education (Hunt, Grable, Clemmons & Clark, 2009).

In the DLC, a class may simultaneously contain students from as many as four different schools from across the state, and technology is set up so that the class that makes the most noise, either by asking questions, socializing, or even just loudly rustling papers, is the class that is displayed on the teacher's screen. One of the participating teachers in a study by Grable, Hunt & Unrue (2008) noted that it was necessary to be especially proactive by calling on individual students at the various sites by name in order to involve all students in the learning. One participant felt the student/teacher relationship was enhanced because students were more "focused on their individual computer screen and paid better attention to the technology and manipulatives I used as a demonstration to teach motion physics" (p.404). The participant described that students were not as attentive to the same lesson taught in a local high school, stating, "It is like the DLC students feel they have one-on-one personal attention through the computer. What I consider to be the biggest problem with a virtual field is that I can't walk around and look over the kids' shoulders, but the trade-off for student attention and participation is worth it (p.404)."

CASE DESCRIPTION

Teacher Evaluation

Teacher education candidates at the University of Arkansas at Little Rock (UALR), a public metropolitan university with an enrollment of over 12,000 students (UALR, 2009), are evaluated in all field placements with a Teacher Performance Internship Assessment that is based on the Pathwise Teacher Performance Assessment created by the Educational Testing Service (ETS, 2006); however, components have been added in the areas of communication and professional ethics in order to align with UALR's College of Education conceptual frameworks.

The State of Arkansas is one of only two states to adopt Praxis III (ETS, 2006) as a method of assessing teacher performance during the first year of initial teacher licensure. Utilizing trained assessors who have passed the ETS test battery, experienced teachers, administrators, and teacher educators complete a one-time evaluation which includes pre-interview, classroom observation, and post-interview to determine whether the novice teacher should continue in the classroom without remediation.

Most teachers at the DLC have been trained in how to use the Teacher Performance Internship Assessment to self-evaluate and/or have been evaluated by Praxis III. This training is used to assess teacher candidates who complete a field placement in their classes. The training gives the teachers a foundation to evaluate their own performance with little bias. Domain B of the Teacher Performance Internship Assessment Evaluation covers five areas related to classroom management: creating a climate that promotes fairness, establishing and maintaining rapport with students, communicating challenging learning expectations to students, establishing and maintaining consistent standards of classroom behavior, and making the physical environment as safe and conducive to learning as possible. A survey based on this instrument was created that addressed the previously listed five areas, but specifically for teachers in online and F2F settings.

The survey was administered to 24 secondary education teachers who teach at the DLC in central Arkansas. Fourteen of these teachers had traditional classroom experience, whereas the remaining 10 teachers had no experience teaching face to face. The intent was to examine whether these two groups of teachers (those with traditional experience and those without) varied regarding their perception of classroom climate and classroom management of online or distance learning.

The survey consisted of 10 forced-choice (Likert) items and 2 open-ended items. The 10 items consisted of two sets of questions: one set focusing on online teaching and the other on F2F teaching. Each set asked the teachers to rate the ease with which they could create a climate of fairness, establish rapport with students, establish standards for behavior, communicate learning expectations, and establish a safe learning environment. The items included a five-point scale ranging from "Extremely Easy," "Somewhat Easy," "Neutral," "Somewhat Difficult," and "Extremely Difficult." The teachers with traditional classroom experience completed the items for both F2F teaching in addition to online teaching. Those without traditional classroom experience only completed the items related to online teaching. A summary of the responses for these items is presented in Figure 1. The open-ended items asked the teachers to include any additional comments regarding their experiences of classroom management in online classrooms (C1), and in traditional F2F classrooms (C2).

The experience and background of the teachers in both groups is summarized in Figure 2. The F2F teachers accumulated an average of 9.71 years of experience in the traditional classroom and 3.79 years of teaching online. The Online Only teachers accumulated 3.10 years experience teaching online. Across both of the groups, most of the

Figure 1. Frequencies (n) of survey responses by teachers with online experience only and teachers with both face to face (F2F) experience and online experience

Items completed by F2F Teachers and Online Only Teachers	Very Easy	Somewhat Easy	Neutral	Somewhat Difficult	Very Difficult
How easy is it to...					
...create a climate that promotes fairness in your online classroom?					
Online Experience Only	5	5	0	0	0
F2F and Online Experience	3	9	0	2	0
Total	8	14	0	2	0
... establish and maintain rapport with students in your online classroom?					
Online Experience Only	2	3	1	4	0
F2F and Online Experience	3	6	2	3	0
Total	5	9	3	7	0
... communicate challenging learning expectations to students in your online classroom?					
Online Experience Only	3	5	1	1	0
F2F and Online Experience	3	5	3	3	0
Total	6	10	4	4	0
... establish and maintain consistent standards of classroom behavior for students in your online classes?					
Online Experience Only	2	4	1	3	0
F2F and Online Experience	3	4	3	4	0
Total	5	8	4	7	0
... make the physical environment as safe and conducive to learning as possible in your online classes?					
Online Experience Only	5	1	0	4	0
F2F and Online Experience	3	2	5	3	1
Total	8	3	5	7	1
Items completed by the F2F Teachers only:					
How easy is it to...					
... create a climate that promotes fairness in your face to face classroom?	2	9	1	2	0
... establish and maintain rapport with students in your face to face classroom?	7	5	1	0	0
... communicate challenging learning expectations to students in your face to face classroom?	3	6	3	2	0
... establish and maintain consistent standards of classroom behavior for students in your face to face classes?	2	6	3	3	0
... make the physical environment as safe and conducive to learning as possible in your face to face classes?	5	3	3	3	0

teachers are in Foreign Languages (n = 10). The remaining participants were distributed across the Performing and Visual arts (n = 5), English (n = 2), History (n = 2), Math (n = 2), Marketing/Finance (n = 2), and Science (n = 1).

Teachers with F2F Experience

The responses of the F2F Teachers were examined across the two sets of items: teaching online and teaching F2F. There were no significant differences in their perception of the difficulty with which to establish a positive learning environment online or F2F. In other words, they thought the two environments posed similar difficulties with respect to building rapport, communicating expectations, and managing behavior.

Transferring Experience from F2F to Online Environments

The responses of the F2F teachers were compared with those of the Online Only group for the items addressing the online environment. It

Figure 2. Experience and background of participants

Teaching Experience		
Experience teaching face to face (F2F) (Mean)		
F2F Teachers	9.71 years	
Online Only Teachers	0 years	
Experience teaching Online (Mean)		
F2F Teachers	3.79 years	
Online Only Teachers	3.10 years	
Curriculum Area		
Foreign Languages	10	41.70%
Arts	5	20.80%
English/Composition	2	8.30%
History	2	8.30%
Math	2	8.30%
Management/Finance	2	8.30%
Science	1	4.20%

was hypothesized that the F2F group would be able to transfer their experience in the classroom to the online environment and find it easier to establish a positive learning environment when compared to the Online Only group. The results did not support this hypothesis as there were no significant differences between the two groups. Whatever experience the teachers acquired F2F before teaching online did not seem to offer an advantage for those teachers. They found it to be as difficult to establish a positive learning environment online as those with no prior F2F experience.

Qualitative Findings

The narrative comments contributed by the participants in the final items on the survey were analyzed using SPSS Text Analysis for Surveys. The software's statistical and linguistic algorithms were used to cluster and classify the data and to identify trends through concept maps or constellations. Key concepts were extracted from the data using the language processing text analysis technology. Once the concepts were extracted, they formed the foundation for constructing larger category terms. A combination of statistics based and linguistics-based methods were used to determine how frequently terms occurred in the data and established a semantic network which created a probabilistic analysis of the co-occurrence of terms. Finally, a constellation of terms was produced showing the relationships and relative importance of the categories of terms identified across the responses.

Twenty of the twenty-four participants' responses were included in this dataset. Four of the participants neglected to offer comments on items C1 and C2. The extraction results from the SPSS TAS 2.1 yielded 160 terms from the participants' comments on classroom management in online classrooms. These extractions were then used to build the categories using a linguistic algorithm. A category, in this study, refers to a group of closely related terms or concepts described by a short phrase or label that captures its meaning. For example, the category Classroom Management is comprised of several terms and concepts generated from the data (i.e., "discipline," "behavior," "behavioral expectations," "behavior policy," and "challenges to discipline").

The 160 terms were reduced to 9 categories: Physical Distance, Teacher/Facilitator Connection, Communication, School Environment, Technology Issues, Teacher/Student Connection, Teacher Behaviors, Facilitator Behaviors, and Classroom Management. These resulting categories along with their defining terms are presented in Figure 4. In addition to reporting the frequency of terms and categories, the data were examined for co-occurrences of categories resulting in a category web demonstrating the strength of influence and the strength of relationships among these categories (Figure 3). The web consists of nodes representing categories connected by lines representing co-occurrences. The size of the node

Figure 3. Category web demonstrating the strength and frequency (n) of co-occurring categories resulting from participants' comments about classroom management in online environments

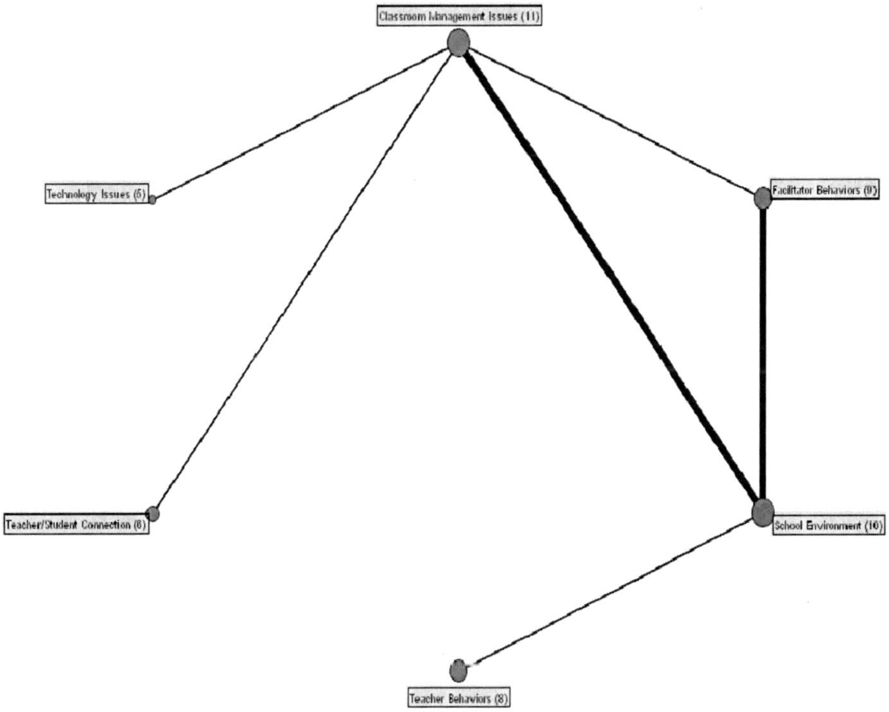

indicates the relative size of the category based on the number of times it occurred in the data. The thickness of the line between two categories denotes the number of common occurrences they share.

The strongest category co-occurrences were Classroom Management – School Environment; and Facilitator Behavior – School Environment; comprising 15% of the co-occurrences. Other categories that co-occurred with Classroom Management included Facilitator Behavior (6%), Teacher/Student Connection (6%), and Technology Issues (6%). These 5 co-occurrences comprised 33% of the total 25 co-occurrences detected.

School Environment

A common theme among the participants was the role of the school in the success of managing classroom behavior. In one class, a teacher might have several schools represented, each with its respective policies and expectations for discipline and student behavior. Issues arose when the students' school policies conflicted with or even contradicted those of the online teacher. The following is a comment from one of the F2F teachers regarding this issue.

> *Because I may be teaching for several different classrooms at one time there may be a variety of school based expectations for student behavior and participation. It is a challenge to establish standards for students who attend schools that do not emphasize the same educational values I set for my classrooms. When I have schools with different education values in class together, I expend great effort creating an environment that meets the needs of all my students in the distance format. (F2F Teacher #14)*

Figure 4. Categories and defining terms extracted from the narrative data resulting from the question, "Please write any additional comments regarding your experience of classroom management in a synchronous online classroom."

Teacher/Facilitator Connection	**Communication**
working together	maintaining open communication
maintaining open communication	expectations
establishing a good relationship with facilitator	communication
faciltator as extra pair of eyes	expectation factor
Technology Issues	**Teacher/Student Connection**
Internet as a distraction for students	connect with the students
volume	build rapport with the students
view only one school at a time	establish and maintain rapport in the classroom
camera	IM a student about a problem
positioning of the cameras	teacher cannot be an involved due to distance
	time
	face time
Teacher Behaviors	**School Environment**
education values in class	key to the environment
educational values	variety of school
online teacher	schools block
teacher	daily procedures in our class
lesson format	school in a class
teaching	environment
lesson	handbook for our class
educator	class
teaching experience	school
face-to-face teachers	structured class
	class period
Facilitator Behaviors	**Classroom Management Issues**
adversarial facilitator	discipline
skills of the adult facilitator	challenges to discipline
facilitator	behavior
true facilitator	prevent behavioral problems
	strict discipline policy
	behavioral expectation
	bear witness to the behavior

This comment is echoed across all of the co-occurrences of these categories. This shared concern of the teachers emphasizes the importance of a shared set of policies between the online teacher and the participating schools. This would establish a common set of values that could be enforced and upheld by both parties.

Facilitator Behavior

The role of the facilitator in the success of online teaching was considered critical by the teachers included in this study. This category co-occurred strongly with both Classroom Management and the School Environment and thus will be addressed together. The teachers indicated that an effective facilitator meant the difference in the quality of learning on the part of the student. Just as behavior policies vary by school, so does the quality of facilitators. The teachers rely on an engaged facilitator in the room to help manage behavior and to keep the students on task.

The best approach is to have an active facilitator in each school, constantly monitoring what the students are doing. If the students know that the facilitator is looking over their shoulders, they are much more likely to stay on task. (Online Only Teacher #9)

The role of the facilitator is very important. They can be a true facilitator or they can be an impediment to the learning process. Establishing a good relationship and maintaining open communication with your facilitators is essential. (F2F Teacher #1)

Classroom management can vary depending on the rapport we establish with our facilitators. If we're working together, it's much easier, but if you have an un-involved or adversarial facilitator, it can become impossible. (F2F Teacher #4)

The F2F Teachers indicated that having a facilitator in the class with the students in many ways made classroom management for online teaching easier than in the traditional classroom. They viewed that supervision as "another set of eyes" that watched over the students' behavior.

The issue of the facilitator behavior and the importance this role takes in classroom management was a prominent theme. Its co-occurrence with Classroom Management and School Environment accounted for 13.5% of the occurrences in the data. This indicates how much care must be taken in training or orienting someone to that role. How a facilitator is chosen and placed can mean the difference between a successful and an unsuccessful student learning experience.

Teacher/Student Connection

The participants all expressed concern about connecting with their students and establishing a rapport with them. This was particularly true for the F2F Teachers who were concerned that the quality of the online rapport was poor compared with their F2F experience. Two teachers (Online Only Teacher #15 & F2F Teacher #20) attempted to use technology in an effort to establish personal communication mimicking that of a traditional classroom.

I can also maintain rapport and control because in certain instances I could simply IM [instant message] a student privately to have them stop a particular behavior or to find out if something is wrong in the classroom. (Online Only Teacher #15)

One way I have connected the most with my students is by starting to use a closed social network called edmodo.com where students can post and reply to messages from me and their fellow classmates. (F2F Teacher #20)

However, most of the F2F Teachers simply expressed frustration that they could not get to know their students better or interact with them in the same manner they did in their traditional classrooms. Nevertheless, the exchange of easier classroom management for less teacher/student connection seemed to be a trade-off these teachers were willing to make.

Technology Issues

The final significant theme related to Classroom Management in synchronous online classes was that of Technology Issues. Most of the issues were centered around the setup and sensitivity of the camera in the classrooms. The cameras were sound sensitive and focused on whoever was talking or making noise to the exclusion of all other sites. As a result 'louder' schools were viewed more frequently than 'quieter' schools. This caused several of the teachers concern that quieter students did not have equal opportunity to participate in discussions and activities as more assertive students.

... the teacher sees whichever school is currently talking or is making the loudest noise (this could be air conditioning, background noise, or students' talking). So, if the teacher is seeing one loud school and not another, it is difficult to know if the more quiet school is on task or not. (Online Only Teacher #24)

IMPLICATIONS AND CHALLENGES

The results of this case study have far reaching implications for teacher education programs seeking to better prepare teachers to adapt to the challenges of online learning environments by presenting a clear picture of the current challenges of online classroom management. This research fills a critical gap to help educators be more effective in a technologically modern world by adapting classroom management skills to distance learning.

This study indicates that one of the major factors impacting a successful synchronous online class is the actual technology itself. When the technology is limiting, such as computer screens only showing the teacher one class at a time, or cameras automatically focusing on student noise, this creates limitations for instruction that would not be found in a traditional F2F classroom. It is essential that teachers inform technology development in these areas to ensure that technology supports distance learning in the best way possible.

Looking toward the future, a major concern for teacher education programs is finding a way to address the growing need for more teachers who have been trained specifically for the challenges of teaching online. It is vital to develop strategies to effectively train teachers not only for the traditional classroom, but also for non-traditional classroom environments including online. The need for qualified online teachers leads to many further challenges that should be explored with future research on issues related to field experiences and field supervision in online classroom environments.

SOLUTIONS AND RECOMMENDATIONS

More teachers will be needed to teach the growing number of online classes; however, teacher preparation programs are inadequately prepared with research regarding effective online teaching. First, teacher preparation programs should add experiences specifically addressing online teaching skills, and integrate these skills into all methods classes. These experiences would include multiple forms of non-traditional environments including completely online (i.e., synchronous and asynchronous) as well as hybrid courses (i.e., combination traditional and non-traditional). Skills that need to be acquired by the teacher preparation students include assessment, student engagement, as well as classroom management.

Second, teacher preparation programs need to integrate online teaching into field experiences for pre-service teacher candidates, whether through observations or through formal internships. Requiring online field experiences in addition to traditional F2F field experiences will help prepare pre-service teachers for the possibility of teaching online, prepare them to learn to effectively integrate technology into F2F classes, and provide more flexibility for pre-service teacher candidates to complete field experience requirements.

Third, distance learning centers should work to establish a shared set of values and expectations with participating schools to better support the online teacher in classroom management. This may indicate a need for improved communication between distance learning centers and the on-site school administrators. As a result, students will know that expectations for behavior in the online classroom are the same as in their traditional F2F classrooms.

Another important recommendation is to emphasize the training and quality of the facilitator who works in the room with the students. As the findings of this study strongly suggest, the role of the facilitator is critical to successful classroom management. Facilitators need to be fully briefed on the expectations of student behavior in addition to the content of the curriculum. They must be actively engaged with the students.

Finally, the authors call for more research regarding the many aspects of effective online teaching, from classroom management, instructional design, and effectively using and integrating current technology. Moving forward, it is essential to have a better understanding of the ways in which online teaching is similar to and different from F2F teaching. Armed with further knowledge, teacher preparation programs will be called upon to keep pace with the demands of technology in a changing world.

REFERENCES

Arkansas Department of EducationDistance LearningCenter. (2009). Retrieved May 26, 2009, from http://dlc.k12.ar.us/

Barbour, M. K., & Reeves, T. C. (2009). The reality of virtual schools: A review of the literature. *Computers & Education*, *52*, 402–416. doi:10.1016/j.compedu.2008.09.009

Davis, N. E., & Roblyer, M. D. (2005). Preparing teachers for the "schools that technology built": Evaluation of a program to train teacher for virtual schooling. *Journal of Research on Technology in Education*, *37*(4), 399–409.

Dede, C., Ketelhut, D. J., Whitehouse, P., Breit, L., & McClosky, E. M. (2009). A Research Agenda for online professional development. *Journal of Teacher Education*, *60*(1), 8–19. doi:10.1177/0022487108327554

Educational Testing Service. (2006). Pathwise Series of Professional Development Programs.

Grable, C., Hunt, A., & Unrue, E. (2008). Comparing digital to traditional field experience in pre-service teacher education. In K. McFerrin, et al. (Eds.), *Proceedings of Society for Information Technology and Teacher Education International Conference* 2008 (pp. 400-405). Chesapeake, VA: AACE.

Hunt, A., Grable, C., Clemmons, K., & Clark, A. (2009). Digital field experiences in teacher education: Teaching and supervision in distance education. In C. Crawford et al. (Eds.), *Proceedings of Society for Information Technology and Teacher Education International Conference 2009* (pp.389-391). Chesapeake, VA: AACE.

Jonassen, D. H., Howland, J., Marra, R. M., & Crismond, D. (2008). Meaningful learning with technology. Upper Saddle River, NJ: Pearson.

National Center for Educational Statistics. (2009). *Numbers and types of public elementary and secondary education agencies from the common core of data: School year 2006-07* [Data file]. Retrieved from http://nces.ed.gov/pubs2009/pesagencies07/tables/table_06.asp

Robinson, S. P. (2008). Settings for teacher education: Challenges in creating a stronger research base. In M. Cochran-Smith, S. Feiman-Nemser, & D. J. Mcintyre (Eds.), Handbook of research on teacher education: Enduring questions in changing contexts. New York: Routledge.

Schlager, M., Farooq, U., Fusco, J., Schank, P., & Dwyer, N. (2009). Analyzing online teacher networks: Cyber networks require cyber research tools. *Journal of Teacher Education*, *60*(1), 86–100. doi:10.1177/0022487108328487

Simpson, M. (2006). Field experience in distance delivered initial teacher education programmes. *Journal of Technology and Teacher Education*, *14*(2), 241–254.

Skylar, A. A., Higgins, K., Boone, R., & Jones, P. (2005). Distance education: An exploration of alternative methods and types of instructional media in teacher education. *Journal of Special Education Technology*, *20*(3), 25–33.

University of Arkansas at Little Rock. (2009). Retrieved May 28, 2009, from http://ualr.edu/www/

Web-Based Education Commission. (2000, December). *The power of the Internet for learning: Moving from promise to practice.* Retrieved June 2, 2009, from http://www.ed.gov/offices/AC/WBEC/FinalReport/

Zeichner, K. (2008). Settings for teacher education. In M. Cochran-Smith, S. Feiman-Nemser, & D. J. Mcintyre (Eds.), Handbook of research on teacher education: Enduring questions in changing contexts. New York: Routledge.

ADDITIONAL READING

Barbour, M., & Reeves, T. (2009). The reality of virtual schools: A review of the literature. *Computers & Education, 52*(2), 402–416. doi:10.1016/j.compedu.2008.09.009

Cennama, K. S., Ross, J. D., & Ertmer, P. A. (2010). Technology integration for meaningful classroom use: A standards-based approach. Belmont, CA: Wadsworth.

Recesso, A., & Orrill, C. (2008). Integrating technology into teaching: The technology and learning continuum. Boston, MA: Houghton Mifflin.

KEY TERMS AND DEFINITIONS

Asynchronous Online Learning: Learning that uses technology to include learners from a variety of different locations, though interaction does not necessarily occur at the same time.

Classroom Management: The practices and procedures that allow teaching and learning to proceed smoothly with minimal interruptions.

Distance Learning: Learning that uses technology to include learners who are not at the same location, as in a traditional classroom.

Online Teaching: Technology supported learning in which learners may not be in the same location, as in a traditional classroom.

Teacher Preparation: Coursework and training designed to provide teachers with the knowledge, skills, and disposition to successfully facilitate learning.

Synchronous Online Learning: Learning that uses technology to include learners from a variety of different locations at the same time.

Virtual School: A school that uses technology to teach entirely through online methods.

Chapter 6
Safe Motherhood Clinical Skills:
A Self-Paced Learning Intervention in Ghana

Nancy Kiplinger
University of North Carolina at Chapel Hill, USA

Wallace Hannum
University of North Carolina at Chapel Hill, USA

ABSTRACT

This case explores the challenges of providing training to health care personnel in Ghana that is appropriate 1) in terms of training content to enable them to perform well in their positions, and 2) in terms of training delivery to take into account the geographic, social, and economic circumstances in Ghana. The approach taken uses self-paced learning modules, paired learning teams, clinical practice with feedback, and supervision. The strategy is illustrated through an example of a learning package that was evaluated for effectiveness, efficiency, and acceptability. The evaluation demonstrated that this approach produced greater learning gains than a traditional approach and was cost-effective. The case proposes solutions to strengthen pedagogy and a strategy for ensuring that the learning design is effective before it is deployed via technology.

ORGANIZATION BACKGROUND

This case study is based on a public health project undertaken in Ghana by the Ghana Ministry of Health (MOH) and a non-governmental organization (NGO) based in the United States. The project was developed to improve health outcomes for mothers and babies by improving the skills of Ghanaian nurses and midwives in remote areas of northern Ghana.

As in many developing countries, Ghana's economic and social progress depends upon adequate health care. The Ministry of Health is the governmental organization with responsibility to improve the health status of all people living in Ghana, thereby contributing to the government's vision of transforming Ghana into a middle-income country by 2015. The Ministry of Health works in partnership with its agencies and stakeholders to improve human capital, thus "creating wealth through health" through the development and implementation of

DOI: 10.4018/978-1-61520-749-7.ch006

proactive policies that will ensure improved health and vitality among Ghanaians.

Government policies and strategies aim at contributing to the socioeconomic development of the country by ensuring access to quality health, population, and nutrition services for all people living in Ghana and by promoting the development of the local health industry. The Ministry of Health also ensures that services are delivered in a humane, efficient and effective manner by well-trained, friendly, highly motivated, and client-oriented personnel (Ghana Ministry of Health, 2009).

The NGO involved in planning and executing is based in the United States but at the time of the project described in this case had an office and operations in Accra, Ghana. This NGO has served the public health needs of developing countries for 30 years from its beginning at the School of Medicine at the University of North Carolina through its incorporation as an independent non-profit NGO in 2003. It has worked in more than 50 countries, with the support of the U.S. Agency for International Development, foundations, corporations and individuals. The NGO provided technical support and assistance to ministries of health in several developing nations with a focus on improving the performance of health care providers, especially those focusing on reproductive health, as a means to enhancing the overall health status of these countries.

SETTING THE STAGE

Ghana's Ministry of Health (MOH) was committed to scaling-up post abortion care/life-saving skills/family planning (PAC/LSS/FP) services as part of the National Safe Motherhood Program to reduce high levels of maternal and neonatal mortality and morbidity. Maternal mortality was estimated at 740/100,000 live births in 1998, according to the Ghana Demographic and Health Survey (DHS), (2003). The risk of unwanted pregnancy in Ghana is also high. Although the use of modern contraceptive methods has increased substantially over the last decade, unmet need for family planning was still 34 percent for women of reproductive age. In addition, 36 percent of women interviewed for the DHS stated that their last pregnancy was either unwanted or mistimed, with increased percentages among younger women.

The strategy for expanding and scaling up PAC/LSS/FP services in Ghana was built on a pilot project implemented in three regions and several key lessons learned during the pilot about training health care providers. Notably, in traditional training, trainees were away from their facilities for a substantial amount of time (at least 3 weeks, all at once), thus restricting access to services at their clinics, and many trainees were not able to complete their practical training due to a combination of low numbers of appropriate clients/patients and the presence of multiple trainees at the training sites at one time. A Self-Paced Learning (SPL) approach was designed to address these issues, as well as the significant challenge of sustainability. The goal was to establish an effective approach to preparing health care providers to offer PAC/LSS/FP services consistent with performance expectations and service standards that could be sustained within the social and economic realities of Ghana. Traditional training approaches had failed at doing this, and the need for this training remained.

The project that is described in the next section of this article was developed as a paper-based prototype to test a pedagogical approach. At the conception of the project, it was planned that the instructional content could eventually be deployed via technology that was not yet widely available in rural Ghana, Africa, where improved knowledge and skills were needed by nurse-midwives providing prenatal, labor and delivery, postpartum, and newborn care in rural clinics and hospitals. Technologies considered for eventual use were laptop computers and PDAs.

An alternative approach for the future would be to use mobile learning (mLearning) to deliver portions of this training, as mLearning technologies are becoming widely accepted and available, as well as highly portable. mLearning is often an appropriate choice for training when:

- there is a need to reduce time away from the job
- more flexibility for learner and/or instructor is desired
- some participants live in distant or rural areas with poor transportation systems
- it is important to reduce the costs of delivering training to large numbers of people
- people need to access instructional content 24 hours a day, seven days a week, or "just in time" while on their jobs

In addition, mLearning can support collaborative and group learning (Vavoula, Lefrere, O'Malley & Sharples, 2003). mLearning is usually self-paced and can be cost-effective over time, especially as enrollment increases and the cost per student decreases. It can be updated easily if Internet based, and it can enable learners to apply new skills immediately in their jobs.

CASE DESCRIPTION

The development and implementation of the SPL approach in Ghana was a collaborative process between an NGO, the Ministry of Health, and other in-country partners. In addition to the lessons learned during the pilot mentioned above, the approach built upon the three-week residential Safe Motherhood course that was in use in Ghana, and applied principles of learning theory and sound instructional design practice to ensure that service providers would acquire the knowledge and develop the clinical skills they needed to provide quality Safe Motherhood services.

Highlights of the Approach

The Safe Motherhood SPL approach combined the following:

- self-directed learning; print-based modules; effective facilitation and a strong learner support system, including learning teams
- sufficient opportunities for learners to practice, receive feedback, and become competent in Safe Motherhood clinical skills
- follow up and supportive supervision by Regional Resource Teams (RRTs) to ensure providers' application and retention of skills on the job

Logistics

Up to 20 learners were invited to participate in the SPL approach in each of two intervention districts based on established criteria (physicians, midwives, and community health nurses doing deliveries). There were an additional 20 learners in each of two comparison districts who participated in the traditional 3-week residential course.

Intervention

The SPL learner support system paired learners into learning teams who would support and motivate each other. Learners formed teams by agreement and were encouraged to consider geographic proximity and anticipated ability to work well together. Learners worked individually and then came together as per an agreed upon schedule to study, discuss, solve problems, role play, and generally encourage each other's progress. The SPL program was designed to take approximately 6-9 months to complete, per learner. The SPL program was implemented and monitored by the RRT members, as well as members of District Health Management Teams, Regional Health Management Teams, and other administrators, who received orientation and preparation for their roles in learner support and program management before learners began their learning activities.

The Learning Materials and Learning Cycle

The SPL materials were adapted with permission from *Life-saving Skills Manual for Midwives*, 3rd edition (1998) and reflected the same content being used in the traditional three-week course. The materials included six units with an accompanying facilitators' guide, tests and answers, grading and tracking tools, a guide for orienting RRTs and managers, and other supporting and reference materials. The six units were: Foundations; Providing Quality Antenatal Care; Providing Quality Care During Normal Labor and Delivery; Complications of Labor; Providing Quality Postabortion Care; and Providing Quality Postpartum and Newborn Care.

At the start of the program, learners gathered as a group with facilitators and received an orientation to the approach and the materials and worked through the first unit (*Foundations*) in a group-based learning session. Learners then received the second unit, returned home, studied on their own, and completed self-assessments and exercises. In meetings with their learning partners, they completed role-plays and other learning activities and worked collaboratively to help each other resolve any learning challenges encountered. Working with their RRT facilitator, learners completed a post-unit questionnaire that assessed readiness for the clinical experience that accompanies Units 2-6. They participated in demonstrations and practice. They then participated in a supervised clinical practice at a regional hospital. As part of the practice, learner competence was assessed via clinical checklists and a post-unit test. The learning cycle started again as learners then began a new unit. This cycle continued until all units and related clinical practices were completed.

The Ghana Safe Motherhood Self-Paced Learning Cycle appears as below:

- *Step 1*: First group of learners receives an orientation and completes the *Foundations* unit, led by a trained facilitator, at the district hospital:
    - How the SPL approach works
    - Roles of facilitators, learners, District Directors of Health Services (tracking), district hospital staff, regional hospital staff
    - Learners review the time line/action plan
    - Learners select a learning partner; this creates the learning team (could be 3 learners together)
    - Learners sketch a learning plan with a facilitator
    - Learners receive the first self-paced module and are assigned a facilitator who will be responsible for mentoring them and then checking them off for the theory and demonstrations
- *Step 2*: Working through the units:
    - Each learner returns to his/her site and works through the current module. (During each cycle, each learner travels [at least] once to work with her learning partner, and learners can be reimbursed for 2 such additional trips during the course of the program.)
    - When the module is complete, or if the learner has difficulties, the learner will travel to the site where the facilitator responsible for the module is located, or by agreement, to a regional training site to receive extra support
- *Step 3*: Working through exercises/post-unit questionnaire/demonstrations/return demonstrations:
    - When the learning team has completed the module, they travel to the site

  - where the facilitator for the module is located
  - Learners complete the post-unit questionnaire. With the facilitator, the learners work through the exercises and demonstrations/return demonstrations, and the facilitator checks that the learners are ready to go to the clinical area at the regional hospital
- *Step 4*: Working through clinical practice at the regional hospital:
  - When the learning team has been "checked off" on the exercises and demonstrations/return demonstrations, they travel to the regional hospital where they are assigned to the unit where they can acquire the skill they have just learned about
  - Staff on the unit serve as clinical instructors, and the learners are assisted by supervising clinical instructors (refreshed by group-based training; are on duty at all times)
  - Learners are assisted as they practice, and when they are deemed competent in the skills practiced, they are "checked off"
  - The District Director and the learner's advisor are informed that the learner has completed the module
  - The next module is given to the learners, and the learners are assigned to a facilitator who is responsible for helping them work through the module and then checks them off for the theory and demonstrations

[As each module is completed, learners go back to Step 2.]

Evaluation

Because of the significant investment by the MOH and its partners in moving into a national scale-up of the Safe Motherhood Program, it was critical that implementation of this approach was well monitored and documented so results would be available for decision-making about further scale-up. Moreover, there was widespread interest in Ghana and elsewhere in the feasibility and effectiveness of alternative in-service training approaches. To ensure a strong and well-documented evaluation, quantitative data, including test scores, were collected to assess learner accomplishments. Learners were asked about the usability and acceptability of the learning materials. Data were also collected from all categories of participants about the implementation of the SPL approach. In addition, costs and impacts of the SPL and traditional training approaches were compared.

Knowledge Gains

Learner performance improved from the pre-unit test to the post-unit test. The average percent gain on those units was 14.1%. When learners did not achieve an 80% cut-off score on the post-unit tests, they reviewed their materials and were then retested. On 55 of 58 occasions that learners were retested, they achieved the 80% cut-off score. The data also demonstrated a reduction in the range of scores from the pre-test to the post-test, indicating that learners were more alike in performance following instruction than before. The average range of scores for the pre-test was 49.7, while the average range for the post-test was 27.3. This is an important finding in terms of consistent care of patients; the SPL approach reduced the variation in knowledge among providers. Evaluative data indicated that learners in the SPL approach had greater gains in knowledge and skill (34%) when compared with the traditional training approach where learners actually experienced a slight loss (-6.8%) in knowledge and skills during the course of the training.

Cost Data

A cost-effectiveness analysis showed that the average cost to obtain a 1% gain in knowledge and skill was $57 (U.S.D.) for the SPL group and $416 for the traditional group. This demonstrates that despite higher development and startup costs for SPL, the average costs to produce learning gains were lower in the SPL group. While the cost per participant was slightly higher for the SPL group than the traditional group ($1,287 vs. $1,133 U.S.D.), the achievement of knowledge and application of skills were considerably higher in the intervention group, resulting in a better cost-effectiveness result.

Skill Development

The primary goal of the SPL approach was to improve job performance and health practices. When examining client outcomes and service delivery before and after training, the SPL group showed relatively high increases, ranging from 34.5% for new and continuing use of injectable contraceptives to 314.5% for new and continuing use of condoms. The traditional training group showed an increase only for use of condoms (17.6%), while all other categories showed a decline following traditional training. The average gain for SPL was 101.4% while the average gain for the traditional group was -38%, indicating a loss from baseline to endline in client outcomes and service delivery. The cost-effectiveness analysis for the measure of new and continuing use of condoms shows that each percent gain by the SPL group was obtained, on average, for an expenditure of $7 U.S.D., while each percent gain by the traditional group cost $76.

Learner Satisfaction

Focus-group meetings at the conclusion of the SPL approach were led by a local moderator using a set of questions to prompt discussion. Questions were prepared by the evaluation team. Focus-group participants responded to questions and prompts and were encouraged to freely express their perceptions and experience with the SPL approach. Learners expressed satisfaction with the content of the SPL training units. Each was able to mention particular areas of benefit to their practice as service providers. Most indicated that the number of activities in the units was also right and helped them to acquire the necessary knowledge and skills. Learners from both regions unanimously expressed that the clinical practice sessions were very useful and helped them to respond to situations for which they previously would have called for a doctor. The learners said that their partners were very supportive and contributed significantly to their successful completion of the program. This arrangement, they said, resulted in sharing and learning from their varied experiences. Some of the learners indicated this collegial support sustained their interest to a large extent. The following comments were typical:

For me as a trained midwife, I found all the units very appropriate for my needs. They helped me to expand my knowledge about some of the things I did not know, so I think the units were appropriate. So I am particularly happy that I [was] involved in this self-paced learning program.(Learner, Northern Region, Ghana)

Now I feel I am competent because of the way I went through the SPL. Recently I had a case in the ward that I was able to manage... before the doctor came._(Learner, Northern Region, Ghana)

Those who were slow in picking up learned from their partners. This happened during the practical sessions and the demonstrations._RRT, Upper West Region, Ghana (Bonku, Sampson, Aboagye, Combary, Engelbrecht, & Kiplinger, 2004, ¶).

CURRENT CHALLENGES FACING THE ORGANIZATION

As a descendant of distance learning and e-learning, mLearning has its limitation and challenges, too. Organizations wishing to use mLearning will face a predictable set of challenges. Like e-learning, mLearning requires more development time than traditional classroom methods. It requires a planned system of learner support to meet learners' needs for feedback and interaction and to address the tendency for learners to feel isolated. With mLearning, learners need to take more individual responsibility for their learning, and some may not be ready for this. Poorly designed instruction and lack of sufficient learner support can lead to greater attrition and lower levels of achievement than are typical in face-to-face instruction. Attrition for these reasons has broader implications than a student leaving one mLearning course: She may think the experience is typical of all mLearning and decide to avoid future mLearning opportunities. She will likely tell others, who may also decide to avoid enrolling in mLearning courses. Problems such as these can prevent mLearning instruction from achieving its full potential, but a positive outcome can be achieved using learning theory and sound instructional design principles and practices.

If an organization plans to use distance learning, perhaps in the form of mobile learning, to improve the knowledge and skills in its workforce, the organization must adhere to established principles and practices of instructional design so that they are able to create and deliver effective lessons. The following are some of these:

Focus the Content

Experts in the field of instructional design recommend using evidence-based principles for curricula design and learning. Several of these suggestions relate to how to focus the content. These include:

- creating learning objectives that are derived from job tasks or a description of a gap in performance
- using the learning objectives to develop performance indicators and help learners meet their learning goal
- specifying only the essential knowledge and skills
- leaving out content that is "nice to know" and including only content that is "need to know"
- focusing on what learners absolutely must know or be able to do to complete a task and on what they will do to demonstrate the knowledge and skills

Design for the Audience

Developers of learning experiences can more effectively target instruction if they first identify the characteristics of the learners. These characteristics can include how many learners are anticipated, their age, gender, language fluency, literacy, background, experience, prior training, their experience with technology, and current and future job responsibilities. Most important of all is the learners' existing level of knowledge and skill vis-à-vis the intended outcomes.

If the developer is designing work-related training, the work context should be considered. Contextual factors include the type of work learners do, where and under what working conditions they do it, and degree and quality of supervision (or lack thereof). Developers must help learners connect with the reason they are learning. That is, developers should help learners link the new learning with knowledge and skills they already possess and ensure learners can describe how the learning challenge they are about to take on will prepare them for their future learning needs or work (Hannum & Hansen, 1989).

Apply Instructional Design Principles

Instructional design principles and practices ensure effective instruction for distance learning. These promote the development of:

- Training methods and techniques that encourage the active involvement of learners
- Exercises and activities that build on the knowledge and experience of participants; opportunities are provided during learning activities for participants to apply learning to their real-life situations
- Curricula and individual components that follow a logical order (from simple to complex, from known to unknown, sequential according to task).
- Materials that use validated layout and presentation methods and techniques
- Instructional content that is sequenced in a way that facilitates learning. Robert Gagne (Gagne, Wager, Golas, & Keller, 2005) recommended a sequence for designing and presenting instruction according to the following nine instructional events:
    1. gain the learner's attention
    2. inform the learner the objective(s)
    3. stimulate recall of prerequisite knowledge and skill
    4. present the new learning material
    5. provide learning guidance
    6. provide opportunity for practice
    7. provide feedback
    8. assess the learning effectiveness
    9. promote transfer and retention of learning

Build a Learner Support System

Effective instruction is learner-centered. It relies on:

- correctly identifying the learner's performance gap and cause
- linking training with the learner's actual job responsibilities and/or educational need
- appropriate instructional design or delivery
- adequate supervised practice of new skills
- individual assessment and feedback, and
- a learner support system to help transfer new skills and knowledge to performance on the job.

Learner support is a carefully designed and maintained system created specifically to minimize the separation between instructor and learner and to connect learners to the learning experience. It involves the learner as well as the key individuals who might have an impact on the learner's performance. Depending on whether the context is education or job training, the individuals who might have an impact may include instructors, other students, trainers, managers, supervisors, and co-workers (PRIME Insights, 2003; Murphy, Harber, & Muhuhu, 2000). Learner support is critical to the success of distance learning interventions and should be the responsibility of all distance learning program staff. Learner support helps implement the constructivist principles that give students an active role in learning. It links learners with instructors, facilitators, and mentors and, where possible, with other learners in the program. Learners are guided to construct knowledge and skill by working to solve realistic problems through interaction and collaboration with instructor/mentors and peers. A planned system of support ensures that learners receive coaching to facilitate learning and are not isolated. Learner support can be designed into the materials and can be provided by facilitators and/or other learners through face-to-face interactions, telephone, fax, e-mail, and regular mail, in addition to mobile devices. Some of the most effective support will be personal and will come from tutors, advisors/counselors, mentors, and other students. (Kiplinger, 2003; Murphy, Harber, & Muhuhu, 2000). Colleagues also may be good sources of support. Support may especially be needed if work, family, or financial concerns distract the attention of the learner. The following are some other needs that distance learners have and some ways of meeting those needs when designing and implementing distance learning. Table 1 shows what instructional developers can provide in response to the needs of mLearners.

Evaluate Learning Gains and Acceptance of the Technology and Learning Approach

Monitor training and make any 'in-flight" adjustments that are necessary. Develop pre- and post-tests that are linked to the desired post-training performance outcomes. Pre-test learners to find out what related knowledge and skill they had before taking the course; give them a post-test to find out what they learned from the course. Compare the results of the two tests to assess the learning gains. If possible, assess learners again at some time after they have completed the course and after they have had an opportunity to apply their knowledge and skills. This information, too, can be used to make adjustments and revisions before the course is offered again.

Ask learners about their perceptions of the technology, ease of use, and appropriateness for the instruction they received. Ask them about the learning approach: Did they understand what they were to do as learners? Were the objectives clear? Was the content logically sequenced and organized? Was there too much content or not enough? Were learners able to get help in a timely manner if they needed it? Would they recommend the course, the approach, and the technology to other students? Then, if any learners did not complete the course, ask them what their reasons were for this.

Revise

The development of effective instruction is an iterative process that is strengthened by making practical use of information gained from monitoring and evaluating a course. Use evaluation data of the learning process and outcomes to identify elements for revision.

One aspect that often needs revision is the amount of content. Subject matter experts often

Table 1. Learner needs for successful instruction (Long & Kiplinger, 1999)

Learners need...	You can provide...
help organizing their time and developing study skills	an activity plan that learners complete to indicate what tasks or activities they will work on and when they will work on them; estimated time for each unit of study
control over their learning experiences	choices of objectives, examples, practice exercises, length of exposure to the material, order and sequence (Avoid overwhelming learners with choices.)
feedback about their cognitive achievement and skill development	self-assessments (pre- and post-tests), role plays with the facilitator or other learners, case studies
"hands-on" activities to allow them to practice new skills	guided practice, supervised experiments, collaborative projects, or skills practice with other learners
prompt feedback so they know immediately how they are doing	examples and samples of correct responses to assessments and case studies; quick responses to learners' questions and requests for help
reassurance, help and support from others	encouragement, opportunities for communication, and information about their progress or changes in the program
incentives and motivation	recognition; course credit or continuing-education credit; credit toward certification, if appropriate

want to include more content than is necessary to meet the desired learning outcomes, and course developers can be hard pressed to hold the line on "content creep." Revisions that are based on data from learners can help with this issue—one that is extremely important in the confined spaces of mLearning technologies—and will ensure that the instruction is more effective and acceptable to learners the next time it is used.

SOLUTIONS AND RECOMMENDATIONS

The evaluation showed that the SPL approach is a viable alternative to the traditional, group-based approach to in-service training of service providers in Ghana. Orientation of the members of the learner support system prepared them adequately for performing their expected roles in the program and was crucial to the successful implementation of the approach. All learners who began the SPL approach completed it. At the end, the majority of learners indicated a preference for the SPL approach over typical classroom training. Generally, there were no serious constraints in resource provision for the program, although there were a few organizational challenges with its management.

Some of the lessons learned based on the quantitative and qualitative evaluation include:

- self-paced learning is effective for in-service training of service providers
- adequate orientation of all stakeholders to program content and activities, as well as to their roles and responsibilities, is essential for successful implementation of the SPL approach
- learner partnerships provide mutual benefit for learner study and comprehension of the learning materials, and
- an SPL approach can stimulate an increase in additional professional reading among service providers who for a long time have felt unchallenged to do so (Bonku, Sampson, Aboagye, Combary, Engelbrecht, & Kiplinger, 2004)

After making revisions identified by the evaluation, this paper-based prototype can be redesigned for deployment via technology-based delivery such as mLearning. Collaborative aspects of the SPL approach could be handled remotely via mobile devices, which are now quite common in most African countries. Trying out the learning materials and the learner support system in print form before deployment via technology helps ensure that the learning approach will produce the desired learning gains, positively impact changes in practice, and meet learner satisfaction—before going to the expense of converting to technology delivery.

Other recommendations include:

- provide training for service providers only in areas relevant to their jobs and duties
- pre-test and exempt prospective learners who already have the necessary knowledge and skills
- ensure effective partnership arrangements for learners by partnering learners with less experience with learners who have more experience and/or training; ensure that managers of the SPL approach have a solid understanding of what makes learning happen and can articulate the rationale for certain instructional practices
- ensure that managers and other members of the learner support system clearly understand their roles and responsibilities
- ensure that participants in SPL receive payments for expenses as expected and on time
- review certain units for non-essential content that is not needed by service providers in their jobs, and

- explore additional ways to ensure learners have adequate client cases for practice, especially in PAC

Technology makes careful instructional design more important than ever, including initial field-testing and revision. Technology-based programs such as mLearning will require re-orientation from traditional, group-based instruction, including:

- more responsibilities for learners (e.g., collaboration, and group learning activities, time management, independent study)
- peer support/tutoring
- new roles for instructors (e.g., mentors and facilitators of the learning process rather than purveyors of knowledge and skills)
- additional key team members for developing and supporting the program (e.g., designers with experience in distance learning and technical support specialists for the selected delivery method)
- planning for management support during implementation (e.g., communication systems for providing feedback and making adjustments to the program)

Recommendations for Developing mLearning

There are over a billion mobile phones in the developing world and approximately 200 studies of using mobile phones in the developing world (Donner, 2008). Several of these studies argue for mobile phones as a resource for learning in developing nations due to their portability, simplicity, and affordability. Rashid and Elder (2009) suggest that mobile phones can play a major role in promoting development for several reasons. Mobile phones are increasingly assessable to lower-income groups in developing countries. Mobile phones require only a basic literacy, not extensive training, in order to use them. Mobile phones do not require an extensive physical infrastructure of phone wires, thus they can allow a developing nation to leapfrog older technologies. Mobile phones support both voice and data, and thus can support educational purposes. Viewing mLearning as a subset of e-learning (online learning), Boyinbode and Akinyede (2008) suggest that mLearning has an advantage for providing education in Africa because it can be used anytime and anywhere, it has lower costs, mobile devices are smaller and lighter and thus more portable, and it is more flexible than e-learning. The definition of mLearning used by Boyinbode and Akinyede (2008) includes cell phones, smart phones, PDAs, notebook computers, and tablet computers. Their views are consistent with what Brown (2005) expressed earlier about m-learning in Africa. He saw mLearning as a natural extension of e-learning that has the potential to make learning more widely available while maintaining the essential role that communication and interaction play in learning. We believe that mLearning is the appropriate next step in the project that is the basis for this case study for the reasons noted above.

mLearning, like all types of learning with and without technology, is more likely to be successful if it follows a systematic instructional design process (Hannum, 2007). An advantage is that instructional design relies on empirically-based pedagogical principles. The widely used instructional design model gathers these principles and sorts them into five phases: Analyze, Design, Develop, Implement, and Evaluate. This model has become known as the ADDIE model. The work described in this case followed the instructional design model, with emphasis on some of these key steps:

Assess the Learning Need and Context

In the analysis phase, instructional developers should find out as much as they can about the learners and the learning and/or work context. A learning needs assessment ensures that the goals and content of a training intervention are based on a documented need of learners for specific knowledge and skills. Needs assessment keeps instructional developers from 1) having to guess at what the learning outcomes should be, 2) basing instruction on a list of topics, or 3) relying solely on a subject matter expert to select the content. Instruction should be based on what learners need to know or be able to do in order to perform a task. After analysis, instructional developers can select an appropriate learning approach that is based on the learning situation, learner needs, setting, and performance context. As part of the analysis phase, instructional developers and program managers should also investigate issues that can affect training success—especially when an unfamiliar or relatively new technology will be used to deliver all or some of the instruction. Factors such as an organization's orientation to training and to change, the degree of alignment between goals and performance, available resources, and the extent to which the organization has systems and structures that support transfer of learning should be considered.

Put Together a Development Team

To fully exploit the benefits of the ADDIE model, an mLearning development team should be assembled. The team should include at least one person who knows the technology, its potential, and its limitations. It is advisable to enlist someone for this role who has experience using technology to deliver instruction. The team will need a subject matter expert and an instructional designer. These people will work closely together and need to respect each other's roles and expertise. If graphic design is needed, this expertise should be acquired, too. Evaluation expertise is also advised; this may come from the instructional designer or an evaluation specialist. Someone to manage funding and reporting requirements is desirable. Most teams have a project manager who is responsible for keeping the project on target and on time. Roles and responsibilities need to be clear to everyone on the team, and problems and frictions should be discussed when they come up.

Identify and Acquire Resources

Sufficient human and financial resources are required for technology-based learning to succeed. It is best to ensure a commitment at the outset of appropriate funds to pay for the project. Work almost always costs more than anticipated, especially if the managers and developers are new to using technology for instruction. It may be better to turn down a project than to take one on for which funds are known to be insufficient or time constraints too limited. Funding may be available from grants or other sources. The project manager should avoid submitting a budget that cannot possibly cover costs in order to avoid having to "cut corners" after the project in underway. It is best to secure commitments in writing and maintain regular communication with the funding source about the project's status.

Prototype the Learning Package

Time and money can be saved and instructional effectiveness made more likely if an instructional package is tried out, or prototyped, before it is deployed using technology. Doing this allows instructional developers to "de-bug" the pedagogy, structure, organization, content, activities and exercises, visuals, and assessments. A paper-based instructional package is a logical step for getting feedback from learners and those responsible for implementation.

The SPL approach is an innovative and effective alternative to group-based training for Safe Motherhood skills and responds to challenges inherent in the residential, traditional, group-based approach. Evaluation results demonstrate the feasibility of using SPL as an alternative to traditional training. SPL was shown to produce greater learner gains and improved service delivery when compared with traditional training.

Cost-effectiveness analysis documented that gains in learning and in service delivery are accomplished in a less costly manner through SPL rather than through traditional training. An approach to learning such as this shows promise for responding to some of the challenges faced by developing countries in providing necessary training for health care personnel.

REFERENCES

Bonku, E., Sampson, W., Aboagye, P., Combary, P., Engelbrecht, S., & Kiplinger, N. (2004). Evaluation of an Alternative Self-paced Learning (SPL) Approach for Training Safe Motherhood Service Providers in the Upper West and Northern Regions of Ghana. PRIME II/IntraHealth International.

Boyinbode, O. K., & Akinyede, R. O. (2008). Mobile Learning: An Application of Mobile and Wireless Technologies in Nigerian Learning System. *International Journal of Computer Science and Network Security*, *8*(11), 386–392.

Brown, T. H. (2005). Towards a Model for m-Learning in Africa. *International Journal on E-Learning*, *4*(3), 299–315.

Donner, J. (2008). Research Approaches to Mobile Use in the Developing World: A Review of the Literature. *The Information Society*, *24*(3), 140–159. doi:10.1080/01972240802019970

Gagne, R. W., Wager, W. W., Golas, K., & Keller, J. M. (2005). Principles of Instructional Design, (5th ed.). Belmont, CA: Thomson/Wadsworth.

Ghana Statistic Service (2004). *Ghana Demographic and Health Survey, 2003.*

Hannum, W. H. (2007). When computers teach: A review of the instructional effectiveness of computers. *Educational Technology*, *47*(2), 5–13.

Hannum, W. H., & Hansen, C. (1989). Instructional Systems in Large Organizations, (pp. 115-122). Englewood Cliffs, NJ: Educational Technology Publications.

Kiplinger, N. (2003). Learner Support for Distance Learning. PRIME/IntraHealth.

Long, P., & Kiplinger, N. K. (1999). Making It Happen: Using Distance Learning to Improve Reproductive Health Provider Performance. PRIME/IntraHealth.

Murphy, C., Harber, L., & Muhuhu, P. (2000). Innovations in Learning to Improve Performance: Learner Support Systems. PRIME/IntraHealth.

Rashid, A.T., & Elder, Laurent. (2009). Mobile Phones and Development: An Analysis of IDRC-Supported Projects. *The Electronic Journal on Information Systems in Developing Countries*, *36*(2), 1–16.

Vavoula, G. N., Lefrere, P., O'Malley, C., & Sharples, M. (2003). Providing Guidelines for Learning, Teaching, and Tutoring in a Mobile Environment. In *Proceedings of the 2nd IEEE International Workshop.*

ADDITIONAL READING

Ally, M. (2009). Mobile Learning: Transforming the Delivery of Education and Training. Edmonton: Athabasca University Press.

Bates, A. W. (2005). Technology, e-learning and distance education (2nd Ed.). London: Routledge.

Beldarrain, Y. (2006). Distance education trends: Integrating new technologies to foster student interaction and collaboration. *Distance Education*, *27*(2), 139–153. doi:10.1080/01587910600789498

Dick, W., Carey, L., & Carey, J. (2008). The Systematic Design of Instruction (7th Ed.). Boston: Allyn & Bacon.

Donner, J. (2008). Research Approaches to Mobile Use in the Developing World: A Review of the Literature. *The Information Society*, *24*(3), 140–159. doi:10.1080/01972240802019970

Gagne, R. M., Wager, W., Golas, K., & Keller, J. (1992). Principles of Instructional Design (5th Ed.). Belmont, CA: Wadsworth/Thomson Learning.

Hannum, W. H., & Hansen, C. D. (1989). Instructional Systems Development in Large Organizations. Englewood Cliffs, NJ: Educational Technology Publications.

Keegan, D. (2002) *The Future of Learning: From eLearning to mLearning*. Retrieved from: http://www.fernuni-hagen.de/ZIFF

Kukulska-Hulme, A., & Traxler, J. (2005). Mobile Learning: A Handbook for Educators and Trainers. London: Routledge.

Long, P., & Kiplinger, N. (1999). Making It Happen: Using Distance Learning to Improve Reproductive Health Provider Performance. PRIME/IntraHealth.

Low, L., & O'Connell, M. (2006). *Learner Centric Design of Digital Mobile Learning*. Learning-on-the-Move Conference. Queensland University of Technology. Australia. 2006.

Morrison, G. R., Ross, S. M., & Kemp, J. E. (2006). Designing Effective Instruction, 5th Edition. NY: John Wiley & Sons.

Rothwell, W. J., & Kazanas, H. C. (1998). Mastering the Instructional Design Process (2nd Ed.). San Francisco: Jossey-Bass.

Sharples, M., Taylor, J., & Vavoula, G. (2005). Towards a Theory of Mobile Learning. In *Proceedings of mLearn Conference*, Cape Town, South Africa.

Smith, P. L., & Ragan, T. J. (2004). Instructional Design (3rd Ed.). Hokoben, NJ: John Wiley.

Traxler, J., & Kukulska-Hulme, A. (2005). In (G. Chin, Ed.), Mobile Learning in Developing Countries Vancouver, BC: Commonwealth of Learning.

Wright, C. R., Dhanarajan, G., & Reju, S. A. (2009). Recurring Issues Encountered by Distance Educators in Developing and Emerging Nations. *International Review of Research in Open and Distance Learning*, *10*(1).

KEY TERMS AND DEFINITIONS

Distance Learning: Refers to any training approach where learners and trainers are not together in a classroom for most of the training time.

Instructional Design: A methodology that uses a systematic, empirically based approach to the development of training and learning.

LSS (Life-Saving Skills): Iinformation, skills, and practices that birth attendants need to routinely provide to after delivery to prevent postpartum hemorrhage.

Ministry of Health (MOH): The agency with oversight for health programs within a country.

Mobile Learning (M-Learning): An e-learning approach in which learning is delivered via a wireless electronic device such as an iPod, a mobile phone, PDA, or other portable or hand-held device.

Non-Governmental Organization (NGO): In this chapter, this term refers to IntraHealth International, a U.S.-based NGO that works in developing countries.

PAC (Post Abortion Care): Care provided when a medical problem develops following a spontaneous or induced abortion.

PDA (Personal Digital Assistant): A portable handheld computer. Newer PDAs have color screens and audio capabilities, enabling them to be used as mobile phones (smart phones), web browsers, or portable media players. Many PDAs can access the Internet wirelessly. Many have touch screens.

RRTs (Regional Resource Teams): In Ghana, teams of medical doctors and nurse-midwives who provide training, oversight, and support to nurses and midwives working in clinics.

SM (Safe Motherhood): An initiative focused on reducing and eliminating maternal mortality and morbidity.

Self-Paced Learning: Refers to a training approach in which, at least to some degree, learners determine when and where they will complete the components of their training.

Chapter 7
An Integrated Framework for Personalized T-Learning

Francesco Bellotti
DIBE, Italy

Stefanos Vrochidis
ITI-CERTH, Greece

Matteo Pellegrino
DIBE, Italy

Ioannis Tsampoulatidis
ITI-CERTH, Greece

Pascal Lhoas
Tudor, Luxemburg

Giancarlo Bo
Giunti, Italy

Alessandro De Gloria
DIBE, Italy

Ioannis Kompatsiaris
ITI-CERTH, Greece

ABSTRACT

Broadcasting interactive learning applications through the digital TV promises to open new pedagogical perspectives given the wide penetration of the medium. This case deals with an open, flexible learning oriented technological framework for interactive digital TV. The framework is divided into two main parts: the production side, where the course is created and the client side, where it is presented on interactive digital television (iDTV) through an interactive learning environment. The course production is supported by an ad-hoc designed authoring tool, which has been thought for a use by pedagogical experts, while the runtime user interaction on iDTV is managed by a Course Multimedia Player. Experimental television learning (t-learning) courses were created by pedagogical experts and served as an important test and evaluation bench for the framework.

BACKGROUND

Television has had a long history of performing an educational function for the mass audience, broadcasting edutainment, documentaries and news as well as educational programmes. The arrival of interactive television has the potential to expand the power of the medium by providing interactive learning opportunities. TV-based interactive education promises a huge potential due to its ability

DOI: 10.4018/978-1-61520-749-7.ch007

to support interactivity while compensating for the low penetration of Internet-enabled computers in comparison with the penetration of a TV in a household. "T-learning" was the new term, which introduced for the definition of TV-based interactive learning (Aarreniemi-Jokipelto, 2005).

Interactive learning services (usually known as e-learning) have provided important solutions and advantages, in particular for Intelligent Tutoring Systems (Shute and Psotka, 1996; Wenger, 1987) that provide personalized support to users, lowering the typical barriers of space, time and availability of contents and services for learning. In this context, t-learning may provide a further specific contribution, thanks to the pervasivity and popularity of TV (especially among a demographic that is not keen on using computers), and exploit typical traditional TV features, such as relaxed and easy use, mix of education and entertainment, media driven proposal of contents, important role of authors/directors in the preparation/delivery of contents.

In this section we will present the history of television as an educational medium and the technologies of the digital interactive TV (iDTV). Subsequently, in the next sections, the methodology for designing t-learning services will be discussed and a personalized technological framework for t-learning will be described and evaluated.

History of TV as an Educational Medium

The use of television as a learning device has a long history since its potential as a learning tool was almost immediately recognized. The first attempts to employ television for educational purposes are reported back to 1930s, when the State University of Iowa prepared the first televised educational programmes. Less than a decade later, elementary and secondary schools used commercial TV educational programs (Leslie, 1980). As the penetration of TV at home was increasing, more learning services were provided. By 1960 more than 50 educational stations were operating in the USA, and by the beginning of the 1960s and the 1970s the development of educational TV was further accelerated by the launching of communication satellites and the growth of cable TV. However, the overall quality of the educational programs produced at that time was mediocre, since most of them focused only on presenting lectures.

Traditional television broadcasts provided only one way information transmission with no possibility to interact immediately with the instructor or a remote co-learner. In the next years, technological developments helped to overcome some of these limitations. One of the first attempts to engage viewers and to add interactivity to educational TV was "Winky Dink and You", which is considered to be the first interactive program. During the 1970s, a number of interactive television experiments were organized, including projects targeting to education and training. In the next few years many different services were developed including combination of TV and telephone line (Jack & Tsatsoulin, 2002) to deliver text and graphic data to the TV screen, as well as cable interactive services that supported quiz answering with the remote control.

During the 1980s and before the advent of personal computers, TV sets were often used as precursors of online service terminals. At the same time telecommunication technologies and infrastructures were developing rapidly and provided more interactivity in media applications both at home and in school. These new technological devices required better interactive skills from users. Increased user literacy, in turn, paved the way for more interactive projects during the 1990s. Most of them were short-lived, mainly because the technology that was required to implement them was too costly for average consumers. Some companies attempted to simplify user technologies and offer cheaper services; while others diversified their products (Carey, 1996).

The latest technological developments promised to enhance realism of instructional programs by applying High Definition TV (HDTV), multi-channel sound, and virtual realities. To overcome some inherent limitations, television technology was often combined with telephone, fax, video recording, and later with internet and mobile technologies. Although the research and development in iDTV-based t-learning is rather limited up to date, some interesting approaches have been presented. Some basic ideas regarding t-learning were expressed in (Aarreniemi-Jokipelto & Tuominen, 2004), while in (Aarreniemi-Jokipelto, 2005) a t-learning model was proposed based on MHP, which included personalization and interaction features. An interesting approach was the technological framework for TV- supported collaborative learning, which was proposed in (Lopez-Nores, et. al 2004). In this work, t-learning contents were developed with appropriate tools and delivered, however personalization was not supported. In a more recent work (Vrba, Cvrk, & Sykora, 2006) a more general framework was presented with content creation serving general purposes. Although the aforementioned approaches were promising they still haven't been tested thoroughly in iDTV or simulation environment.

iDTV Basic Technologies

From the technological point of view, digital television mostly relies on the Digital Video Broadcasting (DVB) standard, characterized as DVB-T for terrestrial, DVB-S for Satellite and DVB-C for Cable transmissions. DVB has been defined by a consortium of public and private organizations in the iDTV sector (Digital Video Broadcasting, 2007).

In the DVB schema, the digital TV signal is transmitted as a stream of MPEG-2 data known as a transport stream. This stream consists of a set of sub-streams (elementary streams), where each sub-stream can contain MPEG-2 encoded audio, MPEG-2 encoded video or data encapsulated in MPEG-2 stream. Hence, the interactive applications are included as part of the MPEG 2 broadcast stream and information about the structure of such interactive applications (application signaling, which is necessary for making them run on the STB) is also broadcast.

Then, the transport stream is fed to the multiplexer and subsequently to a Radio Frequency (RF) transmitter in order to be broadcast. The overall broadcasting system for digital TV is illustrated in Figure 1. The received signal is demodulated and afterwards it is decoded appropriately. As most of the common TV sets are manufactured to deal with analogue signals, a device called Set Top Box (STB) is utilized to transform the digital signal. This devise provides also a middleware, based on an embedded Operating System (OS), which is an execution environment for running the interactive applications that are broadcast in a channel together with the main audiovisual stream. Execution environments are standard and the most common are: the European Multimedia Home Platform (MHP), the American Open Cable Application Platform (OCAP) and DTV Application Software Environment (DASE), the Japanese STD-B23/STD-B24. Since MHP is the standard in Europe and a subset of it, the Globally Executable MHP (GEM), is becoming the common reference world-wide, in this article we focus on MHP.

MHP is the middleware system for interactive TV development designed by the DVB Project (Interactive TV Web 2007). The first draft of MHP was released in August 1999 and the first version of MHP 1.0 was approved by DVB in February 2000. MHP offers a standard platform for application developers. Applications are written in Java and HTML, so they don't depend on any single hardware platform or operating system. Due to the iDTV's special context, MHP-Java applications are slightly different from normal Java applications, however due to the similarities with Java applets, MHP-Java applications are called Xlets. There are 2 main types of DVB applications: "Interactive" applications (e.g. games, interactive advertising), which are based on Java, and "declarative" applications (e.g. SuperTeleText),

Figure 1. Digital TV broadcasting system

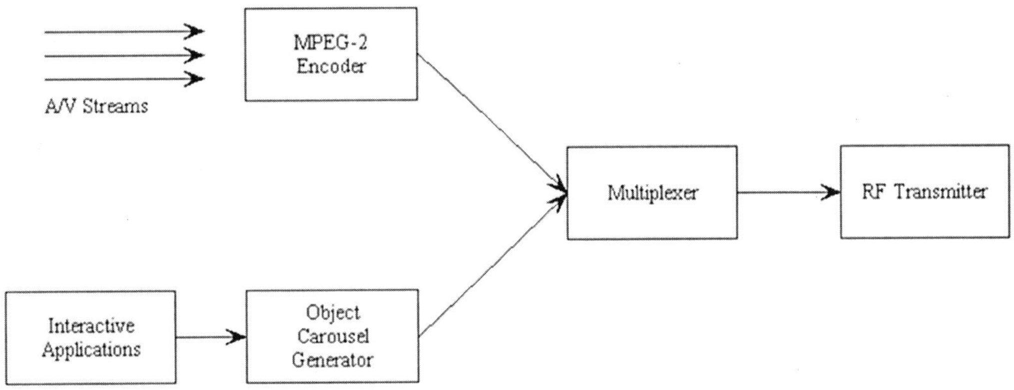

which are based on HTML. Actually, since MHP specifies several restrictions and integration to the standard version of such programming languages, the actual MHP versions are named DVB-J and DVB-HTML, which we sketch in the following subsections.

MHP provides support for those features which are required for digital TV as low-level access to the transport stream, service information access, and support for the specialized graphics model of the digital TV. The introduced limitations of MHP are mainly related to the constraints given by the STB's hardware and OS in terms of computational power, memory size, storage, communication facilities, screen resolution, font and colour availability and their size is severely constrained by the limited bandwidth available. MHP can be extensively exploited by t-learning as it offers the proper middleware for learning interactive applications.

SETTING THE STAGE

Nowadays, the introduction of remote education systems in the computer world with the help of internet has had a significant growth rate. On the contrary, the development of similar services in the TV media is in the initial phase of study and the technical capabilities of the medium to support such services have still to be deeply investigated. For that reason, the design and implementation of t-learning services constitutes a major challenge as it implies the adaptation of e-learning services to TV. The critical differences that can be observed between the t-learning and e-learning world are as given below:

- TV users have a lower level of preparation and predisposition to learn new technologies than Internet users;
- The way to access information in TV is traditionally passive, unlike the more active role that Internet users use to play;
- The information distribution mechanism of digital TV is much more complex than the Internet model, principally by the packing of the course information and the signaling of the transport stream;
- The data formats of the Internet courses have text and graphics as a central axis, while TV should promote audio and video in a natural way. In any case, the greater level of fluidity present in the contents in this media demands a greater interrelation among contents and a temporal reference;
- The STB largely differs from a Personal Computer (PC) as it has less computing

power and local storage and it supports lower resolution.

For these reasons, the architecture of a system, which could create, distribute and execute learning courses by digital TV, is still an open field, with multiples uncertainties to resolve. The MHP standard could represent a suitable technology to develop an iDTV platform able to provide and arrange new services that combine video and data and give viewers greater control over what they see, in comparison with other traditional services. Moreover, iDTV permits consumers to combine the full motion TV with the interactivity and personalization offered by the Internet.

The main characteristics of iDTV can be summarized as follows (Baker, Pulles & Sasno, 2004):

- *Personalization:* in iDTV refers to the use of technology and viewer information, in order to tailor interactive content to each individual viewer profile.
- *Digitization:* refers to the technological advancements that allow better quality of sound and picture.
- *Interactivity:* the control moves away from the networks and is directly placed into the hands of the potential consumer. iDTV can be considered as the convergence of two different technologies: television and computer technology (and more specifically the Internet).

This case will deal with the creation of advanced learning services within the iDTV environment exploiting the existing technologies in a pedagogical way and adapting e-learning features accordingly. More specifically, we will propose an open flexible platform for the development and presentation of personalized interactive t-learning courses. To design such a platform, we first analyze t-learning from a pedagogical point of view and also discuss the opportunities of personalized learning. Subsequently we will discuss the most important strategic issues related to learning on TV.

T-Learning Pedagogy and Methodology

Interactive Digital TV (iDTV) is considered as the convergence of television and computer technologies by encompassing three important features typical of computer-based technologies (Lytras, et al. 2002): interactivity, personalization and digitization.

First of all, the biggest opportunity for the development of learning services is likely to be through personalized TV – as content on-demand or through "personal" delivery services. These new interactive digital TV services have already started to emerge and change the way the viewer interacts with the TV from a passive to a more active mode. This is creating new opportunities for increasing its role in learning. Therefore, ICT policies that are aimed at encouraging increased and widening participation in learning should consider the role that interactive digital TV solutions have in creating new learning opportunities in the home. Such forms of interactive services will become integrated into hybrid developments with more personalized TV, possibly being used as "hooks" to capture interest and pull people towards more engaged learning opportunities.

The TV environment includes features that differentiate it from PCs. First of all, TV is usually watched by more than one person (co-viewing), and usually triggers social interactions that are very useful for a more effective experience and interiorization of the contents. Secondly, the logic of broadcasting to a wide population enables social mass mechanisms that typically enhance the impact of the broadcast program. In defining a t-learning pedagogy it is, thus, crucial to deal with an active learning model, the constraints imposed by the actual development of the technology and the nature of the allowed interactions.

In this context, the challenge is to exploit the added value of providing an interactive learning environment and the potential of allowing people to access learning activities and contents directly in their house, at distance, through media easy to access and simply to use.

This reflection produces a twofold vision that aims at balancing learning and teaching strategies:

1. Guide the learner with proper contents.
2. Leave interaction control to the learner.

Thus, to draw pedagogy for t-learning experiences two dimensions have to be explored and taken into account as the drivers of the design process:

- The context where learning happens and the behaviour of learners in this environment;
- The specific features of the medium, in particular the contents and the pace of the audiovisual (AV) stream.

The interactivity, audio/video-based experiences, narrative learning environment and informal learning/edutainment are the key points that emerged from this exploration. In order to deliver such services to the viewer, a learning oriented technological framework has to be developed to support efficiently the creation and presentation of t-learning courses.

Personalization in T-Learning

In general, the actual purpose of personalized learning is to provide a learning path that is matched to the learner's needs and abilities, resulting in a more efficient and high quality learning process. In order to obtain this matching of learner's profile and objectives, current learning context and available pedagogical resources, a well-defined description of each component involved in the process is needed, with specific focus on the user model. An additional interesting aspect of the personalization process is that, once the user model has been identified, the accuracy of the personalization can be iteratively improved with time, as more dynamic data are collected and stored regarding the ongoing interactions of the user with the system and the continuous monitoring and re-assessment of the user's satisfaction. This also allows for a classification and "clustering" of learners (Blanco-Fernandez et al, 2004). Personalization in terms of t-Learning implies that a potential iDTV learner can easily be offered on his/her TV equipment a selection of available pedagogical contents and services according to his/her interests, skills and preferences.

Personalization involves several technological aspects of the developed system. We describe them in detail in the subsection on the client side of the system running on the STB, where a specific module is responsible for tracing the user activity, keeping a profile and adapt delivery of contents accordingly. As for other services, also for the personalization module the system provides the tools, while it is the responsibility of the course author to exploit them according to a proper educational methodology.

CASE DESCRIPTION

The purpose of this case is to propose a technological framework, which could support an efficient development and deployment of t-learning applications. Such applications represent a novel educational iDTV format that can be applied in a variety of fields not limited to education. In order to satisfy the pedagogical requirements implied by the aforementioned methodology, a technological framework has been designed and built in order to support an efficient development and deployment of personalized t-learning applications. Such applications represent a novel educational iDTV format that can be applied in a variety of fields in education.

Figure 2. Technological Framework

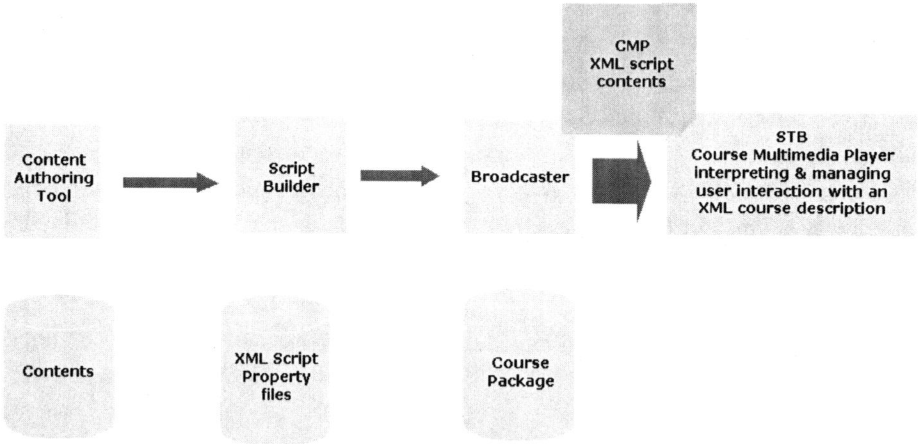

The general philosophy of the approach involves:

- A linear A/V stream (the traditional TV program, on which the user has no control)
- Non-linear interactive contents (on which the user has control)

This schema is realizable through existing TVs, equipped with Set Top Boxes (STBs), thus reaching a wide share of population. Although internet connection (even broadband) is not required, additional services included in the system are capable of exploiting it, in order to enhance the user interaction and experience. On the other hand, non-linear Audio-Visual (A/V) stream contents would require (at least with present technologies) broadband connectivity, which is not supported by the majority of current TVs.

The proposed architecture, which is illustrated in Figure 2, is split into two parts: the production side where the content is prepared and the reception side where the course is presented to the viewer through the appropriate terminal.

The production side is the area where the course content is created. As the course development is based on the requirement of reusability, the content is structured in the appropriate format so it is playable by a Course Multimedia Player which is also transmitted with the course package.

From a pedagogical point of view, this schema involves an important role of the author, who defines the learning space and provides strong guidance by defining the A/V stream, the scheduling and the contents, and of the user, who has a certain freedom in exploring this knowledge space (e.g. deciding whether to perform an interactive test/quiz/game or not, decide which branch of the course to follow). For any course's implementation, the author can decide the desired level of freedom/customization (e.g. by preparing contents for various categories, setting user-performance-based triggers for more information cards, quizzes, letting a number of parameters variable for personalization, etc.). The technological framework is based on the idea that the course consists of resources that can be presented at runtime by the proper course player software. Modularity, re-usability, customizability, flexibility, extensibility and homogeneity are the keywords of such an approach.

T-Learning Course Structure

The course creation is based on the structure of a Learning Object (LO) (Marta Rey, et al., 2006). A Learning Object can be defined as both the basic unit of a learning experience and as a small, atomic chunk of learning that can be reused in different context. In other words, the LO structure is actually an aggregation of items, which grants a customizable and flexible reuse. Following this definition and by adopting the LO model specifically developed for t-learning courses, it is possible to integrate several multimedia components and thus create educational material and content suitable for distribution through an iDTV infrastructure. Thanks to this model the content author can manage separately the various components, as well as the parameters that define their behavior, and then generate in a simple way the final LO (course).

A t-learning course is considered to be composed of the broadcast video and the interactive application, which are running in parallel. The interactive application is divided into the static and the dynamic part. The static includes a set of highly customizable multimedia educational units, which are called cards, while the dynamic defines the flow of the course in time by the different condition-based paths, the synchronization with the A/V stream and the interactions.

In the static part, each card provides one or more services, which are author-customized instances of service templates. Such services include: multimedia pages and presentations, interactive edutainment elements and support for ancillary devices. These items can be presented at runtime by using specific MHP-java classes, which read the property files that are created at the production side. This means that several different instances of the same item can be presented with the support of the same classes that will read different property files at runtime. This is very important for the runtime environment of the STB as one of the major constraints is the limited bandwidth of the transmitted applications.

Figure 3. Instance of a Multimedia Page

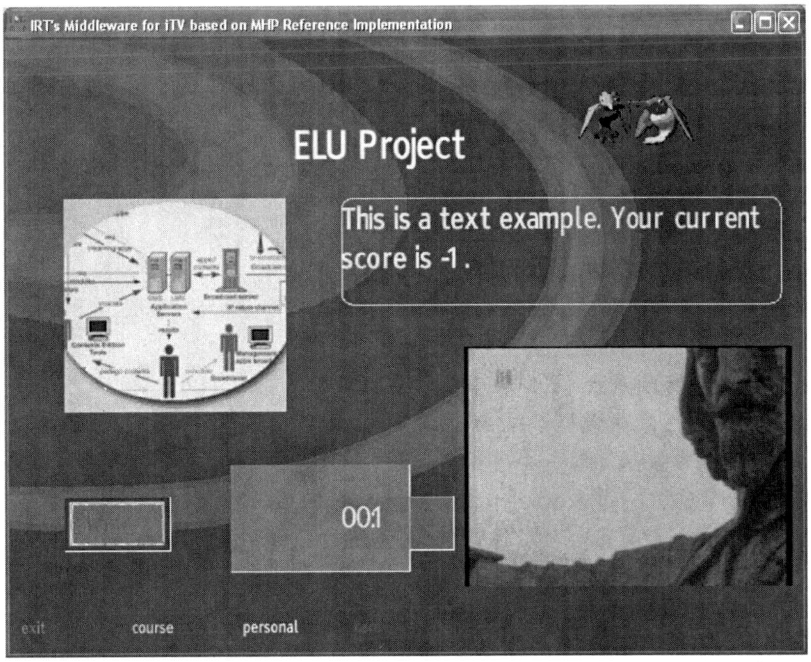

Figure 4. Instances of Games

The main objects nested in the script are called cards and can contain either a multimedia page (MPage), which may consist of texts, images, audios and buttons accompanied by the TV stream in various formats (e.g. inside a quarter frame), or an interactive edutainment unit, such as a game. As multimedia page is considered a normal page that could appear in the TV screen while games include quizzes, puzzles and so on. Multimedia page and games instances are illustrated in Figures 3 and 4 respectively.

In order to support reusability, the above items (Mpage and interactive edutainment units) are implemented as specific templates, which are fully configurable in terms of contents and appearance. These templates can thus be instantiated one or more time in a course. Configuration files also support personalization. That is, the properties of a single template instance can further be parameterized according to the dynamic (i.e. evolving even during the course) profile of the end-user. This is achieved through the introduction of parametrical tags that can be parameterized by the course content author on the parameters defined by the Personalizer's module which is described in the next section.

The dynamic part of the course, which represents the actual flow of the cards (Figure 5), is encoded in an XML script which is called "course script" and it is interpretable at runtime. This script includes the following information:

- Declaration and synchronization of the cards with the underlying iDTV A/V stream (thus directly enhancing the current TV program) with time stamp definition.
- Declaration of asynchronous cards which are accessible at any time during the course. Such cards could be general information or help related multimedia pages.
- Links to the corresponding property files of each card to load the properties of a multimedia page or a game.
- Declaration of navigation bars, that consist of 4 sets of menus (one per each remote control's colored buttons) that provide the user access to additional functions (e.g. personalization services, more-in-depth info, helps, etc.). The navigation bar, which

Figure 5. Dynamic part of the Course, where three different user categories are represented

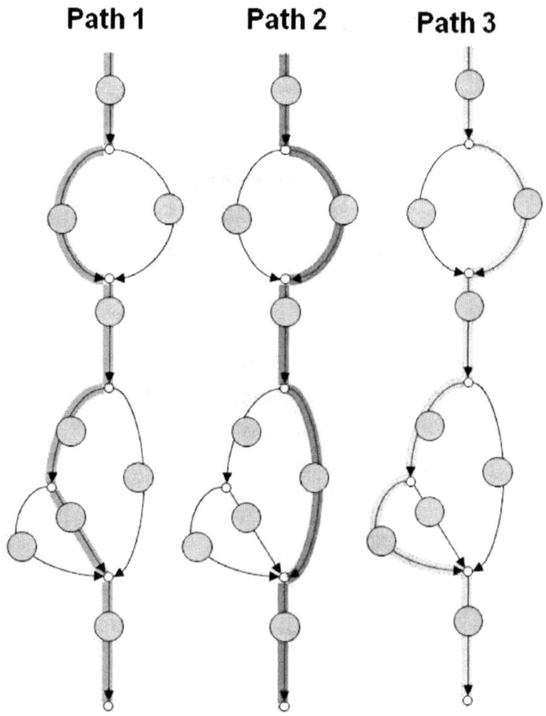

is displayed as a stripe at the bottom (or top) of the screen and is controlled through the 4 iDTV colour buttons (red, green, yellow, blue). Sample functionalities that can be offered by the navigation bar include: personalization settings, choice of course categories, exit/hiding/restoring of cards, helps, further info and other advanced services. Functionalities are grouped in 4 clusters, each one of which is mapped to (and accessed through, by end-users) one the four colored buttons. A course may have several different navigation bar configurations that change dynamically during the course itself in order to provide the most suited, context-aware support. These different configurations are to be specified by the author in the course script.

- Condition-based flow control of the course. Such conditions are based on the real-time value of dynamic (e.g. score, status etc) and/or static personalization variables (e.g. age, sex, etc), that are tracked and managed by the system.
- Categorized flow of the course. Different user categories can be defined by the author either regarding the difficulty level (e.g. hard, easy) or specifying different approaches according to the user's skills and the context of the course (e.g. history profile, architecture profile, etc).

This XML script describes adequately the t-learning course and is interpreted at runtime by the Course Multimedia Player on the STB. It is Object Oriented, which is close to human reasoning, easy to agree and specify. Moreover, Object Orientation is well supported through powerful development tools (e.g. UML). The script is event-oriented as well, which is particularly suited for the TV environment, where an application may be synchronized with the underlying A/V stream.

Dealing with the user's cognitive load is a fundamental aspect when designing a multimedia educational system. This involves contents, timing and user interaction. The script features a time-line, where the author specifies the time events. The scheduling definition approach allows the author to specify sequences and loops of cards, and the *maxDuration* and *latestStartTimes* parameters that are fundamental for a proper synchronization of an interactive application with the underlying AudioVisual (A/V) stream. Synchronous interactive enhancements should help the viewer to have a better experience of the underlying A/V stream. They should be well contextualized in the A/V stream and not distract the viewer from the A/V, which is supposed to be already interesting by itself. Consequently, the amount and type of information in the video should be compatible with the user interaction and cognitive load (Bernhaupt et al. 2007). In general, our tests results show that synchronous information and services should be limited and oriented to support the user in better understanding the A/V stream. On the opposite, more in-depth information should be freely available after the end of the A/V stream.

Production Side

The main component involved in the production side is the authoring tool (AT). The AT is a visual development environment where the author is supported in the creation educational courses for iDTV. It consists mainly of two logical parts which are integrated in a common user interface:

- The script builder, which is the part for writing the course script (scheduling of the cards, definition of alternative course paths) that corresponds to the dynamic part of the course
- The card configurator part for the creation and the configuration of the instances of the service templates (e.g. Edutainment Templates) which are included in the static part of the course.

Figure 6. Authoring Tool architecture

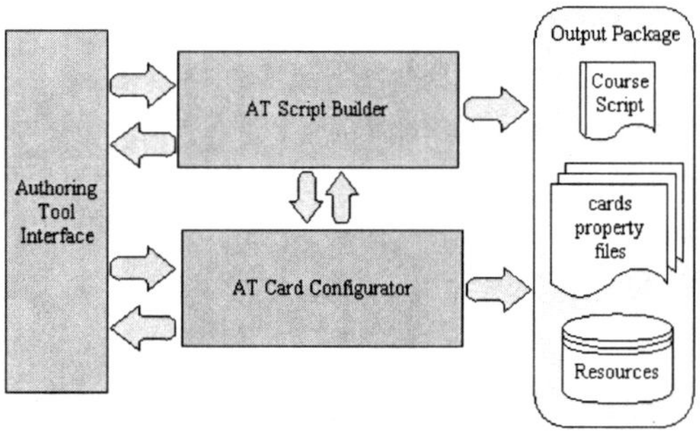

The architecture of the AT is illustrated in Figure 6.

The AT provides a clear graphical interface (Figure 7) which supports visual composition features as drag and drop, content previews and object designing. The tool provides a user friendly environment where authors can focus on the contents and the logic of their course without having to concern about the internal structure and the constraints imposed by the XML script.

The AT script builder, which is dedicated to the definition of the user categories and the scheduling of the cards, provides authors with an intuitive way for defining events lists (temporal or logical) and consequent actions, with the support of personalization as well. Timeline bar proved an easy medium for content authors to use since it is more comprehensible comparing to event triggered-based flow charts. The tool handles the definition of all the supported operations/instructions by using an XSD schema in a "secure" mode, thus avoiding the risk for the author to generate invalid XML files.

The AT card configurator (Figure 7) is responsible for the configuration of the cards and provides a user friendly environment where existing templates can be configured. These templates include Multimedia pages with images, buttons and text, multimedia presentations and edutainment tem-

Figure 7. Authoring Tool card configurator

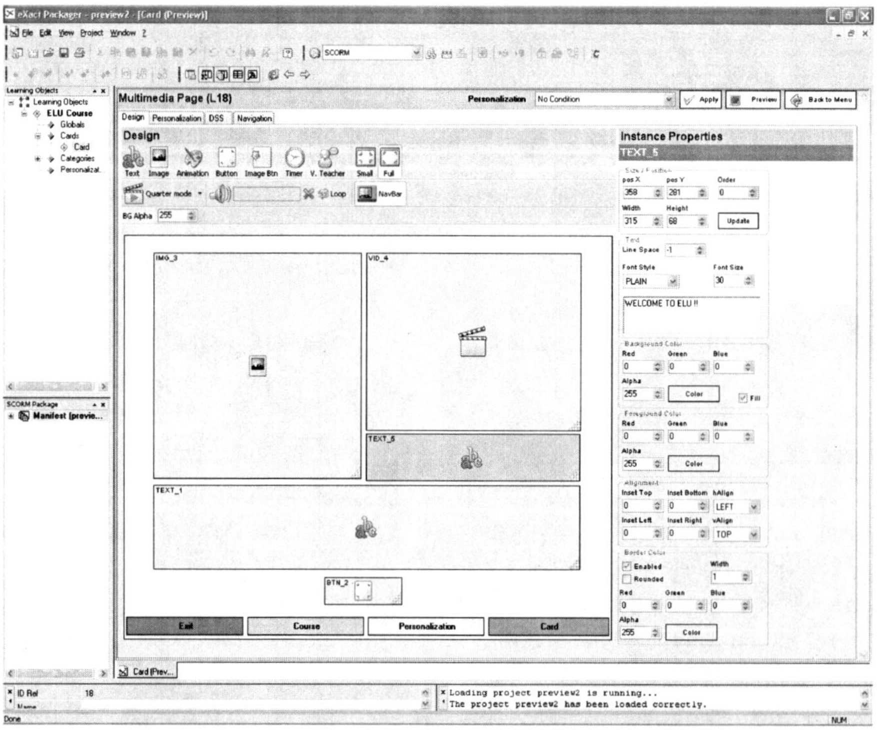

plates, which can be customized appropriately in terms of appearance, fonts, score computation modalities, content etc..

The tool supports two modalities of configuring a newly instantiated service: full configuration, which gives the author full access to all the configurable parameters of the service, and the Style configuration, where the graphics are pre-defined and the author has to insert the contents (e.g. questions and answers, images to be manipulated, graphs, etc.). The first approach is suitable for high customizable solutions, but may be time-consuming and addresses mostly to experienced authors, while the second approach is more efficient since the author can focus more on content than appearance while authoring process becomes more rapid and homogeneity insured.

Client Side

The Course Multimedia Player (CMP) is the t-learning client software that reads the data generated by the authoring tools to present the course to the end-user and manage her/his interaction in front of the TV.

As explained in previous section, the course script file contains all required data to instantiate a course. By reading this xml description file, the multimedia player creates the static part of the course (each page/card) and the dynamic part where navigation, personalized path based on the user profile, and synchronization with the TV-program are involved. When a T-Learning application is launched by a TV viewer, the Course Multimedia Player parses the corresponding scripts to instantiate the T-learning course. Subsequently, the following components are involved:

1. Graphical Rendering Manager: This part is responsible for the graphical interface. It displays all the course components and manages the video stream rendering. For instance, following the course creator choice or according to the Personalizer's values, each course screen can be displayed in 3 different modes: full Screen (FS), full Screen with TV picture (FSTV) and Stripe (S).
2. Navigation Manager (personalized): Interpreted at runtime, the course path can change following several rules from the personalization manager. This path can also be influenced by the synchronization manager or the user interaction. It allows a dynamic adaptation of the learning path.
3. Synchronization Manager: Synchronization is realized between the TV-program and the application. Indeed, regarding the timeline, some time triggers (they may correspond to events such as beginning of the first part, end of the second part) are listened by the synchronization manager in order to take adequate actions. For instance, start an application or change the section in a course.
4. Personalization Manager: The Personalizer keeps track of the dynamic user profile (e.g. current values of the user interaction, such as score, what pages have already been visited, what quizzes, etc.) and of the persistent user profile (e.g. preferences, age, etc.). Consistently with the overall organization of the system, the Personalizer exploits the profile information to operate at two levels: (1) Personalization of the scheduling of the cards. (2) Personalization of the configurable parameters of the services (Multimedia pages and interactive edutainment units) – typical configurable parameters concern the look and the contents of each service.
5. Interactivity Manager

Finally, the Course Multimedia Player manages Interactivity. Interactivity is considered in two levels:

- Local interactivity: it is provided by programmable components that enable the action of the user on visible parts of the screen and change the behavior/settings/

appearance of the objects that are displayed, without the need of a return channel. The user can access local interactivity simply through her/his remote control.

- Server interactivity: same as local interactivity but the actions of the user are sent to a server as "requests" via a physical return channel and the behavior of the displayed objects is modified through the reception of "commands" from the servers, application servers or broadcast server. For instance, the server interactivity can be used to store general data in a centralized way or also to request additional information on a given topic.

Results

In order to validate the above framework and also preview the courses that are developed through the authoring tool, an iDTV simulation environment was employed. We have selected the MHP analyzer from IRT software, which is capable of running MHP applications.

During these tests it was possible either to preview the performance of the static parts of the course independently or the complete course synchronized with the video. Using the AT, the author could iteratively design and implement the cards, fix their scheduling in the timeline and check the preview. The preview functionality provides two levels: single card level and course level. The first one allows immediate inspection of any card, just after its development, while the second one allows analyzing the whole course, checking also the overall scheduling, navigation and learning paths alternatives. The integration inside the AT allowed an instant preview of the course making the testing procedure easier. This intensive testing proved itself to be useful also to signal bugs of the CMP and of the AT, and highlighted the need for improvements and additional functionalities as it emerged from the concrete experience of the course developers. These iterations were important to complete a fully functional t-learning framework comprising of a runtime multimedia player and an offline authoring tool that satisfies the requirements of the pedagogues and the content creators.

Using the authoring tool, an interactive enhancement of the "Snow White and the Seven dwarfs" animated film from Disney has been implemented, in order to support the study of English as a foreign language. This experimental course was created in order to further test and evaluate the framework also from a more technical perspective, considering most of the supported functionalities and realizing multiple course paths with complex sequences and conditions. In addition, the system has been tested in the context of the ELU project (Enhanced Learning Unlimited 2007) by over 170 users in 7 European countries and in a variety of course contexts and educational domains, such as: cultural tourism, basic business, MBA statistics, driving license, computer basics and basic statistics (Bellotti, Vrochidis et al. 2008). These experimental t-learning courses were created by pedagogical experts in various knowledge domains and served as a significant test and evaluation bench for the framework.

Figures 8 illustrates a Couples game from this application. Functional tests have been successfully run in real context of use settings, where the course run on commercial STB and is displayed on TV set and users can interact through a remote control.

CHALLENGES

The main challenges we faced during the implementation of the aforementioned framework had to do with the enhancement and possible integration of various technological advancements, in order to promote more advanced t-learning practices and enhance the interaction in an online t-learning application, as well as with the adaptation of the knowledge and the technology from e-learning

Figure 8. Couples Game preview

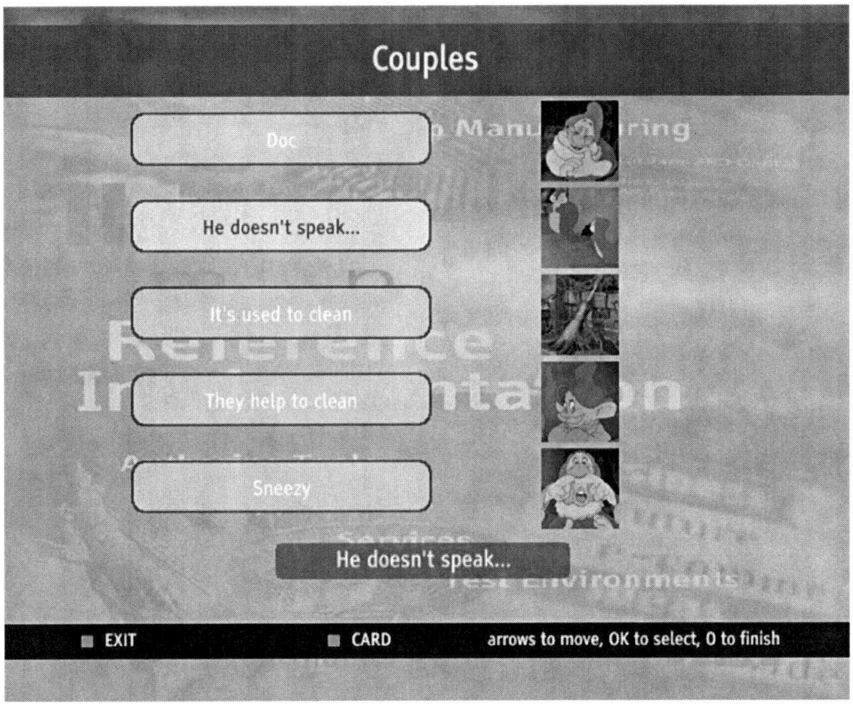

to t-learning world.

More specifically, we had to deal with t-learning courses that included different formats of information (video, audio, text, images, graphics, software applications to provide animations and interaction, etc.). Furthermore, each piece of information was interacting with the others, depending on the events it can produce, its invocation capabilities and the capability to refer to other components in the system. This involves the evaluation of adequacy to the iDTV characteristics of new information formats as MPEG-4 or MPEG-7 (MPEG, 2002), not quite used in e-learning yet. When using an MHP-based platform, the downloaded applications (DVB-J applications) must obey a set of restrictions related to the execution environment and to the capabilities of the STB.

For that reason the design and the implementation of such tools that would deal with content declaration, automatic checking of restrictions existing in the model, automatic generation of software applications following the MHP standard, integration and information packing, generation of the configuration files for signaling the course information and management of the courses was considered a very complicated task.

The receiver side was also complicated as the set of information defined in the production side had to be received in the Set Top Box through an object carrousel, as defined in the DVB-MHP standard. This information had to be rendered and visualized by a software application in charge of the coordination of course execution. In the Set Top Box could be performed by a DVB-J application, periodically transmitted through the same data channel of the iDTV service used to broadcast the course. Such application should be able to accesses all the course structure in order to obtain the proper information to locate within the transport stream all the objects belonging to a specific course and to coordinate their execution and representation, as well as the user interaction.

SOLUTIONS AND RECOMMENDATIONS

The possibility of augmenting video streams with interactive data and services has opened new important perspectives for digital TV that still have to be better investigated and exploited, in several application domains. Important issues concern the computational power of the STBs and the communication capabilities (especially for the return channel), and the Human-Computer Interaction modalities (both considering the remote control and the need to synchronize interactive applications with the underlying A/V stream).

The case proposed in this chapter contributes to this research scenario by suggesting an integrated personalized learning environment for the development, delivery and presentation of educational material. The main challenge involved is to exploit and enhance the technologies from digital TV and computer domain so that they are useful for education. The presented approach to iDTV is evolutionary, rather than revolutionary. That is, it still considers the TV program as a linear audiovisual stream that may be enhanced through simple interactivity. This is due to the prevailing popularity and pervasiveness of the TV as medium for supplying relaxed/informal information and stories.

The approach employs a media-driven strategy (i.e. it is the A/V stream that dictates the flow) and stresses the role of the author/director in proposing contents, as in the TV tradition. Interactivity helps the viewer to better contextualize/understand the video stream and to go more in depth about the touched items at the end of the stream. This is an evolution inside the TV tradition and is complementary to the typical e-learning solutions that have been developed in a computer and network-centered environment.

During the course creation, a clear structure for the content is defined, while the template logic allows reusability, which is a big advantage at the iDTV world where the available bandwidth and the storage capabilities of the STBs are limited and the production costs are high and the time-to-market short. Moreover, the configurability option allows the insertion of personalization, which is considered as an added pedagogical value. This template-based approach allows the creation of flexible and standard courses that are interpreted by a multimedia course player running on a STB. The player interprets the course configuration script and accordingly presents the structure content to the viewer and manages her/his interaction through the remote control. Another advantage of the proposed framework is the extensibility as it is possible to support services on demand, also by exploiting the return channel of the STB, and including other kinds of contents, such as virtual avatars and more complex games.

ACKNOWLEDGMENT

This work was supported by the project ELU (Enhanced Learning Unlimited) (Enhanced Learning Unlimited 2007), which was funded by the European Commission.

REFERENCES

Aarreniemi-Jokipelto, P. (2005). *T-learning Model for Learning via Digital TV*. Paper presented at the 16th EAEEIE Annual Conference on Innovation in Education for Electrical and Information Engineering (EIE), Lappeenranta, Finland.

Aarreniemi-Jokipelto, P., & Tuominen, J. (2004). Experiences with an Interactive Learning Environment in Digital TV. In *Proceedings of the 4th IEEE International Conference on Advanced Learning Technologies, ICALT 2004,* (pp. 296-300).

Baker, K., Pulles, R., & Sasno, P. (2004). *Terminal Architecture Issues for Interactive and Reactive TV media using MHP-Java and MPEG4*. Paper presented at the IEEE International Symposium on Consumer Electonics, University of Reading, UK.

Bellotti, F., Vrochidis, S., Ramel, S., Tsampoulatidis, I., Lhoas, P., & Pellegrino, M. (2008). A Technological Framework for the Authoring and Presentation of T-learning Courses. [iJET]. *International Journal of Emerging Technologies in Learning*, *3*(4), 10–19.

Bernhaupt, R. Obrist, M. Tscheligi M. (2007): Usability and usage of iTV services: lessons learned in an Austrian field trial. *Computers in Entertainment, 5*(2).

Blanco-Fernandez, Y., Pazos-Arias, J. J., Gil-Solla, A., Ramos-Cabrer, M., Barragans-Martinez, B., & Lopez-Nores, M. (2004). A multi-agent open architecture for a TV recommender system: A case study using a Bayesian strategy. In *Proceedings of the Sixth IEEE International Symposium on Multimedia Software Engineering*, Miami, FL.

Carey, J. (1996). *Winky Dink To Stargazer: Five Decades Of Interactive Television*. Paper presented at the Interactive Television 1996, Edinburgh, Scotland.

Digital Video Broadcasting. (2007). Retrieved October 18, 2007, from http://www.dvb.org

Enhanced Learning Unlimited. (2007). Retrieved October 18 2007, from http://www.elu-project.com

Interactive, T. V. *Web*. (2007). Retrieved October 18, 2007, from http://www.interactivetvweb.org

Jack, K., & Tsatsoulin, V. (2002). Dictionary of Video Television Technology. New York: Elsevier Newnes.

Leslie, N. P. (1980). The history of television and radio in continuing education. *New Directions for Adult and Continuing Education*, *5*, 15–29.

Lopez-Nores, M., Elexpuru-Eguia, A., Blanco-Fernandez, Y., Pazos-Arias, J., Gil-Solla, A., Garcia-Duque, J., et al. (2004). A Technological Framework for TV-supported Collaborative Learning. In *Proceedings of the IEEE Sixth International Symposium on Multimedia Software Engineering (ISMSE'04),* Miami, USA.

Lytras, M., Lougos, C., Chozos, P., & Pouloudi, A. (2002). *Interactive Television and E-learning Convergence: Examining the Potential of T-learning*. Paper presented at the European Conference on e-learning, Brunel University, UK.

Rey-Lopez, M., Fernandez-Vilas, A., Diaz-Redondo, R. P., Pazos-Arias, J., & Bermejo-Munoz, J. (2006). *Adaptive Learning Objects for T-learning*. Paper presented at the 5th International Conference on Web-based Learning (ICWL), Penang, Malaysia.

Shute, V. J., & Psotka, J. (1996). Intelligent Tutoring Systems: Past, Present and Future. In D. Jonassen (ed.) Handbook of Research on Educational Communications and Technology. New York: Scholastic Publications.

Vrba, V., Cvrk, L., & Sykora, M. (2006). Framework for digital TV applications. In *Proceedings of the International Conference on Networking, International Conference on Systems and International Conference on Mobile Communications and Learning Technologies*, (pp. 184-184).

Wenger, E. (1987). Artificial Intelligence and Tutoring Systems: Computational and Cognitive Approaches to the Communication of Knowledge. San Francisco: Morgan Kaufmann.

ADDITIONAL READING

Aarreniemi-Jokipelto, P., & Kalli, S. (2005). *Open Standard-Based Digital TV Browser in T-learning*. Paper presented at the EuroITV Conference (http://www.euroitv.org/), Aalborg, Denmark.

Aarreniemi-Jokipelto, P., Tuominen, J., Kalli, S., & Rikonen, T. (2005). *Experimenting with Digital Television Learning Environments*. Paper presented at the 16th EAEEIE Annual Conference on Innovation in Education for Electrical and Information Engineering (http://www.it.lut.fi/eaeeie05/), Lappeenranta, Finland.

Ahonen, A., Turkki, L., Saarijarvi, M., Lahti, M., & Virtanen, T. (2006). *Guidelines for designing easy to-use interactive television services: experiences from the ArviD programme*. Paper presented at the 4th European conference on Interactive television (http://uitv.info/euroitv2006/), Athens, Greece.

Bates, P. J. (2005). *Learning through iDTV – results of t-learning study*. Paper presented at the European Conference on Interactive Television, (http://www.euroitv.org/), Aalborg, Denmark.

Belovics, B., & Kirk, J. (2006). *The Use of Video Games as an Instructional Strategy in Education*. EAEEIE Conference, Western Carolina University, USA.

Brecht, R., & Kunert, T. (2005). *User requirements and design guidance for interactive TV news applications*. Paper presented at EuroITV 2005, (http://www.euroitv.org/), the 3rd European Conference on Interactive Television User-Centred ITV Systems, Programs and Applications, Aalborg, Denmark.

Cronin, G. (1995). Marketability and social implications of interactive TV and the information superhighway. *IEEE Transactions on Professional Communication*, *38*(1), 24–32. doi:10.1109/47.372390

Ferretti, S., & Roccetti, M. (2006), *MHP Meets The Web: Bringing Web Contents to Digital TV for Interactive Entertainment*. Proceedings of the Eighth IEEE International Symposium on Multimedia (ISM'06), San Diego, USA.

Frantzi, M., Moumoutzis, N., & Christodoulakis, S. (2004). *A Methodology for the Integration of SCORM with TV-Anytime for Achieving Interoperable Digital TV and e-Learning Applications*. Paper presented at the IEEE International Conference on Advanced Learning Technologies, Joensuu, Finland.

Geerts, D. (2005). *Towards a Framework For Evaluating the Sociability of Interactive Television*. Paper presented at the European Conference on Interactive Television, (http://www.euroitv.org/), Aalborg, Denmark.

KnowledgebaseM. H. P. (http://www.mhp-knowledgebase.org/).

Lekakos, G., & Giaglis, G. (2002). *Delivering personalized advertisements in digital television: A methodology and empirical evaluation*. In Proceedings of the AH 2002 Workshop on Personalization in Future TV, Malaga, Spain.

Lopez-Nores, M., et al. (2005). *Bringing Standard into T-learning*. Paper presented at EuroITV 2005, (http://www.euroitv.org/), 3rd European Conference on Interactive Television, User-Centred ITV Systems, Programmes and Applications, Aalborg, Denmark.

Masthoff, J., & Pemberton, L. (2003). *Adaptive Learning via Interactive Television*. Paper presented at the PEG 03 conference, St Petersburg, Russia.

Ortiz, A., Aizpurua, I., Oyarzun, D., Arizkuren, I. & Posada J. (2003). *ASEDUC – E-Learning Course Delivery Using 3D Conversational Avatars*. Computer Graphik topics Issue 4.

Ozolina, A., Kapenieks, A., Zuga, B., Jirgensons, M., Bellotti, F., Vrochidis, S., et al. (2007). Designing Attractive T-Learning Courses Applications for Interactive Digital TV, Annual Proceedings of Vidzeme University College, "ICTE in Regional Development", Valmiera, Latvia, pp. 87-95, ISBN 9984-633-10-1.

Santos, D. T., Vale, T., D., & Meloni, L., G., P. (2006). *Digital TV and Distance Learning: Potentials and Limitations*. Paper presented at the 36th ASEE/IEEE Frontiers in Education Conference, (http://fie-conference.org/fie2006/), San Diego, USA.

Santos, D. T., Vale, D. T., & Meloni, L. G., P.(2006). *Digital TV and Distance Learning: Potentials and Limitations*, 36th ASEE/IEEE Frontiers in Education Conference, (http://fie-conference.org/fie2006/), San Diego, USA.

Seels, B., Fullerton, K., Berry, L., & Horn, L. J. (2004). Research on Learning from Television. In D. Jonassen (Ed.), A Handbook of Research for Educational Communications and Technology - Second Edition (pp. 249-334). Mahwah, New Jersey, London: Lawrence Erlbaum Associates, Publishers.

Soares, L., & Filho, G. (2007), *Interactive Television in Brazil: System Software and the Digital Divide*, EURO ITV 2007, (http://old-www.cwi.nl/events/2007/euroitv2007/), Amsterdam, the Netherlands, May 24-25.

Sperring, S., & Strandvall, T. (2006). *The experience of entertainment in an interactive television show*. Paper presented at the 4th International Conference on Communication and Mass Media, Athens, Greece.

Vrochidis, S., Bellotti, F., Bo, G., Napoletano, L., & Kompatsiaris, I. (2008), T-Learning Technologies, in Mehdi Khosrow-Pour (Ed.), Encyclopedia of Information Science and Technology (2nd Edition), IGI Global, vol. VIII, pp. 3765-3771.

KEY TERMS AND DEFINITIONS

Authoring Tool: Environment for applications creation without the need of programming and technical skills.

E-Learning: Distance learning with the aid of Personal Computer.

Framework: A basic conceptual structure of interconnected modules that is used to address complex issues.

iDTV: Interactive Digital TV is the evolution of the traditional TV set based on digital transmission and has the capability of running interactive applications.

MHP: Multimedia Home Platform is the common middleware for running applications for iDTV.

Personalization: The customization and categorization procedure of a viewer-learner.

STB: Set Top Box is the device that decodes and processes the digital received signal.

Synchronization: This term is used to specify the time-matching between the t-learning content and the respective video so that the t-learning course could be presented in the proper way to the viewer-learner.

t-Learning: Term that defines the TV based interactive learning.

t-Learning Course: A set of educational modules that comprises a course for iDTV.

Chapter 8

E-Learning in Higher Education in China and Belgium:

Student, Teacher, Contextual Variables

Chang Zhu
Ghent University, Belgium

Martin Valcke
Ghent University, Belgium

Tammy Schellens
Ghent University, Belgium

ABSTRACT

This case study aims at examining issues related to the adoption and implementation of e-learning in the Chinese and Flemish context, and identifying the similarities and differences regarding the student, teacher and contextual variables. A parallel e-learning design was set up at Ghent University, (Flanders) Belgium and Beijing Normal University, China. A series of variables were considered at the student, teacher and contextual level. Chinese and Flemish students differed in many aspects in their perceptions of and satisfaction with the e-learning environment. Chinese and Flemish teachers were clearly in different stages regarding technology adoption for education. These disparities are related to the specific contexts (both institutional and cultural). Linkage is made to the current status quo of the two contexts and the cultural dimensions, such as individualism/ collectivism, power distance and competition.

BACKGROUND (ORGANIZATIONAL, THEORETICAL AND EMPIRICAL)

Ghent University in (Flanders) Belgium and Beijing Normal University (BNU), in China are both comprehensive and research-oriented universities, and both have a long history in its own setting. At Ghent University, an e-learning system called Minerva has been implemented from the early 2000s, and since 2003 it has been adopted institution-wide. All teaching staff uses this system to support their teaching activities to a certain degree. All registered students have automatic and personalized access to the system. At Beijing Normal University, there is an e-learning system available, but the staff and students have to apply and register for the access to the system. There is no institution-wide policy and

DOI: 10.4018/978-1-61520-749-7.ch008

requirements for the teaching staff to implement this e-learning system. The teachers apply it only on voluntary basis. Some teachers apply it for the purpose of competing for "elite courses" and some others for experimental purposes.

The e-learning system at Ghent University brings these advantages to its staff in view of convenient delivery of information and the facilitation of ways to communicate and share knowledge between teachers and students, and among students. At Beijing Normal University, e-learning is playing a relatively limited role in facilitating teaching and learning, communication, and sharing knowledge in blended learning settings. However, it has started to play a major role in offering degree-based distance education and in-service training. In this case study, we focus on the use of e-learning in blended learning environments, and especially the adoption of e-learning as a collaborative learning and knowledge sharing tool for university teachers and students.

In many Western countries, higher education has transformed tremendously with the implementation of e-learning technologies. E-learning brings a lot of advantages for students and teachers, such as the flexibility of time and space, and convenient communication and interaction. However, the adoption of e-learning is much more than a technology issue (Robertson, 2004). E-learning readiness is related to its connectivity, capability, content, and culture of an institution (Economist Intelligence Unit, 2003). Next to infrastructure issues, policy of integrating the use of Information and Communication Technology (ICT) in education, teachers' course design, communication requirements, teacher and student technology literacy, and institutional support are among the challenges that institutions, teachers and students are facing (Educause, Centre for Applied Research, 2003).

E-learning is essentially a network-enabled transfer of skills and knowledge. Two main functions of e-learning are often discussed: the *distribution* of course material, and *interactive* learning. Underneath these two basic functions, we can distinguish two different pedagogical views of teaching: one is oriented towards the delivery of information and the other is based on the social constructive perspective that teaching and learning foster active and interactive learning processes. The latter is also in tune with the criteria of meaningful learning and can demonstrate the potential of technology-enhanced learning (Löfström & Nevgi, 2007).

Although technological advances have led to global communications across national boundaries and geographical limitations, we cannot ignore the influences of culture on people's perceptions and behavior, such as adoption of technology, and preferences for the way of teaching and learning. Segall, Dasen, Berry & Poortinga (1990) point out that "we are what we are because of our culturally based learning". Culture is a shared, learned, symbolic system of values, beliefs and attitudes that shapes and influences perception and behavior (Bodley, 1994; Douglas, 1992). In brief, culture refers to "the shared way of life of a group of people" (Berry, Poortinga, Segall & Dasen (2002, p.1). However, we need to bear in mind that culture is dynamic and can be taught and learned (Geertz, 1993).

Chinese culture is traditionally regarded as part of the Confucian-heritage cultures (CHC) (Baron, 1998; Smith & Smith, 1999; Watkins & Biggs, 2001). Flanders is the Dutch-speaking part of Belgium. Building on previously available literature and empirical data, the Flemish culture is linked to an individualist culture, characterized by a less power distance, stronger individualism and higher uncertainty avoidance compared to the Chinese culture (Hofstede, 1986) (see Figure 1). However, we have to note that the empirical data to ground these qualifications have been collected more than 30 years ago, and calls for more recent analysis of the cultural dimensions due to the globalization and internationalization process, especially in the higher education arena.

Figure 1. The 5D model of Hofstede: China vs. Belgium

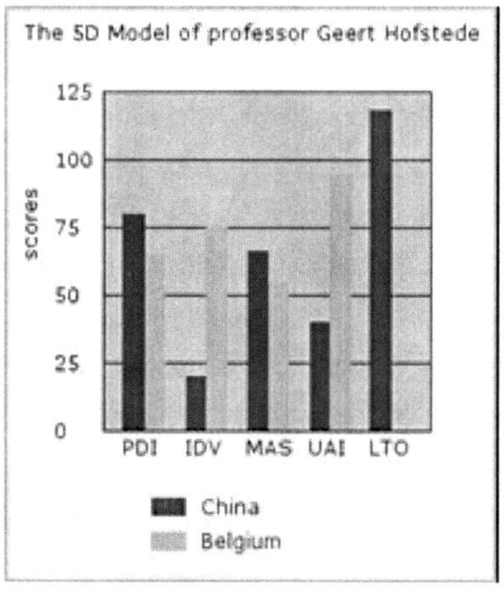

In collectivistic cultures, people tend to avoid conflict and build more on intermediaries. Effort, persistence and obligations are considered as determinants of what a person achieves. People are encouraged to conform to the societal demands (Pratt, 1991; Triandis, 1990). The salient characteristics of learning in the Confucian-Heritage Cultures include social-achievement orientation, diligence, attributing success to effort, a competitive spirit and a strong belief in the maxim "practice makes perfect" (Bond, 1996; Ho, 1986; Watkins & Biggs, 1996). In individualistic cultures, individual differences are respected, people are encouraged to stand out, be unique and express themselves, and to develop the tendency to question and evaluate. The latter are considered essential for learning. It also has to be stressed that the two polar positions in the cultural dimension need to be considered as two positions on a continuum.

Higher education systems in China and Flanders reflect both similarities and differences. As to the differences, first of all, the entry into Chinese universities is based on the outcomes of a competitive national entrance examination, while in Flanders access to higher education is mostly free. This implies a difference in the student composition of university students in these two cultural contexts. Secondly, Chinese bachelor's education is organized during four years, while the Flemish system follows the European Bologna guidelines and takes three years at bachelor level. This implies that the first year of the university curriculum in Flanders is very focused and oriented towards specific subjects; while in Chinese universities, the curriculum of the first two years covers a wider theoretical base (including philosophy, politics, languages, etc.). Thirdly, the class size is different. In China, it is quite often to have a class of 40-80 students (for each lecture). Some courses may have an audience of 100-200 students. In the Flemish setting, it is quite often to have 200-300 students for each lecture. Despite these differences, we found that there are similarities in the main content of the subject matter in many disciplines.

During the last three decades, learning and instruction in Chinese school have been highly exam-oriented (Gu, 2008). Many Chinese parents value education as a stepping stone to develop economic opportunities and society status (Matthews, 2000). Compared to Chinese students, Flemish students are more likely to choose their study programmes following their personal interests. The current innovation of university education in China focuses on structural reforms or a system reform and aims at adjusting the educational objectives (Ma, 2005). This reform has yet not resulted in a prevalent impact on teaching and learning practices. Chinese teachers still stress systematic knowledge transmission, and teacher-centred approaches are the norm in many Chinese universities. In Flemish universities, the social constructivist learning approach has been accepted in various ways since the late 1990s, especially when adopting innovative teaching and learning approaches such as e-learning in general and computer-based collaborative learning more specifically.

The social constructivist learning theory stresses that learning as an active and social process. Meaningful learning occurs when individuals are engaged in social activities (McMahon, 1997).

This trend has been influential to transform higher education in many Western settings, especially in combination with the application of collaborative technologies (Duffy & Jonassen, 1992). It also emphasizes the importance of the relationship between the student and the instructor in the learning process. The development of computer supported collaborative learning (CSCL) is based on this learning principle that students learn – construct knowledge – through group interaction (Gerlach, 1994). Educational research has shown that more effective learning takes place if learners are actively involved, rather than passive listeners (e.g. Van Merrienboer & Paas, 2003). Previous research also reports that students in collaborative learning conditions adopted to a higher extent constructive learning processes (Curtis & Lawson, 2001).

More than two decades ago, the teaching and learning approaches in Flemish universities were rather teacher-centered. Teachers exercised high authority on the students. And the distance between teacher and students was rather big. Nowadays, with the modernization in education and the use of Internet-based learning, students have more autonomy, and have access to more sources of information and knowledge. The teachers are no more considered as "the" authority. In the Chinese context, the same trend is also observed, however, recent studies have pointed out that there does not seem to have much change in the approach to teaching in the last two decades (Liu, 2007; Ma, 2009). Therefore, this case study aims to understand how Chinese and Flemish teachers and students will respond to the implementation of e-learning, with a focus on computer supported collaborative learning; and how these responses are related to their institutional and cultural contexts.

SETTING THE STAGE

The e-learning system "Minerva" implemented at Ghent University is based on the open-source Dokeos/Claroline system, which has been developed by a university consortium. Ghent University is one of the co-developers of this system. At Beijing Normal University, based on a collaborative research agreement, the Chinese version of the same Dokeos e-learning system has been implemented. In order to compare student characteristics and feedback (such as satisfaction), a parallel e-learning design was implemented for a population of Chinese and Flemish students. The parallel design has been set up for three consecutive years for the course of "instructional sciences". In each term the course lasted for about three months. Each year, the participants were first-year students in Educational Sciences. In both settings, student average age was similar (between 18-20); and a majority of students were female (65-85%).

The experimental course, implemented in the e-learning context focuses on major learning and instructional theories and concepts of Educational Psychology, such as behaviorism, cognitivism, constructivism, and meta-cognition. Next to the face-to-face lectures during which the major theories were presented to the students, a collaborative e-learning environment was provided to students as a communication and collaboration tool. In order to ensure a comparable course design, the same handbook on "Instructional Sciences" (Dutch and Chinese version), the same group formation, procedures and similar online asynchronous discussion tasks were implemented in both contexts. In the Chinese setting, each year there were about 100 students. In the Flemish setting, there were about 300 students. In order to promote student collaboration, students were assigned into groups of six to ten students to work on discussion tasks online.

The research study was based on student participation in the academic year 2007-2008. Before and after the implementation of the e-learning, all students responded to a series of questionnaires. The Motivated Strategies of Learning Questionnaire (MSLQ) (Pintrich, Smith, Garcia & McKeachie, 1993) and a questionnaire of perceptions of e-learning environment were used in the pre- and post-test. In the post-test, students also reported their (dis-) satisfaction with the e-learning environment and online collaborative learning.

Additionally, in order to understand –the views of the teacher about the adoption of e-learning and their perspectives on teaching and learning principles, 60 Chinese and 30 Flemish teachers were interviewed. All the teachers were from similar knowledge domain, such as educational science, psychology or sociology. The teacher participants were interviewed separately, each for about 40 minutes to 1 hour. In the Chinese setting, some teachers have already applied e-learning in their teaching practice, and some have not tried yet. When choosing the teacher participants, considerations were made to have a proportionally balanced teacher representation of gender and age groups. Teachers were also asked about what institutional factors influence their adoption of e-learning and CSCL. Furthermore, a questionnaire adapted from the Cultural Environment Inventory of Wang (2004) focusing on student-teacher power distance, collaboration, and competition orientation, and a questionnaire on Teaching Style Survey was administered to all teacher participants. The Teaching Style Survey was based on the questionnaire developed by Grasha & Riechmann (1990) reflecting five scales that centre on specific teacher roles: expert, authority, personal model, facilitator and delegator (See Figure 2).

CASE DESCRIPTION

Ghent University has started to implement the Minerva e-learning system from the year 2000. The University considers up-to-date education as an answer on the changing needs from the knowledge and information society (source: educational development plan). The implementation of the e-learning system is a response to the University's strategy to promote high-quality education, facilitate contacts between students and professors, active acquiring of knowledge and skills by students, encouraging a optimal mixture of educational forms (blended learning), introducing interactive technologies that react adaptively and intelligently to immediate learning needs. Information and Communication Technologies (ICT) is implemented as an enrichment of the learning process and the learning environment. The university educational development plan clearly states that e-learning plays a complementary role to the more traditional education forms. Next to the open-source Dokeos system as the main learning management system, Ghent University has adapted and incorporated some other self-developed functions, such as the Curios for online test/examination environment. All teachers and employees and all officially registered students can use Minerva. The students can register themselves for courses online. Teachers can announce course activities, deliver course materials and assignments to students; more importantly, teachers can manage student groups and organize group activities for case studies, discussions or problem-solving activities.

Beijing Normal University has started to use the Blackboard Academic Suite as a pilot system to provide e-learning for some courses. Due to the high cost and technical agreements with the service provider, it has not been widely applied across the University. Wide applications have been encouraged since 2007; however, there is no university-wide implementation of this e-learning system. In 2007, a rough estimation provided by the Office of Teaching and Student Affair was about 20%-30% of the teachers have registered for the use of the Blackboard e-learning system. However, among these registered users, some have not actively used this system yet. No accurate figure could be obtained at the moment of inquiry. The relevant personnel pointed out that the figure can be changed each year as more training will be organized, and the server size will be enlarged. Some faculties have also applied some alternative e-learning systems at the faculty level,

Figure 2. The Chinese version of the e- learning system and the Dutch version of the e-learning system

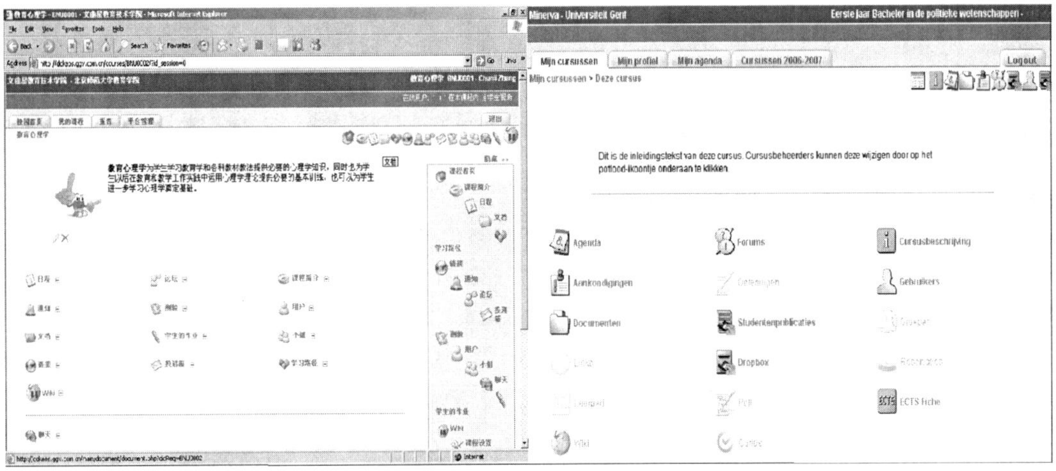

e.g., a web collaborative learning tool (WebCL) was implemented at the Faculty of Educational Technology. Under the framework of a collaborative research agreement between Ghent University and BNU, the Chinese version of Dokeos system was installed and implemented for the course of "instructional sciences" from 2007.

As introduced above, a parallel design of e-learning environment with similar group assignments was implemented for a population of first-year students in Educational sciences who follow the course of "instructional sciences". Next to the face-to-face lectures, students were randomly assigned to a group of 6-8 students with an authentic task for each group. For example, students were asked to jointly design a Wiki page (web content with hyper links that each group can jointly edit). The e-learning system displays the latest version of the Wiki document on the main page and on the "history" page, it tracks all the changes made by the group members. Each group could only view their own content. In addition, each group also had its own discussion forum to discuss the procedure, their comments and the changes they've made in the group task.

Student perceptions of the e-learning environment focus on their perceptions of the learning design in terms of group discussions, peer learning, problem-based learning, critical thinking, and interaction. Student satisfaction of the e-learning environment focuses on their satisfaction with the e-learning functions, online collaborative learning, peer interaction and contribution, interaction, etc. Student learning process was analyzed based on the level of knowledge construction through social interaction using the coding scheme of Gunawardena, Lowe & Anderson (1997) and the coding scheme of Veerman & Veldhuisdiermanse (2001).

Below, we report only the main research findings regarding characteristics and feedback of Chinese and Flemish students with regard to learning strategies, motivation, perceptions, satisfaction with the e-learning system, and student communication types, and level of knowledge construction. In addition, teachers' perceptions of teaching and learning principles, adoption of e-learning, and some institutional variables and cultural dimensions will be presented and discussed.

Characteristics of Chinese and Flemish students

Computer Competence and Online Participation of Flemish and Chinese Students

The Flemish and Chinese students differed significantly in computer competence before the study and actual use of the e-learning environment. Compared to the Chinese students, the Flemish students had easier access to computer and Internet, and they were more familiar with the use of computers; considering their experience with e.g., word processing ($p<.001$). The Flemish students spent on an average more time online and used more frequently emails than the Chinese students. Most Flemish students had computer access at home, but most Chinese students had computer access only at the university PC rooms, and some students had computers in their dormitories. As a result, the Flemish students were more familiar with the use of the e-learning environment than the Chinese students ($p<.001$). The Flemish group on an average posted more messages in the asynchronous group discussions than the Chinese group ($p<.01$).

No gender differences were found regarding student prior knowledge of computer and Internet use. But significant differences were found between Chinese students from urban and rural areas regarding their prior knowledge of computer and Internet use. Students from urban areas reported a higher level of computer competence. Female students posted slightly more messages than male students and student from urban areas posted slightly more messages than students from rural areas, but the differences were not significant ($p>.05$).

Perceptions of the E-Learning Environment

The perception of the Chinese student towards the e-learning environment was compared to their perceptions of the conventional learning environment. The results showed that the Chinese students reported less positive perceptions of the actual e-learning environment compared to their perceptions of previous conventional learning environment. This was clear in relation to the characteristics regarding group discussion, interaction, peer learning, and critical thinking. However, they perceived the e-learning environment more positively regarding problem-based-learning ($t=3.97, p<.05$). The results also showed that the Chinese students reported to a higher level of preferences for peer learning, critical thinking, and problem-based learning ($p<.05$) after one semester of their e-learning experience. No significant differences were found between students from urban and rural areas and between boys and girls regarding their perceptions of the learning environments ($p>.05$).

The Flemish students reported more positive perceptions of the e-learning environment compared to their perceptions of the conventional learning environment ($p<.05$). In other words, the Flemish students reflected positively towards the e-learning environment regarding facilitating group discussion, peer learning, interaction, problem-based learning and critical thinking. The results indicate that the Flemish group was more positive towards the e-learning environment than the Chinese group.

The latter might be related to the fact that Chinese students were less familiar with the e-learning environment as the e-learning system has been less widely implemented at BNU at we pointed out earlier. About half of the Chinese students stated that they were normally used to *acquiring* knowledge from teachers or learning materials. Furthermore, many Chinese students reported that there was a lack of teacher guidance and feedback to their contributions in the e-learning environment.

These results are in line with the findings of Gijbels et al. (2006) that student perceptions are not only based on the actual learning environment, but are also strongly influenced by their prior learning experiences and recent experiences. The results indicate that it is possible that student learning styles were not completely in line with the characteristics of the e-learning environment (Schellens & Valcke, 2000). Prior studies also show that students reflect a more positive attitude towards the learning environment when there is greater congruence between the learning environment and student characteristics (Beard et al., 2004).

Student Motivation and Learning Strategies

At the pre-test level, we found that Flemish and Chinese students did not differ in their level of intrinsic and extrinsic motivation. But Chinese students reported a higher level of control of learning beliefs and self-efficacy ($p<.01$), while the Flemish students reported a higher adoption of learning strategies, such as elaboration, rehearsal, self-regulation, and peer learning ($p<.05$). At the post-test level after the e-learning experience, no significant changes were detected in Flemish students regarding their motivation and learning strategies, except a significant decrease in the learning strategy dimension 'peer learning' ($p<.01$). However, the Chinese group reported a higher adoption of the different learning strategies and higher motivation levels. The results showed that the Flemish students adopted to a larger extent the learning strategies regarding critical thinking, elaboration and peer learning ($p<.05$). The Chinese students adopted to a larger extent meta-cognitive self-regulation compared to the Flemish students ($p<.05$).

Student Satisfaction and Dissatisfaction with the E-Learning Environment

There were significant differences between Chinese and Flemish students regarding their satisfaction and dissatisfaction with the e-learning environment. Compared to the Flemish students, the Chinese students reported a higher level of satisfaction with online collaborative learning and peer contribution ($p<.01$). The Chinese group was more satisfied with the equal contribution of group members compared to the Flemish group ($p<.01$). However, the Flemish students were more satisfied with the final results of the online group work compared to the Chinese group ($p<.01$); and they spent more time on an average on the online group collaborative learning, 4.87 hours per week versus 2.10 hours per week for the Chinese students. As to the dissatisfaction of students, the Chinese group reported that the lack of interaction between students and teacher in e-learning was a big problem for them. The Flemish group reported to a larger extent that it was time-consuming compared to the Chinese group ($p<.001$).

Both Chinese and Flemish students found it an advantage to be able to work at their own pace and time, and appreciated online collaborative learning as each group member can contribute his/her part in the group assignments. Both groups reported that online collaborative learning helped them to gain more knowledge than if they would have studied alone. They also stated that they had learned a lot considering the time they've put into the online collaborative learning assignments. The Chinese and Flemish students were similarly satisfied with the peer interaction and with the technical help they received from the course coordinators. Both groups of students reported similar technical problems, such as losing a contribution after submission, downloading or uploading documents, etc.

For the Flemish students, what they liked most of the e-learning environment was working at their own pace and time, while the Chinese students liked most that they could work together with others on the assignments. What the Flemish students disliked the most was that it was so time-consuming, whereas the first problem the Chinese group reported was the lack of interaction between students and teacher.

The dissatisfaction of the Chinese students might be due to their expectations about teacher involvement. Teachers play a very important role in Chinese educational contexts. Observations of the current e-learning programs in China indicate that e-learning tends to be heavily instructor-centered, for example using video lectures online. Other studies also comment that Chinese e-learners found it problematic when teacher presence is low (Friesner & Hart, 2004). This could also be because of the low ambiguity tolerance of Chinese students who expect the presence of expert and certain knowledge (Zhu, Valcke & Schellens, 2008), which leads for a stronger need for feedback and teacher help in the learning environment (Anderson, 2000).

Content Analysis of Student Knowledge Construction through Social Interaction

Student asynchronous group discussions were analyzed to understand the message types and social interaction. The data set comprised the transcripts of all messages posted during group discussions by student groups during one semester. We applied the coding scheme of Veerman & Veldhuis-diermanse (2001) to analyze the distribution of communication types, and the coding scheme of Gunawardena, Lowe & Anderson (1997) to analyze the level of social construction of knowledge. The messages in the transcripts were coded by four independent coders for the Flemish students and three independent coders for the Chinese students. The Chinese and Flemish coders received training by the same researcher to get acquainted with the coding schemes using the same sample data. The inter-rater reliability was checked by determining percent agreement between the raters. For the raters of the Flemish group, the percent agreement was .91; for the raters of the Chinese group, the percent agreement was .86.

In an average, the Flemish students posted weekly more messages per person (7.5 messages) in asynchronous group discussions compared to those posted by the Chinese students (3.9 messages). For both groups, there were no significant differences as to the number of messages posted by male and female students. The types of messages posted by both groups were rather similar, with a majority of task oriented messages. The results show that the pattern of both groups was rather similar, with a majority of messages at the first level-sharing and comparing information (Table 1); however, Flemish students contributed a much higher frequency of messages at the second level-exploration of dissonance; This means that the Chinese students expressed much less of disagreement with group members. This might be linked to Chinese students' preferences of not expressing their personal opinions especially disagreement in public.

Although Flemish and Chinese students differ in their level of knowledge construction, we found that the majority of messages were centered on the lower levels of knowledge construction. There were fewer messages reaching the higher levels of knowledge construction. This distribution of students' contributions corresponds with previous findings that few messages reach the fourth and fifth level, and a majority of messages were at the first level (Gunawardena et al., 1997; McLoughlin & Luca, 2002). This could be explained by the learning habits of students. Students, especially freshmen, are not yet used to test syntheses, summarize agreements, and to apply newly constructed knowledge. They applied more often the first level of knowledge construction which is a prerequisite for a discussion and maintaining the interaction flow. These contributions are in a way indispensable in order to elicit contributions at a higher level of knowledge construction.

Table 1. Types of messages and levels of knowledge construction based on the interaction analysis model

	Chinese	Flemish	x^2	p^c
Types of messages[a]				
Task oriented	95.9%	94.2%	0.35	.505
Non-task oriented	4.1%	5.8%	11.25	.006
Irrelevant	0.3%	1%	11.58	.005
Technical	0.1%	0.5%	10.16	.052
Planning	0.7%	1.2%	10.11	.053
Social	3%	3.1%	0.27	.641
Levels of knowledge construction[b]				
1. Sharing and comparing information	79.5%	63.7%	1.65	.121
2. Exploration of dissonance	5.4%	19.7%	50.32	.000
3. Negotiation of meaning	11.3%	12.6%	3.88	.054
4. Testing synthesis	1.7%	2.8%	15.77	.005
5. Agreement statements and applications of newly-constructed meaning	2.1%	1.2%	12.10	.006

a. Coding based on Veerman et al., 2001.
b. Coding based on Gunawardena et al., 1997.
c. Adjustment for multiple comparisons: Bonferroni correction is applied.

Teachers' Perspectives and Adoption of E-Learning

All teacher participants teach at least one course to undergraduate students in educational sciences, and some teach both at undergraduate and post-graduate level. Among the interviewed teachers, almost all of the Flemish teachers use the Minerva e-learning system to a certain degree. Some may only use for course management (e.g. student registration for the course) and distribution of teaching materials. About one third of the Flemish teachers seem to have adopted more extensively the e-learning functions, such as discussion forums and student online collaborative group work. However, some other teachers have not tried the interactive or collaborative functions due to lack of time, or lack of knowledge and experience on how to organize and monitor online group work.

In the Chinese context, among the interviewed teachers, only about one third of them have had experience in using an e-learning platform, among them only five teachers have tried to apply student online discussions and collaborative learning. About two thirds of the Chinese teachers have thus far not adopted e-learning.

Using Rogers (2003) model of five stages in the innovation-decision process as a reference, it is clear that Chinese and Flemish faculty are situated at a different stage. The majority of Chinese teachers can be positioned at the first stage ('knowledge' level), and only a very small proportion at the 'implementation' stage; while others are still at the pre-stage ('no knowledge' level). A large proportion of Flemish staff already functions at the 'knowledge' and 'implementation' stage. During the interview, we found that a few Flemish teachers have reinforced the adoption of e-learning and online collaborative mode during the last decade, thus have reached the 'confirmation' stage.

Teachers' Perspectives on the Social Constructivist Approach to Teaching and Learning

The interview results show that the Flemish teachers seem to be more supportive of the social-constructivist approach to teaching and learning compared to the Chinese teachers. A majority (24 out of 30) of the Flemish teachers supports the social-constructivist principles and say they apply them extensively in their teaching practice. For example, one Flemish teacher said, "*I support this learning theory; I leave the students to read, explore, research, and work together*"; *and I give new directions and involve students in discussions*". Some teachers support the social-constructivist principles, but apply them in a limited way. This was due to some practical restrictions, as one Flemish teacher put forth, "*I'm in favor of small group collaboration, but it is not easy to organize when there are more than 300 students*". Only one Flemish teacher doubted the relevance of the social-constructivist principles.

A small part (9 out of 60) of Chinese staff supports the social-constructivist principles and applies it extensively during teaching. About half of the Chinese teachers expressed agreement to the social-constructivist principles and support for collaborative learning modes, but they apply them only in a limited way due to student background, feature of the class, the teaching subject, etc. One Chinese teacher said that "*Undergraduate students, especially in their first two years, hardly have the knowledge base to be able to be involved in a social-constructivist approach to learning. It is the teacher's responsibility to provide them with the knowledge base*." The other Chinese teachers stated they did not consciously consider these principles and were comfortable with their conventional lecture-based approach. "*I have been teaching this subject for more than 20 years. I have already developed my systematic way of teaching,*" one Chinese teacher gave her view when talking about new teaching modes. A few of them expressed doubt about the social-constructivist approach.

Although the Flemish teachers seemed to be much more supportive of the constructivist learning principles, both Flemish and Chinese teachers pointed out some practical limitations, such as large class size, teaching subjects, limited infrastructure (e.g. classroom layout), student interests and perceptions (e.g. towards group work). Compared to their Flemish counterparts, the Chinese teachers seemed to face a wider gap between their theoretical beliefs and teaching practices. Some of the constraints seem to be related to the educational and cultural context, as one Chinese teacher mentioned, "*students are tied up with exams; some students do not like spending time to discuss things, they want to know the conclusion; they are used to work individually, due to the influences they got from primary and secondary schools*".

Teachers' Perspectives about Teacher Roles

From our case study, we found that the Chinese teachers stress to a larger extent the teacher as an expert, an authority and a model as compared to Flemish teachers ($p<.01$). There were no significant differences in the perception of teacher role as a facilitator, or a delegator between the two cultural groups ($p>.01$). In both cultural contexts, "elder" teachers (> Mean age) seemed to stress more the expert and authority roles ($p<.01$). There seem to be no differences between elder and younger teachers regarding the facilitator role. No significant differences were found between male and female teachers in both Chinese and Flemish context. Both Chinese and Flemish teachers stressed the adoption of different roles depending on the course objectives, student capabilities, class size, etc.

Factors that Affect Teacher Adoption of E-Learning and Online Collaborative Learning

Through the interviews of the teachers, we identified that computer skills, familiarity with the use of an e-learning system, willingness to learn, and perceived need for innovation were factors related to teachers' adoption of innovations. In addition, institutional factors, such as infrastructure/ affordances, incentive policies, and proper training were regarded as relevant factors for adopting technology enabled learning and teaching. High workload and lack of time seemed to be obstacles for teachers in adopting new technology for teaching and learning. Lack of experiences on how to organize and monitor student online work was also an obstacle. Some teachers were skeptical about online interaction and communication and expressed preference for face-to-face communication. This was especially prominent among Chinese teachers. Furthermore, social and economic pressure also seemed to make the Chinese teachers focus only on funded research projects or teaching activities that were directly linked to professional assessment and remuneration.

It is found that teachers who expressed a need or interest in innovation and willingness to learn were more willing to adopt e-learning and online collaborative approach. Teachers who used computers more frequently and were more familiar with computer/Internet technologies also expressed a stronger interest in e-learning. Sound infrastructure, institutional incentives and relevant technical training were also considered important conditions for e-learning adoption.

We found that teachers who are supportive of the social constructivist learning principle tend to be more willing to adopt teaching innovations. The teaching subject and class size are also considered as relevant factors. Faculty members teaching application-oriented or reality-related subjects were more active in their adoption of online collaborative learning as compared to staff teaching general introductory and theoretical courses. Teachers in smaller classes more often embrace group work as compared to teachers responsible for larger classes. Teachers who are in favor of the facilitator and delegator roles also tend to be more willing to adopt the online collaborative learning approach.

In both settings, the potential of online collaborative learning is still relatively under-exploited. Besides the practical constraints, such as resources and time, teachers' perceived need of innovation is an important factor. Teachers, who do not experience a concrete necessity to look for an innovation, hold to old teaching habits. This conforms to the position of Rogers (2003) that one of the factors that influence the adoption of innovations is whether or not the innovation meets a perceived need. Teachers' attitude towards online communication is another influencing factor. Previous studies shed light on the benefits of online asynchronous communication as it offer time to present a more measured and considered view (Ramsey, 2005); however, these benefits were not recognized by all teachers. The results of this case study also echo previous finding that teachers who are eager to learn are more open for innovative teaching methods (van Eekelen, 2005).

Contextual Variables

Institutional Variables

The Chinese and Flemish student participation and their feedback as to the e-learning environment might be related to the different levels of e-learning implementation at the Chinese and the Flemish universities. The implementation of the e-learning system in the Chinese university was only at an experimental phase. The university administration provided a platform for those advanced adopters to try out the system. However, there were still no comprehensive policies to promote the integrated use of e-learning throughout the whole campus.

Furthermore, the capacity for technical support and maintenance of the e-learning system was also limited at BNU, which restrains the system to be implemented at a broader level. Different from the Chinese scenario, Ghent University responded to the use of Information and Communication Technology in education in a more efficient and systematic manner. Since 2003, a dedicated department ICTO (department of ICT and education technology) and the ICT& O Service Centre has been established to support technology use in education. ICTO is responsible for the maintenance of the infrastructure and providing training and spreading "best practice" about the e-learning environment Minerva to the users. Furthermore, each faculty has a contact person for Minerva related issues.

The institutional environment also seems to influence teacher perspectives. In the Flemish setting, the use of ICT and interactive learning promoting knowledge construction is promoted by university education development and strategic plans. The Flemish teachers, in general, are more in favor of a social-constructivist learning approach and interactive technologies in education. In the Chinese setting, the use of e-learning platform is encouraged for pilot application and some specific programs, but there is no university-wide policy for the use of e-learning platform or interactive technologies in education. Many Chinese teachers have never tried it and have no motivation or incentives to use technology-enhanced learning.

Workload and the evaluation system for teachers seem to be also a relevant factor for teacher adoption of e-learning. Both teachers from the Flemish and Chinese universities report big challenges and pressure on research and teaching. In both settings, there is an evaluation system for academic staff. The Chinese teachers seem to be unhappier with the strictness and the evaluation approach of their institution. The use of e-learning or technology-enhanced learning is not included in the evaluation system. Therefore, many are rather unwilling to adopt any teaching innovation that is not included in the evaluation system. The Chinese teachers also mentioned that the heavy pressure of teaching and research gave them no time to think about teaching innovations. Furthermore, there are not enough resources to invest for the content development of e-learning; for example, most Chinese teachers have no teaching assistants. The learner-centered and social-constructivist learning approach has been more widely applied in the Flemish educational system. In the Flemish academic evaluation system, more emphasis is put on rewarding investments in educational activities and innovations.

The current innovation of university education in China focuses on a structural reform or system reform and the adaptation of educational objectives (Ma, 2005). The educational reform in China also drives university teaching to encourage students do more reflective thinking and active learning. This could explain that Chinese teachers think of the facilitator and delegator roles similarly important as the Flemish teachers. However, instructional innovations in universities are hardly found. The traditional way of teaching that emphasize the systematic knowledge transmission and teachers being authoritarian of the subjects they teach is still prevalent (Wang, 2006). This is especially related to teachers' teaching principles, the way how they were taught and their own learning behaviors (Gordon, Dembo & Hocevar, 2007). Therefore, the diffusion of e-learning and interactive technologies depends on more than just their technical readiness.

Cultural Variables

Individualism versus collectivism is one of the ways to operationalize cultural categories. We argued earlier that considering a dynamic evolution of a culture and globalization of education, it is worthwhile to reexamine the current status of the cultural dimensions of specific cultures. Based on our survey, the perspectives of Chinese and Flemish teachers on power distance, collaboration and competition were analyzed. The results show that *power distance* between teacher-student and *student collaboration* appear to be similar between the two cultural groups ($p>.01$). However, compared to the Flemish teachers, Chinese teachers put more emphasis on *competition* among students ($p<.001$). Quite a few Chinese teachers stressed that they encourage competition among students. As one Chinese teacher stated, "*our traditional collectivism is under the pressure of competition*." A Chinese teacher who has implemented online learning said, "*I support student collaboration, but the real implementation among students is not so good. Some students prefer to finish the assignments individually.*" Contrary to the Chinese counterparts, none of the Flemish teachers said they support competition among students. Most of them support student collaboration, as one Flemish teacher stressed, "*Collaboration is important, it help students understand the contents and principles*".

In the Chinese educational context, the traditional collectivist disposition is countered in a learning environment due to the high level of competition. Chinese tradition values normally mutual help and support. Considering the lower level of participation of Chinese students in online collaboration, Phuong-Mai, Terlouw & Pilot (2005) argued that referring to collectivism is insufficient to explain the nature of Chinese group learning. Collectivism is no panaché for everything related to the adoption of group learning. The adoption is often dependent on the nature of the educational system; whether instructional and assessment practices encourage independent or collaborative forms of learning and collaboration. For example, it is often observed that when students are not expected to work together, they often tend to work independently. Furthermore, entry into higher education in China is quite competitive, which brings a series of requirements to the teachers and students. The competitive nature of education in the Chinese system often forces teachers and students to adopt more teacher-centered methods.

Openness and daring to think, in principle, is encouraged in the Flemish educational system and its culture. The Flemish teachers clearly stress the importance of collaborative learning and do not support competition among students. However, due to the open access of higher education, the first year education often practically acts as a screening for students. The rigid examination system in a way enhances student strategic learning approach. Furthermore, student individual learning preferences are very diverse; some Flemish student learning 'styles' are not completely congruent with the requirements of the constructive and collaborative learning environment (Schellens, 2004).

CURRENT CHALLENGES

This case study presents to policy makers and university administration a number of challenges for the instructional innovation in higher education institutions, among them the adoption of new teaching principles, the adaption of changing teacher roles, stimulating the need to innovate and providing institutional incentives and support are critical.

At the current stage, for many administrators and policy makers of Chinese universities, the provision of e-learning as a learning platform is not of high importance. Restructuring universities and competing for national important universities (such as the 211 project and the 985 project) and building "world-class" universities already require much financial and human resources for research, etc. In the past few years, Chinese universities have gone through different systems of university ranking at both the national and international level. Many Chinese teachers interviewed commented that they don't have time to reflect on instructional innovations, as they are over-loaded with both teaching and research responsibilities. Qin (2008) commented that some universities have misguided their staff by motivating faculties to produce more articles; Publications are awarded by many Chinese universities; but there is a lack of incentives for developing better teaching approaches. When one observes what happens in the classrooms, there is hardly change in what and how teachers teach; the lecturing approach is the dominant instructional approach in many Chinese universities (Liu, 2007). Ma (2009) commented that although systematic restructuring reform in higher education has taken place in China, curriculum and pedagogy change are the hard part for the reform.

Additionally, due to the rigid national university-entrance examinations, many high schools do not spend much time on training in problem-solving, but on preparing students for the national examinations. Therefore, e-learning that focuses on problem-solving and collaborative and interactive learning faces challenges from a cultural and educational viewpoint. Chen (2006) mentioned that there are four critical factors that influence modern Chinese education: authority, face, harmony, collectivism. First, compared to Western students, Chinese students seem to expect more teacher presence in the e-learning environment. This might be related to the higher expectation of Chinese students that teachers with expert knowledge are present in the learning environment as compared to Flemish students (Zhu, Valcke & Schellens, 2008). Observations of the current e-learning programs in China indicate that e-learning tends to be heavily instructor led, for example, by using video lectures online. Secondly, Chinese students tend to be more restrained in formal or open discussions. Therefore, an online task such as expressing different views on one issue might be more difficult for Chinese students than Flemish students. Often Chinese students prefer to submit a "safe" response or a "quotation" from the literature instead of developing their own thoughts. The group members hardly criticized each other's input. This can be explained by a tendency to preserve *harmonious* group communication.

Teacher-centered approaches are prevalent in Chinese universities. Chinese students are lacking experience to become independent, active and interactive learners. Online learning can offer some opportunities to foster active and interactive learning. However, it may face cultural obstacles. It has been argued that Chinese students need activities that are culturally tailored to avoid putting them on the spot as individuals where they may not be able to present themselves as knowledgeable (Dunn & Wallace, 2004). This case study suggests that an adaptation to provide more structure and guidance to students in asynchronous online group discussion could be welcomed by the Chinese students.

The Flemish teachers seem to have largely adopted e-learning. However, also for them a number of clear challenges and questions remain unanswered; e.g., how to benefit from online collaborative and interactive technologies. First, often they lack time and resources to organize, guide and give feedback to group activities online. Secondly, some of them lack relevant experiences in monitoring students in online group communication contexts.

Another challenge for some teachers to apply e-learning as part of a blended instructional approach, is how it can be an integral part of teaching next to the lectures. Usually students come to universities and expect a structured way of teaching and learning. By shifting part of the lecture or face-to-face learning activities online, this seems to create uncertainty, at least for some teachers and students. Therefore, universities need to enable teachers to draw upon experience from early adopters and be informed about "best practices" about the integrated use of e-learning tools within their conventional teaching and learning approach. University administration policies should also be adapted to allow, e.g., flexibility and independence of teachers and students. The important question about e-learning remains: "do we teach in the same way?" The answer is that teachers need to adapt their perceptions of teaching and learning in order to better benefit from e-learning environments for increased interaction, immediacy, communication and collaboration.

SOLUTIONS AND RECOMMENDATIONS

In summary, technological, social, economic and policy factors matter in view of the adoption and implementation of technology in teaching and learning. In addition, individual and cultural differences need to be considered when involving students and teachers in technology enhanced learning, especially online collaborative learning. Technologies themselves cannot transform the university or create new cultures of learning. It is the university, the teachers and students that need to adapt and make relevant use of available technologies to facilitate teaching and learning in line with the needs of the new era. New learning designs can be made based on the diversity of learner needs and cultural backgrounds. Teacher approaches to teaching and perceived teacher roles need to be adapted accordingly. Therefore, professional development of teachers becomes crucial to support this transformation process. Given the changes from a conventional learning environment to a social and networked learning environment, both teachers and students have to be reoriented to learn to cope with the demands of e.g., task-based learning, online communication and a more flexible learning experience. In order to cater for different student cultural backgrounds, learning needs and individual characteristics, e-learning needs to create an online learning community to connect learners to share experience and to construct knowledge through interaction with peers and teachers. A pedagogical pluralism should be promoted.

The study provides recommendations for university policy makers, teachers and e-learning designers to support at least the following:

The university administration should make sure that all the students and teachers from the institution know about the e-learning system and can easily access it. The university policy makers need to make sure that the information infrastructure is adequate to support the planned delivery system. International e-learning developers should understand the importance of the complex cultural context of the target learners. The educational strategies used via the e-learning system should be culturally appropriate. E-learning designers need to create learning tasks that can enable students to present multiple perspectives and diverse views, and to stimulate interaction, debate and critical analysis of ideas. A training system needs to be set up to help teachers to develop a repertoire of online teaching and monitoring skills, and be prepared to take up different roles such as co-learner, guide, mentor, facilitator or coach. Teachers need to understand that the Internet does not make distance disappear, and should provide effective help to students in e-learning. And last but not least, incentives are necessary for both faculty and students.

REFERENCES

Anderson, M. (2000). Individual Characteristics and Web-based Courses. In C. R. Wolfe (Ed.), Learning and teaching on the Word Wide Web (pp. 47-73). San Diego: Academic Press.

Baron, J. (1998). Teaching on-line across cultures. In A. Gooley, C. Pearson, & S. Towers et al. (Ed.), *Proceedings of the 3rd International Conference on Open Learning* (pp. 67-72). Brisbane: Queensland Open Learning Network.

Beard, L. A., Harper, C., & Riley, G. (2004). Online Versus On-Campus Instruction: Student Attitudes & Perceptions. Tech Trends. *Linking Research & Practice to Improve Learning, 48*(6), 29–31.

Berry, J. W., Poortinga, Y. H., Segall, M. H., & Dasen, P. R. (2002). Cross-cultural psychology: Research and applications. Cambridge, UK: Cambridge University Press.

Bodley, J. H. (1994). Cultural Anthropology: Tribes, states, and the global system. Mountain View, CA: Mayfield Pub. Co.

Bond, M. H. (Ed.). (1996). The Handbook of Chinese Psychology. Hong Kong: Oxford University Press.

Chen, Z. (2006, July). *Cultural Influence on Learner's Behaviour in an On-line English Teacher Training Course*. Paper presented at the 2nd International Chinese Learners Conference, University of Portsmouth.

Curtis, D. D., & Lawson, M. J. (2001). Exploring Collaborative Online Learning. *Journal of Asynchronous Learning Networks, 5*(1), 21–34.

Douglas, M. (1992). Risk and Blame: Essays in Cultural Theory. London: Routledge.

Duffy, T. M., & Jonassen, D. H. (1992). Constructivism: New Implications for Instructional Technology. In T. M. Duffy & D. H. Jonassen (Eds.), Constructivism and the Technology of Instruction: A Conversation (pp. 1-16). Hillsdale, NJ: Lawrence Erlbaum Associates, Inc.

Dunn, L., & Wallace, M. (2004). Australian academics teaching in Singapore: striving for cultural empathy. *Innovations in Education and Teaching International, 41*(3), 291–304. doi:10.1080/14703290410001733285

Economist Intelligence Unit. (2003). *The 2003 e-readiness rankings, A white paper from the Economist Intelligence Unit.* Retrieved September 3, 2008 from http://graphics.eiu.com/files/ad_pdfs/eReady_2003.pdf

Educause Centre for applied research. (2003). Impact and challenges of e-learning. *Supporting e-learning in higher education, 3*, 39-47.

Friesner, T., & Hart, M. (2004). A cultural analysis of e-learning for China. *Electronic Journal of eLearning, 2*(1), 81-88.

Geertz, C. (1993). The interpretation of cultures. London: Fontana Press.

Gerlach, J. M. (1994). Is this collaboration? In K. Bosworth & S. J. Hamilton (Eds.), Collaborative learning: Underlying processes and effective techniques. San Francisco: Jossey-Bass.

Gijbels, D., Van De Watering, G., Dochy, F., & Van Den Bossche, P. (2006). New learning environments and constructivism: The students' Perspective. *Instructional Science, 34*, 213–226. doi:10.1007/s11251-005-3347-z

Gordon, S. C., Dembo, M. H., & Hocevar, D. (2007). Do teachers' own learning behaviors influence their classroom goal orientation and control ideology? *Teaching and Teacher Education, 23*(1), 36–46. doi:10.1016/j.tate.2004.08.002

Grasha, A. F., & Riechmann-Hruska, S. (1990). *Teaching Style Survey.* Cincinnati, OH: University of Cincinnati. Retrieved January, 3 2008 from http://longleaf.net/teachingstyle.html

Gu, Y. (2008). Chinese learner: My lived experiences of studying in Mainland China and Australia. *Critical Perspectives on Accounting, 19*(2), 217–221. doi:10.1016/j.cpa.2006.09.006

Gunawardena, C. N., Lowe, C. A., & Anderson, T. (1997). Analysis of a global online debate and the development of an interaction analysis model for examining social construction of knowledge in computer conferencing. *Journal of Educational Computing Research, 17*, 397–431.

Ho, D. Y. F. (1986). Chinese patterns of socialization: A critical review. In M.H. Bond (Ed.). The Psychology of the Chinese People. Hong Kong: Oxford University Press.

Hofstede, G. (1986). Cultural Differences in Teaching and Learning. *International Journal of Intercultural Relations*, *10*, 301–320. doi:10.1016/0147-1767(86)90015-5

Liu, J. (2007). Effective measures to Chinese general education. [Social Sciences]. *Journal of North China Electric Power University*, *4*, 113–117.

Löfström, E., & Nevgi, A. (2007). From strategic planning to meaningful learning: diverse perspectives on the development of web-based teaching and learning in higher education. *British Journal of Educational Technology*, *38*(2), 312–324. doi:10.1111/j.1467-8535.2006.00625.x

Ma, C. (2005). Some Ideas on System Reform and Innovation in China's Higher Education. *Science Education in Higher Education,* (Vol.2). Retrieved August 19, 2008 from http://scholar.ilib.cn/A-gdlkjy200502010.html

Ma, W. (2009). The prospects and dilemmas in Americanizing Chinese higher education. *Asia Pacific Education Review*, *10*, 117–124. doi:10.1007/s12564-009-9006-3

Matthews, B. M. (2000). The Chinese Value Survey: An interpretation of value scales and consideration of some preliminary results. *International Education Journal*, *1*(2), 2000.

McLoughlin, C., & Luca, J. (2002). A learner-centred approach to developing team skills through web-based learning and assessment. *British Journal of Educational Technology*, *33*(5), 571–582. doi:10.1111/1467-8535.00292

McMahon, M. (1997, December). *Social Constructivism and the World Wide Web - A Paradigm for Learning*. Paper presented at the ASCILITE conference, Perth, Australia.

Phuong-Mai, N., Terlouw, C., & Pilot, A. (2005). Cooperative learning vs Confucian heritage culture's collectivism: confrontation to reveal some cultural conflicts and mismatch. *Asia Europe Journal*, *3*, 403–419. doi:10.1007/s10308-005-0008-4

Pintrich, P. R., Smith, D. A. F., Garcia, T., & McKeachie, W. J. (1993). Reliability and predictive validity of the Motivated Strategies for Learning Questionnaire (MSLQ). *Educational and Psychological Measurement*, *53*, 801–813. doi:10.1177/0013164493053003024

Pintrich, P. R., Smith, D. A. F., Garcia, T., & McKeachie, W. J. (1993). Reliability and predictive validity of the Motivated Strategies for Learning Questionnaire (MSLQ). *Educational and Psychological Measurement*, *53*, 801–813. doi:10.1177/0013164493053003024

Pratt, D. D. (1991). Conceptions of self within China and the United States. *International Journal of Intercultural Relations*, *15*(3), 285–310. doi:10.1016/0147-1767(91)90003-Y

Qin, S. (2008, May 13). *The People's Daily*.

Ramsey, C. (2005). Narrative from learning in reflection to learning in performance. *Management Learning*, *36*(2), 219–235. doi:10.1177/1350507605052558

Robertson, I. (2004). *Teachers at the interface: A model of implementation*. Paper presented at the AARE conference, Melbourne. Retrieved August 3, 2008 from http://www.aare.edu.au/04pap/rob04192.pdf

Rogers, E. M. (2003). Diffusion of innovations, (5th Ed.). New York: The Free Press

Schellens, T. (2004). *Studying in a blended learning environment: researching congruency between learning environment and student characteristics and the impact of CSCL on knowledge construction*. Ph.D dissertation, Ghent University, Belgium.

Schellens, T., & Valcke, M. (2000). Re-engineering conventional university education: Implications for students' learning styles. *Distance Education*, *21*(2), 361–384. doi:10.1080/0158791000210210

Segall, M. H., Dasen, P. R., Berry, J. W., & Poortinga, Y. H. (1990). Human behavior in global perspective. New York: Pergamon.

Smith, P. J., & Smith, S. N. (1999). Differences between Chinese and Australian students: some implications for distance educators. *Distance Education*, *20*(1), 64–80. doi:10.1080/0158791990200106

Triandis, H. C., McCusker, C., & Hui, C. H. (1990). Multimethod probes of individualism and collectivism. *Journal of Personality and Social Psychology*, *59*, 1006–1020. doi:10.1037/0022-3514.59.5.1006

Van Eekelen, I. M. (2005). *Teachers 'will and way to learn: Studies on how teachers learn and their willingness to do so*. Unpublished doctoral dissertation, Maastricht University, The Netherlands.

Van Merriënboer, J. J. G., & Paas, F. (2003). Powerful learning and the many faces of instructional design: Toward a framework for the design of powerful learning environments. In E. de Corte, L.Verschaffel, N. Entwistle, & J. J. G. van Merriënboer (Eds.), Unravelling basic components and dimensions of powerful learning environments (pp. 3-20). Oxford: Elsevier Science.

Veerman, A., & Veldhuis-Diermanse, E. (2001). Collaborative learning through computer-mediated communication in academic education. In P. Dillenbourg, A. Eurelings & K. Hakkarainen (Eds.), *European Perspectives on Computer-Supported Collaborative Learning. Proceedings of the First European Conference on CSCL.* Maastricht: McLuhan Institute, University of Maastricht.

Wang, M. (2007). Designing online courses that effectively engage learners from diverse cultural backgrounds. *British Journal of Educational Technology*, *38*(2), 294–311. doi:10.1111/j.1467-8535.2006.00626.x

Wang, M. J. (2004). Correlational analysis of student visibility and learning outcomes in an online setting. *Journal of Asynchronous Learning Networks*, *8*(4), 71–82.

Watkins, D., & Biggs, J. (1996). (Eds.). The Chinese learner: Cultural, psychological, and contextual influences. Victoria, Australia: Comparative Education Research Centre, University of Hong Kong and the Australian Council for Educational Research Ltd.

Watkins, D., & Biggs, J. (Eds.). (2001). Teaching the Chinese Learners: Psychological and Pedagogical Perspectives. Melbourne, Australia: Australian Council for Educational Research / Comparative Education Research Center.

Zhu, C., Valcke, M., & Schellens, T. (2008). The Relationship between epistemological beliefs, learning conceptions, and approaches to study: a cross-cultural structural model? *Asia Pacific Journal of Education*, *28*(4), 411–423. doi:10.1080/02188790802468823

ADDITIONAL READING

Edmundson, A. (Ed.). (2007). Globalized E-learning Cultural Challenges. Hershey, PA: Information Science Publishing.

Elgort, I. (2005). E-learning adoption: Bridging the chasm. *Proceedings of Ascilite 2005*. Retrieved June 15, 2008 from: http://www.ascilite.org.au/conferences/brisbane05/blogs/proceedings/20_Elgort.pdf

Ess, C., & Sudweeks, F. (2005). Culture and computer-mediated communication: Toward new understandings. *Journal of Computer-Mediated Communication, 11*(1), Retrieved May 5, 2009 from http://jcmc.indiana.edu/vol11/issue1/ess.html

Gilbert, P., & Dabbagh, N. (2005). How to structure online discussions for meaningful discourse: A case study. *British Journal of Educational Technology*, *36*(1), 5–18. doi:10.1111/j.1467-8535.2005.00434.x

Gunawardena, C. N., Nolla, A. C., Wilson, P. L., López-Islas, J. R., Ramírez-Angel, N., & Megchun-Alpízar, R. M. (2001). A cross-cultural study of group process and development in online conferences. *Distance Education*, *22*(1), 85–121. doi:10.1080/0158791010220106

Häkkinen, P., Arvaja, M., & Mäkitalo, K. (2004). Prerequisites for CSCL: Research approaches, methodological challenges and pedagogical development. In K. Littleton, D. Miell & D. Faulkner (Ed.), Learning to collaborate, collaborating to learn. New York: Nova Science Publishers, Inc.

Hara, N., Bonk, C. J., & Angeli, C. (2000). Content analysis of online discussion in an applied educational psychology course. *Instructional Science*, *28*, 115–152. doi:10.1023/A:1003764722829

Hewling, A. (2005). Culture in the Online Class: Using Message Analysis to Look Beyond Nationality-Based Frames of Reference. *Journal of Computer-Mediated Communication*, *11*(1). doi:10.1111/j.1083-6101.2006.tb00316.x

Hofstede, G. (1986). Cultural Differences in Teaching and Learning. *International Journal of Intercultural Relations*, *10*(3), 301–320. doi:10.1016/0147-1767(86)90015-5

Hung, D., & Chen, D. T. (2003). Online Learning and Information Technology in the Asia-Pacific Region: Perspectives, Issues, and Divides. *Educational Technology*, *43*(3), 5–9.

Joo, J. E. (1999). Cultural issues of the Internet in classrooms. *British Journal of Educational Technology*, *30*(3), 245–251. doi:10.1111/1467-8535.00113

Kreijns, K., Kirschner, P. A., & Jochems, W. (2004). Determining Sociability, Social Space, and Social Presence in (A)synchronous Collaborative Groups. *CyberPsychology & Behaviour*, *7*(2), 155–172. doi:10.1089/109493104323024429

Mercer, N. (2000). Words and minds: how we use language to think together. London: Routledge.

Morse, K. (2003). Does one size fit all? Exploring asynchronous learning in a multicultural environment. *Journal of Asynchronous Learning Networks*, *7*(1), 37–55.

Stone, C., & Goodyear, P. (1995). *Constructivism and Instructional Design: Epistemology and the Construction of Meaning*. Retrieved April 12, 2008 from: http://domino.lancs.ac.uk/edres/csaltdocs.nsf

Thompson, L., & Ku, H.-Y. (2005). Chinese graduate students' experiences and attitudes toward online learning. *Educational Media International*, *42*(1), 33–47. doi:10.1080/09523980500116878

Tiong, K.-M., & Yong, S.-T. (2004). *Confucian heritage culture learners' and instructors' expectations and preferences in collaborative learning: convergence or divergence?* Retrieved June 24, 2007, from http://www.herdsa.org.au/conference2004/Contributions/NRPapers/A055-jt.pdf

Tu, C. H., & Isaacs, M. (2002). An examination of social presence to increase interaction in online classes. *American Journal of Distance Education*, *16*, 131–150. doi:10.1207/S15389286AJDE1603_2

Vatrapu, R. (2008). Cultural Considerations in Computer Supported Collaborative Learning. *Research and Practice in Technology Enhanced Learning*, *3*(2), 159–201. doi:10.1142/S1793206808000501

Vatrapu, R., & Suthers, D. (2007). Culture and Computers: A Review of the Concept of Culture and Implications for Intercultural Collaborative Online Learning. In T. Ishida, S. R. Fussell & P. T. J. M. Vossen (Eds.), Intercultural Collaboration I: Lecture Notes in Computer Science (pp. 260-275): Springer-Verlag

Veldhuis-Diermanse, A. E. (2002). *CSCLearning? Participation, learning activities and knowledge construction in computer-supported collaborative learning in higher education*. PhD dissertation, Veenendaal, Wageringen University.

Wang, M. (2007). Designing online courses that effectively engage learners from diverse cultural backgrounds. *British Journal of Educational Technology, 38*(2), 294–311. doi:10.1111/j.1467-8535.2006.00626.x

Wang, Q. (2004). Online Learning Communities Where East Meet West - A Cross Cultural Encounter. In C. Crawford et al. (Eds.), *Proceedings of Society for Information Technology and Teacher Education International Conference 2004* (pp. 3078-3082). Chesapeake, VA: AACE.

Watkins, D., & Biggs, J. (1996). (Eds.). The Chinese learner: Cultural, psychological, and contextual influences. Comparative Education Research Centre, University of Hong Kong and the Australian Council for Educational Research Ltd., Victoria, Australia.

Watkins, D., & Biggs, J. (2001). (Eds.). Teaching the Chinese Learners: Psychological and Pedagogical Perspectives. Australian Council for Educational Research / Comparative Education Research Center: Melbourne / Hong Kong.

Wilson, M. S. (2001). Cultural considerations in online instruction and learning. *Distance Education, 22*(1), 52–64. doi:10.1080/0158791010220104

Zhu, C., Valcke, M., & Schellens, T. (2008). A cross-cultural study of Chinese and Flemish university students: Do they differ in learning conceptions and approaches to learning? *Learning and Individual Differences, 18*, 120–127. doi:10.1016/j.lindif.2007.07.004

KEY TERMS AND DEFINITIONS

E-Learning: In this case study, it refers to computer and Internet delivered learning in blended learning environments, with a special focus on online collaborative learning.

Computer Supported Collaborative Learning: More than one learners communicate and collaborate to work on common or shared learning activities using computer-based communication technologies, either asynchronously or synchronously.

Educational and Cultural Context: The comprehensive environment where teaching and learning is situated, including the cultural background, the educational system, the institutional environment, etc.

Dokeos/Claroline System: It is an open source online learning suite that provides various features needed for e-learning, such as learning management, authoring, interacting and reporting. Claroline and Dokeos started in Belgium and today both are supported by their community of developers and university consortia.

Minerva: It is the e-learning platform of Ghent University based on the Dokeos system, but also continuously updated and extended by its own developers. At the same time, Ghent University is one of the major contributers of the Dokeos community.

Individualistic and Collectivistic Cultures: individualism versus collectivism is one of the ways to operationalize cultural categories. In individualistic cultures, individual differences are respected, people are encouraged to stand out, be unique and express themselves, and to develop the tendency to question and evaluate. In collectivistic cultures, people tend to avoid conflict and use more intermediaries. People are encouraged to conform to the societal demands and maintain the harmony of a group. However, it has to be stressed that the two polar positions need to be considered as two positions on a continuum. Most cultures combine elements of both collectivist and individualistic orientations.

Power Distance: Power distance (high vs. low) is an important cultural dimension, which specifies the degree to which less powerful people in a society accept inequality in power.

Teacher Role: The main functions that teachers choose to perform in relation to their students in learning environments.

Social Constructivist Learning: It is an important learning theory, which stresses that learning is an active and social process and the need for collaboration between learners. It also stresses the importance of taking into account the background and culture of the learner throughout the learning process.

Chapter 9
Impact of Spatial Ability Training in Desktop Virtual Environment

Ahmad Rafi
Multimedia University Cyberjaya, Malaysia

Khairulanuar Samsudin
Sultan Idris University of Education, Malaysia

ABSTRACT

This case study reports an experimental research based on pretest-post test design that was carried out to investigate the extent of Spatial Visualization (SV) and Mental Rotation (MR) training improvement, differential impact attributed to gender and training method, and training transfer to engineering drawing task. The participants of the study were 101 eight graders comprising 42 girls and 59 boys (mean age = 15 years) and were randomly assigned into two experimental groups and one control group. The first experimental group employed interaction-based training in a desktop virtual environment trainer, the second group used animation-based training, and the control group trained using printed materials and all the three groups were trained for 8 weeks. Data were collected through spatial ability tests and a survey and were analyzed using SPSS version 14. Analysis of data reveals that there were substantial performance gains in SV and MR accuracy, but not in MR speed. Main effects of training in SV and MR accuracy were found where those trained by novel methods especially the interaction-enabled method outperforming the control group. Interaction effects were observed where differential improvement gain in SV and MR accuracy only involved male participants but not their female counterparts. Transfer of training to performance in solving engineering drawing task was observed by differential performances of groups, where those with higher spatial ability managed to perform the task better than those with lower spatial ability after spatial training. This transfer was qualified by the multiple linear regression procedure revealing that spatial visualization was a significant factor in predicting performance in basic engineering drawing task.

DOI: 10.4018/978-1-61520-749-7.ch009

INTRODUCTION

Technology has impacted and continues to transform almost every sphere of human endeavors in social, political and economic fields. The use and diffusion of technology has taken place very rapidly in line with the current thinking of learning emphasizing the role of pupils as active participants in the teaching and learning process. Training to improve one's performance involves a complex web of issues entailing careful analysis of factors that can result in either success or failure. The tools and resources for training are aplenty and more are becoming integrated and embedded in IT technology particularly Web technology. Choosing the right and effective tools will be quite a challenge as to create training environment that is not only conducive but also efficient. One of the human intelligence that has fascinated researchers and scientists is spatial ability or spatial intelligence. Notwithstanding the differences of opinions, all agreed that this cognitive ability is importance for humans to function effectively in everyday chores and it becomes more pronounced in performing tasks in specialized domains such as engineering and science. Spatial ability is multi-facet rather than unitary being conceptualized as a cognitive construct built upon several independent sub-abilities or sub-skills. Linn & Petersen (1985) categorized this ability into three components namely spatial visualization, mental rotation and spatial perception. Earlier on, this ability was regarded as innate not amendable to training. However, evidence from experimental studies suggests that improving spatial ability is possible through proper and specific training (Khairulanuar & Azniah, 2004; Olkun, 2003; Rafi, Khairulanuar, & Said, 2008; Turos & Ervin, 2000). One of the important discoveries emerging from studies involving psychometric testing of spatial ability was the revelation of gender differences favoring boys. Generally, boys were consistently found to perform better than girls on these tests suggesting that the former possess greater spatial skills than the latter. Male advantages in spatial ability have been established in reviews by Maccoby & Jacklin (1974), Linn & Petersen (1985), and Voyer, Voyer, & Bryden (1995). Age was also found to mediate gender differences where spatial ability was relatively higher among girls at young age, but began to favor boys as individuals approached adolescence (Maccoby & Jacklin, 1974). Given the diverging orientations or preferences in engaging spatial activities such as games, sports and types of educational enrolment, it can be inferred that environmental or experiential factors may influence the development of this ability. The more spatial experience one has the higher his/her spatial ability which reinforces the notion that this ability can be trained. Various training methods have been employed in spatial training to improve spatial ability namely spatial visualization and mental rotation focusing on the use of current technology and gender (Moyer, Bolyard & Spikell, 2001; Rafi et al,,2008; Rafi & Khairulanuar, 2009; Turos & Ervin, 2000). These studies indicate that the improvement of spatial ability was achievable but the level of performance gain was mediated by training specificity, gender, practice duration and condition.

Spatial ability has been established to be a strong predictor of success in engineering and science disciplines or majors (Olkun, 2003; Rafi & Khairulanuar, 2007; Sorby & Baartmans, 2000; Strong & Smith, 2001). One such course for these engineering majors is the engineering drawing or engineering graphics where strong positive correlation was found between engineering drawing performance and spatial ability particularly spatial visualization. Engineering drawing is a prominent component in technology education curriculum in major countries such as United States, Europe and in Asia, notably Japan and Korea. In general, students need to utilize two perceptual processing when learning the subject matter which falls into two categories utilizing these two processes. In the first category, students are required to represent a three-dimensional object on a two-dimensional plane surface through multiple-view drawings and the other category involves creating three-dimensional perspectives by working from the two-dimensional representation of the object (Davies, 1973; Olkun, 2003). The former requires students to perceive the respective principal orthographic views namely the front, right and plan views from a given or imagined object whilst the latter involves the integration of a number of different views into a single spatial image representation mainly perspective drawing, particularly the isometric representation. Both categories of learning require a high degree of spatial ability or spatial skills to complete the tasks.

The importance of these skills is an integral part of the successful learning of graphics and engineering as a whole. Studies that have been carried out (Kajiyama, 1996; Rafi & Khairulanuar, 2007; Scales, 2000; Shaw, 2001; Wiebe, 1993) highlighted a multitude of conceptual, pedagogical, and technological issues in learning engineering drawing among secondary school pupils, college students and adult learners. Some students exhibited a pattern of having problems completing spatial tasks as noted in a research by Shaw (2001). Subjects comprising adult learners taking technology education distance learning were tested in several spatial tasks. The findings revealed that majority were experiencing difficulty in understanding orthographic projections than isometric projections. This concurs with the widely accepted assumption that mental synthesis of orthographic views into a three-dimensional form can be a difficult skill to learn (Wiebe, 1993). Further study by Potter and Van Der Merwe (2003) also strengthens the argument that level of spatial ability at the time of intake into the university is an important indicator of academic performance and reinforces the value of this cognitive skill or ability for engineering drawing or technical graphics courses at secondary school level. Similar study by Kajiyama (1996) in a university in Japan has shown that freshman engineering students made numerous and different errors in interpreting multi-view drawings. Cited problems were freshmen inability to put a given view on its plane of projection accurately, lacking the ability to imagine spatial coordinates and inability to calculate a geometrical relation of the point of intersection and vertex of an object. All these errors were attributed to low spatial ability in reading multi-view drawings. Some of these studies also revealed that in general male students tend to outperform their female counterparts. All these findings bear a serious implication especially for technology education where spatial thinking is important for students to learn and understand spatial concepts and designs that need to be analyzed and solved where the results and reports are to be communicated mostly through graphical means. Consistent findings indicate gender bias favoring males especially in engineering drawing or graphics performance owing to their greater spatial skills than females (Gorska, 2005; Williams, Sutton & Allen, 2008). Apparently, these findings align with the notion that poor female representation in technical fields is due to gender difference in this ability (Newcombe, 2006). However, on a positive note, many researchers believe that spatial ability is malleable not immutable and both the low spatial and female students can benefit from spatial training. Various methods have been employed and of late spatial training based on specific spatial skills and prolonged practice have been found to be effective (Newcombe, 2006). Thus, the extent of spatial ability improvement, impact due to training methods and gender, and training transfer were the focus of this case study to further illuminate discussion pertaining to spatial intelligence and engineering graphics literature.

THE DEVELOPMENT OF THE DESKTOP VIRTUAL ENVIRONMENT TRAINER

The utilization of available technologies for training must be carefully considered in relation to two vital issues: one relating to the need for appropriate level and style of content; and the other relating to the need to use the right software and delivery mechanisms (Fernie & Richards, 2002). Most importantly, the development of any training program or application is to be informed by current theories of learning to ensure the implementation of such educational or training program will be able to achieve its stated goals through optimizing training or learning process. The use of web-based application comprising instructional activities in the form of tutorials enhanced with virtual environment containing virtual training objects was designed along the constructivist principles to improve learners' spatial visualization and mental rotation. In this study, the authors adopted a theoretical approach informed through a review on the literature of current theories of learning and psychometric testing. The former will guide the development of instructional setting or training environment that helps learners maximize their learning or training potentials whilst the latter will ensure that relevant spatial tasks are put in place using appropriate learning objects or training tools than taps on spatial ability.

The training application was designed based on the framework espoused by the constructivist view of learning. Dalgarno (2002) outlined three broad principles of this view based on previous studies namely endogenous, exogenous, and dialectical constructivism. Endogenous constructivism stresses on individual nature of each learner's knowledge construction process relegating the role of teachers to facilitators. Exogenous constructivism underscores the formation and refinement of knowledge representations through learning by instructions with support from exercises entailing active cognition. Dialectical constructivism espouses learning through realistic experience coupled with social interactions among teachers, experts, and peers providing the essential scaffoldings (Dalgarno, 2002). The appropriate use of training or learning objects to be utilized was informed by reviewing the items in the psychometric test battery. The development of training objects for spatial visualization was based on test items under the category of 'count touching blocks' that measures the ability to visualize forms in space and to manipulate them mentally (Wiesen, 2004). This ability is also a strong component of mechanical aptitude deemed vital in learning technical and industrial fields. For mental rotation training, novel training objects were developed and participants are required to determine whether a displaced object is congruent or incongruent with a given object.

A desktop virtual environment based on Virtual Reality Modeling Language (VRML) was adopted capitalizing on two important criteria; three-dimensionality and practicality. The former is very important in engendering 3D-space learning environment that inherently is spatial and visual allowing training in spatial knowledge or skills that hinges on spatial properties and relationships of objects and space. The latter is more concerned with ease of development, implementation and maintenance in typical Malaysian schools that are invariably affected by limited financial budget. Desktop VR technology emerged in formats such as using mouse-controlled navigation through a 3D-environment on a graphics monitor under computer control that are now realistically available, both financially and technically, for general classroom use (Ausburn & Ausburn, 2004). The spatial trainer contains a series of exercises in which participants are required to solve by choosing the correct solution for a particular question. In the process of problem solving, they can interact with the training objects, use animations, and receive feedback. Figure 1 shows a snapshot of the spatial trainer for mental rotation exercise.

Figure 1. The conceptual framework of the spatial trainer

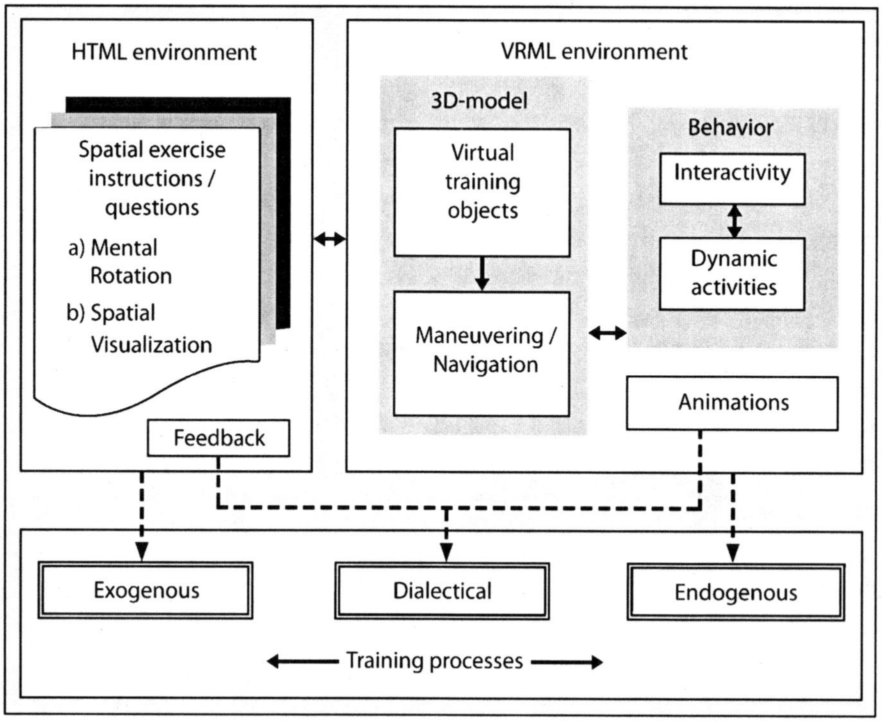

THE PURPOSE OF THE CASE STUDY

The purpose of this case study was to investigate the extent of improvement in spatial visualization and mental rotation (accuracy and speed) by spatial training involving lower secondary school pupils (8th graders). The differential impact of spatial training attributed to gender and training methods that employed different tools or features was examined in this case study given the evidence from the literature that suggests training effectiveness is mediated by such factors. Given the lack of study to determine whether spatial training effect could be carried over to engineering drawing performance, this study also sought to determine whether there was a training transfer from spatial ability training to solving engineering drawing task. In addition, the components of spatial ability were also examined to determine which is/are most predictive in explaining the basic engineering drawing performance. Five research questions have been formulated to address the issues as discussed in the main body of the preceding section. The research questions are as follows:

i. Are the improvements in spatial abilities (spatial visualization, mental rotation accuracy, and mental rotation speed) after training significant?
ii. Is training method a significant factor in influencing the training outcomes?
iii. Is gender a significant factor in influencing the training outcomes?
iv. Is there a training transfer from spatial training to solving engineering drawing task?
v. If there was a training transfer, which component/s of the spatial ability is/are significant for the transfer?

Answering the five research questions above entails the following research hypotheses as follows:

i. The will be significant differences in spatial abilities (spatial visualization, mental rotation accuracy and mental rotation speed) of the participants before and after training.
ii. Participants that trained in novel methods will outperform those trained using conventional method in spatial abilities (spatial visualization, mental rotation accuracy and mental rotation speed)
iii. Male participants will outperform female participants in spatial abilities (spatial visualization, mental rotation accuracy and mental rotation speed) after spatial training.
iv. There will be a training transfer from training domain to engineering drawing task domain where the higher spatial ability group will outperform those of other lower spatial ability groups in solving an engineering drawing task.
v. Spatial visualization will be the significant factor for the training transfer.

METHODS

Participants

The participants of this case study were 101 lower secondary school pupils comprising of 42 girls and 59 boys with a mean age of 15 years who volunteered to participate. The participants were randomly assigned into two experimental groups and one control group. The first experimental group, consisting of 14 girls and 20 boys, used interaction-based training in a desktop virtual environment spatial trainer. The second experimental group comprising 14 girls and 20 boys used animation-based training. The control group of 14 girls and 19 boys used printed materials having similar contents with the other groups in their training.

Instrument and Instructional Materials

The desktop virtual environment spatial trainer is an integrated web-based application developed on desktop virtual environment containing virtual objects that serve as training objects for the spatial exercises. Instructions and information were organized with questions and presented on the lower half of the screen and objects for training were presented on the top half of the same web page. The spatial trainer contains features that support training namely interaction via mouse-controlled VRML client, animations and response feedbacks. The first training condition was set to allow only navigation and exploration (operationalized as interaction) with the virtual objects and response feedbacks. The second experimental condition involved training with animation and response feedback features. The control condition employed similar questions of the spatial exercise in the conventional way supplemented with drawing. Pretesting and post-testing of the SV and MR measures were performed using the Spatial Visualization Test (Middle Grade Mathematical Project, 1983) and Chay's (2000) Mental Rotation online test respectively. This first test comprises 30 items, with each showing a target object and a comparison (displaced) object. Participants are required to determine whether the two objects are congruent or incongruent and performance is based on accuracy and reaction time (measured in seconds). Performance measure for SV is based on the correct answers to 32 SV questions with each carrying one mark. A task was employed that serves as a measure of student understanding in orthographic projection where this discernment will strongly affect their ability to perform in engineering drawing (Kang, David, Jean & Jan, 2004). Hence, a basic engineering drawing task

Table 1. Means and standard deviations of spatial ability measures

	Pre-testing		Post-testing	
Spatial measures:	**Means**	*SD*	**Means**	*SD*
Spatial visualization (max. 32)	14.45	4.52	19.49	5.53
Mental rotation accuracy (max. 30)	19.44	2.12	22.81	2.31
Mental rotation speed (in seconds)	111.35	25.90	113.65	24.38

in the form of a multi-view orthographic drawing exercise was assigned for each student to determine their level of performance that could be explained or attributed to enhanced spatial ability acquired after the training program.

Procedure

The study used multi-factorial pre-test post-test experimental design procedure comprising of two independent variables namely training method (3 levels: interaction-based training, animation-based training, and control) and gender (2 levels: female and male). The mean scores for the spatial measures serve as the dependent variables in the study. Participants trained for eight sessions, evenly spaced in eight weeks, with each session lasting for 2 hours. Two computer labs and a classroom were used for training sessions and training began with simple spatial exercises, then continued with moderately difficult exercises and finally completed with complex spatial tasks.

FINDINGS

Participants' spatial visualization (SV), mental rotation accuracy (MRA), and mental rotation speed (MRS) prior to training were measured revealing mean scores of 14.45, 19.44, and 111.35 respectively. Three independent samples t-tests were performed to detect if there were any gender differences among the participants in the study. The tests performed indicated that there were no gender differences for the three measures. ANOVA procedure was performed to detect group differences prior to training which revealed that there were no differences between the three groups in spatial ability. After training, the mean scores for SV, MRA and MRS were 19.49, 22.81 and 113.65 respectively. Table 1 summarizes the mean scores for the measures of spatial ability before and after training.

Paired t-tests were used to compare the mean scores of the SV, MRA and MRS before and after spatial training. The participants had an average difference of pre-test to post-test spatial visualization scores of 5.05 ($SD = 4.73$) indicating that spatial training resulted in a highly significant increase in spatial visualization level, $t\,(100) = 10.74, p < .001$. The average difference of pre-test to post-test mental rotation accuracy mean scores was 3.37 ($SD = 2.01$) which was significant, $t(100) = 16.25, p < .001$. For mental rotation speed, the average difference of pre-test to post-test mean scores was 2.31 (SD = 16.38) which was not significant, $t\,(100) = 1.42, p > .05$.

A series of analysis of variance (ANOVA) procedure were used to determine whether there were main effects due to training method and gender and their interactions. Results of ANOVA revealed a statistically significant main effect for training condition in spatial visualization, $F\,(2,100) = 13.13, p < .001$. Bonfferoni post hoc test to detect for significance of the differences in the training methods showed that interaction-enabled

Table 2. Analysis of variance for model regressing on engineering drawing scores

Source	Sum of Squares	df	Mean Square	F	R	R^2
Regression	300.454	4	75.113	41.618**	.796	.634
Residual	173.264	96	1.805			
Total	473.718	100				

method outperformed the other two methods. On the other hand, there was no significant main effect of gender, $F\ (1,100) = 1.31, p > .05$ suggesting that both gender improved after training. The interaction between training condition and gender was found to be statistically significant, $F\,(2,100) = 8.00, p < .001$, indicating that the training effectiveness depends on gender. Analysis revealed that boys were better at spatial visualization tasks than girls in interaction-based training condition. On the contrary, girls outperformed boys in the control condition. In addition, both genders were equivalent in their spatial visualization in the second experimental training condition. For mental rotation accuracy, ANOVA revealed a statistically significant main effect for training condition, $F\ (2,100) = 15.38, p < .001$. Bonferroni post hoc test showed that both the experimental groups were equivalent and outperformed the control group. The main effect of gender was not significant, $F\ (1,100) = .61, p > .05$ suggesting that both gender improved after training. Interaction effect between training condition and gender was found to be statistically significant, $F\,(2,100) = 5.60, p < .01$, indicating that the training resulted in differential improvement revealing that boys were more accurate at MR tasks than girls in both the first and second experimental training conditions. On the other hand, girls outperformed boys in the control condition.

A 2-way ANOVA was used to determine if there were differences in the engineering drawing performance arising from the gender and training condition. Results of ANOVA indicated that there was main effect of the training condition, $F\,(2,100) = 8.67, p < .001$. Bonferroni post hoc test confirmed interaction-based training outperformed those in the second experimental and control groups. A significant main effect of gender was also found, $F\ (1,100) = 12.91, p < .05$, indicating that males outperformed females in the engineering drawing task. The interaction between training condition and gender was not significant in this study, $F\,(2,100) = 1.96, p > .05$. The Multiple Linear Regression (MLR) procedure was employed in order to predict accurately which factors have significant influence on the participants' performance in solving engineering drawing task. The use of Multiple Regression for prediction is entailed when one is using a sample to create a regression equation that would optimally predict a particular phenomenon within a particular population (Osborne, 2000). The main objective here was to create the best equation so that, for example, teachers could predict their students' performance in undertaking engineering drawing task in the future, and hopefully intervene with those students identified as at risk for lacking the necessary skills to learn the subject matter. The linear combination of gender and the measures of SV, MRA and MRS was significantly related to the performance of engineering drawing task, $F\ (4,96) = 41.62, p < .001$, accounting 63% ($R^2 = .63$) of the variance of the performance in engineering drawing task as summarized in Table 2.

With other variables held constant, the performance of engineering drawing task was positively related to spatial visualization and mental rotation accuracy factors, and negatively related to mental rotation speed factors. In general, those who had better spatial visualization ability and mental rotation ability (more accurate and faster)

Table 3. Standard Regression Model summaries for gender and spatial ability variables

Variable	B	*SE* B	β	*t*
Post SV.	.278	.028	.707	10.063**
Post MRA	-.061	.062	-.064	-.989
Post MRS	-.008	.006	-.091	-1.300
Gender	1.171	.281	.266	4.170**

tended to perform better than others lacking these abilities. Male participants tended to outperform their female counterparts in undertaking such engineering drawing task.

The effects of spatial visualization (t_{96} = 10.06, $p < .001$) and gender (t_{96} = 4.17, $p < .001$) were the only significant factors in predicting the performance in such task as showed in Table 3. The effects of other factors were found not to be statistically significant to account for the variance in the performance of such engineering drawing task. Stepwise multiple linear regression was also conducted to evaluate whether the gender and spatial ability factors were necessary to predict performance of basic engineering drawing task. At step 1 of the analysis, post spatial visualization measure entered into the regression equation and was significantly related to basic engineering drawing task performance, $F(1,99) = 129.12$, $p < .001$. The multiple correlation coefficient was .752, indicating that approximately 57% (R^2 = .566) of the variance of the performance in basic engineering graphic task can be accounted for by the spatial visualization factor where the main effect attributed to this sub-skill of spatial ability was statistically significant, (t_{99} = 9.21, $p < .001$). Gender factor entered into the regression equation at step 2 of the analysis, where both the spatial visualization and gender factors were significantly related to basic engineering graphic task performance, $F(2,98) = 81.75$, $p < .001$. The multiple correlation coefficient was .791, indicating that approximately 63% (R^2 = .625) of the variance of the performance of basic engineering graphic task can be accounted for by the linear combination of the spatial visualization and gender factors. The R square change in the second step was .06, indicating that gender explained approximately 6% of the variance in basic engineering drawing task performance in the analysis as summarized in Table 4.

The stepwise MLR analysis revealed that, in general, those having superior spatial visualization ability of skill were better in solving the basic engineering drawing task than those with relatively inferior spatial visualization ability.

Table 4. Analysis of variance for stepwise regression models regressing on engineering drawing scores

Model	Variation	Sum of Squares	df	Mean Square	F	R	R^2
1: post SV	Regression	268.133	1	268.133	129.120**	.752	.566
	Residual	205.585	99	2.077			
	Total	473.718	100				
2: post SV	Regression	296.184	2	148.092	81.750**	.791	.625
+ gender	Residual	177.534	98	1.812			
	Total	473.718	100				

Table 5. Stepwise Regression Model summaries for gender and spatial ability variables

Model	Variable	*SE* B	β	*SE* B	t
1: post SV	Post SV	.512	.056	.685	9.205**
2: post SV	Post SV	.489	.052	.654	9.463**
+ gender	Gender	7.729	1.858	.288	4.161**

Male participants were more able to achieve better performance in similar task compared to their female participants. The effects due to spatial visualization ($t_{95} = 9.46, p < .001$) and gender ($t_{95} = 4.16, p < .001$) were statistically significant in predicting performance in such task in this study based on the stepwise MLR analysis as summarized in Table 5.

Other psychometric variables namely the mental rotation accuracy did not enter into the regression at the second step of the analysis as these factors did not have significant effects in accounting for the variance in the performance of basic engineering drawing task.

At the end of the training session, a questionnaire was administered to every participant. The information elicited from the comments and feedbacks for the open-ended question provided a qualitative measure of the spatial training experienced by the participants. Their comments were examined and classified according to several themes or issues namely spatial cognition, training effectiveness and application usability. Thirty-two respondents out of 101 have recorded their comments as summarized in Table 6. Fifteen respondents (4 girls and 11 boys) reported that training by means of interaction with the virtual objects helped them visualize better the various parts of objects and their spatial configuration in solving the spatial tasks. For animation-based training, 13 respondents (3 girls and 10 boys) reported that animations provided them with effective clues during problem solving where only one respondent reported otherwise. Three respondents (1 girl and 2 boys) in control group indicated that spatial cognition experienced by them was somewhat deficient. Thirteen respondents (5 girls and 8 boys) that used interaction-based training reported that training was effective. Likewise, 11 respondents (4 girls and 7 boys) indicated that training aided by animations was effective but only one respondent indicated otherwise. On the other hand, only 6 respondents in the control group (5 girls and 1 boy) reported that training was effective in improving their spatial skills whilst 4 male respondents indicated otherwise. For usability factor such as navigation of the virtual environment, 10 respondents (1 girl and 9 boys) expressed better control in using the interface. On the contrary, 6 female respondents did indicate that they were experiencing some difficulties when using this novel environment in training

These qualitative data provided some clues regarding the participants' opinions on perceived improvement of spatial cognition, training effectiveness and usability of the spatial trainer after training. Those reported having improved their spatial thinking were mainly trained in the novel methods. Apparently, through interactions and animations they were able to visualize training objects that led to better mental manipulations in solving the spatial tasks. On the other hand, spatial training based on printed materials was not effective as evident from the comments made by a few participants who indicated having troubles visualizing the training objects. Overall, spatial training was perceived to be effective especially by those who trained in interaction- and animation-based training. A few respondents of the control group reported that training had no significant impact in improving their spatial skills. For the application usability of the interaction-enabled

Table 6. Comments regarding the cognitive, effectiveness of training, and usability aspects after spatial training

Themes	Some examples of typical responses ('+' and '—' refer to positive and negative comments respectively)		Training Conditions								
			interaction-based			*animation-based*			*control*		
			Girls	*Boys*	*All*	*Girls*	*Boys*	*All*	*Girls*	*Boys*	*All*
Cognitive	+	"...I understand better when I could 'sense' the object / I could rotate an object making it easier to see hidden parts (planes) / I could understand better with more trials (practice) / I was able to figure out the planes of objects with ease / Steps to solve problems were made clear through animations / I like the feedback after each attempt "	4	11	15	3	10	13	0	0	0
	–	"...I could hardly visualize objects even I tried many times / Still, the objects were not easily to capture in mind "	0	0	0	1	0	1	1	2	3
Effectiveness of training	+	"...I think I can solve spatial problems better after training / My skill has improved / I could handle spatial problems with less errors through constant practice"	5	8	13	4	7	11	5	1	6
	–	"...It makes no difference as I was still struggling to solve the problems / The training has no impact on me / It was not that interesting "	0	0	0	1	0	1	0	4	4
Usability	+	"...interacting with objects seemed similar to other games / moving around was confusing but it gets better later / the instructions are easy follow"	1	9	10	n/a			n/a		
	–	"...sometimes the navigational tools produced unexpected responses / it was quite a struggle to control this environment / Occasionally, I clicked the wrong buttons "	6	0	6	n/a			n/a		

training, an interesting finding was revealed in that there seemed to be a gender difference where boys were more adept than girls in navigating and interacting the virtual environment.

CASE DISCUSSION

Spatial Visualization and Mental Rotation Prior to Spatial Training

Prior to the spatial training experiment, all the groups were established to be statistically equivalent in terms of their spatial visualization and mental rotation abilities in the study. This is very crucial in ensuring that resultant outcomes of the spatial training which may differ among the three groups can be confidently explained from the premise and contexts of the effects of the training methods the participants received. Otherwise, the training effects are likely to be confounded by their prior differences in these abilities. Further examination of the groups based on gender revealed an interesting finding where there were no gender differences in spatial visualization and mental rotation abilities indicating that both male and female participants were equivalent. This is quite surprising given ample evidence that highlights spatial ability superiority of males over females in most literature, especially in mental rotation (Halpern, 2000; Linn & Petersen, 1985; Maccoby & Jacklin, 1974; Robert & Bell, 2000; Sanz de Acedo & Garcia, 2003). It is highly probable that there were no superiority of spatial abilities of one gender over the other since both genders were of similar level in mathematics which correspondingly translate into equivalent level of spatial ability as confirmed by the statistical analysis of their differences in means of the spatial pretests. Seen from a wider perspective, this finding may not be unique as gender differences on cognitive and psychosocial tasks are getting smaller and declining (Linn & Hyde, 1989). Likewise, a study by Hyde (2005) that focused on the effect size of gender differences from meta-analyses of research revealed that males and females are alike on most - but not all - psychological variables.

The Improvement in Spatial Visualization After Spatial Training

In general, the comparison of mean differences of spatial visualization before and after spatial training for all groups indicated that the participants achieved considerable gain. Hence, the extent of spatial training was significant that supports the first research hypothesis for this spatial measure. In other words, there was an effect of training where participants' spatial visualization ability improved after engaging in solving spatial problems which entails the utilization of this component of spatial ability or skill. Participants made fewer errors in solving spatial visualization tasks compared to their previous commission of errors indicating that they had gained greater performance after training in this component of spatial ability. Both female and male participants were observed to attain statistically equivalent performance in spatial visualization in this study that further qualifies the extent of improvement in spatial visualization.

The Impact of Training Method and Gender in the Improvement of Spatial Visualization

Further examination using the two-way analysis of variance revealed that significant differential performance gain in spatial visualization resulted from training in three methods of spatial training that verifies the second research hypothesis for this measure. The main effects of treatment observed in spatial visualization showed higher improvement in the first experimental condition (interaction-enabled), moderate improvement in the second experimental condition (animation-enhanced but without interaction), and low improvement in the control condition. Post-hoc test analysis revealed that the greatest performance was attained by first experimental group that was far outperforming the other two groups which were found to perform at par. In solving the spatial visualization tasks, users in the first experimental group were able to interact with the virtual objects representing the objects of interest through the mouse-controlled VRML client interface by panning, twisting, and rolling in the interactive desktop virtual environment giving a multiple viewpoint facilitating the visual perception and processing of objects in 3D space. Viewing at close up and at distance interactively to examine specific and holistic features of objects enhances spatial visualization skills that concur with Smith's (2001) study which suggests that alternating between interaction and observation is the best way to learn spatial visualization. Larger training gain in this condition can be attributed to the availability of features that encourage users to actively process information (Ali & Ferdig, 2002; Brady, 2004).

The second most effective in spatial visualization training was the condition of training in the second experimental condition comprising animations, which suggests that participants utilizing these features gained better insights and understanding of tasks that demand visual perception and cognitive processing based on spatial visualization. Animations are used to fulfill a cognitive function where in this role they support students' cognitive processes that ultimately result them understanding the subject matter (Love, 2004). The set of spatial tasks designed in this study requires participants to solve problems associated with stack configurations composed of regular rectangular block. In determining the number of blocks making contact with a target block entails participants to mentally visualize the blocks in terms of their positions and relations in the 3D space. The animations when activated will cause the relevant virtual blocks to change color highlighting their positions in relations to the target block. Then the virtual blocks will move into space to allow the participants to observe the target block positioned in space and its relation to the moved blocks. Effectively, animation helps the externalization of internal visualization process that the participants would invoke in solving these spatial visualization tasks that support participants' cognitive process in the problem solving of complex configuration of objects in 3D space (Klein & Koroghlanian, 2004; Tversky, Morrison & Betrancourt, 2002).

The main effect of gender on training was not significant to support the third research hypothesis for this spatial measure. However, there was a substantial interaction between the training method and gender in the study. Boys tended to gain differential level of improvement gain based on the methods of training received where girls were more likely to improve irrespective of methods of training they experienced. The former gained high performance in the first condition, moderately in second condition and performed relatively low in control condition. Girls however fared almost equally in the three conditions. Qualitative data seems to reinforce this finding where female respondents' comments from the three groups were almost consistent but male respondents' gave opposite views of training effectiveness between the novel and conventional methods.

The Extent of Improvement in Mental Rotation Accuracy after Spatial Training

Comparison of mean differences of mental rotation for accuracy measure before and after spatial training for all groups indicated that the participants achieved considerable gain which supports the first research hypothesis for this spatial measure. The extent of spatial training in mental rotation accuracy was significant as verified by the significant improvement in this measure. There was an effect of training where their mental rotation accuracy improved substantially after engaging in solving spatial problems that taps on cognitive processing based on this component of spatial ability or skill. The participants made fewer errors in solving mental rotation tasks than before indicating that they had gained greater performance accuracy after training in this component of spatial ability. Both female and male participants were observed to attain statistically equivalent performance in mental rotation in terms of accuracy in this study that further qualifies the extent of mental rotation accuracy training.

The Impact of Training Method and Gender in the Improvement of Mental Rotation Accuracy

Post-hoc analysis conducted revealed that there substantial gains in mental rotation accuracy particularly in the first and second training methods exceeding that of the conventional method which supports the second hypothesis for this spatial measure. No significant gain differences were found between the two experimental groups signifying that the effects of interaction in the first experimental condition and animation in the second experimental conditions were equivalent. In the first experimental condition, the process of solving the mental rotation tasks typically demand the learners to perceive the objects on the screen, visualizing them in 3D space in their minds, and then mentally rotating them along the imaginary axes. Interacting with the object via the mouse-based VRML client interface engenders continuously changing viewpoints of the onlooker with respect to the object. These actions when executed in controlled and structured manner enables the onlooker to perceive the orientations of the virtual object in relation to its axes. Effectively, these interactions in the virtual environment facilitate better visual perception of virtual objects that subsequently aids the process of spatial information processing involving mental rotation operations.

On the other hand, the animation in the second experimental condition when invoked causes the rotation/s of a comparison object about the axis/axes in sequential and timely motion. Animations proved to be effective when the participants tried to solve mental rotation tasks involving more than one rotation along an axis where several steps, in this case rotations, were required to transform the comparison object into the correct orientation that perfectly matches the target object. This particular outcome indicates the effectiveness of animation-enhanced training over conventional training using static pictures concurs with the notion that animation facilitates learning when it presents the micro steps of processes that static drawing do not present (Tversky et al., 2002). Surprisingly, the effect of gender in training did not materialize which leads to the conclusion that the extent of gender effect in mental rotation accuracy training was not significant Thus, the third research hypothesis for this spatial measure was not verified. That this study produced gender parity in mental rotation in accuracy measure after training contradicts findings from previous studies (Khairulanuar & Azniah, 2004; Rafi & Khairulanuar, 2009, Turos & Ervin, 2000) that favored males over females entails closer examination. Arguably, both girls and boys participants were equivalent in terms of mental rotation at the outset of spatial training.

There was no gender group having an advantage over the other group that may exacerbate gender differences in mental rotation after training. Both gender benefited equally from spatial training in mental rotation in the study. A substantial interplay between training method and gender was found where boys in both the experimental conditions fared higher than girls trained in the same conditions. Interestingly, boys in control group were outperformed by girls trained in the same group. On the other hand, girls in general performed equally well in all the three training conditions. Females' psychological traits such as differential level of interest (Heeter, 1994) where males were more enthusiastic and differential level of appeal favoring males in using learning materials and games based on virtual and 3D environments (Ziemek, 2006) may explain gender differential performances in the experimental conditions. Inferring from the respondents' comments, it seems that motivational factor might explain boys' poor performance in the control condition relying on printed materials as they reported low enthusiasm in training compared to girls in the same group.

The Extent of Improvement in Mental Rotation Speed after Spatial Training

Overall, there were no significant differences in terms of mental rotation improvement for speed measure for all the three groups of spatial training based on the comparison of mean differences before and after spatial training. This led to the conclusion that the effect of training for the improvement in mental rotation speed was not significant to support the first research hypothesis for this spatial measure. In other words, all the participants' speed or reaction times after training in solving mental rotation tasks did not differ substantially from their prior mental rotation in terms of speed measure.

The Impact of Training Method and Gender in Mental Rotation Speed

There were no significant differences in mental rotation speed measure among the three groups based on the different methods of training. Irrespective of training condition, the participants did not improve substantially by becoming faster compared to their initial reaction times in mental rotation tasks. This finding effectively verifies that the extent of training condition in influencing the training outcomes was not significant to support the second research hypothesis for this spatial measure. In addition, there were no significant gender differences after training in the reaction time of mental rotation implying that the extent of gender factor in influencing training outcome was not significant to support the third research hypothesis for this spatial measure. In this study, both female and male participants were on par in this measure indicating that neither gender made substantial gain by becoming faster after training in mental rotation. In contrast to earlier findings for spatial visualization and mental rotation accuracy measures described earlier, this particular finding suggests that the types of training utilized to improve mental rotation reaction times had little impact. The result of this insubstantial improvement in reaction times may be a product of various interactions of psychological and methodological variables affecting the training outcome beyond the control in this study.

The finding of no improvement gain in speed factor of mental rotation in this study reflects the traditional assumption in the perception literature that the speed of the imagined rotation is a fixed capability of an individual thus immune from training. This assumption took shape from Metzler and Shepard's (1974) study indicating that individual '...can perform the mental rotation at no faster than some limiting rate' (quoted from Shepard & Cooper, 1982). If this holds, it means that the participants in the study were already operating at this optimal level where training had little impact for improving speed in mental rotation tasks. However, some researchers had challenged the limiting rate criterion such as Cohen and Blair (1998) that found mental rotation speed can increase in certain conditions. Partly, this result could also be attributed to methodological approach adopted in the study. Time restriction imposed by school administration precluded longer training session. The duration of this experimental study spanned over eight weeks with only 2-hour session per week that may not be sufficient for the participants to enhance their reaction times. Apparently, to become faster in solving mental rotation tasks entails greater training exposure by having more practice than encountered in this study. Through longer engagement in spatial activities tapping on mental rotation ability may result in learners developing efficient strategy to solve the tasks quicker.

The Impact of Method of Training and Gender on the Performance of Engineering Graphic Task

It was observed that there were main effects of training condition on the performance of basic engineering drawing task. Those trained in first experimental condition were found to outperform the other two groups substantially. On the other hand, there were no significant differences between the latter two groups. Closer examination revealed that this group achieved higher spatial ability improvement. This finding supports the fourth research hypothesis of training transfer as evidenced from the better solving performance of the task by the high spatial ability group compared to other groups of lower spatial ability. Also observed was gender difference in the performance of basic engineering drawing favoring males thus verifying the extent of gender factor in solving this task to be significant. Male advantage was observed in this study where male participants committed less error compared to female participants concurring with earlier studies (Rafi &

Khairulanuar, 2007; Scales, 2000). The gender difference in the performance could be partly explained by differential level of spatial ability where boys in this study were found to possess relatively higher spatial visualization and mental rotation abilities than girls. Solving an engineering drawing task necessitates an individual to engage in mental processing tapping on spatial visualization (Olkun, 2003; Rafi, Khairulanuar & Azniah, 2006) suggesting that the former would have a slight advantage compared to the latter. Seemingly, those trained in first experimental group and males in particular possessed higher spatial ability that led to better problem solving in tasks that tap on this skill.

The Prediction of Performance in Engineering Drawing Task Based on Spatial Visualization and Mental Rotation

This study also examined the impact of spatial visualization and mental rotation of the participants in solving an engineering drawing through the regression analysis. In addition, the analysis also sought to determine which particular component is most critical and whether gender plays a role in the similar task. It was found that almost 63% of the variance in engineering graphic performance was accounted for by the combined effect of spatial visualization and gender. Spatial visualization accounted 57% and gender explained 6% of the performance variance. Other measures of spatial ability namely mental rotation accuracy and speed were not significant in the analysis suggesting that their impact in engineering drawing performance were not substantially strong. Hence, spatial visualization was established as the factor more critical than mental rotation in the performance of basic engineering drawing that supports the fifth research hypothesis of the study. This is hardly surprising given the concept of a quasi-hierarchical relation in the network of the different intellectual capacities. Based on this premise, a spatial visualization test would contain several aptitudes of lower rank, including rotation, despite this ability being a vital aptitude (Carroll, 1993). This means that spatial visualization ability is much more complex than the mental rotation ability where the former will be more engaged by learners in solving an engineering drawing task.

The universally adopted convention of engineering drawings comprising drawing of 2D multi-view of orthographic projection and 3D isometric representation entails the visualization of 3D objects and the corresponding mental transformation to 2D representations or vice versa requiring mental operations akin to spatial visualization. This result also replicates other findings (Olkun, 2003; Rafi, Khairulanuar & Azniah, 2006) indicating that the ability to solve an engineering graphic task is dependent on one's level of spatial visualization ability more than one's mental rotation. These studies suggest that high spatial individuals would likely to perform better than low spatial learners. Engineering drawing or technical drawing is a means of communicating technical ideas using graphical images. Understanding and producing these drawings necessitates engineers or drafters to visualize those graphical images in their minds and perform mental manipulation to understand spatial relationships and layouts of the drawing elements. An adequate level of spatial ability, in particular spatial visualization, is thus vital to enable students learn the concepts an engineering drawing or technical drawing effectively.

Parallel to the regression analysis above, comparison of performance score means among the three groups were analyzed through an analysis of variance. Any group differences in the engineering drawing performance could be explained from their differential level of spatial visualization and mental rotation abilities. It gives some measure on the transfer of spatial ability skills acquired from the spatial training to solving an engineering drawing where a group with better spatial ability will outperform groups of relatively lower spatial ability. The analysis revealed that the first experimental group outperformed the other two groups. Performance of second experimental group was at par with the control group. The order of groups in terms of improvement gain of spatial ability in ascending order are the control group, second experimental group, and first experimental group indicating that spatial ability is a detrimental factor influencing the ability of the participants to solve the task. There was a transfer of spatial ability namely spatial visualization gained in training to engineering drawing problem solving as qualified by the group of higher spatial ability outperforming groups of relatively lower spatial ability.

CONCLUSION

Overall, this study revealed that spatial ability particularly spatial visualization and mental rotation accuracy to a lesser extent could be nurtured or trained for improvement. However, training of mental rotation speed may require longer and constant practice to produce the desired effect. The finding suggests that training in spatial ability using novel method such as desktop virtual environment may be mediated by several learner characteristics such as gender. Mantovani (2001) cautions that a number of factors have been identified: age, gender, domain experience, spatial ability, and computer experience that may influence training in virtual environment. Apparently, computer-mediated spatial training in desktop virtual environment may be of greater advantage to male participants as demonstrated in this experimental study. In particular, qualitative data derived from respondents' comments provided some evidence revealing potential gender differences in navigational skills where more girls reporting difficulties using the interface. This warrants further study focusing on this issue to determine whether navigational experience may result in performance differences in training. Evidential signs of constructivist learning were quite apparent from a few respondents' comments indicating that they achieved better spatial cognition through trial-and- error practice in solving the spatial exercises by engaging in the virtual environment supported with animations and feedback. Another major finding of this study is that there was a training transfer from spatial training to solving basic engineering drawing task. This training transfer was more pronounced for spatial visualization than mental rotation. This should inform practitioners, instructors and technology education teachers that successful learning of engineering drawing depends on the level of students' spatial visualization skills. Students with low spatial ability namely spatial visualization taking engineering drawing or technical graphics are most likely at risk in learning the subject matter thus impeding their success. Interventional treatments through interaction-based and animation-based training programs could be deployed to help low spatial students train in spatial visualization to acquire the essential skills required in learning the subject matter.

REFERENCES

Ali, N., & Ferdig, R. (2002). Why not Virtual Reality?: The barriers of using virtual reality in education. In C. Crawford et al. (Eds.), *Proceedings of Society for Information Technology and Teacher Education International Conference 2002,* (pp.1119-1120). Chesapeake, VA.

Ausburn, L. J. & Ausburn, F. B. (2004). Desktop virtual reality: A powerful new technology for teaching and research in industrial teacher education. *Journal of Industrial Teacher Education, 41(4).* Retrieved March 2, 2007, from scholar.lib.vt.edu/ejournals/JITE/v41n4/ausburn.html

Brady, L. (2004). The role of interactivity in web-based educational material. *Usability News, 6* (2). Retrieved December 15, 2006, from http://psychology.wichita.edu/surl/usabilitynews/62/interactivity.htm

Carroll, J. (1993). Human cognitive abilities: A survey of factor-analytic studies. New York: Cambridge University Press.

Chay, J. C. (2000). *3D Mental Rotation Test*. Retrieved August 16, 2004, from http://www.uwm.edu/People/johnchay/mrp.htm

Cohen, D. J., & Blair, C. (1998). Mental rotation and temporal contingencies. *Journal of the Experimental Analysis of Behavior*, *70*, 203–214. doi:10.1901/jeab.1998.70-203

Dalgarno, B. (2002). The potential of 3D virtual learning environments: A constructivist analysis, *E-JIST, 5*(2). Retrieved July 20, 2008, from http://www.usq.edu.au/electpub/e-jist/docs/Vol5 No2/Dalgarno/Final.pdf

Davies, T. N. (1973). Visual perception of engineering drawings. *Engineering Designer,* 21- 31.

Fernie, K., & Richard, J. D. (Eds.). (2002). *Creating and using virtual reality: A guide for the arts and humanities*. AHDS. Retrieved February 3, 2008, from http://vads.ahds.ac.uk/guides/vr_guide/

Gorska, R. (2005). Spatial Imagination - an overview of the longitudinal research at Cracow University of Technology. *Journal for Geometry and Graphics*, *9*(2), 201–208.

Halpern, D. (2000). Sex differences in cognitive abilities (3rd ed.). Mahwah, NJ: Lawrence Erlbaum Associates.

Heeter, C. (1994). Gender differences and VR. *Virtual Reality World*, March/April. Retrieved May 26, 2006, from commtechlab.msu.edu/randd/research/gender.html

Hyde, J. S. (2005). The gender similarities hypothesis. *American Pyschologist, 60,* 581-589. Retrieved May 24, 2006 from http://www.apa.org/journals/releases/amp606581.pdf

Kajiyama, K. (1996). Towards a generative theory of freshmen graphics reading errors. In *Proceedings of 7th International Conference on Engineering Computer Graphics and Descriptive Geometry,* (pp 493-497). Cracow, Poland.

Kang, F. M., David, W. S., Jean, C. L., & Jan, B. J. (2004, February). *The study on development of spatial ability scale for vocational high school students.* Paper presented at the 7th UICEE ANNUAL Conference on Engineering Education, Mumbai, India.

Khairulanuar, S., & Azniah, I. (2004). The improvement of mental rotation through computer based multimedia tutor. [MOJIT]. *Malaysian Online Journal of Instructional Technology*, *1*(2), 24–34.

Klein, J., & Koroghlanian, C. (2004). The effect of audio and animation in multimedia instruction. [Norfolk, VA: AACE]. *Journal of Educational Multimedia and Hypermedia, 13*(1), 23–46.

Linn, M. C., & Hyde, J. S. (1989). Gender, mathematics and science. *Educational Researcher*, *18*, 17–19.

Linn, M. C., & Petersen, A. C. (1985). Emergence and characterization of sex differences in spatial ability: a meta-analysis. *Child Development*, *56*, 1479–1498. doi:10.2307/1130467

Love, R. K. (2004). Animations and learning: Value for money? In R. Atkinson, C. McBeath, D. Jnas-Dwyer, & R. Phillips (Eds.), *Beyond the comfort zone: Proceedings of the 21st ASCILITE Conference, Perth, Australia.* Retrieved on 11 June, 2006, from http:www.ascilite.org.au/conference/perth04/procs/lowe-r.html

Maccoby, E. E., & Jacklin, C. N. (1974). The psychology of sex differences. Stanford, CA: Stanford University Press.

Mantovani, F. (2001). VR learning: Potential and challenges for the use of 3D environments in education and training. Towards CyberPsychology: Mind, Cognitions and Society in the Internet Age. Amsterdam: IOS Press.

Middle Grade Mathematical Project. (1983). Spatial visualization test. Department of Mathematics, Michigan State University.

Moyer, P. S., Bolyard, J. J., & Spikell, M. A. (2001, August). *Virtual manipulatives in the K-12 classroom*. Paper presented at the International Conference on New Ideas in Mathematics Education, Palm Cove, Queensland, Australia.

Newcombe, N. S. (2006). A Plea for Spatial Literacy. *The Chronicle of Higher Education, 52*(26).

Olkun, S. (2003). Making connections: Improving spatial abilities with engineering drawing activities. *International Journal of Mathematics Teaching and Learning,* 1-10.

Osborne, J. W. (2000). Prediction in multiple regression. *Practical Assessment, Research, and Evaluation, 7*(2). Retrieved June 15, 2005, from tp://pareonline.net/getvn.asp?v=7&n=2

Potter, C. S., & Van Der Merwe, E. (2003). Perception, imagery, visualization and engineering graphics. *European Journal of Engineering Education, 28*(1), 117–133. doi:10.1080/0304379031000065216

Rafi, A., & Khairulanuar, S. (2007). The relationship of spatial experience, previous mathematics achievement and gender with perceived ability in learning engineering drawing. *Journal of Technology Education, 18*(2), 52–66.

Rafi, A., & Khairulanuar, S. (2009). Practising mental rotation using interactive desktop mental rotation trainer (iDeMRT). *British Journal of Educational Technology, 40*(5), 889–900. doi:10.1111/j.1467-8535.2008.00874.x

Rafi, A., Khairulanuar, S., & Azniah, I. (2006). On improving spatial ability through computer-mediated engineering drawing instruction. *Educational Technology & Society, 9*(3), 149–159.

Rafi, A., Khairulanuar, S., & Said, C. S. (2008). Training in spatial visualization: The effects of training method and gender. *Educational Technology & Society, 11*(3), 127–140.

Robert, J. E., & Bell, M. A. (2000). Sex differences on a mental rotation tesk: Variations in EGG hemispheric activation between children and college students. *Developmental Neuro-psychological, 17*, 199–224.

Sanz de Acedo, M. L., & Garcia, J. M. (2003). Improvement of mental rotation in girls and boys. *Sex Roles, 49*(5-6), 277–286. doi:10.1023/A:1024656408294

Scales, A. Y. (2000). *The effect of learning style, major, and gender on learning computer-aided drawing in an introductory engineering/technical graphics course*. Unpublished doctoral dissertation, North Carolina State University.

Shaw, R. (2001). *Information design and distance learning for international develoment*. Unpublished Master's thesis, Water, Engineering and Development Centre, Loughborough University, UK.

Shepard, R., & Cooper, L. (1982). Mental images and their transformations. Cambridge, MA: MIT Press.

Smith, G. G. (2001). Interaction evokes reflection: Learning efficiency in spatial visualization. *Interactive Multimedia Electronic Journal of Computer-Enhanced Learning, 3*. Retrieved March 17, 2006, from http://imej.wfu.edu/articles/2001/2/05/index.asp

Sorby, S. A., & Baartmans, B. J. (2000). The development and assessment of a course for enhancing the 3D spatial visualization skills of first year engineering students. *Journal of Engineering Education, 89*(3), 301–307.

Strong, S., & Smith, R. (2001). Spatial visualization: Fundamentals and trends in engineering graphics. *Journal of Information Technology*, *18*(1), 1–13.

Turos, J., & Ervin, A. (2000). Training and gender differences on a Web-based mental rotation task. *The Penn State Behrend Psychology Journal*, *4*(2), 3-12. Retrieved from http://viz.bd.psu.edu/viz/conferences/Training-and-Gender

Tversky, B., Morrison, J., & Betrancourt, M. (2002). Animation: Can it facilitate? *International Journal of Human-Computer Studies*, *57*, 247–262. doi:10.1006/ijhc.2002.1017

Voyer, D., Voyer, S., & Bryden, P. (1995). Magnitude of sex differences in spatial abilities: A meta-analysis and consideration of critical variables. *Psychological Bulletin*, *117*(2), 250–270. doi:10.1037/0033-2909.117.2.250

Wiebe, E. N. (1993). Visualization of three-dimensional form: A discussion of theoretical models of internal representation. *Engineering Design Graphics Journal*, *57*(1), 18–28.

Wiesen, J. P. (2004, June). *An in-depth, content review of spatial ability tests*. Paper presented at the 28th Annual IPMAAC Conference on Personnel Assessment, Seattle.

Williams, A. P., Sutton, K. J., & Allen, R. J. (2008). Spatial ability: Issues associated with engineering and gender. In *Proceedings of the 19th Annual Conference for the Australasian Association for Engineering Education*. Yeppoon, Queensland, 7- 10, December, 2008.

Ziemek, T. R. (2006, March). *Two-D or not Two-D: Gender implications of visual cognition in electronic games*. Paper presented at the 2006 Symposium on Interactive 3D Graphics and Games, Redwood City, CA.

ADDITIONAL READING

Barker, P. (2008). Re-evaluating a model of learning design. *Innovations in Education and Teaching International*, *45*(2), 127–141. doi:10.1080/14703290801950294

Basham, K. L., & Kotrlik, J. W. (2008). The effects of 3-dimensional CADD modeling on the development of the spatial ability of technology education students. *Journal of Technology Education, 20 (1)*. Retrieved July 19, 2009 from http://scholar.lib.vt.edu/ejournals/JTE/v20n1/kotrlik.pdf

Caplan, P. J., Crawford, M., Hyde, J. S., & Richardson, J. T. E. (1997). Gender differences in human cognition. New York: Oxford University Press.

Dede, C., Salzman, M., Loftin, B., & Ash, K. (2000). Using Virtual Reality Technology to Convey Abstract Scientific Concepts. In M. J. Jacobson, & R. B. Kozma (Ed.), Learning the Sciences of the 21st Century: Research, Design, and Implementing Advanced Technology Learning Environments. Hillsdale, NJ: Lawrence Erlbaum.

Feng, J., Spence, I., & Pratt, J. (2007). Play ing an action video game reduces gender differences in spatial cognition. *Psychological Science*, *18*(10), 850–855. doi:10.1111/j.1467-9280.2007.01990.x

Gabrielli, S., Rogers, Y., & Scaife, M. (2000). Young children's spatial representations developed through exploration of a desktop virtual reality scene. *Education and Information Technologies*, *5*(4), 251–262. doi:10.1023/A:1012097322806

Grasso, R., Ivanenko, Y. P., McIntyre, J., Viaud-Delmon, I., & Berthoz, A. (2000). Spatial, not temporal cues drive predictive orienting movements during navigation: a virtual reality study. [My Copy]. *Neuroreport*, *11*(4), 775–778. doi:10.1097/00001756-200003200-00024

Gunzelmann, G., & Lyon, D. R. (2007). Mechanisms for human spatial competence. In T. Barkowsky et al. (Eds.), Spatial Cognition (pp. 288 - 307). Berlin Heidelberg: Springer-Verlag.

Hart, W. J. (2003). *Effect of computer animation instruction on spatial visualization performance*. Unpublished master's thesis, North Carolina State University, North Carolina, USA.

Jansen-Osmann, P. (2002). Use of virtual environments to investigate the development of spatial behavior and spatial knowledge of school age children. *Psychological Reports, 100*, 675-690. Retrieved July 21, 2009 from http://www.uni-duesseldorf.de/home/Fakultaeten/math_nat/WE/Psychologie/abteilungen/aap/Dokumente/Psychological_Reports.pdf

Mohler, J. L. (2007). An instructional strategy for pictorial drawing. *Journal of Industrial Teacher Education, 44 (3)*. Retrieved July 20, 2009 from http://scholar.lib.vt.edu/ejournals/JITE/v44n3/mohler.html

Popovici, D. M., & Marhan, A. N. (2008). Virtual reality-based environments for learning and training. In D. Talaba & A. Amditis (Eds.), Product Engineering: Tools and Methods based on Virtual Reality (pp. 123 – 142). B.V.: Springer Science.

Rauterberg, M. (2004). Positive effects of VR technology on human behavior. *Proceedings of the 14th International Conference on Artificial Reality and Telexistence- ICAT 2004*(pp. 85-88). Korea Advanced Institute of Science and Technology and Virtual Reality Society of Japan.

Sebok, A., Nystad, E., & Helgar, S. (2004). Navigation in desktop virtual environments: an evaluation and recommendations for supporting usability. *Virtual Reality (Waltham Cross), 8*, 26–40. doi:10.1007/s10055-004-0133-1

Shaffer, J. (2002). Virtual reality in education. *New Horizons for Learning*. Retrieved July 21, 2009 from http://www.newhorizons.org/strategies/technology/shaffer.htm

Shelton, A. L., & Pippitt, H. A. (2006). Motion in the mind's eye: Comparing mental and visual rotation. *Cognitive, Affective & Behavioral Neuroscience, 6*(4), 323–332. doi:10.3758/CABN.6.4.323

Terlecki, M. S., & Newcombe, N. S. (2005). How important is the digital divide? The relation of computer and videogame usage to gender differences in mental rotation ability. *Sex Roles, 53*(5), 433–441. doi:10.1007/s11199-005-6765-0

Van Garderen, D. (2006). Spatial Visualization, Visual Imagery, and Mathematical Problem Solving of Students with varying abilities. *Journal of Learning Disabilities, 39*(6), 496–506. doi:10.1177/00222194060390060201

Fournier-Viger, P., Nkambou, R., & Mayers, A. (2008). Evaluating Spatial Representations and Skills in a Simulator-Based Tutoring System [My Copy]. *IEEE Transactions on Learning Technologies, 1*(1), 63–74. doi:10.1109/TLT.2008.13

Wexler, M., Kosslyn, S. M., & Berthoz, A. (1998). Motor processes in mental rotation. *Cognition, 68*, 77–94. doi:10.1016/S0010-0277(98)00032-8

KEY TERMS AND DEFINITIONS

Animation: The illusion of movement resulting from the rapid display of a sequence of images of two-dimensional or three-dimensional objects.

Desktop Virtual Environment: A computer generated world displayed on personal computer screen that can be manipulated through mouse-controlled interface that provides a sense of interaction.

Engineering Drawing: A type of technical drawing primarily consisting of a series of two dimensional views representing the top, front and side elevations of a three-dimensional object.

Interaction: The sense of translating and/or rotating an object in a three-dimensional space as one navigates through the virtual environment.

Mental Rotation: The ability to quickly and accurately rotate two- or three-dimensional objects in one's mind.

Spatial Ability: A cognitive construct representing an individual's ability to process, organize and manipulate visuo-spatial information in the mind.

Spatial Visualization: The ability to manipulate complex spatial information through several and sequential stages in order to derive a correct solution.

Training Transfer: Skills and/or knowledge acquired during training that are successfully applied in other activities.

Chapter 10
Collaborative Knowledge Construction in Online Learning Environment:
Why to Promote and How to Investigate

Rikki Rimor
Open University of Israel, Israel

Yigal Rosen
Open University of Israel, Israel

ABSTRACT

The current study is based on academic on-line course and examines the effectiveness of collaborative learning vs. individual learning. Fifty eight graduate students in the Open University participated in course entitled "From information to knowledge" collaborating in a Google Docs environment as their final task of the course. The purpose of the study was to examine whether students with a collaborative learning orientation differ from students with an individual learning orientation, as was measured through their contribution to the process of knowledge construction in a collaborative online database environment. The students' contribution to the database was analyzed through personal and collective criteria of knowledge construction. The results showed differential achievements among learners with different learning orientations. While the 'collaborative learners' contributed more collective knowledge, the 'individual learners' focused on constructing their own personal knowledge. These findings have important implications on planning, coordinating and evaluating collaborative learning environments.

ORGANIZATION BACKGROUND

Distance teaching and the self-study method, developed specifically for the Open University, provides conditions that meet the constraints of individuals who work or raise a family. The method is not space-or time-dependent as it is not based on a central campus where lecturers and students gather, or on an established and uniform schedule. Courses offered by the Open University are fundamentally different from courses offered at other universities. The customary image of a course - a classroom with a teacher on the podium facing a group of students - does not apply to the Open University, or

DOI: 10.4018/978-1-61520-749-7.ch010

only partially. A course at the Open University is first and foremost a printed scholarly or scientific work: one or more volumes written and produced especially for Open University students. Thus, learning at the Open University is primarily conducted through self-study of written material, supported by advanced technologies rather than face to face instructor-student interaction.

SETTING THE STAGE

The Open University utilizes advanced technologies to improve its distance teaching. It provides a wealth of learning materials and technological platforms to facilitate continuous contact with faculty and students in various courses (e.g. video conferences, synchronic sessions, online tasks' system, online forums, blogs, wiki, google collaborative database). Most of the courses offer websites on the internet. The websites include, among other things, additional materials, links to databases and Internet sites related to the course material, multimedia materials, as well as individual and group communication between students and tutors, and among the students themselves. In some of the courses, computer-mediated tutorials alternate with the tutorial sessions in various study centers. These aspects of distance education developed by The Open University, along with the university's open admission policy, aim to open the world of higher education to all, irrespective of age, sex, prior achievements' certificate or occupation, in order to enable every individual to realize and fulfill his or her academic ability.

CASE DESCRIPTION

Collaborative knowledge construction refers to mutual engagement of peers of equivalent learning prerequisites in learning tasks with intertwined layers of socio-cognitive processes (e.g. Berieter, & Scardamalia 1989). Creating effective collaborative learning environment may entail cognitive challenges and social dilemmas which involves processes of reflection and argumentation. The purpose of this study was to examine whether learners with a collaborative learning orientation differ from learners with an individual learning orientation, as was measured through their contribution to the process of knowledge construction in a collaborative online database environment. The study examined students' contribution to the database using personal and collective criteria of knowledge construction. Students' collaborative learning orientation was measured by their previous contribution to the forum of the e-learning course. This paper presents the rationale for collaborative knowledge construction in online learning environments and discusses the results of the study regarding collaborate knowledge building. Measures of individual and collective knowledge are presented. The relationship between these measures and their contribution to e-learning environments are further discussed and challenged.

Theoretical Background

The use of Instructional Technologies enables collaborative learning and has become a popular topic for research within the field of education. Computer technologies enable intellectual partnership between the learner and cognitive tools (Jonassen, 2000). These tools are mainly intended for activities and intellectual partnerships that encourage thinking and support learning in a social context. The theoretical basis for learning as a social process was developed by Vygotsky, who placed great emphasis on the social context of the learning process. This concept became particularly relevant in relation to learning processes involving computer mediated communications (CMC). Vygotsky stressed the importance of the interaction between the learner and his or her environment, and presented the gap created between the learners' level of performance and the level of their own potential. He claimed that personal potential can be realized through a process of interaction with and support from the human environment and from various tools. This defined the optimal conditions in which reciprocal interpersonal activity could lead to intrapersonal mental development, in other words, the connection between cognitive functioning and social functioning. When trying to solve a problem in collaboration through an exchange of ideas, learners construct shared meanings which extend beyond the individual performance. The collaborative parameter and the social context of a meaningful learning process are expressed through group discussion based on prior knowledge and allow ongoing development of thinking (Vygotsky, 1978). In light of this concept, social constructivist researchers claim that interpersonal views internalized by the individual to serve personal-cognitive functions, may further refer to shared meaning appropriation. Intelligence is not a matter of (individual) ownership, but a quality that grows out of intrapersonal negotiation (Salomon, 2002).

Sharing may take place at different stages of the learning such as: data search, data collection, data processing, and outcome assessment (Hathorn & Ingram, 2002). An effective task enables all participants to express themselves and make significant contributions to the final results (Ingram, 2006).

Web-based communications, especially in the Web 2.0 era, contribute to the advancement of collaborative learning. It appears that the online learning environment serves as a platform that promotes and encourages collaborative learning and might thus help close the gap between the learner's level of performance and the level of personal potential due to the collaborative and interactive learning process. The online learning environment allows activities involving debate, argumentation and reflection (Weinberger & Fisher, 2006), and hence develops teamwork orientation, group cohesiveness as well as a sense of belonging (Rovai, 2002). It encourages students to generate new knowledge for rapid distribution and improves their sense of learning and achievements (Williams et al., 2006; Rollett et al., 2007). Apparently the view of learning as a social process is also linked to the constructivist view of learning as a construction of knowledge. While combining effective individualized and group online learning, the emphasis shifts to interactive learning through cooperation and collaboration among all participants in the process. This is a significant extension of the learning and discussion framework which enriches the knowledge construction in an online environment. (Stahl et. al., 2006; Rollett et. al., 2007; Little et. al., 2009; Weinberger & Fischer, 2006). On the other hand, collaborative learning in online environment also arouses some difficulties and constraints among participants as it demands a certain degree of technical literacy, which in turn might require further investment in the acquisition of the necessary technical skills (Frank, Reich & Humphreys, 2003; Yan, 2006). Distance learning requires often elusive self-discipline (Winters et al., 2008). Moreover, researchers claim that personal traits which are essential for collaborative learning, such as a sense of belonging and mutual trust, are lacking in the transition to virtual space (Kreijns et. al., 2003; Frank et. al., 2003). Yet, identification with a group or group cohesiveness may play an important role in an online learning environment with a social setting (Caspi & Blau, 2008). In order to succeed in online team work, participants need to cultivate and preserve shared norms and work procedures. Peer pressure may not be optimal for collaboration and might not allow for original independent thought. The need to fit in with the group's learning pace or level of discussion might sometimes adversely affect personal aspirations and achievements and increases mutual dependency. Similarly, because of the complexity of tasks in this environment, the odds of increased cognitive load causing problems of understanding among the learners and consequently might lead to conflicts and drive participants to seek easier shortcuts (Webb, et. al., 1986; Kreijns et.

al., 2003; Puntambekar, 2006). The difficulty of collaborating and reaching consensus might thus constitute a source of problems and difficulties. Conversely, other researchers claim that one must place more emphasis on the challenge of these experiences alongside the aspiration to reach shared understanding, and that the very participation in the learning process, with all the problems inherent in reaching consensus about the results, is highly important for enhancing learning in social contexts (Chen & Chiu, 2008).

Our research focuses on social activity within knowledge construction process, through group discussion in an online database environment. We investigate a learning environment where rules and norms of participation and negotiation were predefined, as well as the role of each individual in the group. The Google database provides the study with a platform that supports interactive learning characterized by collaboration and facilitates mutual feedback as well as real-time argumentation and debate through social interaction. The unique structure and rationale of the database allowed and triggered the participants' individual and collaborative knowledge on one hand and its investigation on the other hand (Rosen & Rimor, 2009; Rimor, 2001).

Method

Fifty eight graduate students participated in an online course which dealt with search for information and construction of knowledge in technology-rich environments. The final assignment of the course was to construct a database representing various types of knowledge. The students selected items from the course forum and added the items to the database according to categories of knowledge types: declarative, procedural, structural, metacognitive. The spreadsheets application of Google Docs was chosen as an online collaborative database environment for this study. Learning activity in a Google spreadsheet enables organization, classification and representation of data in a collaborative environment. The students defined and classified items from the course forum according to four types of knowledge and assigned each statement to the proper field of the database accordingly. This process was accompanied by explained confirmation or disagreement by the participants for each classification performed in the database. The course participants were divided into groups of 3-4 students who were required to reach collective consent for each classification within their group. The participants were assessed according to each student's success in correctly classifying the forum's statements ("individual knowledge"), and according to the index of accuracy of the group assignment ("collective knowledge"). Additionally, the participants were divided into two groups ("active", "less active"), based on the rate of activity in the course forum, according to three quantitative criteria: 1. Number of items provided by the student in the forum's discussions. 2. Number of queries initiated by the student in the forum. 3. Number of proposed additional information and links contributed to the forum.

Results

Thirty four students were categorized as "more active" and twenty four as "less active" on the basis of the activity in the online course forum. The finding of the study showed that the more active participants were more successful in the group index of knowledge construction, compared to the less active participants (average grade of 17.0 versus 15.2; $t=5.1$, $p<0.1$). Accordingly, it was found that the less active participants in the course forum were more successful in the personal index of knowledge construction (individual knowledge), compared to more active participants (average grade of 14.9 versus 13.9; $t=2.1$, $p<0.5$). These findings demonstrate the differential nature of the process of knowledge construction and the differential type of achieve-

Table 1. Effects of online database learning on individual and collective knowledge construction among more and less active groups

Group	Individual knowledge (Mean)	Collective knowledge (Mean)	t(df)
More active	13.9	17.0	5.1** (53)
Less active	14.9	15.2	2.1*(53)

$p < .05$* $p < .01$, **

ments among learners with a different learning orientation (See Table 1).

Discussion

The purpose of this study was to examine whether learners with a collaborative learning orientation differ from learners with an individual learning orientation, as was assessed through their contribution to the process of knowledge construction in a collaborative online database environment. Our research investigated a learning environment where rules and norms of participation and negotiation were pre-defined, as well as the role of each individual in the group. The collaborative online learning environment provided the participants with a virtual space for argumentation and negotiation in their process of database construction. Researchers claim that learners should increase their accountability and their sense of ownership over the solutions submitted. This conclusion is supported by their findings related to individual assessment and a higher degree of students' involvement, motivation and achievements (Yadin & Or-Bach, 2008). In our research, the students shared a common goal to complete the construction of the database which represented the knowledge they built during the course. Yet, the role of each participant to individually contribute data and classify it in the common database was determined as part of his/her own final grade. The other part of the task was composed of the participants' contribution to the common discussion and debate as a team which accompanied the construction of the collaborative database. All participants were required to respond in writing and to relate to each other's performance. Consequently, misconceptions, misunderstanding, or disagreements became explicit on one hand and resolvable through a process of negotiation and consent, on the other. The instructor intervened online to prompt rules and procedures of the task. The content of the task and its accuracy was examined and assessed at the end through individual and collective indices (see Method).

We claim that this unique structure and rationale of the task, as described above, enabled the participants to demonstrate their own individual knowledge on the one hand, and to demonstrate their social ability to share their knowledge and views and to collaborate on the other. Recent researches have promoted the feasibility of collaboration in various online learning environments (Dillenbourg, 1999, 2002; Scardamalia & Bereiter, 1993; Hathorn & Ingram 2002; Constantino-Gonzalez, Suthers & Escamilla, 2003; Tal & Tal 2006). Evidently, an online platform supports and scaffolds collaborative learning environments technically and pedagogically. Yet it is recommended to include students' individual contributions, along with the group product, as vital components of their learning environment.

The concept of collaborative learning addresses different operational meanings. Collaboration may imply sharing common sources of information, working together on a search for information, distributing collective effort to process data and or its evaluation, as well as assigning different roles aimed at a completion of a mutual goal. Therefore it seems plausible to pre-define the kind of collaboration desired for each task and to clarify its rationale. An effective task allows each participant self expression as well as a significant contribution to a common goal (Hathorn & Ingram, 2002).

In this research, students were required to develop their own understanding as a result of intensive social interaction. They all shared a previous common background (online forum and face-to-face meetings, e-textbook and readings), along with mutual feedback and written dialogues with team members within the database environment. Previous studies of online collaborative learning provided evidence for the effect of reflection as a core process in group learning, enabling students to construct their own knowledge through meta-cognitive processes (Rimor, Reingold & Heiman, 2008; Yukawa, 2006).

The results of the study show that more active participants were more successful in collective knowledge' construction, compared to the less active ones. On the other hand, it was found that relatively less active participants had more success in the personal knowledge construction. Possible explanations for these findings can be a differential motivation of learners with different learning orientations. Learners with collaborative orientation focused on the group's achievements, while learners with individual orientation focused on constructing their own personal knowledge.

Innovative methodology was developed during the study relating to the ability of the student to distinguish between individual knowledge construction and collective knowledge construction. In addition, an index of collaborative learning orientation was developed. The findings show that students with less collective orientation exceeded the more oriented ones in the parameters of individual knowledge. The students who were less active in the previous forum constructed their own knowledge in the database environment significantly more than the active ones. These findings may challenge the collaborative aspects of the social constructivist approach to learning. It shows that individual knowledge can be effectively constructed without social interaction as well. This was achieved through individual contribution to the construction of a collaborative database. Evidently the contribution of argumentation to the process of knowledge construction in an online database has to be further investigated, along with a study of the patterns of social interaction and their contribution to the construction of individual and collective knowledge in online collaborative environments.

CONCLUSION

The findings of the current study suggests that learners have different level of achievements depending on their learning orientation. The learners who have individual learning orientation tend to enhance personal knowledge construction as compared to the learners who increase group knowledge by collaborative learning orientation.

Two major inferences can be drawn from the findings of the study in the environment of an online collaborative database and these are:

1. Learners who are having an orientation towards collaborative learning tend to achieve differently in person or in group as compared to those having orientation to individual learning.
2. The educational implications of this study elicit the importance of creating balance between learners in their online collaborative learning environments which largely depends upon how they orient themselves to group learning or individual learning. In order to achieve higher level of effectiveness in the learning process of the learners, we need to consider the learner's prior tendencies towards group and individual work, and to balance the groups accordingly. The results of our research emphasize the importance of considering learner's different disposition

and tendencies towards individual or collaborative style of learning as a vital part of designing and evaluating online learning environments.

Further studies can be undertaken in the process of collaborative knowledge construction in online learning environments. In this investigation various learning orientation of learners for collaborative learning and applying argumentation mechanism for knowledge construction may help furthering the studies.

REFERENCES

Caspi, A., & Blau, I. (2008). Social presence in online discussion groups: testing three conceptions and their relations to perceived learning. *Social Psychology of Education*, *11*, 323–346. doi:10.1007/s11218-008-9054-2

Chen, G., & Chiu, M. (2008). Online discussion processes: Effects of earlier messages' evaluations, knowledge content, social cues and personal information on later messages. *Computers & Education*, *50*(3), 678–692. doi:10.1016/j.compedu.2006.07.007

Constantino-Gonzalez, M., Suthers, D., & Escamilla, J. (2003). Coaching web-based collaborative learning based on problem solution differences and participation. *International Journal of Artificial Intelligence in Education*, *13*(2-4), 263–299.

Dillenbourg, P. (1999) What do you mean by collaborative learning? In P. Dillenbourg, (Ed.), Collaborative-learning: Cognitive and Computational Approaches (pp. 1-19). Oxford, UK: Elsevier.

Frank, M., Reich, N., & Humphreys, K. (2003). Respecting the human needs of students in the development of e-learning. *Computers & Education*, *40*(1), 57–70. doi:10.1016/S0360-1315(02)00095-7

Hathorn, L. G., & Ingram, A. L. (2002). Online collaboration: Making it work. *Educational Technology*, *42*(1), 33–40.

Ingram, A. L. (2006). *Combining effective individualized and group online larning*. Paper presented at the Innovative Learning Conference, Kent State University, Kent, Ohio.

Jonassen, D. H. (2000). Computers in the classroom: Mindtools for critical thinking. Englewood Cliffs, NJ: Prentice Hall, Inc.

Kreijns, C., Kirschner, P., & Jochems, W. (2002). The sociability of computer-supported collaborative learning environments. *Journal of Educational Technology & Society*, *5*(1), 8–22.

Kreijns, C., Kirschner, P., & Jochems, W. (2003). Identifying the pitfalls for social interaction in computer-supported collaborative learning environments: a review of the research. *Computers in Human Behavior*, *19*(3), 335–353. doi:10.1016/S0747-5632(02)00057-2

Little, J., Page, C., Betts, K., Bonne, S., Faverty, P., & Joosten, T. (2009). Charting the Course and Tapping the Community: The EDUCAUSE Top Teaching and Learning Challenges 2009. *EDUCAUSE Review*, *44*(3), 30–45.

Rollett, H., Lux, M., Strohmaier, M., Dosinger, G., & Tochtermann, K. (2007). The Web 2.0 way of learning with technologies. *International Journal of Learning Technology*, *3*(1), 87–107. doi:10.1504/IJLT.2007.012368

Perkins, D. N. (1993). Person-plus: A distributed view of thinking and learning. In G. Salomon (Ed.), Distributed cognition: Psychological and educational considerations (pp.88-110). New York: Cambridge University Press.

Rimor, R. (2001). Database as a cognitive tool. *Educational Researcher*, *20*(3), 2–9.

Rimor, R., Reingold, R., & Heiman, T. (2008). Instructor's scaffolding in support of students' meta-cognition through an online course, In J. Zumbach, N. Schwartz, T. Seufert & L. Kester (Eds.), Beyond Knowledge: the Legacy of Competence- Meaningful Computer-based Learning Environments (pp. 43-53). Upper Saddle River, NJ: Springer.

Rosen, Y., & Rimor, R. (2009). Using collaborative database to enhance students' knowledge construction. *Interdisciplinary Journal of E-Learning and Learning Objects*, *5*, 187–195.

Rovai, A. P. (2002). Building sense of community at a distance. *International Review of Research in Open and Distance Learning*, *3*(1), 1–16.

Salomon, G. (2002). Technology and pedagogy: Why don't we see the promised revolution? *Educational Technology*, *42*(2), 71–75.

Scardamalia, M., & Bereiter, C. (1993). Technologies for knowledge-building discourse. *Communications of the ACM*, *36*(5). doi:10.1145/155049.155056

Stahl, G., Koschmann, T., & Suthers, D. (2006). Computer-supported collaborative learning: An historical perspective. In Cambridge Handbook of the Learning Sciences. Cambridge, UK: Cambridge University Press.

Tal, M. H., Tal, E. H., & Yair, Y. (2006). Wikis in Academic Courses: An Institutional Perspective. In Y. Eshet-Alkalai, A. Caspi, & N. Geri (Eds.) *Proceedings of the Chais conference on instructional technologies research 2008: Learning in the technological era,* (pp. 79 – 83). Raanana, Israel: The Open University of Israel.

Vygotsky, L. (1986). Thought and language. Cambridge, MA: MIT Press.

Webb, N. M., Ender, P., & Lewis, S. (1986). Problem-solving strategies and group processes in small groups learning computer programming. *American Educational Research Journal*, *23*(2), 243–261.

Weinberger, A., & Fischer, F. (2006). A framework to analyze argumentative knowledge construction in computer-supported collaborative learning. *Computers & Education*, *46*(1), 71–95. doi:10.1016/j.compedu.2005.04.003

Williams, E., Duray, R., & Venkateshwar, R. (2006). Teamwork orientation, group cohesiveness, and student learning: A Study of the use of teams in online distance education. *Journal of Management Education*, *30*, 592–616. doi:10.1177/1052562905276740

Winters, F., Greene, J., & Costich, C. (2008). Self-regulation of learning within computer-based learning environments. *Educational Psychology Review*, *20*(4), 429–444. doi:10.1007/s10648-008-9080-9

Yadin, A., & Or-Bach, R. (2008). Fostering individual learning – when and how. *ACM's Inroads –. SIGCSE Bulletin*, *40*(4), 83–86. doi:10.1145/1473195.1473227

Yan, Z. (2006). Different experiences, different effects: a longitudinal study of learning a computer program in a network environment. *Computers in Human Behavior*, *22*(3), 364–380. doi:10.1016/j.chb.2004.09.005

Yukawa, J. (2006). Co-reflection in online learning: Collaborative critical thinking as narrative. *International Journal of Computer-Supported Collaborative Learning*, *1*(2), 203–228. doi:10.1007/s11412-006-8994-9

ADDITIONAL READING

Andriessen, J. E. B., Baker, M., & Suthers, D. (Eds.). (2003). Arguing to learn: Confronting cognitions in computer-supported collaborative learning environments. Dordrecht: Kluwer.

Baker, M., & Lund, K. (1997). Promoting reflective interactions in a CSCL environment. *Journal of Computer Assisted Learning, 13*, 175–193. doi:10.1046/j.1365-2729.1997.00019.x

Brown, A. L., & Palincsar, A. S. (1989). Guided, cooperative learning and individual knowledge acquisition. In L. B. Resnick (Ed.), Knowing, learning, and instruction. Essays in the honor of Robert Glaser (pp. 393-451). Hillsdale, NJ: Erlbaum.

Chi, M. T. H., DeLeeuw, N., Chiu, M. H., & LaVancher, C. (1994). Eliciting self-explanations improves understanding. *Cognitive Science, 18*, 439–477.

Chinn, C. A., O'Donnell, A. M., & Jinks, T. S. (2000). The structure of discourse in collaborative learning. *Journal of Experimental Education, 69*(1), 77–97. doi:10.1080/00220970009600650

Cooke, N. J., Salas, E., Cannon-Bowers, J. A., & Stout, R. (2000). Measuring team knowledge. *Human Factors, 42*, 151–173. doi:10.1518/001872000779656561

Dillenbourg, P. (2002). Over-scripting CSCL: The risks of blending collaborative learning with instructional design. In P. A. Kirschner (Ed.), Three worlds of CSCL: Can we support CSCL? (pp. 61-91). Heerlen: Open University Netherland.

Dreyfus, Hershkowitz, R., & Schwarz, B. B. (2001). Abstraction in context: The case of peer interaction. *Cognitive Science Quarterly, 1*, 307–358.

Fischer, F., Bruhn, J., Gräsel, C., & Mandl, H. (2002). Fostering collaborative knowledge construction with visualization tools. *Learning and Instruction, 12*, 213–232. doi:10.1016/S0959-4752(01)00005-6

Gol, O., & Nafalski, A. (2007). *Collaborative Learning in Engineering Education,* 10th UICEE Annual Conference on Engineering Education. Retrieved January 2009 from: http://eng.monash.edu.au/uicee/gjee/vol11no2/GolNafalskis.pdf.

Keefer, M. W., Zeitz, C. M., & Resnick, L. B. (2000). Judging the quality of peer-led student dialogues. *Cognition and Instruction, 18*(1), 53–81. doi:10.1207/S1532690XCI1801_03

King, A. (1999). Discourse patterns for mediating peer learning. In A. M. O'Donnell & A. King (Eds.), Cognitive perspectives on peer learning (pp. 87–115). Mahwah, NJ: Erlbaum.

Kuhn, D., Shaw, V., & Felton, M. (1997). Effects of dyadic interaction on argumentative reasoning. *Cognition and Instruction, 15*, 287–315. doi:10.1207/s1532690xci1503_1

Roschelle, J., & Teasley, S. D. (1995). The construction of shared knowledge in collaborative problem solving. In C. O'Malley (Ed.), Computer supported collaborative learning (pp. 69–96). Berlin: Springer.

Salomon, G., & Perkins, D. N. (1998). Individual and social aspects of learning. *Review of Research in Education, 23*, 1–24.

KEY TERMS AND DEFINITIONS

Collaborated Learning: Joint intellectual effort by students or students and teachers, refers to methodologies and environments in which learners engage in a common task in which each individual depends on and is accountable to each other.

Differentiated Learning: The process of ensuring that what a student learns, how he/she learns it, and how the student demonstrates what he/she has learned is a match for that student's readiness level, interests, and preferred mode of learning. Differentiation stems from beliefs about differences among learners, how they learn, learning preferences and individual interests (Anderson, 2007).

Online Learning Environment: A planned teaching/learning experience that uses a wide spectrum of technologies, mainly Internet or computer-based, to reach learners. In most Universities, online-learning is used to define a specific mode to attend a course or programs of study where the students rarely, if ever, attend face-to-face for on-campus access to educational facilities.

Cognitive Tools: Tools that are intended to engage and facilitate cognitive processing. Cognitive tools can be thought of as a set of tools that learners need in order to serve cognitive apprenticeships.

Google Collaborated Database: Use of Google Documents to create, store and share database instantly and securely from any computer, and collaborate online in real time.

Knowledge Construction: A process by which learners construct their own knowledge through exploration, feedback, evaluation and reflection. Knowledge construction is based on pedagogical concepts which promote active and self-regulated learners who are able to search, manipulate and organize data, based on previous knowledge.

Database: Database is a computerized tool for storing and retrieving massive amount of data. It allows quick access to loads of data items and convenient retrieval of different data combinations, through search and queries.

Chapter 11
Training of Teachers in Virtual Scenario:
An Excellence Model for Quality Assurance in Formative Programmes

Olga M. Alegre-Rosa
University of La Laguna, Spain

Luis M. Villar-Angulo
University of Seville, Spain

ABSTRACT

The integration of Information and Communication Technology (ICT) into higher education instruction is receiving growing attention from university scholars and administrators. The Canarian Government funded the Faculty Professional Development project (FPD) to enhance the quality of formative programmes. Political and socioeconomic forces are inundating the two institutions with more strenuous demands for student competence and teaching accountability. FPD aims at developing and implementing online courses for training faculty members. Thus, understanding what makes faculty development effective is critical to understanding the success or failure of the FPD innovation. The arguments in this chapter response the following needs: (a) an explanation of the potential impact of e-development on faculty and agency staff members' learning, and (b) electronic training for quality assurance specifications.

ORGANISATIONAL BACKGROUND

The Canary Islands comprise seven major islands and are situated on the north-west African coast. They have been one of the seventeen Spanish autonomous communities in 'ultra-peripheral regions' of the European Union since 1982. The regional parliament exercises political power and oversees educational policy.

DOI: 10.4018/978-1-61520-749-7.ch011

The expansion of the universities and training industry in the Canary Islands was brought about by the increase in distance education and better quality management and accountability. The first university in this case under reference was founded in 1701 on the island of Tenerife. Nowadays, the university is composed of 25,000 students, 1,700 faculty members belonging to 63 departments, and 819 University Administration and Services Personnel. It offers 56 official three- and four-year degrees, 43 master's degrees and 33 postgraduate degrees. Nine institutes of the university carry out research activities.

The second university of this case under reference was founded by Canarian government in 1989 for students who could not afford to leave their homes and jobs to pursue higher education on the island of Gran Canaria. The university has 24,145 students, 1,554 faculty teachers and researchers, and offers 55 grades of study in both liberal arts and professional studies and 41 doctoral programmes. The most prominent research areas are cybernetics, telecommunications, medical technology, oceanography, marine crops, renewable energy and environmental conservation. In addition, the university has a moodle-based virtual campus primarily providing a service to five fully online formative programmes and four postgraduate programmes.

Today, the two higher education institutions are providing online courses in formative programmes and postgraduate degrees. These universities therefore focus on the transfer of relevant knowledge and learning competences to their students, and that is the product result exchanged in online education. In this context, it is an educational aim, or even mission, to promote 'transferable skills' – discipline content with learning competences – such as 'problem-based learning', and 'communication technological skills', which are certainly forms of learning mastery and proficiency.

Course digitalisation requires an extra faculty design effort. In addition, students must participate more, and be far more actively engaged, in order to communicate and respond to learning tasks. Hence, most distance learning needs face-to-face and web trained faculty on an amalgamation of new technologies. In addition, online faculty training programmes for learning curriculum and teaching and assessment capacities require a rigorous audit.

Higher education ministers responsible for higher education from 29 European countries signed the Bologna Declaration (1999). Later, the Bergen Communiqué (2005) welcomed "the principle of a European register of quality assurance agencies", and underlined "the importance of cooperation between nationally recognised agencies with a view to enhancing the mutual recognition of accreditation or quality assurance decisions" (p. 3).

The National Agency for Quality Assessment and Accreditation (ANECA) was funded in 2002. At the same time, Canarian regional government was taking strong action to solve major social and community problems such as the quality of higher education services, that is, the educational principles that must be met and maintained to attain specific university goals. This led to the creation of the regional Canarian Agency for University Evaluation and Accreditation (ACECAU) for quality assurance in 2002: in other words, an institutional procedure to check whether the set of university objectives was adequately achieved. ACECAU's further goal was to pioneer quality assessment of the university system according to regulated standards, also known as 'standards', 'criteria', 'guidelines', 'subjects', 'facets', 'principles', according to Aelterman (2006, p. 228), which had been subject to consultation with stakeholders. This written mission statement made it clear that external quality assurance was a major activity of the ACECAU, and it was translated into a clear policy or management plan, recognising that quality assurance was primarily the responsibility of the two Canarian higher education institutions themselves. The ACECAU also had its own criteria for the selection, appointment and training of experts, and for establishing legal frameworks, procedures, forms, and other documents (e.g. codes of ethics). Furthermore, this agency promotes quality in higher education, through courses and training stages for faculty and for other agency and community personnel involved in quality assurance processes.

These universities and ACECAU agreed on important joint objectives for the development of a coherent and cohesive European Higher

Education Area by 2010. Also, they adopted the *Standards and Guidelines for Quality Assurance in the European Higher Education Area* (ESG) (Aelterman, 2006), which includes, inter alia, the following:

a. Internal quality assurance within higher education institutions.
b. External quality assurance of higher education institutions.

Therefore, ACECAU initiated a systematic and independent evaluation of the two university system actions (institutions, degrees, teaching, research, faculty, and so on), and applied quality assurance to measure the effects of university policy and regional government strategies created to improve the quality of the educational services offered.

Assessing the impact of formative programmes is difficult and complex in the two Canarian universities. Nevertheless, these universities agreed to strategic plans in 2008, which included the following actions:

(a) Universities are required to take responsibility for all stakeholders (i.e. students, faculty members, and administration and service personnel).
(b) Adaptation of university formative programmes to committees' review results, including new standards, such as students' competences.
(c) Course evaluations by students, complaint procedures, and standards of student achievement; in other words, 'a focus on outcomes', which is one of the axes of external quality assurance processes (Harvey, 2006, p. 289). Selection of a communication information approach to understand the total composition of the institution with comprehension of visible statements.
(d) Design of major strategies to address technological issues/goals.
(e) Developing and authorising budget for positive discrimination of services.
(f) Focus on organic planning (i.e. learning organisation), articulating the groups' vision for the organisation, which includes institutional leadership.

In this context, the Canarian regional government funded a research project for reliable quality improvement: the 'Faculty Professional Development' (FPD) (Villar & Alegre, 2006a) as a regional staff training programme. This two-year project (2004-2006) was an effort to improve the quality teaching and assessment expertise to support internal quality management systems so that teaching personnel make full use of quality competences for delivering and analysing formative programmes comparable in standard in the two universities.

SETTING THE STAGE

FPD is composed of descriptions and evaluations of blended training courses, usually represented as case studies. FPD online courses focus on two general themes: Curriculum and Teaching Capacities (CTC) and Quality Assurance in Formative Programmes (QAFP) with varying degrees of specificity, and various monographic and particularly mini-courses (for example, short-time courses about evaluative capacity, student and faculty portfolios, educational innovations, reflective teaching, and so on). (The QAFP case study is discussed in more detail in the case description section of this chapter.)

The main e-development course focus on is how faculty members can be supported in gaining an excellent university perspective on university quality teaching management. Other case study courses have focused on CTC in other Spanish universities (Villar & Alegre, 2007). Generally speaking, e-development courses begin with a face-to-face workshop and online content modules that are one of the moodle types of course organisation (see the open source software project that has no licensing costs in www.moodle.org). All e-development courses use the moodle platform for documentation and knowledge management, as, for example, in one physics course (Martín-Blas & Serrano-Fernández, 2009).

The first effort at ensuring FPD quality was to develop an e-development model that had six dimensions, namely:

(a) Ensuring coherence in the structure of the online course (i.e. goals, content concepts, and quizzes).
(b) Ensuring the quality of the web platform (e.g. study materials to be put on the web: http://gid.us.es:8083).
(c) Encouraging faculty to test the web-based materials (i.e. organisation, materials, tutoring and communication system, feedback, etc.).
(d) Giving confidence to faculty members that online course adjustments are made during the training process as appropriate (i.e. facilities, teaching management, assessment, and so on).
(e) Reflecting as the heart of good practice (in other words, it shows the professoriate how to demonstrate 'evaluation capacity building' through reflective writing).
(f) Obtaining a certificate. Awarded upon completion of online course requirements.

In moodle, all course information is arranged in modules. Moodle features used in FPD courses are:

(a) Virtual areas for group work, which are easier to manoeuvre (fewer clicks).
(b) Self-assessment quizzes and online testing (in other words, faculty could enter answers multiple times without penalty, and are able to obtain immediate feedback and hints until the due date).
(c) Sequential learning objects, which are customised by date/time programming for lessons and learning activities (for instance, the 'Human resources' lesson and its seven activities lasted a week).
(d) Tracked specific faculty members' activities (thus providing them with individualised feedback easily for all assignments. Mentors return graded assignments to faculty). It is also easier to track each faculty member's activity in class, when and how often parts of class accessed, or from where a faculty member accessed the course.
(e) Register attitude votes (a built-in scale for each learning activity or weekly lesson is included).
(f) Glossary (i.e. it contains more than 100 educational terms and over 500 reference articles).
(g) Survey (e.g. 'Perceptions of Teaching Success Inventory (PTSI)'.
(h) Discussion forums (i.e. asynchronous communication to discuss specific issues, such as the so-called theme 'Critical analysis of an internal formative programme evaluation').
(i) Chat communication functionality (e.g. synchronous dialogue between the mentors and faculty members at a scheduled weekly slot).
(j) Links to external web pages (one serving as a pattern was the following: http://www.wmich.edu/evalctr/checklists).
(k) Quick mail (in other words, it allows emailing all or selected faculty teachers in a given course with attachments and a history).

FPD Management Philosophy is a system of minimum principles for guiding e-development practical affairs in QAFP. As FPD designers, we contend that faculty members' professional development is composed of a core of quality features, instructors' learning experiences and conceptual frameworks, based upon research and policy documents (Desimone, 2009). We hypothesise

Figure 1. FPD management philosophy

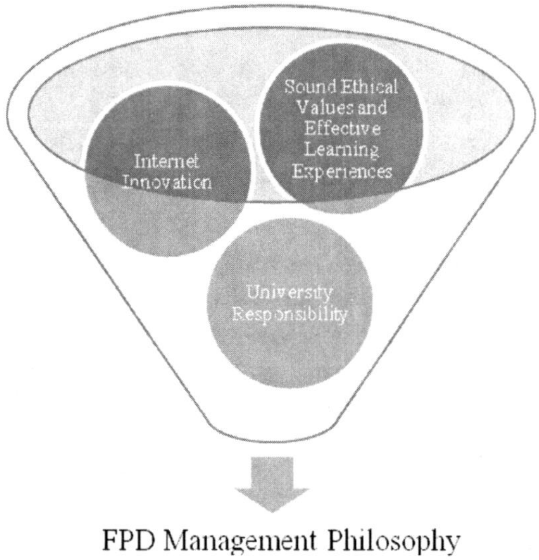

that the standards of evidence concerning FPD effectiveness should use the core features we describe herein. The social, technological and institutional e-development core quality attributes are summarised in Figure 1.

(a) *Sound Ethical Values and Effective Learning Experiences.* We describe FPD in QAFP as an array of activities that are intended primarily to prepare staff members for improved performance in present or future roles of assessment capacities. It also counts as appropriate documentation of university formative programme knowledge (books and articles). Training mentors interact with university and agency staff agents that reflect fair and honest professional development knowledge and attitudes. University and agency staff agents' course performance is reviewed, and feedback is immediately provided. Also, financial report evidence relates to management activities, processes and impact evaluation indicators. Educational considerations and technological software and strategies for university students with mild to moderate developmental disabilities are included as course aims and content. Finally, the complex, interactive and formal faculty learning opportunities are explained by measuring critical features: assessment criteria or content focus.

(b) *Internet Innovation.* Staff members ordinarily face Internet challenges (e.g. time schedule for courses is usually long). In QAFP, staff members need from ten to eleven weeks to complete the training programme. One of the personal issues in online training courses is technology accessibility and literacy. Some mature and untenured professors and agency staff members are unable to develop online materials, navigate in the Internet, and deliver well-designed online activities and appropriate messages in online communication experiences. Consequently, we provided demo guides and tutorials in QAFP. We proposed situated and cognitive views of learning in two assessment forums. Also, we suggested that social learning was based on personal discourses and scientific disciplines (i.e. community of practice). FPD in QAFP was temporarily an informal learning community that acted as a mechanism for faculty growth and development.

(c) *University Responsibility.* There is social and commercial pressure to use online components in courses, assuming student learning benefits. Also, some philosophical controversies are under consideration, such as the commodification of knowledge perspective or the automation of instruction. FPD keeps differences in course formats, according to staff members' diagnosed needs. Also, faculty and staff members use FPD in QAFP to reflect on content and instructional practices. To understand faculty and staff members' learning, we assume that the learning processes are an individual active construction and a matter of enculturation into the expected quality society. Specifically, we contend that institutional support for further online teaching acceptance and continued participation in e-development FPD courses must be fostered. This type of FPD in QAFP took the form of mentoring, co-teaching and group discussions.

In one of the QAFP course all the respondents were full-time faculty at the two public Canarian Universities: eight from the first university (38.1%), six from the second university (28.6%) and seven contracted personnel of the ACECAU (38.1%). Twelve instructors had a doctorate (57.1%) and eight (38.1%) a bachelor's degree and only one had a lower different degree. Three (or 14.3%) held the rank of full professor, and seven (33.3%) held other rank as a contract appointment, reflecting the fact that a large number of participants held a contract status. Teaching experience ranged from nothing to more than nine years. Of the respondents, thirteen (61.9%) had three years of experience, and six (28.6%) between four and six years of experience. When these disciplines were collapsed into scientific areas, five participants (23.8%) taught in the social sciences; three (14.3%) of them in technical sciences and health care sciences, while 33.3% were personnel of the ACECAU. Participants taught disciplines in twelve knowledge areas.

Nine participants (42.9%) indicated their programme evaluation preparation was rated as low, and fifteen (71.4%) indicated that their practical experience in European Convergence was very low. Ten participants followed the course at home (47.6%), eight at work (38.1%), and three in other places (14.3%). We used personal data as independent variables in analyses.

CASE DESCRIPTION

Technology Concerns

The practice of e-development actions is based upon information transformation that has learning values for stakeholders. Consultations with colleagues at the two Canarian universities, and our own FPD project experiences in other Spanish universities, form the basis of the list of technology-related concerns summarised in three codes below:

(a) *Organisation concern.* University and agency staff members perceive the use of technologies (i.e. web-based course management systems) as an extra teaching burden. Whereas all forms of high-quality teaching require mastery of the discipline and practice, technology-based teaching and learning are particularly time-demanding; in parallel with this concern, staff members demand the provision of sufficient time for participation in online actions. From the ICT viewpoint, the social and cultural contexts of two Canarian universities have not conceptualised and theorised the histories and discourses of multiple media, computer technologies, research methodologies, and epistemological positions concerning the digital representations of reality. Management teams are now being committed to improving learning and using ICTs. Leaders are modelling the process of collaboration among disciplines, across departments and colleges and within the community. This professional worry is also supported by empirical findings (Nijhuis & Collis, 2003; Galanouli, Murphy & Gardner, 2004).

(b) *Infrastructure concern.* ICT equipment and media resources should reflect the diverse nature of the learning community. There are several aspects to this individual concern. E-development, like e-learning, typically involves substantial financial investments in infrastructure. Technological resources are distributed to departments following administrative processes, which are sometimes inefficient and frustrating. Equipment also needs annual maintenance costs, and total replacement of hardware every four years or fewer, which means an additional budgetary concern. E-development is a new environment of self-renewal, and activities need to be realised mainly in various and different community contexts (i.e. home, university, different Canarian islands, foreign countries, etc.). This can occur not only with staff members who are geographically distanced from the university and might not have access to high-speed Internet, but also staff on campus who might not have laptops or cannot access overcrowded labs. This professional frustration is also supported by empirical research reports (Nijhuis & Collis, 2003; Galanouli, Murphy & Gardner, 2004; Ajjan & Hartshorne, 2008). Faculty demands good technical support for making up-to-date resources available. Faculty needs access to the plethora of online resources and support services of institutions. In many e-development courses, there is reluctance to use learning technologies in effective pedagogical training practice, because maintaining driver licence agreements and security procedures to safeguard available resources is complex and patching software vulnerabilities is tiring. These hardware and software management tasks have become even more burdensome with the use of technology in e-learning and e-training than they were with traditional forms of teaching professional development (Galanouli, Murphy, & Gardner, 2004).

(c) *Personal concern.* It is timely to examine e-development trainees' ICT needs in order to ensure that faculty professional e-development supports the integration of media and technology programmes across all university curriculum areas. Individual faculty needs and levels of ICT competence depend on many factors, the most important being 'attitudes to ICT' (Galanouli, Murphy & Gardner, 2004, p. 66), and Internet literacy. As Hamilton & Feenberg (2005) pointed out: 'Even where networked educational technologies are concerned - technologies that can and do support human interaction - the tendency has been to understand them in terms of the representational capacities of the computer rather than as redefining or resituating these capacities in the context of new forms of mediated communication' (p. 104). When faculty members believe that e-learning is working better than F2F (face-to-face) instruction, a 'refocusing' stage of personal concern happens. Also, when needs for new and renovated facilities are expressed by staff members, then ICT renewal seems to start. Finally, faculty is concerned about the intellectual property rights of online materials. Questions such as 'who will have access to lesson information?' are another obvious and important concern.

(d) *Curriculum concern.* Computer/technology competency continuums should be integrated with classroom instruction in all college curriculum areas in a flexible delivery model for different students' meta-cognitive competences and learning styles (Galanouli, Murphy, & Gardner, 2004), owing to the fact that 'analytics performed better in the long-page format than the wholistics' (Tallent-Runnels, Thomas, Lan, Cooper, Ahern, Shaw & Liu, 2006, p. 110). Interplay between course design, delivery in computer labs or distance contexts, and user characteristics refines e-learning and level of use. Curriculum materials are not semi-automated educational 'products' (Hamilton & Feenberg, 2005, p. 114). Determination of the authentic activity for students implies avoiding routinised and customary practices; contrarily, it assumes 'increasing refinement of strategies' (i.e. the teaching methodology continuously differentiates cognitive actions, from simple to complex, or solves problems) (Vovides, Sanchez-Alonso, Mitropoulou & Nickmans, 2007,

p. 71). Nevertheless, how to achieve the goal of introducing students to disciplines' complexities is a real teaching and learning concern (Bruning, Siwatu, Liu, PytlikZillig, Horn, Sic & Carlson, 2008). For example, the design resources for arts-based disciplines offer numerous theories, methods, and evaluative principles for the creation of texts. How to embody the students' emotional experiences and other learning devices (e.g. questionnaires, interview transcripts, test scores, video and audio data, computer logs) in a learning portfolio is, however, a 'direct concern of interface design' (Voithofer, 2005, p. 10). (This thought has occurred to us in FPD portfolio mini-courses given at the first university: art faculty instructors were concerned with uploading art artefacts to data bases, and were worried about new artistic knowledge construction.)

(e) *Social and legal concerns*. Social networks may be a potential risk when personal information is posted on these sites (Ajjan & Hartshorne, 2008). When the relationship among students is cooperative and is based on common values and mutual respect, social networks are desirable. QAFP courses are also concerned with legal requirements. This approach is reasonable because they are planned and organised around preset guidelines and measurable standards. Moreover, QAFP courses are connected to policy issues related to the use of computers and the Internet. Specially, FPD courses have concentrated on two areas of legal concern: access to effective communication by all people, and legal issues regarding integrity violations: disclosure (i.e. violations of privacy and confidentiality, electronic communication and fairness, free speech in cyberspace, etc.), copying (i.e. violations of intellectual property on the Internet, copyrights, etc.), modifying (i.e. unauthorised modification of data), and masquerading (e.g. activity or existence of someone under false pretences such as being the course service mentor or provider, online dispute resolution, or other litigation).

Technology Components

Quality Assurance in Formative Programmes (QAFP) is a web-based case study instruction supported by the attributes and resources of the Internet. QAFP teaching strategies that utilise the moodle platform (http://gid.us.es:8083) can be classified according to several categories, as outlined in a-b below.

(a) *Lesson or standard rational framework.* The moodle lesson is a way to come into contact with the European Foundation for Quality Management (EFQM) standard concepts – supported by primary courseware that presents information. The course is structured around six criteria and twelve lessons or standards. Each lesson or standard follows a constructivist perspective. Constructivism is an approach to university learning founded on the assumption that, by reflecting on our teaching experiences, we build our own understanding of the university world we live in (McAlpine, Weston, Beauchamp, Wiseman & Beauchamp, 1999; Rogers, 2001). Thus, each lesson is a deliberate and purposeful act, which is formed by putting four parts together. We constructed each part as a piece of a four-stage reflective cycle as shown in Figure 2.

a. Functional analysis (that is, anticipatory reflection) is an instructional stage that claims that assessment thoughts are organised, criteria are consistent, and readers may come up with insights about assessment standards.
b. Experiential learning (i.e. thoughtful action with reflection) is the process

Figure 2. Lesson or standard rational framework

of making meaning from direct or vicarious experience.

c. Reflection as meditation (e.g. reactive reflection) or the philosophical reflection on the relationship between causal determinism and reactive attitudes.
d. Compromise construction (i.e. proactive reflection) is a reflection for action or the outcome of the previous types of reflection.

Other researchers have also considered stage cycles for treating adult practitioners as learners (Schön, 1987). Another example is the cyclic framework that describes three stages of learning associated with resources: 'conceptualisation', 'construction' and 'integration' (Littlejohn, Falconer & Mcgill, 2008, p. 758), which represents contact with concepts, the building of new knowledge, and the externalising of accurate performance. Again, grounded on experiential learning (Kolb, 1984) and inquiry-based, the QAFP course is an innovative approach for the design and delivery of online learning.

Each evaluative capacity has the same intratextual coherence: it offers pedagogical theories, case studies, proposals for tasks, and a range of resources to enable a participant to reflect and build their own continuous assessment. Each evaluative capacity is associated with its corresponding evaluative model, with thick or deep concepts, in order to solve the underlining assumptions of any given teaching programme action. The learning cycle, as an intratextual invariant, belongs to the QAFP online course discourse and runs concurrently with the twelve course lessons or standards.

(b) *Substantive strategies*. Substantive strategies are interventions that deal directly with training issues. They imply that QAFP critical issues support the theoretical analysis of the EFQM processes. Therefore, the prototype QAFP is an adaptation of the EFQM model, a root from which come the evaluative criteria. In QAFP we put emphasis on how faculty and agency staff members learn and practise evaluation capacities, and declare its specific aim to be as follows: to assess whether faculty and agency staff members learn evaluation capacities to analyse and improve formative programmes. Thus, we remark an important aspect of professionalism in the field of evaluation. As Modarresi, Newman, & Abolafia (2001) write: 'There is an obvious need for theoretical underpinnings when studying the profession of programme evaluation' (p.10). Next, we report the strategies developed in QAFP:

a. *Discussing*. Faculty and agency members examine by argument, comment, and comparing perspectives with other participants, who are tasked with reading common case study data, evaluation of theoretical meta-analyses and discussion of perspectives. Participants use e-mail and chat software for discussion purposes.

b. *Mentoring, supporting participants.* We have acted as mentors to review participants' activities and provide feedback or scaffold processes. We interviewed participants partnered with and helping one another succeed; multi-directional communications were used (i.e. faculty to faculty, and mentor to faculty). It helped to have moodle platform e-mail, synchronous chat rooms, and forums for file sharing and written critiques.

c. *Accessing tutorials with exercises, quizzes, questions, online drill-and-practice.* Participants reviewed content material online, and then accessed interactive exercises to practise or apply the material presented. Each participant read one lesson or standard and solved seven learning tasks for a week. For example, in order to learn standard 3, course participants needed to read two book chapters: 5 (Villar & Alegre, 2004) and 3 (Villar & Alegre, 2006b), and to follow one online hypertext lesson. Also, seven activity tasks were required (that is, generic tasks organised around preparation, monitoring, communicating, and grading). As an example, we cite the following problem-solving preparation task activity: users read an improvement plan report, and apply a twelve-item improvement control list to the report in order to identify and quantify improvement textual evidences.

d. *Exploring real-world cases or evaluation plans.* Course participants explore real cases; use web data (e.g. intern programme evaluation reports, external programme evaluation reports) to practise decision-making or utilise virtual simulations with participants testing personal hypotheses or assessment plans.

e. *Looking for, collecting, organising, and synthesising online information (research).* Participants are specifically tasked with accomplishing some end goal with the resources (e.g. compile, sort, or answer probing questions).

Management and Organisational Concerns

Here we analyze central issues for the QAFP field in the domain of managing:

(a) *Evaluation Capacity Building.* In QAFP, evaluation capacity is the goal of the training course (Table 1). We frame evaluation capacity within a three-component framework:

   a. It involves developing general awareness, skills, resources, and infrastructures to support university internal and external formative programme evaluation.

   b. External evaluation agencies, like ACECAU, see evaluation capacity as a core function. This sort of institution wants to use and develop an intellectual human capital of staff and promote evaluation knowledge inquiry and evaluative ethical behaviour. Consequently, evaluation capacity is an organisational responsibility.

   c. University faculty is intrinsically motivated to learn the evaluation capacity, because it has to use evaluation standards to select and accredit university personnel for promotion and tenure. Also, it conducts quality postgraduate degrees following EFQM models and procedures.

Building knowledge, beliefs and competences of faculty and agency members in evaluation is often viewed as FPD. Few faculty members have a background in evaluation, though many are

Table 1. QAFP criteria and standards

Criterion I. Teaching Programme
Standard 1: How are the objectives of a formative programme designed?
Standard 2: How is the curriculum flexibility adjusted to the objectives of a formative programme?
Criterion II. Teaching Organisation
Standard 3: How is the continuous formative programme improvement planned?
Standard 4: How is effective communication established?
Criterion III. Human Resources
Standard 5: How are the academic personnel involved in investigation, development and innovation activities?
Standard 6: How is the academic personnel's teaching assessed?
Criterion IV. Material Resources
Standard 7: How are the library and documental archives made more convenient and accessible for the formative programme process?
Standard 8: How are media and resources adapted to the formative programme?
Criterion V. Formative process
Standard 9: How are student competences developed in the teaching-learning process?
Standard 10: What is the teaching-learning methodology?
Standard 11: How is the student guided and motivated in a tutorship within the formative programme process?
Criterion VI. Results
Standard 12. How is the student's satisfaction measured in a formative programme process?

experts in discipline research. Given the diversity of university faculty and agency members, we propose a type of curriculum menu that meets all participating staff members' needs. We consider that evaluation capacity learning is best integrated into practice when standards are understood by all and when the training process includes time for reflection.

Other authors have arranged the set of evaluation competences into six distinct categories. Thus, Stevahn, King, Ghere & Minnema (2005) have proposed the following six evaluation competences, namely: '(a) professional practice, (b) systematic inquiry, (c) situational analysis, (d) project management, (e) reflective practice, and (f) interpersonal competence' (p. 52).

(b) *Structural Aspects*. QAFP is composed of disturbing issues for participants - knowledge tests about the twelve standards - reflecting the validity of this core feature (i.e. how course evaluative structure is aligned with the mastery of standards). Managing QAFP evaluation towards explicating a professional learning practice and conducting evaluation of learning and programme is focused around three purposes:
   a. Disentangling participants' assessment needs through a questionnaire. In this respect, other authors have considered questionnaires as effective tools for diagnosing needs. Thus, Ballantyne, Borthwick & Packer (2000) designed a questionnaire to ask teachers to comment on the major problems they experienced and their professional development needs.
   b. Summarising the formal structure of the online course through the *QAFP Questionnaire* applied to each standard; therefore, participants respond to twelve questionnaires to capture their attitude change towards the course quality (for example, the item 'the standard is relevant to an evaluator's formation').
   c. Knowing participants' learning by means of twelve *standard self-assessment* multiple-choice questionnaires.

(c) *QAFP Managing Implementation*. The evaluation standards synthesise various types of evaluation management knowledge (i.e. management of evaluation propositional knowledge, principles of evaluation practice, etc.); understand a faculty instructor or an agency member as an evaluation manager (i.e. an individual who is able to answer questions such as 'what must I do today in the evaluation process?'), and enhance the practice of evaluation managing (i.e. evaluation management expertise, or the individual belief that an individual is managing evaluation issues as a manager). In this way, QAFP realised a technical specification of an evaluation model for adult learners moving from management (i.e. abstract and theoretical evaluation concepts) to managing (i.e. concrete, practical and specific situations, cases and sceneries). The effective managing of evaluation means the practical praxis of theory, concepts, and action in the service of the organisational mission. In managing evaluation as in e-learning, faculty and agency members, 'need assistance both during the development of the courses and during delivery' (Tallent-Runnels, Thomas, Lan, Cooper, Ahern, Shaw, & Liu, 2006, p. 114). This evaluation-managing vision was realised with the help of task activities and resources (i.e. lessons, resource directories and evaluation repositories available in a wide variety of formats), authority, and time. QAFP included 84 task activities (analysis of descriptive reports, identification of good practices, checking standards, etc.).

(d) *Adaptive Assessment System*. QAFP structure is engaged in value-guided action. Consequently, it involves faculty members in eloquent representation of assessment actions. Participants are tied to contexts in either simulated or real worlds to convey certainty about the learning of standards that are essential evaluation competences to describe, judge and communicate a formative programme. These evaluation competences are learned through formative feedback, because 'feedback that has negative effects on learning is not formative' (Shute, 2008, p. 156). We assumed that the degree of ownership felt by course participants was likely to increase when we adapted resources for use within the specific QAFP context. The verification of the responses of multiple-choice tests is done automatically. In one QAFP course, we responded immediately to faculty and agency members' 1,654 task activities. As a general rule, assessment produces feedback for the other preceding FPD principles.

(e) *Quality Assurance Process Use*. There are changes in thinking and behaviour whether at the individual or organisational level as a consequence of participating in QAFP courses. The validity of the evaluation competences refers to its intentional consequences for enhancing shared understanding among faculty and agency staff members about quality assurance. QAFP course participants' learning needs show that they were increasingly engaged, and that their conceptual schema changed owing to the course. The two editions of the 'Evaluation Expert' Postgrade (EEP) developed at the second university keep the same evaluation competences, although the course content and time length have been considerably modified (about 500 hours) (Alegre & Villar, 2007). Again, they were affected by their participation in the online course. Our hypothesis was that the second university in which the EEP course was delivered was the strongest predictor of evaluation process uses, as Malikowski (2008) has also predicted. Finally, the EEP included the following training process: content design, development, implementation, evaluation, and revision, as other web-based courses have outlined (Georgina & Olson, 2008).

CURRENT CHALLENGES FACING THE ORGANISATION

Given that the notion of need is a dynamic force within programme planning, our focus is the investigation of which formative programme evaluation needs are most important for faculty and agency staff members, which it is most reasonable to meet, and which should be the main priority when we determine how QAFP resources (such as mentors, facilities, and instructional methodologies) should be allocated. We emphasised the importance of faculty needs assessments to ensure that QAFP aims are pertinent to the needs of participants and are practically achievable through task activities. Therefore, we designed a questionnaire for addressing faculty and agency staff members' assessment needs. This assessment procedure has also been followed by other authors (Pololi, Dennis, Winn, & Mitchell, 2003). Although there is some debate concerning the definition of need, we used the concept of need as a gap that must be closed between the current formative programme evaluation knowledge and the highly desirable end result. This definition seems pertinent to our case study (Lenning, 1980). Consequently, we assumed the functionalist approach as philosophical orientation in faculty needs assessment. The functionalist approach is positivistic in nature and assumes that needs are identified objectively and are measurable.

(a) *First University Participants' Assessed Needs*. The focus of our needs-assessment study was on the institution: individual clients (faculty and agency staff members). The types of needs were concerned with the broad assessment standards presented in Table 1. The questionnaire asked faculty to rate each item in terms of the importance of learning the skill for themselves. The twelve-item online *Faculty Needs Assessment Questionnaire* (FNAQ) was answered on the first course day. A five-point scale was used to rate the items, where 1 = 'not at all important for me' and 5 = 'very necessary for me'. The SPSS programme was used to support data analysis. Frequencies and percentages were calculated for each question.

In our university study, participants needed professional development in all formative programme evaluation capacities (Villar & Alegre, 2007). The highest percentage (90.5%) indicated that all participants believed that the standard 'how is the academic personnel's teaching assessed?' was very relevant to their professional and academic needs. Participants considered other assessment capacities as very important. They perceived, however, that the assessment standard 'how to measure student satisfaction in a formative process?' was of little priority for them. Half of the participants indicated that their formative programme evaluation was low.

(b) *Second University Participants' Assessment Commitment*. Distance education has become a fast-growing delivery method in higher education at the second university. In the EEP developed at the second university, quality assurance was the training goal for faculty instructors. At the time of this EEP the 'verification' of degrees and master's degrees to be introduced was the new buzzword at Spanish universities. Agencies like ACECAU are selecting university teachers who ultimately make up the evaluation committees to undertake the degree and master's degree evaluation reports. This small-scale initiative is worth 20 European Credit Transfer System (ECTS) credits, and involves the creation of faculty portfolios.

Faculty wanted to succeed in EEP. In fact, for university teachers the EEP was a study course about formative programme evaluation. Therefore, we wanted to identify the areas of faculty concern, in order to determine the relative priorities of needs and to design solutions. Therefore, need-assessment was composed of three phases:

a. Pre-assessment. It involved finding out what faculty already knew about formative programme evaluation standards.

b. Needs assessment. Conducting a study and determining the relative priorities of faculty members' needs.
c. Post-assessment. Designing and implementing solutions within the EEP course and university organisation frameworks and the results of the solution(s) (Figure 3).

During the pre-assessment phase of this EEP course, an overview of the content was considered for university board members and executives. The initial decision was to start with professional staff who would be expected to implement formative programme evaluation practices. The need-assessment survey also contained a Likert-type scale. Figure 3 shows the different aspects of needs (before and after the EEP course).

We also assessed faculty commitment in evaluation and created a thirteen-item instrument that provided functionality for this type of course. The commitment of faculty to formative programme assessment is valuable to higher education institutions. The respondents were closely involved in the EEP's e-learning aspects and it would be realistic to assume that their answers were biased towards a deep interest in evaluation competences. Faculty's need assessment showed adequately detailed information to help faculty consider the strengths and weaknesses of specific assessment standards and plan revisions of the EEP course. As evaluators of e-training courses, we were challenged to find a comprehensive evaluative framework that embraced the faculty perceptions in a university context (Alegre & Villar, 2007).

Figure 3 identifies and documents assessment competences needed/required for participants, particularly: 'How are the objectives of a formative programme designed?' (Standard 1), 'How is an effective communication established?' (Standard 4), 'How are student competences developed in the teaching-learning process?' (Standard 9), 'What is the teaching-learning methodology?' (Standard 10), and 'How is the student's satisfaction measured in a formative programme process?' (Standard 12). It maintains the importance of a current inventory of basic assessment standards, and, finally, it shows the need for results to determine where assessment training is still needed.

Figure 3. Faculty members' need assessment before and after the EEP course

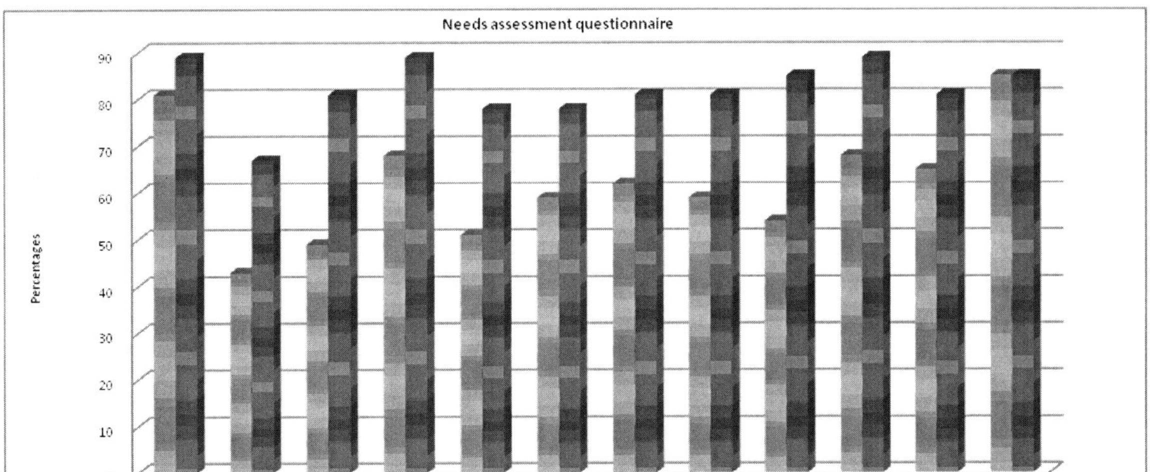

	Standard 1	Standard 2	Standard 3	Standard 4	Standard 5	Standard 6	Standard 7	Standard 8	Standard 9	Standard 10	Standard 11	Standard 12
Before	81	43	49	68	51	59	62	59	54	68	65	85
After	89	67	81	89	78	78	81	81	85	89	81	85

The comments reported should be used to a great or very great extent by quality assurance and accreditation bodies and agencies like ACECAU.

(c) *The Mentoring Function is Worthy of Evaluation.* As mentors, we made a valuable contribution to the FPD. E-mentoring, however, needs university personnel to be self-aware, knowing own and others' traits, feelings, and behaviours, technologically competent and knowledgeable about online strategies. E-mentoring is of basic significance when attempting to answer assessment task-oriented needs and in addressing issues of assessment to produce solutions. Gilbreath, Rose, & Dietrich (2008, p. 379) conceived mentoring as a complex activity and mentoring assessment instruments as a key technical endeavour: 'Human resource development (HRD) practitioners have the potential to increase the quality and effectiveness of mentoring by taking a purposeful evaluative approach'. We put into practice several e-mentoring competences in QAFP, such as providing corrective feedback, opening doors to new evaluation models, managing formative programme evaluation risks, and instructing/developing assessment standards. E-mentoring is an interactive and dynamic process, and instruments that focus on both quality and frequency of core competences should be developed. Thus, Villar & Alegre (2006a) practised a simulated mentor-protégé relationship that enhanced the online course effects. Nevertheless, a relevant educational concern for practitioners and online developers remains: the validity of e-mentoring instruments.

(d) *QAFP's Impact on Higher Education Institutions and on the Learning Community.* The study of the consequences of online training, or more specifically of QAFP, represents a significant portion of the body of our own research on evaluation (Alegre & Villar, 2006). QAFP's impact can be measured in multiple ways, intentionality or 'process use' being possible targets for faculty e-development (Patton, 2007). There are more training outcomes (Brown & Reed, 2002). As an example, the immediate effect of QAFP should be to change faculty and agency staff members' beliefs and assessment competences, although the ultimate outcome is student learning. Nevertheless, we discuss the outcomes that might occur from involvement in QAFP:

a. Enhancing assessment understandings about the course aims among participants (i.e. formative programme improvement as main objective).
b. Increasing participants' commitment with learning (i.e. regular, systematic measurement of formative programme standards).
c. Online content and organisational development (i.e. evaluation logic model as key online course component).

SOLUTIONS AND RECOMMENDATIONS

In this section we present some reflections on possible strategies for targeting those challenges.

(a) *Strategic E-development QAFP Guide.* The following will help to give a more objective view of the strategies that most online QAFP course planners have to choose from. The following strategies may be helpful with online evaluation course change process:

a. Provide trainees with the flexibility to choose among different QAFP training delivery methods (i.e. blended learning is a feasible form for FPD) (Owston, Wideman, Murphy & Lupshenyuk, 2008).

b. Consider combining different online training methods (for example, developing effective e-learning activities within the same QAFP, such as playing roles in evaluation groups) (Watkins, 2005).
c. Make available embedded QAFP training, that is, the more contextual learning is to the job or task, the more a faculty or agency staff member is motivated (i.e. providing learning tasks related to formative evaluation programmes; assessing learning tasks and giving immediate feedback) (Dunlap, 2005).
d. Design and deliver QAFP training in core and essential assessment competences (i.e. offer a combination of skills, abilities, and knowledge needed to perform an assessment tasks in a course model) (Stevahn, King, Ghere & Minnema, 2005).
e. Build QAFP courses using reusable learning theories (i.e. behaviourism, information processing, social cognitive, and constructivism) (Christensen, 2008).
f. Establish collaborative learning relationships in e-mentoring QAFP (i.e., communities of evaluation practice) (Gabriel & Kaufield, 2008).

(b) *QAFP Evaluation Capacity Building (ECB).* Its goal is defined as supporting a QAFP's capacity to (1) plan, implement, and supervise online courses, resources and supports; (2) access, and use assessment knowledge standards and skills; and (3) build consciousness for self-evaluation as an organisational environment that promotes improvement outcomes (leadership, incentives, structures, and policies and procedures) (Taylor-Powell & Boyd, 2008).

Figure 4. Conceptual framework of QAFP as an E-development FPD system

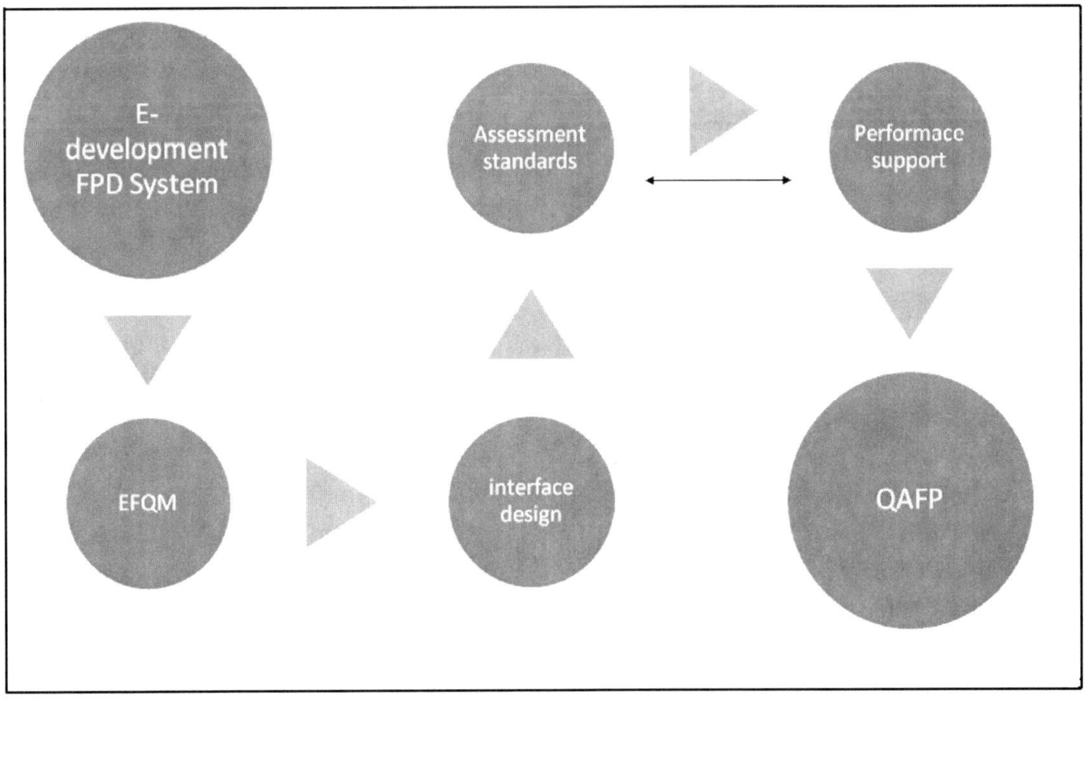

(c) *Guidelines for Higher Education Institutions*. In Higher Education institutions, QAFP courses can also guide decision-making:
   a. Good quality teaching programme evaluation is made possible by well-educated faculty and agency personnel (Ghere, King, Stevahn, & Minnema, 2006; Knight, Tait, & Yorke, 2006).
   b. Make full use of assessment competences for stakeholders such as academic staff and administrators, and take full responsibility for delivering higher education formative programmes comparable in standard.
   c. Develop and maintain networks and partnerships of quality teaching programme evaluation to facilitate the process of recognition.
   d. Provide information on faculty performance improvement (Fang, 2007).
   e. Incorporate faculty incentives to adopt models and procedures that will attain the administration's mission (Comeaux & McKenna-Byington, 2003).

(d) *Our online QAFP Self-assessment Approach.* Let us see what we can identify as QAFP's strengths:
   1. Emphasis on outcomes (i.e. participants' learning).
   2. Formative programme improvement as primary motivator.
   3. Makes some assessment standards practical.
   4. Time frame for assessment standard implementation in months.
   5. EFQM model as important assurance tool.
   6. Emphasises importance of participants' daily progress.
   7. Sufficient links to quality tools and references.
   8. Accessible, ubiquitous format.
   9. Intelligible representations in terms of language, etc.

Also, QAFP's limitations are:

a) Underestimated challenges of outcome measurement for faculty and agency staff members.
b) Too little guidance on how ACECAU should use data.
c) Too little guidance on using participants' qualitative narratives to identify and illustrate learning outcomes.

Finally, Figure 4 seeks to differentiate among concepts used in this chapter by depicting their interrelationships with quality actions. FPD is a research project. EFQM is the starting-point of quality assurance. Interface design refers to the assembly of training features. Assessment standards are the content. Performance support is the mentoring of learning activities. QAFP is the logic model for online learning of assessment competences.

REFERENCES

Aelterman, A. (2006). Sets of Standards for External Quality Assurance Agencies: A comparison. *Quality in Higher Education*, *12*(3), 227–233. doi:10.1080/13538320601050996

Ajjan, H., & Hartshorne, R. (2008). Investigating faculty decisions to adopt Web 2.0 technologies: Theory and empirical tests. *The Internet and Higher Education*, *11*(2), 71–80. doi:10.1016/j.iheduc.2008.05.002

Alegre, O. M., & Villar, L. M. (2006). Evaluación de la formación en línea del profesorado universitario. Evaluation of online faculty development. Madrid: Visión libros.

Alegre, O. M., & Villar, L. M. (2007). *Experto Universitario en Evaluación de la Calidad en la Enseñanza Superior. Segunda Edición*. Expert Degree of Evaluation at ULPGC. Unpublished Evaluation Report.

Ballantyne, R., Borthwick, J., & Packer, J. (2000). Beyond Student Evaluation of Teaching: Identifying and Addressing Academic Staff Development Needs. *Assessment & Evaluation in Higher Education, 25*(3), 221–236. doi:10.1080/713611430

Bergen Communiqué. (2005). *The European Higher Education Area: Achieving the goals: Communiqué of the Conference of European Ministers Responsible for Higher Education, Bergen, 19-20 May 2005*. Retrieved May 10, 2009, from http://www.bologna-bergen2005.no/Docs/00-Main_doc/050520_Bergen_Communique.pdf

Bologna Declaration. (1999). *The European Higher Education Area: The Bologna Declaration of 19 June 1999. Joint Declaration of the European Ministers of Education*. Retrieved May 10, 2009, from http://www.bologna-berlin2003.de/pdf/bologna_declaration.pdf

Brown, R. E., & Reed, C. S. (2002). An Integral Approach to Evaluating Outcome Evaluation Training. *The American Journal of Evaluation, 23*(1), 1–17.

Bruning, R., Siwatu, K.O., & Liu, X., PytlikZillig, L.M., Horn, C., Sic, S., & Carlson, D. (2008). Introducing teaching cases with face-to-face and computer-mediated discussion: Two multi-classroom quasi-experiments. *Contemporary Educational Psychology, 33*(2), 299–326. doi:10.1016/j.cedpsych.2006.11.002

Canarian Agency for the University Evaluation and Accreditation (ACECAU). (n.d.). Retrieved May 7, 2009, from http://www.acecau.org/en/actividades.html

Christensen, T. K. (2008). The Role of Theory in Instructional Design: Some Views of an ID practitioner. *Performance Improvement, 47*(4), 25–32. doi:10.1002/pfi.199

Comeaux, P., & McKenna-Byington, E. (2003). Computer-mediated communication in online and conventional classrooms: some implications for instructional design and professional development programmes. *Innovations in Education and Teaching International, 40*(4), 348–355. doi:10.1080/1470329032000128387

Desimone, L. M. (2009). Improving Impact Studies of Teachers' Professional Development: Toward Better Conceptualizations and Measures. *Educational Researcher, 38*(3), 181–199. doi:10.3102/0013189X08331140

Dunlap, J. C. (2005). Workload reduction in online courses: Getting some shuteye. *Performance Improvement, 44*(5), 18–25. doi:10.1002/pfi.4140440507

European Association for Quality Assurance in Higher Education (ENQA). *Current Trends in European Quality Assurance*. Retrieved May 7, 2009, from http://www.enqa.eu/

Fang, B. (2007). A performance-based development model for online faculty. *Performance Improvement, 46*(5), 17–24.

Gabriel, M. A., & Kaufield, K. J. (2008). Reciprocal mentorship: an effective support for online instructors. *Mentoring & Tutoring: Partnership in Learning, 16*(3), 311–327. doi:10.1080/13611260802233480

Galanouli, D., Murphy, C., & Gardner, J. (2004). Teachers' perceptions of the effectiveness of ICT-competence training. *Computers & Education, 43*(1-2), 63–79. doi:10.1016/j.compedu.2003.12.005

Georgina, D. A., & Olson, M. R. (2008). Integration of technology in higher education: A review of faculty self-perceptions. *The Internet and Higher Education, 11*(1), 1–8. doi:10.1016/j.iheduc.2007.11.002

Ghere, G., King, J. A., Stevahn, L., & Minnema, J. (2006). A Professional Development Unit for Reflecting on Programme Evaluator Competences. *The American Journal of Evaluation, 27*(1), 108–123. doi:10.1177/1098214005284974

Gilbreath, B., Rose, G. L., & Dietrich, K. E. (2008). Assessing mentoring in organizations: an evaluation of commercial mentoring instruments. *Mentoring & Tutoring: Partnership in Learning, 16*(4), 379–393. doi:10.1080/13611260802433767

Hamilton, E., & Feenberg, A. (2005). The Technical Codes of Online Education. *Techné: Research in Philosophy and Technology, 9*(1), 97–123.

Harvey, L. (2006). Impact of Quality Assurance: Overview of a discussion between representatives of external quality assurance agencies. *Quality in Higher Education, 12*(3), 287–290. doi:10.1080/13538320601051010

Knight, P., Tait, J., & Yorke, M. (2006). The professional learning of teachers in higher education. *Studies in Higher Education, 31*(3), 319–339. doi:10.1080/03075070600680786

Kolb, D. A. (1984). Experimental learning: experience as the source of learning and development. Englewood Cliffs, NJ: Prentice Hall.

Lenning, O. T. (1980). Needs as a Basis for Academic Programme Planning. *New Directions for Institutional Research, 1980*(28), 9–25. doi:10.1002/ir.37019802803

Littlejohn, A., Falconer, I., & Mcgill, L. (2008). Characterising effective eLearning resources. *Computers & Education, 50*(3), 757–771. doi:10.1016/j.compedu.2006.08.004

Malikowski, S. R. (2008). Factors related to breadth of use in course management systems. *The Internet and Higher Education, 11*(2), 81–86. doi:10.1016/j.iheduc.2008.03.003

Martín-Blas, T., & Serrano-Fernández, S. (2009). The role of new technologies in the learning process: Moodle as a teaching tool in Physics. *Computers & Education, 52*, 35–44. doi:10.1016/j.compedu.2008.06.005

McAlpine, L., Weston, C., Beauchamp, J., Wiseman, C., & Beauchamp, C. (1999). Building a metacognitive model of reflection. *Higher Education, 37*(2), 105–131. doi:10.1023/A:1003548425626

Modarresi, S., Newman, D. L., & Abolafia, M. Y. (2001). Academic evaluators versus practitioners: alternative experiences of professionalism. *Evaluation and Program Planning, 24*, 1–11. doi:10.1016/S0149-7189(00)00041-0

National Agency for Quality Assessment and Accreditation (ANECA). *Educational Programme Assessment and Institutional Assessment.* Retrieved May 7, 2009, from http://www.aneca.es/

Nijhuis, G. G., & Collis, B. (2003). Using a web-based course-management system. An evaluation of management tasks and time implications for the instructor. *Evaluation and Program Planning, 26*, 193–201. doi:10.1016/S0149-7189(03)00005-3

Owston, R., Wideman, H., Murphy, J., & Lupshenyuk, D. (2008). Blended teacher professional development: A synthesis of three programme evaluations. *The Internet and Higher Education, 11*(3-4), 201–210. doi:10.1016/j.iheduc.2008.07.003

Patton, M. Q. (2007). Process use as usefulism. *New Directions for Evaluation, 2007*(116), 99–112. doi:10.1002/ev.246

Pololi, L. H., Dennis, K., Winn, G. M., & Mitchell, J. (2003). A Needs Assessment of Medical School Faculty: Caring for the Caretakers. *The Journal of Continuing Education in the Health Professions, 23*, 21–29. doi:10.1002/chp.1340230105

Rogers, R. R. (2001). Reflection in Higher Education: A Concept Analysis. *Innovative Higher Education, 26*(1), 37–57. doi:10.1023/A:1010986404527

Schön, D. (1987). Educating the Reflective Practitioner. San Francisco: Jossey-Bass.

Shute, V. J. (2008). Focus on Formative Feedback. *Review of Educational Research, 78*(1), 153–189. doi:10.3102/0034654307313795

Stevahn, L., King, J. A., Ghere, G., & Minnema, J. (2005). Establishing Essential Competences for Programme Evaluators. *The American Journal of Evaluation, 26*(1), 43–59. doi:10.1177/1098214004273180

Tallent-Runnels, M. K., Thomas, J. A., Lan, W. Y., Cooper, S., Ahern, T. C., Shaw, S. M., & Liu, X. (2006). Teaching Courses Online: A Review of the Research. *Review of Educational Research, 76*(1), 93–135. doi:10.3102/00346543076001093

Taylor-Powell, E., & Boyd, H. H. (2008). Evaluation capacity building in complex organizations. *New Directions for Evaluation, 2008*(120), 55–69. doi:10.1002/ev.276

Villar, L. M., & Alegre, O. M. (2004). Manual para la excelencia en la enseñanza superior, [Handbook for Excellence in Higher Education]. Madrid: McGraw-Hill.

Villar, L. M., & Alegre, O. M. (2006a). Online Faculty Development in the Canary Islands: A Study of E-mentoring. *Higher Education in Europe, 31*(1), 65–81. doi:10.1080/03797720600861243

Villar, L. M., & Alegre, O. M. (2006b). Competencias para la formación de evaluadores. [Competences for training evaluators]. Málaga, Spain: Aljibe.

Villar, L. M., & Alegre, O. M. (2007). Online Programme of Excellence Model (OPEM). *International Journal of Social Sciences (IJSS), 2* (2). Retrieved May 10, 2009, from http://www.waset.org/ijss/v2/v2-2-14.pdf

Voithofer, R. (2005). Designing New Media Education Research: The Materiality of Data, Representation, and Dissemination. *Educational Researcher, 34*(9), 3–14. doi:10.3102/0013189X034009003

Vovides, Y., Sanchez-Alonso, S., Mitropoulou, V., & Nickmans, G. (2007). The use of e-learning course management systems to support learning strategies and to improve self-regulated learning. *Educational Research Review, 2*(1), 64–74. doi:10.1016/j.edurev.2007.02.004

Watkins, R. (2005). Developing Interactive E-Learning Activities. *Performance Improvement, 44*(5), 5–7. doi:10.1002/pfi.4140440504

ADDITIONAL READING

Aisbitt, S., & Sangster, A. (2005). Using internet-based on-line assessment: A case study. *Accounting Education, 14*(4), 383–394. doi:10.1080/06939280500346011

Altschuld, J. W. (1999). The Case for a Voluntary System for Credentialing Evaluators. *The American Journal of Evaluation, 20*(3), 507–517.

Baizerman, M., & Compton, D. W. (2009). What did we learn from the case studies about managing evaluation? *New Directions for Evaluation, 2009*(121), 79–86. doi:10.1002/ev.287

Bennett, S., & Barp, D. (2008). Peer observation - a case for doing it online. *Teaching in Higher Education, 13*(5), 559–570. doi:10.1080/13562510802334871

Bruning, R., Siwatu, K.O., & Liu, X., PytlikZillig, L.M., Horn, C., Sic, S., & Carlson, D. (2008). Introducing teaching cases with face-to-face and computer-mediated discussion: Two multi-classroom quasi-experiments. *Contemporary Educational Psychology, 33*(2), 299–326. doi:10.1016/j.cedpsych.2006.11.002

Carpenter, B., & Tait, G. (2001). The rhetoric and reality of good teaching: A case study across three faculties at the Queensland University of Technology. *Higher Education*, *42*(2), 191–203. doi:10.1023/A:1017514502456

Chen, R. T.-H., Bennett, S., & Maton, K. (2008). The adaptation of Chinese international students to online flexible learning: two case studies. *Distance Education*, *29*(3), 307–323. doi:10.1080/01587910802395821

Cook, J., & Oliver, M. (2002). Designing a toolkit to support dialogue in learning. *Computers & Education*, *38*(1-3), 151–164. doi:10.1016/S0360-1315(01)00076-8

Garrote, R., & Pettersson, T. (2007). Lecturers' attitudes about the use of learning management systems in engineering education: A Swedish case study. *Australasian Journal of Educational Technology*, *23*(3), 327–349.

Hammond, M., & Wiriyapinit, M. (2005). Learning through online discussion: A case of triangulation in research. *Australasian Journal of Educational Technology*, *21*(3), 283–302.

Hara, N., & Kling, R. (2000). Student Distress in a Web–Based Distance Education Course. *Information Communication and Society*, *3*(4), 557–579. doi:10.1080/13691180010002297

Holt, D., & Challis, D. (2007). From policy to practice: One university's experience of implementing strategic change through wholly online teaching and learning. *Australasian Journal of Educational Technology*, *23*(1), 110–131.

King, K. P. (2002). Identifying success in online teacher education and professional development. *The Internet and Higher Education*, *5*, 231–246. doi:10.1016/S1096-7516(02)00104-5

Kock, N., Aiken, R., & Sandas, Ch. (2006). Isolated versus integrated case studies: A comparison in the context of teaching complex and domain-specific IT applications. *Computers & Education*, *46*(4), 446–457. doi:10.1016/j.compedu.2004.08.015

Loddington, S., Pond, K., Wilkinson, N., & Willmo, P. (2009). A case study of the development of WebPA: An online peer-moderated marking tool. *British Journal of Educational Technology*, *40*(2), 329–341. doi:10.1111/j.1467-8535.2008.00922.x

Macdonald, J., & Mcateer, E. (2003). New Approaches to Supporting Students: Strategies for Blended Learning in Distance and Campus Based Environments. *Journal of Educational Media*, *28*(2-3), 129–146. doi:10.1080/1358165032000165662

Mäkitalo, K., Häkkinen, P., Leinonen, P., & Järvela, S. (2002). Mechanisms of common ground in case-based web discussions in teacher education. *The Internet and Higher Education*, *5*(3), 247–265. doi:10.1016/S1096-7516(02)00112-4

Marriott, P. (2009). Students' evaluation of the use of online summative assessment on an undergraduate financial accounting module. *British Journal of Educational Technology*, *40*(2), 237–254. doi:10.1111/j.1467-8535.2008.00924.x

McDonald, J., McPhail, J., Maguire, M., & Millett, B. (2004). A Conceptual Model and Evaluation Process for Educational Technology Learning Resources: A Legal Case Study. *Educational Media International*, *41*(4), 287–296. doi:10.1080/09523980410001680914

McGorry, S. Y. (2002). Online, but on target? Internet-based MBA courses: A case study. *The Internet and Higher Education*, *5*(2), 167–175. doi:10.1016/S1096-7516(02)00089-1

Nichols, A. J., & Levy, Y. (2009). Empirical assessment of college student-athletes' persistence in e-learning courses: A case study of a U.S. National Association of Intercollegiate Athletics (NAIA) institution. *The Internet and Higher Education*, *12*(1), 14–25. doi:10.1016/j.iheduc.2008.10.003

Nijhuis, G. G., & Collis, B. (2003). Using a web-based course-management system. An evaluation of management tasks and time implications for the instructor. *Evaluation and Program Planning, 26*, 193–201. doi:10.1016/S0149-7189(03)00005-3

Olapiriyakul, K., & Scher, J. M. (2006). A guide to establishing hybrid learning courses: Employing information technology to create a new learning experience, and a case study. *The Internet and Higher Education, 9*(4), 287–301. doi:10.1016/j.iheduc.2006.08.001

Omeaux, P., & McKenna-Byington, E. (2003). Computer-mediated communication in online and conventional classrooms: some implications for instructional design and professional development programmes. *Innovations in Education and Teaching International, 40*(4), 348-355.

Patton, M. Q. (2005). Diverse and Creative Uses of Cases for Teaching. *New Directions for Evaluation, 2005*(105), 91–100. doi:10.1002/ev.146

Pearson, J., & Trinidad, S. (2005). OLES: an instrument for refining the design of e-learning environments. *Journal of Computer Assisted Learning, 21*(6), 396–404. doi:10.1111/j.1365-2729.2005.00146.x

Price, L., Richardson, J. T. E., & Jelfs, A. (2007). Face-to-face versus online tutoring support in distance education. *Studies in Higher Education, 32*(1), 1–20. doi:10.1080/03075070601004366

Rawazik, W., & Carroll, M. (2009). Complexity in Quality Assurance in a Rapidly Growing Free Economic Environment: A UAE Case Study. *Quality in Higher Education, 15*(1), 79–83. doi:10.1080/13538320902731443

Ritter, L. A., & Sue, V. M. (2007). Case studies. *New Directions for Evaluation, 2007*(115), 57–64. doi:10.1002/ev.237

Sensiper, S. (2000). Making the Case on Line. Harvard Business School Multimedia. *Information Communication and Society, 3*(4), 616–621. doi:10.1080/13691180010002134

Tucker, B., Jones, S., Straker, L., & Cole, J. (2003). Course Evaluation on the Web: Facilitating Student and Teacher Reflection to Improve Learning. *New Directions for Teaching and Learning, 2003*(96), 81–93. doi:10.1002/tl.125

Viitanen, E. (2001). Learning to Manage Welfare and Health Services. Evaluating a Three-Year Academic Training Programme in Professional Development. *Evaluation, 7*(1), 79–97. doi:10.1177/13563890122209531

Villar, L. M., & Alegre, O. M. (2007). Measuring the learning of university teachers following online staff development courses: a Spanish case study. *International Journal of Training and Development, 11*(3), 200–213. doi:10.1111/j.1468-2419.2007.00281.x

KEY TERMS AND DEFINITIONS

Accreditation of a Formative Programme: A process of quality assurance through which accredited status is granted to a university formative programme if it has met predetermined standards.

Basic Information and Communication Technology (ICT) Skills: The skills necessary to use the functions of information and communication technologies.

Competence: The ability to apply learning outcomes adequately in a defined context (i.e. university education programme).

Digital Literacy: The competence to use information and communication technology (ICT).

E-Learning: Learning supported by information and communication technologies (ICT).

Learning Community: A community that promotes a culture of learning (e.g. assessment)

by developing partnerships between sectors of the university and social community, and motivates individuals and higher education institutions to learn.

Mentoring: Guidance provided in a variety of ways to a faculty or agency staff member by a colleague who acts as a tutor or coach.

Standard: A series of assessment criteria whose content is defined by training planners.

Chapter 12
Real Time Internet-Based English as a Foreign Language Learning

Ruth Reynard
Educational Consultant, USA

ABSTRACT

The purpose of this case was to explore the potential for using simple real time technology to connect native language speakers of English and foreign language learners of English. The intended design of the study was to explore the successes and challenges of language and cultural exchange within a real time technology-mediated class. Of particular interest was the effectiveness of connecting authentic language speakers as teachers and foreign language learners as students. The authors' query was to evaluate how effective this methodology is in increasing the understanding of meaning and appropriate language use.

INTRODUCTION

This case study provided an English language teaching and learning opportunity for 40 grade 8 students in Hunan Province, S. China and five pre-service teachers studying in a Masters of Teaching course at a university in Tennessee, USA. The purpose of the study was to explore the possibilities of providing language learning from "authentic" speakers directly to in-class foreign language students using new real-time technology. Most English teaching with authentic English speakers in China is costly and involves teachers who have relocated there for that specific purpose. We were trying to find a more cost effective but efficient way to provide the same opportunity for students of English in China to be taught the language by mother-tongue speakers in the USA using new technology and through the local school system. Specifically, we were interested in finding out if the cultural and language exchange could take place at a distance and if the students understood appropriate language use as a result.

DOI: 10.4018/978-1-61520-749-7.ch012

SETTING THE STAGE

The major theories of second language learning focus on various aspects of the learning process. Krashen (1981) distinguishes between what he sees as the process of acquisition and the more complex processes of learning, where the learner not only becomes familiar with language parts and structures, but also becomes proficient in authentic use and application of the language learned. This distinction is similar to a previous distinction made by Chomsky (1965) between linguistic competence and performance, or input and output as later promoted and developed by Canale & Swain (1979). Other theorists have identified the complexities of attaining and evaluating communicative competence (Hymes, 1971; Canale & Swain, 1980) as it is seen in terms of ability to perform in a language, while Widdowson (1978) distinguishes between use and usage, emphasizing the difference between using language within set and familiar parameters and using the language authentically and creatively.

In terms of learning distinctives, Canale and Swain (1980) identified grammar, sociolinguistics, discourse and strategic competence as four main ability areas that relate to language knowledge. That is, an ability to learn a language accurately through an understanding of the grammar of the language, as well as an authentic use of the language within sociolinguistic conventions is crucial to the language acquisition process. In addition, Canale and Swain (1980) emphasized a distinction between language discourse and the strategic use of the language, or the communicative complexities of conversation and other intentional uses of the language to persuade, influence and inform. Krashen's (1985) simplified the acquisition process to a theory of comprehensible input theory, which suggests that, as a result of comprehending input, learners can acquire morphological language features in a natural order. In other words, if the input is comprehensible to the learner, the acquisition of the target language becomes a natural learning process. Swain (1985), however, promoted the notion that comprehensible output, or 'pushed output' is necessary for effective language acquisition. Learners, according to this theory require opportunities for demanding output in order to learn appropriate language use. Additionally, in a chapter by Fanny Meunier in Granger, Hung and Petch-Tyson (Eds.) (2002), discusses the benefit of frequent use of authentic language in identifying specific grammar uses and language parts uses such a vocabulary and syntax; "grammatical patterns", p. 121., and more specifically, "Grammatical signatures", p. 122.

English grammar is…no longer seen as a monolithic entity (i.e. basically the grammar of written educated English) but rather as being comprised of several specific grammars: the grammar of written, spoken, narrative, argumentative texts, types etc. Many grammatical features are found in a wide range of text types but the main difference lies in their frequency of occurrence (p. 122)

Other theorists have built on notions of authentic use in the context of social construction and community. Wenger (1998) discusses the notion that a focus on identity through language helps to situate and include learners rather than exclude and distance them. This idea also increases the likelihood that individual students will participate in the learning collective by being empowered in the process. A chapter by Joybrato Mukherjee in Granger and Petch-Tyson (Eds.) (2003) discusses the notion of "talk" and "tone" units derived from various speech corpora and argue that while spoken and written language patterns differ, sometimes greatly, listeners and participants can learn those patterns even when letters and word endings are missing because the context of use dictates the pattern. What is interesting about this is the dynamic nature in which language communicates meaning as well as use.

Also of interest in this context is the discussion of situated practice in language learning proposed by Lave and Wenger (1991) in which the notion of practice must be socially and practically engaging in order for students to learn. Their discussion of "peripheral participation" (p. 35) not as a stagnant state but transitory in the process of learning is relevant to this approach of authentic language learning. That is, the idea that the authentic practice and use of language captures the social engagement in ultimately effective language production.

Computer-mediated distance education (CMDE) demonstrates, just as in conventional educational environments, the interconnectedness of all aspects of the teaching and learning field. It is interesting to note, however, that often in CMDE research and professional discourse, as in conventional educational research, the interconnectedness of the process is lost in an attempt to more closely analyze the effectiveness of specific areas. Current CMDE research tends to divide itself into two areas–technical (programming, software and hardware) and pedagogical (how the teaching and learning will happen- instructional design). What is most often missing, however, is an examination of the intent and application of the learning taking place: that is, a critical look at the main purpose and the wider significance to personal and societal growth. Intention or the purpose in learning should not only refer to learning objectives in the conventional sense, but should also address issues of individual intention and the wider significance of societal or global intentions in terms of application of what has been learned. The key to intention or purpose, then, is active, equal, and dynamic participation of both learner and teacher.

The possibilities of multi-dimensional connectivity[1] and Haughey's and Anderson's (1998) vision of "networked learning" mean that conventional boundaries of preset classrooms and content are no longer the only option. People of all ages, cultures, languages and socio-economic status can learn together. However, the expanding potential of electronic learning environments means that content should be inclusive and equitably accessible. If the learner's individual context is excluded from the process, then, constructive learning cannot take place. Therefore, content and content selection involves the active participation of the learner and involves the learner and instructor cooperatively in constructing meaning and producing a relevant application of the learning that has taken place. Cooperation of all participants is truly a collaborative, constructionist process of integration. Collaboration between learner and instructor in second language learning is a way to provide students with integrating more authenticity in their assigned tasks, as well as learning in a more global context about other cultures, as well as helping to maximize learning styles and differences (Braunstein, Meloni & Zolotareva, 2000; Bada & Okan, 2000).

Cummins (2000) in his chapter called "Transformative Pedagogy: Who needs it?" discusses the implications of technology in the negotiation of cultural and linguistic difference in the teaching and learning process. Often in traditional classroom delivery, individual culture and language can be ignored, and, the student can be left at a disadvantage. Mainstream cultures and languages tend to dominate learning communities unless intentionality informs the course design and delivery to accommodate diversity and integrate all learners equally into the process. This is also crucial to distance learning, especially in regards to the self-directed nature of the environment. Cummins cites the New London Group's (1999) theoretical framework for the designs of meaning, which they advance as including the following:

- **Situated practice:** immersion in meaningful practice and experience within a community of learners;
- **Overt instruction:** intentional instructional strategies to demystify skills and content and scaffold learner progress through-

out; (Its goal is systematic, analytic and conscious understanding);

- **Critical framing:** a focus on the historical, cultural, sociopolitical, and ideological roots of systems of knowledge and social practice;
- **Transformed practice:** application of transformed meaning gained from previous practice, instruction, and critical reflection to work in other contexts or cultural sites.

Building on these main points, Cummins (2000) advances a framework of instruction for language learning and academic achievement that has three main aspects:

1. **Focus on Meaning:** making input comprehensible [both for mother tongue speakers and second language speakers] and developing critical literacy;
2. **Focus on Language:** awareness of language forms and uses and the critical analysis of language forms and uses;
3. **Focus on Use:** using language to generate new knowledge, create literature and art and acting on social realities.

Within his framework, Cummins identifies five phases of learning that he regards as necessary to move education beyond merely the transmission of information to knowledge generation or transformative pedagogy:

- **Experiential Phase:** where the prior knowledge of the student is accessed and is essential given that "Our prior experience provides the foundation for interpreting new information";
- **Literal Phase:** where basic content questions can be asked and answered from a superficial readings of texts;
- **Personal Phase:** where students are encouraged to relate the basic information to their own experiences and feelings;
- **Critical Phase:** where students engage in more abstract processes of critically analyzing the issues or problems raised in the text;
- **Creative Phase:** where students translate the results of the previous phases into concrete action.

Therefore, whether a learner is a first or second language speaker, the language development should accommodate critical inquiry and transformative pedagogy. Instructional technology has the potential of helping the learning process by providing necessary scaffolds to the learning, presenting critical context to meaning, encouraging clearer understanding of texts, and creating learning spaces where learners can build on the learning of each other to increases their own understanding of the text. In a very real sense, then, learners can negotiate an individual learning space within the larger framework of a course and, as a result, maximize their own learning experience.

In applying the theory to this case study, my aim was to create a social exchange within a cultural setting that has meaning for both teachers and students. Given the brevity of the study we were able to realize the experiential, literal and personal stages of Cummins (2000) framework but not to the final stages of creativity and critical analysis.

CASE DESCRIPTION

The case study was a synchronous instructional experience connecting teachers of English in TN, USA and school children in China. The teachers of English were graduate students studying to complete an ESL specialization as school teachers in TN. The course included a practicum component and this study was included as that practicum for those students who agreed to participate. Additionally, I worked with teachers in China who were already EFL teachers in the local school systems and who welcomed the idea of having "authentic" speakers of English as tutors for their class of students. The choice of technology was made based on lack of funds for the study which resulted in our using free options (Skype© and Microsoft Instant Messenger©) rather than technology that may have operated better for the real time connection. It was important to have the US teachers work with the Chinese teachers in formulating assignments and language exchanges so that the students could be prepared by their local teachers and then practice language exchange with the distant teachers in the US.

The approach was to bring together all participants in a dynamic language exchange that focused on an agreed upon "foreign culture" context but allowed for students to not only answer questions posed by the teachers but also ask questions of their own about the cultural information presented to them. The content was provided via a website beforehand which allowed the on-site teachers to overview the lessons and prepare the students before the real time exchanges took place. The content included graphics and text. The real time sessions included social and informational exchanges as well as singing and, what was particularly interesting, cultural information from the students to the teachers in the US about Chinese culture and expressions.

Case Objectives

In response to the theory as well as the financial challenges of school language programs in general, a blended approach was identified that combined the comprehensible contextualization of the on-site learning environment and the authentic language use provided by the real time sessions. The following were the central objectives of the study:

1. To effectively connect authentic language speakers and foreign language learners in real time and provide an opportunity for information and language exchange to take place within a set context of meaning.
2. To explore the effectiveness of practicing real language use at a distance providing various supports and resources to both on-site teachers and students.
3. To provide an authentic and "sustainable" language learning opportunity for foreign language speakers in their own country without additional cost and interruption to the regular flow of classes and curriculum.
4. To provide foreign language teaching experience to language teachers in their home country and challenge them to think about cultural exchange as well as language practice.

The Process

Early conversations with the Chinese teachers gave me an opportunity to review their existing curriculum which was quite prescriptive without "free" conversational practice. While I did not want to interrupt the flow of their curriculum, I designed the real time sessions to augment their existing work. Therefore, we established a topic of "foreign culture" in order to situate the language use and practice. Language practice content was prepared as PowerPoint© presentation slides and with online downloadable resources such as images and text and sent to onsite Chinese language teachers who then worked with the school students and with local technicians to set up the necessary technology. The Chinese teachers also reviewed the material on order to prepare the students for the sessions. Therefore, the teachers introduced maps of the US and the state of Tennessee and located the city of Nashville. The website contained downloadable statistical information on Nashville to support the teachers. The pre-service teachers were tasked to create interactive lessons that included socializing (conversation), target language practice, and language-in-context (i.e. from the language practice) conversation. Because of the time difference, the teachers met at 7 p.m. local time in Tennessee which was 8 a.m. local time in China. There were five lessons in total addressing the content of three modules. Each lesson lasted for one hour and involved teachers having general conversation with the whole class: asking questions and receiving answers. For that part of the lesson, the on-site teachers in China were not directly involved. The second part of each lesson involved specific language use practice and this was co-facilitated by the on-site teachers in China.

Case Guidelines

It was important to fit the experience within the pre-service program for the American teachers. The teachers were not paid for this and, therefore, wanted to receive course grades for their participation. As I was their professor, this worked well. I contextualized the opportunity as a practicum for the teachers. Additionally, we did not want to create any artificial circumstances for the Chinese teachers and students. We therefore worked within their daily schedule and provided language sessions when they would normally have those sessions in their school day. We also worked directly with language teachers in China as a result - that is, those teachers gave up their class with their students for this online, real-time experience with the American teachers. The content was also developed in collaboration with the Chinese teachers' input so that we were not providing language practice that the students were not ready for or that the teachers could not facilitate.

Student Learning Outcomes

The grade 8 students in China were regular school students who were participating as English as a Foreign Language (EFL) students in which this project was part of their regular curriculum. The students were required to learn about the language (sociolinguistic and cultural implications of use), learn grammar, practice the pronunciation of the language, and participate in conversational exchange as preparation for the online session. The students were also required to demonstrate their language knowledge through written assignments which were created by their local teachers using the language used in the online sessions. The real time sessions addressed the pronunciation practice and conversational exchange. Before the session, the teachers in China were sent PowerPoint slides which included a graphic of the content area (e.g. food or clothes of Tennessee) and practice words and phrases(See Figure 1).

The teachers were sent structured sentences for practice within written assignments and the cultural context of the language which was then presented to the students in their Chinese language (See Figure 2).

The contextual information was presented before the online session and the written assignments followed (See Figure 3).

The teachers on-site in China were responsible to teach the grammar of the module and prepare the students culturally in terms of geographical information and some general USA cultural information. They also evaluated the students in terms of learning outcomes and I evaluated the US teachers as their professor.

Lastly, all of the module information, the PowerPoint© slides and the graphics were uploaded to a web site that included supporting audio files

Figure 1. Sample slide for teacher use

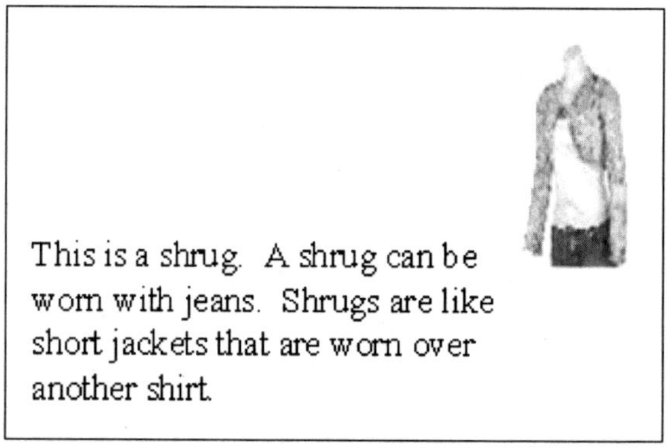

Figure 2. Sample writing assignment for students

Matching – clothes

Draw a line from the words to the corresponding picture:

A shrug

Pair of overalls

Denim jeans

Pair of boots

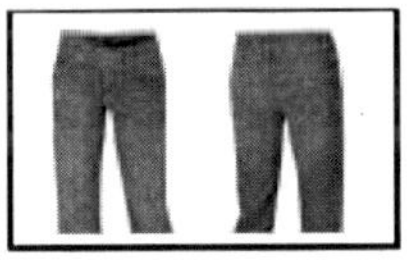

What are your favorite clothes?

1. ____________________
2. ____________________
3. ____________________
4. ____________________

Figure 3. Flow of the instructional process

Diagram A – Flow of the instructional process

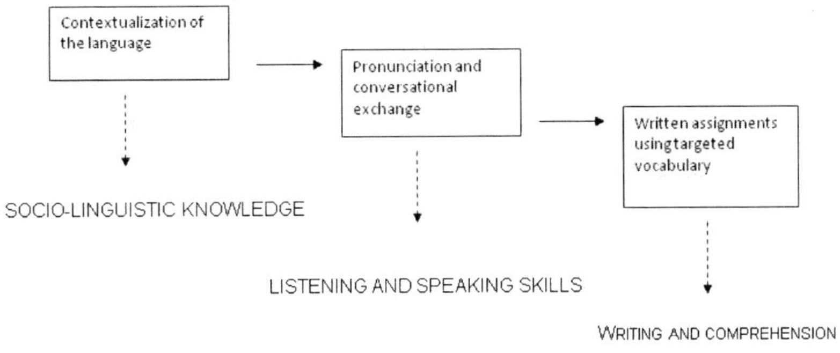

so that the teachers in China could reference their pronunciation before presenting to the class.

Teacher Learning Outcomes

The pre-service teachers were involved in a graduate program of study in which they were specializing as ESL instructors for the K-12 system in TN. The program required some practicum experience and rather than ask each of the students to set up separate practicum experiences I asked if they would be willing to participate in this pilot endeavor with Chinese school children. The teachers were very excited about the idea and enjoyed the whole project immensely. As language instructors in training, they were assigned three modules to design and teach focusing on vocabulary learning, pronunciation practice and conversational exchange. Each teacher divided the work into specific tasks for completion and sent their work to the Chinese teachers about 1 week before each online session, taking turns with the sections of the online sessions.

The teachers in China were responsible to break down the module content into weekly lessons with their students in preparation for the online session that included grammar. The teachers were then required by their school administration to hold several preparation classes in which the students were provided explanations in their own language regarding the socio-linguistic and cultural uses of the vocabulary, terms, and phrases. Additionally, the teachers in China also identified several students to hold conversational exchanges with the online instructors. This was an approach familiar with the Chinese methodology rather than a requirement of the pilot study. The idea of having "representative" students speak with the online instructors may have been due to the "public" nature of the technology. The idea that the school was "on show" internationally seemed to be a motivator for this approach. Unfortunately, it meant that not every student benefited from the experience directly although they were included as a group in the lesson. The US teachers were evaluated on their preparation and delivery as well as the resources they provided for ongoing learning to the students.

Module Content

The content of each module was selected in negotiation with the on-site teachers in China. That is the topics were chosen in keeping with their local language curriculum and also within the framework of a foreign rather than second language approach. Additionally, as the students were "meeting" authentic speakers of English speaking about their home culture, basic cultural topics were chosen: Tennessee food, clothing and weather. In each topic an explanation was sent to the teachers in China along with the presentation slides illustrating a topic item graphic and target vocabulary and sentences. Each online session was construed to provide an introductory greeting and warm up by the US teachers, a pronunciation practice of the target words and phrases, and an interactive exchange.

Interestingly, one teacher chose a TN school song to teach the children rather than a conversational exchange. This became popular with the children in China who then desired to teach the US teachers a song from their home culture, this completing the cultural exchange flow very effectively. Another addition to the planned session was the exchange of conversational idioms. Partly because the US teachers were unfamiliar with this mode of connectivity and partly because their basic instinct as teachers was to engage their students, they began introducing more familiar conversational idioms. This resulted in both a problem/challenge for instruction and an excitement for the teachers in China (who felt they were learning something new) and the students who enjoyed the "off-plan" interruptions. As a result, the next online session included the idioms introduced the session before so that they could be practiced. The actual result of this was to full engage the students in a more natural conversation flow and thus more fully benefit from the connection with authentic language speakers.

CURRENT CHALLENGES

The majority of challenges we experienced was with the technology and the time lag created in the exchange flow. The result of this was some of the authenticity of tone and phrasing was lost, which was detrimental to our project. Additionally we had methodological differences that meant we could not create a totally "free" conversational exchange, although some of the exchange took place naturally and was permitted to continue. The major set back was that this was the last class I taught at the institution and so I was not able to maintain continuity and build on the previous experience.

SOLUTIONS AND RECOMMENDATIONS

The technology challenges could have been solved with better equipment and more funding. More funding would also have permitted a repeat study immediately following this one with the same group of participants. In terms of future work, it would be beneficial to have several classes of students of different ages working with teachers over a longer period of time in order to truly evaluate the benefits of this approach.

REFERENCES

Auerbach, E. (1992). Making meaning, making change: participatory curriculum development for adult ESL literacy. Washington DC: Center for Applied Linguistics; McHenry, IL: Delta Systems.

Bada, E., & Okan, Z. (2000). Students'Language Learning Preferences. *TESL-EJ, 4*(3), May 2000.

Benson, P. (2000). Autonomy as a learner's and teacher's right. In B. Sinclair, et al. (eds), Learner Autonomy, Teacher Autonomy; Future Directions, (pp. 111-117). London: Longman.

Braunstein, B., Meloni, C., & Zolotareva, L. (2000). The U.S. –SiberLink Internet Project. *TESL-EJ, 4*(3), May 2000.

Campbell, J. K. (1998). The WWW for the students: a theoretical basis for using the WWW in Foreign Language Instruction. Paper for American Council of Foreign Languages, Chicago.

Canale, M., & Swain, M. (1979). Theoretical bases of communicative approaches to second language teaching and testing. Toronto: Ontario Institute for Studies in Education.

Chapelle, C. A. (1999). Theory and Research: Investigation of 'Authentic' Language Learning Tasks. In J. Egbert, & E. Hanson-Smith, (Eds.), CALL Environments: research, Practice and Critical Issues. Alexandria, VA: Teachers of English to Speakers of Other Languages.

Chomsky, N. (1965). Aspects of the Theory of Syntax. Cambridge, MA: MIT Press.

Cummins, J. (2000). Language, power and pedagogy: bilingual children in the crossfire. Buffalo, NY: Multilingual Matters.

Hymes, D. (1971). On Communicative Competence. Philadelphia: University of Pennsylvania Press.

Kitade, K. (2000). L2 Learners' Discourse and SLA Theories in CMC: Collaborative Interaction in Internet Chat. In Computer Assisted Language Learning. Oxford, UK: Intellect.

Kramsch, C., A'Ness, F., & Lam, W. S. E. (2000). Authenticity and authorship in the computer-mediated acquisition of L2 literacy. *Language Learning & Technology*, *14*(2), 78–104.

Krashen, S. 1981. Second Language Acquisition and Second Language Learning. Oxford, UK: Pergamon Press.

Krashen, S. (1985). The Input Hypothesis: Issues and Implications. London: Longman.

Lave, J., & Wenger, E. (1991). Situated Learning; Legitimate peripheral participation. New York: Cambridge University Press.

Meunier, F. (2002). The Pedagogical Value of Native and Learner Copora in EFL Grammar Teaching. In S. Granger, J. Hung, & S. Petch-Tyson, (Eds.), Computer Learner Corpora, Second Language Acquisition and Foreign Language Teaching. Philadelphia: John Benjamins Publishing Co.

Mukherjee, J. (2003). From corpus data to a theory of talk units in spoken English. In S. Granger & S. Petch-Tyson, (Eds.), Extending the scope of corpus-based research; new applications, new challenges. New York: Rodopi. Haughey, M., & Anderson, T. (1998). Networked Learning: The Pedagogy of the Internet. Montreal, Toronto: Cheneliere/McGraw-Hill.

Reynard, R. (2003). Internet-based ESL for Distance Adult Students – A Framework for Dynamic Language Learning. *Canadian Modern Language Review*, *60*(2).

Wenger, E. (1998). Communities of Practice; learning, meaning, and identity. New York: Cambridge University Press.

Widdowson, H. (1978). Teaching Language as Communication. Oxford, UK: Oxford University Press.

ADDITIONAL READING

Carmona, J. A. (2008). Perspectives on Community College ESL, Craig Machado, Series Editor. Chapter by Ruth Reynard, "Technology, Innovation, and Teacher Change in an ESL Program." (pp. 127-137). TESOL Inc. Virginia, USA.

Center for Advanced Research on Language Acquisition. http://www.carla.umn.edu/technology/

Computer Assisted Language Learning - An International Journal

Curricular Resources in ESL. http://www.cln.org/subjects/esl_cur.html

Distance Education, Network and Learning Technologies: http://node.on.ca/

Enhancing Authentic Language Learning Experiences Through Internet Technology Jean W. LeLoup & Robert Ponterio, SUNY Cortland; Moderators, FLTEACH, May 2000

Interactive Language Learning on the Web Sally Morrison, ERIC Clearinghouse on Languages and Linguistics, December 2002.

JournalE. L. T.http://eltj.oupjournals.org

Language Learning and Technology – a refereed journal for second and foreign language educators: http://llt.msu.edu/

MattersM.http://www.multilingual-matters.com/

Promoting Synchronous Interaction in an e-Learning Environment: http://thejournal.com/articles/2005/09/01/promoting-synchronous-interaction-in-an--elearning-environment.aspx

Reynard, R. (2003). Internet-Based ESL for Distance Adult Students - A Framework for Dynamic Language Learning. *Canadian Modern Language Review*, *60*(2), 123–143.

Reynard, R. (2003). *Using the Internet as an Instructional Tool: ESL Distance Learning.* ERIC # ED479246 http://www.eric.ed.gov/ERICWebPortal/custom/portlets/recordDetails/detailmini.jsp?_nfpb=true&_&ERICExtSearch_SearchValue_0=ED479246&ERICExtSearch_SearchType_0=no&accno=ED479246

Reynard, R. (2007). Hybrid Learning: Challenge for Teachers. *T.H.E. Journal.* http://thejournal.com/Articles/2007/05/17/Hybrid-Learning-Challenges-for-Teachers.aspx?Page=1

TechKnowLogia. is at http://www.TechKnowLogia.org/

Vol. 3, Iissue 6, November/December 2001 is on Technologies and Language Acquisition

Using Chat to move the thinking process forward (Ruth Reynard, 2008): http://www.campustechnology.com/Articles/2008/10/Using-Chat-To-Move-the-Thinking-Process-Forward.aspx

KEY TERMS AND DEFINITIONS

Real Time Technology: Technology that provides connection in real time between participants and material. Some examples of this would be Microsoft's Net Meeting© or MSN Messenger©; chat connections within course delivery systems, or Skype©.

Situated Language Practice: Language practice that involves using language within an actual and real context of use rather than a hypothetical situation. In this sense, practice conversations in a class about hypothetical exchanges with, say, a doctor, are not situated language practice. Rather a conversation with an actual doctor either in person or using real time technology provides a real situation of use.

Cultural and Language Exchange: Exchange language for meaning often implicates culture. That is, language is not vacuous of culture and is really a form of cultural representation. As such, culture must be recognized in establishing the meaning.

Authentic Language Use: Authentic language use is when language is used by native speakers or exchanged with native speakers.

Computer-Mediated Distance Learning: Instructional mediation with technology is when, in this case, a computer mediates the connection between student and teacher, student and student, and student and content.

ENDNOTE

1 'Connectivity' here is referring to the electronic connections and interactivity of learner to learner, learner to content, learner to teacher and learner to the world.

Chapter 13
Meeting the Realities in Technology Enhanced Learning

Sibitse Mirriam Tlhapane
Tshwane University of Technology, Republic of South Africa

Sibongile Simelane
Tshwane University of Technology, Republic of South Africa

ABSTRACT

The case discusses the challenges of introducing technology-enhanced learning in geographically dispersed learners, most of who are situated in rural areas. These are post-diploma nursing learners with minimal computer literacy. They also have limited or even no access to computers at the university because they attend part time, have full-time jobs and stay far from the university and so cannot even visit computer labs after hours. Despite these challenges, these students end up being motivated to learn computers so that they can access learning material and also use them for lifelong learning. The case also covers computer training, e-applications used, online learning, studies done, partnerships between faculty and the directorate and teaching and learning with technology. The value of simple, cheap technologies like an interactive CD-ROM in initiating students to e-learning and overcoming their bandwidth problems is emphasised, including the gains made from the project. Both staff and managerial challenges are discussed and recommendations are made.

INTRODUCTION

Technologies are a reality in education and so too are their challenges. Information technology, or its incorporation into educational programmes, is often presented as an ideal and practical solution to *inter alia* contemporary problems in teaching methodologies, demands for innovation and dealing with large groups of students. It is indeed true that it does address these problems, but what is rarely mentioned are the challenges of incorporating e-learning into educational practices and maintaining an e-learning environment that meets the needs

DOI: 10.4018/978-1-61520-749-7.ch013

of both faculty and students. Burchell (2001) elaborates on various studies which consistently report on the problem of computer illiteracy, computer availability and access to computers by post-graduate students. Challenges of using the web are listed by Alessi and Trollip (2001) and these will be addressed later in this chapter. These challenges are not unique to Tshwane University of Technology as studies from other institutions in different parts of the world reveal. Hence, one refers to them as realities.

The main focus of this case study is on the introduction of technology-enhanced learning in geographically dispersed, post-diploma nursing students who study part time and are at the same time in full-time employment. Tan (2004) defines a case study as a research strategy involving in-depth empirical investigation of a particular phenomenon and states that a "case" may be an organisation, city, country or person. Gwele (2000) refers to these geographically dispersed students as returning African students whose learning needs can best be addressed through e-learning. Though the returning, geographically-dispersed students are used as a basis for the discussions, these are not necessarily the only students affected by the e-learning challenges. The reader can identify other similar situations in various parts of the world where these challenges occur.

This chapter will address some of these challenges, based on our experiences in technology-enhanced learning. These challenges include students' challenges before implementing technology-enhanced courses: the technology-enhanced course as an intervention strategy, challenges faced by both staff and the institution in this regard; the benefits of technology-enhanced learning and, lastly, the introduction of an interactive CD-ROM as a strategy of addressing some of these realities in e-learning. In this study the technologies referred to include CD-ROMs, computers, the Internet, networks and bandwidth.

RATIONALE FOR THE TECHNOLOGY-ENHANCED EDUCATION PROJECT

The Nursing Department offers the programme B.Tech Occupational Health Nursing on a part-time basis. This is an outreach programme to make continuing nursing education programmes available to nurses in remote areas of the country. The course runs for two years. The learners are professional nurses employed full time in either public and private healthcare institutions or industries. Nursing in this country is still a predominantly female profession, so males make up less than 1% of the total population of 120-150 per year of study. Being female, most of the students have to cope with the multiple roles of being a wife, a mother, a professional, a community member and a student. But as adult learners, they know what they want. They desire to be involved in their learning and wish for knowledge which is of immediate use.

There is minimal lecturer-leaner contact, three days a month for three subjects in the first year, and in second year they do only two subjects. Lecturing venues include Polokwane, Nelspruit, EMalahleni, Klerksdorp, where the majority of the students stay and work in rural areas, and Pretoria, which is more urban. In our case, the context is not that of complete separation between lecturer and learner in space and time. It is partially because lecturers do go to learners periodically and they meet at educational venues with minimal infrastructure. The e-learning project in this case was implemented to augments the part-time, face-to-face modality. Each lecturing venue has at least one part-time lecturer who also acts as an onsite mentor for the learners.

The teaching and learning approach used here is Problem-based Learning (PBL). Problem-based Learning (PBL) is a curriculum design and a teaching learning strategy. According to Yin Ho (1999) PBL develops higher-order thinking skills, disciplinary knowledge bases and practical skills by placing students in the active role of problem solvers, confronted with ill-structured problems that mirror real-life problems. The absence of learning resource centres at off-campus venues and students' distance from the main campus previously made it impossible for students to get enough learning material. Technology-enhanced learning was seen as the best way of addressing this issue. "Technology-enhanced learning, in its basic form, involves the use of some form of electronic media to enhance the learning process" (Kante, 2003, pp. 15-16). The author says it allows for the efficient transfer of knowledge anywhere and anytime, regardless of subject matter. It opens up a world of learning unavailable in most corners of the world. Both PBL and e-learning facilitate self-directed learning and lead to lifelong learning.

In addition to the problem of the absence of learning resource centres, communication with learners during the inter-contact periods was very minimal because of the costs involved of both cell phones and landline telephones. It was difficult to keep track of learners' performance and also to keep records like test and assignment marks up to date. The heavy workload of lecturers made it impossible to give individual attention to learners, especially those with learning problems. Satellite campuses do have computer laboratories, but these are small and are available on weekdays only. There was also the issue of time and money spent on travelling, and this affected both lecturers and learners. All of the issues mentioned above were enough motivation for e-learning facilities for both the learners and the instructors. All these made the needs of geographically dispersed learners unique, so they needed special attention.

STUDENTS' TECHNOLOGICAL CHALLENGES

As practice, we did a survey of students' experiences with computers before commencing with the technology-enhanced course. Over a period of three years, we have had similar results from geographically dispersed learners.

In all our studies, we found that students who came to the course with e-learning experience made up less than 2% of the participants, and these came from universities and university of technologies. They reported high use of electronic materials, including CD-ROMS, data projectors and computers. Most participants, specifically those from nursing colleges and nursing schools, reported an absence of computers at their libraries. Books were searched and issued using cards, or, in some cases, the librarian did the search for them. Most said they walked about searching for books in the library. Some said there were computers in the libraries, but they were unused and always covered. A similar study was carried out in nursing schools in Greece by Koutsojanis, Kontomina, Margari, Doulias and Katsardi (2007), and researchers found that 73% of the nurses had never used the internet before.

In our studies, we found that most participants did not have computers at home. A few of the participants had computers, and they indicated that the use of computers at home is by their children. This is seen as largely a cultural issue or trend amongst women: that of placing the needs of children before those of the parents. Some participants saw the computer as a source of crime. They said the way computers are stolen in this country, owning one is just one way of inviting criminals into ones' house. Few mentioned internet costs as a problem, but lack of internet cafés in the rural areas was seen as a greater set back.

In our study most participants said they had computers at work, but these were used by administration staff. This was specific to nurses employed in the public sector. Some participants stated that the fear was that if nurses were allowed access to computers at work, they would neglect patients and concentrate on computers. The use of computers in nursing practice is a controversial issue. Participants employed in private sector reported free access to computers at work. Internet accessibility was seen as a problem due to costs of installing and maintaining it for home use. In an online discussion on this issue, some participants reported that it was a common practice for nurses to neglect patients and play cards on the computer. The majority of the participants who had access to computers either at home or work reported spending less than three hours on the computer per week, hence the minimal level of computer literacy. Others had no access to computers.

Computer illiteracy amongst both faculty and students in South Africa is a reality which needs to be confronted. What conceals this problem in South Africa is the fact that the country has features of both highly-developed and developing communities. The country has highly industrialised areas in urban areas, but a lot of underdevelopment in rural areas. In our study on students' exposure to multimedia before enrolment to the course, few of them rated their computer literacy level as average. Most participants reported minimal computer literacy, but the reality became apparent during empowerment in the computer laboratory where many students could not click nor hold a mouse and needed much reassurance that they will succeed.

Sinkovic, Stottinger, Schlegelmilch and Ram (2002) list a number of synonyms for the concept technophobia including: reluctance or resistance to use technology, computer aversion, computer anxiety, negative psychological reaction to technology and less openness to innovative technology. In our study, students were asked to express their fears and aspirations with regard to computers, and most said they were scared of the computers. On explaining what caused their fears, most said they feared that the *information might be wiped off*, with some even mentioning computer viruses. Others indicated that they were *scared of computer viruses,* with some revealing that *viruses will infect* their computers. Few participants said they were scared of *computer language*, which is a real problem for somebody who is not trained in information technology. The majority said they were afraid of *failing to master computer skills*. Others just said they *had a fear of the unknown*. In the end, all said they were keen to learn how to use computers for learning. In the study by Koutsojanis et al. (2007), they also looked at participants perceptions of other medical related technology such as electro-cardiograms. Overall, 32% of the participants reported being comfortable with the use of healthcare technology whilst 90% of the nurses considered the use of biomedical technology as an 'obstacle' in their relation with patients.

In the study by Koutsojanis, et al. (2007) they also looked at participants' perceptions of other medical related technologies such as electro-cardiograms. Overall, 32% of the participants reported being comfortable with the use of medical-related technologies, while 90% of the nurses in the study considered the use of biomedical technology as an 'obstacle' in their relationship with patients

PROFESSIONAL DEVELOPMENT PROGRAMME IN UTILISING EDUCATIONAL TECHNOLOGY

Nationally, the government issued a directive on e-education in the form of a White paper. Section 2.5 (Republic of South Africa, 2004) states that e-education provides learning for the real world. According to the paper, information communication technology can enhance higher-order thinking skills such as comprehension, reasoning, problem solving and creative thinking, and enhance employability. The Department of Education (DoE) believes that information communication technology creates access to learning opportunities, redresses inequalities, improves the quality of teaching and learning and delivers life-long learning. Information communication technology can accommodate differences in learning styles and remove barriers in learning. Hence, the policy framework of the DoE (Republic of South Africa,

2004) is equal access and equal competencies.

Twigg (2003) argues that higher education institutions should improve and supplement their traditional courses by taking advantage of the Internet, technology and multimedia. This statement is the starting point for the justification for the educational-technology professional-developing programme. Empowering lecturers in educational technology is the aim of a Tshwane University of Technology project known as the Partners@Work programme. Empowerment is done by the Directorate of Teaching and Learning with Technology (DTLwT). The duration of the empowerment programme is one year. Empowerment is done at the well-equipped Directorate of Teaching and Learning with Technology (DTLwT) centre. Each trainee lecturer is assigned an instructional designer who offers empowerment, guidance and support even after the empowerment programme is completed. In addition to this, there are other professionals for designing graphics, developing CD-ROMs and maintaining the technology during the empowerment project. Though the DTLwT is responsible for the programme, other directorates like Curriculum Development and Support, Research and Innovation and Library Services are involved. Without this team, e-learning would still be just a wish.

For the first six months a replacement lecturer is appointed and he/she is paid by the DTLwT. The remaining six months, the partner comes back to the department to implement the educational technology course developed. Each partner is given a laptop, a 3G card for 24-hour internet connection, headphones and all the necessary software. After the empowerment programme, the laptop remains with the partner and it belong to the partner's department. The 3G-card cost becomes the responsibility of the partner's department.

In other departments, the sustainability of this online connection remains the lecturer's responsibility, so this becomes a financial liability for the lecturer. There is also the problem of sustaining the software after the programme. During the Partners@Work programme the DTLwT is responsible for maintaining the technology. After the project, the maintenance is done by the university's information and technology support services. It is difficult sometimes to get a technician who can attend to the problems that you encounter with your laptop as well as software. One can say this is a grey area. So the problem of sustainability is real and varies from department to department.

IMPLEMENTATION OF THE TECHNOLOGY ENHANCED COURSE

Technology-Enhanced Course

As part of the educational-technology professional project, in January 2007, the Adelaide Tambo School of Nursing at Tshwane University of Technology made part of the programme B.Tech Occupational Health Nursing available to students on-line. This was to supplement the face-to-face module. Bates (2001) refers to this as the mixed mode consisting of reduced face-to-face and online content. The advantage of this model is that it allows the benefits of both the campus and online to be combined. The main reasons for using the web can be aligned to those listed by Bates (2001, p. 23) and these include:

- Access to educational resources from outside the university in an instant and a global village
- Increased and flexible interaction with students
- 24/7 availability of course notes, diagrams and lists
- Ability to combine text, graphics and limited amounts of multimedia, enabling a wide range of educational applications
- Content links on an international basis for research and teaching purpose

- Opportunities for cross-campus collaboration
- Use of low-cost, off-the-shelf software such as myTUTor
- Creating a one-stop educational shopping centre for students

The technology-enhanced course was developed on the Blackboard learning management system, known as "myTUTor" at Tshwane University of Technology. This meant that all students registered for the subjects Nursing Research and Occupational Health could now receive learning material online. Due to logistical problems, the practical implementation started at the Pretoria, EMalahleni and Polokwane campuses. In 2008, this was extended to the Klerksdorp campus. Presently, there is still one learning site outstanding with implementation. As this was a first-time experience, we had to conduct studies on various aspects of implementation, including learners' perceptions of the various technologies, and effects of various e-learning strategies on their learning. Below is an illustration of a technology-enhanced course in myTUTor. The online course consists of content from blocks one to four, which is done in the first year. The second year content is from block five to block 9. Block one is the main theme of the course (See Figure 1).

Student Training

The technology-enhanced course was first developed online using the myTUTor learning management system with links to various sources on the internet. When we first started, the training consisted of the basic computer skills as taken from Gibson and Silverberg (2000) course for medical students. The training included two days training in:

Figure 1. Schematic representation of course content for B.Tech Occupational Health © 2007 Tshwane University of Technology. Used with permission

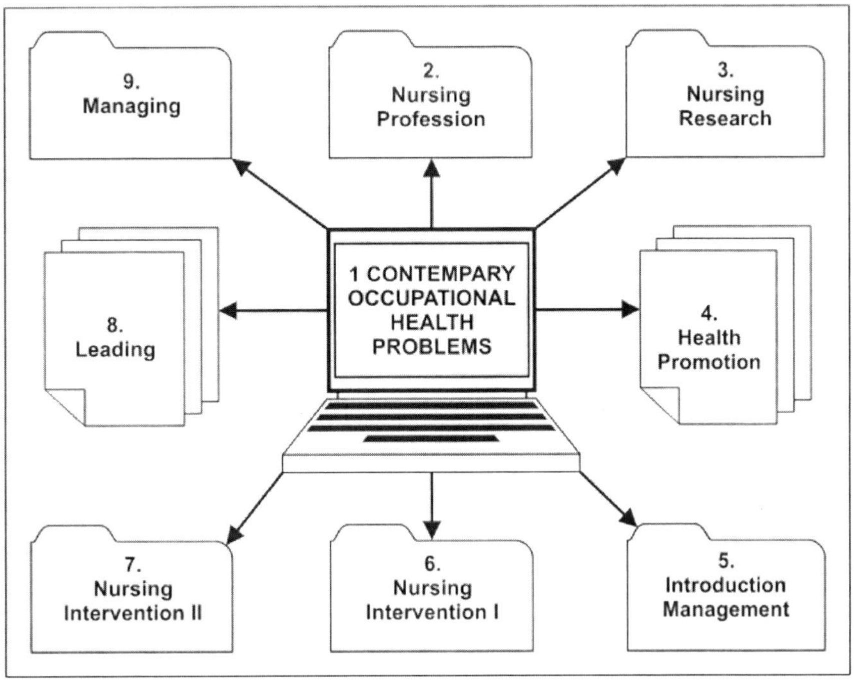

- Basic computer skills; e.g., logging on and logging off to the myTUTor and navigating through the course
- Accessing files in the course
- Saving files from the internet
- Downloading a document from the internet
- Using tools on the course; e.g. e-Games, assignment and discussion tool.
- Searching the internet directly or using hyperlinks

The above programme has since improved, taking into consideration the following role of the nurse with regard to information:

Nurses in their day-to-day work deal with volumes of information. They generate information about patients, equipment, supplies and various other activities related to healthcare. They store the information and even pass the information to other healthcare professionals and agencies and organisations. In view of this, any training programme on computers must put more emphases on the skilled use of the keyboard, including creating messages (typing), posting and accessing information on the computer. Patients' information is kept confidential, so all information about the patient's condition is handled by health professionals and not clerks. This has prompted us to include a discussion forum as part of computer training. The results of training in this skill will be discussed later.

The training is followed by real activities including sending and receiving e-mail and assignments. Information literacy is provided by the library for main-campus students, and the other campuses' students get a booklet on that. The log-on page for the myTUTor program has a telephone number of the helpdesk in case students encounter problems. This facility is provided by

Figure 2. Students' usage of the technology-enhanced course over a three-month period. © 2007 Tshwane University of Technology. Used with permission

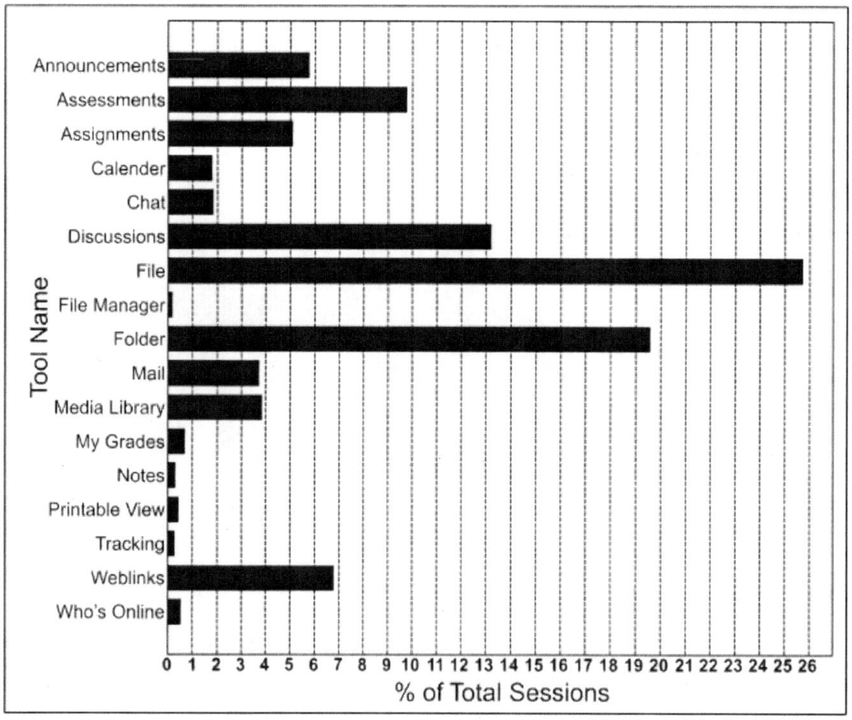

the DTLwT. Students are also encouraged to have an off-campus computer mentor referred to as a 'computer buddy' for further support. The buddy can be anybody including a colleague, neighbour, friend or one's child. This has helped most students, but some reported that their children were not good mentors because they had the tendencies of doing the work for them instead of showing them. Figure 2 is a tracking tool for recording students' activity.

Some of the findings on the training were discussed in the discussion forum. Upon evaluation of the training, most participants said they were happy with the training. One participant stated this in quote: "*It is exciting.*" Another said, "*It is better to struggle at your own pace*", whilst another said, "*A new experience*". One participant said, "*What a day! I wish we could have more of these*".

Initially, students' training was the sole responsibility of the lecturer. At the main campus, this was done at the students' internet cafe which could accommodate about 30 students at a time. For the other learning sites, the lecturer's laptop was used for training. The sites do have computer laboratories, but these were always fully booked and closed after hours. Attempts to secure after-hours facilities failed. What happened was that after the initial demonstration with a data projector, students would come in two's or three's to the lecturer's laptop to practice logging on and navigation. This took a long time, and with subsequent contacts this would continue after tutorial sessions.

Presently, the faculty has acquired a large computer laboratory at the main campus. This computer laboratory can take 100 students at a time. Training for all students, including those from the other three learning sites, is done at this laboratory. The laboratory has a full-time technician. This has been a great gain for the geographically dispersed learners.

STUDENT CENTRED APPLICATIONS

myTUTor Learning Management System

As mentioned earlier, the teaching methodology used is Problem-based Learning (PBL) which forces students to go to the web in search of information. PBL is associated with constructivist learning. Wilson and Lowry (2000) explain constructivism as a meaning-centred approach to teaching and learning. Learners do more than process information. Students build an understanding through interacting with their environment. In addition to the recommended websites found on the web links tool, students are motivated to search for information on the web, using search engines like Google Scholar, Yahoo e-Books and many others. In addition, students can register with online libraries like the Africa Digital Library or publishing houses. The reality is that the web opens up new opportunities for students once they get acquainted with it.

Wilson and Lowry (2000) describe the web as a fairly powerful source of information that needs to be processed and understood and which is especially valuable to self-directed learners. They further state that users of the web quickly learn that they must judge the quality of conflicting sources. This has not been so much the case with our students, some of whom seem to be just happy to find a lot of information on the web even if some of it is not scientific. According to Koutsojanis, et al. (2007) nurses lack the skills for verifying the quality of information available online. What one finds difficult to control is the high rate of plagiarism by some students, even after being warned against doing this. Before going online, students used to submit their work with proper referencing techniques and acknowledgements, but with the introduction of technology-enhanced learning this has somehow changed. In some cases, students just download information as it is and present it as own work. What makes one realise that it is not students' own work was the perfect work with content sequencing and referencing too good for the student level.

Though applications like Turn-it-in and Safe-assign can be used to check plagiarism, it is not always possible to use it, due to the large numbers of students and the large amount of information on the web. It becomes tedious to track down the large quantities of the allegedly plagiarised work. Though Turn-it-in does identify plagiarised work, the report needs to be verified. The other thing with the application is that its reliability and accuracy is questionable. The reality is that the rich online environment does not minimise the role of the lecturer. Instead, it poses new challenges for the lecturer, such as the importance of monitoring every student's activity thoroughly. Technology has brought with it many advancements and developments, yet at the same time it has made it easier to cheat and more difficult to detect plagiarism when it occurs. Lester and Diekenhoff (2002) state that it is important that university administrators work together with faculty to encourage efforts to detect cheating and punish those that are found guilty of such an offence. Concluding the survey that they took, Lester and Diekenhoff (2002) further state that the majority (68.04%) of the students who participated in their survey reported that they do cheat. One can say cheating cannot be completely eradicated but can be minimised.

Discussion Tool

The discussion tool in e-learning is used, *inter alia*, to promote interaction between lecturers and students and amongst students themselves. In this space, students are brought together to form a community. The other term used for this online interaction is 'presence'. According to Picciano (JAL, 2002) the simplest definition of presence refers to a student's sense of being and belonging in a course and the ability to interact with other students and an instructor even though physical contact is not available. In addition to forming a community, students learn how to log on, navigate through the course and also post messages. This has proved to be useful. The online discussion is also graded so that students, as they gain more competence with the web, can access scientific information even after the training. The following is a report on a study done after an online discussion with students, but before that, one can summarise the online discussion (debate). Participants had to respond to the notion that "nurses should not be given access to computers at work".

Students were divided on the issue. Few students were against the above notion, but they were very emphatic in their deliberations. Here are the reasons they forwarded:

- The use of computers suppresses creativity
- Nurses neglect patients and play cards
- Computers are demanding so they would steal valuable time which should be dedicated to patient care
- Much time will be wasted teaching nurses how to use computers
- The patients' environment has a lot of microorganisms so technicians coming to repair computers would be infected.
- Nurses are supposed to be with the patients and not with computers

The majority were in favour of computers with valid reasons and responded to the above by saying:

- With or without computers, patient care still suffers due to poor nurse-patient ratio.
- Neglect of patients is due to poor management.
- Managers must address issues and not use defence mechanisms like fearing technology, denying change and neglecting the advancement of technology

There was a third group which was in the middle. Some actually used the words "yes and no". Here are some of their reasons:

- Nurses need to be computer literate, but this should not be done at the expense of the patient. Training nurses in the use of computers should be done during off duty time
- There is nothing wrong with playing cards during on duty time. It is one way of reducing stress on keeping night nurses awake.
- Nurses should be allowed access to computers at work, but programs for games should be blocked

Two weeks after the above discussion, a study was undertaken to get the students' perceptions about the online discussion. Data was collected using semi-structured interviews. The reason for this method was that the topic was an emotional one, so non-verbal communication would be prevalent. Interviewees were instructed to also observe the non verbal communication. The following results indicate the students' perceptions and experiences with the activity:

- Most students said it was the first time that they used computers. This contradicts what they had said earlier, that they had minimal experience with computers. Others said it was difficult for them to type their messages and post them because they had never typed before. But most participants reported that by the end of the day they were enjoying it because their typing had improved. They expressed the same with logging on, opening other participants' messages and responding. Few said they found it easy to log on create messages and post them. One participant expressed this, "*It was difficult at first but at the end it was easy because I learned more things about the computer in a short time*" Most participants shared this sentiment. One participant stated that she never succeeded in logging on, so she never participated in the discussion. She said, "*I did not learn anything because I never logged on. I was bored.*" The other participants who did not succeed in logging on said they participated by partnering with those who succeeded in logging on.
- All participants who logged on said the topic was stimulating, so it kept them busy. Others described the topic as exciting. One participant stated, "*I wish I could have time to practice so that I can express my feelings well*", and the other said, "*It was stimulating because you had to critically analyse the topic and respond.*" According to another, "*It was challenging because people held different views on the topic.*"
- Most participants said they felt good when others responded to their postings. But one participant said, "*I felt small and embarrassed because some questions were not clear.*" One participant said, "*I realised that some participants' reasoning capacity was more than mine because they had facts*". Another one said, "*I was shocked at the number of nurses who are computer illiterate*".
- Most participants expressed satisfaction with the general attitude of participants in the discussion. They said the behaviour was ethical. This is surprising because one student referred to another as '*comrade*' and even used the expression "*viva computers viva*". Ethics is an important subject in nursing, but in this case nurses were tolerant. This seems not to have offended other participants.
- Most participants said they would be willing to participate in future discussions. In fact, some requested more online discussion sessions. One participant reported that after the discussions, she went and bought

her own computer. Others said they saw the need to have their own computers. Participants appreciated the activity very much. They said with online discussion they were able to get information and help from students at other campuses. One said, "*I am able to get more and different information from others*. Most said, "*It made communication very easy and fast*".

- Participants claimed to have learned the following from the activity: "I *have learned that it is important to have a computer"*. The following was mentioned by most participants*: "I must improve my computer literacy so that I can be able to communicate with other learners and teachers*". Others reported to have already bought themselves laptops and were in the process of getting internet connection. Most participants welcomed the intercampus communication.

Participants' Reflections

The activity helped the students to reflect on who they are, where they are and where they need to be with regard to technology. One participant said, "*I have learned that without computer literacy, the course is going to be difficult.*" Another said, "*I have learned that the computer is simple it just needs practice*." Another stated:

This experience has opened my eyes. I used to use the computer for playing cards only but now I use the computer for work and learning. I have learned that instead of playing cards we can send messages through the internet. This helped me a lot because previously I used to get somebody to get something on the internet for me

The overall perception was that students felt the need for them to have access to computers, be it at home or at work. They felt technologically disempowered, but some saw it as their responsibility to empower themselves whilst others saw it as the responsibility of their employers to empower them.

Assignments Tool

The assignment tool follows the online discussion. At this stage, students are familiar with the keyboard, logging on and navigating through the course. Most importantly, students can now type up their assignments and post them on the assignment tool. This is a valuable tool for both students and the lecturer. It gives students immediate and accurate feedback. In our course, students have to submit at least one assignment using this application. This is in a form of a web quest where all the information is found online. Dodge (1997) defines a web quest as an inquiry-oriented activity in which some or all of the information that learners interact with comes from resources on the internet. At first, the response rate to this activity was low, but after grading the assignment, the response rate increased to 99%. Students have access to the grading form. Those who had technical problems with uploading the assignment submitted them by email. With the first group only one student failed to submit the assignment due to other reasons. This has subsequently improved because with subsequent groups the assignment follows the online discussion activity, when students are familiar with the posting process.

One can recall one incident where at one stage, all students from a certain town complained that they could not access the course from the only internet café in that town. On my way to Pretoria, I stopped at that internet café and discussed the problem with the manager there. This was possible because this is a small town. After this intervention, students from that town started posting their assignments on the myTUTor. This shows that help comes only if someone takes the initiative. Three of our learning sites are situated in the more rural provinces with small towns where establishing a rapport with internet cafés or other organisations like town council libraries is possible.

Assessment Tool

For every block in a technology-enhanced course there is a student self assessment exercise. The assessments are designed using the program Respondus. Most students describe these assessments as useful. In our studies students said these about the assessments in quote: "*I used the assessments to test my knowledge*". "*The self assessments helped me prepare for the examination*".

THE INTERACTIVE CD-ROM

Though the myTUTor project was a success, some participants in our study expressed certain frustrations with the web. These included slow connectivity and the lack of internet cafés in rural areas. As a result, an interactive CD-ROM was developed to support online learning. According to Reid-Searle and Moxham (2005) CD-ROMS are the best way of developing learning material because a CD-ROM can hold over 650 megabytes of data, sound, graphics and video and are portable, durable and inexpensive to reproduce. In our institution reproducing the CD-ROM contents costs only R8.00 each. Because it is a support for myTUTor, the CD-ROM contains all the files available in myTUTor course, except for the communication tools. The media types used in the CD-ROM include text, still pictorial images and motion images.

Both myTUTor and CD-ROM require the Front Page program for encoding the information for easy application to the CDROM. In addition to the files, each module has the e-Games, a highly interactive application for students to test their mastery of concepts. The e-games are developed on a software program called StudyMate (See Figure 3).

The lectures notes are summarised on PowerPoint form and some are in pictorial form for the student to interpret, understand and construct knowledge out of. The unpacking of content is

Figure 3. Homepage of a CD-ROM © 2007 Tshwane University of Technology. Used with permission

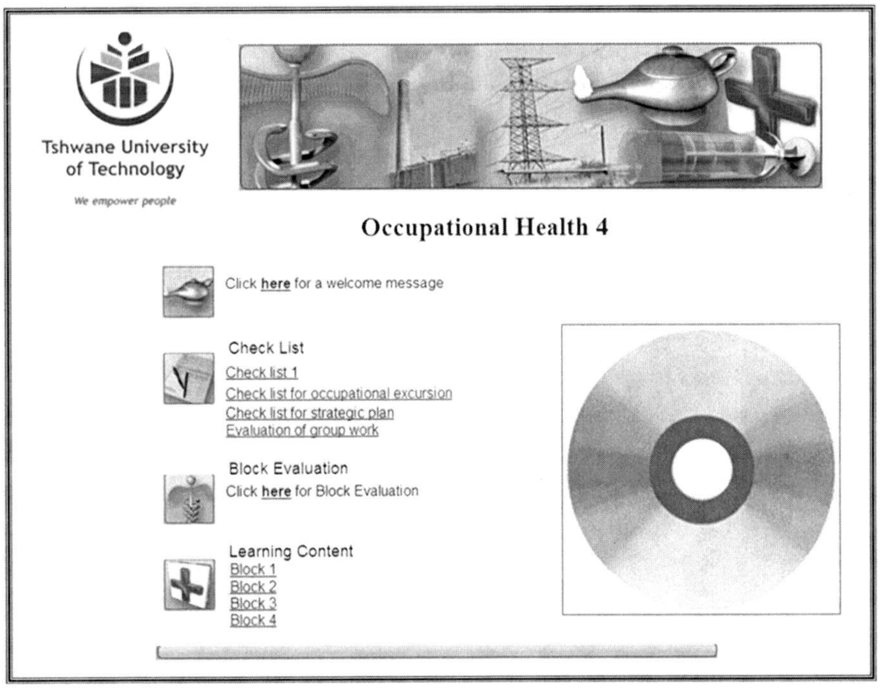

typical of constructivist learning. CD-ROM is less complex, and its information is easily accessible to students. What a CD-ROM does lack compared to myTUTor is communication tools, and these include: e-mail, assessments, media library, discussion tool and assignment tools. There is no internet, so there are no web links. It is for this reason that we say the CD-ROM supports the myTUTor and does not replace it.

DISCUSSION AND FINDINGS ON THE CD-ROM

User-Friendliness

Participants in our study found the interactive CD-ROM more user friendly than the myTUTor. Most participants said: "*It is easy and quick.*" Others said, "*It is simple It is easy to understand.*" Remarkable are those who said, *"With the CD-ROM I learned how to go to myTUTor* and *before I did not know how to use a computer but since studying for this course I have the interest to even go to myTUTor for more information."* Some participants (2) still reported problems in opening the CD-ROM. On following up, it was found that they did not check their computers for devices like a media player and Java Script without which the CD-ROM cannot work.

The e-Games

During an online discussion session, learners complained about nurses using computers in the ward for playing cards. Some said card games were good for keeping them awake during night duty, while others said they were good for relieving stress. All these point to the power of games over peoples' behaviour. Now in our course, both the CD-ROM and the myTUTor have e-Games. The games are developed using the program StudyMate. We use the e-games mostly for promoting the mastery of concepts and objective item testing. Clarke (2006) says about e-games that they motivate, accelerate and reinforce learning. They are personalised and give the student immediate feedback. One participant in our study had the following to say about e-games: "*I used the e-games to test my knowledge*". Another said, "*I enjoyed the games.*" Some said, "*But the e-games are addictive.*" The e-game is an effective student-centred application.

Lecture Notes

With myTUTor, some students reported problems with accessing the PowerPoint lecture notes, but with the CD-ROM this problem was not there. Participants said this about the PowerPoint lecture notes, "*It is a summary. I enjoyed the pictures. They are informative. You cannot miss any part of the syllabus. The notes are self explanatory. They give enough guidance.*" One participant complained that the notes were *too brief.* This above experience with PowerPoint has led to some students to also use PowerPoint for their PBL presentations. This was enhanced by our recent move to an auditorium for lectures. The availability of a data projector and a laptop in this venue has motivated students to, on their own; decide to use the PowerPoint as a medium for their presentations. They are beginning to accept the use of technology as a reality in education.

Use of an interactive CD-ROM helps students with the development of computer skills. It reduces the problem of slow connection and internet costs because it can contain a lot of information, thus lessening students' time on the internet. It is less frightening than the web, and students describe it as being user-friendly. After introducing the CD-ROM to support online learning, students, as stated in the preceding discussion, said they found it easier to go to the myTUTor. The ultimate aim of e-learning is to enhance students' learning activities and this is attainable

Offline Applications

The few students who still have problems with the web or CD-ROM download PowerPoint lectures notes to a memory stick for easier access. The myTUTor program has an email tool for communication between lecturers and students, but this is underutilised. Sending messages through the myTUTor email has also proved futile because students do not respond to this. Interestingly, some students use the tool only when they want to send an apology for not coming to class. Instead, they prefer using their mobile phones for communication with the lecturer. The simple reason for this is that the mobile phone is something they carry with them, so it is easily available and accessible. Most mobile phones have internet connections, so some students access some web content using this devise. What still needs to be explored is the possible use of mobile applications like MXIT for geographically dispersed learners. There are some reports on the effective use of MXIT in academic programmes, and these need to be explored because the student should be able to choose from a variety of applications to access learning material.

Other mobile technologies available in our institution are e-testing mobile applications like clickers. These can ease the lecturers' load of marking test and examination scripts.

EVALUATION

E-Learning

To reflect on the success of the project, one can refer to Kante (2003). He identifies three fundamental principles of the successful implementation of e-learning in developing communities, and these include:

- The existence of an established community of learners
- Delivery through a blended face-to-face/ electronic mechanism
- The offering of learner incentives

The first one we have in place in the form of both the face-to-face interaction in each campus and the inter-campus learning communities. The second one, blended learning, is quite evident in this case. The last one, which is incentives for students, we do not have in place, so the following suggestion can be considered:

As stated earlier, our students are professionals and are working, so they should be motivated to buy their own laptops or computers. Some of them indicated in the study that they were motivated to buy their own computers. What needs to be done is to make some arrangements so that if they buy computers they would be subsidised (e.g. 50%) in getting 3G cards for the duration of the course, i.e., two years. This seems to be feasible because they study in groups, as demanded by the PBL methodology, so each group can be given a 3G card. Each learning site has three student groups, so we would need 15 3G cards. Geographically dispersed learners need internet facilities at their disposal. Again, students can be given material incentives for best practices in e-learning. At the moment, the only incentive they have is the marks for incorporating technologies in their work.

Improved Problem-Based Learning Tutorial Sessions

The use of technology has improved the quality of PBL methodology. As stated earlier, in PBL, students work in groups to solve problems and meet specific learning outcomes. This is a face-to-face method consisting of tutorial sessions. It is in this methodology where a lot of scholarly information is required. Each group presents information gathered to the whole class. It is in these tutorial sessions where the impact of technology is being realised. Before incorporating technology to our programme, students' presentations were boring. Some would use the chalk board whilst others resorted to outdated technology like the overhead projector and transparencies. This has since changed. Students are beginning to use PowerPoint presentations, and this has been strengthened by our recent move from a lecture hall to an auditorium for tutorial sessions. More and more students are taking advantage of the availability of a laptop, data projector and screen in the auditorium. One group even used video material for their presentation.

The above is a great achievement because the choice of teaching aids in students' presentation is left to the students' own initiative. Because these presentations are graded, students put great effort into them. There is usually competition in terms of the quality of presentations. The only problem is that the department has not yet introduced incentives for quality presentations, especially those involving technology. Having incentives for both staff and students is something lacking in our institution. The DTLwT has incentives for best practices in e-learning; however, this is limited to staff members only.

Effects of E-Learning on Students' Performance

All participants with the exception of one agreed that e-learning enhanced their learning experience. They said it contributed a lot to their success in the summative evaluation. A comparison was made between campuses where students received the CD-ROM and a campus where students did not receive the CD-ROM. The findings were that, although the difference in the pass rate was very minimal, the grades on the campuses where CD-ROM was used had improved. There were more students on the 60-80% score, whilst the other campus had more on the 50-60% score.

As a follow-up on students' comments about, *inter alia,* the effects of pictures in the PowerPoint lectures, an analysis of the examination question which included the history of occupational health was done. This was a compulsory question consisting of 25 multiple choice items from all sections of the syllabus, measuring all level domains. This is usually a difficult section of the examination. The results of the students' performance in that question showed that students in the learning site where the CD-ROM was introduced had a 65% pass rate, and those on the campus where the CD-ROM was not introduced achieved a 35% pass rate.

So far, the e-learning course has helped students to reflect on their development both personally and professionally. It has stimulated students to reflect on themselves both as learners and professionals. Through online collaboration, students have learned to identify their shortcomings or gaps in knowledge regarding both computers and subject content. They see the value of technology in both patient care and overall management of the healthcare service. They can also think of strategies to curb the abuse of computers by nurses.

MANAGEMENT ISSUES

Sustaining E-Learning

Sustaining the programme remains a challenge due to some grey areas in the management of technology. The institution's IT support is geared towards general IT support for the whole institution and this places great pressure on the technician. With such pressure, it is virtually impossible for this department to maintain the e-learning technology. On the other hand the technician at TLT is also responsible for IT support during training only. This is understandable because the centre also runs e-learning staff development programmes for the entire institution.

Coping with latest developments with both the hardware and the soft ware is a daunting task. Computers do have automatic updates, but educational applications need a technician. Programs like Endnote, Respondus, and StudyMate come with guidelines, but, speaking from experience, there are always some technicalities that make it difficult for lecturers to download and install them

Often, good physical infrastructure with inadequate human technological support weakens the sustenance of e-learning. Bates (2001) says the reason for this is that human technology support, as an operational cost, often competes with research and teaching. The author concludes by saying human technological support is often under-funded in most institution. In our institution, both the directorate for research and that for teaching and learning with technology do get additional funding from outside the institution. As mentioned earlier, geographically dispersed learners have to compete with residential students who are in the majority.

The institution has challenges with regarding bandwidth, network and internet access. This problem is common to most developing countries.

Need for Marketing E-Learning

There is an urgent need to market e-learning to both faculty and students. Technophobia exists in both teachers and students. Policy alone is not enough to motivate staff to incorporate e-learning into their programmes. One's experience is that introducing e-learning to one subject in the whole course works only, to the disadvantage of the students. It splits the students into two camps: those who want e-learning in all subjects and those who want traditional methods in all subjects. The suggestion is that all subjects have a component of e-learning so that there is balance in teaching methods across the board. E-learning is just like PBL. Once students have adjusted to it, they can only tolerate a minimal amount of traditional teaching methods.

The situation described above can only happen if all lecturers are trained in the basics of e-learning and that would take a long period. What could work is marketing e-learning so that staff members who are computer literate can take the initiative in incorporating technology into their teaching, with minimal assistance from the directorate TLT. Or alternatively, TLT can have shorter programmes for people with computer skills. In other words there would be different training packages according to lecturers' needs. One year's training is ideal, but not attainable when looking at staff availability. Another way of marketing e-learning can be incentives for any staff member who introduces web- based learning for the first time.

The importance of staff training cannot be over-emphasised. In our case, we have seen that putting a course online without training staff does not accomplish anything. This happened with our other learning site where the technology-enhanced course has not been implemented. Lecturers at this site were made aware of the online material. Tracking tool results shows that learners at this site are not using the online learning material, even after being made aware of it. Both these students and their lecturers need training.

As stated earlier, our part-when time lecturers are onsite mentors for the students, but they can only do this with the face–to-face part of the course. For the online material, students have to phone the e-learning facilitator at the main campus, which becomes costly for them. Students are advised to use the e-mail tool on Blackboard, but, as mentioned earlier, they do not use it. They would rather wait for the contact day when the e-learning facilitator comes around.

BENEFITS FROM THE TECHNOLOGY ENHANCED LEARNING PROJECT

Fletcher (2003) states that technology allows students to proceed as rapidly or as slowly as needed. Each student can skip what they know and concentrate on what they do not know. The author further mentions that this substantiates the students' ability to apply knowledge. He applies the rule of three, which states that technology-based instruction reduces costs by one third, and either increases achievement by one third or reduces the time needed to reach learning objectives by one third. In our case, the first one, which is reducing costs, has not yet been assessed. The second and third rules have been realised through the following:

- Enhanced student learning experiences due to student-centred e-learning material
- Improved student performance
- More satisfied students
- Improvement in communication with students
- Improvement in tracking students and record keeping
- Manageable workload for the lecturer
- Improved self-esteem for both lecturers and students
- Digitally competent professional nurses (graduates)
- Improved research skills and output

Although our institution gets the bulk of its funding from the government, it does get funding from private organisations. Most of these organisations target certain faculties from which they recruit prospective employees like engineers, etc. Still research gets most of the funds. Recently the institution has received funding for e-learning. This is a major boost for technology-enhanced learning. Most of the challenges mentioned earlier will, hopefully, be addressed.

IMMEDIATE SOCIO-ECONOMIC SPINOFFS FROM THIS PROJECT

When talking about community development, most people think of the injection of large sums of money by other governments or big business, accompanied by huge projects. Little do they realise, it is the small empowerment projects like technology-enhanced learning whose impact can be immediately realised. Development is about people, and if everybody can make a small contribution more will be achieved.

For example, in the small rural town mentioned previously, the first year we had six students from that area, followed by others in subsequent years. At the end of each year, all these students were computer literate. They used the only internet café in that town and so not only brought income to the owner but also life to the café. The café is situated inside a restaurant and seemed to be underutilised because on that day and for the time that I was inside there was only one customer there. If other institutions, including nursing colleges serving communities in that area, could also embark on e-learning, the internet café would expand to the level of having its own premises. Ever since we started with technology-enhanced learning, our students in all these rural towns have learned to go and look for internet centres and reported finding ones, mainly at other academic institutions, church organisations, libraries or NGO offices.

In our studies, some participants, especially those in urban areas, reported that the computers they had at home were being used by their children. It is a known fact that children, if unsupervised, spend most of their leisure time or even time when they are supposed to be doing home work watching pornographic material. Computer literacy will empower mothers to monitor their children with regard to the use of the internet, thus enhancing their parenting skills. If all of the participants in the study buy own computers as promised, then they will, together with those who have already purchased them, be contributing to the economic growth of their (rural) towns. Internet connections and software have to be maintained, not forgetting the culture of sharing within Black communities especially those in townships and villages. Most children in these communities learn about computers from neighbours and relatives.

Participants stated that they will use computer skills to improve the standards of care in their healthcare institutions. Most healthcare institutions do have computers, but due to digital illiteracy, these are being underutilised. As stated earlier, computers are only used by ward clerks and for limited periods only. It is for our graduates to demonstrate to their seniors the computer skills they have acquired so that they can be used appropriately and improve the standard of care. This will mitigate the problem of nurses using computers for playing cards only. The problem of underutilised computers at nursing colleges and schools needs to be investigated by some higher authority in both healthcare and education.

MANAGEMENT OF TECHNOLOGY-ENHANCED LEARNING FOR GEOGRAPHICALLY DISPERSED LEARNERS: SUGGESTIONS

Though the institution does have ICT infrastructure, a lot still needs to be done to make sure that this is optimally utilised by all. This includes,

- Staff training to include two to three lecturers per department. This will not only minimise the isolation of the e-learning lecturer, but will also ensure that more people benefit
- Giving priority to student training by allocating an IT person to do that
- As stated earlier, when competing for funding, both technology and geographically dispersed learners are in weak positions, so, for the sake of fairness, faculty management needs to have a person solely responsible for the learning needs of geographically dispersed learners. This must be a senior staff member whose voice would be listened to. She/he would see to it that computer labs at other learning sites accommodate our students including making sure that these are open on weekends.
- There should be incentives for lecturers involved in e-learning. There should be criteria set for such incentives, for an example, a reward for first-time implementation of e-learning and research in e-learning.
- Ideally, each department should have its own e-learning infrastructure even if it is on a small scale. The University is too big for centralisation of infrastructure.

CONCLUSIONS AND RECOMMENDATIONS

Technology-enhanced learning has reached out to touch both the personal and professional lives of geographically-dispersed learners. From the findings discussed so far, it is evident that students would in future use the knowledge gained to use computers appropriately and improve patient care. Through these geographically dispersed learners, the standards of patient care would hopefully improve. The programme is also seen as contributing towards curbing the high rate of digital illiteracy, technophobia and lack of access to information in Sub-Saharan Africa. Through this programme, communities' perceptions about computers will also improve in that computers will be used not just for entertainment but also for accessing, storing and passing on information. More families would purchase computers, and these would not just be for use by children but also by their parents. It is hoped that these learners, as members of geographically-dispersed communities, will also motivate other people to strive for digital literacy. The saying that if you teach a man you teach one person, but if you teach a woman you teach the entire nation is applicable in this case. The following recommendations are made:

- Training and implementing of technology-enhanced learning to target a minimum of 50% of students for better impact and sustainability

- The technological issues of challenges of geographically-dispersed learners to be prioritised
- Technology sustainability should be part of the total plan
- Incentives for both students and lecturers to make use of e-learning to be part of the total plan.

REFERENCES

Alessi, S. M., & Trollip, S. R. (2001). Multimedia for learning: methods and development (3rd edition). Boston: Allyn and Bacon.

Bates, T. (2001). National strategies for e-learning in post secondary education and training. In Fundamentals of Educational Planning, (No. 70). Paris: UNESCO.

Burchell, J. (2001). Online Education: a viable role in postgraduate nursing curricula. Nursing Monographs, (pp. 30-35). Darlinghurst, Australia: St Vincent's Health Care Campus, Sisters of Charity Health Service Darlinghurst.

Clarke, D. (2006). *Games and e-learning.* Retrieved on February, 12, 2008 from CaspianLearning.co.uk/whtp_caspian

Dodge, B. (1997). *Some thoughts about WebQuests*. San Diego, CA: San Diego State University. Retrieved April, 7, 2009 from http://webquest.sdsu.edu/about_webquests.html

Fletcher, J. D. (2003). Does this thing work? A review of technology used to learn. *International Journal of Technologies for the Advancement of Knowledge and Learning*, *5*(1), 10–13.

Gibson, K.E. & Silverberg, M. (2000). A two year experience teaching computer literacy to first year medical students. *Bulletin of Medical Library Association, April 88*(2), 157-164.

Gwele, N. S. (2000). Online teaching and learning in a graduate course in nursing education. *Curationis*, ▪▪▪, 20–25.

Kante, C. (2003). eLearning, The New Frontier in the Developing world. *TechKnowLogia*, (January – March). Retrieved on December, 10, 2008 from www.TechKnowLogia.org

Koutsojanis, C., Kontomina, I., Margari, G., Doulias, E., & Katsardi, M. (2007). Education in Computers Conquers Health Care Professionals Technophobia. *Social Applications of Technological Advances, 11th Panhellenic Conference on Informatics*, (pp. 406-413). Retrieved on December, 14, 2008 from http://pci2007.upatrs.gr.proceedings/PCI2007

Lester, M. C., & Diekenhoff, G. M. (2002). A comparison of traditional and internet Cheaters. *Journal of College Student Development*, *43*(6), 906–911.

Picciano, A. G. (2002). Beyond student perceptions: issues of interaction, presence, and performance in an online course. *Journal of Asynchronous Learning Networks*, *6*(1), 21–32.

Reid-Searle, K., & Moxham, L. (2005). Promoting the students' practicum, a CD-ROM for nursing preceptors. *Studies in learning, evaluation, innovation and development, 2*, 20-28. Retrieved on November, 20, 2007 from http://sleid.cqe.edu.au

Republic of South Africa. (2004). *White Paper on e-Education: transforming learning and teaching through information and communication technologies.* Pretoria, South Africa: Government Printers.

Sinkovics, R. R., Stottinger, B., Schlegelmilch, B. B., & Ram, S. (2002). Reluctance to use Technology Related Products: Development of Technophobia Scale. *Thunderbird International Business Review*, *44*(4), 477–494. doi:10.1002/tie.10033

Tan, W. (2004). Research Design 1: Case studies In Practical Research Methods, (2nd ed). Jurong, Singapore: Prentice Hall.

Twigg, C. (2003). *Change: Improving quality and reducing cost; design for effective learning.* Retrieved on November, 20, 2007 from http://proquest.umi.com/pdweb?did=592388111&sid=10&Fmt=3&clientld=21888&RQT=309&VName=PQD

Wilson, B., & Lowry, M. (2000). Constructivist Learning on the Web. *New Directions for Adult and Continuing Education*, *2000*(88), 79–88. doi:10.1002/ace.8808

Yin Ho, N. (1999). Teaching and Learning via IT: Higher Order Thinking Skills in English Language, English Literature and Mathematics, (pp. 2-3).

ADDITIONAL READING

Bezuidenhout, J., & De Beer, K. (2006). A preliminary literature overview of open learning at the Central University of the Free State. *Progression*, *28*(1&2), 64–81.

Black, E. W. (1999). Academic Dishonesty in Traditional and Online Classrooms: Does the Media Equation Hold True? *Journal of Asynchronous Learning Networks*, *12*(3-4).

Brodeer, R. (2002). *Changing Computer Literacy and its Effect on Engineering Education.* Paper presented at the International Conference on Engineering Education, 19-21, Manchester, UK

Catney, C.M., & Currie, J.D. (1999). Implementing Problem Based Learning with www support in an introductory Pharmaceutical pp., 97-104 Iowa City; University of Iowa

Eggins, H. (2000). Costing technology based education. Phoenix: Orynx Press

Elhert, M. E. (2004). An evaluation of Problem Based Learning: Application in an undergraduate supply chain management course. Technical Report. North Western University. Chicago.

Erickson, M. (2002). Assessing the perceived impact of Computer assisted instruction on Physical therapy education. Unpublished doctoral dissertation, Morgantown, West Virginia.

Glazer, E., Hannafin, M. J., Glazer, E., & Song, L. (2006). Promoting Technology Integration through Collaborative Apprenticeship. [Retrieved from ProQuest Educational Journals.]. *Educational Technology Research and Development*, *53*(4), 57. doi:10.1007/BF02504685

Henning, E. Van Rensburg., W., & Smit, B. (2004). Finding your way in qualitative research. Pretoria: Van Schaik.

Jang, K. S. (2005). Effects of web-based learning on undergraduate students' learning of electrocardiogram. *Nurse Educator*, *44*(1), 35–39.

Kenny, A. (2002). Online learning: Enhance nurse education? *Journal of Advanced Nursing*, *38*(2), 127–135. doi:10.1046/j.1365-2648.2002.02156.x

Knebel, E. (2002). The use and effect of distance education in Health Care. *The Quality Assurance Project*, *2*(2).

Long, L. K., Janas, D. L., & Kay, L. (2009). Introducing Online Learning at a Small College through a Faculty Learning Community. *Online Journal of Distance Learning Administration, XII.* Retrieved January, 12, 2009, from http://www.westga.edu/distance

Meyer, S. (2001). Telematic education: A reality in post-basic nursing education. [Johannesburg: Rand Afrikaans University.]. *Health SA Gesondheid*, *6*(4), 66–71.

Palloff, R. M., & Pratt, K. (2005). *Online Learning Communities Revisited*. Paper presented at the 21st, Annual Conference on Distant Teaching and Learning, Wisconsin. Retrieved, December, 20, 2008 from http://www.uex.edu/disted/conference

Parker, D., & Gemino, A. (2001). Inside Online Learning; Comparing Conceptual and Technique Learning Performance in Place-based and ALN formats. *Journal of Asynchronous Learning Networks*, *5*(2), 64–74.

Phillip, K., & Watters, J. (2006). Transforming Pre-Service Teacher Knowledge in Science and Education through Multimedia and ICT, proceedings of the *National Association for Research in Science and Teaching, Annual Meeting* San Francisco.

Ray, C., & Day, J. (1998). Students' attitude towards electronic information resource. *Information Research*, 4. Retrieved November, 20, 2007 from http://informationr.net.ir/4-2/paper54.html

Savery, J. R., & Duffy, T. M. (1995). Problem Based Learning: An instructional model and its constructivist framework B. Wilson (Ed.). Constructivist Learning Environments: Case Studies in Instructional Design. Educational Technology. New Jersey: Publications: Englewood Cliffs.

Smith, J. C., & Diaz, R. (2002). *Evolving Uses of Technology in Case-Based Teacher Education*. Paper presented at Society for Information Technology and Teacher Education International Conference (SITE), Nashville, Tennessee, USA, (905-909).

Sturgess, P., Reaburn, P., Toft, Y., Marsh, P., Stehlik, D., & Moxham, L. (2002) *Problem Based Learning: Making the Technology work*. Paper presented at the 2002 WebCT Conference, Central University of Queensland.

Teghe, D., & Knight, B. A, & Knight, C. (2003). The SWIMS CD-ROM pilot: Using community development principles and technologies of the information society to address identified informational needs. *Progression* Retrieved November 20, 2007 from http://www.proceedings.information-science.org/InSITE2004/074teghe.pdf

Tellis, W. (1997). Introduction to Case Studies. *The Qualitative Report*, 3(2). Retrieved January, 3, 2007 from http://www.nova.edu/ssss/QR/QR3-2/tellis1.html

Tergan, S., & Schenkel, P. (2003). *Assessing the Instructional Power of eLearning Applications: A Learner Centred Checklist Approach*. ED-Media World Conference on Educational Multimedia, Hypermedia and telecommunication, Honolulu, (pp. 604-609).

Tlhapane, M., & Simelane, S. (2007). *Using Multimedia to enhance the cost-effectiveness of geographically dispersed learners*, Proceedings of the 9th Conference on World Wide Web applications in Education, Johannesburg, RSA

KEY TERMS AND DEFINITIONS

Technology Enhanced Course: It is technology designed and developed teaching and learning material that incorporates various software applications.

Professional Development Program: An empowerment program that trains lecturers to integrate technology in their teaching practices.

Geographically Dispersed Learners: This refers to students who are scattered around the country but attend classes at one common venue.

Problem Based Learning: This is a teaching and learning strategy where learners are divided into small groups and solve structured problems in order to meet their learning objectives.

CD-ROM: This is a compact disc with read only memory. It takes massive volumes of data and does not need internet connection.

eLearning: An electronic learning environment where students interact with the learning content, the facilitator and one another in pursuit of achieving their learning objectives.

Chapter 14
Bracing to Teach Online in Teacher Education

Omiunota N. Ukpokodu
University of Missouri-Kansas City, USA

ABSTRACT

This case study documents one teacher educator's successful adaptations of traditional pedagogies in online teaching. Specifically, using data from a graduate online course, it examines the general concern and beliefs that online teaching is an inadequate and inappropriate substitute for the traditional face-to-face instruction in a teacher education course aimed at transformative learning. Both quantitative and qualitative data revealed that online teaching evidenced successful student quality learning and adaptability of traditional pedagogies. It discusses the promises and challenges associated with designing and implementing an online teacher education course.

SETTING THE STAGE

As we move further into the 21st century, it is clear that technology is increasingly revolutionizing our lives and how we conduct businesses and education especially teaching and learning. Technology now offers the possibility of higher education to a variety of students who otherwise would not have the opportunity to advance themselves due to geographical and time barriers of the traditional face-to-face classroom instruction and learning. Additionally, vast and diverse multimedia resources now make it possible to engage learners in interactive and community-based online learning similar to traditional face-to-face setting. Given this availability, many institutions are creating and offering online courses and programs. A review of the literature indicates that online degree programs and courses are increasingly gaining popularity among students in higher education (NCES, 2003). Unfortunately, many faculty including teacher educators are reluctant to embrace online teaching (Taylor & Maor, 2000; Ukpokodu, 2008). Even when studies suggest that most traditional pedagogies can be successfully adapted and applied in online teaching (Beach & Lundell, 1998; Brooks et al., 2001; Chickering

DOI: 10.4018/978-1-61520-749-7.ch014

& Ehrmann (1996); Chong, 1998; Merryfield, 2000; Palloff & Pratt, 1999; Ukpokodu, 2008; Maor, 1999, Maor & Hendriks, 2001; Bonk & Cunningham, 1998; Von Glasersfeld, 1995), many teacher educators are still skeptical and reluctant to embrace it because of concern about its efficacy to promote student quality learning (O'Quinn & Corry,2002) and the perception that best practices evidenced in traditional pedagogy are not adaptable in online teaching. More importantly, they fear compromising the specific acts of teaching that model for preservice and inservice teachers—the communal and collective act of teaching and learning—and loss of control and power. For example, only 6 percent of the faculty in my department has embraced online teaching. This is not to say that some faculty members have not integrated technology into their courses, but such integration is limited to posting of handouts, grades, quizzes, announcements, and frivolous blogging.

Like many teacher educators, I too harbored some concerns and fears about online teaching. Then I braced the challenge! Now that I have taught the online course for four consecutive years, how valid are my concerns? Is the quality of student learning compromised in an online course? Are best practices evidenced in traditional, face-to-face teaching adaptable in an online course? This case study examines these questions and documents my journey toward bracing to teach a critical teacher education course online. The case study is designed to debunk fears and concerns about online teaching in teacher education, and hopefully, will encourage teacher educators to embrace technology-enabled teaching and learning.

The case study explores three critical questions:

1. How well does an online course promote quality student learning in a critical teacher education course?:
2. To what extent, are best practices evidenced in traditional teacher education courses adaptable in online teaching?: and
3. What are the promises and paradoxes associated with designing and implementing online teaching in teacher education?

CASE DESCRIPTION

Research documents that online instruction is a relatively new phenomenon in teacher education, that only a few faculty engage in online teaching (Sunal, et al., 2003). It is also suggested that even when online teaching can be successfully achieved (Mckeon, 2001; Merryfield, 2000; Ukpokodu, 2008), fewer faculty embrace the challenge of technology-enabled teaching because of concerns of student quality learning and effective online pedagogies. Researchers have reported that social constructivist approaches to online teaching have the capability to create and enhance high quality, interactive online learning environments (Hara, Bonk & Angli, 2000; Garrison, et al., 2000). In fact, recent studies have revealed that the teaching and learning environment can foster interaction, collaboration and negotiation of meaning among participants (Maor, 1999; Maor & Hendriks, 2001; Bonk & Cunningham, 1998; Von Glasersfeld, 1995). These researchers and others suggested that the key elements in successful e- learning include: affective support, the creation of a community of learners, peer learning, reflective discourse, and student-centered learning with the instructor taking the role of facilitator (Maor, 2003; Jonassen, 2000). Generally, research suggests that online teaching is an "intellectually challenging forum which elicits deeper thinking on the part of students," and "has some definite advantages that may make. .. the work worth the effort" (Smith, Ferguson & Caris, p. 67). Given this development, various studies have been undertaken to compare the effectiveness of e-teaching/learning versus traditional, face-face-to format. However, most studies have focused on aspects of e-teaching/learning, such as time, workload, dropout rates, and performance of students in online discussions and face-to-face discussions, rather than fully on-line teaching. For example, Althaus examined the academic performance of students who had face-to-face discussions versus those who used on-line discussions. Althaus (1997) found that students who were involved in online discussions created responses that were more thoughtful because they had more time to read and think about their responses compared to students in a face-to-face setting. Althaus also found that the student in the online class earned higher grades than that of the student in the traditional classroom (Christopher, Thomas & Tallent-Runnels, 2004). Some studies have specifically compared online to in-class formats and found that online courses were no less effective than traditional in-class formats when looking at the learning results of students (Lim 2002; Neuhauser 2002; Ngu 2002), that students were generally satisfied with online learning (Allen et al., 2002; Moore, 2002). Other studies have suggested that, the online learning environment has a unique potential to promote an in-depth dialogue and a framework of openness to new knowledge and ideas (Thomas, 2002; Wolfe, 2001). In other studies comparing two sections of a course, one face-to-face and one online, the findings showed that online learning was as effective as face-to-face learning. For example, Blocher and Tucker (as cited in Fuller & McBride, 2001) reported that more students taking the online course found the course to be better than expected than those who found the course to be what they expected or less than they expected. Karen Hughes Miller (2006) in her study of graduate two sections of a course (online and face-to-face), she found that online learning can be every bit as effective as teaching and learning face-to-face. However, other studies have been inconclusive regarding the quality of student learning in online courses.

Context and Data Sources

I teach at a university located in a large urban community. For the past seventeen years, I have taught courses in teacher education that prepares prospective and inservice teachers to become highly qualified and competent teachers. In particular, I have taught courses on diversity, multicultural education with an emphasis on culturally responsive social justice pedagogy. I work with prospective and inservice teachers who fit the national profile described in the literature—predominantly European Americans (whites), middle-class, suburban, rural, female, conservative, and often culturally and racially encapsulated (U.S. Department of Education, 2003; Ukpokodu, 2003; Villegas and Lucas, 2002), as well as those of color. My courses are aimed at fostering student reflective processes and transformative learning. In this context, my scholarship of teaching is grounded in literature on critical reflection (Dewey, 1933; Loughran, 2002), transformative learning (Mezirow, 2000; Clark, 1993; O'Sullivan, 2003), critical pedagogy (Freire, 1970; Giroux, 1988; Greene, 1998), constructivism and socio-cultural learning theory (Bonk & Cunningham, 1998; Collins & Berge, 1996; Vygotsky, 1978), multicultural education (Banks, 2007; Nieto, 2000) and social justice (Ayers, 1998; Oakes, 1995; Oakes & Lipton ;2007). Most of these theorists have been mostly concerned about issues of educational equity and social justice and the value of education for humanization and empowerment, and change agency and the link to teacher quality.

Interestingly, five years ago, my concern for quality learning in my traditional, face-to-face courses made me to reconsider and brace online teaching. While students often appreciated the interactive and experiential classroom learning experiences I facilitated, I often felt dissatisfied with their lack of self-regulated learning behavior, critical knowledge and scholarship development, and lack of high-level intellectual development.

How ironical! While a decade and half ago I felt that online teaching/learning produced low quality student learning, it would now be a possible solution to the low quality learning I perceived among my students. However, I still agonized over the potential of online teaching to promote students' quality learning. How would I foster interactions, collaboration, discussion, and collective learning that often characterize my face-to-face courses? This would change. A year before the design and implementation of my first online course, I had the opportunity to attend a session at a conference on technology integration in a methods course. I was impressed, inspired, convinced and so, on my way to developing and teaching my online course. In the fall semester of 2005, I developed and taught the online course entitled "Teaching for equity and social justice" to K-12 teachers. It is one of the courses that fulfill the diversity requirement in our graduate program.

The course objectives include the examination of the connection between education for social justice and democratic citizenship; comprehending and analyzing teachers' role in a multicultural democracy and issues of educational equity and social justice; developing skills for self-critique and transformative intellectualism and practice; examining models of curricular and pedagogical practices of social justice education; and designing personal plans that integrate social justice into their development and practice. The broad goal of the course is to move teachers beyond mere recognition of diversity and shallow multicultural practices (Nieto, 2000) to raising and heightening their awareness about teaching as a political activity and social responsibility. The course goals listed above align closely with my teacher education program dispositions that include: teachers who are open-minded regarding divergent worldviews; are aware of and actively confront their own biases, prejudices; take responsibility for positive change; commit to and advocate for educational equity and social justice; display professional ethics and universal human values and teachers who are reflective and conscientious about their professional responsibility.

The course utilized the Blackboard Management System Software. Although the course was a full online course, it also involved a mandatory three face-to-face class meetings. The first two meetings occurred in the first two weeks of the semester and designed to provide orientation and overview of the course and to engage students in initiatory and stimulating cultural and get-to-know-you activities, community building and completion of pre-course instructional surveys. The orientation meeting focused on Blackboard navigation, discussion and negotiation of course expectations, requirements, location of materials, assignment for partnership learning, discussion board topics and participation expectation, use of electronic reserves, video links, etc. Like a traditional course, students were provided hard copies of the syllabus, which was also posted on Blackboard. Second class meeting was a follow-up to the first meeting and focused on answering questions, taking pictures for self-introduction that were posted on Blackboard for reference. The third class meeting met two weeks before the end of the semester. The purpose of this meeting was to bring the students back to share perspectives about their learning experiences and for oral presentation of their of research investigation.

The course was divided into an introduction section and five learning modules. Each module listed the topic for examination followed by a listing of resources/materials that included textbook reading materials, supplemental articles, videos (in some cases); required assignments, due dates and module assessment. The online course has been taught for the past four years (2005-2008) with a total enrollment of sixty-five students. The students who have enrolled in the course have varied in terms of race, gender, teaching positions and experience. About 95 percent of the students who have enrolled in the course were taking a full-fledged online course for the first time and could barely navigate the Blackboard. However, most had engaged in Blackboard blogging. The central questions explored in this study are:

1. How well does an online course promote quality student learning in a critical teacher education course?
2. To what extent, are best practices evidenced in traditional teacher education courses adaptable in online teaching?
3. What are the promises and paradoxes associated with designing and implementing online teaching in teacher education?

The data for this case study were drawn from the 2005 and 2008 courses—the first and last time the course had been taught. A combined student enrollment in both classes was twenty-nine. There were twenty Caucasians (70%), four African Americans (14%), five international (17%), eight males (41%), and seventeen females (59%). Both quantitative and qualitative data were collected. The primary data sources include formal student end-of-course evaluation, alternative anonymous course evaluations (constructed by me, the course instructor), written student surveys, student email correspondences, and the researcher's field notes. The formal end-of-course evaluations were administered two weeks prior to the end of the semester. The alternative course assessment and surveys were administered the last day of the course. The alternative anonymous assessment was titled, "how can I improve: I need your help!" Students were asked to provide specific feedback for course improvement and were asked to not identify themselves on the form.

Analysis and Findings

Both quantitative and qualitative data were used for analysis. To address the first question, how well an online course produces quality student learning, I analyzed data from formal student end-of-course evaluations administered by my institution. The evaluation instrument known as "IDEA" and student anonymously rated the course based on their experience. The instrument lists learning objectives related to student quality learning that their perception of it is summarized in Table 1 below. Students are asked to list their progress on the objectives (1-low to 5-high). For example, students identify their progress on learning fundamental principles, generalizations, or theories. In both 2005 and 2008 evaluations, students' ratings of the courses were high, denoting satisfaction and the quality of learning. Students rated highly their development in significant areas such as learning fundamental principles related to the course; learning to analyze and apply course materials to improve thinking and solve problems; developing skills, competencies, and points of view needed by professionals in the field; learning to analyze and critically evaluate ideas, arguments, and points of view, among others. The summary evaluation of the overall excellence of teacher and course was 4.4. The high ratings of these specific objectives and overall course effectiveness should be viewed as a measure of students' satisfaction with the quality of learning and the course.

The second data involved two informal, alternative anonymous assessment surveys. The first informal assessment was a self-constructed open-ended questionnaire that I administered for students to rate their perceptions about the course content, the quality of learning, opportunities for interactions, comparison between online learning versus face-to-face learning, communication and interaction between instructor and students, feedback on assignments, and overall learning experience (see Table 2). The students' ratings were based on a Likert Scale of 1 (low) to 5 (high).

The second informal assessment was a questionnaire with open-ended items entitled "I need your help: How can I improve!" The survey questions asked students to identify their perceptions of what they liked best and least about the course and its organization, experiences and activities that were most beneficial, learning activities that enhanced their learning, changes I should make,

Table 1. Student end-of-course evaluation

Fall Semester 2005		**Fall Semester 2008**	
% of Students Responding (12) 100%		% of Students Responding (17) 100%	
Overall Measures of Effectiveness On a Scale of 1-5 (1=low; 5 =High)	Raw Score Average	Overall Measures of Effectiveness On a Scale of 1-5 (1=low; 5 =High)	Raw Score Average
A. Progress on Relevant (Essential and Important Objectives)	4.4	A. Progress on Relevant (Essential and Important Objectives)	4.5
B. Overall Excellence of Teacher	4.3	B. Overall Excellence of Teacher	4.4
C. Overall Excellence of Course	4.2	C. Overall Excellence of Course	4.7
D. Average of B & C	4.3	D. Average of B & C	4.6
E. Summary Evaluation (A & D)	4.4	E. Summary Evaluation (A & D)	4.6
Student Ratings of Progress on Relevant Objectives		**Student Ratings of Progress on Relevant Objectives**	
Essential Objectives	Raw Score Average	**Essential Objectives**	Raw Score Average
Learning fundamental principles	4.5	Learning fundamental principles	4.6
Learning to apply course materials (to improve thinking, problem solve)	4.6	Learning to apply course materials (to improve thinking, problem solve)	4.5
Acquiring skills in working with others	4.3	Acquiring skills in working with others	4.4
		Developing skills, competencies, and points of view needed by professionals in the field	4.7
Important Objectives	Raw Score Average	**Important Objectives**	Raw Score Average
Developing skills in expressing myself orally or in writing	4.4	Developing skills in expressing myself orally or in writing	4.4
Learning how to find and use resources for answering questions or solving problems	4.3	Learning how to find and use resources for answering questions or solving problems	4.3
Developing a clearer understanding of, and commitment to, personal values	4.4	Developing a clearer understanding of, and commitment to, personal values	4.4
Acquiring an interest in learning more by asking my on questions	4.5	Acquiring an interest in learning more by asking my on questions	4.5
Learning to analyze and critically evaluate ideas, arguments, and points of view	4.5	Learning to analyze and critically evaluate ideas, arguments, and points of view	4.7
Developing skills, competencies, and points of view needed by professionals in the field	4.7		

the effectiveness of online learning, and the ways specific pedagogies and activities benefitted them (see Table 3). Students' responses were.

Additionally, given that I have taught the course both from a traditional and asynchronous mode, I found it pertinent to reflect on both courses to discern some comparisons especially in terms of learning quality. I first taught the course "Teaching for equity and social justice" in 2003 in a traditional, face-to-face format and online in 2005. First, in my assessment, both in the traditional and online format, student end-of-course evaluations (formal and informal) revealed that the course was well received and students unanimously agreed that the course was an eye-opening experience, that they were exposed, for the first time, to the concepts of educational equity and social justice. Most of the students stated, that prior to their engagement in the course, they had never considered the values and politics that pervade education especially the

Table 2. End-of-course survey

Criteria	SA (5)	A (4)	NS (3)	D (2)	SD (1)
1. The course raised my awareness about educational equity and social justice	27 (93%)	2 (7%)	0	0	0
2. I know and understand more about issues of educational equity and justice than I did at the start of the course	27 (93%)	2 (7%)	0	0	0
3. The course challenged me to think about issues of educational equity and social justice	27 (93%)	2 (7%)	0	0	0
4. The course materials enhanced my knowledge of the course discourse	27 (93%)	2 (7%)	0	0	0
5. The course challenged me to think about my professional role in a new way	27 (93%)	2 (7%)	0	0	0
6. The course helped me to reflect on who I am	27 (93%)	2 (7%)	0	0	0
7. The course helped me to think about my students (**1 student didn't answer**)	25 (86%)	3 (10%)	0	0	0
8. I gained diverse perspectives about others' thinking of issues about educational equity and social justice	26 (90%)	3 (10%)	0	0	0
9. The quality of learning in this course was high	26 (90%)	3 (10%)	0	0	0
10. The quality of learning in this course was as high as in a traditional course	27 (93%)	2 (7%)	0	0	0
11. The quality of learning in this course was higher compared to a traditional course	26 (90%)	3 (10%)	0	0	0
12. I grew more scholarly in this online course than in a face-to face course	23 (79%)	5 (17%)	1 (3%)	0	0
13.Opportunity was provided for peer interaction in this course	22 (76)	5 (17%)	2 (7%)	0	0
14. The quality of interaction in this course was high	15 (52%)	10 (34%)	4 (14%)	0	0
15. I had as much interaction with my peers in this course as in a face-to-face course	9 (31%)	12(41%)	4 (14%)	3 (10%)	1(3%)
16. I was prepared for the demand of this online course	3 (10%)	1 (3%)	3 (10%)	19(66%)	3 (10%)
17. Taking this course online course was valuable	6 (21%)	17 (58%)	4 (14%)	2 (7%)	0
18. This course should not be taught as an online course	1 (3%)	0	3 (10%)	9 (31%)	16 (55%)
19. As an online course, the assignments were adequate	15 (52%)	10 (34%)	2 (7%)	2 (7%)	0
20. Feedback on assignments was prompt and meaningful	25 (86%)	4 (14%)	0	0	0
21. I received prompt response to my inquiries	26 (90%)	2 (7%)	1 (3%)	0	0
22. I received adequate assistance when I needed it	25 (86%)	3 (10%)	0	1(3%)	0
23. The professor was flexible	21(72%)	5 (17%)	2 (7%)	1 (3%)	0

(SA = Strongly Agree, A = Agree, NS = Not Sure, D = Disagree, SD = Strongly Disagree)

examination of inequities associated with student race, class, gender, language, sexual orientation in their own practices and thought that issues of equity and social justice stemmed from funding and resources due to districts' tax allocation and formula) and had nothing to do with their teaching. Thus, for students both in the asynchronous and synchronous courses, the course has been overwhelmingly a positive experience.

However, in terms of the quality of learning, students in the online course definitely evidenced a more deepened understanding, critical thinking, and high-level scholarship than those in the traditional course. This conclusion is drawn from

Table 3. Student perceptions of online course experience

What did you like best about the course and its organization? List/ explain	• High expectation for learning (24, 83%) • On-line discussion (29, 100%) • Clarity of assignments (29, 100%) • Prompt and detailed feedback (29, 100%) • Partner sharing learning (24, 83%) • Variety of reading materials (23, 79%) • Liked the scoring rubrics in advance (25, 86%)
What did you like least about the course and its organization? List/ explain	• Amount of reading (25, 86%) • Too much work in a semester (27, 93%) • Writing for every assessment (5, 17%) • Too much to read and write in a short time (15, 59%)
What experiences/activities were most beneficial? List/explain	• On-line discussion (29, 100%) • Partner shared learning (24, 83%) • Teachers feedback (29, 100%) Blackboard discussions, because other students views were interesting and helpful (26, 90%) The readings, reflective papers and final project (23, 79%), Rigor (21, 72%) • Pre/post narratives (29, 100%) • None

a comparative analysis of the top-scoring papers on assignments from each group. In both course formats I required identical assignments such as reading response papers, pre-post self-reflective narratives, and threaded online discussions, among others. In addition, identical textbooks were required for both course formats. For example, one identical assignment that was analyzed for comparison purpose was the reading response paper. This assignment required students to develop a response to a module scenario on teaching for equity and social justice. Angela was enrolled in the traditional, face-to-face course and her introductory response paragraph is as follows:

The inequity of Eurocentric curriculum was mentioned such as tracking, high stake testing, educational profiling, language inequalities, race, and sex inequities. Since Eurocentric curriculum which is patriarchal in nature does not address or respond to all the microcultures in our society, therefore, we must try to reach all students irrespective of their cultural, economic, gender, ability, and racial background. (Student, 2003)

Mindy, who enrolled in the 2005 online course, introduced her response with more sophistication and scholarship.

In their book, Teaching to Change the World (2007), Oakes and Lipton address the issues of educational inequity and injustice of diverse students who are "underserved" in urban schools. The authors assert that many urban schools have a lack of adequate resources, teachers with low expectations of their students, tracking (race, class, gender, and language), unresponsive Eurocentric curriculum, high-stakes testing, and large class sizes due to lack of teachers. As a result of such scenarios, students are conflicted with low academic achievement. Given the previous scenario, Oakes and Lipton (2007) challenge teachers as to what qualifies a teacher to be socially just in efforts to provide equal access of educational opportunities to students in urban schools (Oakes and Lipton, 2007, p. 4). (Student, 2005).

In addition, as I compared the discussion threads from both courses, students in the online course evidenced more sophisticated, reflective and scholarly responses than those in the traditional course who provided simplistic, less reasoned and uninformed comments.

The reasons for the high-level performance of the students enrolled in the online course are not far-fetched. In an online course, students must be actively involved, be self-disciplined and directed. They must be active to learn and perform. Because the students primarily direct their own learning, it forces them to engage and interact with course materials and therefore forges a high cognitive response. On the other hand, based on my personal experience and conversations with some colleagues, in traditional courses, most graduate students rarely read assigned materials and textbooks. At best, they skim the material for a general view of the materials and do not read for understanding. As one student stated in an email correspondence to me, "I am concerned about my poor performance on the reading response papers. I know now that I must challenge myself to fully absorb the readings to gain a deeper knowledge of the materials instead of skimming." Additionally, in traditional classes, students always rely on the professor to provide the lecture points that they should learn, answer questions on the spot (Lankbeck & Mugler, 2000; Smith, Ferguson & Caris, 2002). They expect the professor to come prepared with what they should know—the lectures, and so do not bother to read. Most graduate students are teachers who work full time, which leaves them with less time to do the readings.

In all my courses I expect students to read assigned materials and to be prepared to raise questions for class discussion, but they often fall short of it. In fact, recently, I have started administering in my traditional classes what I call "quick writes" to test students' engagement and understanding of assigned readings. Most students do poorly in them because they either do not read the materials or fail to read for understanding and retention. Students have confessed in class, actually complained, that because of their busy work schedules—writing lesson plans, teaching, testing, and conferencing with parents and living their personal lives—they are left with no time to read and submit quality work. This does not happen in an online course. Students enrolled in an online course recognize and know that they are held accountable for all module materials and expected to demonstrate evidence of interaction and engagement with the readings when they submit their reading response papers. For example, students' comments provided in an anonymous, alternative course assessment entitled "I need your help; How can I improve!" when asked to list what they liked best about the course and its organization, noted: "the elaborate readings, the reading response papers which required full engagement with the reading in order to write quality papers." In addition, when asked to describe the quality of learning in the online course, students described the course as "rigorous, active, challenging, enriched, meaningful and gratifying."

Regarding the course goal of transformative learning, how well did students in the online course experience it? Transformative educators have defined transformative learning, as learning that produces a significant impact, or paradigm shift, which affects the learner's subsequent experiences (Clark, 1993). As Mezirow (1997) also explains, to foster transformative learning, students would have to change their frames of reference by critically reflecting on their assumptions and beliefs and consciously making and implementing plans that bring about new ways of defining their worlds and understanding. Through the varied forms of assignment in the course, students constantly reflected on their pre-post course experience. Overwhelmingly, all students reported that the course was transformative. For example, most students reported naivety about issues of educational equity and social justice in their pre-narrative but noted developing better knowledge and understanding of issues of inequities and injustice including their manifestation in their own classroom practices and discovering their own passive role in functioning as transformative intellectuals and agents of change (Giroux, 1988). Most students in the course described various practices that they thought were good teaching practices such as ability grouping, but realized were actually inequitable and unjust, and discussed plans to do things differently to ensure equity and social justice for their students. As previously explained transformative learning occurs when individuals reflect on their prior experiences and are able to alter their preconceived perspectives about society, institution and practice (Ukpokodu, 2008). This was evident in the students' writings across the course.

Data from the course survey also attests to students' perception of the quality of learning. Students' ratings of the items were very positive. Specific questions related to their perception of the quality of learning and as compared to courses in a traditional face-to-face courses, were very positive (see Table 2). Specific items reflected student perception of the (a) knowledge of the course content (items 1-3). For example, students overwhelmingly responded positively (100%) that the course helped them to gain knowledge about the course discourse—issues of educational equity and social justice (b) quality of learning (items 9-12). These items specifically asked students to rate the quality of the learning in the course. Students also unanimously agreed that the quality of learning was high. Additionally, the students reported that the quality of learning was as great as the traditional face-to-face learning they had experienced and even greater in the online course. All items in this category received a 100% rating (c) opportunity for peer interaction (items 13-15). Students also agreed that the course provided for peer interaction (93%) and that the quality of interaction was high (86%).

Research question #2 explored the extent to which best practices evidenced in traditional teacher education courses are adaptable in online teaching? There has been a substantial amount of literature regarding principles and practices that promote effective teaching practices that promote student quality learning (Chickering & Gamson, 1987; Chickering & Ehmann, 1996). Most of these essential principles include student active engagement, high interactivity, cooperative and collaborative learning, and the changing role of the instructor from the sage on stage to facilitation (Jonassesn, 2000; Tobin, 1993; Von Glasersfeld, 1995). In most teacher education programs, because of the importance of modeling best practices for prospective and inservice teachers, most teacher educators engage in these pedagogical practices. This is particularly so with courses on multicultural education, designed to foster critical dialogue, reflective thinking, collective learning, perspective consciousness and transformative learning. In teaching the face-to-face 2003 course on "teaching for equity and social justice," I promoted these practices such as, establishing high expectation for student learning; creating a learning community that fosters open spaces for dialogic and dialectical relationship, active, interactive, collaborative learning; learner engagement in experiential activities;, critical reflection, and rational discourse.

These practices have been classified into four clusters determined to promote quality online teaching and learning—learner-instructor interaction, learner-learner interaction, learner-content interaction, course organization, instructor as facilitator, and delivery method (Roberts et al., 2005). In teaching the online course, given the data analysis, I would say that I successfully adapted these pedagogical practices. High expectation was fostered through requiring rigorous, active, and challenging assignments; a learning community was fostered through collaborative learning involving three threaded discussion boards, partnership learning for learning support, and collaborative project; critical reflection through writing pre-post self-reflective narratives and writing four reading response papers in which they examined their prior conceptions and practices. Most students, overwhelmingly expressed valuing and benefitting from these learning experiences (for details, see (Ukpokodu, 2008). However, a minor challenge I encountered in adapting traditional pedagogies was the use of videos to enhance students' learning. The lack of a face-to-face meeting prevented active discussions of the videos among students. Students individually viewed, constructed meaning, although some did use the information from the videos to support their perspectives on discussion threads and post-self-reflective narrative.

Finally, research question #3 examined the strengths and challenges associated with teaching a critical teacher education course online. For this question, I drew on my field notes/journal and email correspondences. Like teaching and learning in a traditional classroom format, teaching an online course has its strengths and challenges. In my reflection, the major strength of teaching an online course is the high quality of student learning that is influenced by course rigor, challenge, high expectation, and opportunity for collaborative, reflective, and critical reflection. The high level of scholarly work and higher-order thinking, knowledge synthesis and integration, and connection to praxis is unsurpassed. In teaching the online course, upon the inception of the course, most students quickly became aware of the lack of rigor and challenge in their past learning and their dependency on professor for their learning. This was the case for Andrianne, who took the online course (2005) for the first time and struggled through the first few assignments. As she expressed in an email correspondence to me:

Thank you for taking the time to help me understand what I am supposed to be doing in the course. It was difficult to understand at first, but I think I now have a wider view of the topics and assignments. The course has opened my eyes to the fact that perhaps I have not been challenged enough by my self and other professors. Thank you! (Student, 2005)

Another strength I discovered was the opportunity for increased and intimate interaction between students and me. In a traditional course, students rarely seize the opportunity to actively interact with the professor outside of class, unless their grades are at-risk. In the online course I found that students and I were constantly communicating and interacting about the course discourse, sharing insights and perspectives. Although I have always considered myself a facilitator of learning regardless of the classroom setting, in a traditional teaching setting, it is impossible for the professor not to control both the content and learning environment, which fosters student dependency. On the other hand, in an online course, students are totally dependent on themselves for learning, which changes the role of the professor from that of information dispenser to a facilitator of learning.

In teaching online, I experienced the true meaning of being a facilitator of learning—designing the curriculum, setting goals and objectives, creating the environment for collaborative, contextual and active learning and guiding students toward realizing the course goals. In order for online learning to be successful, teachers as well as learners must take on new roles and I found myself experiencing a new role. Another strength of online teaching is the opportunity to improve my teaching practice—becoming more responsive and responsible in my communication and provision of feedback to students. I developed a new love for responding and providing feedback on assignments. I learned to provide prompt, typed, detailed, personalized and informative feedback (Berge, 2002; Chickering & Gamson, 1987; Vrasidas & McIsaac, 2000) on assignments. More importantly, I learned to be more thoughtful when I provided feedback by highlighting strengths, areas of challenge and suggestions for work improvement. In both formal and informal course evaluation and assessment, students expressed appreciation for the prompt and meaningful feedback and communication (see Table 2, items 20 - 23). In addition, I developed a habit of responding promptly to emails from students in the online course. In fact, I realized that when I was away to conferences I made a conscious effort to regularly check emails and respond to emails of students in the online course than I did my traditional courses. Definitely, my email response rate for students in the online course was higher than the traditional course. Another major strength I found with the online course is the diminished tension between students and professor and display of student defensiveness and hostility often encountered in a course on diversity taught in a traditional, face-to-face setting especially when the professor is that of color (Alqhuist, 1990; Ukpokodu, 2002).

Some of the major challenges that I faced teaching the online course include time, workload/assignment appropriateness, students' unpreparedness for a rigorous online course especially lack of self-regulatory learning behavior, and assessment. First, I must say that teaching an online course is not less challenging than teaching it synchronously (Butcher, 2002; Young, 2002). Often the assumption that the professor of an online course does not have to prepare weekly lectures, go to class to teach and deal with complex classroom/student situations, makes an online course relatively easy. On the contrary, I found myself constantly working 24/7 when teaching online courses. This is the challenge that time poses. There is always the need to check for student emails and Blackboard for assignment submission especially late submissions. Providing immediate individualized detailed and collective feedback on assignments and responding to emails expeditiously (although a great teaching practice) can be overwhelming and takes a heavy toll on the professor's time. Designing the online course in itself is very demanding and challenging. Creating guidelines, the learning modules, selecting resources (videos and supplemental articles), constructing completion and scoring guides, takes time. Grading voluminous papers on several assignments, monitoring discussion threads on Blackboard, adjusting assignments and due dates, re-grading assignments and managing student correspondences can be overwhelming and time consuming.

Determining coursework/workload appropriateness can be extremely challenging and agonizing. In a course such as teaching for diversity, equity and social justice where the goal is to foster transformative learning, the temptation is to expose students to an array of resources that help develop knowledge, construct critical understanding, thinking, and reflection. As previously noted, the online course consisted of five learning modules with a lot of reading materials, videos that students must interact with in order to successfully complete the assignments especially the reading response papers. As I constructed the modules I agonized over how best to challenge students to develop the knowledge base on teaching for equity and social justice (discourse), curriculum, pedagogy, self-transformation and change agency. Understandably, I required four reading response papers with the option of dropping the lowest score. The dilemma about balancing quality and empathy can be difficult. From the student perspective, was requiring four reading response papers too much? I also required participation in three threaded discussions, partner-shared learning and submission of reflection paper, pre-post-self-reflective narratives and a final. Where these assignments too many for one semester? Was I sensitive to the demand on students' time? I struggled with this and as I read students' comments on the end-of-course evaluation about too much work and information overload, my dilemma continues.

Most students who enrolled in the course had never taken an online course. Even though students are cautioned about the demands and the self-discipline needed in an online course, some students still take it only to feel overwhelmed and sometimes frustrated especially when assignments are due. Students taking an online course often think it is easier because they do not have to attend class. However, they rarely understand that they must discipline and self-pace themselves to be successful. Unlike the traditional class where students would receive reminders in class about assignment due dates, students in an online course must regulate their learning and schedules. So I have faced a few students who initially lacked the self-regulatory learning behavior and who were not prepared for the demands of the course. There have been a few situations where students would email to say, what chapter are we supposed to be reading this week? What assignments are due? In other times, in an attempt to meet the deadline, students would submit unsatisfactory work with an excuse—"I am closing on a house this week, teaching four classes, stressed, so I cannot produce the kind of quality work I know you expect" and yet expect not only a passing grade but a decent grade.

The most challenge I have faced relates to assessing the work of students who are often unprepared for high-level and scholarly work, although this is not that different from the traditional, face-to-face course since all my courses whether online or traditional, are writing-intensive. The only difference is that the online course requires more written assignments than the traditional courses. In my observation, the nature of online course is that it works successfully for students with sophisticated linguistic skills. I have had students with limited linguistic skills (both domestic and international) who are challenged by the standard of work and scholarship expected in the course. Rocky explains, "I guess what I really gained from this course aside from learning about issues of educational equity and social justice is learning to write scholarly essays. I guess my past instructors had never challenged me in this way and I never had to write this much in any course." These students are also particularly challenged in the threaded discussion assignments as they fail to develop comprehensive, coherent and intelligent responses to the discussion threads. However, by the end of the course, most students do rise to the challenge and learn to write more quality papers but it takes several re-reading, providing detailed feedback. In some cases, I have been able to allow oral demonstration of knowledge over the phone but I struggle with the equitability of this practice.

The final and most difficult challenge is the inability to engage students more effectively in experiential learning activities such as simulation/role-playing especially, the "privilege walk," I now facilitate it on the last day of the course when the class meets face-to-face. But in spite of these challenges, the reward of online teaching makes it worthwhile. These students' comments illuminate the value and worthiness of online teaching.

Excellent way to create an online course. I like that she practiced what she preached.

One of the most challenging courses I have ever taken, but one of the most rewarding super insights gained.

This was a great course that enhanced a lot of knowledge. In spite of the work load, I felt like I was really in graduate school. Very knowledgeable instructor and works really hard.

This course was very insightful and a wonderful learning experience. All future or current teachers should attend this course.

SOLUTIONS AND RECOMMENDATIONS

This case study has documented my journey toward teaching online and examining my concerns about student quality learning in an online course in a critical teacher education course. The study dispelled my concern and fears that online teaching is inadequate and inappropriate substitute for the traditional, face-to-face teaching format. I not only found that quality learning can be effectively fostered in an online learning, but also that transformative learning, an important goal in teacher education for preservice and inservice teachers is possible. I also found that traditional pedagogies are adaptable in an online course especially that communal learning and high-level interactions are possible and easily facilitated. However, facilitating technology enhanced learning in a teacher education course must be well conceptualized, planned, orchestrated in order to be successful.

First, the course construction must be carefully planned to provide for an array of learning resources that actively and cognitively engage students. This includes using multiple texts that are diverse in perspectives, videos that provide for iconic learning, discussion boards that provide for collective learning and learner interaction. More importantly, structure the online learning environment around constructivist principles.

Second, establish high expectation for students' learning to foster a high sense of responsibility, accountability, self-regulated learning, and intentional learning. This also involves establishing due dates, clear expectation for quality work, providing completion and scoring guides (rubrics) for assignment completion.

Third, the learning environment must provide for high-level interactivity that involves learner-content, learner-learner, learner-instructor, and learner-interface (Chen, 2002; Moore & Kearsley, 1996). Collaborative learning has been noted as an effective element for promoting active student involvement with the course and more engagement in the learning process (Harasim, 1990)

Fourth, be proactive and scaffold student learning by anticipating problems and building partner-shared learning for learning support.

Fifth, the course instructor must be prepared to assume a new role of serving primarily as a facilitator rather than the traditional role of the sage on the stage.

Sixth, the instructor must be disciplined to provide prompt, informative, individualized and collective feedback on student learning. Timely feedback is one of the important variables in student learning (Berge, 2002; Chickering & Gamson, 1987; Vrasidas & McIsaac, 1999). Closely related to this, is the instructor's presence online and availability to student through responsiveness to student inquiries, providing individual feedback on assignments and rendering support and encouragement and exercising flexibility especially for revision and resubmit of unsatisfactory work.

REFERENCES

Ahlquist, R. (1991). Position and imposition: Power relations in a multicultural foundations class. *The Journal of Negro Education*, *60*(2), 158–169. doi:10.2307/2295607

Allen, M., Bourhis, J., Burrell, N., & Malbry, E. (2002). Comparing Student Satisfaction With Distance Education to Traditional Classrooms in Higher Education: A Meta-Analysis. *American Journal of Distance Education*, *16*(2), 83–97. doi:10.1207/S15389286AJDE1602_3

Althaus, S. (1997). Computer-mediated communication in the university classroom: An experiment with on-line discussion. *Communication Education*, *46*, 158–174. doi:10.1080/03634529709379088

Ayers, J. A. Hunt, & T. Quinn (Ed.), Teaching for social justice (xxvii-xlvi). New York: The New Press.

Ayers, W. (1998). Popular education: Teaching for social justice (xvi-xxv). In W. Ayers, J. A. Hunt, & T. Quinn (Ed.), Teaching for social justice. New York: The New Press

Banks, J. A. (2006). Cultural diversity and education: Foundations, curriculum, and teaching. Boston: Allyn & Bacon.

Beach, R., & Lundell, D. (1998). Early adolescent's use of computer-mediated communication in writing and reading. In P.D. Pearson & A. Iran-Nejad (Ed.), Review of Research in Education, 23, (pp. 235-275). Washington, DC: American Educational Research Association.

Berge, Z., & Collins, M. (1995). Computer-mediated communication and the Online classroom in distance learning. *Computer-Mediated Communication Magazine, 2*(4). Retrieved June 7, 2009, from http://www.ibiblio.org/cmc/mag/1995/apr/berge.html

Bonk, C. J., & Cunningham, D. J. (1998). Searching for learner-centered, constructivist, and sociocultural components of collaborative educational learning tools. In C. J. Bonk & K.S. King, (Ed.), Electronic collaborators: learner-centered technologies for literacy, apprenticeship, and discourse (pp25-50). Mahwah, NJ: L. Erlbuam Associates.

Brooks, M. (1997). Beyond teaching and learning paradigms: Trekking into the virtual university. *Teaching Sociology, 27*, 1–14. doi:10.2307/1319107

Butcher, D. (2002, May). Six professors discuss time online. *The Chronicle of Higher Education*, A32.

Chen, H. (2002). *Interaction In distance education*. Retrieved June 25, 2009, from http://seamonkey.ed.asu.edu/~mcisaac/disted/week2/7focushc.htmlhttp://seamonkey.ed.asu.edu/~mcisaac/disted/week2/7focushc.html

Chickering, A. & Ehrmann, S. C. (1996, October). Implementing the seven principles: Technology as lever. *AAHE Bulletin*, 3-6.

Chong, S. M. (1998). Models of asynchronous computer conferencing for collaborative learning in large college classes. In C. J. Bonk & K. S. King (Ed.), Electronic collaborators (pp.157-182). Mahwah, NJ: Lawrence Erlbaum.

Christopher, M., Thomas, J., & Tallent-Runnels, M. (2004). Raising the Bar: Encouraging High Level Thinking in OnlineDiscussion Forums. *Roeper Review, 8*(3), 166171.

Clark, M. C. (1993). Transformational learning. *New Directions for Adult and Continuing Education, 1993*(57), 47–56. doi:10.1002/ace.36719935707

Freire, P. (1970). Pedagogy of oppressed. New York: Continuum.

Fuller, F. D., & McBride, R. (2001). Distance Education: Section Introduction. Technology and Teacher Education Annual. Ames, IA: Society for Information Technology in Teacher Education.

Giroux, H. (1988). Teachers as transformative intellectuals: Toward a critical pedagogy of learning. North Hadly, MA: Bergin & Garvey.

Greene, M. (1998). Introduction: Teaching for social justice. In W.

Hara, N., Bonk, C. J., & Angeli, C. (1998). Content analysis of online discussion in an applied educational psychology. Bloomington, IN: Center for Research on Learning and Technology, Indiana University.

Harasim, L. E. (1990). On-Line Education: Perspectives on a new medium. New York: Praeger/Greenwood.

Jonassen, D. (2000). Toward a design theory of problem solving. *Educational Technology Research and Development, 48*(4), 63–85. doi:10.1007/BF02300500

Lankbeck, R., & Mugler, F. (2000). Distance learners of the South Pacific: Study strategies, learning conditions, and consequences for course design. *Journal of Distance Education, 15*(1), 63-80. Retrieved June 19, 2009 from http://www.jofde.ca/index.php/jde/article/view/159/359

Lim, D. H. (2002). Perceived Differences Between Classroom and Distance Education: Seeking Instructional Strategies for Learning Applications. *International Journal of Educational Technology, 3*(1), 20–32.

Loughran, J. J. (2002). Effective reflective practice. *Journal of Teacher Education, 53*, 33–34. doi:10.1177/0022487102053001004

Maor, D. (1999). Teacher and student reflections on interactions in an internet- based unit. In K. Martin, N. Stanley, & N. Davison (Ed.), *1999 Teaching* and Learning Forum: Teaching in the Disciplines/Learning in Context, The *Proceedings of the 8th Annual Teaching and Learning Forum,* (pp. 257–261). Perth, Australia: University of Western Australia.

Maor, D. (2003). Teacher's and students' perspectives on on-line learning in social constructivist learning environment. *Technology, Pedagogy and Education, 12*(2), 201–218. doi:10.1080/14759390300200154

Maor, D., & Hendriks, V. (2001, December). *Peer learning and reflective thinking in an on-line community of learners*. Paper presented at the Australian Association for research in Education (AARE), Fremantle, Australia. Retrieved from http://www.aare.edu.au/index.htm

Mckeon, C. A. (2001). Email as a motivating literacy event for one struggling reader: Donna's case. *Reading Research and Instruction, 40*, 185–202.

McLaren, P. (1998). Life in schools: An introduction to critical pedagogy in the foundation of education, (3rd Ed.). New York: Longman.

Merryfield, M. (2000). Using electronic technologies to promote equity. *Education, 26*, 342–36.

Metiri, Group. (2006). *Technology in the schools: What the research says.* Cisco Systems. Retrieved from http://www.cisco/web/strategy/docs/education/technologyinSchoolsReport.pdf

Mezirow, J., & Associates. (2000). Learning as transformation: Critical perspective on a theory in progress. San Francisco: Jossey-Bass.

Miller, K. H. (2006). One course, two ways: Lessons learned from teaching the same graduate course online and face-to-face. *E-learn Magazine*. Retrieved from http://www.elearnmag.org/subpage

Moore, M. G. (2002). Editorial: What Does Research Say About the Learners Using Computer-Mediated Communication in Distance Learning? *American Journal of Distance Education, 16*(2), 61–64. doi:10.1207/S15389286AJDE1602_1

Moore, M. G., & Kearsley, G. (1996). Distance Education: A systems View. Belmont, CA: Wadsworth Publishing Company.

NCES, National Center for Education Statistics. (2003). *Distance Education at Degree-Granting Postsecondary Institutions: 2000-2001.* U.S. Department of Education, National Center for Education Statistics Report. Retrieved June 20, 2009 from http://nces.ed.gov/pubsearch/pubsinfo.asp

Neuhauser, C. (2002). Learning Style and Effectiveness of Online and Face-to- Face Instruction. *American Journal of Distance Education, 16*(2), 99–113. doi:10.1207/S15389286AJDE1602_4

Ngu, B. H. (2002). Online Instruction Versus Face-to-Face Instruction At UNIMAS. *International Journal of Educational Technology, 3*(1), 1–19.

O'Quinn, L., & Corry, M. (2002). Factors that deter faculty from participating in distance education. *Online Journal of Distance Learning Administration, 5*(4). Retrieved from http://www.westga.edu/~distance/ojdla/winter54/Quinn54.htm

O'Sullivan, E. (2003). Bringing a perspective of transformative learning to globalized consumption. *International Journal of Consumer Studies, 27*(4), 326–330. doi:10.1046/j.1470-6431.2003.00327.x

Oakes, J. (1995). Keeping track: How schools structure inequality. New Haven, CT: Yale University Press.

Oakes, J., & Lipton, M. (2007). Teaching to change the world. Boston: McGraw- Hill.

Palloff, R. M., & Pratt, K. (1999). Building learning communities in cyberspace: Effective strategies for the online classroom. San Francisco: Jossey-Bass Publishers.

Smith, G. G., Ferguson, D., & Caris, M. (2002). Teaching online versus face-to- face. *Journal of Educational Technology Systems*, *30*(4), 337–364. doi:10.2190/FFWX-TJJE-5AFQ-GMFT

Sunal, W. D., Sunal, C. S., Odell, M. R., & Sundberg, C. L. (2003, Summer). Research-Supported Best Practices for Developing Online Learning. *Journal of Interactive Online learning, 2*(1), 1- 40.

Taylor, P., & Maor, D. (2000). Assessing the efficacy of on-line teaching with the Constructivist On-Line Learning Environment Survey. In A. Herrmann & M. Kulski (Ed.) Flexible Futures in University Teaching, (pp. 207-218). Perth, Australia: University of Western Australia

Ukpokodu, O. N. (2002). Breaking through preservice teachers' defensive attitudes in a multicultural education course. *Multicultural Education Magazine*, *9*(5), 25–33.

Ukpokodu, O. N. (2003). Teaching multicultural education from a critical perspective: Challenges and Dilemmas. *Multicultural Perspectives*, *5*(4), 17–23. doi:10.1207/S15327892MCP0504_4

Ukpokodu, O. N. (2008, November). Teachers' reflections on pedagogies that enhance learning in an online course on teaching for equity and social justice. *Journal of Interactive Online Learning*, *7*(3), 227–255.

U.S. Department of Education, Center for Education Statistics. (2003). Digest of education statistics, 2002 (NCES 20003-060). Washington, DC: Author.

Villegas, A. M., & Lucas, T. (2002)... *Journal of Teacher Education*, *53*(1), 20–32. doi:10.1177/0022487102053001003

Vrasidas, C., & McIsaac, M. S. (2000). Principles of pedagogy and evaluation for web-based learning. *Educational Media International*, *37*(2), 105–112. doi:10.1080/095239800410405

Vygotsky, L. (1978). Mind in society: The development of higher psychological processes. Cambridge, MA: Harvard University Press.

ADDITIONAL READING

Baugh, I. W., & Baugh, J. C. (1997). Global classrooms e-mail learning communities. *Learning and leading with Technology*, *25*, 38–41.

Beach, R., & Lundell, D. (1998). Early adolescents' use of computer-mediated communication in writing and reading. In P.D. Pearson & A. Iran-Nejad (Ed.), Review of Research in Education: Vol. 23 (pp.235-275). Washington, DC: American Educational Research Association.

Bennett, L. (2001). Online journals to reflect on teaching in an elementary social studies education course. *The International Social Studies Forum*, *1*, 17–32.

Berge, Z. L., & Muilenburg, L. Y. (2003). Barriers to distance education: Perceptions of K-12 educators. *Issue 1.Proceedings of the Society for Information Technology and Teacher Education International Conference* (pp. 256-259). Albuquerque, New Mexico USA, March 24-29. Retrieved July 14, 2009, from: http://www.emoderators.com/barriers/barriersk12.htmlRetrieved

Brown, E. L. (2004). Overcoming the challenges of stand-alone multicultural education courses: The possibilities of technology integration. *Journal of Technology and Teacher Education, 12*(4), 553–559.

Bullock, L. M., Gable, R. A., & Mohr, J. D. (2008). Technology-Mediated Instruction in Distance Education and Teacher Preparation in Special Education. *Teacher Education and Special Education: The Journal of the Teacher Education Division of the Council for Exceptional Children, 31*(4), 229–242. doi:10.1177/0888406408330644

Caywood, C., & Duckette, J. (2003). Online vs. On-Campus Learning in Teacher Education. *The Journal of the Teacher Education Division of the Council for Exceptional Children, 26*(2), 98–105. doi:10.1177/088840640302600203

Chen, S. (2007, Spring). Instructional design strategies for intensive online courses: An objectivist-constructivist blended approach. *Journal of Interactive Online Learning, 6*(1), 72–85.

Chickering, A. W., & Ehrmann, S. C. (1996). Implementing the seven principles: Technology as lever. *AAHE Bulletin*, 3-6.

Conrad, R., & Donaldson, J. A. (2004). Engaging the online learner. San Francisco, CA: Jossey-Bass.

Crowe, A. R. (2007). Learning to teach with mobile technology: A teacher educators' journey. In M. van't Hooft & K. Swan (Ed.), Ubiquitous Computing in Education: Invisible Technology, Invisible Impact (pp. 127-144). Mahwah, NJ: Erlbaum.

Damarin, S. K. (1998). Technology and multicultural education: The question of convergence. *Theory Into Pratice, 37*(1), 11–19. doi:10.1080/00405849809543781

Diem, R. A. (2000). Can it make a difference? Technology and the social studies. *Theory and Research in Social Education, 20*, 493–501.

DiRamio, D., & Wolverton, M. (2006). Integrating learning communities and distance education: Possibility or pipedream. *Innovative Higher Education, 31*(2), 99–113. doi:10.1007/s10755-006-9011-y

Dove, M. K., Fisher, S. C., & Smith, D. L. (2000). Internet learning connections between second graders and university teacher education electronic mentors. In D. L. Johnson, C.D. Maddux, & L. Liu (Ed.), Integration of technology into the classroom (pp.59-72). The Haworth Press.

Garner, R., & Young, M. D. (1999). Internet communication in six classrooms: Conversation across time, space, and culture. Mahwah, NJ: Erlbaum.

Harasim, L., Hiltz, S. R., Teles, L., & Turoff, M. (1995). Learning networks: A field guide to teaching and learning online. Cambridge, MA: MIT Press.

Harrington, H. (1997). Technology's second level effects: Fostering democratic communities. *Journal of Technology and Teacher Education, 5*, 203–222.

Harrington, H. L. (2002). Using computer conferencing to foster and assess prospective teachers' moral sensitivity. *Journal of Technology and Teacher Education, 10*(3), 323–342.

Howard, J. (2002). Technology-enhanced project-based learning in teacher education: Addressing the goals of transfer. *Journal of Technology and Teacher Education, 10*(3), 343–364.

Jonassen, D. H. (1996). Handbook of research for educational communications and technology. New York: Simon & Schuster.

Kinzer, C., & Risko, V. (1998). Multimedia and enhanced learning: Transforming preservice education. In D. Reinking, M. M. Mckenna, L. D. Labbo, & R. Kieffer (Ed.), Handbook of literacy and technology: Transformation in a post-typographic world (pp. 185-2002). Mahwah, NJ: Erlbaum.

Merryfield, M. (2001). The paradoxes of teaching a multicultural education course online. *Journal of Teacher Education*, *52*(4), 283–299. doi:10.1177/0022487101052004003

Palloff, R. M., & Pratt, K. (2003). The virtual student: A profile and guide to working with online learners. San Francisco, CA: Jossey-Bass.

Privateer, P. M. (1999). Academic technology and the future of higher education. *The Journal of Higher Education*, *70*, 60–79. doi:10.2307/2649118

Reinking, D., Mckenna, M. M., Labbo, L. D., & Kieffer, R. (1998). Handbook of literacy and technology: Transformation in a post-typographic world). Mahwah, NJ: Erlbaum.

Rodriguez, M. C., Ooms, A., & Montañez, M. (2008, Summer). Students' Perceptions of Online-learning Quality given Comfort, Motivation, Satisfaction, and Experience. *Journal of Interactive Online Learning*, *7*(2), 105–125.

Romiszowski, A. J., & Mason, R. (1996). Computer-mediate communications. In D. H. Jonassen (Ed.). Handbook of research for educational communications and technology (pp. 438-456). New York: Simon & Schuster.

Shapiro, N. (1998, Spring). Learning communities: Moving beyond classroom walls. *Metropolitan Universities*, 25-34.

VanFossen, P. J. (2006). The electronic republic? Evidence on the impact of the Internet on citizenship and civic engagement in the U.S. *The International Journal of Social Education*, *21*(1), 18–43.

Willis, J., & Mehlinger, H. (1996). Information technology and teacher education. In J.Sikula (Ed.). Handbook of research on teacher education (pp. 978-1029). New York: Macmillan Library Reference USA.

Zong, G. (2002). Can computer mediated communication help to prepare global teachers. An analysis of preservice social studies teachers' experience. *Theory and Research in Social Education*, *30*(4), 589–616.

KEY TERMS AND DEFINITIONS

Teacher Educator: A college/university faculty preparing future teachers in a teacher education program.

E-Teaching, E-Learning: Teaching or learning that is grounded in cyberspace and technologically mediated.

Traditional Pedagogy: Instructional practices used in a face-to-face teaching.

Prospective and In-Service Teachers: Future teachers in training and teachers currently teaching.

Diversity: A concept that exemplifies all cultural and human differences that include but not limited to, race, nationality, ethnicity, sex/gender, class, cultural heritage, language, exceptionality/disability, sexual orientation, etc.

Quality Student Learning: Achievement of high standard of academic goals within a defined course.

Pedagogical Adaptation: Successful application of traditional instructional strategies and activities in online learning environment.

Reflective Processes: A system of learning to think deeply and critically about one's learning and cognitive development.

E-Pedagogies: Electronic pedagogies that include content, activities, interactions, and relationships.

Transformative Learning: Learning that results in a shift in perspective as a result of critically reflecting on one's assumptions and frame of reference.

Chapter 15
Authentic Assessment Contribution to Competence Based Education:
Questions and Challenges

Alda Pereira
Universidade Aberta, Portugal

Luís Tinoca
Universidade Aberta, Portugal & Universidade de Lisboa, Portugal

Isolina Oliveira
Universidade Aberta, Portugal & Universidade de Lisboa, Portugal

ABSTRACT

The new adopted pedagogical model (Pereira et al., 2007) at a European distance teaching university called for the use of new assessment strategies aligned with the most recent paradigm for assessment design in online learning. This new scenario supported the introduction of new authentic assessment strategies (Gulikers, Bastiaens, & Kirschner, 2004) that allow learners to attain deeper levels of knowledge, professional development skills and thinking processes. In this case, the authors' explored a tool (the Learning Contract) to facilitate assessment authenticity as a way to promote student learning. They explored the use of the Learning Contract to increase student's responsibility and commitment for their own learning, while at the same time facilitating its alignment with their professional practice, and contributing to the development of their life-long learning competencies.

ORGANIZATION BACKGROUND

Pioneer in distance education in Europe, our university was founded in the mid 1980's and has been promoting formal actions related to higher education and continuous training, as well as actions concerning life-long learning aiming different sectors of population. It has also contributed to the active dissemination of the national language and culture. With its legal entity recently adapted to Higher Education National Law, it is currently

DOI: 10.4018/978-1-61520-749-7.ch015

managed by a structure composed by Rector, General Council (teachers and researchers, students, technical staff, Rector and external experts) and Management Council, and funded through a governmental budget, direct sales and student fees. The university is organized in four departments: Education and Distance Teaching; Humanities; Science and Technology; and Social Sciences and Management.

It is the main national centre of expertise, in the area of distance education, having developed the know-how that allows it to be the largest provider of on-line higher education degrees in the country. During the last three years, significant changes took place in the institution due to external causes – namely the Bologna Process -, but also due to an internal process of re-identification.

The current reorientation of the educational and training activities of the university implied the migration from an industrial distance education model, to a model focused on the development of competencies fully supported by information and communication tools. This transition resulted, not only from the current technological developments, but also from the construction of a European higher education space (Pereira, Quintas-Mendes, Morgado, Amante &Bidarra, 2007).

The university, being a distance teaching university, is particularly suited to tackle some of the recommendations, concerning the assurance of accessibility to education, expressed in the "Education and Training 2010" goals (European Commission, 2008a). The university decided to implement a fully virtual innovative teaching and learning methodology as envisaged in the Strategic Plan for 2006-2010 having four strategic priorities:

1. Institutional re-identification – it was recognized the need to adjust pedagogical offerings to the scale and demands of university level distance education, as it ought to be practice by a public university, leading to the redefinition of the university's pedagogical model.
2. Development and Innovation – this two independent notions in the same priority are justified by the fact that distance education has undergone (and continues to undergo) a refinement and a diversification of its methods and instruments which are largely a direct consequence of the rapid evolution of the information and communication technologies.
3. Openness – to develop the university on the principle and practice of openness in reaffirming its specific mission, namely, investing in the promotion of education as a mean to affirming citizenship. Another distinct dimension of openness concerns the process of internationalization.
4. Cooperation – the geo-cultural and linguistic area of the African countries in which Portuguese is the official language is a factor of strategic relevance. Cooperation must also be thought in terms of the existing or future expectations of civil society and its different social and professional groups. Distance education can and must play a decisive role in the processes of life-long learning and professional re-qualification.

Following this Strategic Plan, some actions have been developed:

- The establishment and application of a pedagogical model which intends to serve as an indispensable point of reference for a distance education university, paying particular attention to the increasing relevance of on-line education.
- The development of a continuing plan for the professor professional development in the area of e-learning.
- The development of the Virtual Student Kit.
- The attempt to promote the electronic inclusion of students, leading to the carrying out of administrative processes (applications,

enrolment, etc) in digital formats and through on-line communication.

- The creation of distance learning in the areas of life-long learning and professional re-qualification.
- The establishment of concerted actions (mainly Conferences and Seminars) with other institutions and political agents aimed at broadening cooperation with the Portuguese speaking world.
- The creation of a new research unit - the Distance Education Laboratory. Some of its goals include: applied research focused on virtual pedagogies; the development and testing of pedagogical and technological innovative solutions; gathering, sharing and disseminating knowledge in the area of E-learning; promotion of advanced professional development for course designers and e-tutors.
- In the international context, the university has been participating in a considerable number of projects, namely the ones co-founded by EU programs.

SETTING THE STAGE

The new adopted pedagogical model (Pereira et al., 2007), in use since 2007, resulted from a reflection carried out by a multidisciplinary team of teachers and researchers from the university under reference, who mobilized all their experience and know-how accumulated in more than half a decade of successful teaching in formal online courses. This model is "strongly dominated by the valuing of students' social and communal integration, personalized monitoring of their learning and the respect for the particular life experience of each student" (p.8). The four cornerstones of the model are: student-centered learning, flexibility, interaction and digital inclusion, aligned with the key competences required for learners in this knowledge-based society (Directorate for Education, Employment, Labour and Social Affairs, 2002). The cornerstone of digital inclusion is particularly important in the context of a fully virtual learning environment, such as the one offered at university. In this way, the University is promoting the development of competences in the use of information and communication technologies (ICT), especially in the case of adults who, even without having such ITC competences, want to enroll in a higher education institution. In this context, being a student at the university is a factor for social inclusion, contributing to digital literacy.

The university's presented pedagogical model is supported through the use of a free Learning Management System (Moodle®). Learning Management Systems (LMSs) are essential tools to modern teaching institutions. Moodle is an open source LMS, widely used by open and distance teaching universities, as well as to support face-to-face courses. There are almost 40,000 registered Moodle sites, all over the world (Coelho & Rocio, 2008). Moodle can be installed in a wide range of environments: operating systems (Linux, Windows), supporting databases (MySQL, PostgreSQL, ...), and hardware. Moreover, Laboratory researchers developed adaptations to Moodle's configurations and features in order to better adjust it to the University pedagogical model. For instance, the learning card is a device where students' continuous assessment grades are recorded for each course. It uses the credit card metaphor, whereby students accumulate points throughout the course, as established in our pedagogical model for online learning. This gives both teachers and students the feeling of granting and scoring points in a card, as a reward for accomplishing the goals proposed in particular activities, as opposed to globally compute a final grade as a function of its components. Additionally, code changes to the standard assignment module software were necessary, to allow finer-grained grading (Rocio, Coelho & Pereira, 2008).

At the university, the professors are responsible for the curriculum design and implementation, as well as the interactions established within each course. Moreover, the presented pedagogical model introduced new teaching and learning methodologies, supported by new forms of interaction, particularly the interaction among students, that were absent in the industrial models for distance learning and required a substantial change in the professors' practice.

This strategic choice for a highly virtual institution required a significant professional development effort for all of the university's professors. For that reason, a three-step professional development program was created and all professors required to enroll (Morgado, Quintas-Mendes, Oliveira & Goulão, 2008). The first training level required all professors to complete a fully online course, aimed at making teachers understand distance education students; how distance education differs from face-to-face instruction or traditional distance education; understanding the new learning model of the university; and to make participants develop the skills they need to design, implement and deliver online courses. The program also included guidelines for clear communication and netiquette.

The pedagogical design of the teacher's training course was based on the needs and principles described above. Online education involves, naturally, the mastering of some technical skills and tools, but the real challenges for an online teacher are of a pedagogical and didactical nature, not technological. The course structure, pedagogical principles and main activities are described in Table 1. The training was certified, corresponding to 4 European Credit Transfer System (ECTS) points, and all the activities were assessed.

Table 1. Course structure and activities

Course Modules	Pedagogical principles underlying each module	Main Activities in each module
1) Welcome, Self-Presentation Online Communication and Online Learning Work in Groups and Online Discussion	Immersive Experiential learning Embedded approach	Using the Web/Search in the Web Retrieving useful sites for e-teachers Decide/Negotiate in Group Discussion
2) Distance Education and Online Education	Immersive Experiential learning Conceptual & Reflexive learning Embedded approach	Online Debate (Forum)
3) Online Teacher and the e-teacher	Immersive Experiential learning Conceptual & Reflexive learning Embedded approach	Problem Based Learning Working in Teams; Moderating a Discussion Teaching in a Online Learning Context Communication and Collaboration in Online Learning
4) Designing an Online Activity	Immersive Know How To Experiential learning Embedded approach	Design an e-tivity
5) Design of a Curricular Unit Project	Immersive Know How To Embedded approach Conceptual & Reflexive learning	Design of a curricular unit project Reflective journal

CASE DESCRIPTION

New Learning Environments - New Assessment Strategies

The implementation of the new pedagogical model forced, and at the same time called for, the use of new assessment strategies aligned with the most recent paradigm for assessment design in online learning (Bates & Pool, 2003; Birenbaum, 2003; Birenbaum et al. 2006; Black, Harrisson, Lee, Marshall & Wiliam, 2003; Brown, Bull & Pendlebury, 1997; Mateo & Sangrà, 2007; Orvis & Lassiter, 2007). To implement this change, it is necessary that all teachers become knowledgeable in these new alternative approaches to assessment in higher education (Maclellan, 2004). According to Maclellan (2004), alternative assessment is characterized by:

- Student involvement in setting goals and criteria for assessment;
- performing a task, creating an artifact/product;
- Use of higher level thinking and/or problem solving skills;
- measuring metacognitive, collaborative and intrapersonal skills as well as intellectual products;
- measuring meaningful instructional activities;
- Contextualization in real world applications;
- Use of specified criteria, known in advance, which define standards for good performance. (p. 312)

The Bologna Process (European Commission, 2008b) challenged Higher Education to promote learning environments that go beyond an objectives based instruction to a new paradigm centered on the development of competencies. This shift requires not only a change in the perceived goals of the higher education system and on the selection of methodological approaches to be used, but also a drastic change in the assessment strategies to be used in order to foster and assess a competence-based learning curricula. As Baartman, Bastiaens, Kirschner, and Vleuten (2007) put it "if European countries want to reform their curricula, assessment must have an important place in the reform process and assessment approaches need to focus on the integrated assessment of knowledge, skills and attitudes". To attain this goal, we propose to share our Competency Assessment Program (Baartman et al., 2007) for an online Masters course where the main objective was to further the students understanding about "how to learn", particularly when learning is mediated through technological tool. This new scenario calls for authentic assessment strategies that allow learners to attain deeper levels of knowledge, professional development skills and thinking processes (Elwood & Klenowski, 2002; Gardner, 2006; Gulikers, Kester, Kirschner & Bastiaens, 2008), closer and more relevant to their professional practicum. On the one hand, several authors refer to the relevance of assessment authenticity (Gulikers, Bastiaens, & Kirschner, 2004; Macdonald, 2004; Maclellan, 2004), focused on the way that knowledge, skills and attitudes are used in order to reflect real world contexts. On the other hand, Mateo and Sangrà (2007) emphasize the importance of authentic experiences to build mental structures that work in significant situations, defining the concept of authenticity "as a function of the type of cognitive challenge proposed by the activity more than the genuine character of the context" (p. 6).

As part of university's new Pedagogical Model for online learning (Pereira et al., 2007) participants are required to work collaboratively with their peers, participating in online forums where they debate and (re)construct collectively their knowledge. Moreover, if we intent to promote the participants active engagement in their learning, we must also adopt the same posture regarding their participation in their own and their peers assessment (Lave & Wenger, 1991; Linn, 2000;

McConnell, 2006; Nightingale & O'Neil, 1994). Moreover, participants are expected to work in small groups and to find the best solutions for the problems and cases that they are confronted with. This strong emphasis in student-centered interaction is also supported by new approaches of authentic assessment strategies (Gulikers et al., 2004; Oliveira, Pereira & Tinoca, 2009) that are expected to have a positive effect on the participants learning and better prepare them, for their professional life. A very important component of these new authentic assessment strategies is the partaking of students in their own assessment, through self and peer-assessment, of their participation in small group projects. This is also aligned with the new approach to competency assessment (Baartman et al., 2007) contributing to the students' active participation and shared responsibility for their learning process. From our perspective, this contributes to the shortening of the gap between teaching in academic settings and the real world, and between assessment tasks and professional life. Furthermore, by creating the conditions for student's self-regulatory processes through self-monitoring and self evaluation strategies, we are promoting the development of their own self-efficacy (Schunk & Pajares, 2001; Zimmerman, 2000)

Since 2006, our research group already has a significant amount of work exploring how assessment strategies can support e-learning development, whatever the subject or level of the course, namely: the establishment of Learning Contracts (Morgado Pereira, Quintas-Mendes & Aires 2006; Pereira, Tinoca & Oliveira 2009a); the use of online portfolios (Pereira et al, 2009); online group work (Tinoca, Oliveira & Pereira, 2007; Pereira, Tinoca & Oliveira 2008); the use of Weblogs (Monteiro & Pereira, 2007).

For this case, we propose to describe, analyze and discuss the concept of authentic alternative assessment strategies in an online environment, supported by our experience and the student data gathered through online discussions records, student's artifacts, and from questionnaires applied at the end of the semester. Data was collected in the context of several courses offered by the Department of Education and Distance Teaching. In particular, we analyze and discuss the use of specific strategies such as the Learning Contract and its relevance for authentic assessment. Within this framework, we analyze and discuss strategies potentialities and shortcomings to promote authentic assessment. The Learning Contract is introduced as subject to negotiation and debate with the students in order to define its final format.

The Learning Contract as a Mediator for Authentic Assessment

The Learning Contract (LC) is introduced as a structuring element for all graduate courses (Pereira, et al., 2007). According to these authors, the LC:

Acts as a mediator between the academic requirements ... and the students' needs and interests. In effect, it defines the necessary level of structure in the context of a group learning environment and, at the same time, incorporates a certain degree of flexibility adjustable in function of student's personal rhythm and needs (Pereira et al., 2007, p. 29).

This way, the LC functions as a nuclear document that mediates the communication between teacher and students and is socially shared by the group. In the beginning of each curricular unit, the LC is introduced and "should be negotiated between the teacher and the students, allowing for some adjustments that take into account needs or relevant issues raised by the students" (Pereira et al., 2007, p. 29).

In the LC the teacher designs a learning path where moments of interaction are defined: within the class, within small groups and between teacher and students. This learning path is based on tasks, such as "problem-solving, guided reading, discussion on given topics, case studies and analysis (…)" (Pereira et al., 2007, p. 29). In addition, the LC should include a sequence of work units, with the competencies to develop, the sequence of tasks, the description of the methodologies to be used, the assessment strategies and criteria, the scheduling of activities and the list of resources to be used. Each professor is responsible for structuring the implemented assessment strategies; being the only requirement present in the LC that the results achieved through continuous assessment should represent at least 60% of the students' final grade.

Important emerging questions from this research that we intend to answer include: 1) how does the discussion/negotiation of the LC with the students contribute to their perception of authenticity of the proposed assessment strategies? 2) How can higher education students be motivated to become active participants in the assessment process? 3) How can the LC contribute to the authenticity of the assessment strategies?

The Study

One of the Distance Learning Laboratory's goals is to research the assessment strategies being used at the university, as a consequence of the new pedagogical model currently in place. Part of this research effort has been directed towards the development of multiple case studies focused on the assessment strategies being used in a variety of courses. This particular study was developed in the context of a Course called Educational Research that is part of the degree plan for the Master level program in Pedagogical Supervision at the university. This Course was based on the Pedagogical Model for online learning developed by a group of researchers from the university. Based on this model, the adopted methodology is structured around two completely asynchronous and complementary work strategies. Firstly, it is based on the participants' independent study and reflections of the presented documents. It requires the participants to read critically, to identify the main thesis defended by the authors, and elaborate their own opinion. Secondly, it requires that the participants work collaboratively with their peers, participating in online forums where they debate and (re)construct collectively their learning. The participants are expected to work in small groups and to find the best solutions for the problems and cases that they are confronted with.

The goals of this Course incorporated the development of the participants' metacognitive, argumentative and evaluative competencies. The participants were assessed based on four different tasks: a) their participations on the online discussion forums; b) group activities; c) a reading review; and d) a personal online portfolio. The assessment of the group activities was entirely the responsibility of the participants, who had to explicitly argue their attributed classifications based on the previously negotiated criteria. Online group work was presented as an ill-structured real-life problem (Gulikers et al., 2004; Resnick, 1987) framed by an authentic environment. The online portfolios provided the students with an opportunity to demonstrate their progress, where knowledge, attitudes and skills emerge in an integrated way from their work. The online discussions contributed to the students sharing, negotiation and construction of knowledge under a collaborative umbrella, so enhancing this strategy's authenticity.

The participants were 17 graduate students from the Master on Pedagogical Supervision. 7 were male and 10 female. All of the participants were employed professionals, 8 were 5-12th grade teachers (from a variety of subjects: Portuguese; History; Physics; Geography and English); 3 were 1st-4th grade teachers, 2 were kindergarten teachers; 2 were special needs teachers; 1 was a professional development trainer / consultant; and 1 was a psychologist. The ages ranged from 23 to 50.

The Focus of the Analysis

This research is based on qualitative case study methods (Merrian, 1998; Stake 1999; Yin, 2003). It aims to produce a qualitative description of the application of the new pedagogical model, in use at the university in a variety of courses, as a response to new educational policies. This account was based on several triangulated sources of data, including written artifacts of student work; online student portfolios; open-ended questionnaires of the students perceptions and experiences; and transcripts from the students online discussion forums. Triangulation was also achieved through the cross comparison of the developed categories by the three main researchers.

The analysis was conducted using Strauss and Corbin (1998). "grounded theory" approach. For these authors the theoretical interpretation of the data emerges from the systematical analysis of the data, implying a very close relationship between them. The project does not start with a predefined or preconceived theory that is instead allowed to emerge from the data. Precisely because of this relying on the data, it is extremely important to aim for a deep understanding of all phenomena, situations, and events in order to enable an orientation towards action.

It is important to clarify that this interpretation of the theory is sustained by a set of well defined categories (concepts or themes) that are systematically interrelated through statements of relationship originating a theoretical framework that explains the situation being studied (Strauss & Corbin, 1998). However, the creativity and professional experience of the researchers are also pointed as essential, since the analysis is the result of the iteration of both objectivity and sensitivity, "objectivity is necessary to arrive at an impartial and accurate interpretation of events. Sensitivity is required to perceive the subtle nuances and meanings in data and to recognize the connections between concepts. Both objectivity and sensitivity are necessary for making discoveries" (Strauss & Corbin, 1998, p. 43). In this method, posing questions, making comparisons, and confronting the derived theoretical concepts are core procedures that force the analysis and the constant immersion in the data.

The analysis of both the participants online postings and questionnaire responses involved: a) reading and questioning the data taking into account the posed research questions; b) identification of the main concepts/themes where both the LC and the developed competencies were discussed; c) subsequent refinement of the analysis to identify the emerging sub-themes and consequent data coding with the support of NVIVO®; d) final data analysis taking into account both the identified similarities and the variability among the study participants.

In this study, the researchers are also online professors, with experience in the conception and implementations of courses, and when this investigation was started had already a set of questions to guide their analysis. This way, the initial reading of the participants' interventions was guided by these initial questions, later emerging the themes that were then used as references.

This case study illustrates one possible way of developing a competence-based learning program supported by authentic assessment strategies, aligned with the Bologna Process recommendations, and contributing to the university's change process. The definition of authentic assessment used in this study is: an assessment requiring students to use the same competencies, or combinations of knowledge, skills, and attitudes, which they need to apply in the criterion situation in professional life. The level of authenticity of an assessment is thus defined by its degree of resemblance to the criterion situation. This idea is extended and specified by the theoretical framework that describes that assessment can resemble a criterion situation along a number of dimensions (Gulikers et al., 2004)

In the next section, we present the four main themes emerging from the participants' online interactions and their questionnaire answers, which illustrate how the LC and its discussion shape the level of assessment authenticity attained in this particular Course. These themes include the LC as a promoter of authenticity; issues raised by the negotiation of the LC; and competence development.

The Learning Contract as a Promoter of Authenticity

The LC is proposed as a mediator between the professor's proposals and the students' interests and needs. However, from our previous research (Pereira, Tinoca & Oliveira, 2009) it becomes clear that simply presenting a LC is not enough to engage the participants in its discussion. For this reason, in the beginning of the semester, the professor initiated a debate about the LC with three clear lines of discussion: the overall proposals and how they meet the participants' expectations; the group work activity and its implications for both peer and self assessment; and the assessment criteria proposed for the portfolio that the participants are expected to build throughout the semester. Furthermore, data gathered from the questionnaire was also used to elaborate and complement the analysis and support the emerging themes.

The Advantages of Negotiating the Learning Contract

The participants' first reaction to the discussion of the LC was one of surprise. Nevertheless, all of them subscribed the proposed LC. The first major finding from this analysis was that all the participants recognized as important the opportunity to discuss the proposed LC. There were four main types of advantages identified by the participants:

Clarifying the Assessment Strategies

All of the participants participated in the LC debate and expressed their opinion about the proposed assessment criteria with the goal to better clarify them and even to advance suggestions regarding their relative weights, originating a proposal that was then translated into the LC final version. We can see an example of this negotiation when Victor's questions his colleagues, "taking into account the assessment criteria defined for the group work, how much should their relative weight be? Which should we value more?" This originated a very productive discussion that ended up with a final proposal that was then included in the LC.

53%[1] of the participants stress the importance of the LC and its discussion to clarify the course objectives, used assessment strategies and criteria, as we can see from these excerpts:

The assessment process is seen as commonly constructed, not imposed. Another advantage is that we can raise any other questions about that we don't fully understand so that they can be clarified (Q. 1, I .5).

The main advantage is that we can clarify and adjust the structure, learning path and assessment of this course, we can understand better both the assessment strategies and criteria (Q.1 I.7).

Participation in the Decision Process

Also, 53% of the participants emphasize that the opportunity awarded by the LC discussion to participate in the decision process, and so fine-tune contents, schedules, assessment strategies and criteria, and so adjust the course to the participants' needs and interests contributes to their ownership and responsibility for their learning. This recognition for their contribution to the decision process was particularly evident in the following quotes:

I think we benefited from the fact that the portfolios presentations were not scheduled for the last week of May, as initially planned, but that taking into account their weight in the final grade, and the time they take to prepare, it was much better to do it only in mid June (Q. 2, I .3).

It was great to be able to adjust the contents to our own needs and interests, and to be able to anticipate managing issues, and request minor changes and adjustments. To participate in the decision process in general and in the assessment in particular really helped to make us more responsible for our learning (Victor, LC debate).

The negotiation allowed us to voice our opinions, share our professional constraints (particularly regarding timings), and better adjust the various courses we were enrolled in and so facilitate our own learning experience (Q. 2, I .5).

Commitment

35% of the participants recognize that the fact that they can negotiate the LC is then reflected into its revised version. This way, the possibility to debate the proposed the LC allowed them not only to clarify it, but also to present alternatives and promote this collaborative endeavor resulting from everyone's perspective. This will, in turn, contribute to their commitment (McConnell, 2006), as a result from the fact that all participants were responsible for the final LC version. The following excerpts can illustrate this commitment:

It was very important to be able to negotiate the LC, it increased everyone's commitment, and reflected what was actually valued during the negotiation (Q. 2, I .1).

Having a chance to have a final version of the LC that is the result of the collective negotiated intentions, such as in the case of the blog use for the portfolio presentation, helped us to feel more responsible for our learning and become more attentive and participative in our own learning process (Q. 2, I .12).

The LC assures the knowledge, discussion and acceptance of the principles and competences prescribed in it. It makes students responsible for their learning, and helps them to better gage their efforts (Q. 2, I .14).

Managing the Learning Process

Also interesting was the value attribute by the participants to the LC discussion contribution to the management of their learning trajectory process and to their study planning, particularly the scheduling of activities and time management issues. 45% of the participants emphasized the benefits of the LC form the management of their learning process with comments such as these:

The details of the LC allowed us to know ahead of time the "who, what, when, where, for what, and how" perfectly describing the course, in terms of objectives, resources, and learning path. Knowing what was expected from us made it easier to understand our learning process, and, at each moment, to confront our learning with what as initially presented (Q. 2, I .15).

I consider the LC a fundamental tool for this type of learning as it allows us to control and manage our learning and the tasks. It allowed me to make an effective study plan of all my work, that translated into the control of my anxiety, since I knew from the beginning of the semester what we were expected to do (Q.2, I. 3).

The LC forces us to critically reflect, since the beginning of the semester, about what is expected from us. This way, it contributes to our learning since it lets us know very precisely what we are going to learn about, what tasks we'll have to complete, and their schedule (Q.2, I.12).

It made clear what competences we were going to develop, the tasks that we had to do, and their schedule, and so contributed to our anticipation of work strategies, fields of study, and ways to organize the tasks we had to fulfill (Q.2, I.9).

Time Management

41% of the participants also shared their concerns about time management taking into account their own professional life, particularly the tasks that they are responsible for in their own schools, and on the other hand the expectations that they are confronted with as presented by the professor proposals in the LC. This was particularly clear in Carla's quote from the debate:

given our own professional complications and commitments, the time we need to spend at school, and the little free time we have during the week, it will be helpful to adjust the tasks calendar so that we can maintain the same level of proficiency as we had during the first semester and so accomplish the expectation that the professor has from us!

Even though all of the participants were able to share their support for the LC and its discussion, and identify the advantages associated with it, one of the participants was also able to share his desire that his colleagues had been more actively engaged in the negotiation. He advanced that this may be due to a gap in their democratic participatory habits, resulting from the innovative nature of this type of strategy. According to this perspective, he also points outs the participants fear for: originating disruptive conflicts; exposition; and judgment by their peers and professors.

I wish the students had participated more in the LC negotiation, but I feel that we are the ones to blame, due to the fact that we are not used to a very active citizenship.

Negotiation may provoke conflicts amongst the participants, again because there are not used to this type of participatory system, and to manage the emerging divergences.

Students do not participate enough, maybe because they fear to expose themselves and that the professors will judge them (Q.2, I. 8).

Issues Raised by the Learning Contract Discussion

The analysis of the participants' interactions revealed their need to clarify, debate and contribute to certain aspects, that translated into a range of questions that fueled the discussion and negotiation among them, under the supervision of the instructor that acted only as a trigger, co-expert, and facilitator. Four main types of issues emerged from the triangulation of this analysis with the participant's responses to the questionnaires:

Assessment

When asked what kind of questions they considered important to raise about the proposed LC, 41% of the participants mentioned assessment issues. On the one hand, the participants took advantage of this opportunity to discuss the proposed assessment criteria and adjust their relative weights. On the other hand, the innovativeness of some of the proposed assessment strategies also prompted the participants to clarify what was intended with each of them, and how they would be implemented, as we can see from these excerpts:

It was great to clarify assessment questions, particularly how it would be implemented, what would be valued, and what would be expected from the students (Q.3, I.12).

Peer assessment was something new to me, it was fundamental to define the criteria and better learn how to operationalize its use. I think that because it was something new, for most of us, it was good to understand how it would work and what the underlying goals were (Q.3, I,8).

Procedures

Another theme, raised by 47% of the participants, was related to procedural concerns, particularly, the scheduling of activities. This degree had four Courses per semester, for that reason, the participants also used the LC negotiation to manage their time, and adjust their own learning schedule, and time slots devoted to each Course activities. The participants explicitly identified this possibility, and given their professional activity, it is understandable their concern for discussing and coming to a compromise concerning this issue. Several quotes can be used to illustrate this theme:

More than questioning, I think that negotiation may contribute to adjust scheduling issues presented in the LC (Sara, LC debate).

The clear explicitness in the LC of the amount of time that we were expected to need for each particular task (even though it fell way short!) was very important for my own work organization. I believe that without that indicator I would have had a much harder time to keep up with the required work rhythm (Q.3, I.3).

... it helped with time management, and in the definition of which moments I needed to invest more. Moreover, it allowed me to better manage my time and study methods (q.3, I.13).

At the time we questioned a lot of issues related to time and work demands. I think that because most master students have a professional activity that require a lot of his time, and the lack of fluency in technology use by some of us, lead us to expose these concerns (Q.3, I.1).

As we can also notice from the last excerpt, the participants also used this occasion to clarify some of the new technologies being used. This was clear on both the LC debate analysis and the questionnaire answers. 35% of the participants took advantage of this opportunity to clarify some of their procedural concerns, some related to the development and presentation of an online portfolio such as Ana when she asked, "What media will we use to make the online synchronous portfolio presentation? And how much time will each of us have?" Moreover, participants' also used this opportunity to inquire about how to implement the peer assessment necessary for the group work activity such as João when he said "how are going to operationalize the peer-assessment? Will the professor define the rules? What will our role be? Each team will have four students assessing each other, do we calculate the average?"

Relation to Real-life

The participants were able to closely relate the competences and assessment strategies being used in this course with their own life experience. Presently, most of the course participants, who are 5th-12th grade teachers, are in the process of discussing their own assessment process. Maybe for this reason, in the LC discussion it is explicitly mentioned their recognition for the importance of being master students participating in a peer-assessment process.

I think that this is a very interesting idea, particular in the current context, where the teachers are being assessed by the government, it is very timely! (Susana, LC debate)

In a phase where peer assessment is required more than ever, it is very important that we also do it here (Carlos, LC debate).

Moreover, the participating teachers also consider the analogy to their own practice and assessment strategies used with their own students

I agree with peer-assessment, and believe that it is very interesting for us to implement it here since it is something that we often use with our students but not among us – and that is changing! (Sandra, LC debate)

Furthermore, the presented concept of authenticity as an assessment strategy that requires students "to use the same competencies, or combinations of knowledge, skills, and attitudes, that they need to apply in the criterion situation in professional life" (Gulikers et al., 2004) was also evident when Victor said:

This LC clearly mirrors the importance of this course for any education/training professional, in general, and for any master degree student in particular. I think it was especially interesting the sharing of the assessment in the group project, making everyone responsible for such an important task, now more than ever given our current context, we may function here as a small "laboratory" in the very important area of assessment.

Also emergent form this quote is Victor's recognition for the importance of collaboration and responsibility also mirrored in the participants professional life and consequently further enhancing this assessment strategy authenticity.

Competence Development

Fundamental for the LC's role in the promotion of authenticity are also the competences that are intended to be developed and their relationship with the proposed assessment strategies. This theme was only present in the participants' responses to the questionnaire. Even though, the participants could have also raised it during the LC discussion, no one opted to do so; they focused mainly on broad comments and on assessment and procedural issues.

Regarding this issue, the participants were able to identify the existing relationship between the proposed assessment strategies, and the competences that they were developing. Moreover, they were able to identify and reflect on the competences that they developed and on its relevance for their professional practice. Three types of competences emerged from the participants answers to the final questionnaire: fluency in ITC use; metacognitive; and group work (Pereira et al., 2009).

Fluency in ITC use entails the efficient use of ITC tools and the ability to plan/create products to be available online. This was particularly clear when the students identify the creation of a blog as a new tool that they learned how to use and continued doing so.

I developed a parallel or secondary learning experience in the use of ITC, for example when I had to create and maintain a blog, a tool that I keep on using! (Q.4, I.7)

Metacognitive competences are related with the capacity to reflect upon one's learning process, with the ability to analyze gaps of knowledge/wrong turns, and also with self-questioning habits. This was recurrent on the students' responses particularly when they said:

... it contributed for my learning when, both individually and in group, we were prompted to reflect about the proposed themes (Q.4, I. 10).

"It was great to make such a deep self-assessment, and reflection about the developed research and our own learning. It helped me to look-inside! (Q.4, I.6)

I developed greater reflection habits that accompanied me throughout my learning process, making it more conscious and with greater depth (Q.4, I.3).

I consider that the main focus was the learning process itself, making it a much more reflexive experience (Q.4, I.7).

Group work competences are related with the ability to share information and resources, with the exhibition of solidarity habits towards one's peers, and the promotion of group's actions/interactions. This competence was present in the participants' responses, particularly in the form of their communication/collaboration concerns:

... the chance to cooperate with our colleagues and share different points of view, open our eyes to other ways of conceptualizing. Individual work is also important, since it contributes to the consolidation of learning, but for me the main message was that "I learn more when I share my knowledge with others (Q.4, I.2).

Several aspects were valued, namely, collaboration and group work, critical reflection, communication (both written and orally), and analyzes and synthesis competences (Q.4, I. 14).

Collaborative learning was something new for me and the most stimulating part, even though it required extra work, since that confronting our thought process with that of our colleagues is not easy, it translated into more and better learning (Q.4, I.5).

I tried different resources and tools that I had never experimented with before, like the online portfolio or the Moodle platform that are now very important tools in the interaction with my own students, and the blogs where I share my work, or even the negotiation of a LC in the beginning of the school year (Q.4, I.9).

These three types of competences do not appear as disconnected in the participants' responses, but related to each other. This can be illustrated by the latest quote, where we can see competences that he recognizes has having developed and is currently using in his daily work. Moreover, this participant also illustrates the close relationship between the proposed learning tasks (such as the blogs that was the tool chosen by the participants to develop their online portfolios) and the developed competencies recognized by them as relevant for their professional life.

Discussion

This study was focused on the analysis of the LC and its role as a mediator between the professors' proposals and students the students' expectations and needs. With this goal we adopted a three step procedure. We started by the analysis of what a LC is, in particular in the case of an Educational Research course, and what it should include. Next, we examined the students' interactions when the LC was open to discussion, and their responses to an open ended anonymous questionnaire. Four main advantages in the LC negotiation are stressed by the participants: to clarify the proposed assessment strategies; the participation in the decision process; the commitment; and the learning process management. Moreover, the participants also took advantage of the LC negotiation to debate issues pertinent to them such as the assessment strategies, procedural concerns, and the proposed competencies relationship to their real life.

There is not a consensus in the literature concerning the concept of authenticity. Some authors privilege a concept focused on the degree of cognitive challenge (Mateo & Sangrà, 2007). Others, give a greater emphasis the adaptability of the learning experiences to the students' professional needs and interests (Kischner, Strijbos, Kreijns & Beers, 2004; Gulikers et al., 2004). In this study we build from these initial perspectives and advance that the concept of authenticity is anchored in several complementary components or dimensions. Moreover, we argue that it is closely related to the merging of both the professor's initial perspectives concerning the competences that should be developed and the students' professional life. Furthermore, we also emphasize the importance of assessment authenticity as a cornerstone to warrant the development of competencies, given that "the assessment process can be central to the way that students engage with learning" (McConnell, 2006, p.104)

In this study, we aimed to understand how the LC as a cultural tool included in university's pedagogical model can mediate different modes of participation that are promoters of an adequate level of authenticity. We agree with Gulikers et al. (2004, p. 69) when they say that "what students perceive as authentic is not necessarily as what teachers ... see as authentic". Being authenticity a subjective concept it is important to learn about the students' perceptions in order to adjust authentic assessment so that it can influence learning. The set of competences initially identified by the professor should not only be focused on the students real and professional life, but also further them and present the students with cognitive challenges that will promote their learning. Consequently, the proposed assessment strategies must also be aligned with both the students' life and their cognitive plane, to be seen as promoters of their learning while assessing it at an adequate level.

It is clear that the discussion and negotiation of the LC in its different component, some more related to the procedures and others more conceptual, promoted the participants reflection and commitment concerning the responsibility for their own learning process. McConnell (2006) emphasized the importance of reflection for the production of new forms of knowledge, metacognition and "the development of a 'deep' approach to learning" (p. 137). In our case, the participants were able to mention that through their reflection and discussions achieved new learning and understandings. The opportunity to discuss the LC, in writing, creates the necessary records that will allow the participants to confront their points of view, with those of their colleagues and the professor, enabling the consequent reflection. However, it should be noted that this is not a strictly cognitive process. It results from a socially mediated and technologically supported process. This is what, in turn, will promote their commitment to the negotiated and agreed learning path. Moreover, Kischner et al. (2004) also consider the need for student ownership and control over the task development (context, content, sequencing, pacing, and presentation style). This approach to task control is now facilitated through ITC technologies as they allow the student to take over the "depth of study, range of content, number and type of delivery media, and time spent on learning" (p. 56). This way, the participants are empowered to manage and take control of, and responsibility for, their learning process, also promoting the participants self-efficacy (Schunk & Pajares, 2000; Zimmerman, 2000). The results from this research show that the discussion of the LC prompted the participants to exercise responsibility for their own learning. This agrees with the previous work of Vonderwell, Liang and Alderman (2007), these authors advocate that "student self-determination and responsibility influenced the degree that the students took advantage of the asynchronous nature of online discussions" (p. 320).

One of the goals, that was behind the development of the LC, according to the used pedagogical model, was the promotion of the students individual learning process. This was clearly reflected and recognized by the participants as one of the positive outcomes from the LC discussion, further justifying its use. Not only do they use the LC as a tool to design their study plan, taking into account the requirements of the different courses that they are enrolled in, but also, in each particular course they are able to contribute and suggest changes to better adapt the sequence of activities to their own needs and interests (Rovai, 2004). This opportunity was also used by the participants to further assume their responsibility and so clarify time management and scheduling adjustments. This is particularly relevant in our case, since we are working with an employed, adult population, who are only part time students. The LC and its discussion, empower students to make advanced planning decisions concerning both their professional and academic commitments. This is typical of lifelong learning contexts that are mainly self-determined and require participants to carefully manage their time.

Furthermore, the proposed assessment strategies, which were framed by the intended set of competencies, were innovative and unfamiliar for most participants. Therefore, the opportunity to discuss, clarify and suggest alternative proposals allowed them to further their understanding about what they were being asked to do, and how it was related to their professional life. What is more, the suggested and negotiated assessment strategies were also recognized as usable and appropriate cognitive challenges to their practice.

Other concerns emergent from the confrontation between the participants discussion about the LC and their answers to the questionnaire, were related with time management, scheduling adjustments, and procedural concerns. The participants took advantage of the LC discussion to clarify

Figure 1. Authenticy components perceptions analysis (in percentage points)

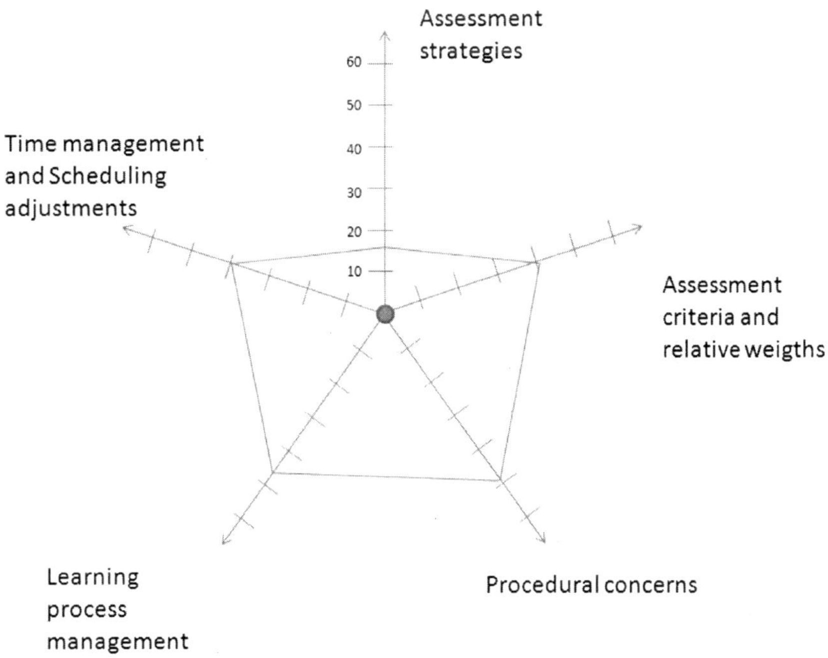

procedures related to the use of new ICT that they were required to use and to the operationalization of the proposed peer-assessment strategies.

It becomes apparent from our analysis that authenticity is influenced by several different dimensions. To reflect the level of authenticity, we propose a multi-component approach as illustrated in figure 1. In this figure one can see the perceptions of authenticity related to each of the proposed components for this particular case study. The participants gave great emphasis to the learning process management and the definition of assessment criteria and their relative weights.

Even though some participants exposed procedural concerns, this was not a very important factor, probably because of their recognition of the shared expertise in the community that helped to reduce their apprehensions. At approximately the same level we also find the participants references, to time management and scheduling adjustments. The participants did not question much the proposed innovative assessment strategies, such as peer assessment and portfolio assessment, probably because they recognize the advantages put forward by them for their professional life.

Authenticity is a subjective concept that cannot be unilaterally defined since it is always influenced by students' perceptions. This way, it becomes crucial to take them into account. In our case, we have introduced the LC as a promoter/mediator to merge both students perceptions, expectations needs, interests, concerns and real/professional life issues, with the professor's targeted competences, sequence of activities, assessment strategies and schedule (see figure 2). This fusion is possible thanks to the negotiation promoted by the Learning Contract that acts as a mediating tool for: the learning process management, assessment strategies, assessment criteria and relative weights, time management and scheduling adjustments, and procedural fine-tuning. We argue here that this process, where professor and students interact and

Figure 2. The Learning Contract as a mediator between professor and students to promote authentic assessment

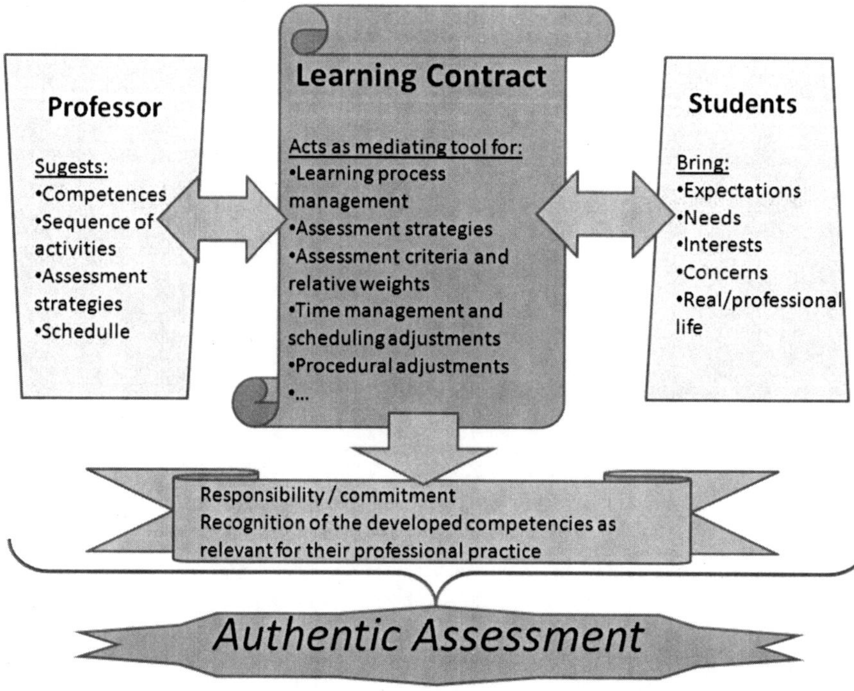

negotiate, results in a greater commitment of both parties and on an increased sense of responsibility. Moreover, it enables the students' recognition of the developed competencies as relevant for their professional practice, particularly in the case of metacognitive competencies, fluency in ITC use and group work.

The LC itself, by proposing a variety of assessment strategies, is recognized by the participants as aligned with their professional practice. What is more, the participants identified this assessment proposal as authentic when, during the negotiation, they justify its importance saying that it mirrors what they experience in the workplace. Furthermore, the fact that the LC is open to negotiation allows the participants to share their ideas, not only about the assessment strategies, criteria and instruments being used, but also to further their knowledge about assessment, making explicit their concerns and doubts rooted in their professional life. This process also allows the instructor to further review its assessment practices and so contributes to the authenticity of the assessment strategies.

CURRENT CHALLENGES FACING THE ORGANIZATION

A big part of the research efforts currently in place at the Distance Learning Laboratory are focused on the development of strategic design-based research targeted at the evaluation of university's Pedagogical Model (Pereira, et al., 2007). As part of that effort, one of our major concerns has been the development and implementation of sound assessment practices aligned with the latest recommendations from educational research about competence assessment, alternative assessment, and authentic assessment. Concerning this area of our research, several challenges are still facing us.

It is fundamental to keep on pushing for further research in the areas of alternative assessment, inquiring about ways to develop its validity and reliability in Higher Education virtual environments. Even more, it will be necessary to broaden the variety of assessment strategies and instruments being used, as well as the approaches to promote student engagement and participation in their negotiation, definition and implementation, to continuously improve assessment authenticity. This is no easy task, and will require significant efforts, not only on the research side, but also because of the professional development implications for all the professors involved.

On the technological side, all this innovations will need to be seamlessly included into our university's learning and management systems, to facilitate and encourage its use by both students and professors. Moreover, it will also be necessary to investigate the class size for master Courses that is better suited to these new strategies. If we are advocating a negotiation model for the LC to which most participants should contribute, the question becomes: what will be the costs of increasing class size? For that reason class size must be a carefully controlled variable so that it is not so small that it lacks critical mass, nor to big that it strips participants of their voice.

SOLUTIONS AND RECOMMENDATIONS

There is no easy fix for the validation of these new assessment strategies. The problem is currently being debated in traditional face-to-face education, and needs, naturally, to also be discussed in online, technologically enhanced environments. That is one of the main goals of the Distance Learning Laboratory, and only with such continuous efforts can we hope to keep furthering our knowledge. However, one important recommendation clearly emerges from the value of the LC as a tool to promote assessment authenticity. Moreover, the need to foster a community of learners that is willing to be part of, participate in, and go through their learning process together is also decisive. We argue here that such a community plays a fundamental role in promoting participants commitment towards their learning, for that reason, class size needs to be a carefully controlled variable. Finally, even though the LC, as presented, seems to be a very powerful tool to promote student involvement in their learning and assessment authenticity, the professor's role is fundamental to promote its discussion and negotiation. Particularly, when we are faced with a context where participants do not have participatory citizenship habits. In order to take full advantage of the LC and its benefits, it is crucial to foster and nurture its negotiation, and that is one of the professor's tasks.

REFERENCES

Baartman, L. K. J., Bastiaens, T. J., Kirschner, P. A., & Vleuten, C. P. M. (2007). Evaluating assessment quality in competence-based education: A qualitative comparison of two frameworks. *Educational Research Review*, *2*, 114–129. doi:10.1016/j.edurev.2007.06.001

Bates, T., & Poole, G. (2003). Effective Teaching with Technology in Higher Education: Foundations for Success. San Francisco: Jossey-Bass.

Birenbaum, M. (2003). New insights into learning and teaching and their implications for assessment. In M. Segers, F. J. R. C. Dochy, & E. Cascallar (Eds.), Optimising new modes of assessment: In search of qualities and standards, (pp. 13–36). Dordrecht, The Netherlands: Kluwer Adademic Publishers.

Birenbaum, M., Breuer, K., Cascallar, E., Dochy, F., Dori, Y., & Ridgway, J. (2006). EARLI position paper. A learning integrated assessment system. *Educational Research Review*, *1*, 61–67. doi:10.1016/j.edurev.2006.01.001

Black, P., Harrisson, C., Lee, C., Marshall, B., & Wiliam, D. (2003). Assessment for Learning: Putting it into practice. Berkshire, UK: Open University Press.

Brown, G., Bull, J., & Pendlebury, M. (1997). Assessing Student Learning in Higher Education. New York: Routledge.

Coelho, J., & Rocio, V. (2008). A Study on Moodle's Performance. EDEN annual conference. Lisbon, Portugal, June 12-14, 2008.

Directorate for Education, Employment, Labour and Social Affairs (2002). *Definition and Selection of Competences (DESECO): Theoretical and Conceptual Foundations Strategy Paper*. Paris: OCDE.

Elwood, J., & Klenowski, V. (2002). Creating communities of shared practice: The challenges of assessment use in learning and teaching. *Assessment & Evaluation in Higher Education*, *27*(3), 243–256. doi:10.1080/02602930220138606

European Commission. (2008a). *Education and Training 2010*. Retrieved May 20, 2009, from http://ec.europa.eu/education/policies/2010/et_2010_en.html

European Commission. (2008b). *The Bologna Process*. Retrieved May 20, 2009, from http://ec.europa.eu/education/policies/educ/bologna/bologna_en.htmlU

Gardner, J. (Ed.). (2006). Assessment and Learning. London: Sage.

Gulikers, J. T. M., Bastiaens, T. G., & Kirschner, P. A. (2004). A Five-Dimensional Framework for Authentic Assessment. *Educational Technology Research and Development*, *52*(3), 67–86. doi:10.1007/BF02504676

Gulikers, J. T. M., Kester, L., Kirschner, P. A., & Bastiaens, T. G. (2008). The effect of practical experience on perception of assessment authenticity, study approach, and learning outcomes. *Learning and Instruction*, *18*, 172–186. doi:10.1016/j.learninstruc.2007.02.012

Kirschner, P., Strijbos, J. W., Kreijns, K., & Beers, P. J. (2004). Designing Electronic Collaborative Learning Environments. *Educational Technology Research and Development*, *52*(3), 47–66. doi:10.1007/BF02504675

Lave, J., & Wenger, E. (1991). Situated learning: Legitimate peripheral participation. Cambridge, UK: Cambridge University Press.

Linn, R. (2000). Assessments and accountability. *Educational Researcher*, *29*(2), 4–16.

Macdonald, J. (2004). Developing competent e-learners: the role of assessment. *Assessment & Evaluation in Higher Education*, *29*(2), 215–226. doi:10.1080/0260293042000188483

Maclellan, E. (2004). How convincing is alternative assessment for use in higher education? *Assessment & Evaluation in Higher Education*, *29*(3), 311–321. doi:10.1080/0260293042000188267

Matteo, J. & Sangrà, A. (2007). Designing online learning assessment through alternative approaches: facing the concerns. *European Journal of open, distance and E-learning*.

McConnell, D. (2006). E-learning Groups and communities. Berkshire, UK: Open University Press.

Merriam, S. B. (1998). Qualitative research and case study application in education. San Francisco, CA: Jossey-Bass.

Monteiro, V., & Pereira, A. (2007). O blog como elemento agregador numa comunidade de aprendizagem. Actas do 2º Colóquio Luso-Brasileiro de Educação a distância e online, Lisbon, Portugal.

Morgado, L., Pereira, A., Quintas-Mendes, A., & Aires, L. (2006). Towards a pedagogy of elearning: the contract as an instrument to mediate learning. In A.J. Mendes, (Eds.), Computers and education – towards educational change and innovation. Amsterdam: Springer Science.

Morgado, L., Quintas-Mendes, A., Oliveira, I., & Goulão, F. (2008). Empowering distance teachers – training teachers to teach online. In *European Distance E-Learning Annual Conference*, Lisbon, Portugal.

Nightingale, P., & O'Neil, M. (1994). Achieving quality learning in higher education. London: Kogan Page.

Orvis, K. L., & Lassiter, A. R. L. (2007). Computer-supported collaborative learning: best practices and principles for instructors. Hershey, PA: The Idea Group.

Pereira, A., Mendes, A. Q., Morgado, L., Amante, L., & Bidarra, A. (2007). Universidade Aberta's Pedagogical Model for Distance Education: A University for the Future. Lisboa: Universidade Aberta.

Pereira, A., Oliveira, I., Tinoca, L. F., & Amante, L. Relvas, M.J., Pinto, M.C. & Moreira D. (2009). Evaluating continuous assessment quality in competence-based education online: the case of the e-folio. In *European Distance and Elearning Network annual conference*. Retrieved May 20, 2009, from http://sites.google.com/site/luistinoca/Home/papers-1/EDEN09.pdf?attredirects=0

Pereira, A., Tinoca, L., & Oliveira, I. (2008). Processes of Group Work Collaboration Online. In *European Distance and Elearning Network Annual Conference*. Lisbon: Portugal. Retrieved May 20, 2009, from http://sites.google.com/site/luistinoca/Home/papers-1/EDEN08.pdf?attredirects=0

Pereira, A., Tinoca, L., & Oliveira, I. (2009). Answering Bologna's challenge: How authentic assessment strategies can be used to promote competency based education in an online course. In *23rd ICDE/EADTU World Conference*, Maastricht, Netherlands.

Pereira, A., Tinoca, L., & Oliveira, I. (2009). The contribution of the Learning Contract for authentic assessment in online environments. Accepted for the *European Association for Research on Learning and Instruction 13th Biennial Conference*, Amsterdam, Netherlands.

Resnick, L. B. (1987). Learning in school and out. *Educational Leadership, 16*(9), 13–20.

Rocio, V., Coelho, J., & Pereira, A. (2008). Implementation of a Learning Card in Moodle. In EADTU annual conference, Poitiers, France.

Rovai, A. P. (2004). A constructivist approach to online college learning. *The Internet and Higher Education, 7*, 79–93. doi:10.1016/j.iheduc.2003.10.002

Schunk, D. H., & Pajares, F. (2001). The Development of Academic Self-Efficacy. In A. Wigfield & J. Eccles (Eds.), *Development of achievement motivation*. San Diego: Academic Press. Retrieved July 3, 2009, from http://www.des.emory.edu/mfp/SchunkPajares2001.PDF

Stake, R. E. (1995). The art of case study research. London: Sage Publication

Strauss, A., & Corbin, J. (1998). Basics of Qualitative Research: Techniques and Procedures for Developing Grounded Theory. London: SAGE Publications.

Tinoca, L., Oliveira, I., & Pereira, A. (2007). Group work peer-assessment in an online environment. In *European Association of Distance Teaching Universities Conference*. Retrieved May 20, 2009, from http://www.eadtu.nl/conference-2007/files/SAA4.pdf

Vonderwell, S., Liang, X., & Alderman, K. (2007). Asynchronous discussions and assessment in online learning. *Journal of Research on Technology in Education, 39*(3), 309–328.

Yin, R. K. (2003). Case study research design and methods, (3rd ed.) Thousand Oaks, CA: Sage Publications.

Zimmerman, B. J. (2000). Self-Efficacy: An Essential Motive to Learn. *Contemporary Educational Psychology, 25*, 82–91. doi:10.1006/ceps.1999.1016

ADDITIONAL READING

Falchikov, N. (2005). Improving assessment through student involvement: Practical solutions for aiding learning in higher and further education. London: RoutledgeFalmer.

Falchikov, N., & Goldfinch, J. (2000). Student peer assessment in higher education: A meta-analysis comparing peer and teacher marks. *Review of Educational Research, 70*, 287–322.

Gardner, J. (Ed.). (2006). Assessment and Learning. London, England: Sage.

Garrison, R., & Anderson, T. (2003). E-Learning in the 21st Century: A framework for research and practice. Routledge.

Kidd, T. (Ed.). (2007). Handbook of Research in Instructional Systems and Technology, Idea Group Inc., Hershey, PA.

McConnell, D. (2006). E-learning Groups and communities. Berkshire: Open University Press.

Mendes, A. J. (Ed.). (2006). Computers and education – towards educational change and innovation. Amsterdam: Springer Science.

Morgado, L., Quintas-Mendes, A., Oliveira, I., & Goulão, F. (2008). Empowering distance teachers – training teachers to teach online. *European Distance E-Learning Annual Conference*. Lisbon, Portugal.

Segers, M. Dochy, F. & Cascallar, E. (2003). Using new modes of assessment. In search of qualities and standards. Dordrecht, the Netherlands: Kluwer Academic Publishers.

Topping, K. (2003). Self and peer assessment in school and university: Reability, validity and utility.In M. Segers, F. Dochy, & E. Cascallar (Eds.), Optimising new modes of assessment: In search of qualities and standards. Dordrecht, The Netherlands: Kluwer Adademic Publishers.

KEY TERMS AND DEFINITIONS

Authentic Assessment: An assessment requiring students to use the same competencies, or combinations of knowledge, skills, and attitudes that they need to apply in a criterion situation in professional life.

Learning Contract: "It is constituted by a sequence of work units, with competencies to develop, the sequence of tasks, the methodology, assessment strategies and criteria, the scheduling of activities and the recourses. Defines the necessary level of structure in the context of a group learning environment and, at the same time, incorporates a certain degree of flexibility adjustable in function of student's personal rhythm and needs" (Pereira et al., 2007, p. 29).

Competency-Based Assessment: Involves the use of multiple forms of authentic assessment, that are carried out without time pressure and using the tools or other helping materials that are also used in real life.

Cognitive Challenge Task: A task targeted at the development of the students competencies, related to their Professional practice and requiring higher order thinking skills.

Learning Contract Negotiation: Is characterized by the involvement/collaboration of the students in their learning process, particularly in the negotiation of the Learning Contract, not only in issues related to the clarification of goals, and assessment strategies and criteria to be used; but especially in the presentation of adjustments and alternative proposals targeted at the definition of their learning process.

Level of Assessment Authenticity: Is defined by its degree of resemblance to the criterion situation, this idea is extended and specified by the theoretical framework that describes that an assessment can resemble a criterion situation along a number of dimensions. One of the dimensions that should be taken into account is the alignment promoted by the negotiation between the targeted competencies and the used assessment strategies.

Student Commitment: Is characterized by the active participation of the students, who shares responsibility for his learning process, practices self-evaluation and reflection, and collaborates with the teacher and other students.

ENDNOTE

1 Even though the sample for this case study was small, and no generalizability is intended, percentages were used to facilitate the readers' perception of the participants' distribution.

Chapter 16
Project Learning, the Linked Course, and Ramifications for Global Research

Ruth Robbins
University of Houston Downtown, USA

Merrilee Cunningham
University of Houston Downtown, USA

ABSTRACT

In a regionally accredited urban university, high risk students enrolled in a freshman English course are simultaneously enrolled in a freshman level computer information systems class where project learning is taking place. This linkage allows faculty for both courses to design course instructional objectives which will complement what students are learning in the other linkage course as well as cover the objectives of their respective discipline's course.

ORGANIZATION BACKGROUND

The regionally accredited urban university which is the setting for this case is located in the center of downtown in a large metropolitan area located in the southwestern part of the country. The commuter university is an open admissions institution with over twelve thousand students. The university is recognized for its diversity. Students vary from traditional high school graduates to less traditional students who are working with families to support. Less than 40 years in existence, the university is a majority minority institution with Hispanic, Black, and Asian students comprising the majority. The university has numerous majors, masters programs, and is one of the fastest growing universities in the state.

DOI: 10.4018/978-1-61520-749-7.ch016

SETTING THE STAGE

The university requires all students enrolled in a degree seeking program to include in their studies a general education core curriculum. This core curriculum includes courses such as: English, history, government, computer literacy, sciences, psychology, math, and more. The courses linked and described in this case, were two of these required general education core curriculum courses: the second semester freshman English course and the computer literacy course. The two faculty teaching these courses have worked together teaching this linkage for several semesters. The English faculty member routinely teaches the second semester freshman English course as well as upper division and graduate English courses where computer skills are required for successful research projects. The computer literacy faculty member routinely teaches the computer literacy classes and upper division computer information systems courses. Each has numerous years of experience in their respective disciplines.

In a regionally accredited urban university, high risk students enrolled in a freshman level, second semester English course are simultaneously enrolled in a freshman level computer information systems class where project learning is taking place. This linkage allows faculty to design course instructional objectives which will complement what students are learning in the other linkage course as well as cover the objectives of each course. In the English course portion of the linkage, topics such as public policy and the problems of the global megalopolis; issues of transportation, health, housing, clean air and water in the most populated cities of the world, and poverty and the nation state are just some of the themes used to aid the student who is learning to do research in library databases on the web, think tanks, world organizations such as the World Health Organization, The United Nations, On-line publications like the Country books available from the CIA, and Think Tank consolidators like Docuticker (http://www.docuticker.com.) The scholarly elements of the World Wide Web are used to investigate world wide issues and solve global problems using global research.

In the computer information systems portion of the linkage, basic computer literacy topics are covered and then students utilize HTML to develop web pages that present research results for an online presentation, word processing and presentation software are used to fully explore the presentation of research conducted for the English linkage course, spreadsheet software is used as an analytical tool to examine and graphically present the results, and database software is used to provide an organized way to store results.

CASE DESCRIPTION

The linked courses described in this case were initially established as a teaching model within the Learners' Community which was launched by the university under the auspices of the freshman year experience and the Dean of the University College. Numerous linkages were introduced. Faculty from different disciplines within different colleges were paired to more efficiently blend and provide a wider array of skills and knowledge areas to enhance the learning experience. The university continues to support this effort because of the success that students have demonstrated after they have participated in these linkages.

As a model for global research, the linked course serves as a excellent example of what can happen when two educators in diverse disciplines work together to blend, syncretize, and synergize the learning experience. Rimmington, O'Reilly & Gibson (2003) made it clear that "global learning is best achieved through project-based or other active approaches to learning by teams of people living in countries with vastly different cultures … using modern communication technologies" (pp. 247-248). Learning key competencies enables new populations of student-researchers to see themselves in perhaps a completely new way as they learn at warp speed or at least experience accelerated learning because a classroom world of accelerated learning possibilities of "know where the research is" is provided to them. Building fluency in language is finally so complimentary to building fluency in writing skills.

Students are required to sign up for briefing services on their problem with media companies that offer free briefing services like *The Financial Times* (http://www.ft.com/home/US) and *Foreign*

Policy Magazine (http://www.foreign-policy.com). Both these companies offer free specific briefing services to anyone who simply signs up. The very idea of being important enough to be briefed on a subject, encourages the student to take his or her research seriously as information on the subject is coming to his or her email, often on a daily basis. Like a real decision-maker, the student has a briefing service on the specific subject and thus is kept up-to-date on the changing status of the issue. But more importantly, for the sake of learning, students visit their email on a regular basis and are thus forced into considering the subject of their research paper also at much more regular intervals than those that they might normally consider necessary for good research. The emailed briefings thus focus their work on their larger project appear on their I-phones and Blackberries.

Way before both project learning and Eraut & Holes's suggestion concerning the importance of expanding the amount that students learn, John Dewey in his 1939 work "Education and Experience" experimented with "action learning" but it is as old as Archimedes's "Eureka" of 212 B.C. John Seeley Brown's "Growing Up Digital: How the Web Changes Work, Education, and the Way People Learn" (*Change,* March/April 2000, pp. 10-20) suggests a new learning paradigm and bridge research and practice through project learning is part of that new paradigm where computers become mind tools using the written word as well as critical thinking and putting theory into learning-centered practice in a computer intense environment is not just a technology enhanced learning environment. The world wide web comes with a world wide epistemological stance opportunity, but it is more likely an epistemological necessity. Lodge (1995) described globalization as a process that is both technological and human (*International Journal of Intercultural Relations Creating the Global Learning Organization*, Amy Tolbert et al, 1-15), though the human must absorb elements of the technological in this linked class system and elsewhere.

One thing that we have learned about learning from our own earlier data-driven research is that one size does not fit all and one style does not either. Allowing the student choices so that students can play to strengths and the interests that they bring into the course at the beginning of the course while learning enough to do sophisticated research using on-line library databases and think tank consolidators is what computers in the classroom facilitate. Using the same "know where" skills in different instructional settings and for content and skill linked courses facilitates reusing the same new skill in very different instruction contacts and thus reaffirms process learning in that recombined situation. Even in our modern world, a student who is not engaged in the research that he or she is doing, is a student who would rather be somewhere else doing something else and is in danger, via their lack of concern and engagement in the subject, of seeking development of their felt interests elsewhere. Linked courses combine assignments in dramatically different ways than a traditional class and require additional transforming of learning and additional performing and are, de facto, an eclectic and accelerated approach. The skills learned in a student's CIS class are immediately confirmed as they are used in the English class as the student builds an information matrix with a skill matrix and the skills learned in an English class are used in the CIS classroom to make a nodal matrix of skills and talents. In some ways, perhaps, this is just a continuance of B.F. Skinner's 1958 assertions that students learn at a much higher rate if their environment is systematically controlled. However, it is Eraut & Holes(1998) who have done the most impressive work on insetting collaborative patterns into a variety of systematically controlled, benevolent, challenging learning environments or building those learning environment constructs.

Mark Warschauer, (1997) suggests that diversity of learning methods approaching the globalization/diversity process allows a diverse student population to create a maximized, globally inclusive, problem solving environment where this very diversity is an asset (pp. 470-481). Right now, it is still debatable whether or not there is even a sense that globalization in the classroom is even desirable or respected. Until globalization in the classroom becomes a goal and supported, or at least tolerated, all the theoretical constructions in the world will not cause its implementation.

Linked courses, like project learning, are a pattern of a learning system. In a linked, computerized classroom, you have a new form of multi-agent learning with two very differently trained instructors-agents, and the computer-agent with its re-enforcement possibilities creating an environment in which people both want to perform at optimum level and can. Culminating team events get the continental, neighboring mega-cities together for an evaluation of desirable public policy events in that geographic and cultural real place, privileging core global justice values such as eliminating famine and genocide, basic horses of the Apocalypse stuff at the base of Maslow's hierarchy of human needs. Arguably one of the most important learning moments in the course is when the students realize that there are different value systems available as the starting point of their selection of the most urgent or most important (sometimes not the same) problem in their continental area. If the students use the criteria of Failed States available in the Failed State Index of *Foreign Policy Magazine* (and available for free on the website), then they get one system, and that system is closely related to Maslow's hierarchy of individual human needs. If they refuse to convert Maslow's hierarchy into FP's Failed States criteria, they have made a personal values decision on their own. If they go to other values available at some of the think tanks that reproduce their political perspective, then their criteria change as well. It is not in the interest of the professors in this course, to judge their criteria, but rather to judge how they implement their criteria in their problem solving program, how they develop effective partnerships with viable players in the problem solving program, and how they place their tiered, multi-pronged chess-like moves in ways that allow for the realities of the complexity of the problems as well as the focus on solving the problem. The instructors repeatedly remind the students that they will need partners, that they will need information, data, help, that they must build relationships with organizations that can take a part of the problem away from them, and that they must give birth to some of their partners if those agencies do not already exists, so it is fair to invent organizations that do not already exist, but that there is a felt need for.

Accountability for globalization in a linked CIS/English course can create an organizational culture that is the epitome of global inclusiveness if the instructors select assignments using a global array of mega cities. Thus the assignments are learning inclusive in both theory and practice and shift the learning parading from a provincial ethnocentric, almost narcissistic world view to a challenging geocentric paradigm through globalizing assignments which encourage globally conscious mind sets. Diversity is advantaged. A comfortable attitude toward differences among students develops as assignments will parallel classroom student diversity as an asset. Empowerment opportunities are seized like norming through experts in the field who become outside coaches for mentors moving work through applications such as the Model United Nations Program or our in-house student research conference, providing extensive team building practice by organizing students into continental problem solving groups, but performance management plays a large role in any classroom in any part of the globe and one of the basic rules of performance management is to create challenging, clear, interesting expectations that allow the student to participate in the planning process at times when that is possible. Announced course objectives, planning forms and help sheets as well as a clear rubric go far to help a student organize his or her class activities, but how the student relates new knowledge to existing knowledge and that the learner relates new knowledge to existing knowledge are also very important in both project learning and globalized learning and depend, in part, on instructional design. Abstract thinking is required when the student determines a grid of problems to tackle in the mega city. Teams using computers to solve problems have been studied (Eraut & Holes, 1998) and students are amazed at the better results and greater skill and knowledge gains. Internationalizing the curriculum works very well with the kind of diverse student body we have at our urban university for that reason, Learning is at least in part a self-organizing processes. As early as 1987, Cole & Griffin suggested that, in part, at least, instructors are "orchestraters" of computer-based activities.

Working with computers in a classroom to acquire research as well as to write up your research, requires levels of multimediality, great stimulation of the senses, more visual recognition and greater involvement. The person to person interactivity is shared with the person – machine relationship and these, electronic texts, along with course books that are not electronic texts, allow a level of information confluence, reinforced outcomes, and problem-solving results. The design of the learning project may be the professor's greatest contribution to competencies in the classroom as this sort of intercultural engagement suggests global citizenship and attitudes once only imagined by Homi Bhaba, but they also contribute to another goal, that of globally transferable competencies. Socio-environmental change (distopic to utopic in extreme) and environmental deterioration are documented just by using an image search such as Google or Yahoo offer for free. Justice-based decision-making, such as Homi Bhaba suggested decades ago, can be used in instruction design as well as meliorism and pragmatism (Berger & Kam). Students are encouraged and/or required to run anti-plagarism software on their own papers and adjustments are made at a pre-grading point, rather than tragically later.

Teaching the students how to gather and process enough relevant information ("Know-where") to write a good research paper requires that they combine computer information systems with English anyway, and sequencing the instruction in the first few weeks of this linkage must be fine tuned as well. Rapid prototyping of a public policy plan for the mega city's transportation needs is followed by extensive re-evaluation using best practices models. Thus the instructors use a Vista-enhanced site that the students may go to supplement the handouts that they receive in class. There, they can find every website that we take the students to in-class: websites like the World Health Organization, The African Union, Docuticker, Wikipaedia's amazing list of think tanks, the United Nations, The International Monetary Fund, The World Bank, The World Court in the Hague, and other useful partnerships that are suggested by the tools within the Vista Enhancement software. Computer Supported Collaborative Learning (Scardamalia & Bereiter, 1994) creates powerful communities of collaborative learning which actually link CIS and English anyway and encourages on-line use of both computer accessible library databases and think tank search engines (CSCL Resources; CSCL theories of Jy Wana Daphne Lin Hsiao) are instructional design models that result in a surge of learning when applied to global public policy initiatives using theorists of the student's selection.

Simply put, the student's new technical abilities change the learning model that the teacher has been using into one that must be replaced. Diffusions of technical ability change learning model possibilities for the better as the student comes to realize the extent of the mind tools available and, perhaps more importantly, to participate in his or her own knowledge management with skill and selectivity. It is hard to over evaluate how much a student is grateful for being encouraged to participate actively in his or her own knowledge management. Somewhere in the class, things change and, to remain challenging, the assignment ante must be upped. Project or problem based learning allows for learner-centered classrooms, rather than teacher-centered classrooms. Learner supports or learning scaffolding while participating in learning that is so challenging that without this special scaffolding, this level of information attainment and high quality decision-making would be out of a student's reach. A linkage which combines CIS and English can provide the kind of scaffolding that can relate tasks and subtasks that have been accomplished through policy changes and partnerships in one mega city to the problems confronted in Rio, Mexico City, or Cairo. Simulations of making public policy can be very exciting business in the classroom so that students are eager to get the skills that are necessary for doing this. Problem-solving modeling or simulations are part of what an education is about.

Scaffolding strategies are vital to our work in these courses. Clay and Cazden(1992) did early important work on scaffolding strategies in teaching reading and the importance of seeing the correct parts of answers that are only partially correct and encouraging the student to develop the work from those correct segments. Scaffolding strategies become extremely important when one is working with massive quantities of new knowledge, or massive new knowledge or massive inabilities to properly edit the grammar problems of one's own paper. Without self-consciously prioritized scaffolding strategies, we doubt that the learning matrix required in these courses could be achieved by t he end of the course. Each assignment must feed into the next, and each skill learned must immediately be reused in order to solidify the learning process. The student's ability to perform the activity must be reasserted and the teacher must model the appropriate epistemology of the problem solving process as well as the working computer and research skills. The desired learning or scaffolding strategy allows the student to see what he already knows in a problem as well as to see what he does not already know and to begin to build what he does not know from what he does. Like metacognition, scaffolding needs to be supported, literally and figuratively. It is support, but it must be supported. Vista Enhanced websites are great places to support required scaffolding strategies because the student can return to visit any time that the professors are not available to redirect them to the places that they might need to go to learn what they do not already know. If they know where to get the knowledge, then they are more likely to be able to navigate themselves enough to get that knowledge. Knowing where is close to knowing how. Achieving active consideration of a problem is a wonderful first step. Sometimes, however, one must return to this early step when active consideration of a problem has given way to a student's impatience with a sustained argument, and, however old school, a sustained argument is still a very desirable achievement in a research document of any kind. The student participates in, in fact, somewhat controls his or her own knowledge management.

Solving problems based on a Model United Nations simulation is used in the classroom. Students decide how to strategically plan, design, and continue to work on the problem that they have selected in the mega city of their choice using the theories of Janice Perlman as they are found on the web in her Cities model (Perlman, Megacity Project: http://www.megacitiesproject.org/default.asp)... Creating an improved model of Cairo, for instance, is motivating as the student discovers that there are literally millions of quasi-homeless people there, that traffic kills 40 times the number as in American cities and that the air is toxic and the water disease ridden. Partly because it is both challenging and actually necessary for the real survival of Cairo's 20 million people that the world engage in attempting to help them solve some of their problems, the student can easily select a problem that needs to be worked on. Computer available data as well as process guides like Janice Perlman's scaffold the complex solution grid for the student. Sustained engagement in the process of making the world' mega cities more livable results from the real difficulties these social constructs are actually facing and the massive data available on the web about them.

Through the yoking of global learning, written language skills and technology, the learner's own correct perceptions of his or her now recently prior experiences change the kind of student that he or she is, as well as the kind of self-perception that conforms to reality. Global learning is not linear. Global learning suggests an ability to sustain an overview. Global learning gives you at least a skeletal structure of the macrocosm first -- the world and its cities; you are seeing the big picture. Then you can return to the microcosm – a person in Cairo who needs housing according to Maslow's hierarchy of human needs and does not have it. Then once you have the global format, you can return to a world where there are organizations which specialize in eliminating homelessness, although in England it may be called "rough sleeping" and in other agencies and countries it may have other names. The matrix construct is created, via public policy, one step at a time, just as surely as the original problem followed what becomes now linear.

In learning theory, connectivism was developed by George Siemens to explain how learning has been changed by technology. In connectivism, the ability to understand connections among disciplines, concepts, ideas, is a vital ability necessary, even critical to capacity learning. Seeing through the "noise" of massive amounts of information and managing the information, is also vital in connectivism, as is understanding the dangers of residual imaging: of not being able to see the changed world as it presently actually is today. This learning theory, more than others, is appropriate to globalized topics and linked courses with English and CIS (*The Theory and Practice of Online Learning*, Terry Anderson, ed. May 2008). In "A Learning Theory for the Digital Age" (*International Journal of Instructional Technology and Distance Learning*, 2[1], Jan. 2005) motivation is clarifying in connectivistic learning as elsewhere saving the mega cities population from the distopic, however matrix-like, is stimulating, motivating, and emotional. Rewarding enough about computers and the internet to get trained enough to do a difficult assignment and research a difficult subject is all of the above as well. Forming a network to get the job done is also stimulating. Increasing one's sense of competence because one is more competent is easy compared to starting with a small rogue node of academic confidence because one has no competence.

Turning that conflicting rogue node of confidence in the matrix of academic despair into a network of confidence through true competencies in a semester of linkage between CIS and English 1302 can be done. It's almost a microcosm of the "Save the Mega city One Problem at a Time" assignment. Connectivism's learning as network creation, as George Siemens imagined it, builds a construct of amplified skill sets and that skill set construct is not common. Learning resides in many places in a classroom. It resides in the professor, in the students, in books and articles, papers, but learning also resides in the computers in a computer classroom and facilitating the rapid movement toward that learning is what our linkage does in order to create a highly adaptive, transforming learning network. After all, they still call it the World Wide Web and every time we put that WWW somewhere, we are affirming the global nature of the machine we take with us into a linkage between CIS and English.

Instructional design is a process. The creators of that process, at best, systematically develop an instructional matrix using code and learning theory to promote learning. It is, in a crude sense, a delivery system, but way before the delivery process begins, after the analysis of learning needs, massive work must be done creating and sequencing assignment. Caroline Crawford, our colleague from the University of Houston Clear

Lake, writes in her article in the *British Journal of Education Technology* (Col. 35, 4, pp. 413-420, 20 July 2004) as follows concerning thoughtful instructional design: "The Addie generic instruction design model emphasis five basic steps with the instructional design process: analyze, design, develop, implement and evaluate: emphases the non-linear nature of the instructional design process." She also emphasizes the continuous nature of modern education. Formal education is still an important part of our learning experience and we need to teach those things in formal education that are not easily acquired in other venues. While it may no longer be the place where one gets the majority of his or her knowledge, it plays an important, if changing role in our learning matrix.

A combination of learning that is in the center of a course and the learning that the student seeks out should be part of knowledge management. Siemen's "Connectivism: A Learning Theory for the Digital Age" first suggests that "Know-how and know-what are being supplemented with Know-where." "Know where" is the knowledge of where to find the knowledge for which you are searching. In our CIS/English linkage, CIS aids the student in the learning process of both "know-how" and "know-where." And this is very important to do as part of a university experience and influences what the student will do outside the university and after the training of the freshman curriculum; the learning which we now know is the majority of that of a lifelong learner. P. Ginsparg (1996) discusses the formal and informal availability of knowledge on the internet and the new availability to even non-matriculated students on university websites and other open forums for learning. Rather like that old Matt Damon movie, *Good Will Hunting*, about the young janitor at M.I.T, Will Hunting, doing math problems in his spare time, the intellectually ambitious with a home computer or a library card with internet access, can be a new source of intellectual leadership for problem-based work. In a better world, one just needs to be in the place where knowledge is accessible to gain access. Bulletin boards, blogs, and even conference papers provide the interested with a level of learning possibilities that should remind professors that the point is not that the teacher teaches, but that the student learns. At some point, if the student can learn without the teacher teaching, then that is the result that we are after. As Ginsparg notes, "the conventional journal system had always been much less fair to the underprivileged."(P.3). The scholarly journal was always more difficult for the reader to get to than a computer article and cost more in time as well. But as Brown notes, the scholarly internet and the world wide web serve as an amazingly transformative medium as information on global issues comes to us through our electronic mail from briefing services as well as from purposeful library searches and offers individuated matches between "a medium and how a particular person learns" (Brown, 2000).

Data Analysis and Findings

As computer support knowledge-building communities we learn to learn in a new way and that new way in project learning is purposefully and intentional. The classroom becomes filled with cognitive apprenticeships, experts and expertise that the instructor may not be able to duplicate as the levels of problem solving often reach a place on the scaffolding that the instructor has not reached, so the students are thrilled with their new positions in the classroom, in knowledge-building activities, and on the learning scaffolding (Hsiao, 2007). And these cognitive apprenticeships and their advantages do not go unnoticed by the student in the classroom.

In Spring 2009 semester, the two professors in the linkage asked the students a series of questions about what they had learned, in terms of computer skills in the classroom. These students had already had 100% of their research projects accepted by the Student Research Conference judges, so now it was time to ask them how they personally felt

Table 1. Surveyed students' future plans for websites

I would add any other coursework and keep updating my resume information.
I will add any data that is appropriate in order to continue gaining knowledge from website
I might add more about me.
I plan to add all my current course work.
Further course work as well as updating my resume, future essays or major accomplishments.
I would like to add a different picture and change my resume
Much more interesting information about me.
The poster for the Scholars Academy from my English 1302 class
I am planning on adding more of my previous assignments.
I plan to add a little of everything. Meaning that as I go along with school tacking courses here at XXX I will add recent stuff until I finally graduate.
If anyone in general ask for my assistance to create a web page; I will definitely help him/her because it is a really cool thing to know and learn from.
Yes, any other work I do with Microsoft, I will add
Yes, I plan to maintain the website by adding any sort of electronic assignments in order to easily access them.
I do plan on adding more pages for example like adding some of my best essay that I write or important projects
I plan to add everything I do till I graduate
Yes I plan to add any more important work in the future

about what they had learned to do, not just what they had learned about their megacity, or their rhetorical sophistication or their knowledge of air pollution in general. We asked the simplest of questions and got very consistent answers. Table 1 is a table of the surveyed students, the questions and their answers to those questions.

Students in the linked CIS/English class created websites to serve as the initial structure for an e-portfolio, using HTML (Hypertext Markup Language) and Microsoft Office web page tools to display and include work from both of these classes. Upon completion of their websites, a brief survey was given and the results were very positive. The survey results follow. Of the 16 students in the class, 14 students completed the survey and 12 of those 14 students identify themselves as students in the Learners' Community linked classes. Of the students completing the survey, 86% indicated that they had never created web pages before. All (100%) of the students indicated that they had enjoyed working with the HTML and creating their websites. 86% of the students indicated that they felt that they could now make minor changes to their websites and upload new web pages to the server without assistance. All of the students surveyed indicated that their websites contained 3 or more separate web pages that they created with HTML and, an additional 2 or more, web pages created with the assistance of Microsoft Word, Excel, PowerPoint or Access.

When asked if they had included any material for classes other than a class in the linkage, 14% said "yes". Surveyed students were evenly divided when asked if they had shown their websites to someone outside the class; 50% said "yes" and 50% said "no". When asked if they planned to show their work to a future prospective employer, 57% said "yes" and 43% said "no".

To determine if students felt confident and competent regarding what they had learned in the web building/e-portfolio experience, they were asked if they plan to add additional content in the future and how they plan to utilize the skills they developed in the class. The answers were varied:

Finally, students were asked to describe how they felt about utilizing the ongoing HTML which was completed in this class. Students were very positive, once again. All 14 students responded (Table 2).

Clearly, these students felt that they had walked through a new door in terms of what they are able to do and how they are able to build websites and accomplish technological feats that many of comparable skill are able to use to earn middle-class livings.

Table 2. Students comments on the ongoing html project

I really enjoyed it, it was interesting to learn how to make a webpage.
I felt confident because although parts were a bit challenging, I knew that I would be able to complete the assignment.
it helped me a lot and I like learning about it, but I still need to learn a lot more
I felt it was something new and I would have like to have done more to the website.
It was a great experience and accomplishment
I felt it was challenging and overall interesting seeing as how I had no background in HTML.
I liked that we started with this in the beginning. Now at the end of the semester I feel much more comfortable using HTML, though it definitely took some practice.
It was different, a little had to understand at first but after using it, it has become easier
it was a great experience
I really enjoy it and I learned a lot of useful information
I felt that it was really helpful.
I thought it was beneficial and educating.
I feel very proud of myself because never in my life would I imagine myself creating a web page that I could actually add and delete stuff by myself, without any professional assistance. I am very, but very happy, in completing this assignment in CIS
It was something new for me, and I'm glad I did it

CURRENT CHALLENGES FACING THE ORGANIZATION

This paper has looked at the process of learning in a linked CIS/Freshman English class that studies utopia, distopia, and the megacity and what public policy can do to improve life in the world's megacities. A great deal of learning on these subjects is stored outside of people and accessible through books, libraries and computers. Manipulating the technologies that have that learning is very important in learning management. Siemen understands that learning has changed so dramatically that revisions of earlier learning theories are desperate and finally ineffectual. The new technology requires us to reexamine what we as teachers thought would last throughout our teaching careers, but we were wrong. Where knowledge is abundant is where we want to go with our students. In far too many classrooms, knowledge paucity permeates the environment. We want to move from a knowledge paucity environment to a knowledge abundant environment and our linkage makes it so. We follow learning for in it is veritas. Only where knowledge is abundant, like the computer classroom, is the student able to develop his or her skill of quick knowledge evaluation and the discernment of that veritas.

Sharing a classroom with students on computers means, for the professor in the room, that the accuracy (and veracity) of what that teacher is saying can be checked on a moment-by-moment basis. It also means that the professor is no longer the absolutely centralized source of learning and knowledge. But it provides a literal knowledge nodel system that carries with its own scaffolding system that the professor continues to create. The computer does not create the design, but it does enrich and facilitate the implementation of that design. Obviously, this advantages the student on the computer, giving him or her a partially false sense of what he can say he knows. However, habits of inquiry are brought to the fore. Students are immediately rewarded for knowing the answer to the question, and computer and epistemological roads to get to the answer are traveled so that they may more easily be traveled again, and, as Robert Frost noted, and that will make all the difference. Intellectual curiosity is rewarded for the student who has the willingness to look something up that he or she wants to know the answer to or that does not immediately make sense to him or her.

These linked courses are freshman level and the dangers of the freshman experience are well documented elsewhere and ad nauseum. However, students involved in this linkage, experienced fewer of these problems. Some of the challenges and problems that the linkage experienced are basic ones such as providing the computerized classrooms for all students in the linkage for each of the class sessions, working with department chairs from different departments to schedule linked classes back-to-back, and getting permission from department chairs for allowing freshmen to participate in the Research Conference largely meant for upper classmen.

SOLUTIONS AND RECOMMENDATIONS

In the fullness of time, department chairs became used to the requirement of synchronizing the scheduling of the linked classes and providing the computerized classrooms for all students for each of the class sessions. Additionally, the quality of research undertaken during the pilot year demonstrated the ability of the students to do outstanding work, even while competing with upper classmen.

The long-range effects of our case call for at least a limited ability to look into the future until there are easier ways to transfer software to wetware than are presently available except in science fiction like *The Matrix*. Until we can just have programs installed in us, we will have to use programs to learn the hard way, but perhaps not the hardest way. Through multimediality, careful adjustments to scaffolding strategies, project learning, and sequencing of assignments, the professors in the linked classes come to expect a quantum leap in student skills as well as a highly sophisticated knowledge base in their courses. This quantum leap expectation is surely the wave of the future as the internet offers us knowledge and heretofore unimaginable levels. What we want to know is largely at our fingertips unless we are very imaginative creatures indeed. This problem is even more interesting when we look at the long term future possibilities of global research for classes like ours. Already, at major research universities, significant scholars have been able to make their research partners available to their best students at no additional cost to those students or their parents. The available problem solving, scaffolding-savvy professors could be available on a level heretofore unimagined. Thus both greater elitism -- a wider span between research university students and open door institution students, and, fortunately, greater intellectual democratization – a training democratization, are not only possible, but likely to occur during the same development period. Simultaneous waves of increase in knowledge and skill base for the elite and the democratic makes knowledge management in the twenty-first century the business and concern of us all, but places tremendous responsibility on what are now our public libraries and our institutions of higher learning.

Certainly one of the most profoundly interesting long-term possibilities of global research and linked courses is to link professors from different universities (and even continents and hemispheres) together in an on-line linked problem-based course that would have been absolutely unimaginable just a decade ago. This will give professors an agency separate from their university that might initially be a bit uncomfortably for the university, but it also might open up new opportunities to educate the best and the brightest, and perhaps, with more complex results, the truly great and the good.

Here are just a few of the lessons that the teachers have learned from this project: Allow your students to work from their interests. The first few weeks of class, you are teaching the teachers of the other students, so make sure that there are students who learn fast and teach while you are teaching others. Find forums for the students to present their work. Sign up for free briefing services on research paper topics. Use library databases. Introduce the students to think tanks that they can live with. Finally, introduce the student to think tanks that have ideas and political beliefs that they can live with, even espouse. You will be doing them a great service if you give them a rationale for what they believe, an intellectual background for their social and political perspectives.

REFERENCES

Anderson, T. (2005). A learning theory for the digital age. *International Journal of Instructional Technology and Distance Learning*, *2*(1).

Anderson, T. (2008). The theory and practice of online learning. Athabasca, CA: Athabasca University Press.

Bhabha, H. K. (1994). The location of culture. New York: Routledge.

Brown, J. (2000). Growing up digital: how the web changes work, education, and way people learn. *Change*. Retrieved 5/22/2009, from http://www.usdla.org/html/journal/FEB02_Issue/article01.html

Clay, M., & Cazden, C. (1992). A Vygotskian interpretation of reading recovery. Vygotsky and Education: Instructional Implications and Applications of Socio-historical Psychology, (pp. 206-222).

Crawford, C. (2004). Non-linear instructional design model: eternal, synergistic design and development. *British Journal of Educational Technology*, *35*(4), 413–420. doi:10.1111/j.0007-1013.2004.00400.x

Daphne, J. W., & Hsiao, L. (2009). *CSCL theories: cognitive apprenticeships*. Retrieved September 8, 2009, from http://www.edb.utexas.edu/csclstudent/Dhsiao/theories.html

Eraut, M., & Holes, C. (1988). Groupwork with computers. *Information and Communication Technologies*. Retrieved September 8, 2009, from http://www.virtuallearning.org.uk/virtuallearning/Virtual%20Learning.pdf

Ginsparg, P. (1996). Winners and losers in the Global research village. *1996 UNESCO Conference*, from http://people.ccmr.cornell.edu/~ginsparg/blurb/pg96unesco.html

Perlman, J. (2003). The megacity project. *Assessment Strategies for Global Learning*. Retrieved from http://megacitiesproject.org/default.asp

Scardamalia, M., & Bereiter, C. (1994). Computer support for knowledge-building communities. *Journal of the Learning Sciences*, *3*, 265–283. doi:10.1207/s15327809jls0303_3

Siemens, G. (n.d.). *Connectivism: a learning theory for the digital age*. Retrieved September 4, 2008, from http://www.elearnspace.org/articles/connectivism.htm

Skinner, B. F. (1935). Two types of conditioned reflex and pseudo types. *The Journal of General Psychology*, *12*, 66–77.

Tolbert, A., Mclean, G., & Myers, R. (2002). Creating the global learning organization. *International Journal of Intercultural Relations*, 1–15.

Warschauer, M. (1997). Computer-mediated collaborative learning: theory & practice. *Modern Language Journal*, *81*(4), 470–481. doi:10.2307/328890

ADDITIONAL READING

Avdic, A. (2005). Mediability of knowledge types--planning for a web based forum for knowledge sharing about end user development. *Promote IT 2005 -- Proceedings of the Fifth Conference for the Promotion of Research in IT at New Universities and University Colleges in Sweden,* Ed: Bubenko jr, Janis, Eriksson Owen, Fernlund, Hans & Lind Mikael, Studentlitteratur, Lund.

Boud, D. (1998). The challenge of problem-based learning. New York, New York: Routledge.

Bradley, K., & Bradley, J. (2004). Scaffolding academic learning for second language learners. *The Internet TESL Journal, 10(5),* http://iteslj.org/Articles/Bradley-Scaffolding/

Cooper, J., & Robinson, P. (2000). The argument for making large classes seem small. *New Directions for Teaching and Learning*, *81*, 15–16.

Cooper, J., Smith, K., & MacGregor, J. (2000). Implementing small-group strategies in large classes. *New Directions for Teaching and Learning*, *2000*(81), 17–24. doi:10.1002/tl.8102

Dewey, J. (1933). How we think: a restatement of the relation of reflective thinking to educative process. Boston: Houghton Mifflin.

Elder, L., & Paul, E. (2001). Critical thinking: thinking with concepts. *Journal of Developmental Education*, *24*(3), 42–43.

Fitch, B., & Kirby, A. (2000). Student assumptions and professors' presumptions: creating a learning community for the whole student. *College Teaching*, *48*(2), 47–54. doi:10.1080/87567550009595812

Fritz, M. (2002). Using a reading strategy to foster active learning in content area courses. *Journal of Developmental Education*, *32*(2), 189–194.

Gindis, B. (1998). Scaffolding children's learning and early childhood education. *School Psychology International*, *19*(2), 189–191. doi:10.1177/0143034398192007

Ginsparg, P. (1996). Winners and losers in the global research village. New York: UNESCO.

Gruber, S., & Boreen, J. (2003). Teaching critical thinking: using experience to promote learning in middle school and college students. *Teachers and Teaching: Theory and Practice*, *9*, 5–19.

Gupta, G. (2005). Improving students' critical-thinking, logic, and problem solving skills. *Journal of College Science Teaching*, *34*(4), 48–51.

Hillenius, S. (2008). Global research collaboration. *SRC Annual Report 2008*, doi: http://grc.src.org/Default.asp Indiana University, (n.d.). *Global Research Network Operations Center*, doi: http://globalnoc.iu.edu/

Josefgsen, R. E., & Mark, B. E. (1995). Teaching in the information age: active learning techniques to empower students. *The Reference Librarian*, *51-52*, 105–120.

Josepfson, J., & Casey, K. (2000). Stimulating issue networks in small classes using the world wide web. *PS: Political Science and Politics*, *33*(4), 843–846. doi:10.2307/420927

Kocour, B. G. (2000). Using web-based tutorials to enhance library instruction. *College & Undergraduate Libraries*, *7*(1), 45–54. doi:10.1300/J106v07n01_06

Lorenzen, M. (2000). Active learning and library instruction. *Illinois Libraries*, *83*(2), 19–24.

Magill, M. K. (1988). A computer-assisted system for analysis of interaction in problem-based learning groups. *Evaluation & the Health Professions*, *11*(3), 318–332. doi:10.1177/016327878801100303

Miller, J. S. (2004). Problem-based learning in organizational behavior class: solving student's real problems. *Journal of Management Education*, *28*(5), 578–589. doi:10.1177/1052562903257937

(n.d.). *U.S. Global Change Research Program*. Retrieved from http://www.usgrcrp.gov/usgcrp/default.php

Oswal, S. K. (2002). Group oral presentations as support for writing in large classes. *Business Communication Quarterly*, *65*(1), 71–78. doi:10.1177/108056990206500108

Smith, K. A. (2000). Going deeper: formal small-group learning in large classes. *New Directions for Teaching and Learning*, *2000*(81), 25–46. doi:10.1002/tl.8103

Smith, S. (2004). Designing collaborative learning experiences for library computer classrooms. *College & Undergraduate Libraries*, *11*(2), 65–83. doi:10.1300/J106v11n02_06

Van Der Stuyf, R. R. (2002). Scaffolding as a teaching strategy. *Adolescent learning and development*, 1, 13.

KEY TERMS AND DEFINITIONS

Computer-Mediated Collaborative Learning: This is Mark Warschauer's term which suggests that diversity of learning method approaches configurates a more diverse and thus more successful problem-solving environment.

Linked Courses: Two university courses that meet one after the other, share elements of their syllabi, schedule of readings and assignments, team culminating projects, practices and goals as well as potential external events such as entry into a Student Research Conference or guest speakers.

Multimediability: The interdependency of different media and the absorption of other media by the internet, allowing for the inclusion of international media organizations and global media organization as well as increasing the transparency of public policy decision-making and global problem solving. In our case, mutimediability allowed the student to do specific research relating to the research problem in his or her megacity at a level that would have been unavailable to any but a very few research library in the world. Early internet scholarship understood the internet as a distinct new medium with its own autonomous dynamic. Recent developments have occasioned a more nuanced perception of the internet as media: while the internet does have a number of unique characteristics, it is simultaneously marked by various forms of interaction with other media. http://www.cfi.au.dk/en/research/areas/multimediality

Project Learning: This is learning that is going on while a group of students reproduce a real-life problem such as air pollution in Mexico City or Housing in Cairo. Using best practices models and partnerships with NGO's and other organizations relevant to their place and problems, students create a multilayered, multipronged solution spiral.

Skill Matrix: A set of desired skills that become a real major goal for the linked classes of Computer Information Systems and English. The skill matrix is the skill environment that is desired at the end of the course and one skill's relationship to another skill inside that cultural construct.

Scaffolding: An instructional technique whereby the teacher models the desired learning strategy or tasks and then gradually shifts the responsibility for some or all of those strategies to the students, thus creating a changing scaffold while slipping away from some of the earlier responsibilities so that the teacher can take on other, more complex responsibilities, only to begin to slip away from even those as students become able to fulfill the roles of those tasks. Thus the teacher is building a scaffold, while disappearing from the scaffold and building another section at a higher level. Clay and Cazden (1992) point out two scaffolding strategies in teaching reading: working with new knowledge and accepting partially correct responses. In the first strategy, when a teacher suspects the child does not have the ideas or words needed for a particular text, he/she may explain some part of the story or contrast a feature presented with something he/she knows the child understands from another reading. In the second strategy, the teacher uses what is correct in the student's response but probes or cues the student, so as to suggest good possibilities for active consideration. Another scaffolding strategy is for the teacher to model the appropriate thinking or working skills in the classroom. Such modeling helps children learn to operate in the school culture. Harmin (1994) notes the applicability of Rosenshine's Guided Practice technique for developing student understanding and provides an actual example in language arts instruction in the classroom.

Chapter 17

Web-Based Instructions:
An Assessment of Preparedness of Conventional Universities in Saudi Arabia

Mohammed Saleh Al Balawi
King Fahd Naval Academy, Saudi Arabia

ABSTRACT

Factors affecting faculty decisions in the conventional university setup in Saudi Arabia for participating or not participating sin Web-based instruction (WBI) were investigated in this study. Incentives and barriers to WBI, faculty attitudes, and participants' demographic information were also explored. The study was aimed to investigate the attitudes of the faculty members at three Saudi universities toward WBI in an effort to describe the current status of WBI in the Saudi higher education system. In addition, results of the study could also provide the Saudi universities and the faculty with insight into factors affecting adoption of WBI. Finally, since there have been few implementations of WBI across the country, it was important to explore how WBI is currently used in Saudi universities and to determine critical factors that could affect the implementation of WBI.

ORGANIZATION BACKGROUND

Three Saudi Arabian universities were selected for this study, King Saud University in Riyadh, King Abdul Aziz University in Jeddah and King Fahd University of Petroleum and Minerals in Dhahran. The first being one of the oldest universities in Saudi Arabia established in 1957 in the central region of the country. By 2007-08 the university had a total of 4886 faculty members out of which 1456 were international faculty. A total of 40010 students were enrolled in the different academic programs of the university by 2007-08. The second university in this study was established in 1967 and situated in the prominent commercial city, i.e. ,Jeddah on the west coast of Saudi Arabia. The third university of this study was established as a university in 1975 and situated in the eastern region of the country. All the three universities of this case study are relatively old compared to other Saudi universities, and each has recently started to implement distance learning.

DOI: 10.4018/978-1-61520-749-7.ch017

SETTING THE STAGE

Saudi Arabia is a large country with many of its communities isolated from major cities and established colleges and universities. It was determined that providing higher-education programs through distance education would greatly benefit the people and the nation (Abahussain, 1998). Through the use of distance learning and the integration of Web-based training and technology, information and knowledge can be made available to students in the Kingdom of Saudi Arabia anytime and anywhere. The introduction of additional Web based educational opportunities will help Saudi universities move from formal classroom training and education to a new way of teaching and learning that does not require classrooms.. In addition, new methodologies of teaching and learning can be integrated into practical instruction.

The WWW has provided a new and interesting teaching and learning environment (McCormack & Jones, 1998), which has, in turn, affected higher education. Individual faculty, academic institutions, research centres, colleges, universities, and institutions of all kinds began to develop an Internet presence early in the emergence of the Web in the 1990s. The WWW became a popular teaching and learning tool during this time as well (Christianson, 2001; Crossman, 1997). The development of online or Web-based curricula accessed via the student's computer connected to a college network and the Internet has permitted students to learn from the comfort of their own homes (Cherepski, 2000). Additionally, WBI courses can be convenient for students, instructors, and institutions. With the rapid increase in the number of students in Saudi Arabia graduating from high schools, there is a growing strain on higher-education resources (Al-Mogbel, 2002). Institutes of higher education do not have the necessary resources to provide all of these students with a good education (Al-Mogbel, 2002). In the past decades, many institutions of higher learning in Saudi Arabia were able to respond to the continuing pressure of the growth of the student population by expanding existing colleges and universities or by building new ones (Al-Arfaj, 2001). Although the price of oil is high and the government has a surplus, and universities are being built as fast as possible, resources still are not available to educate all potential students. Some administrators believe that creating education programs that make use of modern technology, such as video and television broadcasting and the Internet, address the financial constraints and limited resources being experienced in the Kingdom (Al-Mogbel, 2002; Al-Rashoud & Al-Abdul-Kareem, 2001).

WBI can also offer opportunities for men and women who, inhibited by cultural and social barriers, desire to pursue higher education. For cultural and religious reasons, the higher-education system in Saudi Arabia is separated by gender, compounding the lack of necessary resources to fulfil the student demands (Abanmie, 2002; Al-Erieni, 1999). In response, Al-Arfaj (2001) stated, "Female students in Saudi Arabia were very interested in distance WBI" (p. 6). The use of WBI could be one method to solve the problem of a lack of access to higher education in Saudi Arabia (Al-Erieni; Al-Mogbel, 2002; Al-Rashoud & Al-Abdul-Kareem, 2001). Several Saudi universities have already realized the significance of this possible solution (Abahussain, 1998; Al-Arfaj, 2001). Understanding the perceptions and attitudes of administrators, faculty, and students (who are the major players) on the subject of distance education in Saudi Arabia is vital because there have been few WBI courses implemented in Saudi Arabia. There is also a need to understand how WBI is currently used (Al-Mogbel, 2002). With the modernization of the higher-education system, Saudi universities have placed a high priority on providing Saudi citizens with the opportunity to obtain a quality education. Around the world, the number of the courses on the WWW has increased; Web-based education has progressed rapidly. The integration of the Web into the educational environment makes it possible for students to study from cities far away from the main campuses. Whereas some professors consider themselves technologically adventurous in putting their syllabi and class notes online, more and more institutions are beginning to make entire degree programs accessible online (Arenson, 1998).

The Saudi education system is shifting gradually from the traditional classroom to Web-based distance learning in higher-education (Al-Erieni, 1999). In Saudi Arabia, as a supplementary delivery system, distance learning is one among many applications the universities are employing to provide educational services to remote cities (Al-Dawood & Al-Kasabi, 2001). Institutions of higher education in Saudi Arabia are facing new levels of competition for resources to educate as many students as possible by implementing more online courses. In response to these initiatives, this study investigated WBI as an effective solution to the many problems related to education in Saudi Arabia. In this study, the attitudes of Saudi faculty members toward development and implementation of WBI were investigated.

Using technology in instruction has been a part of education for decades; however, WBI is still a new pedagogy (Cherepski, 2000; Huang, 2003), especially in countries challenged to provide technology access to all citizens. The role of the faculty in higher education across the world is changing as technology evolves. Faculty attitudes affect the success or failure of the WBI implementation (Cherepski; Huang, 2001); for some faculty members, there is a willingness to participate in offering Web-based courses, while for others, there is not. The differences in the level of willingness may be related to factors such as (a) attitudes, (b) incentives, (c) support, (d) training, (e) policies, (f) time, and (g) tenure problems (Huang, 2001). Understanding these factors, in inhibiting or encouraging faculty members in Saudi universities to participate in distance learning, will facilitate decisions on the use of WBI in the Saudi education system.

Therefore, understanding faculty attitudes and examining the factors that encourage or impede faculty members to participate in WBI would be useful to the implementation of WBI. This study investigated faculty attitudes and the influence of other factors toward adopting WBI or distance learning.

This study was conducted with an objective to investigate the attitudes of the faculty members at three Saudi universities toward WBI in an effort to describe the current status of WBI in the Saudi educational system and to explore how WBI is currently used in Saudi universities and to determine critical factors that could affect the implementation of WBI. Based on the theoretical framework and statement of the problem, the following three research questions were formulated:

1. What are the attitudes of the Saudi faculty toward Web-based instruction?
2. How do the factors related to the barriers influence faculty participation in Web-based instruction?
3. How do the factors related to incentives influence faculty participation in Web-based instruction?

As stated earlier, this study was an investigation of the current use of WBI in Saudi institutions and the facilitating and impeding factors affecting faculty decisions to participate or not to participate in WBI. A survey research design (Pinsonneault & Kraemer, 1992) was used to collect information about the characteristics of the faculty and the effect of those characteristics on participation in developing WBI. Incentives and barriers to WBI, faculty attitudes, and participants' demographic information were also explored in this study. In this study it was assumed that the faculty had the ability to measure attitudes toward WBI.

CASE DESCRIPTION

During the 1990s, distance education changed significantly with the integration of computer-mediated learning, two-way interactive video, and a variety of other technologies (Phipps & Merisotis, 1999). Garrison and Shale's (1987) model presents four generations that can be discussed in terms of a delivery system: (a) Generation 1—print, radio, and television; (b) Generation 2—video and cable television; (c) Generation 3—electronic mail, chat rooms, and bulletin boards; and (d) Generation 4—unlimited with the possibilities of virtual reality or video desktop (two-way audio and video). Al-Arfaj (2001) stated that there are three generations of distance education: (a) correspondence education, (b) broadcast and teleconferencing, and (c) WBI. A wide range of technological options are available to the distance educator. Gutenberg's invention of the printing press was an extremely early example of technology revolutionizing distance-education processes (Spodick, 1996). Print formats including textbooks, study guides, workbooks, and course syllabi form the foundation of distance-education support systems. Technologies have facilitated access to learning opportunities through radio, voice, telephone, audio-conferencing, tapes, television, fax machines, videotapes, two-way video communication (whether through satellites or communication networks), auto-tracking cameras, phonographs, computer networks, and electronic mail (Spodick, 1996; University of Idaho, College of Engineering, 1999). Moore and Kearsley (1996) pointed out that each medium and each technology has its own set of strengths and weaknesses, and one of the worst mistakes an organization or an instructor can make is to become completely focused on delivery by a single medium. Baird and Monson (1992) stated that distance education offers tremendous opportunities as well as challenges to today's educational stakeholders.

WBI is defined as an innovative approach for delivering instruction using the WWW as the delivery system (Khan, 1997). WBI is not simply placing lecture notes online, nor is it creating a library of links to content-related sites. WBI requires instruction, teaching, content, cognitive, visual, and usability design principles to be followed; WBI ensures fulfilment of teachers' and students' needs (Rice, McBride & Davis, 1998). In WBI, content in hypertext, audio, video files, and other multimedia formats are provided. Resources such as chat, threaded discussion, e-mail, and hyperlinks are included (Marsh et al., 2000). The developer of Web-based learning environments uses the resources of the Web to create a context in which learning is supported and fostered (Daugherty & Funke, 1998). WBI is growing faster than any other instructional technology (Cherepski, 2000; Crossman, 1997). In Saudi Arabia, more and more university faculty members are using WBI as an integral part of instructional activities

(Al-Arfaj, 2001; Al-Frieni, 1999). For this study, *WBI* is defined as a comprehensive set of instructional materials available through a browser over the Internet or intranet. Whittington (1990) stated that the rapid growth in the use of telecommunications technologies in higher education during the 1980s stimulated interest in distance learning. In the 1980s, with the availability of personal computers for home and office use, a wide variety of uses of computer-based instruction or computer-assisted instruction were initiated. Since the 1980s, multimedia products have been available, and advancements in Web technologies have permitted educational opportunities to be widely delivered at relatively low costs (Marquardt & Kearsley, 1999).

The capabilities offered through the Web, including Internet tools, multimedia components, content development, authoring programs, servers, and browsers, facilitate active learning in Web-based learning environments (Khan, 1997). Khan indicated that well-designed WBI provides numerous features that together contribute to the learning environment, such as interactivity, online search, online resources, open systems, global accessibility, authenticity, and collaborative learning. Furthermore, Hall (1997) observed that these features encompass pedagogical, technological, organizational, institutional, and ethical issues. Khan concluded that "the more components a WBI program integrates the more features it is able to offer" (p. 7). The use of WBI is growing faster than any other instructional technology, and more and more university faculty are using WBI as an integral part of instructional activities (Crossman, 1997; Fredrickson, 1999; Mwaura, 2003).

The potential collaborative and interactive benefits of WBI are touted. Web assisted and Web-based courses provide the opportunity for students to move from individual to collaborative learning, from the consideration of ideas in isolation to an examination of their meaning in global context (Clayton, 2002; Huang, 2001). WBI has gradually become the current mainstream choice for distance education, especially in higher education (Olgren, 2000; Robinson, 1994). In the U.S., university administrators' interests in non-traditional methods of course delivery (Orwig, 1999) include computer applications such as computer-assisted instruction and computer-managed instruction, in which the computer is used to organize instruction and track students' records and progress. In addition, computer-mediated education facilitates the delivery of instruction and includes (a) electronic mail, (b) fax, (c) real-time computer conferencing, and (d) WWW applications (Glenn, 1999).

Computer-based education and computer-based instruction refer to any kind of computer use in educational settings, including drill and practice, tutorials, simulations, instructional management, supplementary exercises, programming, database development, and writing by using word processors. These terms may refer either to stand-alone computer learning activities or to computer activities that reinforce material introduced and taught by teachers (Cotton, 2003). The use of computer-mediated communication (CMC) in classes creates online-learning opportunities for students at a distance and has become an extremely popular strategy in higher-education institutions (Berge, 1998). Advancements in telecommunication technologies have created opportunities whereby educators in higher-education institutions can expand the educational process beyond the traditional classroom and deliver instruction and training to geographically diverse audiences locally, nationally, and internationally.

In Saudi Arabia, current Internet-based learning is presented through text and graphic images. Some of the universities in Saudi Arabia use Web-enhanced methods as an extension in their teaching processes. Saudi students can download syllabi and course summaries from the Internet and use e-mail to interact with instructors. In Saudi Arabia, the Internet has become a popular way to communicate information to distance students (Al-Rashoud &Al-Abdul-Kareem, 2001).

Factors Inhibiting Faculty Participation in Distance Learning

Several studies have identified a list of factors which inhibit participation of faculty members in online and distance learning instructions. Some of them which have been discussed in detail are Institutional Support and Administrative Issues, Technical issues, Faculty experience, Faculty professional development and Course development needs.

Schifter (2002) suggested in his study of factors that inhibit faculty participation in asynchronous learning networks (ALNs) that "the lack of institutional support for faculty, technical infrastructure and course development needs" (p. 15) are the top three factors that inhibit faculty participation in ALNs. Frequently mentioned barriers include (a) decreased live, face-to-face interaction with students; (b) lack of time to plan and deliver an online course; and (c) the lack of support and assistance in planning and delivering an online course (McKenzie, Mims, Bennett, & Waugh, 2000). In addition, factors such as lack of release time, lack of technical support from the institution, concern about faculty workload, and lack of grants for material expenses have negatively influenced faculty participation (Betts, 1998). The primary factors inhibiting faculty from teaching via distance as identified in the literature include (a) increased workload, (b) the altered role of the instructor, (c) lack of technical and administrative support, (d) reduced course quality, and (e) negative attitudes of colleagues (Clay, 1999a). Instructors have other concerns about distance learning, primarily, how distance will change their role in education (Kincannon, 2000).

Faculty concerns about teaching via distance are related to (a) time, (b) cost, (c) instructional design, (d) instructor-student relationships, (e) reward structure, (f) degree programs, (g) policy, and (h) training (Rockwell, Schauer, Fritz, & Marx, 2000). Bichelmeyer, Misanchuk, & Malopinsky (2000) listed factors that impact the adaptation process of WBI, such as (a) instructor experience and openness to innovation, (b) technological capacity and infrastructure, (c) rationale for adaptation to WBI, (d) fit of course goals with technological capacity, (e) labour force available for course adaptation, (f) technological equipment and sophistication of learners, (g) learner motivation for taking the course, (h) administrative support, and (i) tuition and fees.

Faculty also reported a wide range of challenges in the development and delivery of WBI. The most frequently identified barriers included (a) lack of technical support, (b) lack of software and hardware, (c) lack of faculty and administrative support, (d) lack of preparation time required to create assignments, and (e) student resistance (Daugherty & Funke, 1998). Overcoming these barriers and enabling the ability to teach and learn anytime, anywhere with institutional responsiveness requires three components: (a) administrative leadership, (b) the technical and workforce infrastructure to fulfil the mission, and (c) faculty willing to risk experimentation (Truman-Davis, & Hartman, 1998). Clay (1999b) found that faculty resists teaching distance-education courses because of increased workloads and lack of administrative support. In addition, Clay found the following issues to be important: (a) altered role of the instructor in distance-education instruction, and (b) negative perception of the distance-education instructor by colleagues. He also pointed out that not all of these issues exist at every institution, but that they do exist in various forms at many of them. On the other hand, some studies have indicated why instructors prefer to teach distance education and online courses. Clay (1999b) listed reasons for teaching distance-education courses as (a) opportunities to reach more students, (b) intellectual challenges, (c) opportunities to work with more motivated students, (d) provision of release time, (e) financial rewards, (f) motivation to use technology, (g) opportunities for research, (h) opportunities for recognition, (i) opportunities to use support services, (j) increased course quality, (k) reduced travel, and (l) increased flexibility. In addition to the reasons for teaching distance courses recognized by Clay, Arthur (1998) identified barriers that might prevent distance education from becoming a viable alternative form of education as (a) interactive issues, (b) familiarity with distance education, (c) technology, (d) time, (e) money, (f) the role of the faculty, (g) motivation to change, and (h) curriculum development.

Clark (1993) suggested that faculty support for distance courses was framed within concerns for quality of interaction, administrative support, and rewards. Berge and Muilenburg (2000) indicated that barriers, as perceived by managers and administrators, include (a) organizational resistance to change, (b) lack of shared vision for distance education in the organization, (c) lack of strategic planning for distance education, (d) a slow pace of implementation, and (e) difficulty keeping up with technological changes. Critical barriers and factors can be organized in four general areas: (a) instructional support and administration issues, (b) technical issues, (c) faculty experience and professional development, and (d) course development needs. Exploration of these areas provides context to how faculty and university administrators respond to the challenges of distance learning.

Institutional Support and Administration Issues

Institutional support for faculty involvement in distance education is essential and takes on a variety of forms, especially in terms of the recognition that there is a wide range of faculty motivations and needs (Bower, 2001). Administrators must understand what motivates and inhibits faculty distance-education participation to maximize efforts and ensure that any issues related to the institution culture are taken into consideration (Al-Erieni, 1999; Schifter, 2002). Faculty need administrative support and opportunities to develop effective technology-based courses (Thomson & Stringer, 1998). University administrators often pressure faculty to teach courses online; many faculty have never taught online and, therefore, wonder what they are getting into (Smith, Caris & Ferguson, 2001). As distance education changes the way education is being delivered, administrators should re-examine policies, rules, and regulations (Gilbert, 1996) to make sure that they respond to problems in ways that encourage faculty participation. Availability of the necessary technology resources, including computers and access to telecommunication networks, is also an important issue in making decisions regarding institutional policies (Al-Erieni, 1999).

Faculty and administrators must work together to make a distance program successful (Schifter, 2002). As the use of distance education increases, college and university administrators must develop strategies for successful implementation of online degree programs (Ensminger & Surry, 2002). Rockwell et al. (2000) stated, "For faculty to be successful in distance-education teaching, higher-education institutions must take into account the wants, needs, interests and aspirations of the faculty so they can help faculty develop distance learning educational models and techniques" (p. 10). As an outcome of such initiatives, many administrators are leading efforts to review the extent to which distance education will apply toward awarding tenure and promotion (Wolcott, 1997). Two core challenges are faced by administrators who want to facilitate delivery of courses and programs, especially when preparing faculty to teach in this environment. First, the online environment has created an increased need for faculty with interests and skills in this area, who can master the technology, take advantage of the new pedagogy mandated by teaching in a virtual environment, and maintain their subject area competence. Second, faculty must be sufficiently trained to take advantage of these resources in the design and delivery of Web-based courses (Schweber, Kelly & Orr, 1998). A clear policy will guide faculty toward the use of the technology and aid in achieving the institution's mission (Al-Erieni, 1999).

The need to reform existing educational programs and implement new ones requires understanding of both teachers' and directors' beliefs concerning distance education. Nasser and Abouchedid (2000) found that faculty who were involved in distance-education programs consider literacy, awareness, and interest as powerful agents for change. Abahussain (1998) found that teachers and administrators who were working in higher education in Saudi Arabia favored having courses available to remote areas of the Kingdom of Saudi Arabia and suggested that a sense of change in the traditional environment may already be in process. The evidence of WBI effectiveness can serve as a reference base and as justification for the use of WBI (Berge & Muilenburg, 2000). In addition, such evidence can be the basis for making strategic decisions (Cegles, 1998).

Technical Issues

The faculty have expressed the need for additional support and compensation to meet expectations concerning WBI. The challenge for faculty is to meet the expectations of students and their administration to incorporate this technology into their teaching practice and still retain their own definition of quality teaching (Kincannon, 2000). To integrate technology into teaching and learning processes, two key objectives have been identified: (a) to preserve a sense of community in colleges and universities, especially among teachers and learners, and (b) to sustain or increase the quality and frequency of communication between students and teachers within these groups (Clayton, 2002). Beggs (2000) and Lan (2001), among others, identify technology factors related to the success of online instructional programs as (a) adequate equipment and technological resources, (b) incentives for using technology, (c) comfort level using technology, (d) time for training, and (e) need to change existing instructional methods. Along with the need for current Web technology skills, faculty need the ability to design and deliver their course on the Web using a variety of instructional strategies in interactive formats (Gerlich & Mills, 2003).

From an individual faculty member's perspective, Betts (1998) found that the intrinsic factors (a) intellectual challenge, (b) personal motivation to use technology, (c) ability to reach new audiences who cannot attend classes on campus, and (d) opportunity to develop new ideas were important factors when examining faculty issues. Neglecting faculty beliefs about the rapid developments in technology and uses for instruction often leads to limited implementation (Cuban, 1997).

Cost is a consideration when investing in an organization's new technology or equipment infrastructure (Chute, Thompson, & Hancock, 1999; Greengard, 1999). Acquisition costs for technology are high, and rapid development of new technology reduces the effective life of equipment already in place (Al-Mogbel, 2002). Faculty should be able to identify and recognize strengths and weaknesses of technology and select the most appropriate delivery mechanism for a particular lesson (Gunawardena, 1990). Another issue relates to individual attitudes toward technology. Delcourt and Kinzie (1993) argued that experience and a positive attitude are predictive of self-efficacy for use of computer technologies. A person's individual confidence in his or her ability to complete certain tasks will provide a positive attitude toward technology (Al-Mogbel, 2002). There are also potential technology-related factors that may prevent faculty from pursuing technology innovations, including fear of (a) change, (b) increased time involved, (c) appearing incompetent, (d) failure, (e) not knowing where to start, (f) making bad choices, (g) typing, and (h) reprisals and rejection (Williams, 1996). Addressing these fear factors helps to promote use of distance education in order to meet organizational goals.

Faculty Experience

One of the most important steps in the development of WBI is to obtain a clear view of faculty characteristics. In the U.S., a faculty member's prior knowledge or experience has a potential influence on online delivery (Colley, Gale, & Harris, 1994) and is one of the most important considerations when deciding on the implementation of online delivery (Lyon, 2001). Not only are faculty members' knowledge and skills needed for implementing distance education, but also their perceptions of and attitudes toward the use of technologies for the purpose of education are needed (Tobin, Tippins, & Gallard, 1994). The basic skills required for faculty include understanding of (a) basic educational psychology, (b) basic principles of instructional design, (c) basic principles of effective instructional delivery, and (d) basic Web page design, including use of tools that positively impact learning (Formosa, 1998).

On the issue of faculty experience, Dillon and Walsh (1992) found that faculty involved in distance-education endeavours developed more positive attitudes as their experiences with distance-education projects increased than those faculty who were not involved. Faculty experience changes their teaching practice when faculty transition from face-to-face classrooms to Web-based learning environments (Kincannon, 2000). Understanding the attitudes of faculty, students, and administrators is very important in trying to implement a program of distance education (Al-Mogbel, 2002). Al-Erieni (1999) showed in her study that although many of the faculty in the first university of this study had limited knowledge of computers, they did have positive attitudes regarding distance-education programs as an alternative to on-campus traditional classrooms. The faculty also felt that for distance-education programs to be effective,

good policies and procedures, quality assurance, compatibility, adequate course offerings, appropriate faculty training, necessary staff and administrative support, reasonable faculty workload and satisfactory faculty promotion and rewards were vital (Al-Erieni, 1999, p. 51).

Faculty's lack of knowledge about and experience in distance learning can be major barriers to further development (Al-Mogbel, 2002). Stinehart (1987) provided descriptive information on the factors that affect faculty attitudes toward distance teaching, finding that full-time faculty held concerns about losing control of the teaching and learning process in distance education and that the level of control the instructor perceived was the greatest predictor of the willingness to teach at a distance. Many faculty fear distance learning is just a means of reducing the number of faculty or a means to solve budget problems. Others fear dehumanization and alienation of students and a loss of critical thinking and social skills (Novek, 1996). Faculty experiences color their teaching strategies, but professional development can be a way to expand those experience levels to meet instructional challenges. Keegan (1995) suggested that instructors can prepare for the classroom by including multimedia use, speaking voice, and even font size considerations. Instructors also need to realize that the support systems are a central part of the distance learning experience. Taking advantage of support systems permits faculty to focus on what they do best—facilitate the teaching and learning process.

Faculty Professional Development

Teaching in the online environment requires faculty to have training in how to design and deliver interactive instruction using this online format (Gerlich & Mills,2003). Killian (1997) said, "If we are to serve the faculty well, we need to show them how the computer can help them do what they want to do anyway" (p. 31). Teaching in the online environment also requires faculty to have certain basic technical skills and a technical support infrastructure that may not be as critical in a traditional classroom (Gerlich & Mills). Shaeffer and Farr (1993) proposed that faculty development is a prerequisite to successful distance-education programs. Faculty professional development is critical to the success of any distance education program (Lee, 2001; Willis, 1993). Professional development should be strategically planned and integrated (Al-Erieni, 1999). Faculty are unlikely to request assistance in learning new skills and techniques without institutional motivation and encouragement. Colleges and universities must address how faculty members will be trained in their efforts to integrate technology into instruction, and faculty need to learn how to establish and maintain contact at distance (Lee, 2001). One area that is of prime concern is a lack of knowledge in the areas of instructional development and delivery (Formosa, 1998). Faculty are concerned with the integrity and quality of the teaching and learning process that occurs with their work, including how to best engage their students through interactivity (Yong & Wang, 1996).

Course Development Needs

Two factors viewed as critical in the successful implementation of distance environments are time and interaction. These factors impact faculty, learners, and the institution as a whole.

Preparation time: The factor of time is the most consistent faculty complaint in designing WBI; Web-based teaching takes enormous amounts of preparation time, more time than required for face-to-face teaching (Kincannon, 2000). Hiltz (1997) found that the faculty indicated that their greatest area of concern was the increased workload. This concern was attributed to the increased preparation time needed for each course. In addition, the faculty felt that class size should be limited to 25 students, as any more than that adds significantly to the time necessary to conduct the class. Faculty also identified the grading process as a concern, as projects would arrive at different times and often by different means, adding to time, effort, and confusion (Cherepski, 2000).

Faculty feel they are learning to be more effective teachers online, but it has been a difficult transition (Kincannon, 2000). The increased amount of time necessary to prepare for distance learning adequately takes away from the activities faculty are evaluated on, such as grant writing and publishing (Valentine, 2002). University administrators should recognize this fact and incorporate appropriate compensations when planning distance-education initiatives (Bower, 2001). The faculty is aware of the substantial time required for developing, integrating, and administering interactive elements courses (Clayton, 2002).

Learners' interaction: A second development need involves interaction strategy design, development, and implementation. Moore (1989) proposed three types of interactions for successful distance education: (a) learner-content interaction, (b) learner instructor interaction, and (c) learner-learner interaction. Strategies for all three types should be included in distance learning courses if instruction is to be successful. Mungall, Green, and Skunza (2001) explained that any program must address learner orientation before launching a successful online degree program. Frankola (2001) argued that "the emotional connection between instructor and student may be even more important for online courses than in the classroom" (p. 14). Learners in an online format need curricular, instructional, and technological support. Learners should be actively involved in the evaluation and implementation of the course (Bichelmeyer et al., 2000). Successful distance-education learners are self-motivated and disciplined; they operate well on their own without constant reminders from faculty or peers to meet project deadlines (Feasley, 1993).

Black (1997) cited a study in which online students learned 20% more when compared to the traditional students. The way students are classified may, in some instances, indicate their level of acceptance of online learning, although this may not always be the case (Cherepski, 2000). Most distance-education research literature has centered on methods and learning from the student's perspective (Al-Erieni, 1999). Dillon and Walsh (1992) indicated that most of the research cantered on the learner. In fact, most of the research, according to Dillon and Walsh, has examined "learner outcomes, learner characteristics, and learner attitudes" (p. 5).

Factors Motivating Faculty to Participate in Distance Learning

Faculty participate in distance environments for a variety of reasons. Among the top factors motivating faculty to participate as distance instructors include (a) the opportunity to reach remote students, (b) intellectual challenge and the opportunity to develop new ideas, (c) the opportunity to work with more motivated students, (d) release time, (e) financial reward, (f) opportunities for research, (g) motivation to use technology, (h) the opportunity for recognition,

(i) the opportunity to utilize support services, (j) reduced travel, (k) increased course quality, and (l) increased flexibility (Clay, 1999a). Faculty are motivated to teach online for many other reasons: (a) flexible working conditions, (b) the ability to reach new audiences, (c) the enjoyment of conducting online instruction, and (d) the opportunity to enhance their technology skills while planning and delivering online courses (McKenzie et al., 2000). Additional incentives include (a) faculty recognition, (b) awards, (c) travel supplements, (d) grants for materials, (e) modified teaching assignments, and (f) credit toward advancement (Wolcott & Haderlie, 1995).

Betts (1998) conducted a study at George Washington University in Washington, DC, to identify factors that influence faculty to participate in distance education and found that (a) faculty who have extensive experience in higher education are more likely to participate in distance education than faculty with less experience; (b) faculty are more likely to participate in distance education if inhibiting factors are eliminated by the administration; (c) faculty participation will not increase significantly unless the administration eliminates inhibitors that deter faculty from participating in distance education; and (d) regardless of whether or not faculty feel positive or negative toward distance education, the faculty recognize the value of distance education. Taylor and White (1991) found that the primary benefits of distance teaching include (a) ability to reach new populations of learners, (b) opportunity to work with better prepared and motivated students, (c) flexibility in work schedule, and (d) pedagogical advantages such as the necessity for more efficient organization and the ability to use a broader range of media-based resources. Distance-education researchers reveal a cross-section of incentives that have been used to motivate faculty to participate in distance education; these incentives include (a) salary increases, (b) merit payments, (c) overload payments, and (d) stipends (Al-Erieni, 1999). These concerns are often reflected in the literature as a need for faculty to have incentives for WBI development (Daugherty & Funke, 1998).

The Study

The data for this research study were collected using a survey developed by Cherepski (2000), who examined factors that encourage or discourage faculty participation in teaching Web-based courses in 2-year colleges. The survey was further modified by Huang (2003), who examined critical factors of implementing WBI by Taiwan's higher-education faculty. The researcher of this study modified the survey for use with the study population. Data were collected in two forms, through printed instruments and via an online survey. The returned surveys were analyzed using descriptive statistics methodology to provide descriptive information corresponding to the research questions in this study. Conclusions were collectively drawn from the data sources to answer the research questions. The researcher used a survey research design. This design was chosen because of a need to (a) collect data for testing the research hypotheses and (b) provide answers to the research questions by evaluating the attitudes and perceptions of selected faculty members regarding various aspects of distance education. The way to gather information in a survey research design is to ask participants structured and predefined questions. Descriptive statistics are used to present information about the sample of respondents (e.g., mean, standard deviation). Inferential statistics are used to generalize from the sample results to the population of interest. In this framework, the researcher gathers data from a sample population at one time through use of a survey, summarizes the quantitative data through descriptive and inferential statistical analyses, and then finally decides whether it is reasonable to generalize to a particular population (Leedy & Ormrod, 2001). The survey included closed-ended items. For the closed-ended items, the quantitative approach is used in this study (a) to determine an account of the survey participants based on their demographic factors, (b) to analyze their responses to the measurable items of the survey, and (c) to examine the significance of the selected variables in the attitude of the survey participants.

The 531 faculty members who comprise the sample in this study were randomly selected from faculty member lists provided to the researcher by each of the three selected Saudi universities. The provided lists included all the faculty members, male and female, of all departments. The items of the survey were divided into four sections. The first section related to basic demographic information and general WBI questions. The second section included questions concerning factors that inhibit faculty participation in WBI, or barrier factors. The third section included statements of factors that encourage faculty participation in WBI, or incentive factors. The final section included statements about faculty attitudes toward the value of WBI. Three of the response variable items pertaining to faculty participation were embedded within the second section while the other was embedded within the third section. For Sections 2, 3, and 4, questions were all measured on a 5-point Likert scale ranging from 1 to 5 with 1 being *strongly agree,* 2 being *agree,* 3 being *neutral,* 4 being *disagree,* and 5 being *strongly disagree.* Where appropriate, items were reverse-scored such that low numbers represented the least amount of that being measured (e.g., least agreement with something as a barrier) and high numbers represented the greatest amount of that being measured. Of the 531 identified participants, a total of 154 responses were received and of these responses, 67 (43.50%) were from the university based in Jeddah, 56 (36.40%) were from the university located in Riyadh and 31 (20.10%) were from the university based in eastern city of Dhahran. There was an overall 29% response rate.

The most reported teaching experience range was more than 15 years (n=58, 37.70%). The most common academic degree reported was the doctorate degree (n = 106, 68.80%). The most common position attained was assistant professor (n = 49, 31.80%). The gender of faculty was 70.10% male (n = 108) and 29.90% female (n = 46). The most reported age range was from 41 to 45 years (n = 43, 27.90%). Of the faculty, 74.70% were Saudi citizens (n = 115) and 25.30% were non-Saudi residents from other nations (n = 39). Over half of the faculty reported a teaching course load of 1 to 5 courses (n = 83, 53.90%). Most faculty reported daily computer use (n = 112, 72.70%). Most faculty reported never having taught a Web-based class (n = 96, 2.30%). Most faculty had training in e-mail (n = 132, 85.70%). Less than half of the faculty had training in threaded discussions (n = 45, 29.2%), List Servs (n = 39, 25.30%), chat rooms (n = 19, 2.30%), teleconferencing (n = 30, 19.50%), videoconferencing (n=48, 31.20%), and a Learning Management System such as WebCT (n=22, 14.30%). Faculty displayed a willingness to participate in WBI, with 140 of the respondents (90.90%) willing to participate in WBI.

Willingness and Unwillingness to Participate in WBI

Of the 154 total participants, a total 140 (90.90%) were willing to participate in WBI. Of the 140, 60 (42.90%) were from KAU, 53 (37.90%) had more than 15 years of teaching experience, 97 (69.30%) had doctorate degrees, 46 (32.90%) were assistant professors, 100 (71.40%) were male, 41 (29.30%) were 36 to 40 years of age, 105 (75%) were Saudi, 75 (53.60%) taught 1 to 5 courses, 102 (72.90%) used the computer daily, 49 (35.00%) used the Internet 2 to 3 hours each visit, and 85 (60.70%) had never had a Web based teaching experience. Of the 132 participants who had training in e-mail, 123 (93.20%) were willing to participate in WBI. Of the 45 participants who had training in threaded discussion, 42(93.30%) were willing to participate in WBI. Of the 39 participants who had training in ListServs, 36 (92.30%) were willing to participate in WBI. All participants who had training in chat rooms were willing to participate in WBI. Of the 30 participants who had training in teleconferencing, 29 (96.70%) were willing to participate in WBI. Of the 48 participants who had training in videoconferencing, 44 (91.70%) were willing to participate in WBI. All participants who had training in WebCT were willing to participate in WBI. For a complete presentation of frequencies related to characteristics of faculty who were willing and not willing to participate in WBI. Of the 154 total respondents, 14 (9.10%) were not willing to participate in WBI. Of those 14, 7 (50.00%) were from second university, 5 (35.70%) had more than 15 years of teaching experience, 9 (64.30%) had doctorate degrees, 3 (21.40%) were assistant professors, 8 (57.10%) were male, 6 (42.90%) were 41 to 45 years of age, 10 (71.40%) were Saudi, 8 (57.10%) taught 1 to 5 courses, 10 (71.40%) used the computer daily, 6 (11.10%) used the Internet 30 to 60 minutes per visit, and 11 (78.60%) had never had a Web-based teaching experience. Of the 132 participants who had training in e-mail, 9 (6.80%) were not willing to participate in WBI. Of the 45 participants who had training in threaded discussion, 3 (6.70%) were not willing to participate in WBI. Of the 39 participants who had training in ListServs, 3 (7.70%) were not willing to participate in WBI. Of the 30 participants who had training in teleconferencing, 1 (3.30%) was not willing to participate in WBI. Of the 48 participants who had training in videoconferencing, 4 (8.30%) were not willing to participate in WBI.

Analysis and Findings

The majority of the faculty were willing to participate in WBI (N = 140); over 90% of the respondents were willing to participate in WBI. The highest percentage of responses came from the second university (n = 67, 43.5%); of those 60 (42.90%) were willing to participate in WBI. This finding may be due to the fact that this university implemented WBI before the other two universities. Data from this study indicated that faculty members with more teaching experience were more willing to participate in WBI. Previous research studies have indicated the same finding; that is, most of the faculty who want to teach on the Web had more teaching experience (Cherepski, 2000; Huang, 2003). Of faculty who wanted to teach on the Web, most had master's degrees (n = 32, 22.90%) or doctorate degrees (n = 97, 69.30%). Previous research studies showed the same finding i.e. most of the faculty who want to teach on the Web had either master's or doctorate degrees (Cherepski, 2000; Huang, 2003). The most common position attained was assistant professor (n=49, 31.80%); of those in that position, 32.90% (n = 46) were willing to participate in WBI. Data indicated that faculty with higher positions were more willing to participate in WBI than faculty in lower positions.

Faculty who teach one to five courses (n = 75, 53.60%) appeared to be more willing to participate in WBI than faculty who teach six or more classes. The finding of this research study indicated that faculty who teach fewer courses were more willing to participate in WBI than faculty who teach more courses. This result may be due to a heavier workload that the faculty member faces when teaching more courses. Other researchers have reported the same result (Cherepski, 2000; Huang, 2003; Robinson, 2000).

The finding of this study showed the highest faculty level of those who are willing to participate in WBI were faculty who use the computer daily (n = 102, 72.90%). The finding indicated that the more faculty members used the computer and the Internet, the more willing they were to participate in WBI.

Many faculty who were willing to participate in WBI were those who never had a Web-based teaching experience (n = 85, 60.70%). The openness of these faculty to try WBI suggest that there are opportunities for additional offerings of WBI throughout the Saudi higher-education system. Faculty who had training on how to use Web-based technology were more willing to participate in Web teaching than faculty who had not had training. The majority of participants had training in e-mail, followed by videoconferencing and threaded discussion. In this study, the technology most used by faculty was e-mail; e-mail was the most common technology tool used in teaching. Previous researchers obtained the same finding: The most widespread technology used by faculty in teaching was e-mail (Cherepski, 2000; Huang, 2003). Additionally, in this study, faculty aged 36 to 40 years (n = 41, 29.30%) were the most willing to participate in WBI. The result of this finding indicated that the older faculty members were willing to participate in WBI. Other researchers have reported that younger faculty members were more willing to participate in WBI than older faculty (Huang, 2003; Robinson, 2000).

The findings on first Research question of the study, i.e., the attitudes of the Saudi faculty toward Web-based instruction showed that the faculty attitude toward WBI were positive. Faculty agreed with several attitude statements: WBI offers students enough opportunities for interaction; WBI is the wave of the future in higher education; adopting and developing WBI in the Saudi universities will create a challenge for faculty; WBI provides a valuable service to students; WBI opens higher education to a broader range of students than does traditional education; and adoption of WBI will improve student learning. Respondent faculty strongly agreed with the attitude statement: WBI is a good teaching tool due to gender segregation in the Saudi higher-education system. These results mirror findings of other researchers who found overall positive faculty attitudes in relation to WBI (Al-Erieni, 1999; Al-Mogbel, 2002; Cherepski, 2000; Clark, 1993; Dillon & Walsh, 1992; Huang, 2003).

Faculty also agreed that WBI will create stress for them as an instructor. Faculty disagreed with three attitude statements: Students tend to learn just as much in a Web-based education environment as they do in the traditional classroom; WBI technology is too complicated for both the students and the faculty to be successful; and WBI will put their job at risk. Faculty were neutral toward one attitude statement: Adopting WBI in Saudi universities will encourage students to be more interested in learning. Faculty held generally positive attitudes toward WBI as the wave of the future in higher education. Over half of the faculty (n = 84, 54.60%) indicated that WBI is the wave of the future in higher education. Cherepski (2000) and Huang (2003) found similar results.

In this study, overall faculty attitudes toward WBI were positive. Faculty held positive attitudes toward WBI and believed that online courses are the future of higher education in Saudi Arabia. Faculty agreed that WBI provides a valuable service to students. Faculty held positive attitudes toward WBI because they believed it opens higher education to a broader range of students than does traditional education. Additionally, faculty did not think that WBI would jeopardize their jobs or that WBI technologies are complicated. They did believe, however, that WBI would create more stress for them as instructors. When it came to adopting WBI in Saudi Arabia universities, faculty believed WBI (a) will improve students' learning, (b) will encourage students to be more interested in learning, (c) will be a good teaching tool because of gender segregation in the Saudi higher-education system, and (d) will create a challenge for faculty. Additionally, as previously stated in the data analysis section of Research Question 1, the null hypothesis was rejected.

In the second Research Question factors that might inhibit participation in WBI were explored. Nine main barriers items were identified, including (a) lack of knowledge on how to develop WBI, (b) lack of enough time to develop WBI, (c) lack of clear WBI policies, (d) lack of clear course ownership policies, (e) lack of peer support, (f) lack of technical support, (g) lack of monetary incentive, (h) lack of administrative support, and (i) lack of governmental support. However, faculty did not perceive 2 of the 11 attitudes items as barriers: (a) fear of using new technology and (b) necessary campus network infrastructure.

In Research Question 3 the factors related to incentives influencing faculty participation in Web-based instruction were studied, the factors identified were (a) appropriate knowledge bases, (b) appropriate Web-based courses for teaching, (c) a training program, (d) enough time to develop WBI, (e) clear WBI policies, (f) clear course ownership policies, (g) a campus network infrastructure, (h) tenure and promotion incentives, (i) workload incentives, and (j) governmental support. The campus network infrastructure ranked highest in the area of incentives. Saudi faculty perceived that the campus network infrastructure should be established before implementation could begin. Among the highest ranked incentives were clear course ownership policies and clear WBI policies. This finding of the study was a concern for the Saudi faculty even though the majority of the Saudi faculty had never taught on the Web. Faculty agreed that the following factors are incentives: (a) release time, (b) appropriate Web-based courses, (c) tenure and promotion, (d) workload, and (e) faculty knowledge.The findings show that the majority of faculty agreed that incentives would provide encouragement to engage in WBI; all incentive factors had a mean of 3.55 or greater, indicating positive perceptions of those incentives. Overall, Saudi faculty had positive views about potential incentives when implementing WBI. Saudi faculty agreed that incentive items are available to faculty. With incentives in place, faculty should be inclined to participate in WBI. The evidence from the survey suggests that the great majority of Saudi faculty is, indeed, supportive of WBI.

SOLUTION AND RECOMMENDATIONS

Based on the findings of this research, a series of recommendations were formulated.

First, this study should be replicated and a similar study should be conducted using additional Saudi universities. Further research in Saudi universities is required to determine and evaluate barriers, incentives, and attitudes that could affect the implementation of WBI at the Saudi Universities. Saudi universities that implement Web-based programs in the future could use such results to provide supports for faculty and universities to improve the design, development, and implementation of WBI.

Second, further studies should be conducted to determine if there are other factors affecting the implementation of WBI at Saudi universities beyond those investigated in this research study. The researcher of this study was unable to evaluate all the potential factors that might affect implementation of WBI at the Saudi universities. The survey instrument for this study was close-ended; it is possible that by using open-ended questionnaires, additional factors not mentioned in this research study might be collected.

Third, this research study evaluated barriers, incentives, and attitudes of faculty members only. Further research should be conducted to determine and explore similar areas affecting Saudi students and administrators.

Fourth, it is recommended that the Saudi government and Ministry of Higher Education seek ways to increase faculty participation in developing more Web-based programs. Since the Saudi government and Ministry of Higher Education control the budgeting and planning process of Saudi universities, increasing the Saudi government and Ministry of Higher Education support will help faculty have the resources needed to develop and implement high-quality Web-based programs.

Fifth, this research study focused on faculty of Saudi universities only. It would be interesting to conduct further studies at Saudi community colleges, technical colleges, and industrial businesses institutions, to see if their faculty have the same perceptions of WBI.

Sixth, it is recommended that Saudi universities should develop clear course ownership policies, clear WBI policies, and a training program for faculty in how to use WBI technologies. Additionally, instructors should be given enough time to develop WBI and for administrators to build an up-to-date campus network infrastructure. These kinds of support will encourage faculty to participate in developing WBI.

REFERENCES

Abahussain, S. (1998). Implementation of interactive television technology in distance education higher learning program in Saudi Arabia (Doctoral dissertation, University of Southern California, 1998). *Dissertation Abstracts International, 60*(6), 132B, (UMI No. 9931904).

Abanmie, A. M. (2002). Attitude of high school students in Saudi Arabia toward computers (Doctoral dissertation, Mississippi State University, 2002). *Dissertation Abstracts International, 63*(2), 193B, (UMI No. 3043178).

Al-Arfaj, A. H. (2001). The perception of college students in Saudi Arabia towards distance WBI (Doctoral dissertation, Ohio University, 2001). *Dissertation Abstracts International, 62*(11), 191B, (UMI No. 3032949).

Al-Dawood, K., & Al-Kasabi, S. (2001, February). *ATM-based solution to facilitate distance learning at KSU.* Paper presented at the 16th National Computer and Educational Conference, Riyadh, Saudi Arabia.

Al-Erieni, S. A. (1999). Attitudes of King Saud University faculty toward development and implication of a telecommunications-based distance education program as an alternative to conventional teaching (Doctoral dissertation, George Mason University, 1999). *Dissertation Abstracts International, 60* (10), 248B, (UMI No. 9948544).

Al-Mogbel, A. (2002). Distance education in Saudi Arabia: Attitudes and perceived contributions of faculty, students, and administrators in technical college (Doctoral dissertation, University of Pittsburgh, 2000). *Dissertation Abstracts International 64* (01), 95B, (UMI No. 3078818).

Al-Rashoud, A., & Al-Abdul-Kareem, M. (2001, February). *Interactive distance learning over the Internet and the intranet.* Paper presented at the 16th National Computer and Educational Conference, Riyadh, Saudi Arabia.

American Society for Training and Development. (2001). E-learning glossary. Retrieved February 5, 2004, from http://www.learningcircuits.org/glossary.html

Arenson, K. W. (1998, November 2). More colleges plunging into uncharted waters of online courses. *New York Times,* (p. A14).

Arthur, M. F. (1998, July). *Barriers affecting adoption of distance education programs.* Paper presented at the Pennsylvania State University Fifth Distance Education Symposium, Philadelphia.

Baird, M. A., & Monson, M. K. (1992). Distance education: Meeting diverse learners' needs in a changing world. *New Directions for Teaching and Learning,* (51): 65–76. doi:10.1002/tl.37219925108

Barnes, S. (2003). Computer-mediated communication: Human-to-human communication across the Internet. Boston: Pearson Education.

Beggs, T. A. (2000). Influences and barriers to the adoption of instructional technology. In *Proceedings of the Fifth Annual Mid-South Instructional Technology Conference*, Middle Tennessee State University, Murfreesboro. Retrieved August 21, 2003, from http://www.mtsu.edu/~itconf/proceed00/beggs/beggs.htm

Belanger, F., & Jordan, D. H. (2000). Evaluation and implementation of distance learning: Technologies, tools and techniques. Hershey, PA: Idea Group.

Berge, Z. L. (1998). Barriers to online teaching in post-secondary institutions: Can policy changes fix it? *Online Journal of Distance Learning Administration, 1*(2). Retrieved July 18, 2003, from http://www.westga.edu/~distance/Berge12.html

Berge, Z. L., & Muilenburg, L. Y. (2000). Barriers to distance education: A factor analytic study. *American Journal of Distance Education, 15*(2), 7–22.

Betts, K. S. (1998). Factors influencing faculty participation in distance education in postsecondary education in the United States: An institutional study (Doctoral dissertation, The George Washington University, 1998). *Dissertation Abstracts International, 59* (7), 445B, (UMI No. 9900013).

Bichelmeyer, B. A., Misanchuk, M., & Malopinsky, L. (2000, October). *Adapting a master's course to a Web: Principles, strategies and recommendations.* Paper presented at the 23rd National Convention of the Association for Educational Communications and Technology, Denver, CO, (ERIC Document Reproduction Service No. ED455808).

Black, J. (1997). *Online students fare better.* Retrieved July 15, 2002, from http://www .news.com/News/Item/0,4,7147,00.html

Bower, B. L. (2001). Distance education: Facing the faculty challenge. *Online Journal of Distance Learning Administration, 4*(2). Retrieved June 13, 2003, from http://www.westga.edu/~distance/ojdla/summer42/bower42.html

Cegles, K. A. (1998). Emerging issues affecting distance education research and practice in higher education: A global futures perspective. *Dissertation Abstracts International, 59* (8), 320B, (UMI No. 9901000).

Cherepski, D. D. (2000). *Factors that encourage or discourage faculty participation in teaching Web-based courses in two-year colleges.* Unpublished doctoral dissertation, University of Arkansas, Little Rock, AR.

Christianson, L. (2001). Teaching on the World Wide Web: A descriptive investigation of WBI in nursing undergraduate education (Doctoral dissertation, Kent State University, 2001). *Dissertation Abstracts International, 62*(5), 256B, (UMI No. 3014147).

Chute, A. G., Thompson, M. M., & Hancock, B. W. (1999). The McGraw-Hill handbook of distance learning. New York: McGraw-Hill.

Clark, T. (1993). Attitudes of higher-education faculty toward distance education: A national survey. *American Journal of Distance Education, 7*(2), 19–33. doi:10.1080/08923649309526820

Clay, M. (1999a). *Development of training and support programs for distance education instructors.* Retrieved September 10, 2003, from http://.westga.edu/~distance/ clay23.html

Clay, M. (1999b). *Faculty attitudes toward distance education at the State University of West Georgia.* Retrieved September 10, 2003, from http://www.westga.edu/ ~distance/attitudes.html

Clayton, M. (2002, April). *Communities of learners: Connecting students to maximize learning.* Paper presented at the Seventh Annual Mid-South Instructional Technology Conference, Murfreesboro, TN, ERIC Document Reproduction Service No. ED464628.

Colley, A. M., Gale, M. T., & Harris, T. A. (1994). Effects of gender role identity and experience on computer attitude components. *Journal of Educational Computing Research, 10*, 129–137.

Connick, G. P. (Ed.). (1999). The distance learner's guide. Upper Saddle River, NJ: Prentice Hall.

Cotton, K. (2003). *Computer-assisted instruction.* Retrieved January 10, 2004, from the Northwest Regional Educational Laboratory website http://www.nwrel.org/ scpd/sirs/5/cu10.html

Crossman, D. M. (1997). The evolution of the World Wide Web as an emerging instructional technology tool. In B. H. Kahn (Ed.), Web-based instruction, (pp. 19-23). Englewood Cliffs, NJ: Educational Technology.

Cuban, L. (1997, May 21). High-tech schools and low-tech teaching. *Education Week on the Web, 16.* Retrieved September 7, 2003, from http://www.edweek.org/ew/vol-16/34cuban.h16

Daugherty, M., & Funke, B. L. (1998). University faculty and student perceptions of Web-based instruction. *Journal of Distance Education, 13*(1). Retrieved August 20, 2003, from http://cade.athabascau.ca/vol13.1/daugherty.html

Delcourt, M. A. B., & Kinzie, M. B. (1993). Computer technology in teacher education: The measurement of attitudes and self-efficacy. *Journal of Research and Development in Education, 27*, 35–41.

Dillon, C. L., & Walsh, S. M. (1992). Faculty: The neglected resource in distance education. *American Journal of Distance Education, 6*(3), 5–6, 25–28. doi:10.1080/08923649209526796

Ensminger, D., & Surry, D. (2002, April). *Faculty perceptions of factors that facilitate the implementation of online programs.* Paper presented at the Seventh Annual Mid-South Instructional Technology Conference, Murfreesboro, TN. (ERIC Document Reproduction Service No. ED464622)

Feasley, C. E. (1993). Is distance education right for you? In National University Continuing Education Association, (Ed.), The electronic university: A guide to distance learning (p. viii). Princeton, NJ: Peterson's Guides.

Frankola, K. (2001, June). The e-learning taboo: High dropout rates in online courses. *Syllabus Magazine, 14*(11), 14–16.

Fredrickson, S. (1999). Untangling a tangled Web: An overview of WBI programs. *T.H.E Journal, 26*(11), 67-77.

Garrison, D. R., & Shale, D. (1987). Mapping the boundaries of distance education: Problems in defining the field. *American Journal of Distance Education, 1*(1), 7–13. doi:10.1080/08923648709526567

Gerlich, R. N., & Mills, L. (2003). *The design and delivery of effective Web-based instruction: An analysis of faculty concerns.* Retrieved August 28, 2003, from http://karsenti.scedu.umontreal.ca/pdf/ressources/designDelivery.pdf

Gilbert, S. W. (1996). Making the most of a slow revolution in distance education. *Change, 28*(2), 47–52.

Glenn, A. (1999). *Implications of new educational technologies in community colleges.* Retrieved May 25, 2003, from http://faculty.tamu-commerce.edu/mdennehy/ technologies.htm

Greengard, S. (1999, February). Web-based training yields maximum returns. *Workforce, 78*(2), 95–96.

Gunawardena, C. (1990). Integrating telecommunications systems to reach distance learners. *American Journal of Distance Education, 4*(3), 38–46. doi:10.1080/08923649009526715

Hall, B. (1997). Web-based training cookbook. New York: Wiley.

Hiltz, S. R. (1997). Impacts of college-level courses via asynchronous learning networks: Some preliminary results. *Journal of Asynchronous Learning Networks*, *1*(2), 1–19.

Huang, P. (2001). University faculty perceptions on WebCT for delivering courses (Doctoral dissertation, University of South Dakota, 2001). *Dissertation Abstracts International, 62*(3), 149B. (UMI No. 3007064).

Huang, Y. (2003). *Critical factors related to the adaptation of WBI by higher-education faculty.* Manuscript in preparation, The University of West Florida, Pensacola.

Khan, B. H. (1997). WBI: What is it and why is it? In B. H. Kahn (Ed.), Web-based instruction (pp. 5-19). Englewood Cliffs, NJ: Educational Technology.

Kilby, T. (2000). *What is Web-based training?* Retrieved July 5, 2003, from http://www .wbtic. com/primer_whatiswbt.aspx

Killian, C. (1997). F2F—Why teach online. *Educational Review*, *32*(4), 31–34.

Kincannon, J. M. (2000, April). *From the classroom to the Web: A study of faculty change*. Paper presented at the annual meeting of the American Educational Research Association, New Orleans, LA. (ERIC Document Reproduction Service No. ED467096)

Lan, J. (2001). WBI for education faculty: A needs assessment. *Journal of Research on Computing in Education, 33*, 385–400.

Lee, J. (2001). *Higher education on the Web,* (Report No. 034225). Washington, DC: National Education Association, Higher Education Research Center. ERIC Document Reproduction Service No. ED455751.

Leedy, P. D., & Ormrod, J. E. (2001). Practical research: Planning and design, (7th ed.) Upper Saddle River, N. J. Merrill/Prentice-Hall..

Lyon, E. (2001). Online education: An exploratory study into success factors. Journal of EducationalComputing Research, 24, 77-92.

Marquardt, M. J., & Kearsley, G. (1999). Technology-based learning: Maximizing human performance and corporate success. Boca Raton, FL: St. Lucie Press.

Marsh, G. E., II, Price, B. J., & McFadden, A. C. (2000, February). *An overview of online educational delivery applications.* Paper presented at the 11th Annual Society for Information and Teacher Education International Conference, San Diego, CA. ERIC Document Reproduction Service No. ED444476.

McCormack, C., & Jones, D. (1998). Building a Web-based education system. New York: Wiley.

McKenzie, B. K., Mims, N., Bennett, E., & Waugh, M. (2000). Needs, concerns and practices of online instructors. *Online Journal of Distance Learning Administration, 3*(3). Retrieved July 15, 2003, from http://www.westga.edu/ ~distance/ojdla/fall33/mckenzie33.html

Moore, M. G. (1989). Three types of interaction. *The American Journal of Distance Education, 3*(2), 1-7. Retrieved May 17, 2003, from http://www.ajde.com/ Contents/vol3-2.htm#editorial

Moore, M. G., & Kearsley, G. (1996). Distance education: A systems view. Belmont, CA: Boston Wadsworth.

Mungall, D., Green, C., & Skunza, B. (2001, October). *Challenges of creating an online doctoral program: Panel discussion of the trials and success of the Ohio State nontraditional Doctor of Pharmacy program.* Paper presented at WebNet 2001 World Conference on the WWW and Internet, Orlando, FL. (ERIC Document Reproduction Service No. ED466587).

Mwaura, C. W. (2003). An investigation of the innovation-decision process of faculty members with respect to Web-based instruction. *Dissertation Abstracts International, 65* (05), 1649.

Nasser, R., & Abouchedid, K. (2000). Attitudes and concerns towards distance education: The case of Lebanon. *Online Journal of Distance Learning Administration, 3*(4). Retrieved May 15, 2003, from http://www.westga.edu/~distance/ojdla/winter34/ nasser34.html

Novek, E. M. (1996, August). *Do professors dream of electronic sheep? Academic anxiety about the information age*. Paper presented at the 79th annual meeting of the Association for Education in Journalism and Mass Communication, Anaheim, CA. (ERIC Document Reproduction Service No. ED399594).

Olgren, C. H. (2000). Distance learning in higher education. In K. Mantyla (Ed.), The 2000/2001 ASTD distance learning yearbook, (pp. 19-25). New York: McGraw-Hill.

Orwig, G. (1999, October). *Academic support for Web course development: A successful top-down strategy.* Paper presented at WebNet 99: World Conference on the WWW and Internet, Honolulu, HI. (ERIC Document Reproduction Service No. ED448731).

Phipps, R., & Merisotis, J. (1999). What is the difference? A review of contemporary research on the effectiveness of distance learning in higher-education. Washington, DC: American Federation of Teachers, National Education Association, and The Institute for Higher-education Policy.

Pinsonneault, A., & Kraemer, K. L. (1992). *Survey research methodology in management information systems: An assessment.* Retrieved May, 9, 2003, from http://www .crito.uci.edu/research-archives/pdf/urb-022.pdf

Rice, J., McBride, R., & Davis, J. (1998). *Defining a Web-based learning environment.* Retrieved August 28, 2003 from http://www.byu.edu/ipt/workshops/wbi/text.html

Robinson, J. L. (2000). The new media, faculty, and Web-based instruction at the University of Florida: A study of implementation. Doctoral dissertation, University of Florida. *Dissertation Abstracts International, 61* (06), *2091.* (UMI No. 9976598).

Robinson, M. (1994). Improving science teaching with e-mail. *Computers in the Schools, 11*(1), 95–107.

Rockwell, K., Schauer, J., Fritz, S. M., & Marx, D. B. (2000). Faculty education, assistance and support needed to deliver education via distance. *The Online* Journal of Distance Learning Administration, 3(2). Retrieved August 11, 2003, from http://www .westga.edu/~distance/rockwell32.html

Rosenberg, M. J. (2001). E-learning: Strategies for delivering knowledge in the digital age. New York: McGraw Hill.

Schifter, C. C. (2002). Faculty participation in asynchronous learning networks: A case study of motivating and inhibiting factors [Electronic version]. *Journal of Asynchronous Learning Networks, 4*(1), 15–22.

Schweber, C., Kelly, K., & Orr, G. J. (1998, August). Training, and retraining, faculty for online courses: Challenges and strategies. In *Proceedings of the 14th annual* conference on Distance Teaching & Learning, Madison, WI. (ERIC Document Reproduction Service No. ED422874).

Shaeffer, J. M., & Farr, C. W. (1993). Evaluation: A key piece in the distance education puzzle. *T.H.E. Journal, 20*(9), 79–82.

Smith, G. G., Caris, M., & Ferguson, D. (2001, June). *Teaching over the Web versus face to face.* Paper presented at the ED-Media 2001 World Conference on Educational Multimedia, Hypermedia & Telecommunications, Tampere, Finland. (ERIC Document Reproduction Service No. ED466216).

Spodick, E. F. (1996). *The evolution of distance learning.* Retrieved December 10, 2003, from http://sqzm14.ust.hk/distance/evolution-distance-learning.htm

Stinehart, K. (1987). Factors affecting faculty attitudes toward distance teaching (Doctoral dissertation, Iowa State University, 1987). *Dissertation Abstracts International, 48* (7), 131B. (UMI No. 8721935).

Taylor, J. C., & White, V. J. (1991). Faculty attitudes towards teaching in the distance education mode: An exploratory investigation. *Research in Dance Education, 3*(3), 7–11.

Thomson, J. S., & Stringer, S. B. (1998, August). Evaluating for distance learning: Feedback from students and faculty. In Proceeding of the 14th Annual Conference *on Distance Teaching & Learning*, Madison, WI. (ERIC Document Reproduction Service No. ED422879).

Tobin, K., Tippins, D., & Gallard, A. (1994). Research on instructional strategies for teaching science. In D. L. Gabel (Ed.), Handbook of research on science teaching and learning, (pp. 45-93). New York: Macmillan.

Truman-Davis, B., & Hartman, J. (1998, November). *Online with the future: Web-based* program development at the University of Central Florida: Designing a university *for the 21st century.* Paper presented at WebNet 98: World on the WWW and Internet Conference, Orlando, FL. (ERIC Document Reproduction Service No. ED427739).

University of Idaho, College of Engineering. (1999). *Distance education at a glance: Guide #1.* Retrieved August 15, 2003, from http://www.uidaho.edu/evo/dist1.html Valentine, D. (2002). Distance learning: Promises, problems, and possibilities. *Online* Journal of Distance Learning Administration, 5(3). Retrieved January 29, 2003, from http://www.westga.edu/%7Edistance/ojdla/fall53/valentine53.html

Whittington, N. (1990). Characteristics of good state instructional telecommunications policy for higher education: Some research considerations. In M. G. Moore (Ed.), Contemporary issues in American distance education, (pp. 23-54). New York: Pergamon Press.

Williams, A. E. (1996, June). *Integrating courses with the Internet: Preparing the teacher as well as the learner.* Paper presented at the Association of Small Computer Users in Education Summer Conference, North Myrtle Beach, SC. (ERIC Document Reproduction Service No. ED405839).

Willis, B. (1993). Distance education: A practical guide. Englewood, NJ: Education Technology.

Wolcott, L. L. (1997). *Tenure, promotion, and distance teaching: A study of faculty rewards and incentives.* Unpublished manuscript, Utah State University at Logan. (ERIC Document Reproduction Service No. ED413861).

Wolcott, L. L., & Haderlie, S. (1995, August). *The myth of dangling carrots: Incentives,* promotions, and rewards for teaching at distance. Paper presented at the 11th Annual Conference on Distance Teaching and Learning, Madison, WI.

Wood, P. A. (2001). The U.S. Department of Education and student financial aid for distance education: An update. Washington, DC: ERIC Clearinghouse on Higher Education. (ERIC Document Reproduction Service No. ED457762).

Wu, C. L. (2003). *Web-based training in Taiwan's fortune 500 corporations: Implementation factors*. Unpublished doctoral dissertation, The University of West Florida, Pensacola, FL.

Yong, Y., & Wang, S. (1996). Faculty perceptions on a new approach to distance learning. *Journal of Instruction Delivery Systems, 10*(2), 3–5.

ADDITIONAL READING

Al-Anqari, K. (2003, August 28). The government is giving more attention to the subject of accepting all of the high school graduated students for this year. *Al-Riyadh Daily Newspaper, No. 12851,* p. 24.

Al-Brydi, A. (2006, August 27). We are in need of a higher education that follows the needs of the homeland and the domiciles. *Al-Watan Daily Newspaper, No. 2158,* p. 10. Retrieved June 29, 2007, from http://www.alwatan.com.sa/daily/2006-0827/writers/writers06.htm

Bishop, R. W. (1999). *Training and education program negotiations between Americans and Saudi Arabians.* Unpublished doctoral dissertation, The University of West Florida, Pensacola.

Carliner, S. (2000). Build a business case for online learning projects. In K. Mantyla (Ed.), 2000/2001 ASTD distance learning yearbook (pp. 92-97). New York: McGraw-Hill.

Carlson, R. D., Downs, E., Repman, J., & Clark, K. F. (1998, March). *So, you want to develop a WBI: Points to ponder.* Paper presented at the SITE 98: Society for Information Technology & Teacher Education International Conference, Washington, DC. (ERIC Document Reproduction Service No. ED421097)

Cronbach, L. J. (1951). Coefficient alpha and the internal structure of tests. *Psychometrika, 16,* 297–334. doi:10.1007/BF02310555

DeVellis, M. K. (1991, March). *Reliability test of attitudinal instruments.* Paper presented at the Annual Research Conference, University of Minnesota, Minneapolis.

Field, M. (1994). Inside the Arab world. Cambridge, MA: Harvard University Press.

Formosa, J. (1998, April). *Are you sure you want to train faculty to develop WBI?* Paper presented at the 3rd Annual Mid-South Instructional Technology Conference, Murfreesboro, TN. (ERIC Document Reproduction Service No. ED431387)

Gerrity, T. W. (1976). College-sponsored correspondence instruction in the United States: A comparative history of its origin (1873-1915) and its recent development (1960-1975; Doctoral dissertation, Columbia University, New York, 1976). *Dissertation Abstracts International, 37* (2), 214B. (UMI No. 7617282)

Grinnell, R. M., Jr., (Ed.). (2001). Social work research and evaluation: Quantitative and qualitative approaches (7th ed.). Belmont, CA: Wadsworth.

Hafiz, T. (1976). The potential role of education instructional television in higher education and human resources development for the Kingdom of Saudi Arabia. (Doctoral dissertation, State University of Colorado, Fort Collins, 1976). *Dissertation Abstracts International, 37* (04), 413B. (UMI No. 7623620)

Holmberg, B. (1986). Growth and structure of distance education. London: Croom Helm.

Iken, M. B. (2000). Faculty attitudes toward computer-mediated distance education (Doctoral dissertation, University of South Dakota, 2000). *Dissertation Abstracts International, 61* (10), 138B. (UMI No. 9991647)

Jacobsen, D. M. (1998). Adoption patterns and characteristics of faculty who integrate computer technology for teaching and learning in higher-education (Doctoral dissertation, University of Calgary, Canada, 1998). *Dissertation Abstracts International, 59* (12), 227B. Jeffries, M. (n.d.). *Research in distance education.* Retrieved January 17, 2004, from http://www.digitalschool.net/edu/DL_history_mJeffries.html

Kerlinger, F. N., & Lee, H. B. (1999). Foundation of behavioral research (4th ed.). Fort Worth, TX: Harcourt.

Long, D. E. (1997). The kingdom of Saudi Arabia. Gainesville, FL: University Press of Florida.

Ministry of Higher Education. (2003). *Saudi Arabia higher-education system.* Retrieved August 9, 2003, from http://www.mohe.gov.sa

Ministry of Higher Education. (2007). *The number of students admitted to universities for the academic year 2006-2007.* Retrieved April 2, 2007, from http://www.mohe.gov.sa

Nasseh, B. (1997). *A brief history of distance education.* Retrieved May 10, 2003, from http://www.seniornet.org/edu/art/history.html

Perraton, H. (1988). A theory for distance education. In D. Sewart, D. Keegan, & B. Holmberg (Eds.), Distance education: International perspectives (pp. 34-45). New York: Routledge.

Public Broadcasting Service. (2002). *A brief history of distance learning.* Retrieved August, 18, 2003, from http://www.pbs.org/als/dlweek/history/index.html

Roberts, J. M. (1996). The story of distance education: A practitioner's perspective. *Journal of the American Society for Information Science American Society for Information Science, 47,* 811–816. doi:10.1002/(SICI)1097-4571(199611)47:11<811::AID-ASI3>3.0.CO;2-5

Royal Embassy of Saudi Arabia. (2003). *Saudi Arabia's education system.* Retrieved August 8, 2003, from http://www.saudiembassy.net/Country/Education/edu.asp

SAMEX. (2007). *Ministry of Higher Education.* Retrieved June 29, 2007 from the Saudi Arabian Market Explorer Web site: http://www.saudinf.com/main/c6n.htm

Saudi Arabian Information Resource. (2004). *Saudi Arabia higher education.* Retrieved September 4, 2003, from http://saudinf.com/main/j3.htm

Saudi Arabian Information Resource. (2007). *Saudi Arabia population.* Retrieved April 2, 2007, from http://www.saudinf.com/main/a4.htm

Schreiber, D. A. (1998). Organizational technology and its impact on distance training. In D. A. Schreiber & Z. G. Berge (Eds.), Distance training: How innovative organizations are using technology to maximize learning and meet businessobjectives (pp. 3-18). San Francisco: Jossey-Bass.

Sharaf, A. S. (1991). Distance education: An alternative route to formal college education sin Saudi Arabia. *Dissertation Abstracts International, 52* (11), 3793A. (UMI No. 057318)

Simonson, M., Smaldino, S., Albright, M., & Zvacek, S. (2000). Teaching and learning at a distance: Foundation of distance education (2nd ed.). Upper Saddle River, NJ: Prentice-Hall.

Slavin, R. E. (1992). Research methods in education (2nd ed.). Boston: Allyn & Bacon.

Smith, S., & Benscoter, A. (2000). Implementing an Internet tutorial for Web-based courses. In M. G. Moore & G. T. Cozine (Eds.), Web-based communication, the Internet, and distance education (pp. 131-136). University Park: The Pennsylvania State University, American Center for the Study of Distance Education.

Tiffin, J., & Rajasingham, L. (1995). In search of the virtual class: Education in an information society. New York: Routledge.

Watkins, L., & Wright, J. (1991). The foundations of American distance education: A century of collegiate correspondence study. Dubuque, IA: Kendall Hunt.

Weisburg, M., & Ullmer, E. J. (1995, February). *Distance learning revisited: Life-long learning and the national information infrastructure*. Paper presented at the 1995 Annual National Convention of the Association for Educational Communications and Technology, Anaheim, CA. (ERIC Document Reproduction Service No. ED383345)

Wiesner, P. (1983). Some observations on telecourse research and practice. *Adult Education Quarterly*, *33*, 215–221. doi:10.1177/0001848183033004002

Willis, B. (2000). Glossary of distance education terminology. In K. Mantyla (Ed.), The 2000/2001 ASTD distance learning yearbook (pp. 355-360). New York: McGraw-Hill.

Zigerell, J. (1984). Distance education: An information age approach to adult education. Columbus: Ohio State University, The National Center for Research in Vocational Education.

KEY TERMS AND DEFINITIONS

Asynchronous Delivery: Asynchronous delivery is a method of distance education in which the instructor and students are not required to have real-time contact on a regular basis. It is not time and location dependent (Marsh, Price, & McFadden, 2000).

Attitude: Attitude is the Saudi faculty's belief, disposition, and opinion regarding the implementation of the WBI.

Barrier: Barriers to Web-based training are factors that prevent or hinder university organizations from implementing Web-based training (Wu, 2003).

Computer-Mediated Communication (CMC): Computer-mediated communication is the process by which people create, exchange, and perceives information using networked telecommunications systems (or non networked computers) that facilitate encoding, transmitting, and decoding messages. CMC refers to "a wide range of technologies that facilitate both human communication and the interactive sharing of information through computer networks" (Barnes, 2003, p. 4).

Criteria for Implementing Web-Based Training: The criteria for implementing web-based training are standards on which a judgment or decision about the implementation of Web-based training in business organizations may be based (Wu,2003).

Distance Education: Distance education is an educational process with the instruction often occurring when students and instructors are not in the same place; the method of communication may be synchronous or asynchronous (Huang, 2003).

E-Learning: E-learning is comprised of educational contents delivered through the use of electronic or digital technologies, such as audio-videotape, CD-ROM, interactive TV, satellite broadcasting, intranets, or the Internet. Computer-based training and Web based training are included in the range of e-learning (American Society for Training and Development, 2001).

Faculty: Faculty are the teachers at the three Saudi universities who participated in this study.

Higher Education: Higher education is the courses and degrees offered to students who have completed high school. Higher education includes individual programs, technical training certification, bachelor's degrees, master's degrees, and doctoral degrees.

Online University or College: An online university is the offshoot of the traditional college or university. In this case, the institution may offer some courses and programs on the Internet or WWW, but not all of them (Connick, 1999).

Synchronous Delivery: Synchronous learning takes place when the learner can interact with the instructor and other learners in real time (Belanger & Jordan, 2000). The technology used in synchronous delivery includes two-way interactive video tele-courses, one-way video with two-way audio, audio-conferencing, and audio-graphic conferencing, and may include electronic white boards, radio, television, closed-circuit and satellite (Marsh et al., 2000).

Virtual Learning Environment (VLE): VLE is an Internet-based software program that allows lecturers to create course Web sites quickly and easily. VLE is a set of teaching and learning tools designed to enhance a student's learning experience by including computers and the Internet in the learning process. There are a number of commercial VLE software packages available, including Blackboard, WebCT, Lotus LearningSpace, and COSE (Rosenberg, 2001).

Virtual University or College: A virtual university or college has no physical campus and offers courses and programs exclusively on the Internet and WWW (Cherepski, 2000).

Web-Based Instruction (WBI): According to Khan's (1997) definition, "WBI is a hypermedia-based instructional program which utilizes the attributes and resources of the WWW to create a meaningful learning environment where learning is fostered and supported" (p. 6).

Web-Based Training: Web-based training is instruction or computer-based training that is delivered or transferred over the Internet or intranets through the use of a Web browser. With Web-based training, the Internet or an intranet is the primary medium to deliver instruction anytime, anywhere around the globe (Belanger & Jordan, 2000; Hall, 1997; Kilby, 2000).

Chapter 18
Blended Assessment Methods in Online Educational Programs in Turkey:
Issues and Strategies

Erman Yukselturk
Middle East Technical University, Turkey

Orhan Curaoglu
Middle East Technical University, Turkey

ABSTRACT

This study analyzed eleven online educational programs of different universities in Turkey regarding their assessment methods with several aspects. The results showed that online quizzes and tests, assignments, individual and group projects, participation to the discussions, proctored face-to-face midterm and final exams are major blended assessment methods used in the online programs. All methods have benefits and challenges while preparing and administering in the courses. Therefore, online and traditional assessments methods are used complementarily to overcome their respective disadvantages. The main parts of student success scores are assessed based on human proctored face-to-face final exams at the end of the courses to get accreditation in the programs.

BACKGROUND

Turkey is a country with physical and cultural bridge between Europe and Asia. It has a total area of about 780 sq.km. with a population of 72 million. Children between 0 and 14 age group constituted 29.8% of this estimated population. Population between 6 and 21 age group constituted 29.1%. The primary education was compulsory education which was extended to 8 years in 1997 for children aged between 6 and 14 age groups. Secondary education was also extended to 4 years in 2005 (MoNE, 2007). After the students have graduated from high schools, they have to enter the university entrance examination to be students in the university. There is a great competition for entry into the 68 public and 25 private universities. In the last years over 1.5 million high school graduates took this examination and less than a quarter of these students admitted to conventional higher education institutions. Due to

DOI: 10.4018/978-1-61520-749-7.ch018

the characteristics of educational system, distance education is a rational alternative to increase an overall education level in Turkey.

Distance education has been applied in Turkey since 1980. Although some distance education models were discussed and seen before 1980, as an implementation, Anadolu University began distance higher education in the preserve of its Open Educational Faculty (OEF), OEF started programs in Business Administration and Economics with a student enrollment of 29,479 for the 1982-1983 academic year in 1982 (Ozkul, 2001). Today, Anadolu University comprises 12 faculties, three of which- Open Education, Business Administration and Economics- constitute the Open Education System, 10 vocational schools, 6 graduate schools, and 26 research centres. There are more than 1.000.000 pre-bachelor and bachelor degree students graduated through the Open Education System and it is one of the mega universities of the world.

In addition to Anadolu University, with help of Internet technology, numbers of courses and programs were started to deliver at various universities such as METU, ITU, Sakarya, Fırat, İstanbul Bilgi and Ahmet Yesevi at the end of 1990s. METU has started an experimental distance education course via the Internet in 1997. In the following years, METU developed online certificate and graduate programs. Sakarya University has started an online two years pre-BA program related to computer programming, information management. Also, several courses have been offered both online and on-campus in the following years. ITU established remote classrooms via a microwave link connecting two campuses that were in different locations of Istanbul. Furthermore, Istanbul Bilgi University offered e-MBA program in 2000. Fırat University has broadcasted some educational programs on Fırat RTV. Ahmet Yesevi University has offered some distance learning programs via the Internet (Askar, 2005). Nowadays, several courses and programs (especially graduate courses and programs) have been given over the Internet in many universities in Turkey.

SETTING THE STAGE

With the information era, online education has become more important for lifelong learning. Developments in telecommunication and computer technologies made easily design online courses with establishing networked cultures. Today, there are numbers of courses given online for any subject in higher education institutions. With time, most of the problems with online education have been solved and new ways have been developed for better online learning environment. One of the main problems of the online education is assessment part of the education that is still tough problem in front of the online education. Although there are lots of comments and studies related to advantages of online learning, there have been few evaluations and it is an ongoing challenge for educators since with little known on how assessment is implemented in online courses and how to use computer-mediated tools to monitor and inform performance and progress (Bartley, 2006; Benson, 2003; Liang, & Kim, 2004; Shephard, 2009).

Assessment is a key component of any education systems. The Quality Assurance Agency (QAA, 2006) describes assessment as "any processes that appraise an individual's knowledge, understanding, abilities or skills" (p.4). Also, Suskie summarized assessment as:

the ongoing process of (1) establishing clear, measurable expected outcomes of student learning, (2) ensuring that students have sufficient opportunities to achieve those outcomes, (3) systematically gathering, analyzing, and interpreting evidence to determine how well student learning matches our expectations, and (4) using the resulting information to understand and improve student learning. (Suskie, 2004, p.3)

Suskie mentioned that these four steps are continuous cycle and they are not a once-and-done process. In addition, Hanson, Millington, and Freewood (2001, cited by Benson, 2003) categorized assessments by purpose that is accepted by many researchers: (1) diagnostic assessment, (2) formative assessment, and (3) summative assessment. Diagnostic assessment "provides an indicator of a learner's aptitude and preparedness for a program of study and identifies possible learning problems" (p.2). Formative assessment "provides learners with feedback on progress and informs development but does not contribute to the overall assessment". Summative assessment "provides a measure of achievement or failure made in respect of a learner's performance in relation to the intended outcomes of the program of study".

Assessing learning is difficult process. Both face-to-face courses and online courses use variety of techniques to assess student learning outcomes, but, there are some differences among them. Traditional means of assessment have shifted to nontraditional means in online environments in the last years. For examples, online technologies allow for a wide range of assessment techniques that can be used to assess student performance in online courses: selected response assessments, constructed response assessments, virtual discussions, concept mapping, e-portfolio assessment, writing, field experiences, individual and group projects, informal student feedback, peer assessment, and self-assessment (Jordan & Mitchell, 2009; Benson, 2003; Reeves, 2000). As a result, this study examined several online learning programs in Turkey regarding their assessment techniques to determine how to implement them in the courses. By examining assessment methods in online programs, not only this study will fill a void that currently exists in the research, but it will also be useful for instructors and course designers while selecting and preparing alternative assessment techniques in online courses.

The Research

This study analyzed eleven online educational programs of different universities in Turkey regarding their assessment methods with several aspects. The main purpose of the study was to identify factors relating to using assessment methods (e.g. online and in class) in online programs to better assess students' performance. The benefits and challenges of assessment techniques in online programs were also examined to suggest proper interventions about assessing student learning outcomes.

Procedure

This study was designed to analyze assessment methods in eleven online programs (given in this paper as cases). Firstly, online web pages of each program were analyzed in a detailed way. Then, the coordinators of these online programs were selected to collect the relevant data. The online survey consisting of mainly open-ended questions was developed to gather the data from the coordinators. All coordinators of the programs were contacted via their e-mail in the web pages of the programs. They were informed about the aim of the study and their participation will be voluntary. After that, the survey was sent to the coordinators. The questions in the survey were developed around the central themes related to the assessment methods and some of the major questions were as follows:

- What kinds of assessment methods do you use to measure and evaluate student performance in your online programs? (e.g. assignments, portfolios, projects, exams, etc.)
- What are the advantages of using online assessment methods used in the courses?
- What are the possible reasons for using face-to-face assessment methods used in the courses?

- What kind of suggestions would you make based on your experience on the online programs?

In this study, the data analysis process was started with iterative cycles of examining the patterns and ideas that emerged from the collected data. Then, the researchers explored similarities and differences among the coordinators' replies from the survey. After that they searched for confirming and disconfirming evidences that would be incorporated into the conclusions. In other words, drawing conclusions and verification involved the researcher drawing meaning from the organizing and compressing information based on data at the end of analysis process.

CASE DESCRIPTION

The online programs analyzed in this study are grouped into four categories: certificate, pre-undergraduate, undergraduate and graduate programs.

Online Certificate Programs

Case1

Information Technologies Certificate Program (ITCP) is one of the first Internet Based Education Projects of the technical university based in Ankara. It is based on synchronous and asynchronous communication methods over the Internet offered by cooperation of Computer Engineering Department and Continuing Education Center the University. The online certificate program was started in May 1998, and it is still active. It includes eight fundamental courses of Computer Engineering Department, and comprises of four semesters lasting nine months totally. The courses in the program are given by the instructors from Computer Engineering Department: computer systems and structures, introduction to computer programming with C, software engineering, database management systems, data structure and algorithms with C, operating systems with Unix, web programming and software development project. The main aim of the online ITCP is to train the participants in the IT field to meet the demands in the field of computer technologies in Turkey.

Case 2

Numbers of e-certificate programs (25 different e-certificate programs in Turkey and 7 e-certificate programs in West Europe) have been offered by the University, which is considered pioneer in offering program in open and distance education mode in Turkey. The fields of the programs are accounting, marketing, entrepreneurship, and finance. These programs (all of them given with help of the same strategies) are designed for those who would like to improve their job related skills. Anyone having completed high school, associate, Bachelor's, Masters or doctoral level education can apply for these e-certificate programs. Especially, people who work in banks and small and medium sized enterprises are encouraged for attending to these programs. The certificate programs' duration is three months and three semesters a year. Each program offers three online courses supplemented with textbooks, licensed software, virtual company practices, and videos of applications on CD ROMs, online tutorials, assignments, communication-access services, support service, and examinations. Also, participants who register e-certificate programs can take advantage of textbooks designed based on online the teaching methods and e-practice, e-lessons, e-books, e-television, e-consultancy, e-exam and e-audio books that are provided on the online environment to prepare them for certification exams during the program. Participants that are successful at three courses can get their certificates.

Online Pre-Undergraduate Programs

Case 3

Computer Technology and Programming (CTP) has been an online pre-undergraduate program provided by one of the University since 2004. CTP offers thirty six courses and students have to accomplish thirty courses in two years period. The program instructors continuously monitor industry trends and upgrade their programs to meet the needs of today's employers from the beginning years. In the program, students are able to access their courses, forums, receiving and sending e-mails, loading file, online midterm exam on the e-cukurova that provides platform for communication between lecturers and students. This program associate two years degree that helps their students develop contemporary career skills and find jobs of the 21st century.

Case 4

Knowledge Management is another online pre-undergraduate program and it was launched by Vocational Higher School in 2001. Similar to CTP program, this program composes of thirty compulsory courses which have to be accomplished all of them. E-Learning courses are enhanced in accordance with online education methodology with the text, animation, graphics, audio and video material provided in formal education. In the program, students are able to access their courses, forums, receiving and sending e-mails, loading file, online midterm exam on the SAU-UZEM that provides platform for communication between lecturers and students. The aim of the program is to develop greater knowledge and understanding of the computer businesses and the effective and efficient use of current software, corporate information, new technologies for processing and producing skills.

Online Undergraduate Programs

Case 5

Internet-based Computer Engineering Undergraduate Program is offered by an international university established through collaboration of Turkey and Kazakhstan. Computer engineering program is designed with the aim to educate their students in the appropriate format requirements of today's business and industry at the level of current computer technology. The following course topics are given in this program: computer hardware technology, software development techniques and software, databases and information systems management. Graduates receive four years undergraduate degrees accredited by Higher Education Council. The diploma degrees are equivalent to those of the other universities in Turkey and Kazakhstan.

Case 6

The undergraduate completion Theology Program (ILITAM) is carried out in cooperation with distance education center and faculty of theology at one of the university in Turkey. Program has spread to two years in total, and includes 15 online courses. The students who register the programs can take advantage of textbooks and online facilities that are provided on course website. Upon enrolling, the students are issued with ID numbers, which enable them to access the online materials and support services, CDs, videos, study guides, etc. Orientation, instruction, tutoring, assessment, and feedback are provided through a mix of online and face-to-face methods. The students can join virtual academic and technical forums and coffee shops and exchange ideas with their tutors and peers by email. They can also attend face-to-face classes at centers in many cities. The courses, examinations, and awards are identical to the on-campus programs.

Case 7

Business and Administration program is one of distance undergraduate programs offered by the same university discussed in Case 2 and provides associate degree as well as bachelor degree. Program has included thirty online courses within the four years in total. Teleconferences, which is supported by internet and computer, as well as printed materials and TV broadcasts are mainly offered facilities for its students. In addition, the program aims to help students to adapt these technologies and create technological interaction with the usage of them. In the meanwhile, students who enroll programs profit from textbooks designed based on online the teaching methods and textbooks, virtual company practices, and videos of applications, online tutorials, assignments, communication-access services, support service, and examinations and audio books that are made available on online learning portal to prepare themselves exams. Moreover, there are tutorials at appropriate cities in the country.

Online Graduate Programs

Case 8

Informatics Online is a non-thesis program in which course participation will be exclusively through the Internet at University (same as discussed in Case 1) based in Ankara, Turkey. Courses cover fundamental and current concepts of information technology and systems in depth. This online program aims at providing expertise on the rapidly developing subjects of information technology and systems. It is intended for working professionals who need continuing education at anytime and anywhere without the need to come to the university (METU) campus for lectures. The program is designed and conducted primarily in an asynchronous approach. Collaboration among students and instructors is carried out by using mainly asynchronous (e.g. e-mail, forums/ discussion lists) and rarely synchronous (e.g. chat, exam / review meeting on-campus during a scheduled mid-semester weekend and final) tools. Web based material enriched with interactive animations, simulations and exercises form the basic course content. Personal appearance of students on the campus is required twice in every semester (at the beginning and at the end of the semesters).

Case 9

Information System is another non-thesis online master program by another University based in Ankara and it was launched in 2006. The program is designed in an online format for working adults who want to complete their degree without interrupting their careers. The purpose of this online graduate program is that the students gain deeper knowledge in the utilization of existing knowledge to show and to you how to use it in vocational subjects The 36 credit-hour-degree program consists of seven core courses and four elective courses, with a further requirement of a final project. Master of Information System program uses all available communication tools for educational purposes. During the semesters, students follow course content, homework, discussion and chat on the program's website. Courses are designed based on both asynchronous (e-mail, forums/discussion lists) and synchronous (chat, video conference). Learning management system tracks any activities of students on the system and keeps their records.

Case 10

One of the e-MBA programs (Online Master of Business Administration) offered by university based at Istanbul is an adaptation of a traditional MBA program using distance learning techniques and principles in 2000. Like all program, fully accredited by the Turkish Higher Education Council, e-MBA is designed specifically to meet the contemporary needs of the business world in the strategic arena. The eight core courses are designed in order to prepare managers for dealing with the problems encountered in the business world, along with providing them with the appropriate basis for finding applicable solutions. The students may choose two elective courses that correspond to their interests from among a list of many alternatives.

Case 11

Another e-MBA program offered by one of the University in Turkey is a postgraduate program for Business Administration Major Science Branch, Production/Manufacturing Management and Working Branch, Production/Manufacturing and Service Systems Management Program which is recognized by Higher Education Committee like other programs and provided online through internet

The purpose of the program is to provide specialization to improve analysis and decision-making capabilities in the field of business and management. That is, students learn the basics of business administration and specialize in international business. The Sakarya University-Advancity Academic LMS Project facilitates e-MBA program to engage more effectively in distance education and e-learning delivery, tracking, and evaluation. Courses are delivered through various combinations of online videoconferencing, asynchronous Web-based learning and face-to-face interaction via LMS. Even though the period of program lasts three semesters, it may extend up to six semesters.

DISCUSSION

Assessment Methods in the Programs

The findings showed that the assessment and evaluation of student performance is seen as an important issue in online programs. Both online and traditional face-to-face assessments methods have been used to evaluate the student performances in almost all programs. Although there are several differences in the program types, such as, certificate, undergraduate, and graduate, the assessment methods in these programs show similarities. The student assessments mainly depended on the traditional proctored face-to-face final exams at the end of the courses of the programs. The rest of the assessment part in the programs composed of online assignments, midterms, quizzes, exercises, individual or group project and participation to the online discussions. The assessment methods in the programs are summarized in the Table 1 and it shows both self-assessment techniques prepared for self-study and student assessment techniques prepared for assessing student performance. The major assessment methods in each program/case are given as follows:

- **Case 1:** Assessment methods consist of self-assessment activities (no marked for success score), online assignments during the courses (30% of success score) and the traditional proctored final examination (paper-based test) (70% of success score) at the end of the courses. Program instructors can use student participation to online discussions and individual and group project as an assessment method in some courses.
- **Case 2:** Assessment part of the program is designed based on online self assessment tests and traditional face to face proctored exams. Online self tests are used to check students' level before final exams and they are not used in the student evaluation process. The final face to face proctored exam is administrated at the end of programs. Student success scores are determined by only this final exam result.
- **Case 3:** Assessment of the students consists of online midterm or assignment and traditional face to face proctored exams.

Table 1. The assessment methods in the online programs/cases

Name	Quizzes/ Tests		Participate Discussion		Projects		Assignments		Midterms		Final exams	
	Online	In-class	Online	In-class	Online	In-class	Online	In-class	Online	In-class	Online	In-class
Certificate Programs												
Case1	X		√		√		√					√
Case2:	X											√
Pre-Undergraduate Programs												
Case 3:	X						√		√			√
Case 4:	√						√		√			√
Undergraduate Programs												
Case 5:	√		√		√		√		√			√
Case 6	X									√		√
Case 7:	X									√		√
Graduate Programs												
Case 8:	X		√		√		√		√	√		√
Case 9	X						√		√			√
Case 10	X				√		√					√
Case 11	X				√		√					√

√ = Assessment method included to student success score, X= Assessment method used for only self-assessment

Midterm exam taken online or assignments submitted online are administrated during the courses. Final exam is administrated as a traditional paper-pencil proctored exam at the end of the courses. Students' success score is determined by online midterm or assignment (%20 of success score) and final examination (80% of success score).

- **Case 4:** Assessment methods consist of both online and face-to-face activities. For example, online short tests, assignments, and midterm are administered during the course via online learning environment. To attend midterm exam, students have to complete 60% of online education modules at the web pages of program. Finals exam is also administered as a face to face proctored exam at the university campus. Student success is determined by online tests such as short test, weekly assignments and midterm (%20 of success score) and final exam which is face to face proctored exam (%80 of success score)
- **Case 5:** Both online and face-to-face assessment activities are used in the program. Midterms, assignments, interviews with teachers (guidance) are administrated entirely over the Internet. The final test procedures are administrated as a traditional face to face proctored exam at the university campuses in Turkey and Turkistan. Online activities during the semesters, such as, mid-term exam, homework, discussion, chat, etc. influence 30% of the students' success scores and traditional final exam score at the end of course influence 70% of the students' success. Program instructors can increase student success score little based on student effort during the semesters

- **Case 6:** Assessment methods are designed based on online exercises and traditional face to face proctored exams for both midterm and final. Online exercises are used for student self assessment. Midterm and final exams are administered as a face to face proctored exam in the 10 location in the country. Student success scores are determined by midterm exam (30% of success score) and final exam (70% of success score).
- **Case 7:** Assessment methods are designed based on online exercises and traditional face to face proctored exams for both midterm and final. Online exercises are used for student self assessment. Midterm and final exams are administered as a face to face proctored exam in the several location in the country. Student success scores are determined by midterm exam (30% of success score) and final exam (70% of success score).
- **Case 8:** Assessment methods consist of both online and traditional assessment activities, such as, midterm exams, project, weekly assignments participation to discussion and final exam. The percentage of assessment methods on student success generally depend on course instructors. Generally, final exams as a traditional paper pencil exam (50-70% of success score) have constituted main part of student assessment. In some courses, individual or group project can be the main part of student assessment.
- **Case 9:** Assessment methods consist of self-assessment activities (no marked for success score), online assignments and midterms during the courses (30% of success score) and the traditional proctored final examination (paper-based test) (70% of success score) at the end of the courses. Program instructors can increase student success score little (about %5) based on student effort during the semesters.
- **Case 10:** The student assessment process composes of the results of the final exam, assignments and projects as well as self-tests administered on the web. At least 50% of the passing grade comes from the final examinations that take place under the supervision of academic staff while the rest is determined according to assignments and tests. A passing grade of 70% is required for the students to succeed in the final examination. Also, in the last semester of the program, students are responsible for preparing a final project with the assistance of academic staff.
- **Case 11:** The student assessment process composes of the results of the final exam, homework and projects and self-tests on the web. All types of assessment methods, except for final exams, are administered on online environment. Final exams as a traditional proctored paper pencil exam (50-70% of success score) constitute main part of student assessment. Also, in the last semester of the program, students are responsible for preparing a final project with the assistance of academic staff.

Quizzes and Tests

Quizzes and tests are generally designed by learning management systems in the online programs. They include multiple-choice, true-false, fill-in-the blank, matching questions and short answer. They generally provide automated feedback to the students after each question is answered or after the all questions are answered. With help of assessment methods, students are provided self-study opportunities and they can test their own knowledge regularly. In the programs, students can practice weekly course objectives at their own pace. As a summary, these assessment methods are prepared for students to evaluate their progress themselves, but they do not affect the student achievement scores at the end of the courses in almost all programs.

Participation in Discussions

Participation in online discussions is used for another assessment method of students in some courses of the programs. These discussions may be synchronous (real-time) or asynchronous (delayed). In the programs, generally, synchronous discussions occurs via text based tools like Internet chat and instant messaging, whereas asynchronous discussions occur over web-based bulletin boards and discussion lists. In asynchronous discussions, students can be assessed based on frequency of access and level of participation (such as, posts new ideas, synthesizes and analyzes peers' ideas, make interpretation from course content, reads messages of others). In synchronous discussions, students can be assessed based on arrival time and level of participation (such as, states new ideas, responds when prompted).

Individual and Group Projects

Individual and group project is one of the used assessment methods in the courses of the online programs, especially graduate programs. Students are expected to develop projects individually or as a group in some courses. The projects consist of several components, such as, project descriptions, milestones, design, implementation and presentation. Generally, the project development processes are guided with help of online technologies during the courses. At the end of the project, students come to the campus of the university to present their projects to the instructors and their classmates.

Assignments

Many types of assignments can be done online in the programs. These are literature searches, practice exercises, case studies, reading and writing essays. Online instructors in many courses of the program create several assignments, provide instructions, and give a period of time to the students to complete them. The number of assignments can be changed based on the course instructors. After that, students upload or send e-mail their completed work to the instructors. The instructors assess the students' submissions, mark the works and provide electronic feedback to the students in their courses. This online assessment method is similar to traditional one. Student can not pass the course without completing the assignments in some courses of the programs.

Midterm

Students are assessed and evaluated mainly with face-to-face traditional exams in these online programs. Students come to the campus of the universities or exam centers that nearest them at least one time or two times in each semester. At the middle of the semesters, students come to attend the exams, which are midterm exams, in some courses of the programs. These midterms are generally developed with paper-and-pencil tests. During the exams, the traditional security procedures are used by human proctors.

Final Exam

Final exams are the major assessment method to evaluate student performance in all programs. Similar to midterm exams, students come to the campus of the semesters at the end of the semesters. In some programs, the face-to-face courses are designed for the students before the final exams to review the course content. The time tables of these face-to-face exams are prepared at beginning of the programs and they are announced to the students with the program web pages. At least 50 percentages of student grades are determined by this traditional final examination score. Students have to get enough score to pass the courses in this exam in all programs.

Advantages and Disadvantages of Online and Traditional Assessment Methods

The coordinators of the programs mentioned that there are both advantages and disadvantages of online and traditional assessment methods. Related to first one, online technologies enable learners to attend and continue their education in anywhere and anytime. These benefits also provide easier and more convenient assessment methods. They enable learners to manage and monitor their own learning via self-testing. Moreover, online assessment methods can provide students with immediate automated feedback and they can enable students to identify their weaknesses, reflect on their performance. Also, with help of immediate feedback provided by the online assessment methods, instructors' workload reduces comparing with traditional ones. Moreover, online technologies provide keep records that can be stored and reduce the error rate while evaluating the exam scores. All coordinators emphasized these advantages of online assessment methods.

In addition to advantages of online assessments methods, there are several online assessment challenges. The major challenges are academic dishonesty, cheating and plagiarism. The biggest concern the coordinators stated is that they are not sure whether the students enrolled to the courses is the students who perform the course works. It is too difficult to identify students who are responsible for completing their homework or tests. Moreover, students could copy any information and insert them into their documents easily. The plagiarism is very common in the assignments and homework despite warning of the students. Especially graduate program coordinators who gave more assignments and homework mentioned that they were faced with these problems while assessing student progress in online courses.

The most common assessment method in the programs is traditional face-to-face exams since they are more reliable. In traditional methods, the assessment situation is more under controlled and avoids cheating attempts. In other words, the traditional security procedures are used by human proctors in paper-and-pencil tests. Although the coordinators agreed that this system may not be convenient and feasible for online students who can not attend face-to-face environments easily, it is most preferable assessment methods to determine validity and reliability of assessment systems in the programs.

Accreditation Issues in the Programs

According to the results, the assessment methods in almost all programs are designed based on legislations stated by Turkish Higher Education Council (HEC) to get accreditation. The assessment method criteria in these legislations are mentioned persistently by the coordinators of the programs in the answers of the survey questions. For example, HEC is responsible to coordinate the all the universities (68 states and 25 foundations) and higher education in Turkey. Each university consists of four-year faculties, two year institutes, research and development departments and continuous training departments. The programs and courses offered by these universities should be accredited by the Turkish Higher Education Council (HEC).

The legislation for accreditation related to online programs stated by HEC consists of several issues that universities should follow. One of them is related to assessment and evaluation of students in the online programs. According to HEC, the assignments of the courses can be given on the Internet and the results be announced via Internet. Midterm exams (e.g. take home and short exam) can be done through Internet or communication network. However, the majority of student success (80%) is based on human proctored exams in pre-undergraduate and undergraduate programs.

Similarly, 50% of student success is based on human proctored exams in graduate programs. Students have to get at least 70% of exam scores in human proctored face-to-face exams, otherwise students can not pass the courses (HEC, 2009). As a summary, the findings showed that all programs have been designed based on these legislations to get an accreditation from HEC.

Suggestions for Assessment Systems

The results showed that both online and traditional assessments methods are used complementarily to overcome their disadvantages. These blended assessment methods in the courses are more effective to evaluate the student progress. Although these methods are used commonly, online programs still need more effective assessment methods. According to the results of the study, there are several recommendations that can be used for online program assessment systems. For examples, it is agreed that the measurement and evaluation groups consisting of experts are composed to help online instructors while preparing and using assessment methods in the programs. During the courses, the instructors are dealing with all learning process including assessment methods in the courses and so they might be sometimes overloaded. Also, they have lack of technical skills to develop and apply the online assessment methods. With help of this group in the programs, a variety of assessment methods can be designed and administrated with online contemporary technologies.

In addition, the coordinators stated that current online technologies should be used functionally to assess the students. Learning management systems are helpful to design the affective assessment systems. For example, question pools can be prepared and the quiz and test questions can be created randomly from this tools for each student. Student progress can be analyzed with log files saved in the databases. Moreover, they stated that we need more adaptive systems to assess the student performance since online students are different from traditional ones. They have different educational backgrounds, age levels, learning styles and employment characteristics, and also many of these students have other responsibilities outside of school (e.g., family, job) in online programs. Therefore, adaptive assessment systems should be designed based on students' properties and requirements in the online programs.

SUGGESTIONS AND RECOMMENDATIONS

Assessment is an integral part of teaching and learning process and it is described as a process of gathering, describing, or quantifying information about student performance. Also, it plays a significant role in learning whatever the environment, traditional or online and general principles are similar in both environments (Rovai, 2000). In fact, student assessments are more important in the online environment since students can not be observed and interacted like in traditional face-to-face environment (Rovai, 2000). Moreover, compared to traditional one, research on student assessment in online environments has not been extensive and we need more research to provide guidelines and specific procedures for online instructors (Ross & Ross, 2005). For these reasons, this study examined eleven online learning programs in Turkey regarding their assessment methods.

In the literature, there are a variety of assessment methods and strategies in traditional environments. Many assessment methods have been adapted to the online environments. Also, online technologies allow for several new assessment techniques that can be used to assess student performance in online programs. Similarly, the results of the study showed that quizzes and tests, assignments, individual and group projects, participation to the discussions, proctored face-to-face midterm and final exams are major assessment methods used in the online programs. According to the results, there are not much more differences about using assessment methods among the programs and they are designed based on legislations stated by Higher Education Council (HEC). The student course performances are assessed based on blended assessment methods and mainly traditional proctored assessment activities.

Blended assessment methods combining web-based assessment activities with traditional assessment activities can lead to a comprehensive, reliable and valid assessment system (Hodgson, 2006). According to the results, two major factors, getting accreditation by HEC and reducing barriers of online assessment methods, affect the program coordinators and instructors to use blended assessment methods in the courses. Adams and DeFleur (2006) mentioned that there is a considerable controversy in online degrees regarding the quality of the instruction, educational outcomes, the reputation of the providing institution, and regulatory policies that used to evaluate and manage these important resources due to the steady expansion of online education. In other words, the acceptability of online programs is highly debated issues with increasing number of online programs. Therefore, it is more important to get accreditation for online programs. Actually, the goal of accreditation is to ensure that programs provided by institutions of higher education meet acceptable levels of quality. Program coordinators, especially undergraduate and graduate programs, mentioned that online programs that are fully accredited have earned a widely recognition like traditional ones.

All assessment techniques have both benefits and challenges while preparing and administering in the courses. For example, the benefits of online assessment are similar with those of online learning. The convenience and flexibility of online assessment methods provide that students can arrange when, where, and how often they engage with assessment. Similarly, Brown, Race and Bull (1999) discussed the advantages of computer-assisted assessments include repeatability, reliability, equitability, timeliness, and flexibility. Also, they mentioned that they provide instructors and students with immediate feedback. On the other hand, the key challenges to online assessment are academic dishonesty, cheating and plagiarism (Benson, 2003; Rovai, 2000). Rovai (2000) stated that the online assessment techniques have certain challenges due to the lack of control of assessment conditions, the unique set of available resources, and the isolation of the online learners. The proctored testing is advised by the coordinators to overcome the challenges of online assessment. For example, online learners might be assessed at some proctored location under a controlled assessment setting for summative assessments. Also some coordinators suggested that online instructors might assess discussions with analyzing discourse styles and patterns. Moreover, in the literature, Benson (2003) stated that the availability of online technology tools allows for use of alternative assessment techniques to decrease the challenges, such as, concept mapping, portfolio assessment, individual and group projects, field experiences, and peer assessment.

Blended assessment methods can be applied to both formative and summative assessment as a means of assessing student learning in online programs. Applying these methods in all programs is difficult process for the instructors. Due to a variety of assessment techniques and lack of face-to-face interaction, great attention is being given for successful design and implementation of student assessment in the online courses. Also, Ryan (2000) stated that the design of effective and reliable assessment for online student requires substantial effort for innovation and different approach from traditional practice. The coordinators mentioned that designing effective assessment methods requires combination of instructor experiences and support from measurement and evaluation support staff. In other words, online instructors could not be only person dealing with learning assessment process in the courses. Another factor that might affect assessment process is related to technology used to design and deliver the content, assignments and assessments. For example, learning management systems could be designed properly for several assessment activities that can be integrated into learning process properly. Also, instructors should aware of these online technological facilities since the advent of new assessment tools open new methods to assess student performance before, during, and after the courses take place.

The major suggestions and recommendations stated by the coordinators of programs were summarized as follows:

- Blended assessment methods combining web-based assessment activities with traditional assessment activities should be used to assess student learning in online programs,
- Assessment methods in online programs should be designed based on legislations stated by Higher Education Council,
- Measurement and evaluation support staff could help online instructors for designing effective assessment methods in online programs,
- Alternative assessment techniques, such as, concept mapping, portfolio assessment, individual and group projects, field experiences, and peer assessment could be utilized to assess student performances as well.
- Learning management systems could be designed properly for several assessment activities in online programs.

CONCLUSION

Assessing learning in online programs has still challenging issues. We still need more research about how assessment is implemented in online courses and how to use online technologies to assess student performance and progress. According to this study based on analyzing assessment methods in eleven online programs, blended assessment activities, especially traditional proctored testing, is still common main method to assess the student performance in online courses. Online quizzes and tests are administered for self-assessment methods in many programs. Online assignment and rating the quality of student interactions are alternative assessment methods to monitor student progress during the courses. Individual and group project work is rarely used assessment method to analyze students while constructing projects over time, especially in graduate programs. Proctored face-to-face midterm and final exams are most common summative assessment methods that measure of achievement or failure made in respect of a learner's performance at the end of the courses. New blended assessment techniques, tools, and methodologies will be necessary to assess the student performance in online learning environments.

REFERENCES

Adams, J., & Defleur, M. H. (2006). The Acceptability of Online Degrees Earned as a Credential for Obtaining Employment. *Communication Education*, *55*(1), 32–45. doi:10.1080/03634520500343376

Askar, P. (2005). Distance education in Turkey. In C. Howard, J. Boettcher, L. Justice, K. Shenk, P. L. Rogers & G. A. Berg (Eds) Encyclopedia of distance learning, (Vol 2, pp. 635–640). Hershey, PA, Idea Group Inc.

Bartley, J. M. (2006). Assessment is as assessment does: a conceptual framework for understanding online assessment and measurement. In M. Hricko & S. L. Howell, (eds.), Online Assessment and Measurement Foundations and Challenges (pp. 1-45). Hershey, PA: Information Science Publishing.

Benson, A. D. (2003). Assessing participant learning in online environments. *New Directions for Adult and Continuing Education, 2003*(100), 69–78. doi:10.1002/ace.120

Brown, S., Race, P., & Bull, J. (Eds.). (1999). Computer-assisted assessment in higher education. London: Kogan Page.

Hanson, J., Millington, C., & Freewood, M. (2001). *Developing a Methodology for Online Feedback and Assessment*. Paper presented at the Fifth International Computer Assisted Assessment Conference, Leicestershire, U.K.

HEC. (2009). *Turkish Higher Education Council*. Retrieved May 30, 2009, from http://www.yok.gov.tr/content/view/480/183/lang,tr/

Hodgson, P. (2006, December). *Achieving enriched learning experience through blending computer-mediated and conventional assessment methods*. Paper presented at the Evaluations and Assessment Conference, Australia. Retrieved May 30, 2009, from http://otl.curtin.edu.au/eac2006/papers/hodgson.pdf

Jordan, S., & Mitchell, T. (2009). e-Assessment for learning? The potential of short-answer free-text questions with tailored feedback. *British Journal of Educational Technology*, *40*(2), 371–385. doi:10.1111/j.1467-8535.2008.00928.x

Liang, X., & Kim, C. (2004). Classroom assessment in web-based instructional environment: instructors' experience. *Practical Assessment, Research & Evaluation, 9*(7). Retrieved March 23, 2009 from http://PAREonline.net/getvn.asp?v=9&n=7

MoNE. (2007). National Education Statistics Formal Education 2006-2007. Ankara, Turkey: MoNE.

Ozkul, A. E. (2001). Anadolu University Distance Education System from Emergence to 21st Century. *The Turkish Online Journal of Distance Learning, 2*(1), Retrieved January 12, 2009, from http://tojde.anadolu.edu.tr/tojde3/2/ekremtxt.htm

QAA (Quality Assurance Agency). (2006). *Section 6: Assessment of students. Code of practice for the assurance of academic quality and standards in higher education*. Retrieved February 2, 2009, from http://www.qaa.ac.uk

Reeves, T. C. (2000). Alternative Assessment Approaches for Online Learning Environments in Higher Education. *Journal of Educational Computing Research, 23*(1), 101–111. doi:10.2190/GYMQ-78FA-WMTX-J06C

Ross, J. A., & Ross, M. (2005). Student assessment in online courses: Research and practice, 1993-2004. *The Canadian Journal of University Continuing Education, 31*(2), 43–63.

Rovai, A. P. (2000). Online and traditional assessments: What's the difference? *The Internet and Higher Education, 3*(3), 141–151. doi:10.1016/S1096-7516(01)00028-8

Ryan, R. C. (2000). Student assessment comparison of lecture and online construction equipment and methods classes. *T.H.E. Journal, 27*(6), 78–83.

Shephard, K. (2009). e is for exploration: Assessing hard-to-measure learning outcomes. *British Journal of Educational Technology,40*(2),386-398. doi:10.1111/j.1467-8535.2008.00927.x

Suskie, L. (2004). Assessing student learning. Bolton, MA: Anker Publishing Company, Inc.

ADDITIONAL READING

Aisbitt, S., & Sangster, A. (2005). Using internet-based on-line assessment: A case study. *Accounting Education: An International Journal*, *14*(4), 383–394. doi:10.1080/06939280500346011

Bryan, C., & Clegg, K. (Eds.). (2006). Innovative assessment in higher education. London: Routledge.

Bull, J., & McKenna, C. (2004). Blueprint for computer-assisted assessment. London: Routledge Farmer.

Conole, G., & Warburton, B. (2005). A review of computer-assisted assessment. *ALT-J*, *13*(1), 17–31. doi:10.1080/0968776042000339772

Crisp, G. (2007). The e-assessment handbook. New York: Continuum International Pub. Group.

Dermo, J. (2009). e-Assessment and the student learning experience: A survey of student perceptions of e-assessment. *British Journal of Educational Technology*, *40*(2), 203–214. doi:10.1111/j.1467-8535.2008.00915.x

Dermo, J., & Eyre, S. (2008). Secure, reliable and effective institution-wide e-assessment: paving the ways for new technologies. In F. Khandia (Ed.), *Proceedings of 12th International CAA Conference* (pp. 95–106). Loughborough: University of Loughborough.

Engelbrecht, J., & Harding, A. (2004). Combing online and paper assessment in a web-based course in undergraduate mathematics. *Journal of Computers in Mathematics and Science Teaching*, *23*(3), 217–231.

Howell, S. L., & Hricko, M. (Eds.). (2006). Online assessment and measurement: Case studies from higher education, K-12 and corporate. Hershey: Information Science Publishing.

Hricko, M., & Howell, S. L. (Eds.). (2006). Online assessment and measurement: Foundations and challenges. Hershey: Information Science Publishing.

Nicol, D. J. (2007). E-assessment by design: using multiple choice tests to good effect. *Journal of Further and Higher Education*, *31*(1), 53–64. doi:10.1080/03098770601167922

Nicol, D. J., & Macfarlane-Dick, D. (2006). Formative assessment and self-regulated learning: a model and seven principles of good feedback practice. *Studies in Higher Education*, *32*(2), 199–216. doi:10.1080/03075070600572090

Oosterhof, A., Donald, P. E., & Rita-Marie, C. (2008). Assessing Learners Online. Upper Saddle River: Pearson/Merrill Prentice Hall.

Ricketts, C., & Wilks, S. J. (2002). Improving student performance through computer-based assessment: insights from recent research. *Assessment & Evaluation in Higher Education*, *27*(5), 475. doi:10.1080/0260293022000009348

Rust, C. (2005). Developing a variety of assessment methods. *Enhancing practice: reflections on assessment, 1*, 179–186.

Shephard, K. (2009). e is for exploration: Assessing hard-to-measure learning outcomes, *British Journal of Educational Technology*,*40*(2),386-398. doi:10.1111/j.1467-8535.2008.00927.x

Sim, G., Holifield, P., & Brown, M. (2004). Implementation of computer assisted assessment: lessons from the literature. *ALT-J*, *12*(3), 215–229. doi:10.1080/0968776042000259546

Taras, M. (2008). Summative and formative assessment: perceptions and realities. *Active Learning in Higher Education*, *9*(2), 172–192. doi:10.1177/1469787408091655

Vos, H. (2000). How to assess for improvement of learning. *European Journal of Engineering Education*, *25*(3), 227–233. doi:10.1080/030437900438658

Whitelock, D., & Watt, S. (2007). e-Assessment: how can we support tutors with their marking of electronically submitted assignments? *Ad-Lib Journal for Continuing Liberal Adult Education*, *32*, 7–9.

Williams, D. D., Howell, S. L., & Hricko, M. (Eds.). (2006). Online assessment, measurement, and evaluation: Emerging Practices. Hershey: Information Science Publishing.

KEY TERMS AND DEFINITIONS

Lifelong Learning: It means education to create ability for continuous lifelong development of quality of life.

Assessment: The processes used to collect information and analyze them about student progress toward educational goals.

Self-Assessment: The process of judging one's own teaching performance for the purpose of self-improvement.

Traditional Assessment: It is face-to-face assessment and generally tests given in the paper pencil format to the students by the teachers to measure how much the students have learned.

Proctored Exam: It is a kind of exam which is overseen by an impartial individual (called a proctor) who monitors or supervises a student while he or she is taking an exam.

Accreditation: Recognition by an accrediting organization or agency that a university meets certain acceptable standards in its education programs, services, and facilities.

Plagiarism: The process of copying the work of another without proper citation.

Chapter 19
Generic Themes for Developing Research Skills through E-Learning:
A Case Study from Iran

Abbas Bazargan
University of Tehran, Iran

Amin Mousavi
University of Tehran, Iran

ABSTRACT

Research competencies are considered as a major part of post-graduate programs. With the introduction of new technologies in higher education, there has been particular emphasis to move to an e-learning variant of the teaching-learning process in developing research competencies. Based on the recent experiences, it seems the blended approach is more promising. In this regard, an experimental approach in designing and developing an e-course was adopted at a private e-learning university in Iran. The e-course was organized through a design-based approach. This chapter is a case study which presents an analysis of the factors that affected designing and developing the e-course. It points to the experiences gained through building the community of inquiry and discusses lessons learned.

BACKGROUND

In twenty-first century, information and communication technologies (ICT) have speeded globalization and the move towards "constructing knowledge society" (World Bank, 2002). This has reinforced many countries to build capacities to apply the ICT, in education system in general and higher education and life-long learning in particular. Such a move has been made to realize the new meaning of learning for developing knowledge society (Mashayekh, 2006). In this regard, it is recommended that higher education systems develop more diverse programs to respond to the needs of sustainable development (UNESCO, 2009). It is expected that by applying new technologies in higher education the quality of teaching and learning would be improved. Among the approaches to responding to such needs is e-learning (Bates, 2001; Oliver, 2001).

DOI: 10.4018/978-1-61520-749-7.ch019

"E-learning can be defined broadly as any use of web and internet technologies to create learning experiences" (Horton & Horton, 2003, p. 13). It varies from an entirely online web-supported learning to web-enhanced classroom teaching. There has been research evidence on e-learning which indicates its advantages for adult learning and workforce development (D'Antoni, 2006). Furthermore, it has been argued that e-learning is an effort in meeting the technology challenge (Bates, 2000) and an approach to the removal of barriers that restrict access to university-level studies, relevance of programs to local needs and to increasing equality of educational opportunities for adult learners.

However, there are pre-conditions for success in e-learning programs. These include, among others: needs-based instructional design, appropriate technology, interaction/learner support, tutor/student ratio and local support, efficient administration systems (Bates, 2001). Furthermore, financing, professionals, and technology infrastructure are important to the success of e-learning programs. In developing countries, besides the limited infrastructure, there are social and cultural factors which should be taken into account in e-learning programs (Masoumi & Lindstrom, 2009).

Experiences of establishing e-learning systems in different countries are classified in to four categories. Based on this classification, there are four models of organizational development in e-learning (D'Antoni, 2006, p. 27):

1. newly created institution;
2. evolution of an existing institution;
3. a consortium; and
4. a commercial enterprise.

Although, developing countries try to apply the cutting-edge educational practices, due to structural and human factors, the results are not usually as expected. In Iran, as a developing country, the first model was adopted by private higher education and the second model by the public universities to initiate and develop e-learning systems, a decade ago. But, the expansion of e-learning, so far has been satisfactory.

The Iranian higher education institutions, by source of funding, may be classified into three types: a) public, b) non-public, and c) private. The public institutions are composed of more than hundred government-funded universities. The non-public institutions include Islamic Azad University system which may be partially funded by the government (Bazargan, 2000). The private institutions are not funded by the government.

A decade ago, the Iranian universities were so enthusiastic to apply the ICT for educational programs that more than 40 universities initiated some sort of activities to establish virtual classes or virtual campuses. However, gradually the number of universities that succeeded to offer degree programs through virtual campus decreased to ten. These universities introduced e-courses through the existing university structure. In this regard, the most important Iranian public university (MIPU) created a Deputy Rector for Information Technology (DRIT) in 2004. The DRIT was responsible for establishing and directing activities of the center for e-learning at the MIPU. It was hoped that the DRIT, through applying new learning technologies, would force the existing teaching practices to upgrade the quality and relevance of the educational programs and "meeting the technology challenge" (Bates, 2000). However, such initial over-enthusiasm for e-learning has given way to more cautious practice in Iran. In this regard, after two years when the rector of the MIPU was changed, the deputy-rector position (DRIT) was removed from the university's administrative structure. But, the e-learning center was revitalized; its status and activities were strengthened later on. In the past two years, the E-learning Center of the MIPU has gained momentum, and now it is expected to lead the e-learning activities in Iran (Bazargan & Assadi, 2008).

In 2009, in addition to the most important public university, there are about nine other public universities which are active in offering virtual learning programs and providing learning opportunities through the application of the ICT in higher education in Iran. Besides, five private e-learning institutions have been created to offer degree programs through virtual environments. In this regard, the first private e-learning university (FPELU) in Iran was established in 2005 through official approval of the Ministry of Science, Research and Technology (MAIHE, 2006). The purpose of the FPELU is to provide learning opportunities and offer degree programs to wider communities through the ICT. The challenges such as existing higher education strategies, infrastructure, cultural and social conditions are the factors which have slowed the activities of the FPELU. Despite these factors, the FPELU has been trying hard to face these challenges and overcome them.

Based on this background, the purpose of this paper is to review and analyze the process of designing, developing and implementing an e-course at the FPELU and conceptualize the situation in Iran as a developing country. Towards this end, here we examine the process of designing, developing and delivering the e-course on research skills in the master's program in information technology management. Furthermore, specific factors which have contributed to its success are analyzed.

SETTING THE STAGE

In order for the e-learning to be successful at the national level, there is need for national strategy (Bates, 2001). In addition, connectivity, acceptability, quality learning materials, relevant interactive content and faculty support should be facilitated and strengthened (Allesi & Trollip, 2001; Shroff & Vogel, 2009; van Dam, 2004; Garrison & Vaughan, 2008). Based on this, there has been a tendency to encourage private higher education institutions in Iran to offer quality higher education programs through e-learning.

As mentioned previously, the FPELU has offered a Master's program on Information Technology Management (MITM). Research Methods (RM) is among the courses of the MITM. The RM course was offered in the second semester as an e-course. Research findings have indicated that achievement of learning objectives in a research methods course is best supported by a series of self-paced modules (Bazargan, 2002). In this respect, the RM course was designed, developed and delivered, within a modular framework, through a blended learning approach. Based on this, three teaching-learning processes were combined as follows: face-to-face, self-paced e-learning and live e-learning (Van Dam, 2004).

In developing the modules, Bloom's taxonomy of educational objectives was applied. Therefore, based on the objectives of the RM course, analysis was carried out to find out the specific learning objectives according to the type of knowledge and the cognitive process (Anderson & Krathwohl, 2001). In doing so, four areas of learning experiences were identified as follows:

1. In depth skill buildings in research methods;
2. Supporting applications of the research methods knowledge;
3. Practical aspects of research methods in information and technology management; and
4. Action planning in conducting research project.

After designing the modules, implementation of the blended course was carried out through combination of three processes as mentioned above. There were four sessions of the face-to-face learning, each taking 8 hours through workshop. Furthermore, three sessions of the live e-learning were held, each taking two hours. The types of sessions are described and their impacts on learning performance are analyzed here:

Face- to- Face Sessions

In these sessions the students, towards reaching learning objectives, reviewed the instructional materials related to the modules and interacted through a workshop approach at the FPELU premises.

Self-Paced Sessions

During the self-paced learning sessions, students were expected to review PowerPoint and other files, post messages to the Discussion Board, do assignments as required according to teaching-learning calendar or e-mail the instructor. The files were examples on the process of preparing and conducting research on information technology management. Furthermore, self-study guides recorded e-learning session, online case studies, and online assessment materials provided to students.

Live E-Learning Sessions

In these sessions each participant had a chance to participate in live e-learning, through voice and text with the instructor and the other participants. Towards this end, the instructor through collaborative techniques (Barkley, et al. 2005), based on the students' abilities, involved each of them actively in achieving learning objectives of the modules.

Depending on the above, the RM course (e-course) applied constructivist learning theory with a blended learning approach which combined the face-to-face and online teaching–learning processes for developing research skills. By doing this, the instructional process was made relevant to experiences of students and also to the contextual factors in which they were engaged in everyday life.

CASE DESCRIPTION

Nineteen students were involved in the e-course. Their academic background was mainly distributed among three disciplines as follows: 45 percent in management and business studies, 45 percent in engineering, and 10 percent in mathematics and basic sciences. Two-thirds of students were female. The age distribution of students ranged from 24 to 38 years with a mean of 28. Furthermore, 50 percent of students had a job related to information technology management.

To achieve the objectives of the e-course, the multimedia was utilized in such way to maximize the strengths of face-to-face and computer-mediated communication (CMC) for learning outcomes in research skills. Towards this end, the learning environment was structured with three components: **social presence**, **cognitive presence** and **teaching presence** (Rourke, Anderson, Garrison, &Archer, 2001; Garrison; Anderson; Archer, 2000; Garrison & Archer, 2007; Perry & Edwards, 2005). Hence, learning activities were designed to develop a sense of building a community of inquiry (Garrison &Vaughan, 2008, p. 33) among instructor, teaching assistant and students.

In the design phase of the modules, it was intended that through the use of learning theory, principles and methodologies, engage students in such a way that their learning performance take place in an effective and efficient manner. Through this process, the students were encouraged to collaborate in developing their knowledge and skills. Each student, by selecting a research topic, followed steps to conduct a research project. These steps are delineated in the twelve generic modules. In doing so, she/he identified research approach (quantitative, qualitative, or mixed), stated research problem, reviewed literature, identified required data, prepared research design, collected and analyzed data and prepared research report. This required that students get engaged in critical reflection, discourse and a set of tasks that supported systematic inquiry.

Based on the above, in the teaching-learning process four principles were incorporated: action-oriented approach; anchoring activities in the task domain; supporting error recognition and recovery; and using texts to help students improve their performance through study and locate help. These aspects are described here.

Action-Oriented Approach

As mentioned above, the teaching-learning process included twelve modules as follows:

1. Introduction to philosophical foundations of knowledge and their impact on research methodology and research method
2. Selecting a research topic
3. Statement of research problem
4. Review of literature
5. Statement of research objectives, questions and hypothesis
6. Identification of variables under investigation
7. Selection or construction of measurement instruments
8. Defining population and sampling scheme
9. Identifying a suitable research design
10. Data collection and tabulation
11. Data analysis
12. Preparing research report and communicating the results.

As the majority of students were engaged in information technology management activities, or had in mind to do so, they were motivated to act upon an inquiry related to a real life problem. Therefore, besides theoretical aspects of the above-mentioned modules, which were presented through the sessions, each student selected a topic for inquiry. Then, through hands-on approach, and "instructional interactivity" (Allen, 2007, p. 128) acted upon research steps towards stating questions/hypothesis, selecting/ constructing measurement instrument, collecting and analyzing data and interpretation of findings.

Anchoring Activities in the Task Domain

In presenting each module, authentic tasks, in the process of research, were provided for students to perform. As such, each student, with regard to his/her job experiences identified an "undetermined situation"(problem) and accordingly selected a research topic related to the problem of the world of work. Then, he/she was encouraged to identify keywords for reviewing the research literature and get prepared for defining the research problem. As such, learning activities of students were linked to the process of disciplined inquiry in information technology management.

Supporting Error Recognition and Recovery

Based on the twelve modules, related messages from the instructor were posted in the Discussion Board, asking the students to carry out learning tasks. Depending on the responses of students, systematic feedback process was provided by the instructor and his teaching assistance to students. This made the students discover their mistakes and make corrections.

Using Texts to Help Students Perform, Study and Locate Help

Two texts on quantitative research, qualitative research and mixed methods research were listed as required books in the e-course. These texts helped students in developing knowledge and skills towards achieving learning objectives. The course was scheduled for a semester taking 18 weeks, with a view to the calendar of the FPELU. While covering the twelve generic modules, in all the three types of teaching-learning experiences (face-to- face learning, self-paced e-learning and live e-learning), specific chapters of required texts were marked as reading assignments. This helped students get familiarized with the terminology, concepts, procedures and meta-cognitive knowledge. In addition to printed texts, there was explanation of the process of scientific research through PowerPoints. Furthermore, through community of inquiry the teaching-learning process was supported so that students progress systematically from identifying a problem to resolving it (Garrison & Vaughan, 2008, p. 17).

Towards this end, the presences of cognitive, social and teaching elements were combined in the e-course. As such, the students by selecting "undetermined situations" (research problems) and considering a step-wise approach to finding solutions, aimed at constructing meaning through sustained communication. Then, the instructor and students were acting out the steps through the twelve modules with developing and maintaining personal relationship. In the meantime, instructor-students interaction, student-content interaction, and student-students interaction developed and facilitated learning experiences.

DEVELOPMENT OF THE MODULES THROUGH DESIGN-BASED RESEARCH

There have been many changes in educational computing during the past two decades. However, the question is how computers should be used in blended approach to facilitate learning and instruction. In this regard, towards developing effective modules in the RM course, an interactive approach was adopted in the planning, preparation and implementation of the learning materials. In doing so, a design-based research (DBR) approach was adopted.

Application of Design-Based Research in the Blended Program

Design-based research is an approach which facilitates understanding of how, when and why educational innovations work in practice (DBRC, 2003). As development and implementation of the modules was considered an innovation, it required a whole range of designed innovations, such as activity structures, scaffoldings and instructional materials. Therefore, the DBR approach was adopted in the process of the e-course. In the process of the DBR, researchers, policy makers and practitioners of e-learning would collaborate in understanding how, when and why the e-learning environments work (or do not work) in practice. In other words, by applying design-based research method, continuous cycle of design, enactment, analysis and redesign was applied to achieve the expected outcomes.

Planning the Modules

Towards developing the modules, in the planning phase, scope of the modules, students' characteristics, constraints in implementing the modules were considered. In other words, desired outcomes of the modules were stated in terms of performance objectives. In this respect, before class started, the goals, activities, and resources of the course were listed on the site. In the process of preparing instructional materials, characteristics of students were taken into account. These included the following data: information literacy, age, previous field of study at college, grade point average, familiarity with disciplined inquiry, report writing, motivation, their availability, and their access to computer. This information was collected by going through students' qualifications and personal data provided to the instructor prior to the start of the course. The results, among other things, indicated that about 60 percent of students were at the low end of the research skill range, 30 percent at the middle and 10 percent at the high end.

Development of the Modules

Here, by development it is meant implementation of the modules' design. As mentioned earlier, the course was implemented through three processes of teaching-learning: face-to-face learning self-paced e-learning and lives e-learning. Thereby, the **Moodle** was used as a Course Management System.

A text which described the Twelve Generic Modules (TGM) had already been prepared and its summary, through PowerPoint, was uploaded on the site. As implementation of the course was carried out through blended approach, it helped broader and deeper participation of the students. In the process of implementing the TGM, the instructor presented the first four modules at the first face-to-face session. Then in the second session he presented modules 5 to 8, and finally modules 9 to 12 were presented at the last session. By doing this, in each session which took 8 hours, the instructor first described the objectives of the session and made a quick survey of students' learning difficulties, then, presented the instructional materials in a one-hour long lecture. As face-to-face sessions were held through workshop, after presentation of instructional materials, students, who numbered 19, were divided into four groups. Each group practiced the steps of disciplined inquiry which was already presented by instructor. In other words, each face-to-face session was composed of three interrelated sub-sessions:

a) Presentation of materials by instructor for one-hour;
b) Practice by students and preparing answers to exercises through discussion and group work in a group of 4 to 6; and
c) Presentation of a summary in each group and presenting the summary in the plenary session.

The face-to-face session was followed by self-paced e-learning. Based on the learning experiences that students gained in the face-to-face and self- paced sessions, online sessions were implemented. In the online sessions students participated in a lively interaction and debate. They raised issues and made comments then suggested answers to specific questions. In doing so, the interaction was carried out between instructor and other students and between students themselves. This generated high levels of cognitive activities (Heckman & Annabi, 2005).

Therefore, the implementation of the generic modules through utilization of the three phases, created a community of inquiry (Perry & Edwards, 2005) which strengthened critical reflection and discourse among students.

ASSESSMENT

The assessment component in the generic themes for developing research skills was based on continuous assessment. It gave emphasis to provide information for guiding teaching-learning activities. The process was composed of frequent assessment, self-assessment, and feedback to address inequalities in cognitive skills. The required information was provided through portfolio assessment (Banta, 2003). Therefore, it had two objectives: (a) to collect data for feedback to improve the learning outcomes; (b) to evaluate effectiveness of the program. In other words, the first objective stressed formative evaluation and focused on the principle of ensuring that the teaching-learning activities are congruent with the intended learning outcomes. The second objective emphasized summative evaluation of the program.

By doing this, out of four levels of Kirkpatrick evaluation model (Kirkpatrick, 1995), levels one and two were applied. According to this model, four levels of evaluation may be used for education (training) programs. These are as follows: (1) evaluation of reaction of learners, (2) evaluation of the attainment of learners against the intended learning outcomes, (3) the impact of the learners, on the job performance, and (4) evaluation of the overall results of the program.

In order to use evaluation data for feedback, the first two levels of the Kirkpatrick model were used in each of the three processes. Thus, data was collected from students through interview in the middle of face-to-face session and through three paper-based multiple-choice tests at each of the three face-to-face sessions. These three tests were parallel forms. The multiple-choice test had content validity and the split-half reliability coefficient was calculated as 0.90. While, the interviews focused on reaction of students towards different areas of the e-course, the criterion-referenced multiple-choice tests covered the learning objectives. These three tests were parallel forms with acceptable reliability coefficient and content validity. However, as the e-course in research methods was offered in the third semester, the students were not at the final stage of their studies. Therefore, third and fourth levels of the Kilpatrick's model were not applied.

Considering that the course was conducted as a design-based research project, the evaluation data was collected and used as feedback in a continuous cycle of design, enactment, analysis and redesign (DBRC, 2003, page 5) in the blended program. Therefore, the formative evaluation data was very helpful to methodological adjustments in both face-to-face and online sessions. As the blended program was led towards a community of inquiry, students' reaction was used to make the teaching-learning process more congruent with collaborative and constructivist learning environment.

In addition to the data collected during the face-to-face and online sessions, evaluation data was collected also during the self-paced learning through self-assessment. Besides, in order to assess students' learning outcomes, as mentioned earlier, each student was expected to select a research topic related to information technology management, then design the research process, collect the necessary data and prepare a research report. The objectives of this exercise were: (a) to set the stage for students to gain hands-on application exercises on the twelve generic themes; and (2) to provide further evidence for learning outcomes. In preparing and conducting the research project, two students could have collaborated through virtual interaction. The final report of such project was considered as the first part of summative evaluation of students' learning performance. Results of the paper-based multiple-choice tests, in the three face-to-face sessions, were taken into account as the second part of evaluation data.

Table1. Mean and standard deviation of test scores

Test	No. of students	Mean	S.D.
1	19	10.12	2.89
2	19	12.89	2.10
3	19	16.63	1.25

The results of the three tests are given in table (1). It indicates that, as the e-course moved ahead, the performance of students improved significantly. Furthermore, learning outcomes became more concentrated around the mean performance of the class as the course progressed.

A repeated measures analysis of variance of the three test scores was carried out. The results of this analysis indicated that improvement of learning performance of students during the e-course was statistically significant ($p=0.05$). In other words, the mean change of students' performance over time was significant.

MANAGING STUDENTS THROUGH BLENDED LEARNING

The course was conducted during a semester for 18 weeks from February to June. About 30 days prior to the start of the course, the students received an e-mail regarding the timetable and deadline for registration in the course.

At the end of each face-to-face session in order to get a quick feedback from students, the instructor asked each student to list three concepts that they learned best and three concepts or issues that they felt they had difficulty in understanding and needed more explanation. Besides, during final face-to-face session, students were requested to discuss the knowledge and skills they developed in this course and the areas they will need to develop further understanding in order to plan and conduct research in information technology management. Based on this, the instructor analyzed the responses of students and remedial activities were designed and carried out in the online session. Furthermore, additional instructional materials to strengthen students learning were posted on the site. As such, application exercises were worked out during live e-learning sessions to ensure students' understanding of the concepts and issues relative to disciplined inquiry in information technology management (Wood, 2006).

CURRENT CHALLENGES FACING THE VIRTUAL LEARNING PROGRAMS

National strategies regarding e-learning is one of the major challenges that the e-learning programs are facing (Razaie, 2008; Montazer, 2007). "Policy making bodies and authorities responsible for decision making about e-learning are several and not aligned" (Montazer, 2007, page 12). This may cause difficulties with regard to responding to needs of national development through the application of the ICT in education. Besides, based on a survey of transnational education in Iran (Bazargan et al., 2008), lack of quality assurance mechanism for ensuring the quality of virtual and transnational learning programs is considered as an impediment in the expansion of such programs. It is expected that the policies and decisions related to the e-learning programs encourage potential candidates to enroll in related higher education institutions. Consequently, there is much room for improvement in policy planning, decision making and action towards reaching a desirable situation in this regard.

A recent survey of a virtual learning environment in Iran indicated that 80 percent of students "had experienced a kind of miscommunication with others" in an online classroom (Dolatabadi, & Dillon, 2009, page 34). In this respect, in addition to pedagogical factor and technological infrastructure which are challenging in many virtual learning environments, there are cultural factors that should be taken into consideration in Iran (Montazer, & Bahreinejad, 2007).

Instructor's readiness and commitment to virtual learning environment is also another important challenge. Thus, the challenge is getting academic members to change their ways of work towards building community of inquiry. Therefore, in faculty development programs for virtual learning environments, a strong emphasis should be put on the development of e-skills, including cognitive and communication skills especially ability to develop and maintain human relationship (Crichton & Childs, 2008). Furthermore, pedagogical capabilities necessary for being a "guide on the side" in the online programs should be emphasized. Other challenges include acceptability of e-learning programs.

In general, designing, developing and implementing an e-course, with high learning performance, in a developing country such as Iran is a challenging activity. The amount of time that an instructor is required to spend for facilitating high quality learning performance is considerable. The results of this case study indicate that if the instructor is motivated enough to engage in a virtual learning environment, having pedagogical expertise and capacity of applying new learning technologies, he/she would be able to overcome the shortcomings of a traditional learning environment. Therefore, in this regard the challenge is recruitment of empowered instructors. In this regard, the university reward mechanism should be aligned with such efforts (Kulski & Groombridge, 2004).

SOLUTIONS AND RECOMMENDATIONS

This case study has indicated that blended learning approach, in which three methods: face-to-face, self-paced, and online learning are combined, provides a better opportunity for arriving at the expected learning performance.

As research methods course is generally offered by many degree programs at the post-graduate level, generic modules in research methods through blended approach would help provide a learning environment in which development of research skills with higher performance would be facilitated. Results of this case study indicate that in the blended learning approach, applying workshop method in the face-to-face sessions motivates students to do their best towards achieving the learning objectives.

Application of new learning technologies in higher education has become a reality and it is expanding. Although, public universities in Iran were over-enthusiastic to use e-learning through evolution of existing institutions a decade ago, they gradually lost enthusiasm and became skeptical. Hence, there is need for national policies, strategic planning and management to gain the confidence of faculty members and higher education managers in the virtual learning environments. In doing so, faculty development programs in the application of new technologies should be given high priority. Moreover, there is need for model e-learning programs with high standards of performance as examples of good practice.

As a final point, it should be noted that the proportion of enrollments in higher education to the population of age group 18 to 24 years old is 30 percent in Iran at present (2009). The national development plan has indicated the tendency towards building knowledge society. Furthermore, as there has been a high social demand for higher education, there would be a need to increase the above-mentioned proportion. Towards this end, transnational or cross-border higher education could help increase learning opportunities and also introduce higher quality in teaching-learning activities (Bazargan, 2009). This requires capacity building for quality assurance of higher education system in general and e-leaning institutions in particular (Bazargan, 2004). In order to expand virtual learning environments, it is necessary to ensure the quality of learning outcomes of e-learning programs. In doing so, it is expected that the idea of Iran Universities Quality Network (IUQN) would be realized (Bazargan, 2008). As such, the institutionalization of IUQN would facilitate internal and external quality assurance of programs and institutions in higher education in general and virtual learning environments in particular (Bazargan, 2007 & 2008).

REFERENCES

Allen, M. W. (2007). Designing Successful E-Learning. San Francisco, CA: Pfeiffer.

Allesi, S. M., & Trollip, S. R. (2001). Multimedia for Learning: Methods and Development, (3rd ed.). Boston: Allyn and Bacon

Anderson, L. W., & Krathwohl, D. R. (2001). A Taxonomy for Learning, Teaching, and Assessing: A Revision of Bloom's Taxonomy of Educational Objectives. New York: Longman.

Banta, T. W. (2003) (Ed.). Portfolio Assessment: Uses, Cases, Scoring and impact. San Francisco: Jossey-Bass

Barkley, E. F., Cross, K. P., & Mayor, C. H. (2005). Collaborative learning techniques: A handbook for college faculty. San Francisco: Jossey-Bass.

Bates, A. W. (2000).Managing technological change. San Francisco, CA: Jossey-Bass.

Bates, A. W. (2001). National strategies for e-learning in post- secondary education and training. Paris: UNESCO /IIEP.

Bazargan, A. (2000). Internal evaluation as an Approach to Revitalize University Systems: The case of I.R. Iran. *Higher Education Policy*, *13*(2), 173–180. doi:10.1016/S0952-8733(99)00024-0

Bazargan, A. (2002). *Teaching Statistics to Medical Doctors through Research Methods: A case of Medical Education in Iran*. Paper Presented at the 6th International Conference of Teaching Statistics on Developing Statistically Literate Society, Cape Town, South Africa. Retrieved May 25, 2008 from http://www.stat.auckland.ac.nz/~iase/publications/1/4f1_baza.pdf

Bazargan, A. (2004). Enhancing Institutional Capacity for Evaluation and Quality Assurance in Higher Education Systems: International Experiences and National Requirements for Organizational Development. [in Persian]. *Majlis and Pajouhesh*, *41*, 141–158.

Bazargan, A. (2007). Problems of Organizing and Reporting Internal and External Evaluation in Developing Countries: The case of Iran. *Higher Education Quarterly*, *13*(3), 207–214. doi:10.1080/13538320701800126

Bazargan, A. (2008). A Proposal for Establishing "Iran Universities Quality Network" (in Persian). *Computer Report (Journal of Informatics Society of Iran)*, *180*, 24-27. Retrieved on May 25, 2009 from http://www.isi.org.ir/Magezin/180/24.asp

Bazargan, A. (2009). The Role of e-learning in transnational Medical Education. In *Proceedings of the 2nd Conference of e-Learning in Medical Sciences*. Tehran University of Medical Sciences, Tehran, Iran, January 29-30,2009. (in Persian)

Bazargan, A., et al. (2008). Final Report of a Survey on Transnational Education in Iran. Tehran, Iran: Institute for Research and Planning in Higher Education.

Crichton, S., & Childs, E. (2008). Looking forward: stories of practice. In *Education for a digital world: Advice, guidelines, and effective practice from around the globe.* Vancouver: BCcampus and Commonwealth of Learning. Retrieved on August 8, 2009 from http://www.irrodl.org/index.php/irrodl/article/view/722/1237

D'Antoni, S. (2006). The Virtual University: Modules and messages, lessons from case studies. Paris: UNESCO /IIEP.

Dolatabadi, H. R., & Dillon, P. (2009). Intercultural Discourse in Virtual Learning Environments: A Preparatory Study of the Perceptions of Students in an Iranian university. *International Journal of Information Science and Management, 7*(2), 29-43. Retrieved on May 26, 2009 from http://www.srlst.com/ijist/ijism-Vol7No2/ijism72-29-43.pdf

Garrison, D. R., Anderson, T., & Archer, W. (2000). Critical inquiry in a text-based environment: computer conferencing in higher education. *The Internet and Higher Education*, *2*(2-3), 87–105. doi:10.1016/S1096-7516(00)00016-6

Garrison, D. R., & Archer, W. (2007). A community of inquiry framework for online learning. In M. Moore (Ed.), Handbook of Distance Education. New York: Erlbaum.

Garrison, D. R., & Vaughan, N. D. (2008). Blended learning in higher education (framework, principles and guidelines). San Francisco, CA: Jossey Bass.

Heckman, R., & Annabi, H. (2005). A content analytic comparison of learning processes in online and face-to-face case study discussions. *Journal of Computer-Mediated Communication, 10*(2), article 7. Retrieved May 15, 2009 from http://jcmc.indiana.edu/vol10/issue2/heckman.html

Horton, K. (2003). E-learning Tools and Technologies. Indianapolis, IN: Wiley.

Kirkpatrick, D. L. (1996). Evaluating training programs. San Francisco: Berrett-Koehler.

Kulski, M., & Groombridge. (2004). Aligning Teaching Quality Indicators with University Reward Mechanisms. *Tertiary Education and Management*, *10*, 45–59. doi:10.1023/B:TEAM.0000012236.63005.a2

Mashayekh, F. (2006). Reviewing the Meaning of Learning. In A. Khorsandi (Ed.) *Communication within the Educational System in Iran* (pp.59-71). Tehran: Institute for Cultural and Social Studies, Ministry of Science and Technology. Tehran, Iran (in Persian). Retrieved on May 22,2009, from http://pedagogy.ir/index.php?option=com_content&view=article&id=159&Itemid=99

Mehraborz Institute of Higher Education (MAIHE). (2006). MAIHE Bylaws. Tehran, Iran: MIHE.

Montazer, Gh. A., & Bahreinejad, A. (2007). An Adaptive and Intelligent Framework for Virtual Higher Education in Iran. *Iranian Journal of Information Science and Technology*, *5*(1), 11–26.

Montazer, Gh. A. (2007). Strategic Studies of Informational Development in Higher Education System in Iran (in Persian). *Quarterly Journal of Research and Planning in Higher Education (Special issue on e-learning)*, *13*(1), 1-26.

Oliver, R. (2001). Assuring the Quality of Online Learning in Australian Higher Education. In M. Wallace, A. Ellis, & D. Newton (Eds.), *Proceedings of Moving Online II Conference*, (pp. 222-231). Limore, New Zealand: Southern Cross University. Retrieved on May 20, 2009 from http://elrond.scam.ecu.edu.au/oliver/2001/mocpaper.pdf

Perry, B., & Edwards, M. (2005). Exemplary Online Educators; Creating a Community of Inquiry. *Turkish Online Journal of Distance education, 6*(2). Retrieved on May 20, 2009 from http://tojde.anadolu.edu.tr/tojde18/articles/article6.htm

Razaie, M. (2008, December). *Identifying Necessary Policies for Expanding E-learning in Agricultural Higher Education* (in Persian). Paper Presented at the 3rd E-learning Conference, Tehran, December. Tehran: K.N.T. University of Technology.

Rourke, L., Anderson, T., Garrison, D. R., & Archer, W. (2001). Assessing social presence in asynchronous, text-based computer conferencing. *Journal of Distance Education*, *14*(3), 51–70.

Shroff, R. H., & Vogel, D. R. (2009). Assessing the Factors Deemed to Support Individual Student Intrinsic Motivation in Technology Supported Online and Face-to-Face Discussions. *Journal of Information Technology Education*, *8*, 59–85.

The Design-Based Research Collective (DBRC). (2003). Design-Based Research: An emerging paradigm for educational inquiry. *Educational Researcher*, *32*(1), 5–8. doi:10.3102/0013189X032001005

UNESCO. (2009, July). *2009 World Conference on Higher Education: The New Dynamics of Higher Education and Research for Societal Change and Development.* UNESCO, Paris. Retrieved on August 05, 2009 from http://www.unesco.org/fileadmin/MULTIMEDIA/HQ/ED/ED/pdf/WCHE_2009/FINAL%20COMMUNIQUE%20WCHE%202009.pdf

Van Dam, N. (2004). The e-Learning Field book (Implementation lessons and case studies from companies that are making e-learning work). New York: McGraw-Hill.

Wood, K. (2006). Changing a person: the experience of learning to research in the social sciences. *Higher Education Research & Development*, *25*(1), 53–66. doi:10.1080/13600800500453162

World Bank. (2002). Constructing Knowledge Societies: New Challenges for Tertiary Education. Washington, DC: World Bank.

ADDITIONAL READING

Aldrich, C. (2005). Learning by doing: a comprehensive guide to simulations, computer games and Pedagogy in e-learning and other educational experiences. San Francisco, CA: Pfeiffer.

Anderson, B. (2008). Contemporary Perspectives in E-Learning Research. *American Journal of Distance Education*, *22*(2), 123–125. doi:10.1080/08923640701595399

Bernard, R., Abrami, P., Lou, Y., & Borokhovski, E. (2004). A methodological morass? How we can improve quantitative research in distance education. *Distance Education*, *25*(2), 175–198. doi:10.1080/0158791042000262094

Bonk, C., & Garaham, C. (2006). Future directions of blended learning in higher education and workplace learning centres. In C. Bonk & C.Graham (Eds.). The handbook of blended learning: Global perspectives, local designs. San Francisco: Pfieffer.

Brower, E. W., Dejonge, J. O., & Stout, V. J. (2001). Moving to Online: Making Transition from Traditional Instruction and Communication Strategies. Newbury Park, CA: Corwin Press.

Carayannis, E. C., & Sipp, C. M. (2006). E-development toward the knowledge innovation and entrepreneurship for "smart" development. New York: Palgrave Macmillan.

Cartelli, A. (2008). Web Technologies and Integration of Different E-Learning Strategies in Education. *International Journal of Web-Based Learning and Teaching Technologies*, *3*(2), 23–34.

Cho, V., Lai, W. M. J., & Cheng, T. C. E. (2009). The role of perceived user-interface design in continued usage intention of self-paced e-learning tools. *Computers & Education*, *53*(2), 216–227. doi:10.1016/j.compedu.2009.01.014

Clark, R. C., & Mayer, R. E. (2003). E-Learning and the Science of Instruction; Proven guidelines for consumers and designers of multimedia learning. San Francisco: Pfeiffer.

Cooze, M., & Barbour, M. (2007). Learning Styles: A Focus upon E-Learning Practices and Their Implications for successful Instructional Design. *Journal of Applied Educational Technology*, *4*(1), 7–20.

Ellis, R., Gins, P., & Piggott, L. (2009). E-learning in higher education: some key aspects and their relationship to approaches to study. *Higher Education Research & Development*, *28*(3), 303–318. doi:10.1080/07294360902839909

Flix, U. (2005). E-learning pedagogy in the third millennium: the need for combining social and cognitive constructivist approaches. [the journal of EUROCALL]. *ReCALL*, *17*(1), 85–100.

Grubisic, A., Stankov, S., Rosik, M., & Zikto, B. (2009). Controlled Experiment Replication in Evaluation of E-learning System's Educational Influence. *Computers & Education*, *53*(3), 591–602. doi:10.1016/j.compedu.2009.03.014

Halawi, L., Pires, S., & McCarthy, R. (2009). Viewpoint. An Evaluation of E-Learning on the Basis of Bloom's Taxonomy: An Exploratory Study. *Journal of Education for Business*, *84*(6), 374–380. doi:10.3200/JOEB.84.6.374-380

Iskandar, M. (2007). Innovation in e-learning, instruction, assessment, and engineering education. Dordrecht, Netherlands: Springer.

Khan, B. (2005). Managing E-Learning Strategies: Design, Delivery, Implementation and Evaluation. Hershey, PA: Information Science Reference.

Kidd, T. T., & Song, H. (2008). Handbook of research on instructional systems and technology. Hershey, PA: Information Science Reference.

Mandinach, E. B. (2005). The Development of Effective Evaluation Methods for E-Learning: A Concept Paper and Action Plan. *Teachers College Record*, *107*(8), 1814–1835. doi:10.1111/j.1467-9620.2005.00543.x

Pallaoff, R. M., & Keith, P. (2007). Building Learning Communities (Effective Strategies for the Virtual Classroom). San Francisco, CA: Jossey-Bass.

Ravenscroft, A. (2003). From conditioning to learning communities: implications of fifty years of research in e-learning interaction design. *ALT-J Association for Learning Technology Journal*, *11*, 4–18. doi:10.1080/0968776030110302

Romero, C., Ventura, S., & Garcia, E. (2008). Data Mining in course management systems: Moodle case study and tutorial. *Computers & Education*, *51*(1), 368–384. doi:10.1016/j.compedu.2007.05.016

Shee, D. Y., & Wang, Y.-S. (2008). Multi-criteria evaluation of the web-based e-learning system: A methodology based on learner satisfaction and its applications. *Computers & Education*, *50*(3), 894–905. doi:10.1016/j.compedu.2006.09.005

Shepley, S. E. (2009). Building a virtual campus: Librarians as collaborates in online course development and learning. *Journal of Library Administration*, *49*, 1–20, 89–95. doi:10.1080/01930820802312821

Shimizu, Y. (2007). Current Status of e-Learning in Japan and Networking Learning Objects for Quality Enhancement. *Frontiers in Artificial Intelligence and Applications*, *162*, 7–8.

Stanfield, M., & Connolly, T. (2009). Institutional transformation through best practices in virtual campus development; advancing e-learning policies. Hershey, PA: Information Science Resources.

Wang, Y.-M., & Wang, Y.-S. (2009). Examining the dimensionality and measurement of user-perceived knowledge and information quality in the KMS context. *Journal of Information Science*, *35*(1), 94–109. doi:10.1177/0165551508092260

Wang, Y.-S., Wang, H.-Y., & Shee, D. Y. (2007). Measuring e-learning systems success in an organizational context: Scale development and validation. *Computers in Human Behavior*, *23*(4), 1792–1808. doi:10.1016/j.chb.2005.10.006

KEY TERMS AND DEFINITIONS

Blended Learning: As described in this case study, it is the integration of face-to-face learning, self-paced learning, and online learning experiences.

Collaborative Learning: Is a teaching-learning process that highlights students' abilities and get them involved through interdependence in working towards learning objectives.

Community of Inquiry: A community of students and teachers engaged in the process of disciplined inquiry (identifying a problem, stating research questions, …, reporting the results).

Community of Inquiry Model: Is an instructional design model developed for e-learning which includes three elements: cognitive presence, social presence, teaching presence (Garrison, et al., 2000, 2007, 2008).

Research Skills: Ability to identify an "undetermined situation", define the problem, state research questions (hypothesis), determine required data, select an appropriate disciplined inquiry technique, collect and analyze data, and report the results.

Virtual Learning Environment: An information space in which social interactions facilitates communication towards building learning communities through collaboration with the help of multimedia tools.

Chapter 20
Effectiveness of Interactivity for Enhanced Undergraduate Learning

Luis Palacios
Brunel University, UK

Chris Evans
Brunel University, UK

ABSTRACT

This study focuses on how Technology Enhanced Learning (TEL) can best be used by Brunel University students to enhance their learning. The study considers the impact that different levels of interactivity have on the memory and understanding of the students. In particular, it considers the use of interactive self-assessment questions (ISAQs) as a mechanism to help them learn from an eLearning system. One mechanism that has been employed for over four years is the use of a bespoke multimedia eLearning system available over the Web to first-year undergraduates. A common feature of many eLearning systems is the use of ISAQs to allow students to evaluate their grasp of the material with a view to revisiting it if they feel it necessary. However, ISAQs are time-consuming to develop and implement. This case study considers whether the incorporation of ISAQs has a measurable impact on learning as indicated by their performance in tests.

ORGANIZATION BACKGROUND

Brunel's distinctive mission has always been to combine academic rigour with the practical, entrepreneurial and imaginative approach pioneered by its namesake Isambard Kingdom "Brunel". The name of Brunel University has become as well-known and respected in engineering circles as was the name of Isambard Kingdom Brunel a hundred years ago for British engineers who were famous for the creation of the Great Western Railway, a series of famous steamships, including the first with a propeller, and numerous important bridges and tunnels.

Brunel is one of a number of British universities created in the 1960s following the Robbins Report on higher education that recommended immediate expansion of universities, and that all Colleges of Advanced Technology should be given the status of universities (Wikipedia, 2009). Originally Acton Technical College, based in Acton on the outskirts

DOI: 10.4018/978-1-61520-749-7.ch020

of London, it was decided in 1957 that the college should split into two sections – Acton Technical College continued to cater to technicians and craftsmen, whereas Brunel College of Technology was dedicated to the education of chartered engineers.

In 1961 it was awarded the status of College of Advanced Technology, and it was decided that Brunel College should expand at another site in order to accommodate the extra buildings that would be needed. Uxbridge, Hillingdon was chosen to house the new buildings. From April 1, 1962 it was officially named Brunel College of Advanced Technology – it was only the 10th Advanced Technology College in the country, and the last to be awarded this title. The first buildings were due to be finished in 1967. However, in 1963 it was decided that the College should become a technological university, and the Royal Charter was awarded on the June 9, 1966 giving university status. In 1980, the University merged with Shoreditch College of Education, which was located at Cooper's Hill, Runnymede since 1951.

In 1995 the University expanded again, integrating the West London Institute of Higher Education, and adding campuses in Osterley and Twickenham. This increased the number of courses that Brunel University was able to offer – traditionally its strengths had been engineering, science, technology and social sciences. With the addition of the West London Institute, departments such as arts, humanities, geography & earth science, health and sports science were added, and the size of the student body increased to over 12,000. Then Brunel put together a £250 million master plan, to sell off the sites at Runnymede, Osterley and Twickenham, using the revenue to renovate and update the buildings and facilities at Uxbridge. Works already carried out include the library extension, a state-of-the-art sports complex, renovated students' union facilities, a new Heath Sciences teaching centre, and many more halls of residence.

In the late 1990s, the Departments of Physics, Chemistry, and Materials Engineering were closed. In 2004, the then Vice-Chancellor Steven Schwartz, initiated the reorganisation of the university's faculties and departments into schools, and announced the closure of the Department of Geography and Earth Sciences. The present Vice-Chancellor, the sociologist Christopher Jenks who took office in 2006, may be developing a less rankings-driven approach.

This long succession of developments and mergers has brought the University from modest beginnings to a major force on the UK higher education scene. However, today, Brunel University's influence extends far beyond the fields of engineering, science and technology, which were its traditional strengths.

Brunel University has undergone a dramatic expansion in recent years, partly in response to the UK Government's objective of having 50% of school leavers to enter Higher Education. Moreover, today's students have increased demands on their time due to other social and work commitments. This makes it increasingly difficult for all students to physically attend a lecture, at a particular time and place; as a consequence an alternative to teaching using technology has been seen as an appropriate methodology.

THEORETICAL BACKGROUND

TEL is forecast to be the mechanism by which future students and organizations can facilitate learning practices that are independent of time, place and pace. Learners can select the educational material and study in the style and pace that suits them as individuals, enabling them to be active learners. In general, it involves the support of any learning activity by means of technology. These learning activities should be organised with the intention to improve students' knowledge, skills and competence.

However, the focus on learning alternatively shifts from technology to human cognition in order to take into account our capabilities to assimilate knowledge. Constructivism look at these abilities to explain that humans generate knowledge and meaning from their own experiences. Constructive learning takes place when meaningful mental representations are constructed on top of previous knowledge creating schemas.

The experiment and system design developed in this case study is underpinned by the dual coding theory (Paivio, 1986), the cognitive load theory (Chandler & Sweller, 1992), the cognitive theory of multimedia learning (Mayer and Moreno, 1998), and a constructivist learning approach.

Feinburg and Murphy (2000) define the cognitive load theory as "the amount of mental energy' required processing a given amount of information. As the amount of information increases, so does the cognitive load on our mental resources. If the amount of information and instruction surpasses the capacity and limitations of our mental resources, learning doesn't takes place and our sensors get distorted. Sweller (1988) describes a cognitive model of learning that is built based on three memory types: sensory memory, working memory, and long-term memory. These memories have limited capacity according to Sweller's (1988, 1994; Chandler & Sweller, 1992) cognitive load theory.

Working memory is an area for storage of short term information that includes separate auditory and visual working memories (Baddeley, 1986). In later research, Baddeley (1992) formulates that the working memory is organised into a visio-spatial sketch pad for visual images manipulation, and the phonological loop that handle speech-based information. Long-term memory is the resident knowledge and skills acquired and held in a permanently retrievable area.

Paivio's (1986) dual-code theory establishes that verbal and non-verbal information are represented in different mental systems. These systems use working memory to process the received information.

The cognitive theory of multimedia learning (Mayer, 1997) indicates that meaningful learning takes place when relevant information in each store, is digested into a coherent representation, and makes connections between corresponding representations in each store.

Web-based multimedia eLearning systems are ideal tools to complement or replace traditional delivery. E-Learning can be defined as a combination of technology and the pedagogical approaches required to present and teach a particular subject. E-Learning systems are key delivery components to communicate the educational message by using text and visual images. But the heuristic of using text and visual images is just an element of a series of design principles whose implementation improve the effectiveness of teaching using web-based multimedia e-Learning.

According to Mayer (2001) multimedia theory of learning the information presented in more than one mode e.g. as words or pictures, or both facilitate learning. Mayer establishes that meaningful learning occurs when learners mentally select relevant information and build mental coherent connections. Mayer developed a series of research-based learning techniques where information is integrated and distributed proportionally into the auditory and visual channels to maximize the learner's working memory. Therefore, people learn better when multimedia messages are designed in ways that are consistent with how the human mind works and with research-based principles.

These principles according to Mayer research are as follows:

The multimedia or multiple representation principle establishes that is better to use narration and pictures (two modes) to present an explanation rather than (one mode) narration or pictures alone. This multimedia effect is consistent with the cognitive theory of multimedia learning because those given a multimedia explanation are capable to create two different mental representations related to the auditory and visual channels and make connections between them. In Mayer experiments (Mayer & Anderson, 1991, 1992) students who listened to a narration explaining how a bicycle tire pump works while also viewing a corresponding animation generated twice as many useful solutions to subsequent problem solving transfer questions than did students who listened to the same narration without viewing any animation.

The coherence principle indicates that students learn better when extraneous material is excluded rather than included in multimedia explanations. Based on the cognitive theory of multimedia learning, this is due to the limitations on capacity of the visual and auditory channels. If a narrated multimedia animation presentation is delivered, the narrated component flow in the auditory channel while the animation is processed in the visual channel. Any additional auditory or visual information competes with is counterpart earlier presented with the tendency to overload it. The less capacity available for processing the narration hurt students' learning.

The modality principle recommends use narration with pictures rather than written words with pictures. When students are listening verbal information instead than visually as on-screen text, research showed (Mayer and Moreno's, 1998) that the former outperform those who learn with concurrent on-screen text and animations. This group may have the advantage of being able to attend two channel of information simultaneously: the auditory and the visual channel. On the other hand, the second group may overload the visual channel with two visual sources competing for the same channel.

The spatial and temporal contiguity principles relates to when and how far apart display words should be from pictures. The principle is consistent with the cognitive theory of multimedia learning since corresponding words and pictures must be in working memory at the same time in order to facilitate building the connection between them.

The spatial contiguity principle recommends displaying words adjacent to the parts of the picture to which they relate. When giving a multimedia explanation, present corresponding words and pictures contiguously rather than separately. Research demonstrated that students who learn with verbal and visual explanations integrated outperform those who learn with material that was separated (Mayer, 1997). In a review of ten studies concerning whether multimedia instruction is effective, Mayer (1997) manipulated the ***physical proximity*** of the on-screen text and the animation to conclude that there was consistent evidence for what was called a spatial-contiguity effect.

The **temporal contiguity** principle is that students better understand an explanation when corresponding words and pictures are presented at the ***same time*** than when they are separated in time. For example, students who listened to a narration explaining how a bicycle tire pump works while also viewing a corresponding animation outperforms students who viewed the animation before or after listening to the narration (Mayer & Anderson, 1991, 1992).

The redundancy principle recommends the use of narration and pictures rather than narration, text and pictures if the visual information is presented simultaneously to the verbal information.. There is the misconception when using multimedia learning system than the most material presented such as animations, video, or graphics with simultaneous text and audio the better the message will be delivered. Unfortunately, redundant information presented simultaneously thought different channels only help to overload the channel. This is due to a split- attention effect between the on-screen text and the animation occurs and the redundant message hurts rather than helps students' learning. However, students presented with redundant verbal materials outperformed students who learned with non-redundant verbal materials when the presentations are sequential.

The Split-Attention principle (Chandler & Sweller, 1991; Sweller, Chandler, Tierney and Cooper, 1990) recommends presenting words as auditory narration rather than as visual on-screen text. The principle rationality base on on-screen text and animation can overload the visual information processing system whereas narration is processed in the verbal information processing system and animation is processed in the visual information processing system.

For example, students who viewed an animation while also listening to a corresponding narration outperform students who viewed the same animation with corresponding on-screen text consisting of the same words as the narration (Mayer & Moreno, in press).

The personalisation principle recommends using words in conversational style rather than formal style to increase learning. Conversational style aids learning because people work harder to understand material when they feel they are in a conversation with a partner. In formal style first and second-person is avoided. However, there is research evidence that explains the contrary when designing multimedia systems. E.g., "Caution should be used when opening pyrotechnic containers."

The **segmenting material** principle recommends that learning material be presented in learner-paced segments rather than as a continuous unit (Mayer, 2005). People learn more deeply when a multimedia message is presented in user-paced segments rather than a continuous unit. Segmenting slows the pace of the presentation enabling the learner to carry out essential mental processing.

The **pre-training** learning principle recommends that is better when they know the names and characteristics of the main concepts. (Clark & Mayer, 2003) It equips the learner with prior knowledge that can use to process the next multimedia message with less cognitive effort.

The **Signalling** principle recommends that is better when the words include cues about the organization of the presentation Mayer (2005). The learner attention is taken by highlighting or flashing the appropriate elements in the multimedia message. It helps to reduce extraneous cognitive load in the learning process.

The **voice** principle recommends that is better when words are spoken in a standard-accented human (Mayer, 2005). People learn more deeply from a multimedia message when the narration is made in human natural voice rather than in a computer voice. The human voice triggers a social response in the learner that invites him to make sense of the information presented.

The **image** principle indicates that learning performance is better when the speaker's image is added to the screen.

The individual differences principle indicates that multimedia effects, contiguity effects, and split-attention create largest effect for high spatial or low knowledge learners and depend on individual differences in the learner. Students with high prior knowledge may not require for example to have a contiguous visual presentation because they can generate their own mental images while listening to an animation or reading a verbal text. In addition, students who scored high on tests of spatial ability showed greater multimedia effects than did students who scored low on spatial ability. According to the cognitive theory of multimedia learning, students with high spatial ability are able to hold the visual image in visual working memory and thus are more likely to benefit from contiguous presentation of words and pictures.

For example, students who lack prior knowledge are inclined to show stronger multimedia effects and contiguity effects than students who possessed high levels of prior knowledge (Mayer & Gallini, 1991).

Interactivity is also one of the main factors to take into account when designing a multimedia system. Interactivity in this context refers to the degree of responsiveness established in a two way communication multimedia environment. Evans and Sabry (2002) formulated the interaction model in order to study the process and the effects interaction has in learning. The three-stage model of computer-initiated interactions has been adopted in this case study to define the terminology and methodology that follows. According to the model, an interaction involves a sequence of three actions: initiation, response, and feedback with exchange of information between the two agents involved. In a multimedia system, initiation consists on the system request for input to start the process. The response makes the second agent providing that input. Feedback is the reaction to the first agent input. The three actions are interrelated and they are a direct consequence of each agent response. The term interactivity includes interactions between students (student–student interaction), interactions with the tutor (teacher–student interaction), and interactions with the teaching material itself (student–content interaction) (Moore, 1989; Schrum & Berge, 1997).

In a multimedia computer system, the interaction can be either initiated by the system or by the learner (Scha¨r & Krueger, 2000). When initiated by the student, s/he seeks some information from the content acting in a similar way to any other traditional media. When initiated by the system, it demands some input from the learner, such as pressing a button or answering a question. In the case of computer-initiated interaction, the response action is carried out by the learner and the feedback action by the computer.

As Evans and Sabry (2002) point out, all forms of computer-initiated interactivity can be described in terms of this model. Their example in a navigation or pacing interaction has three actions:

1. Present button or control to learner (computer initiation).
2. Student presses button or uses control (learner response).
3. Present new information to learner (computer feedback).

A lesson in a computer-based learning system can now be described as non-interactive if it requires little or no computer-initiated interactivity in order for a lesson to be completed. By contrast, a computer-based learning system is said to be interactive if it uses computer-initiated interactivity as an intrinsic part of the lesson.

CASE DESCRIPTION

On the other hand, technological innovations triggered by computer and network-based learning have given assessment a new dimension that can change this emotional and highly sensitive activity. Assessment is generally considered a term that involves the process by which we give students tests and assign them grades. It is specifically a mechanism for providing either the teachers (summative assessment) or the learners (formative assessment) with vital information for improving their teaching/learning methodology and determining if accompanied by feedback where mistakes have been made to reflect on them and becoming more effective, self-assessing, self-directed learners. (Angelo & Cross, 1993, p.4).

Assessment has long been categorised depending on the purpose of the evaluation into summative or formative. (Brown & Knight, 1994; Boud, 1995; Black & Wiliam, 1998; Bransford et al., 2000; Buchanan, 2000; Khan et al., 2001; Manogue et al., 2002; Velan et al., 2002). The former looks to measure performer during or at the end of a lesson, unit of study, etc. The latter refers to the help provided to the learner to improve their knowledge and skills. (Morss & Murray, 2005). With technology driven education over the past decades, teachers are focusing more on assessment for learning in which the role of the learner changed from passive to active. Thus, the role of the teachers transform from a dominant to a flexible position where their acting facilitate comprehension of ideas built on learners own cognitive conceptions. Self-assessment provides the pertinent mechanism for enhancing individual performance either on summative or formative evaluation. It is used in courses within the medical profession that implement CPD (continuing professional development) activities to disseminate their expertise and for staff development that is self directed and electronically delivered (Dornan, 2008).

Activities that contribute to assessment for learning include the use of detailed feedback, teacher questioning built on specific learning goals and self-assessment. Self-assessment in this context is formative assessment that provides feedback for reflection on learning activities. Feedback is the process used to indicate to the learner where and how their learning can be improved. This has long been recognized as an important instrument for improving education. Feedback on learning encompasses a great range on activities that provides diagnosis and remedial suggestions for changing future actions. Feedback can make students more effective, self-assessing, self-directed learners. Self-assessment provides the pertinent mechanism for enhancing individual performance. Meaningful feedback takes time to design and implement (Black et al, 2002) but it compensates the effort by actively engaging the learner and increasing the depth of student understanding in terms of increased performance in problem solving transfer questions (Evans & Gibbons, 2007). The experiment relates to Evans & Gibbons (2007) study experiment on the bicycle pump where it was found that the addition of interactivity increased the scores of transfer test but not the scores of retention tests.

Self-assessment is a kind of formative assessment that provides feedback to learners for reflection on learning activities. Interactivity plays a pivotal role in all scenarios. An interactive self-assessment question is a computer-based multiple-choice or text-entry question that requires input from the learner, and provides feedback based on that input (Evans, 2007). Interactive self-assessment questions to be effective must be designed following well established design principles. These principles applied to the design of web learning content create the playground to foster deep learning where interactivity plays a crucial role in student education. Research on the interactivity effect (Evans, 2007; Mayer, 2001) indicates that learner performance increases when they are exposed to a system which interactively reacts to their inputs using self-assessment questions.

However, the technology to work effectively must be embraced to pedagogical methods to elicit performance and provides a well guided element of interactivity. Interactive self-assessment questions to be effective must be designed following well established design principles (Mayer, 2001). These principles applied to the design of web learning content create the playground to foster deep learning where interactivity plays a crucial role in student education (Evans & Sabry, 2002). Basic characteristic of interactivity is learner control of the pace of a multimedia presentation which establishes that students learn better when they were allowed to control the pace of presentation of a narrated animation (Mayer and Chandler, 2001). Studies that allow students the freedom to interact and keep control of their own pace while learning in a computer based simulation shows evidence of higher performance (Mayer, Dow & Mayer, 2003). Research on the interactivity effect indicates that learner performance increases when they are exposed to a system which interactively reacts to their inputs by means of self-assessment questions (Evans & Gibbons, 2007).

This case study considers the effect of adding in a computer-based system used by undergraduate students at Brunel interactive self-assessment questions (ISAQ) described by Evans & Gibbons (2007) as computer-based multiple-choice or text-entry questions that require input from the learner, and provide feedback based on that input. The case involved two different types of ISAQs, designed to engage either memory (retention) or understanding (transfer), in an effort to determine which is the most effective. The study looks at retention and transfer as considered by Mayer (2001) where retention is the power to recognise or recall past learning events (surface learning), and the transfer skill involves recognition but also interpretation and implementation of that knowledge in a different context (deep learning). Two computer-based systems were designed to teach a lesson about how the circulatory system and the heart work in resemblance to others experiment developed by Evans & Gibbons (2007) and Mayer (Mayer, 2001; Mayer, Dow & Mayer, 2003; Moreno, Mayer, Spires & Lester, 2001) on how a bicycle pump works. A non-interactive component is added as a control group for comparison reasons. The experiment looks to measure the retention and transfer learning effects taking place in the learners and provides a degree of its effectiveness by using their scores. The study hypothesis infers that adding interactivity in the form of retention and transfer based self-assessment questions incorporated in a computer-based system will increase learning. The prediction is made on the basis that ISAQ helps the learner to identify misconceptions, create mental schemas that can be added to existing knowledge by providing constructive feedback and integrate them to form new skills or attitudes.

Methodology

Participants

A group of 30 students aged in between 21 and 30 from different ethnic backgrounds and gender participated in this study. Recruitment was made via email notification on a first come first served basis with £5.00 reward for participating in the experiment. Participants were not informed of the subject of the topic and the mechanism for knowledge acquisition. The pre-test exposed that all three groups possessed general prior knowledge about the heart function as can be seen from a mean score of 45% (SD=0.759) and highest score of 100%. Majority (85%) of students rated their knowledge of the heart higher than their knowledge about the circulatory system. Students were randomly divided into three groups: 10 in the ISAQ group (with retention type interactive self-assessment questions), 10 in the ISAQ group (with transfer type interactive self-assessment questions), and 10 in the nISAQ group (non- interactive self-assessment questions). They shared similar educational backgrounds and registered for studying MSc courses at Brunel University.

Materials and Apparatus

Material and apparatus are consistent with previous experiment developed by Evans (2008). Three interactive e-learning systems developed in Adobe Authorware 7 were designed to teach students how the heart and the circulatory system work. Their structure contains: a pre-test to determine student previous knowledge; the lesson explaining the main parts of the heart, the functioning of the circulatory system and how both relates to the process of pumping the blood in the human body; and a post-test to assess what the student learned. A computer laboratory with thirty computers running Microsoft Windows XP was the environment used to implement the study. The three content-identical systems consisted of two containing ISAQ components (retention and transfers interactive self-assessment questions), and one without it (the nISAQ: non- interactive self-assessment question). After a brief **introduction** was given on the procedures to operate the simulation, personal information was collected to keep general statistics about the groups.

The pre-test consisted of four questions designed to check the students' prior knowledge of the heart and the circulatory system. Two **Likert - scale** type questions were made for each topic where the learner required to rate his/her knowledge from very low (1) to very high. (Figure 1). Another two open-end questions were requiring

Figure 1. The Likert-scale pre-test question for each topic was introduced to the learners before starting the lesson

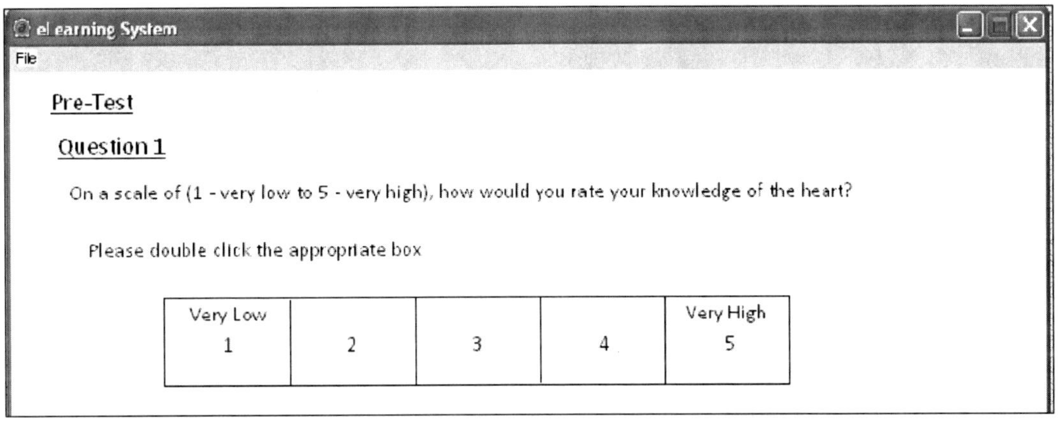

Figure 2. The open-end type pre-test question allows the learners to describe their previous knowledge about the subject

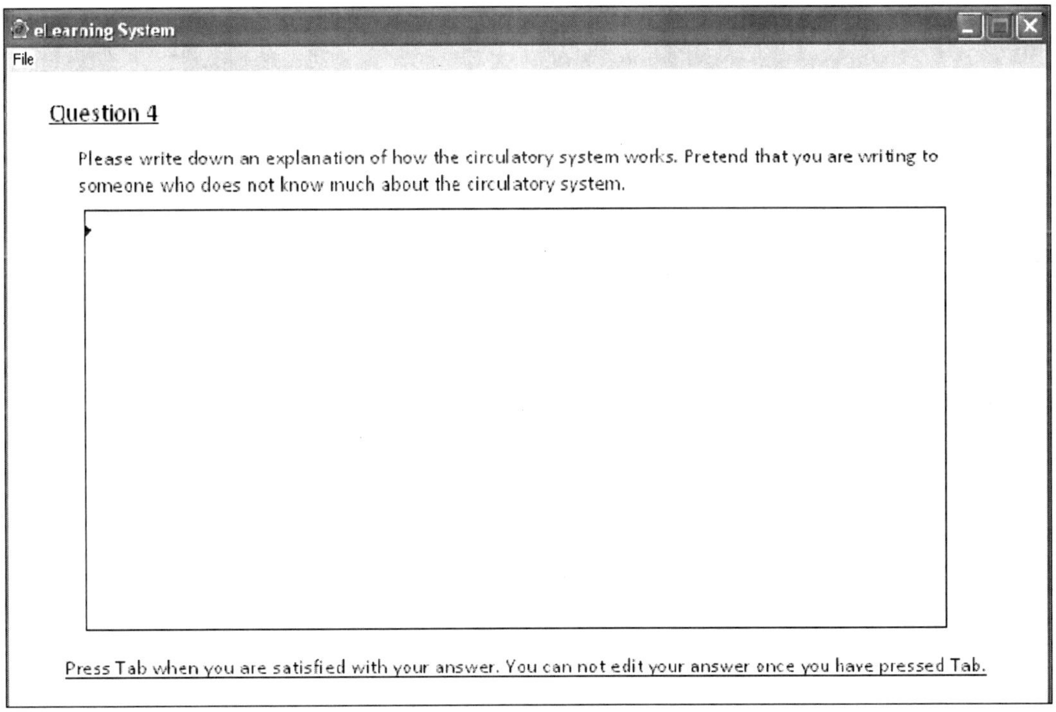

to type in an explanation of how the heart and the circulatory system works (Figure 2).

The lesson consisted of two components one related to the circulatory system and another to the heart. They kept this order during the online presentation. The circulatory system focuses on the 15 stages taken by the heart to pump the blood around the body (Figure 3 and Figure 4).

Figure 3. Screenshot of the animation describing one of the stages performed by the heart to pump blood around the body

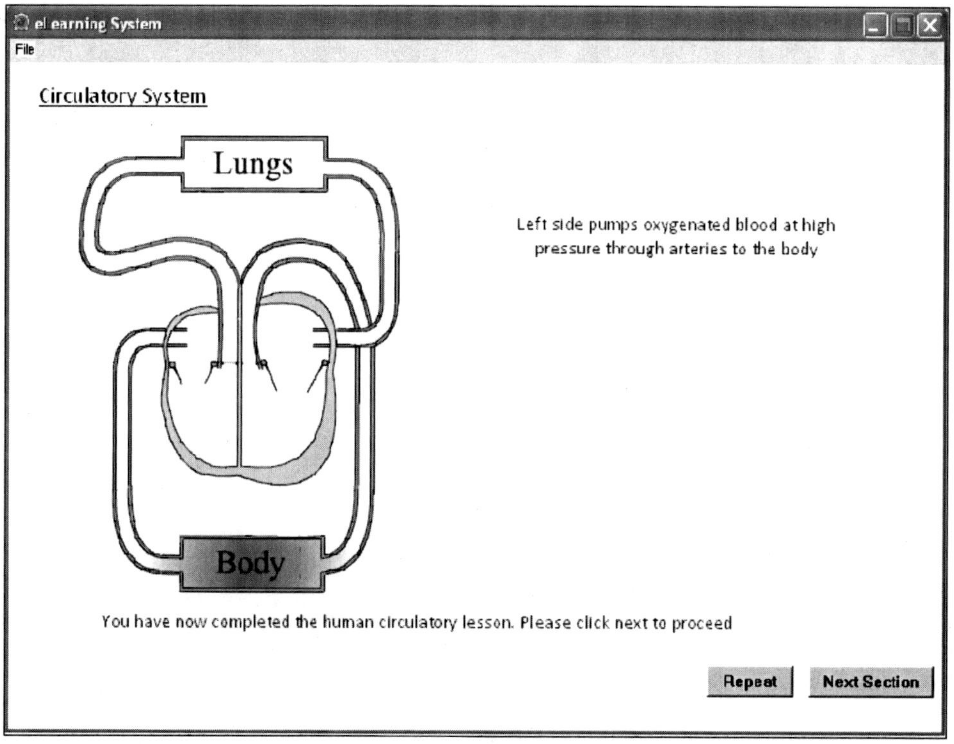

Figure 4. Screenshot of the animation describing parts of the heart

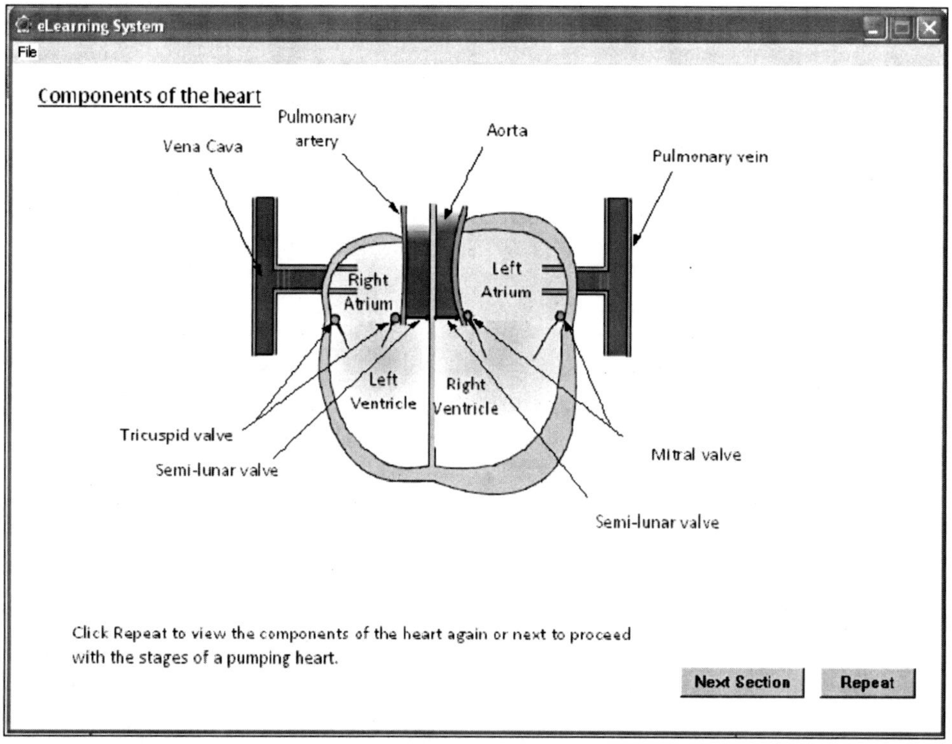

Atria systole

1. the left and right atrial muscles contract
2. the left and right atria decrease in volume
3. the pressure in the atria increases
4. the mitral and tricuspid valve open

Ventricular systole

5. The left and right ventricle muscles contract
6. The left and right ventricles decrease in volume
7. Pressure in valves increases
8. The mitral and tricuspid valves close (muscle)
9. The semi lunar valves opens
10. Blood flows into pulmonary artery and aorta.

Atria and Ventricular diastole

11. both muscles relax
12. atria increases in volume
13. pressure in valve decreases
14. Semi lunar valves close
15. Blood flows into atria.

These stages are related as we can see in the previous list to the four cardiac cycles in the heart: the Atria and Ventricular systole (contraction) and the Atria and Ventricular diastole (dilatation). This corresponds to other studies performed by Evans (Evans & Gibbons, 2007 - twelve-stage operation) and Mayer and Gallini's (Mayer and Gallini's, 1990 - ten-stage description) where the operation of a bicycle pump is used to study the interactivity effect.

The ISAQ mechanism located after the lesson content and before the post-test consisted of 8 multiple choice questions. The pedagogical design used to build them considers constructive feedback for both correct and incorrect answers. The structure of the questions contemplate distracters which are the incorrect answers presented as a choice in a multiple-choice test. The selected item could be dragged and dropped into an answer box (Figure 5). Then, constructive feedback pops up with a related explanation if incorrect the learner is allowed to repeat the question.

The ISAQ questions for the transfer and retention systems differ from one to another for obvious reasons. The retention ISAQs (rISAQ) provides questions pedagogically designed for retention while the transfer ISAQs (tISAQ) provides questions for deep learning. They both differ from the nISAQ system which doesn't include any feedback at all. Either type of ISAQs was kept consistent with the lesson content. In other words, the ISAQs information was formative assessment of the lesson material.

The learner controls the pace by means of two buttons located at the lower right part of the page that was kept identical through the entire system.

The post-test consisted of summative assessment that determines the final score of the student. It measures how much the learner retained or understood the lesson. It is located in the final part of the three systems and consisted of five retention questions and three transfer questions (See Figure 6).

RESULTS

The pre-test indicates that all three groups got low prior knowledge. The mean score average was 1.80 (SD.786) from a total average of a total 25 possible marks. Majority (85%) of students related their knowledge of the heart as (3) and the circulatory system as an average (2) very little knowledge. Students performed better on the transfer than on retention ISAQs setup. The means and standard deviations for the retention and transfer tests are given in Figure 7.

Evidence suggests that students in the rISAQ system had the best (M=1.87) performance compared the tISAQ (M=1.68) compared to nISAQ (M=1.32) in terms of overall scores.

Figure 5. The image here shows the initial interactive self-assessment question for the ISAQ systems. Dragging the right answer into the box triggers the feedback mechanism that allows proceeding to the next question

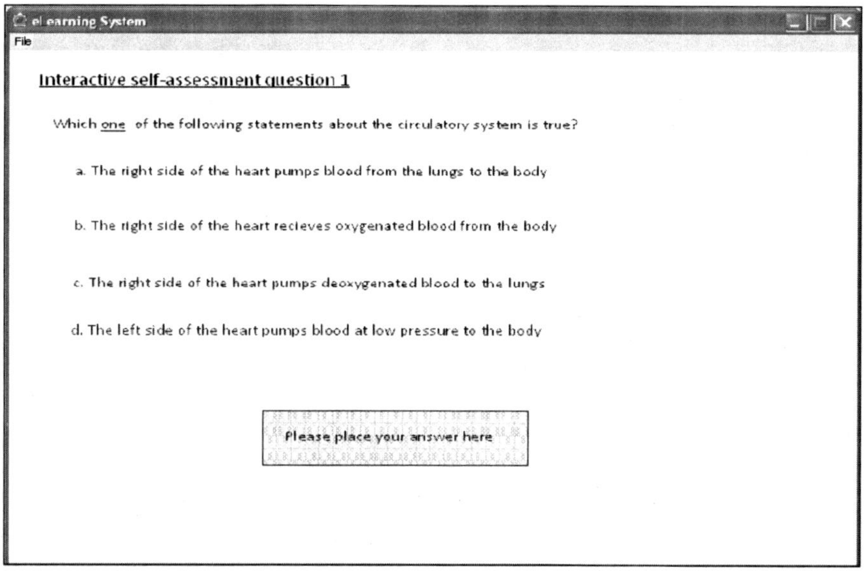

Figure 6. Example of a Post-test question

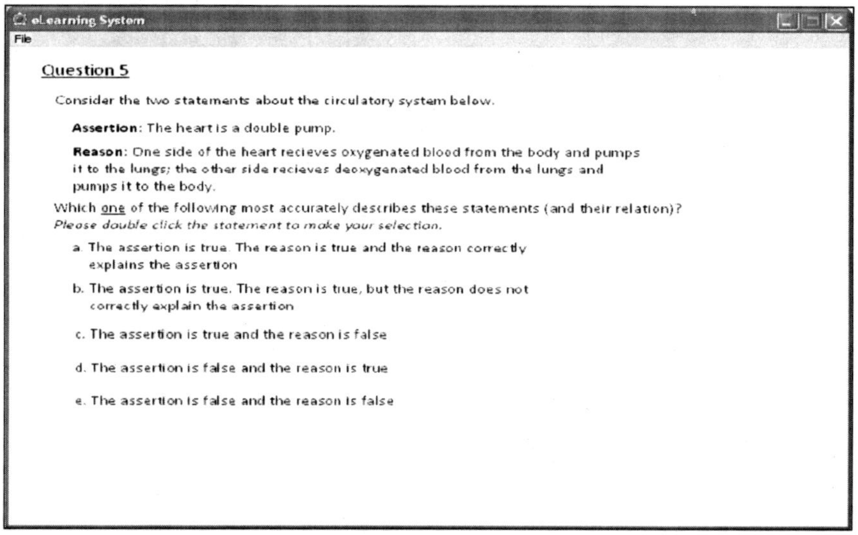

The findings conclude (Mirza, 2008) that overall transfer mean test scores was better in rISAQ (M=37, SD 3.40) as compared to tISAQ (M=32 SD.49) with nISAQ having the lowest mean (M=0.25, SD 0.42). The results are consistent with the interactivity principle which suggests that interactive self-assessment should increase deep learning by actively engaging students in the learning process.

A set of interviews were designed in order to collect the students' feedback (Mirza, 2008) It was deducted from the interviews that participants

Figure 7. Post test scores (Mirza, 2008)

System n=10	Retention		Transfer	
	M (out of 5)	SD	M (out of 3)	SD
rISAQ	1.87	.98	.37	.51
tISAQ	1.68	1.27	.32	.49
nISAQ	1.32	.57	.25	.42

Note: Number of participants (n) = 10 for each group M = mean Standard deviation (SD)

were positive about the help obtained from the navigation mechanism used to control the pace and interaction in the systems. This is consistent with Mayer & Anderson (1992) experiments that found out the negative effect of absent pacing control got on the test scores leading to cognitive overload. Students complain about the lesson structure, clarity of the lesson, but rate the whole experience as positive. All students interviewed indicated that the overall experience exceeded their expectations. They also felt they learned using the systems.

CONCLUSION

The experiment results may be interpreted as an indication that the use of ISAQs questions on eLearning system may promote deep learning. In the context of the experiment, the self-assessment questions clearly emphasize the importance of the interactivity effect as it is well documented in the literature. Evans & Gibbons (2007) for example found out in another experiment that the interactivity effect is clearly connected to increasing learning acquisition and enhancement of the learning experience. The ISAQs provide reflections on the new material and allow the amalgamation of the new and the existing knowledge by providing constructive feedback. The ISAQs have a beneficial impact in student learning performance because they are able to construct their own understanding of the material. The potential for this interactive self-assessment question in fostering students understanding are enormous.

The objective of this experiment was to determine as to what extent learning is increased using interactive self-assessment questions (ISAQs) within two multimedia e-learning systems. Two types of learning were investigated which were retention and transfer. Retention relates more to recognition whereas transfer is related to deep learning. The results are consistent with the interactivity principle which suggests that interactive self-assessment should increase deep learning by actively engaging students in the learning process. This suggests that educational designers, who seek to foster deep- rather than merely surface-learning, should incorporate interactive self-assessment questions in all their e-learning systems.

CURRENT CHALLENGES

Some implementation difficulties were presented due to lack of technical skills of the persons taking the test, students' availability, and small size of the sample that cause a negative impact on the experiment. However, they were overcome. The interviews were conducted manually which demanded considerable time for analyzing them. Future recommendation suggests an online approach for collecting students' opinion.

There are some other issues related to the complexity of the application design used to deliver the material. It was developed in Authorware with flash animations embedded that display interactive controls to navigate through it. Authorware is a popular visual authoring program for Windows and the Mac from Adobe widely used for creating interactive material. These movies were heavy and usually demanded significant time to be loaded in memory.

SOLUTIONS AND RECOMMENDATIONS

Recommendations from the point of view of implementing ISAQs in any other educational material are positive and focus on their pedagogical development. One of the essential elements is the constructive feedback. It must be related to the lesson and the difference between the correct answer and the distracters should be recognised by knowledge gained during the lesson. Future research will incorporate a set of retention ISAQs with another set of transfer ISAQs combined into one system. Retention questions will create a basic knowledge where deeper knowledge will seat over.

Another recommendation is related to the size of material in the lesson and the amount of ISAQ questions. Although they served the purpose of this particular experiment, the size of the lesson and the amount of questions could be increased for rehearsing purposes and for presenting a broader perspective of the same or similar subject being looked at from different angles.

There is also an issue about how long knowledge acquisition remains in memory and how it fades with time. An additional post test could be applied in order to determine how long does the knowledge last that has been learnt from the lesson. Another future recommendation is related to the ISAQ system designs. They need to be improved to target some inconsistencies in the navigation mechanism, loading time that delays some times the normal flow of the lesson; and more ISAQ questions to pedagogically address the lesson content.

ACKNOWLEDGMENT

The authors thank all the students who participated in the study and specially acknowledge contribution to the work done by Peter Spencer and Sabina Mirza.

REFERENCES

Angelo, T. A., & Cross, K. P. (1993). Classroom assessment techniques: A handbook for college teachers. San Francisco: Jossey-Bass.

Baddeley, A. (1992). Working memory. *Science*, *255*, 556–559. doi:10.1126/science.1736359

Baddeley, A. D. (1986). Working memory. Oxford, UK: Oxford University Press.

Black., et al. (2002). *The Global Information Technology Report 2001-2002: Readiness for the Networked World (World Economic Forum), USA*. New York: Oxford University Press Inc.

Black, P., & Wiliam, D. (1998). Assessment and classroom learning. *Assessment in Education*, *5*, 7–74. doi:10.1080/0969595980050102

Boud, D. (1995). Enhancing Learning through Self-Assessment. London: Routledge.

Bransford, J. D., Brown, A., & Cocking, R. (2000). How People Learn: Mind, Brain, Experience and School, Expanded Edition. Washington, DC: National Academy Press.

Brown, S., & Knight, P. (1994). Assessing Learners in Higher Education. London: Kogan Page.

Buchanan, T. (2000). The efficacy of a World-Wide Web mediated formative assessment. *Journal of Computer Assisted Learning, 16*, 193–200. doi:10.1046/j.1365-2729.2000.00132.x

Chandler, P., & Sweller, J. (1991). Cognitive load theory and the format of instruction. *Cognition and Instruction, 8*(4), 293–332. doi:10.1207/s1532690xci0804_2

Chandler, P., & Sweller, J. (1992). The split-attention effect as a factor in the design of instruction. *The British Journal of Educational Psychology, 62*, 233–246.

Dornan, T. (2008). Self-Assessment in CPD: Lessons From the UK Undergraduate and Postgraduate Education Domains. *The Journal of Continuing Education in the Health Professions, 28*(1), 32–37. doi:10.1002/chp.153

Evans, C., & Gibbons, N. J. (2007). The interactivity effect in multimedia learning. In Computers & Education, (pp. 1147 – 1160).

Evans, C., & Sabry, K. (2002). Evaluation of the Interactivity of Web-Based Learning Systems: Principles and Process. *Journal of Innovations in Education and Teaching International, 40*(1), 89–99.

Feinberg, S., & Murphy, M. (2000). Applying cognitive load theory to the design of web-based instruction. Technology & Teamwork, IEEE, 353-360.

Khan, K. S., Davies, D. A., & Gupta, J. K. (2001). Formative self-assessment using multiple true-false questions on the Internet: feedback according to confidence about correct knowledge. *Medical Teacher, 23*, 158–163. doi:10.1080/01421590031075

Manar, A. (2009). Brunel University. *Wiki-pedia.* Retrieved from http://en.wikipedia.org/wiki/Brunel_University

Manogue, M., Kelly, M., Masaryk, S. B., Brown, G., Catalanotto, F., & Delap, E. (2002). Evolving methods of assessment. *European Journal of Dental Education, 6*, 53–66. doi:10.1034/j.1600-0579.6.s3.8.x

Mayer, R., & Gallini, J. K. (1990). When is an illustration worth ten thousand words? *Journal of Educational Psychology, 82*, 715–726. doi:10.1037/0022-0663.82.4.715

Mayer, R. E. (1997). Multimedia learning: Are we asking the right questions? *Educational Psychologist, 32*, 1–19. doi:10.1207/s15326985ep3201_1

Mayer, R. E. (1999). The promise of educational psychology: Learning in the content areas. Upper Saddle River, NJ: PrenticeHall.

Mayer, R. E. (2001). Multimedia learning. New York: Cambridge University Press.

Mayer, R. E., & Anderson, R. B. (1992). The Instructive Animation: Helping students build connections between words and pictures in multimedia learning. *Journal of Educational Psychology, 84*, 444–452. doi:10.1037/0022-0663.84.4.444

Mayer, R. E., Dow, G. T., & Mayer, S. (2003). Multimedia learning in an interactive self-explaining environment: What works in the design of agent-based micro worlds? *Journal of Educational Psychology, 95*, 806–812. doi:10.1037/0022-0663.95.4.806

Mayer, R. E., & Moreno, R. (1998). A split-attention effect in multimedia learning: evidence for dual processing systems in working memory. *Journal of Educational Psychology, 90*, 312–320. doi:10.1037/0022-0663.90.2.312

Mayer, R. E., & Moreno, R. (2000). A Learner-Centered Approach to Multimedia Explanations: Deriving Instructional Design Principles from Cognitive Theory. *Interactive Multimedia electronic of computer enhanced learning, 2*, 2.

Mayer, & Chandler. (2001). When learning is just a click away: does simple user interaction foster deeper understanding of multimedia messages. *Journal of educational Psychology, 93*, 390-397

Mirza, S. (2008). *'Interactivity effect in E-learning systems'*. Unpublished Dissertation for the degree of Master of Science, Brunel University, UK.

Moore, M. G. (1989). Editorial: three types of interaction. *American Journal of Distance Education, 3*, 1–6.

Moreno, R., Mayer, R. E., Spires, H. A., & Lester, J. C. (2001). The case for social agency in computer-based teaching: do students learn more deeply when they interact with animated pedagogical agents? *Cognition and Instruction, 19*, 177–214. doi:10.1207/S1532690XCI1902_02

Morss, K., & Murray, R. (2005). Teaching at Universities: A guide for Postgraduates and Researchers. London: Sage Publications.

Paivio, A. (1986). Mental representation: A dual coding approach. Oxford, UK: Oxford University Press.

Scha¨r, S., & Krueger, H. (2000). Using new learning technologies with multimedia. *IEEE MultiMedia, 7*(3), 40–51. doi:10.1109/93.879767

Schrum, L., & Berge, Z. (1997). Creating student interaction within the educational experience: a challenge for online educators. *Canadian Journal of Educational Communication, 26*(3), 133–144.

Sweller, J. (1988). Cognitive load during problem solving: Effects on learning. *Cognitive Science, 12*, 257–285.

Sweller, J., & Chandler, P. (1994). Why some material is difficult to learn. *Cognition and Instruction, 12*, 185–233. doi:10.1207/s1532690xci1203_1

Sweller, J., Chandler, P., Tierney, P., & Cooper, M. (1990). Cognitive load and selective attention as factors in the structuring of technical material. *Journal of Experimental Psychology. General, 119*, 176–192. doi:10.1037/0096-3445.119.2.176

Velan, G. M., Kumar, R. K., Dziegielewski, M., & Wakefield, D. (2002). Web-based self-assessments in pathology with Questionmark Perception. *Pathology, 34*, 282–284. doi:10.1080/00313020220131372

ADDITIONAL READING

Clark, R. (2007). Developing Technical Training: A Structured Approach for Developing Classroom and Computer-based Instructional Materials, Pfeiffer

Clark, R., & Lyons, C. (2004). Graphics for Learning: Proven Guidelines for Planning, Designing, and Evaluating Visuals in Training Materials. Pfeiffer

Clark, R., Nguyen, F., & Sweller, J. (2005). Efficiency in Learning: Evidence-Based Guidelines to Manage Cognitive Load. Pfeiffer

Clark, R. C., & Mayer, R. E. (2003). E-learning and the Science of Instruction. San Francisco: Jossey-Bass.

Jonassen, D. H., & Reeves, T. C. (1996). Learning with technology: Using computers as cognitive tools. In D. H. Jonassen (Ed.), Handbook of research for educational communication and technology (pp. 693-719), New York: Macmillan.

Lohr, L. (2007). Creating Graphics for Learning and Performance: Lessons in Visual Literacy, Prentice Hall.

Mayer, R. (2005). The Cambridge Handbook of Multimedia Learning. New York: Cambridge University Press.

Mayer, R. E. (1996). Learning strategies for making sense out of expository text. The SOI model for guiding three cognitive processes in knowledge construction. Educational Psychology Review.

Mayer, R. E. (2001). Multimedia learning, New York: Cambridge University Press.

Mayer, R. E. (Ed.). (2005). The Cambridge Handbook of Multimedia Learning. New York: Cambridge University Press.

Tufte, E. R. (1990). The visual display of quantitative information. Cheshire, CT: Graphics Press.

KEY TERMS AND DEFINITIONS

E-Learning: The delivery of a learning, training or education program by electronic means. It involves the use of a computer or electronic device.

Multimedia: A presentation of content that relies on both text and graphics.

Multimedia Design: The art of creating multimedia content by combining sources of multiple media.

Interactivity: Can be considered the degree of responsiveness established in a two ways communication environment.

Interactive Multimedia System (IMS): A multimedia system in which related items of information are connected and can be presented together)

Interactive Self Assessment Questions (ISAQ): A computer-based multiple-choice or text-entry questions triggered by input from the learner, provides feedback based on that input. Self assessment is form of formative assessment.

Retention (Remembering): The ability to reproduce or recognize the presented material and is assessed by retention tests i.e. describe the six stages of atria and ventricular diastole.

Transfer (Understanding): ability to use presented material in novel situations and is assessed by transfer tests i.e. Write down possible consequences of failure of thc tricuspid and mitral valve during ventricular systole.

Chapter 21
The Challenges of Technology-Enhanced Instructional System in Nigeria

O. A. Sofowora
Obafemi Awolowo University, Ile-Ife, Nigeria

A. A. Adekomi
Obafemi Awolowo University, Ile-Ife, Nigeria

J.O.Adeyanju
Obafemi Awolowo University, Ile-Ife, Nigeria

T. A. Bada
Obafemi Awolowo University, Ile-Ife, Nigeria

L.M. Oyewusi
Obafemi Awolowo University, Ile-Ife, Nigeria

A.O. Egbedokun
Obafemi Awolowo University, Ile-Ife, Nigeria

Lanre Idowu
Obafemi Awolowo University, Ile-Ife, Nigeria

F.M Oyeniran
Obafemi Awolowo University, Ile-Ife, Nigeria

ABSTRACT

The development and deployment of innovative Information and Communication Technologies (ICTs) in higher education is being given prominent attention today. This is because of its pedagogical and socio-economic forces that include; greater information access; cost effectiveness, enhancement of collaboration and cooperation; and its ability to solve numerous problems confronting education in the developed and developing countries. It is also essential as it allows learners to acquire and exploit information within every sphere of human activities. However, the integration of technology into teaching and learning is facing some problems and challenges. This case presents an overview of the integration and application of modern technologies in providing higher quality teaching/learning in the Obafemi Awolowo University, (OAU), Nigeria, how to solve the problem of providing equitable access to education and how to improve the teaching and learning of Science and Technology in Post Basic Institutions using Technology Enhanced Instruction. It also highlights the problems, challenges and the lessons learnt from such innovation using OAU Ile-Ife as a case study of Nigeria.

DOI: 10.4018/978-1-61520-749-7.ch021

Table 1. A customer service approach to Distance Learning. Sources: cited from Aworuwa (2009)

Year	Total no of students who sat for UME	Total students admitted	Percentage
2000-2001	550,399	60,718	11%
2001-2002	749,727	9,769	12.1%
2002-2003	994,381	51,845	5.2%
2003-2004	1,o46,950	104,991	10.1%
2004-2005	841,878	122,492	14.5%

BACKGROUND

In Nigeria today, there are greater demands for university education. Every year there is a greater number of students than all the universities in the country can admit. According to Aworuwa (2009) quoting from the OAU Vice Chancellors speech to the Nigerian Tribune of 1st August2008, of the 30,000 qualified students that applied for admission, only 4,000 could be offered admission (0.13%) due to the problems of poor facilities, lack of space, shortage of academic staff, and poor funding. The situation is the same all year round. Aworuwa lamented the denial of educational access to thousands of qualified students (See Table 1).

Other problems facing university education in the country include overstretched facilities due to exponential increase in students enrolment, falling standard, high rates of drop out and failure, decreasing attractiveness of academic career to young and intelligent scholars .In addition to the above are other challenges of brain drain, obsolete equipment, negative attitude on both the part of the lecturers and students and poor economy.

Obafemi Awolowo University is one of the first generation universities established in1962 as University of Ife. It is situated in Ile-Ife (The Cradle of Yoruba Civilization) occupying a vast expanse of land totalling 11,861 hectares. It has 13 Faculties, 2 Colleges and 92 academics Departments. According to Impact (2008, P.1), "the mission of the University is to create a teaching and learning community for impacting appropriate skills, knowledge, behaviour and attitude, advance the frontiers of knowledge that are relevant to national and global development, engender a sense of selfless public service and promote African cultures and traditions." The vision of the university is of a top rated University in Africa, ranked among the best in the world and whose products occupy leadership position in the public and global economy. To achieve this, the University is to harness ICT, modern Technologies and economic strategies, build strong partnerships and linkages within and outside world and whose research works will contribute a substantial proportion of innovations to the Nigerian economy. It was based on the mission and vision statements that made the University seeks the assistance of The Carnegie Corporation and the World Bank to embark on eight projects in the first cycle: enhancement of Information and Communications Technology (ICT) capability and application to distance learning so as to solve the problems of equitable access to quality higher education. In order to solve this problems, Obafemi Awolowo University, decided to apply modern technology (ICT) which led to the inauguration of a committee that came up with a university ICT Policy. The policy includes: developing ICT to serve as the backbone of OAU Ile-Ife development strategies in the 21st century. It involves upgrading the current capability, integration and application of ICT to teaching – learning, research, health and other strategic area. Development of ICT and research in Distance Learning, computerization of the University library and the Bursary Department, development of the Computer Engineering Laboratory, enhancing teaching and learning of Science and Technology through virtual laboratories and remote experiment (INTECU 2006 p.3). This also led to the establishment of a Centre for Distance Learning (CDL), with the objective of providing a teaching -learning community based on technology (Technology Enhanced Instructional System) to provide more access to the teeming qualified students who could not gain admission either as a result of lack of space, distance, finance or physical disability. A sort of collaboration was made with different Departments such as: Educational Technology (DET), Information and Communication Technology Unit (INTECU), Centre for Distance Learning (CDL), Nursing Science, Management and Accounting. INTECU is to provide the necessary technology while DET is to design Technology Enhanced Instructional packages, and to provide the training and skills needed.

The success of the first project eventually gave birth to a new one called Strengthening Information and Communication Technology (ICT) and Educational Technology Infrastructure for Multi-Media Based Learning in Technology and Science. The latter is a new proposal submitted by the University for the STEP-B project sponsored by the World Bank. According to the project publication prepared by the project leaders and Director (Professors Adeniran, BickerSteth and Adagunodo 2007, p. 4) the project will address the problem of gender imbalance, improve the teaching and learning of Science and Technology crucial for the development of Nigeria. According to them, ICT facilities available in OAU Ile-Ife, will be provided through technology enabled instructional systems to students from selected Post-Basic Institutions like: Federal Polytechnic Ede, Adeyemi College of Education, Ondo (ACEO) Federals Science and Technical College, Ilesa (FSTCI), Federal Government Girls College, Ipetumodu (FGGCI) and Obafemi Awolowo University, International School (OAUIS). However the case under review is the former i.e. the collaborative effort between INTECU, DET, CDL and other departments at encouraging Technology Enabled Instructional System to solve the problem of large classroom enrolment, bringing education to those who are denied either because of distance, money, age, gender or the physically challenged. The major problems addressed in this study are presented in form of research questions.

SETTING THE STAGE

There are many crises facing the universities in the developing countries. They include increase in enrolment, overstretched existing facilities, space problem, poor economy and poor access to quality education. Nigeria being one of the developing countries shares similar problems. Nigeria is facing the challenges of providing equitable access to education and how to improve teaching and learning in the universities especially in Science and Technology. Not only this, every year only few of the qualified students seeking admission into the universities could be offered admission because of lack of space, poor facilities, shortage of academic staff and poor funding that are peculiar to all Nigerian universities.

Other problem is the gender disparity in the admission of students especially in the Science and the Technology courses. However, Obafemi Awolowo University, Ile-Ife because of its strategic position and being the foremost ICT university in the country took the lead to apply modern technologies to solve these problems. The integration of modern technologies into teaching and learning has its own problems and challenges especially in a poor economy. This paper therefore presents an overview of how OAU, Ile-Ife solved these problems in the face of bad economy through trans-institutional cooperation in order to reduce the cost.

Implementation Phases

The project of implementing Technology Enhanced Instruction is going to be completed in four different components:

i. Upgrading the ICT and Educational Technology infrastructure;
ii. Establishment of virtual laboratories through remote experimentation;
iii. Recording, production and delivery of web-based instructional modules; and
iv. Capacity building for staff, students and partnering institutions.

The first phase is concerned with provision of ICT facilities in all the units, departments, institutes, students' residential hostels and the main university library. This has been completed since 2003. The university moved into the next phase to upgrade the facilities provided earlier. The upgraded facilities included internet facilities to take care of video streaming, television instruction and video conferencing. It also included complete networking of the university library, the bursary department and the health centre. As of today, the Hezekiah Oluwasanmi Library at OAU, Ile-Ife is completely digitalized making it Virtual. The other phase was the complete overhauling of the Educational Technology facilities. The old analogue television transmitter was replaced with digital television equipment and the area of coverage extended to take care of distance learners who will be using the device when fully operational. A new digital radio transmitter was also purchased and has been installed. The station is called Great FM. It is also to compliment television instruction for large class enrolment and distance education. This was also done in preparation for the transition to the use of web –based instruction for all the university courses by the year 2010. It is hoped that by this year, students will be able to access these facilities on the web. In order to take care of the practical oriented science and technology courses, a virtual laboratory was established in collaboration with MIT in Massachusetts. The university management has also purchased the blackboard e-education platform, which had been installed. Presently the university is conducting a pilot study on the effectiveness of the blackboard for instruction. Training programmes are also being organized for all cadres of staff and students in phases. The last phase is the improvement of the teaching of Science and Technology courses in Post Basic Institutions (STEP-B). This project is on a wider scope as it involves secondary schools, technical colleges and colleges of education.

Managerial, Organizational and Technological Issues Involved

A committee was appointed by the university administration to manage the project. The committee is headed by the Vice Chancellor (Academic) and a Director who is a Professor of Computer Engineering. Others are selected members from the Budget and Bursary Departments responsible for the disbursement of finance. Other members constitute the technical, implementation, monitoring and evaluation units. There are other members outside the academic community, precisely from the Federal Ministry of Education Abuja, National University Commission, the World Bank and Carnegie Corporation. Internal members of the committee were selected from all the faculties, departments while other members were nominees from all the collaborating institutions.

In agreement with the implementation guidelines, many workshops were organized for the purpose of training technical staff, academics and other staff from related disciplines. Among them are: Web-Based Co-Curriculum Development (2003), Micolm-Golf (2004), Paul Bateman and Carnegie (2006), Summit on Distance Learning (2009) and Designing and Developing Web-Based Instruction using Blackboard e-education platform (2009). The Department of Educational Technology in collaboration with the Department of Management and Accounting and CDL have successfully designed an on-line Master Degree course in Business Administration (MBA). Similar programmes are being designed as undergraduate compulsory courses with very large student enrolment. The Department of Educational Technology also successfully carried out a pilot study on the effectiveness of multi-site teaching on second year Education students using one of the compulsory core courses. It was part of the attempt at solving the problem of large enrolment of students and lack of infrastructures.

REACTION FROM THE UNIVERSITY COMMUNITY

There were positive reactions from both the students and the lecturers. The student said the multi-site teaching project was motivating, user friendly and activity based. It was also found that technology enhanced instruction positively influenced student's attitude. While students that were exposed to the mode performed significantly better than those exposed to the traditional method. As a result of the positive impact, there were requests that all the courses in the University be taught using Technology Enhanced Instruction. Overall impact of this project was that problems of space was solved, students behaviour and attitudes improved. This was addressed by providing large plasma screens at strategic centres, halls of residence and lecture halls. Not only these lectures were beamed through television but they were also broadcast through Internet and radio. With this innovation, students do not necessarily need to sit in an over crowded classroom facing their lecturers to receive lectures in an un-conducive atmosphere. With the new method, students learn in relaxed mood and can even access lectures outside the university through television, radio and in text format on the Internet. However because of the limitation of bandwidth, it is not possible to have video conferencing and streaming. This problem is hoped to be addressed in the next phase, so that students any where in the country can receive both text and on-line video instruction through the Internet. From the feed back gathered from the questionnaire distributed and the sample used as case study, the data showed that 78.67% said it was user friendly while 75.34% said it aided their retention and comprehension. On the problem of access to higher education, the university is expanding the Centre for Distance Learning to encourage work place learning. To this end, the university has successfully purchased a blackboard e-education platform; and has put the facilities required in place. It has also established the permanent site at Moro, a satellite town close to O.A.U, Ile-Ife. With these new developments, students whether full-time, residential or part-time can receive lectures through multi-site technology, radio, television or Internet any where in Nigeria.

Technology Concerns and Components

For the purpose of this study, Technology Enhanced Instructional System is a different form of computer-based resources networked together for the purpose of teaching and learning. It includes multimedia teaching packages, Internet and World Wide Web. Adekomi (2004) defines it as the integration and utilization of innovative computer technology for the purpose of organizing, encoding, packaging and disseminating information in any teaching-learning environment without the constraint of time and space. According to the above scholar, it involves a continuous lifelong training process that does not require the physical presence of an instructor but demands constant monitoring. The monitoring process in this kind of system is ICT based. There are different ways of operating technology enhanced instructional system. They include:

(a) Computer Managed Instructional System (CMI) where organization of classroom, instructional materials and electronic evaluation of instruction are the major concerns.
(b) Computer Assisted Instruction (CAI). Here, there is no physical presence of the teacher. The learner individually interacts with the instructional packages in the computer that are designed by experts to meet specific instructional needs.

There are many other forms of technology enhanced instructional system like the e-learning, virtual classroom, on-line instruction, video conferencing, video streaming, web presentation, intelligent tutoring systems, cable television format, tele-lecture, multi-site learning and university digital library. For the purpose of this study, emphasis is placed on e-learning and multi-site learning. E-learning in our context refers to courses that are primarily text based with computer-mediated enhancement and specifically designed for distribution through the Internet. It incorporates a wide variety of learning strategies and technologies. It is also an alternative solution to the problems of accessibility, over population and a compliment to the didactic method of teaching and learning. It utilizes a wide variety of learning modes which includes: virtual laboratory, television and radio, mobile technologies, video conferencing, web-based technologies, and e-learning platforms.

Pedagogical Values of Operating Technology Enhanced Instructional System

There are numerous educational advantages of technology enhanced instructional systems. Among the authors that have been discussed here are; Cisco, Carter and Monaco (1987) speak on the skills needed to learn with ICTs and Chadwick (1994) discusses the future of on-line learning, Tiffin and Rajas Ingham (1995) provides the modalities for virtual classroom, while NGFL (1998) describes what virtual teacher centre is and its implications to teaching and learning, Soloway and His (1998) write on procedure for designing learning using learner centred approach, while Cisco (2000) explains how computers can be networked for quality education and Lukes (2000) and McGraw (2001) prescribe the infrastructures required for e-learning. From the literature, it is therefore evident that if any institution of higher learning and Nigeria is to meet the instructional demands for quality education, it must be technology driven and compliant. Pedro (2001) and Adekomi (2005) also belief that if the library is to provide its effective role as the back bone of any system of learning, then it must be prepared to use ICT to provide a very strong, effective and more reliable library facilities. Other advantages of technology enhanced instructional system are that:

- It encourages and ensures effective distributed learning;
- Technology enhanced instructional system may improve the effectiveness of university education by increasing education benefits and democratization of education;
- It removes distance and time constraint in any learning process;
- It ensures immediate provision of knowledge in relevant areas with ease and speed that could never be gotten from traditional learning system;
- The multiplier advantage of a networked instructional system ensures future educational excellence, expansion and efficiency at reduced cost; and
- It is the issue of the cost benefits that makes technology enhanced instructional system more imperative in Nigeria.

Table 2. E-learning technologies, pedagogical implications, technical implications and costs

e-learning technologies	Pedagogical implications	Technical implications (Technology required by institution and students)	Cost implications
Television/Radio	Effective utilization of either radio or television for instruction depends on the pre-production, production and the post-production. Other factors include learners expectation at the end of each scene	The equipment needed by the institution include transmitters PCs, camera, editing suites/software, audio/video mixers, capturing cards Receivers/white interactive boards, display screens, projectors Lightings of various forms, Animator microphones of different types outside broad casting van etc	Not easy to finance:-procurement, production, Graphics, animation, special effects are very expensive that extra-budgeting allocation is needed.
CD/DVD/CDROM	Necessary for students' self study. Also as backup to support training	Technologies needed include video capturing cards, CD/DVD writer or reader, MPEG 2 cards	The cost is higher than printed text materials. It is more time-consuming
Web-Based Technologies	Computer-with website creation, internet-based learning materials/ tutorials delivered need to be made accessible 24-hours, all days of the week. Fast, direct and interactive delivery of learning	On- line computer plus internet access. Faster band width, reliable and uninterrupted internet connections are required. Team of experts in web-cast/ webmaster, instructional designer, graphic artist, programmer and subject matter experts are also needed.	Internet subscription cost, high band width is required to allow video streaming. Hardware and technical expertise costly. Cost of alternate power generation needed in lieu of the epileptic power failure
Video-conferencing	The new pedagogical methods require interactive delivery. One to one communication/small group or tutor support. Video or telephone conversation	Equipment required include- Television monitors, video projector, cameras, micro phones, video conferencing codec, good lightings, multi- media and higher/faster band with	There are basically two types of costs ; (1) equipment for setting up the video conferencing system. (2) operation/maintenance
The e-learning platforms	- The pedagogical factors include structure of contents - Template for the inclusion of course content. - multi- media support for course presentation	Server - Platform hardware (blackboard e-education platform) - Operating system - Registration, administration/ organization Format should be standard HTML, RTF, MPEG, and JPEG or PDF.	Procurement of hard ware is costly. They are; - cost implications for - operation - maintenance - technical/administrative support annual license fee

COST, TECHNICAL AND PEDAGOGICAL IMPLICATIONS OF OPERATING TECHNOLOGY ENHANCED INSTRUCTIONAL SYSTEM IN NIGERIA

Here emphasis will be placed on television and radio, web-based technologies, video-conferencing and e-learning platforms for multi site teaching.

The table below is an example of the technology adapted at OAU. It explains the factors considered before making the final choice. The table contains the technologies adapted to solve the problems identified. They include: digital television and radio that students can access on the internet, DVD/CDROM and web based technology. The cost implications at every stage and the pedagogical consideration for their adoptions were also stated (see Table 2).

CHALLENGES OF OPERATING TECHNOLOGY ENHANCED INSTRUCTIONAL SYSTEM IN NIGERIA

A physical challenge is one of the many challenges of technology enhanced instructional system in Nigeria. According to Beebe, Kouku, Okeyinka and Rao (2003) physical constraints are not just in terms of a large room and how it is put to use but that of appropriate design and infrastructures. In Nigeria, there is shortage of infrastructure in most of our institutions. The problem has forced the National Universities Commission to peg the admission into universities in Nigeria based on available facilities. Every year millions of qualified youths could not gain admission because of lack of space and infrastructures. It is disheartening to see that in Nigeria, lives of youths who could have contributed to the growth, economy and the development of the country are being wasted due to lack of foresight and proper planning. South Africa and Senegal have successfully used ICT to solve some of these problems. It is hoped that when this programme is implemented nationally the problem of lack of access to higher education will be solved

Inadequate Fund

Financial resources are key factor to the successful integration and implementation of technology enhanced instructional system. It is known that countries that heavily invested on ICTs will reap greater benefits than those with limited investment. Nigeria is a clear example of a country with low financial investment in education. Lack of fund and its inadequacy has been a great challenge to the educational system. In most University today, existing facilities are in deplorable condition. According to Akinsola (2003) Government subvention to the universities is currently lower than the amount requested for over the years. An average of 52% of the requested fund had been released. Kehinde (2003) also says infrastructure and development in universities are static and deteriorating. While funding declined from 99% to 57%. The fund released by the Federal Government is 7.5% and below the UNESCO minimum recommendation of 26%. (See Table 3 and Table 4)

The implication of the above is that if there is not enough fund for staff emolument, teaching and research how then can we develop / integrate ICT into teaching and learning. With the current state of low investment into education, the speed and rate of developing, integrating and utilization of technology enhanced instructional system will be slow and very low as it is the case with us today. The inadequacy of fund for teaching and research in Federal Universities was part of the reasons for incessant strike actions by the Academic Staff Union of Universities (ASUU) in Nigeria over the decades. One of their numerous demands

Table 3. Schedule of fund required for Federal Universities (2003-to date). Source: ASUU Secretariat University of Ibadan, Nigeria

	2003	2004	2005	2006	Total
	(Supplementary)				
Sub Head	N billion	N billion	N billion	N billion	N billion
Recurrent	7	50	55	57.855	169.855
Capital	15	10	12	13.57	50.57
Restoration	10	15	18	22.17	65.17
Stabilization	3	5	5	5	18.00
Total	35	80	90	98.595	303.595

Table 4. Quantum of Funds required for the Universities in Nigeria. Source: ASUU (2003) Document Presented to the Technical Team

Year	Sub-Head Expenditure Recurrent	Amount specified in the 2001 Agreement	Amount Disbursed (D) to/Approved (A) for Universities by Government	Balance
2001	//	N60bn	N28.743bn (D)	N31.257bn
2002	//	N66bn	N30.645bn (D)	N35.355bn
2003	//	N138bn	(N34.757bn) (A)	N103.243bn
		Subtotal		N169.855bn
		CAPITAL EXPENDITURE		
2001	//	N20bn	N5.880bn (D)	N14.12bn
2002	//	N22bn	N2.050bn (D)	N19.95bn
2003	//	24bn	(N7.5bn) (A)	N16.5bn
		Subtotal		N50.57bn
		RESTORATION FUND		
2001	//	N18.6bn	-	N18.6bn
2002	//	N22.17bn	-	N22.17bn
2003	//	N24.4bn	-	N24.4bn
		Subtotal		N65.17bn
		STABILIZATION FUND		
2001	//	N6bn	-	N6bn
2002	//	N6bn	-	N6bn
2003	//	N6bn	-	N6bn
		Subtotal		N18bn
			GRAND TOTAL	N303.595b

has been the demand for better improvement in teaching and learning through the application of modern and improved technology. We are however grateful to the Carnegie Corporation and the World Bank for the present project at Obafemi Awolowo University Ile-Ife which have yielded positive result.

Scarcity of Qualified Network Staff/Staff Development

Panagiotis and Angeliiki (2003) speak on the need to train more ICT specialists because of greater demands for qualified network staff. Bates (1997), Pelgrum and Anderson (1984) and Adekomi (2004) also show the importance of staff professional training to ensure employee commitment to continue service and quality control. Adekomi is also of the view that network standard and quality must be ensured to minimize overdependence on individuals. According to Farrell (1999) training and workshops are not only needed to improve instructors skills, but also as a mean of getting them involved in the process of implementing and integrating ICTs in teaching and learning.

Increasing Security Demand

The Internet has recently become a full fledged commercial environment supporting the routine exchange of huge amounts of money and critical information. There are also individuals who are determined to steal. Today, internet fraud is so rampant; they have developed highly sophisticated tool kits to perpetrate their evil deed. Although higher institutions are not their targets but they are not left out as many of them are now on-line. With student registration, payment of fees and students academic results are now on-line many institutions now see the need for security. The need for security is also very important because research have shown that internet fraud is more rampant among Nigeria students/youths (Sofowora 2007).

Network Standards

There is the need to change/upgrade network standards as we increasingly depend on ICT for instruction. Consideration should be given to the need to upgrade to fast Ethernet, the combinations of IP telephony, and motion digital video. The Obafemi Awolowo University,Ile-Ife faced these challenges by upgrading its bandwidth from 256 to 512KBPS and changed from the wireless radio system to optical fibre-network which is 80% completion. The university decided to opt for fibre cabling though very costly because, it is capable of meeting further challenges of video streaming and voice over-IP which is necessary for the effective delivery of distance learning systems. Just as the World Wide Web (WWW) emerged a decade ago, there is also the likely possibility for "Killer Application" to emerge in the next five years in Nigeria. Killer Application includes Video and voice communication over the data network. New killer application could necessitate change from copper to fibre wiring. This need could be a big challenge. There may be need also to change network electronics, number of cables and possibly network interface equipment in the computer.

Challenges Arising from Participation/Collaboration

Collaboration implies joining hands in the development and utilization of ICT. The development of ICT has never been uniform in all institutions. Besides, the learners who will use it for instruction have their peculiarities, knowledge skills and training needs. Other challenges include non-familiarity with ICT, visual illiteracy and computer illiteracy. Another area is how the collaboration should be interpreted. Other questions that pose challenges are: should the collaboration be just program development, or fully financial collaboration? What will happen to training needs? Who is to handle the development of training packages? All these are factors that can prevent effective collaborations of ICT application in Nigeria. It can also equally reduce the quick growth of digital instruction in almost all of the third world countries. In Nigeria, there has been an attempt of collaboration among O.A.U., Ile-Ife, University of Jos, University of Port-Harcourt and other privately owned universities. The Open University in Abuja Nigeria also made such effort but such integration is facing serious problems and opposition because of attitude to change and lack of financial support. O.A.U., Ile-Ife also had similar experience and also heavy financial costs incurred during the ICT developmental stages.

Human Attitude

In Nigeria, it is not certain that we are fully mature and prepared in our attitude to use ICT for instruction. Many still believe in the conventional method of instruction and sourcing for information. Many still believe that surfing on the Internet is a waste of time while the majority are yet to be computer literate. There are fears among some groups that ICT introduction into the universities may lead to retrenchment of secretariat staff and confidential secretaries. Dirty environment, and epileptic power supply, carelessness and unwillingness to accept/observe and obey digital prompts and ineffective use of artificial intelligent of the computer are some of the additional shortcomings of the academics.

SOLUTIONS AND RECOMMENDATIONS

Relevant solutions to the above challenges demand a change of attitude on the part of all the stakeholders in the use of ICT for instruction. We must employ systems approach to training and implementation rather than the guerrilla approach. We should develop our own local software to meet our local needs with considerable international acceptance. The selection of our hardware must receive the conceptual re-orientation needed to foresee the future. However the most important solution is the need for increase collaboration between institutions of higher learning, the society and even the government. Effective collaboration and participation has enabled the United States to uphold a position of leadership in Sciences, ICT, Engineering and Mathematics. Broadening the reach of advanced networking to include all higher institutions would allow maximum possible participation in our national process of discovery and help to educate all those that can participate in scientific discovery in the next century. Every college that supports research will need to have access to advance networking to attract and retain research faculty.

Participation also promotes the discovery, integration, disseminations and acquisition of new knowledge. A partnership must be made between institutions of higher learning, state government, local industries, and the Internet industries (See Figure 1).

This structure is being proposed because it is not feasible for the federal government alone to single-handedly fund ICT extensively in every college and university in Nigeria. It is therefore recommended that a National Education Network Connections (NENC), leverage between private and various universities be pursued. This presupposes that the Federal government will provide support and funds for 2 years after which individual university will take over. Also each participating university should provide a written plan, commitment and engage in technical and financial cooperation. The institutions are also to provide regional access and key technical leadership for advanced networking.

Figure 1. Proposed participation structure for ICT driven instructional system for Nigeria

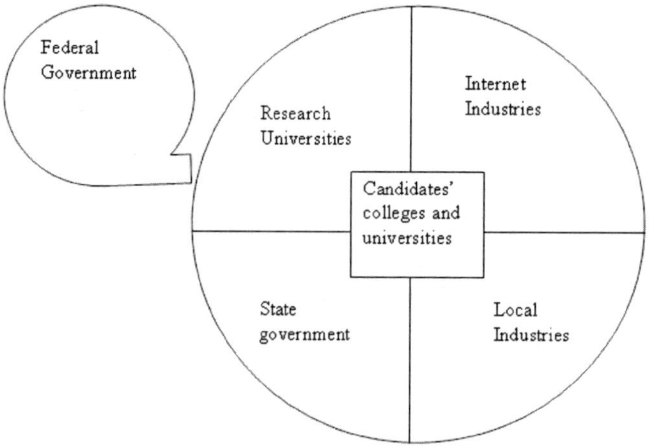

REFERENCES

Academic Staff Union of Universities. (2003). White Paper Document presented by the ASUU Negotiating Team to the Federal Government.

Adekomi, A. A. (2004). Virtual Library, what is it? A lead paper presented to the Nigeria Association of Librarian, Osun State Branch, Held of Obafemi Awolowo University, Ile-Ife, Nigeria.

Adekomi, A. A. (2005). *Using computer as a tool for Multigrade teaching*. Paper presented at the workshop organised by UNESCO in collaboration with National Universities Commission, Abuja.

Akinsola, A. A. (2003). *Distance learning and Information Technology within the context of the University Strategic Plan and Vision*. A Paper Presented During the Conference on African University Day Held at Obafemi Awolowo University Conference Centre, Ile-Ife, November 12, 2003.

Bates, A. W. (1997). Technology, open learning and distance education. London: Routledge.

Carter, C., & Monato, J. (1987). Learning, Information Technology Skills. Library and Information Research Report, 54, London: The British Library.

Castagnetti, C., & Luisa, R. (2007). *Effort allocation in tournaments: The effects of Gender on academic performance in Italian Universities*. Retrieved from http://apura.ub.unimuenchen.de/13441/ mpra.meda.ng13441,posted16thfebruary

Chadwick, N. (1994). The virtual college: An on- line learning future. The role of Technology in education. Glasgow, UK: SCET.

CISCO Systems Inc. (2000). *Reusable learning object strategy*. Retrieved from http://www.cisco.com/warp/public/10/wawtraining/acceping/implement/r/ostrategyv3-1.pdf

Denzin, N. K. (1970). The research acts: A theoretical introduction to sociological methods. Chicago: Aldine.

Farrell, G. M. (1999). The Development of virtual education: A global perspective. An Impact (2009) An appraisal of the impact of Carnegie Corporation grants to Obafemi Awolowo University, Ile-Ife, Nigeria. July 1, 2003- June 30, 2009.

Jbeengut, L. (1998). Quality Assurance in distance education through tutor training at Mauritius College of Air. *Open Praxis, 2*. Retrieved from http// www.org.za/worldbank/management/benefits/m43bmau.html

Kehinde, L.O. (2003). *Obafemi Awolowo University network backbone for open learning and distance Education in O.A. U., Ile-Ife*. A workshop organized by Distance Learning Centre, OAU, Ile-Ife, November 12, 2003.

Kouku, B., Oyeyinka, E. & Rao (Eds.), (2000). *Information Technology opportunity and Higher Education in Africa*. New York: Macmillan.

Laurillard, D. (2002). Rethinking University Teaching: A framework for effective use of learning technologies. London: Routledge.

Lukes, (2000). *Preparing Your Campus for a Network Future: EDUCAUSE Leadership Strategies No. 1* San Francisco: Jossey Bass Publishers.

McGraw, K. L. (2001). *E-Learning strategy and infrastructure*. Retrieved from http://wwlearningcircuits.org/2001/mcgrawhtml

Molla, A., & Licker, P. S. (2005). E-commerce adoption in developing countries; A model and instrument. *Information & Management, 42*, 877–899. doi:10.1016/j.im.2004.09.002

NGFL. (1998). *VTC-Virtual Teacher Centre (Reception)*. Retrieved from http://www.scotland.gov.ulc/library/ict/appendmove3.html

Paragiotis, Z., & Angeliki, P. (2003). Identifying training needs for ICT skills Enhancement in South-Eastern Europe; Implications for designing web based learning courses. *Educational Technology and Society*, *6*(1), 1–7.

Pedro, F. (2005). Comparing traditional and ICT-enriched university teaching methods: evidence from two empirical studies. *Higher Education in Europe*, *30*(4), 339–411.

Pelgrum, W. J., & Anderson, R. E. (1999). "ICT and the Emerging Paradigm for Life Long Learning: A World wide Educational Assessment of Infrastructure, Goals and Practice." International Association for the Evaluation of Educational Achievement. The Hague, The Netherlands: IEA Publications Enschede.

Sofowora, O.A. (2009). Perceived effect of GSM on older adults in south-western Nigeria. *Ethiopian Journal of Education and Science.*

Soloway, E., & His, S. (1998, April). *Learner-Centre design*. Paper presented at the CHI 98 Conference, Los-Angeles, CA.

Telematics Application Programme. (1998). *Project – t3, Telematics for teacher training*. Retrieved from http://www2.echo.lu/telematics/education/en/projects/files/ts.html

Tiffin, J., & Rajasinham, L. (1995). In search of the Virtual class: Education in an information society. London: Routledge.

ADDITIONAL READING

Alessi, S. M., & Trollip, R. S. (2001). Multimedia for learning: methods and development (3rd edition). Boston: Allyn and Bacon.

Bateman, A. (1995). Technology, Open learning and distance education. London: Routledge.

Briggs, J. (1999). Teaching for quality learning at University of Buckingham. Buckingham, UK: SHRE and Open University.

Brooks, D. W. (1997). Web-teaching: A guide to designing interactive teaching for the world wide web. New York: Plenum.

Doolittle, P. E. (2001). Multimedia learning: Empirical and practical applications. Virginia.

Ertmer, P. A., & Newby, T. J. (1996). The expert learner: strategic, self-regulated and reflective instructional science. Netherlands: Kluwer Academic Publishers.

Grugean, D. (1987). Educational Counseling and open learning. In M. Thorpe & D. Grugeon, (Eds.) Learning for Adults. Harlow, UK: Longman Open Learning.

Inglis, A., Ling, P., & Joosten, V. (1999). Delivering digitally: managing the transition to the knowledge media. London: Kogan Page.

Lockwood, F. (1992). Activities in Self-instructional text. London: Kogan Page.

Lockwood, F. (1994). Material production in open and distance learning. London: Paul Chapman Publishing.

Madux, C., Johnson, D., & Willis, J. (2001). Educational computer: Learning with tomorrow technologies. Boston: Allyn and Bacon.

Mayer, R. E. (2001). Multimedia learning. New York: Cambridge University Press.

McGregor, K. W. (2004). The utilization of computer generated animation in Agriculture, Power and Technology courses. Talenton State University.

Moore, M., & Tait, A. (2003). Open and distance learning: trends, policy and strategy considerations. Paris: UNESCO.

Schwartz, J. E., & Beicher, R. J. (1999). Essentials of Educational Technology. Boston: Allyn and Bacon.

Scriven, B. (1993). Trends and Issues in the use of communication technologies in distance education. In G. Davies & B. Semways, (Eds.), Tele teaching. North-Holland: Elsevier Science Publishers.

Seels, B., & Glasgow, Z. (1998). Making Instructional design decisions (2nd ed.). Upper Saddle River, NJ: Merrill.

Smith, P. L., & Ragan, T. (1999). Instructional design. New York: John Wiley & Sons.

Stewart, M. Wangira, K. & Wallace, T. (2009). Bridging the Knowledge divide: Educational technology for development. Charlotte, NC: Information Age Publication (IA).

KEY TERMS AND DEFINITIONS

Animation: This is a simulation of movement created by displaying series of pictures or frame.

Technology Enhanced Instructional System: These are all forms of computer-based resource networked together for the purpose of teaching and learning.

Multi-Site Teaching: It involves the use of multimedia in teaching where students can receive lectures at different locations within or outside the campus.

Intelligent Tutoring Systems: They are new generation of computer systems for supporting and improving learning and teaching. It also provides direct feedback to students.

Killer Application: These are Video conference, extensive network needing higher band width.

Video Conferencing: This is a device that provides a real time video and voice communication to another computer software or hardware device allowing other individuals to participate in a conference.

Virtual Classroom: Virtual classroom refers to a learning environment where the teacher and students are separated by space or time.

Voice Over IP: Technology that allows telephone calls to be made over computer networks. It converts human voice into digital packets and support real time and 2 way transmission of conversation using Internet protocol.

STEPB: This is a project developed by OAU, Ile-Ife to enhance the teaching and learning of Science and Technology in Post Basic Institutions in Nigeria. The programme is sponsored by the World Bank.

Compilation of References

Aarreniemi-Jokipelto, P. (2005). *T-learning Model for Learning via Digital TV.* Paper presented at the 16th EAEEIE Annual Conference on Innovation in Education for Electrical and Information Engineering (EIE), Lappeenranta, Finland.

Aarreniemi-Jokipelto, P., & Tuominen, J. (2004). Experiences with an Interactive Learning Environment in Digital TV. In *Proceedings of the 4th IEEE International Conference on Advanced Learning Technologies, ICALT 2004,* (pp. 296-300).

Abahussain, S. (1998). Implementation of interactive television technology in distance education higher learning program in Saudi Arabia (Doctoral dissertation, University of Southern California, 1998). *Dissertation Abstracts International, 60*(6), 132B, (UMI No. 9931904).

Abanmie, A. M. (2002). Attitude of high school students in Saudi Arabia toward computers (Doctoral dissertation, Mississippi State University, 2002). *Dissertation Abstracts International, 63*(2), 193B, (UMI No. 3043178).

Academic Staff Union of Universities. (2003). White Paper Document presented by the ASUU Negotiating Team to the Federal Government.

Adams, J., & Defleur, M. H. (2006). The Acceptability of Online Degrees Earned as a Credential for Obtaining Employment. *Communication Education, 55*(1), 32–45. doi:10.1080/03634520500343376

Adekomi, A. A. (2004). Virtual Library, what is it? A lead paper presented to the Nigeria Association of Librarian, Osun State Branch, Held of Obafemi Awolowo University, Ile-Ife, Nigeria.

Adekomi, A. A. (2005). *Using computer as a tool for Multigrade teaching.* Paper presented at the workshop organised by UNESCO in collaboration with National Universities Commission, Abuja.

Adler, P.S. & Kwon. (2002). Social Capital: Prospects for a New Concept. *Academy of Management Review, 27*(1), 17–40. doi:10.2307/4134367

Aelterman, A. (2006). Sets of Standards for External Quality Assurance Agencies: A comparison. *Quality in Higher Education, 12*(3), 227–233. doi:10.1080/13538320601050996

Ahamer, G. (2004). Negotiate your Future: Web Based Role Play. *Campus-Wide Information Systems, 21*(1), 35–58. doi:10.1108/10650740410512329

Ahamer, G. (2009). A geo-referenced method to project trends into the long future. In *Proceedings of the Third Central Asia GIS Conference - GISCA'09, Austria-Central Asia Centre for GIScience ACA*GIScience,* Bishkek, Kyrgyzstan, (pp. 85-90).

Ahamer, G., & Strobl, J. (2009). Learning across Social Spaces. In S. Mukerji & P. Tripathi, (Eds.), Cases on Transnational Learning and Technologically Enabled Environments. Hershey, PA: IGI Global.

Ahamer, G., Car, A., Marschallinger, R., Wallentin, G., & Zobl, F. (2009). How to map perspectives: Moving GISc to IISc. In *Proceedings of the ICIT'09 conference in* Amman, Jordan.

Ahlquist, R. (1991). Position and imposition: Power relations in a multicultural foundations class. *The Journal of Negro Education, 60*(2), 158–169. doi:10.2307/2295607

Ajjan, H., & Hartshorne, R. (2008). Investigating faculty decisions to adopt Web 2.0 technologies: Theory and empirical tests. *The Internet and Higher Education, 11*(2), 71–80. doi:10.1016/j.iheduc.2008.05.002

Akinsola, A. A. (2003). *Distance learning and Information Technology within the context of the University Strategic Plan and Vision.* A Paper Presented During the Conference on African University Day Held at Obafemi Awolowo University Conference Centre, Ile-Ife, November 12, 2003.

Al-Arfaj, A. H. (2001). The perception of college students in Saudi Arabia towards distance WBI (Doctoral dissertation, Ohio University, 2001). *Dissertation Abstracts International, 62*(11), 191B, (UMI No. 3032949).

Al-Dawood, K., & Al-Kasabi, S. (2001, February). *ATM-based solution to facilitate distance learning at KSU.* Paper presented at the 16th National Computer and Educational Conference, Riyadh, Saudi Arabia.

Alegre, O. M., & Villar, L. M. (2006). Evaluación de la formación en línea del profesorado universitario. Evaluation of online faculty development. Madrid: Visión libros.

Alegre, O. M., & Villar, L. M. (2007). *Experto Universitario en Evaluación de la Calidad en la Enseñanza Superior. Segunda Edición.* Expert Degree of Evaluation at ULPGC. Unpublished Evaluation Report.

Al-Erieni, S. A. (1999). Attitudes of King Saud University faculty toward development and implication of a telecommunications-based distance education program as an alternative to conventional teaching (Doctoral dissertation, George Mason University, 1999). *Dissertation Abstracts International, 60* (10), 248B, (UMI No. 9948544).

Alessi, S. M., & Trollip, S. R. (2001). Multimedia for learning: methods and development (3rd edition). Boston: Allyn and Bacon.

Ali, N., & Ferdig, R. (2002). Why not Virtual Reality?: The barriers of using virtual reality in education. In C. Crawford et al. (Eds.), *Proceedings of Society for Information Technology and Teacher Education International Conference 2002,* (pp.1119-1120). Chesapeake, VA.

Allbeck, J. M., & Badler, N. I. (2004). Creating Embodied Agents With Cultural Context. In S. Payr, & R. Trappl (eds.), Agent Culture: Human-Agent Interaction in a Multicultural World, (pp. 107—126). London: Lawrence Erlbaum Associates.

Allen, M. W. (2007). Designing Successful E-Learning. San Francisco, CA: Pfeiffer.

Allen, M., Bourhis, J., Burrell, N., & Malbry, E. (2002). Comparing Student Satisfaction With Distance Education to Traditional Classrooms in Higher Education: A Meta-Analysis. *American Journal of Distance Education, 16*(2), 83–97. doi:10.1207/S15389286AJDE1602_3

Allesi, S. M., & Trollip, S. R. (2001). Multimedia for Learning: Methods and Development, (3rd ed.). Boston: Allyn and Bacon

Allport, G. W. (1954). The nature of prejudice. Reading, MA: Addison-Wesley.

Ally, M. (2006). Foundations of Educational Theory for Online Learning. In Theory and Practice of Online Learning. Athabasca, Canada: Athabasca University Publications, Athabasca University.

Al-Mogbel, A. (2002). Distance education in Saudi Arabia: Attitudes and perceived contributions of faculty, students, and administrators in technical college (Doctoral dissertation, University of Pittsburgh, 2000). *Dissertation Abstracts International 64* (01), 95B, (UMI No. 3078818).

Al-Rashoud, A., & Al-Abdul-Kareem, M. (2001, February). *Interactive distance learning over the Internet and the intranet.* Paper presented at the 16th National Computer and Educational Conference, Riyadh, Saudi Arabia.

Althaus, S. (1997). Computer-mediated communication in the university classroom: An experiment with on-line discussion. *Communication Education, 46*, 158–174. doi:10.1080/03634529709379088

American Society for Training and Development. (2001). E-learning glossary. Retrieved February 5, 2004, from http://www.learningcircuits.org/glossary.html

Andersen, P. A. (2000). Explaining intercultural differences in nonverbal communication. In L. A. Samovar, & R. E. Porter (eds.), Intercultural communication: A reader. Belmont, CA: Wadsworth.

Anderson, L. W., & Krathwohl, D. R. (2001). A Taxonomy for Learning, Teaching, and Assessing: A Revision of Bloom's Taxonomy of Educational Objectives. New York: Longman.

Anderson, M. (2000). Individual Characteristics and Web-based Courses. In C. R. Wolfe (Ed.), Learning and teaching on the Word Wide Web (pp. 47-73). San Diego: Academic Press.

Anderson, T. (2005). A learning theory for the digital age. *International Journal of Instructional Technology and Distance Learning, 2*(1).

Anderson, T. (2008). The theory and practice of online learning. Athabasca, CA: Athabasca University Press.

Angelo, T. A., & Cross, K. P. (1993). Classroom assessment techniques: A handbook for college teachers. San Francisco: Jossey-Bass.

Annan, K. (1999). Speech given to the Millennium Assembly. In Gourley, B. (2004). *'The Digital Divide: Solution or Problem.'* Paper Presented at the All Africa Ministers Conference on Distance Education.

Arenson, K. W. (1998, November 2). More colleges plunging into uncharted waters of online courses. *New York Times,* (p. A14).

Arkansas Department of EducationDistance Learning Center. (2009). Retrieved May 26, 2009, from http://dlc.k12.ar.us/

Arnold, M. (2003). Intranets, community, and social capital: The case of Williams Bay. *Bulletin of Science, Technology & Society, 23*(2), 78–87. doi:10.1177/0270467603251297

Arthur, M. F. (1998, July). *Barriers affecting adoption of distance education programs.* Paper presented at the Pennsylvania State University Fifth Distance Education Symposium, Philadelphia.

Askar, P. (2005). Distance education in Turkey. In C. Howard, J. Boettcher, L. Justice, K. Shenk, P. L. Rogers & G. A. Berg (Eds) Encyclopedia of distance learning, (Vol 2, pp. 635–640). Hershey, PA, Idea Group Inc.

Asmal, K. (2004). *Prospects, Possibilities and Perils: Distance education's response to Africa's development needs.* Paper Presented at the *2004 All Africa Ministers Conference on Distance Education*, Cape Town, South Africa. Retrieved November 8, 2007 from http://www.polity.org.za/article.php?a_id=46293

Auerbach, E. (1992). Making meaning, making change: participatory curriculum development for adult ESL literacy. Washington DC: Center for Applied Linguistics; McHenry, IL: Delta Systems.

Auernheimer, G. (2003). Einführung in die interkulturelle Pädagogik [Introduction to Intercultural Pedagogy]. Darmstadt, Germany: Wiss. Buchges.

Ausburn, L. J. & Ausburn, F. B. (2004). Desktop virtual reality: A powerful new technology for teaching and research in industrial teacher education. *Journal of Industrial Teacher Education, 41(4).* Retrieved March 2, 2007, from scholar.lib.vt.edu/ejournals/JITE/v41n4/ausburn.html

Ayers, J. A. Hunt, & T. Quinn (Ed.), Teaching for social justice (xxvii-xlvi). New York: The New Press.

Aylett, R. S., Dias, J., & Paiva, A. (2006). An affectively-driven planner for synthetic characters. In [Cumbria, UK: AAAI Press.]. *Proceedings of ICAPS, 2006*, 2–10.

Baartman, L. K. J., Bastiaens, T. J., Kirschner, P. A., & Vleuten, C. P. M. (2007). Evaluating assessment quality in competence-based education: A qualitative comparison of two frameworks. *Educational Research Review*, *2*, 114–129. doi:10.1016/j.edurev.2007.06.001

Bada, E., & Okan, Z. (2000). Students'Language Learning Preferences. *TESL-EJ, 4*(3), May 2000.

Baddeley, A. (1992). Working memory. *Science*, *255*, 556–559. doi:10.1126/science.1736359

Baddeley, A. D. (1986). Working memory. Oxford, UK: Oxford University Press.

Bailenson, J. N., Blascovich, J., & Guadagno, R. E. (2008). Self representations in immersive virtual environments. *Journal of Applied Social Psychology*, *38*(11), 2673–2690. doi:10.1111/j.1559-1816.2008.00409.x

Baird, M. A., & Monson, M. K. (1992). Distance education: Meeting diverse learners' needs in a changing world. *New Directions for Teaching and Learning*, (51): 65–76. doi:10.1002/tl.37219925108

Baker, K., Pulles, R., & Sasno, P. (2004). *Terminal Architecture Issues for Interactive and Reactive TV media using MHP-Java and MPEG4*. Paper presented at the IEEE International Symposium on Consumer Electonics, University of Reading, UK.

Bales, R. F. (1976). Interaction process analysis: A method for the study of small groups. Chicago: University Press.

Ballantyne, R., Borthwick, J., & Packer, J. (2000). Beyond Student Evaluation of Teaching: Identifying and Addressing Academic Staff Development Needs. *Assessment & Evaluation in Higher Education*, *25*(3), 221–236. doi:10.1080/713611430

Bandura, A. (1973). Aggression: a social learning analysis. Englewood Cliffs, NJ: Prentice-Hall.

Bandura, A., & Adams, N. E. (1977). Analysis of self-efficacy theory of behavioral change. *Cognitive Therapy and Research*, *1*(4), 287–310. doi:10.1007/BF01663995

Banks, J. A. (2006). Cultural diversity and education: Foundations, curriculum, and teaching. Boston: Allyn & Bacon.

Banta, T. W. (2003) (Ed.). Portfolio Assessment: Uses, Cases, Scoring and impact. San Francisco: Jossey-Bass

Barajas, M., & Owen, M. (2000). Implementing virtual learning environments: looking for a holistic approach. *Educational Technology and Society*, *3*(3), 39–53.

Barbour, M. K., & Reeves, T. C. (2009). The reality of virtual schools: A review of the literature. *Computers & Education*, *52*, 402–416. doi:10.1016/j.compedu.2008.09.009

Barkley, E. F., Cross, K. P., & Mayor, C. H. (2005). Collaborative learning techniques: A handbook for college faculty. San Francisco: Jossey-Bass.

Barmeyer, C. (2003). Interkulturelles Coaching [Intercultural Coaching]. In C. Rauen (ed.), Handbuch Coaching (pp. 241 – 272). Göttingen: Hogrefe.

Barnes, S. (2003). Computer-mediated communication: Human-to-human communication across the Internet. Boston: Pearson Education.

Baron, J. (1998). Teaching on-line across cultures. In A. Gooley, C. Pearson, & S. Towers et al. (Ed.), *Proceedings of the 3rd International Conference on Open Learning* (pp. 67-72). Brisbane: Queensland Open Learning Network.

Bartley, J. M. (2006). Assessment is as assessment does: a conceptual framework for understanding online assessment and measurement. In M. Hricko & S. L. Howell, (eds.), Online Assessment and Measurement Foundations and Challenges (pp. 1-45). Hershey, PA: Information Science Publishing.

Bates, A. W. (1997). Technology, open learning and distance education. London: Routledge.

Bates, A. W. (2000).Managing technological change. San Francisco, CA: Jossey-Bass.

Bates, A. W. (2001). National strategies for e-learning in post- secondary education and training. Paris: UNESCO /IIEP.

Bates, T. (2001). National strategies for e-learning in post secondary education and training. In Fundamentals of Educational Planning, (No. 70). Paris: UNESCO.

Bates, T., & Poole, G. (2003). Effective Teaching with Technology in Higher Education: Foundations for Success. San Francisco: Jossey-Bass.

Baylor, A. L. (2001). Permutations of control: Cognitive considerations for agent-based learning environments. *Journal of Interactive Learning Research*, *12*(4), 403–425.

Baylor, A. L., & Ryu, J. (2003). Evidence that multiple agents facilitate greater learning. International Artificial Intelligence in Education (AI-ED), Sydney, Australia.

Bazargan, A. (2000). Internal evaluation as an Approach to Revitalize University Systems: The case of I.R. Iran. *Higher Education Policy*, *13*(2), 173–180. doi:10.1016/S0952-8733(99)00024-0

Bazargan, A. (2002). *Teaching Statistics to Medical Doctors through Research Methods: A case of Medical Education in Iran.* Paper Presented at the 6th International Conference of Teaching Statistics on Developing Statistically Literate Society, Cape Town, South Africa. Retrieved May 25, 2008 from http://www.stat.auckland.ac.nz/~iase/publications/1/4f1_baza.pdf

Bazargan, A. (2004). Enhancing Institutional Capacity for Evaluation and Quality Assurance in Higher Education Systems: International Experiences and National Requirements for Organizational Development. [in Persian]. *Majlis and Pajouhesh*, *41*, 141–158.

Bazargan, A. (2007). Problems of Organizing and Reporting Internal and External Evaluation in Developing Countries: The case of Iran. *Higher Education Quarterly*, *13*(3), 207–214. doi:10.1080/13538320701800126

Bazargan, A. (2008). A Proposal for Establishing "Iran Universities Quality Network" (in Persian). *Computer Report (Journal of Informatics Society of Iran), 180*, 24-27. Retrieved on May 25, 2009 from http://www.isi.org.ir/Magezin/180/24.asp

Bazargan, A. (2009). The Role of e-learning in transnational Medical Education. In *Proceedings of the 2nd Conference of e-Learning in Medical Sciences.* Tehran University of Medical Sciences, Tehran, Iran, January 29-30,2009. (in Persian)

Bazargan, A., et al. (2008). Final Report of a Survey on Transnational Education in Iran. Tehran, Iran: Institute for Research and Planning in Higher Education.

Beach, R., & Lundell, D. (1998). Early adolescent's use of computer-mediated communication in writing and reading. In P.D. Pearson & A. Iran-Nejad (Ed.), Review ofResearch in Education, 23, (pp. 235-275). Washington, DC: American Educational Research Association.

Beard, L. A., Harper, C., & Riley, G. (2004). Online Versus On-Campus Instruction: Student Attitudes & Perceptions. Tech Trends. *Linking Research & Practice to Improve Learning*, *48*(6), 29–31.

Beggs, T. A. (2000). Influences and barriers to the adoption of instructional technology. In *Proceedings of the Fifth Annual Mid-South Instructional Technology Conference*, Middle Tennessee State University, Murfreesboro. Retrieved August 21, 2003, from http://www.mtsu.edu/~itconf/proceed00/beggs/beggs.htm

Belanger, F., & Jordan, D. H. (2000). Evaluation and implementation of distance learning: Technologies, tools and techniques. Hershey, PA: Idea Group.

Bellotti, F., Vrochidis, S., Ramel, S., Tsampoulatidis, I., Lhoas, P., & Pellegrino, M. (2008). A Technological Framework for the Authoring and Presentation of T-learning Courses. [iJET]. *International Journal of Emerging Technologies in Learning*, *3*(4), 10–19.

Bem, S. (1993). The lenses of gender. New Haven, CT: Yale University Press.

Bennett, M. (1986). A developmental approach to training for Intercultural Sensitivity. *International Journal of Intercultural Relations*, *10*(2), 179–195. doi:10.1016/0147-1767(86)90005-2

Bennett, M. (1998). Intercultural communication: a current perspective. In M. Bennett (ed.), Basic Concepts of Intercultural Communication. Yarmouth, MA: Intercultural Press.

Bennett, M. J. (1993). Towards enthnorelativism: A developmental model of intercultural sensitivity. In M. Paige (ed.), Education for the intercultural experience. Yarmouth, MA: Intercultural Press.

Benson, A. D. (2003). Assessing participant learning in online environments. *New Directions for Adult and Continuing Education*, *2003*(100), 69–78. doi:10.1002/ace.120

Benson, P. (2000). Autonomy as a learner's and teacher's right. In B. Sinclair, et al. (eds), Learner Autonomy, Teacher Autonomy; Future Directions, (pp. 111-117). London: Longman.

Berge, Z. L. (1998). Barriers to online teaching in post-secondary institutions: Can policy changes fix it? *Online Journal of Distance Learning Administration*, *1*(2). Retrieved July 18, 2003, from http://www.westga.edu/~distance/Berge12.html

Berge, Z. L., & Muilenburg, L. Y. (2000). Barriers to distance education: A factor analytic study. *American Journal of Distance Education*, *15*(2), 7–22.

Berge, Z., & Collins, M. (1995). Computer-mediated communication and the Online classroom in distance learning. *Computer-Mediated Communication Magazine*, *2*(4). Retrieved June 7, 2009, from http://www.ibiblio.org/cmc/mag/1995/apr/berge.html

Bergen Communiqué. (2005). *The European Higher Education Area: Achieving the goals: Communiqué of the Conference of European Ministers Responsible for Higher Education, Bergen, 19-20 May 2005.* Retrieved May 10, 2009, from http://www.bologna-bergen2005.no/Docs/00-Main_doc/050520_Bergen_Communique.pdf

Berman, S. (1997). Civil society and political institutionalization. *The American Behavioral Scientist*, 40(*5*), 562–574. doi:10.1177/0002764297040005003

Bernhaupt, R. Obrist, M. Tscheligi M. (2007): Usability and usage of iTV services: lessons learned in an Austrian field trial. *Computers in Entertainment, 5*(2).

Berry, J. W., Poortinga, Y. H., Segall, M. H., & Dasen, P. R. (2002). Cross-cultural psychology: Research and applications. Cambridge, UK: Cambridge University Press.

Bersin, J. (2004). The Blended Learning Book: Best Practices, Proven Methodologies, and Lessons Learned. San Francisco, CA: Jossey-Bass.

Betts, K. S. (1998). Factors influencing faculty participation in distance education in postsecondary education in the United States: An institutional study (Doctoral dissertation, The George Washington University, 1998). *Dissertation Abstracts International, 59*(7), 445B, (UMI No. 9900013).

Bhabha, H. K. (1994). The location of culture. New York: Routledge.

Bichelmeyer, B. A., Misanchuk, M., & Malopinsky, L. (2000, October). *Adapting a master's course to a Web: Principles, strategies and recommendations.* Paper presented at the 23rd National Convention of the Association for Educational Communications and Technology, Denver, CO, (ERIC Document Reproduction Service No. ED455808).

Birenbaum, M. (2003). New insights into learning and teaching and their implications for assessment. In M. Segers, F. J. R. C. Dochy, & E. Cascallar (Eds.), Optimising new modes of assessment: In search of qualities and standards, (pp. 13–36). Dordrecht, The Netherlands: Kluwer Adademic Publishers.

Birenbaum, M., Breuer, K., Cascallar, E., Dochy, F., Dori, Y., & Ridgway, J. (2006). EARLI position paper. A learning integrated assessment system. *Educational Research Review*, *1*, 61–67. doi:10.1016/j.edurev.2006.01.001

Black, J. (1997). *Online students fare better.* Retrieved July 15, 2002, from http://www .news.com/News/Item/0,4,7147,00.html

Black, P., & Wiliam, D. (1998). Assessment and classroom learning. *Assessment in Education, 5,* 7–74. doi:10.1080/0969595980050102

Black, P., Harrisson, C., Lee, C., Marshall, B., & Wiliam, D. (2003). Assessment for Learning: Putting it into practice. Berkshire, UK: Open University Press.

Black., et al. (2002). *The Global Information Technology Report 2001-2002: Readiness for the Networked World (World Economic Forum), USA.* New York: Oxford University Press Inc.

Blanco-Fernandez, Y., Pazos-Arias, J. J., Gil-Solla, A., Ramos-Cabrer, M., Barragans-Martinez, B., & Lopez-Nores, M. (2004). A multi-agent open architecture for a TV recommender system: A case study using a Bayesian strategy. In *Proceedings of the Sixth IEEE International Symposium on Multimedia Software Engineering,* Miami, FL.

Bodley, J. H. (1994). Cultural Anthropology: Tribes, states, and the global system. Mountain View, CA: Mayfield Pub. Co.

Bologna Declaration. (1999). *The European Higher Education Area: The Bologna Declaration of 19 June 1999. Joint Declaration of the European Ministers of Education.* Retrieved May 10, 2009, from http://www.bologna-berlin2003.de/pdf/bologna_declaration.pdf

Bond, M. H. (Ed.). (1996). The Handbook of Chinese Psychology. Hong Kong: Oxford University Press.

Bonk, C. J., & Cunningham, D. J. (1998). Searching for learner-centered, constructivist, and sociocultural components of collaborative educational learning tools. In C. J. Bonk & K.S. King, (Ed.), Electronic collaborators: learner-centered technologies for literacy, apprenticeship, and discourse (pp25-50). Mahwah, NJ: L. Erlbuam Associates.

Bonku, E., Sampson, W., Aboagye, P., Combary, P., Engelbrecht, S., & Kiplinger, N. (2004). Evaluation of an Alternative Self-paced Learning (SPL) Approach for Training Safe Motherhood Service Providers in the Upper West and Northern Regions of Ghana. PRIME II/IntraHealth International.

Borde, D. (2007). Psychosoziale Potentiale und Belastungen der Migranten – globale, institutionelle und individuelle Perspektiven [Psycho-social potentials and burdens of migrants – global, instituational and individual perspectives]. In D. Borde, & M. David (ed.), Migration und psychische Gesundheit. Frankfurt am Main, Germany: Mabuse.

Borzak, L. (1981) (ed.). Field study: A source book for experiential learning. Beverly Hills, CA: Sage Publications.

Boud, D. (1995). Enhancing Learning through Self-Assessment. London: Routledge.

Bourdieu, P. (1997). The Forms of Capital. Education: Culture, Economy, and Society, (pp. 46-58). A. H. Halsey, H. Lauder, P. Brown, & A. S. Wells (Eds.). Oxford, UK: Oxford University Press.

Bower, B. L. (2001). Distance education: Facing the faculty challenge. *Online Journal of Distance Learning Administration, 4*(2). Retrieved June 13, 2003, from http://www.westga.edu/~distance/ojdla/summer42/bower42.html

Boyinbode, O. K., & Akinyede, R. O. (2008). Mobile Learning: An Application of Mobile and Wireless Technologies in Nigerian Learning System. *International Journal of Computer Science and Network Security, 8*(11), 386–392.

Brady, L. (2004). The role of interactivity in web-based educational material. *Usability News, 6* (2). Retrieved December 15, 2006, from http://psychology.wichita.edu/surl/usabilitynews/62/interactivity.htm

Bransford, J. D., Brown, A., & Cocking, R. (2000). How People Learn: Mind, Brain, Experience and School, Expanded Edition. Washington, DC: National Academy Press.

Braunstein, B., Meloni, C., & Zolotareva, L. (2000). The U.S. –SiberLink Internet Project. *TESL-EJ, 4*(3), May 2000.

Breen, P. (2006). The Education of Language Teachers in East Asia. *Asian EFL Journal, 13*(1). Retrieved from http://www.asian-efl-journal.com/pta_july_06_pb.php

Breen, P. (2008). Maritime Lessons for the Digital Age. *Research Paper on how online learning can make a positive contribution to British universities - submitted to Association of Learning Technology Conference 2008.*

Brooks, M. (1997). Beyond teaching and learning paradigms: Trekking into the virtual university. *Teaching Sociology, 27*, 1–14. doi:10.2307/1319107

Brown, G., Bull, J., & Pendlebury, M. (1997). Assessing Student Learning in Higher Education. New York: Routledge.

Brown, J. (2000). Growing up digital: how the web changes work, education, and way people learn. *Change*. Retrieved 5/22/2009, from http://www.usdla.org/html/journal/FEB02_Issue/article01.html

Brown, J. D., & Rodgers, T. S. (2002). Doing Second Language Research. New York: Oxford University Press.

Brown, R. E., & Reed, C. S. (2002). An Integral Approach to Evaluating Outcome Evaluation Training. *The American Journal of Evaluation, 23*(1), 1–17.

Brown, S., & Knight, P. (1994). Assessing Learners in Higher Education. London: Kogan Page.

Brown, S., Race, P., & Bull, J. (Eds.). (1999). Computer-assisted assessment in higher education. London: Kogan Page.

Brown, T. H. (2005). Towards a Model for m-Learning in Africa. *International Journal on E-Learning, 4*(3), 299–315.

Brownlow, A. (2005). A Geography of Men's Fear. *Geoforum, 36*, 581–592. doi:10.1016/j.geoforum.2004.11.005

Bruning, R., Siwatu, K.O., & Liu, X., PytlikZillig, L.M., Horn, C., Sic, S., & Carlson, D. (2008). Introducing teaching cases with face-to-face and computer-mediated discussion: Two multi-classroom quasi-experiments. *Contemporary Educational Psychology, 33*(2), 299–326. doi:10.1016/j.cedpsych.2006.11.002

Buchanan, T. (2000). The efficacy of a World-Wide Web mediated formative assessment. *Journal of Computer Assisted Learning, 16*, 193–200. doi:10.1046/j.1365-2729.2000.00132.x

Burchell, J. (2001). Online Education: a viable role in postgraduate nursing curricula. Nursing Monographs, (pp. 30-35). Darlinghurst, Australia: St Vincent's Health Care Campus, Sisters of Charity Health Service Darlinghurst.

Burt, R. S. (2000). The network structure of social capital. *Research in Organizational Behavior*, 22, 345–423. doi:10.1016/S0191-3085(00)22009-1

Butcher, D. (2002, May). Six professors discuss time online. *The Chronicle of Higher Education*, A32.

Butcher, N. (2004). *Financing Distance Education Programmes in African Education: A Guide for Sound Investment.* Paper presented at the All-Africa Minister's Conference on Open Learning and Distance Education.

Byrne, D. (1971). The attraction paradigm. New York: Academic Press.

Cameron, L., Rutland, A., Brown, R., & Douch, R. (2006). Changing children's intergroup attitudes toward refugees: Testing different models of extended contact. *Child Development, 77*(5), 1208–1219. doi:10.1111/j.1467-8624.2006.00929.x

Campbell, J. K. (1998). The WWW for the students: a theoretical basis for using the WWW in Foreign Language Instruction. Paper for American Council of Foreign Languages, Chicago.

Canale, M., & Swain, M. (1979). Theoretical bases of communicative approaches to second language teaching and testing. Toronto: Ontario Institute for Studies in Education.

Canarian Agency for the University Evaluation and Accreditation (ACECAU). (n.d.). Retrieved May 7, 2009, from http://www.acecau.org/en/actividades.html

Carey, J. (1996). *Winky Dink To Stargazer: Five Decades Of Interactive Television*. Paper presented at the Interactive Television 1996, Edinburgh, Scotland.

Carroll, J. (1993). Human cognitive abilities: A survey of factor-analytic studies. New York: Cambridge University Press.

Carron, A. V., Widmeyer, W. N., & Brawley, L. R. (1985). The development of an instrument to assess cohesion in sport teams: The Group Environment Questionnaire. *Journal of Sport Psychology, 7*, 244–266.

Carter, C., & Monato, J. (1987). Learning, Information Technology Skills. Library and Information Research Report, 54, London: The British Library.

Caspi, A., & Blau, I. (2008). Social presence in online discussion groups: testing three conceptions and their relations to perceived learning. *Social Psychology of Education, 11*, 323–346. doi:10.1007/s11218-008-9054-2

Cassell, J., Sullivan, J., Prevost, S., & Churchill, E. (2000). Embodied Conversational Agents. Cambridge, MA: MIT Press.

Castagnetti, C., & Luisa, R. (2007). *Effort allocation in tournaments: The effects of Gender on academic performance in Italian Universities*. Retrieved from http://apura.ub.unimuenchen.de/13441/mpra.meda.ng13441,posted16thfebruary

Castells, M. (1996-8). *The Information Age: Economy, Society and Culture*. Cambridge, MA: Blackwell.

Cegles, K. A. (1998). Emerging issues affecting distance education research and practice in higher education: A global futures perspective. *Dissertation Abstracts International, 59* (8), 320B, (UMI No. 9901000).

Chadwick, N. (1994). The virtual college: An on- line learning future. The role of Technology in education. Glasgow, UK: SCET.

Chandler, P., & Sweller, J. (1991). Cognitive load theory and the format of instruction. *Cognition and Instruction, 8*(4), 293–332. doi:10.1207/s1532690xci0804_2

Chandler, P., & Sweller, J. (1992). The split-attention effect as a factor in the design of instruction. *The British Journal of Educational Psychology, 62*, 233–246.

Chapelle, C. A. (1999). Theory and Research: Investigation of 'Authentic' Language Learning Tasks. In J. Egbert, & E. Hanson-Smith, (Eds.), CALL Environments: research, Practice and Critical Issues. Alexandria, VA: Teachers of English to Speakers of Other Languages.

Chay, J. C. (2000). *3D Mental Rotation Test*. Retrieved August 16, 2004, from http://www.uwm.edu/People/johnchay/mrp.htm

Chen, G., & Chiu, M. (2008). Online discussion processes: Effects of earlier messages' evaluations, knowledge content, social cues and personal information on later messages. *Computers & Education, 50*(3), 678–692. doi:10.1016/j.compedu.2006.07.007

Chen, H. (2002). *Interaction In distance education*. Retrieved June 25, 2009, from http://seamonkey.ed.asu.edu/~mcisaac/disted/week2/7focushc.htmlhttp://seamonkey.ed.asu.edu/~mcisaac/disted/week2/7focushc.html

Chen, Z. (2006, July). *Cultural Influence on Learner's Behaviour in an On-line English Teacher Training Course*. Paper presented at the 2nd International Chinese Learners Conference, University of Portsmouth.

Cherepski, D. D. (2000). *Factors that encourage or discourage faculty participation in teaching Web-based courses in two-year colleges*. Unpublished doctoral dissertation, University of Arkansas, Little Rock, AR.

Chickering, A. & Ehrmann, S. C. (1996, October). Implementing the seven principles: Technology as lever. *AAHE Bulletin*, 3-6.

Chomsky, N. (1965). Aspects of the Theory of Syntax. Cambridge, MA: MIT Press.

Chong, S. M. (1998). Models of asynchronous computer conferencing for collaborative learning in large college classes. In C. J. Bonk & K. S. King (Ed.), Electronic collaborators (pp.157-182). Mahwah, NJ: Lawrence Erlbaum.

Christensen, T. K. (2008). The Role of Theory in Instructional Design: Some Views of an ID practitioner. *Performance Improvement*, *47*(4), 25–32. doi:10.1002/pfi.199

Christianson, L. (2001). Teaching on the World Wide Web: A descriptive investigation of WBI in nursing undergraduate education (Doctoral dissertation, Kent State University, 2001). *Dissertation Abstracts International*, *62*(5), 256B, (UMI No. 3014147).

Christopher, M., Thomas, J., & Tallent-Runnels, M. (2004). Raising the Bar: Encouraging High Level Thinking in OnlineDiscussion Forums. *Roeper Review*, *8*(3), 166171.

Chung, L. H., & Gibbons, P. T. (1997). Corporate Entrepreneurship: The roles of ideology and social capital. *Group & Organization Management*, *22*(1), 10–30. doi:10.1177/1059601197221004

Chute, A. G., Thompson, M. M., & Hancock, B. W. (1999). The McGraw-Hill handbook of distance learning. New York: McGraw-Hill.

CISCO Systems Inc. (2000). *Reusable learning object strategy*. Retrieved from http://www.cisco.com/warp/public/10/wawtraining/acceping/implement/r/ostrategyv3-1.pdf

Clark, M. C. (1993). Transformational learning. *New Directions for Adult and Continuing Education*, *1993*(57), 47–56. doi:10.1002/ace.36719935707

Clark, R. E. (1983). In Taylor, J. (1995), Distance Education Technologies: the fourth generation. *Australian Journal of Educational Technology*, *11*(2), 1–7.

Clark, T. (1993). Attitudes of higher-education faculty toward distance education: A national survey. *American Journal of Distance Education*, *7*(2), 19–33. doi:10.1080/08923649309526820

Clarke, D. (2006). *Games and e-learning*. Retrieved on February, 12, 2008 from CaspianLearning.co.uk/whtp_caspian

Clay, M. (1999). *Development of training and support programs for distance education instructors*. Retrieved September 10, 2003, from http://.westga.edu/~distance/clay23.html

Clay, M. (1999). *Faculty attitudes toward distance education at the State University of West Georgia*. Retrieved September 10, 2003, from http://www.westga.edu/ ~distance/attitudes.html

Clay, M., & Cazden, C. (1992). A Vygotskian interpretation of reading recovery. Vygotsky and Education: Instructional Implications and Applications of Sociohistorical Psychology, (pp. 206-222).

Clayton, M. (2002, April). *Communities of learners: Connecting students to maximize learning*. Paper presented at the Seventh Annual Mid-South Instructional Technology Conference, Murfreesboro, TN, ERIC Document Reproduction Service No. ED464628.

Coelho, J., & Rocio, V. (2008). A Study on Moodle's Performance. EDEN annual conference. Lisbon, Portugal, June 12-14, 2008.

Cohen, D. J., & Blair, C. (1998). Mental rotation and temporal contingencies. *Journal of the Experimental Analysis of Behavior*, *70*, 203–214. doi:10.1901/jeab.1998.70-203

Colley, A. M., Gale, M. T., & Harris, T. A. (1994). Effects of gender role identity and experience on computer attitude components. *Journal of Educational Computing Research*, *10*, 129–137.

Collis, B., & Moonen, J. (2001). Flexible Learning in the Digital Age. London: Kogan Page.

Comeaux, P., & McKenna-Byington, E. (2003). Computer-mediated communication in online and conventional classrooms: some implications for instructional design and professional development programmes. *Innovations in Education and Teaching International, 40*(4), 348–355. doi:10.1080/1470329032000128387

Connick, G. P. (Ed.). (1999). The distance learner's guide. Upper Saddle River, NJ: Prentice Hall.

Constantino-Gonzalez, M., Suthers, D., & Escamilla, J. (2003). Coaching web-based collaborative learning based on problem solution differences and participation. *International Journal of Artificial Intelligence in Education, 13*(2-4), 263–299.

Core, M., Traum, D., Lane, H. C., Swartout, W., Gratch, J., van Lent, M., & Marsella, S. (2006). Teaching negotiation skills through practice and reflection with vVirtual humans. *Simulation, 82*(11), 685–701. doi:10.1177/0037549706075542

Cotton, K. (2003). *Computer-assisted instruction.* Retrieved January 10, 2004, from the Northwest Regional Educational Laboratory website http://www.nwrel.org/scpd/sirs/5/cu10.html

Crang, M. (2000). Public Space, Urban Space and Electronic Space: Would the Real City Please Stand Up? *Urban Studies (Edinburgh, Scotland), 37*(2), 301–317. doi:10.1080/0042098002203

Crawford, C. (2004). Non-linear instructional design model: eternal, synergistic design and development. *British Journal of Educational Technology, 35*(4), 413–420. doi:10.1111/j.0007-1013.2004.00400.x

Crichton, S., & Childs, E. (2008). Looking forward: stories of practice. In *Education for a digital world: Advice, guidelines, and effective practice from around the globe.* Vancouver: BCcampus and Commonwealth of Learning. Retrieved on August 8, 2009 from http://www.irrodl.org/index.php/irrodl/article/view/722/1237

Crossman, D. M. (1997). The evolution of the World Wide Web as an emerging instructional technology tool. In B. H. Kahn (Ed.), Web-based instruction, (pp. 19-23). Englewood Cliffs, NJ: Educational Technology.

Cuban, L. (1997, May 21). High-tech schools and low-tech teaching. *Education Week on the Web, 16.* Retrieved September 7, 2003, from http://www.edweek.org/ew/vol-16/34cuban.h16

Cummins, J. (2000). Language, power and pedagogy: bilingual children in the crossfire. Buffalo, NY: Multilingual Matters.

Curtis, D. D., & Lawson, M. J. (2001). Exploring Collaborative Online Learning. *Journal of Asynchronous Learning Networks, 5*(1), 21–34.

D'Antoni, S. (2006). The Virtual University: Modules and messages, lessons from case studies. Paris: UNESCO /IIEP.

Dalgarno, B. (2002). The potential of 3D virtual learning environments: A constructivist analysis, *E-JIST, 5*(2). Retrieved July 20, 2008, from http://www.usq.edu.au/electpub/e-jist/docs/Vol5 No2/Dalgarno/Final.pdf

Daphne, J. W., & Hsiao, L. (2009). *CSCL theories: cognitive apprenticeships.* Retrieved September 8, 2009, from http://www.edb.utexas.edu/csclstudent/Dhsiao/theories.html

Daugherty, M., & Funke, B. L. (1998). University faculty and student perceptions of Web-based instruction. *Journal of Distance Education, 13*(1). Retrieved August 20, 2003, from http://cade.athabascau.ca/vol13.1/daugherty.html

Davies, T. N. (1973). Visual perception of engineering drawings. *Engineering Designer,* 21- 31.

Davis, A. (2006). Developing an infrastructure for online learning. In T. Anderson & F. Elloumi (Eds.), *Theory and Practice of Online Learning.* Athabasca, Canada: AUPress. Retrieved April 7, 2007 from, http://cde.athabascau.ca/online_book/ch4.html

Davis, M. H. (1996). Empathy – a social psychological approach. Madison, WI: Brown & Benchmark Publishers.

Davis, N. E., & Roblyer, M. D. (2005). Preparing teachers for the "schools that technology built": Evaluation of a program to train teacher for virtual schooling. *Journal of Research on Technology in Education*, *37*(4), 399–409.

de Rosis, F., Pelachaud, C., & Poggi, I. (2004). Transcultural Believability in Embodied Agents: A Matter of Consistent Adaptation. In S. Payr, & R. Trappl (eds.), Agent Culture: Human-Agent Interaction in a Multicultural World (pp. 75-106). London: Lawrence Erlbaum Associates.

Dede, C., Ketelhut, D. J., Whitehouse, P., Breit, L., & McClosky, E. M. (2009). A Research Agenda for online professional development. *Journal ofTeacher Education*, *60*(1), 8–19. doi:10.1177/0022487108327554

Delcourt, M. A. B., & Kinzie, M. B. (1993). Computer technology in teacher education: The measurement of attitudes and self-efficacy. *Journal of Research and Development in Education*, *27*, 35–41.

Dennis, L. (1970). Dewey's Brief for the Fine Arts. *Studies in Art Education*, *11*(3), 3-8. Retrieved from http://www.jstor.org/stable/1319771

Denzin, N. K. (1970). The research acts: A theoretical introduction to sociological methods. Chicago: Aldine.

Derudder, B., Devriendt, L., & Witlox, F. (2007). An Empirical Analysis of Former Soviet Cities in Transnational Airline Networks. *Eurasian Geography and Economics*, *48*(1), 95–110. doi:10.2747/1538-7216.48.1.95

Desimone, L. M. (2009). Improving Impact Studies of Teachers' Professional Development: Toward Better Conceptualizations and Measures. *Educational Researcher*, *38*(3), 181–199. doi:10.3102/0013189X08331140

Dias, J., & Paiva, A. (2005). Feeling and reasoning: a computational model. In *Proceedings of the 12th Portuguese Conference on Artificial Intelligence*, EPIA 2005 (pp. 127-140). Berlin: Springer.

Digital Video Broadcasting. (2007). Retrieved October 18, 2007, from http://www.dvb.org

Dillenbourg, P. (1999) What do you mean by collaborative learning? In P. Dillenbourg, (Ed.), Collaborative-learning: Cognitive and Computational Approaches (pp. 1-19). Oxford, UK: Elsevier.

Dillon, C. L., & Walsh, S. M. (1992). Faculty: The neglected resource in distance education. *American Journal of Distance Education*, *6*(3), 5–6, 25–28. doi:10.1080/08923649209526796

Directorate for Education, Employment, Labour and Social Affairs (2002). *Definition and Selection of Competences (DESECO): Theoretical and Conceptual Foundations Strategy Paper*. Paris: OCDE.

Dodge, B. (1997). *Some thoughts about WebQuests*. San Diego, CA: San Diego State University. Retrieved April, 7, 2009 from http://webquest.sdsu.edu/about_webquests.html

Dolatabadi, H. R., & Dillon, P. (2009). Intercultural Discourse in Virtual Learning Environments: A Preparatory Study of the Perceptions of Students in an Iranian university. *International Journal of Information Science and Management*, *7*(2), 29-43. Retrieved on May 26, 2009 from http://www.srlst.com/ijist/ijism-Vol7No2/ijism72-29-43.pdf

Donner, J. (2008). Research Approaches to Mobile Use in the Developing World: A Review of the Literature. *The Information Society*, *24*(3), 140–159. doi:10.1080/01972240802019970

Dornan, T. (2008). Self-Assessment in CPD: Lessons From the UK Undergraduate and Postgraduate Education Domains. *The Journal of Continuing Education in the Health Professions*, *28*(1), 32–37. doi:10.1002/chp.153

Dörner, D. (2003). The mathematics of emotions. In F. Detje, D.Dörner, & H. Schaub (Eds.), *Proceedings of the Fifth International Conference on Cognitive Modeling* (pp. 75–79). Bamberg, Germany: Universitäts-Verlag.

Dornyei, Z. (2001). Teaching and Researching - Motivation. Upper Saddle River, NJ: Pearson Education Limited.

Douglas, M. (1992). Risk and Blame: Essays in Cultural Theory. London: Routledge.

dSwaan, e, A. (1997). Widening Circles of Disidentification. On the Psycho- and Sociogenesis of the Hatred of Distant Strangers. Reflections on Rwanda. *Theory, Culture & Society, 14*(2), 105–122. doi:10.1177/026327697014002010

Duffy, T. M., & Jonassen, D. H. (1992). Constructivism: New Implications for Instructional Technology. In T. M. Duffy & D. H. Jonassen (Eds.), Constructivism and the Technology of Instruction: A Conversation (pp. 1-16). Hillsdale, NJ: Lawrence Erlbaum Associates, Inc.

Dunlap, J. C. (2005). Workload reduction in online courses: Getting some shuteye. *Performance Improvement, 44*(5), 18–25. doi:10.1002/pfi.4140440507

Dunn, L., & Wallace, M. (2004). Australian academics teaching in Singapore: striving for cultural empathy. *Innovations in Education and Teaching International, 41*(3), 291–304. doi:10.1080/1470329041000173328 5

Dzvimbo, K. B. (2004). *The Challenges and Potential of Distance Teaching and Open Learning in Africa: Experiences from the African Virtual University.* Paper presented at the All-Africa Minister's Conference on Open Learning and Distance Education.

Economist Intelligence Unit. (2003). *The 2003 e-readiness rankings, A white paper from the Economist Intelligence Unit.* Retrieved September 3, 2008 from http://graphics.eiu.com/files/ad_pdfs/eReady_2003.pdf

Eder, K. (2007). Europe as a particular space of communication. On the question of the social integration of a culturally heterogeneous community. *Berliner Journal fur Soziologie, 17*(1), 33-50+140.

Educational Testing Service. (2006). Pathwise Series of Professional Development Programs.

Educause Centre for applied research. (2003). Impact and challenges of e-learning. *Supporting e-learning in higher education, 3*, 39-47.

Elias, M. J., Zins, J. E., Weissberg, R. P., Frey, K. S., Greenberg, M. T., Haynes, N. M., et al. (1997). Promoting social and emotional learning: Guidelines for educators. Alexandria, VA: Association for Supervision and Curriculum Development.

Ellis, R. (1986). Activities and procedures for teacher training. *ELT Journal, 40*(2), 91–99. doi:10.1093/elt/40.2.91

Elwood, J., & Klenowski, V. (2002). Creating communities of shared practice: The challenges of assessment use in learning and teaching. *Assessment & Evaluation in Higher Education, 27*(3), 243–256. doi:10.1080/02602930220138606

Enhanced Learning Unlimited. (2007). Retrieved October 18 2007, from http://www.elu-project.com

ENP. (2009). *European Neighbourhood Policy.* See http://ec.europa.eu/world/enp/

Ensminger, D., & Surry, D. (2002, April). *Faculty perceptions of factors that facilitate the implementation of online programs.* Paper presented at the Seventh Annual Mid-South Instructional Technology Conference, Murfreesboro, TN. (ERIC Document Reproduction Service No. ED464622)

Eraut, M., & Holes, C. (1988). Groupwork with computers. *Information and Communication Technologies.* Retrieved September 8, 2009, from http://www.virtuallearning.org.uk/virtuallearning/Virtual%20Learning.pdf

EU. (2009). *Boosting Co-operation through Twinning.* European Commission, EuropeAid, Retrieved from http://ec.europa.eu/europeaid/where/neighbourhood/overview/Twinning_en.htm

European Association for Quality Assurance in Higher Education (ENQA). *Current Trends in European Quality Assurance.* Retrieved May 7, 2009, from http://www.enqa.eu/

European Commission. (2008). *Education and Training 2010.* Retrieved May 20, 2009, from http://ec.europa.eu/education/policies/2010/et_2010_en.html

European Commission. (2008). *The Bologna Process*. Retrieved May 20, 2009, from http://ec.europa.eu/education/policies/educ/bologna/bologna_en.htmlU

Evans, C., & Gibbons, N. J. (2007). The interactivity effect in multimedia learning. In Computers & Education, (pp. 1147 – 1160).

Evans, C., & Sabry, K. (2002). Evaluation of the Interactivity of Web-Based Learning Systems: Principles and Process. *Journal of Innovations in Education and Teaching International*, *40*(1), 89–99.

Fang, B. (2007). A performance-based development model for online faculty. *Performance Improvement*, *46*(5), 17–24.

Farrell, G. M. (1999). The Development of virtual education: A global perspective. An Impact (2009) An appraisal of the impact of Carnegie Corporation grants to Obafemi Awolowo University, Ile-Ife, Nigeria. July 1, 2003- June 30, 2009.

Feasley, C. E. (1993). Is distance education right for you? In National University Continuing Education Association, (Ed.), The electronic university: A guide to distance learning (p. viii). Princeton, NJ: Peterson's Guides.

Feinberg, S., & Murphy, M. (2000). Applying cognitive load theory to the design of web-based instruction. Technology & Teamwork, IEEE, 353-360.

Fernie, K., & Richard, J. D. (Eds.). (2002). *Creating and using virtual reality: A guide for the arts and humanities*. AHDS. Retrieved February 3, 2008, from http://vads.ahds.ac.uk/guides/vr_guide/

Fletcher, J. D. (2003). Does this thing work? A review of technology used to learn. *International Journal of Technologies for the Advancement of Knowledge and Learning*, *5*(1), 10–13.

Forgas, J. (1994). Soziale Interaktion und Kommunikation, [Social interaction and communication]. Weinheim, Germany: Beltz.

Frank, M., Reich, N., & Humphreys, K. (2003). Respecting the human needs of students in the development of e-learning. *Computers & Education*, *40*(1), 57–70. doi:10.1016/S0360-1315(02)00095-7

Franklin, S., & Peat, M. (2001). Managing change: The use of mixed delivery modes to increase learning opportunities. *Australian Journal of Educational Technology*, *17*(1), 37–49.

Frankola, K. (2001, June). The e-learning taboo: High dropout rates in online courses. *Syllabus Magazine*, *14*(11), 14–16.

Fredrickson, S. (1999). Untangling a tangled Web: An overview of WBI programs. *T.H.E Journal*, *26*(11), 67-77.

Freire, P. (1970). Pedagogy of oppressed. New York: Continuum.

Friesner, T., & Hart, M. (2004). A cultural analysis of e-learning for China. *Electronic Journal of eLearning*, *2*(1), 81-88.

Fuller, F. D., & McBride, R. (2001). Distance Education: Section Introduction. Technology and Teacher Education Annual. Ames, IA: Society for Information Technology in Teacher Education.

Gabriel, M. A., & Kaufield, K. J. (2008). Reciprocal mentorship: an effective support for online instructors. *Mentoring & Tutoring: Partnership in Learning*, *16*(3), 311–327. doi:10.1080/13611260802233480

Gagne, R. W., Wager, W. W., Golas, K., & Keller, J. M. (2005). Principles of Instructional Design, (5th ed.). Belmont, CA: Thomson/Wadsworth.

Galanouli, D., Murphy, C., & Gardner, J. (2004). Teachers' perceptions of the effectiveness of ICT-competence training. *Computers & Education*, *43*(1-2), 63–79. doi:10.1016/j.compedu.2003.12.005

Galileo, G. (1632). Dialogo dei due massimi sistemi del mondo, tolemaico e copernicano. Firenze.

Gardner, J. (Ed.). (2006). Assessment and Learning. London: Sage.

Garrison, D. R. (1997). Computer conferencing: the post industrial age of distance education. *Open Learning*, *12*(2), 3–11. doi:10.1080/0268051970120202

Garrison, D. R., & Archer, W. (2007). A community of inquiry framework for online learning. In M. Moore (Ed.), Handbook of Distance Education. New York: Erlbaum.

Garrison, D. R., & Shale, D. (1987). Mapping the boundaries of distance education: Problems in defining the field. *American Journal of Distance Education*, *1*(1), 7–13. doi:10.1080/08923648709526567

Garrison, D. R., & Vaughan, N. D. (2008). Blended learning in higher education (framework, principles and guidelines). San Francisco, CA: Jossey Bass.

Garrison, D. R., Anderson, T., & Archer, W. (2000). Critical inquiry in a text-based environment: computer conferencing in higher education. *The Internet and Higher Education*, *2*(2-3), 87–105. doi:10.1016/S1096-7516(00)00016-6

Geertz, C. (1993). The interpretation of cultures. London: Fontana Press.

Georgina, D. A., & Olson, M. R. (2008). Integration of technology in higher education: A review of faculty self-perceptions. *The Internet and Higher Education*, *11*(1), 1–8. doi:10.1016/j.iheduc.2007.11.002

Gerlach, J. M. (1994). Is this collaboration? In K. Bosworth & S. J. Hamilton (Eds.), Collaborative learning: Underlying processes and effective techniques. San Francisco: Jossey-Bass.

Gerlich, R. N., & Mills, L. (2003). *The design and delivery of effective Web-based instruction: An analysis of faculty concerns.* Retrieved August 28, 2003, from http://karsenti.scedu.umontreal.ca/pdf/ressources/designDelivery.pdf

Ghana Statistic Service (2004). *Ghana Demographic and Health Survey, 2003.*

Ghere, G., King, J. A., Stevahn, L., & Minnema, J. (2006). A Professional Development Unit for Reflecting on Programme Evaluator Competences. *The American Journal of Evaluation*, *27*(1), 108–123. doi:10.1177/1098214005284974

Giannini-Gachago, D., & Seleka, G. (2005). Experiences with international online discussions. Participation patterns of Botswana and American students in an Adult Education and Development course at the University of Botswana. *International Journal of Education and Development using ICT, 1*(2).

Gibson, K.E. & Silverberg, M. (2000). A two year experience teaching computer literacy to first year medical students. *Bulletin of Medical Library Association, April 88*(2), 157-164.

Gijbels, D., Van De Watering, G., Dochy, F., & Van Den Bossche, P. (2006). New learning environments and constructivism: The students' Perspective. *Instructional Science*, *34*, 213–226. doi:10.1007/s11251-005-3347-z

Gilbert, S. W. (1996). Making the most of a slow revolution in distance education. *Change*, *28*(2), 47–52.

Gilbreath, B., Rose, G. L., & Dietrich, K. E. (2008). Assessing mentoring in organizations: an evaluation of commercial mentoring instruments. *Mentoring & Tutoring: Partnership in Learning*, *16*(4), 379–393. doi:10.1080/13611260802433767

Ginsparg, P. (1996). Winners and losers in the Global research village. *1996 UNESCO Conference*, from http://people.ccmr.cornell.edu/~ginsparg/blurb/pg96unesco.html

Giroux, H. (1988). Teachers as transformative intellectuals: Toward a critical pedagogy of learning. North Hadly, MA: Bergin & Garvey.

Glenn, A. (1999). *Implications of new educational technologies in community colleges.* Retrieved May 25, 2003, from http://faculty.tamu-commerce.edu/mdennehy/ technologies.htm

Gonzalez, C. (2004). The Role of Blended Learning in the World of Technology. In G. Siemens, (2005). *Connectivism: A Learning Theory for the Digital Age*.' Retrieved July 13, 2006 from: http://www.itdl.org/Journal/Jan-05/article01.htm

Gordon, S. C., Dembo, M. H., & Hocevar, D. (2007). Do teachers' own learning behaviors influence their classroom goal orientation and control ideology? *Teaching and Teacher Education*, *23*(1), 36–46. doi:10.1016/j.tate.2004.08.002

Gorska, R. (2005). Spatial Imagination - an overview of the longitudinal research at Cracow University of Technology. *Journal for Geometry and Graphics*, *9*(2), 201–208.

Gourley, B. (2004). *The Digital Divide: Solution or Problem*. Paper presented at the All-Africa Minister's Conference on Open Learning and Distance Education.

Grable, C., Hunt, A., & Unrue, E. (2008). Comparing digital to traditional field experience in pre-service teacher education. In K. McFerrin, et al. (Eds.), *Proceedings of Society for Information Technology and Teacher Education International Conference* 2008 (pp. 400-405). Chesapeake, VA: AACE.

Grasha, A. F., & Riechmann-Hruska, S. (1990). *Teaching Style Survey*. Cincinnati, OH: University of Cincinnati. Retrieved January, 3 2008 from http://longleaf.net/teachingstyle.html

Gratch, J., & Marsella, S. (2005). Evaluating a computational model of emotion. *Autonomous Agents and Multi-Agent Systems*, *11*(1), 23–43. doi:10.1007/s10458-005-1081-1

Greenberg, M. T., Weissberg, R. P., O'Brien, M. U., Zins, J. E., Fredericks, L., Resnik, H., & Elias, M. J. (2003). Enhancing School-Based Prevention and Youth Development Through Coordinated Social, Emotional and Academic Learning. *The American Psychologist*, *58*, 466–474. doi:10.1037/0003-066X.58.6-7.466

Greene, M. (1998). Introduction: Teaching for social justice. In W.

Greengard, S. (1999, February). Web-based training yields maximum returns. *Workforce*, *78*(2), 95–96.

Grosch, H., & Leenen, W. R. (1998). Bausteine zur Grundlegung interkulturellen Lernens [Modules for intercultural learning]. In Interkulturelles Lernen. Arbeitshilfen für politische Bildung. Bonn, Germany: Bundeszentrale für politische Bildung.

Grosch, H., Groß, A., & Leenen, W. R. (2002). Interkulturelle Kompetenz in der sozialen Arbeit [Intercultural competence in social work]. In G. Auernheimer (ed.), Interkulturelle Kompetenz und pädagogische Professionalität. Opladen, Germany: Leske + Budrich.

Gu, Y. (2008). Chinese learner: My lived experiences of studying in Mainland China and Australia. *Critical Perspectives on Accounting*, *19*(2), 217–221. doi:10.1016/j.cpa.2006.09.006

Gudykunst, W. B., & Mody, B. (2002). Handbook of international and intercultural communication. Thousand Oaks, CA: Sage Publications.

Gudykunst, W. B., Hammer, M. R., & Wiseman, R. (1977). An analysis of an integrated approach to cross-cultural training. *International Journal of Intercultural Relations*, *1*, 99–109. doi:10.1016/0147-1767(77)90045-1

Gulikers, J. T. M., Bastiaens, T. G., & Kirschner, P. A. (2004). A Five-Dimensional Framework for Authentic Assessment. *Educational Technology Research and Development*, *52*(3), 67–86. doi:10.1007/BF02504676

Gulikers, J. T. M., Kester, L., Kirschner, P. A., & Bastiaens, T. G. (2008). The effect of practical experience on perception of assessment authenticity, study approach, and learning outcomes. *Learning and Instruction*, *18*, 172–186. doi:10.1016/j.learninstruc.2007.02.012

Gunawardena, C. (1990). Integrating telecommunications systems to reach distance learners. *American Journal of Distance Education*, *4*(3), 38–46. doi:10.1080/08923649009526715

Gunawardena, C. N., Lowe, C. A., & Anderson, T. (1997). Analysis of a global online debate and the development of an interaction analysis model for examining social construction of knowledge in computer conferencing. *Journal of Educational Computing Research*, *17*, 397–431.

Gwele, N. S. (2000). Online teaching and learning in a graduate course in nursing education. *Curationis*, 20–25.

Hall, B. (1997). Web-based training cookbook. New York: Wiley.

Hall, E. T. (1990). The silent language. New York: Anchor Press.

Hall, E. T. (2001). Understanding cultural differences. Yarmouth, MA: Intercultural Press.

Hall, L., Vala, M., Hall, M., Webster, M., Woods, S., Gordon, A., & Aylett, R. (2006). FearNot's appearance: Reflecting children's expectations and perspectives. In J. Gratch, M. Young, R. Aylett, D. Ballin, & P. Olivier (eds.), *6th International Conference, IVA 2006* (pp. 407-419). Berlin: Springer.

Halpern, D. (2000). Sex differences in cognitive abilities (3rd ed.). Mahwah, NJ: Lawrence Erlbaum Associates.

Hamilton, E., & Feenberg, A. (2005). The Technical Codes of Online Education. *Techné: Research in Philosophy and Technology*, *9*(1), 97–123.

Hannum, W. H. (2007). When computers teach: A review of the instructional effectiveness of computers. *Educational Technology*, *47*(2), 5–13.

Hannum, W. H., & Hansen, C. (1989). Instructional Systems in Large Organizations, (pp. 115-122). Englewood Cliffs, NJ: Educational Technology Publications.

Hanson, J., Millington, C., & Freewood, M. (2001). *Developing a Methodology for Online Feedback and Assessment*. Paper presented at the Fifth International Computer Assisted Assessment Conference, Leicestershire, U.K.

Hara, N., Bonk, C. J., & Angeli, C. (1998). Content analysis of online discussion in an applied educational psychology. Bloomington, IN: Center for Research on Learning and Technology, Indiana University.

Harasim, L. E. (1990). On-Line Education: Perspectives on a new medium. New York: Praeger/Greenwood.

Hargittai, E. (2008). Whose Space? Differences Among Users and Non-Users of Social Network Sites. *Journal of Computer-Mediated Communication*, *13*(1), 276–297. doi:10.1111/j.1083-6101.2007.00396.x

Harvey, L. (2006). Impact of Quality Assurance: Overview of a discussion between representatives of external quality assurance agencies. *Quality in Higher Education*, *12*(3), 287–290. doi:10.1080/13538320601051010

Hathorn, L. G., & Ingram, A. L. (2002). Online collaboration: Making it work. *Educational Technology*, *42*(1), 33–40.

HEC. (2009). *Turkish Higher Education Council*. Retrieved May 30, 2009, from http://www.yok.gov.tr/content/view/480/183/lang,tr/

Heckman, R., & Annabi, H. (2005). A content analytic comparison of learning processes in online and face-to-face case study discussions. *Journal of Computer-Mediated Communication*, *10*(2), article 7. Retrieved May 15, 2009 from http://jcmc.indiana.edu/vol10/issue2/heckman.html

Heeter, C. (1994). Gender differences and VR. *Virtual Reality World*, March/April. Retrieved May 26, 2006, from commtechlab.msu.edu/randd/research/gender.html

Herskovits, M. (1955). Cultural anthropology. New York: Knopf.

Hesse, H.-G., & Göbel, K. (2003). *Evaluation and quantitative methods in global learning: A contribution from the field of intercultural sensitivity*. Paper presented at the Global Education Network Europe Seminar: Starting practice and theory in global education. Improving quality and raising standards through evaluation. University of Erlangen-Nürnberg, 29.03.2003.

Hiltz, S. R. (1997). Impacts of college-level courses via asynchronous learning networks: Some preliminary results. *Journal of Asynchronous Learning Networks*, *1*(2), 1–19.

Hinsch, R., & Pfingsten, U. (2002). Gruppentraining Sozialer Kompetenzen (GSK) [Group Training of Social Competencies]. Weinheim, Germany: BeltzPVU.

Ho, D. Y. F. (1986). Chinese patterns of socialization: A critical review. In M.H. Bond (Ed.). The Psychology of the Chinese People. Hong Kong: Oxford University Press.

Hodgson, P. (2006, December). *Achieving enriched learning experience through blending computer-mediated and conventional assessment methods*. Paper presented at the Evaluations and Assessment Conference, Australia. Retrieved May 30, 2009, from http://otl.curtin.edu.au/eac2006/papers/hodgson.pdf

Hofstede, G. (1979). Value systems in forty countries. In L. Eckensberger, W. Lonner, & Y. Poortinga (eds.), Cross-cultural contributions to psychology. Amsterdam: Swets and Zeitlinger.

Hofstede, G. (1984). Culture's Consequences: International Differences in Work-Related Values. Beverley Hills, CA: Sage.

Hofstede, G. (1986). Cultural Differences in Teaching and Learning. *International Journal of Intercultural Relations*, *10*, 301–320. doi:10.1016/0147-1767(86)90015-5

Hofstede, G. (1991). Cultures and Organizations: Software of the Mind. London: McGraw-Hill.

Hofstede, G. (1993). Cultural Constraints in Management Theories. *The Academy of Management Executive*, *7*(1), 81–94.

Hofstede, G. (2001). Culture's consequences: Comparing values, behaviors, institution, and organizations across nations. Thousand Oaks, CA: Sage Publications.

Hofstede, G., & Bond, M. (1984). Hofstede's culture dimensions. *Journal of Cross-Cultural Psychology*, *15*, 417–433. doi:10.1177/0022002184015004003

Horton, K. (2003). E-learning Tools and Technologies. Indianapolis, IN: Wiley.

Huang, P. (2001). University faculty perceptions on WebCT for delivering courses (Doctoral dissertation, University of South Dakota, 2001). *Dissertation Abstracts International*, *62* (3), 149B. (UMI No. 3007064).

Huang, Y. (2003). *Critical factors related to the adaptation of WBI by higher-education faculty*. Manuscript in preparation, The University of West Florida, Pensacola.

Hunt, A., Grable, C., Clemmons, K., & Clark, A. (2009). Digital field experiences in teacher education: Teaching and supervision in distance education. In C. Crawford et al. (Eds.), *Proceedings of Society for Information Technology and Teacher Education International Conference 2009* (pp.389-391). Chesapeake, VA: AACE.

Huntington, S. P. (2000). Cultures count (Foreword). In L. E. Harrison, & S. Huntington (Eds.), Culture Matters. How Values Shape Human Progress. New York: Basic Books.

Hyde, J. S. (2005). The gender similarities hypothesis. *American Pyschologist*, *60*, 581-589. Retrieved May 24, 2006 from http://www.apa.org/journals/releases/amp606581.pdf

Hyden, G. (1997). Civil society, social capital, and development: Dissection of a complex discourse. *Studies in Comparative International Development*, *32*(1), 3–30. doi:10.1007/BF02696304

Hymes, D. (1971). On Communicative Competence. Philadelphia: University of Pennsylvania Press.

Inglis, A. (2001). Selecting an integrated electronic learning environment. In F. Lockwood & A. Gooley (eds.), Innovation in Open and Distance Learning: Successful development of online and web based learning. London: Kogan Page.

Ingram, A. L. (2006). *Combining effective individualized and group online larning*. Paper presented at the Innovative Learning Conference, Kent State University, Kent, Ohio.

Inkeles, A., & Levinson, J. (1969). National character: The study of modal personality and sociocultural systems. In G. Lindzey, & E. Aronson (Eds.), Handbook of social psychology, (Vol. 4, pp. 418-506.). Reading, MA: Addison-Wesley

Interactive, T. V. *Web.* (2007). Retrieved October 18, 2007, from http://www.interactivetvweb.org

Isbister, K. (2004). Building bridges through the unspoken: Embodied agents to facilitate intercultural communication. In S. Payr, & R. Trappl (Eds.), Agent Culture: Human-Agent Interaction in a Multicultural World. London: Lawrence Erlbaum Associates.

Islam, M.T., & Selim, Abu Sadeque Md. (2006). Current Status and Prospects for E-Learning in the Promotion of Distance Education in Bangladesh. *Turkish Online Journal of Distance Education – TOJDE, 7*(1), Article 11.

Jack, K., & Tsatsoulin, V. (2002). Dictionary of Video Television Technology. New York: Elsevier Newnes.

Janis, I. (1982). Groupthink, (2nd ed.). Boston: Houghton-Mifflin.

Jbeengut, L. (1998). Quality Assurance in distance education through tutor training at Mauritius College of Air. *Open Praxis, 2*. Retrieved from http//www.org.za/worldbank/management/benefits/m43bmau.html

Jekel, T. (2007). What you all want is GIS 2.0. Collaborative GI based learning environments: spatial planning and education. In Car, A. et al. (Eds.), GI-Crossroads @ GI-Forum. Heidelberg, Germany: Wichmann.

Jekel, T. (2008). Children Mapping Global Change. Participatory GI-Based Learning. In *Proceedings, Map India*, Noida. Retrieved from http://www.gisdevelopment.net/application/miscellaneous/mi08_227.htm

Jekel, T. (2008), Developing spatial concepts: GI based learning in secondary education. In *Proceedings GIS-CA'08, KSUCTA News*, Bishkek, Kyrgyzstan.

Johnson, D. W., Johnson, R. T., & Holubec, E. J. (1993). Cooperation in the classroom. Edina, MN: Interaction Book Company.

Jonassen, D. (2000). Toward a design theory of problem solving. *Educational Technology Research and Development, 48*(4), 63–85. doi:10.1007/BF02300500

Jonassen, D. H. (2000). Computers in the classroom: Mindtools for critical thinking. Englewood Cliffs, NJ: Prentice Hall, Inc.

Jonassen, D. H., Howland, J., Marra, R. M., & Crismond, D. (2008). Meaningful learning with technology. Upper Saddle River, NJ: Pearson.

Jordan, S., & Mitchell, T. (2009). e-Assessment for learning? The potential of short-answer free-text questions with tailored feedback. *British Journal of Educational Technology, 40*(2), 371–385. doi:10.1111/j.1467-8535.2008.00928.x

Kajiyama, K. (1996). Towards a generative theory of freshmen graphics reading errors. In *Proceedings of 7th International Conference on Engineering Computer Graphics and Descriptive Geometry,* (pp 493-497). Cracow, Poland.

Kang, F. M., David, W. S., Jean, C. L., & Jan, B. J. (2004, February). *The study on development of spatial ability scale for vocational high school students.* Paper presented at the 7th UICEE ANNUAL Conference on Engineering Education, Mumbai, India.

Kante, C. (2003). eLearning, The New Frontier in the Developing world. *TechKnowLogia*, (January – March). Retrieved on December, 10, 2008 from www.TechKnowLogia.org

Kanther, M. (2001). Interkulturelles Lernen [Intercultural learning]. Stuttgart, Germany: ibidem-Verlag.

Keesing, R. (1974). Theories of culture. *Annual Review of Anthropology, 3*, 73–97. doi:10.1146/annurev.an.03.100174.000445

Kehinde, L.O. (2003). *Obafemi Awolowo University network backbone for open learning and distance Education in O.A.U., Ile-Ife*. A workshop organized by Distance Learning Centre, OAU, Ile-Ife, November 12, 2003.

Keniston, K. (2001, December). *IT for the Common Man: Lessons from India, MN Srinivas Memorial Lecture.* Bangalore: National Institute of Advanced Studies, India Institute of Science. [MIT published as a working paper in 2002].

Kenny, P., Parsons, T., Gratch, J., Leuski, A., & Rizzo, A. (2007) Virtual patients for clinical therapist skills training. In *Proceedings of the 7th International Conference on Intelligent Virtual Agents* (pp. 197-210). Berlin: Springer.

Kenworthy, L. (1997). Civic engagement, social capital, and economic cooperation. *The American Behavioral Scientist, 40(5)*, 645–656. doi:10.1177/0002764297040005010

Khairulanuar, S., & Azniah, I. (2004). The improvement of mental rotation through computer based multimedia tutor. [MOJIT]. *Malaysian Online Journal of Instructional Technology, 1*(2), 24–34.

Khan, B. (1997). Web Based Instruction - What is it and why is it? In B.H. Khan, (ed.) Web based instruction (pp. 5-18). Englewood Cliffs, NJ: Educational Technology Publications.

Khan, K. S., Davies, D. A., & Gupta, J. K. (2001). Formative self-assessment using multiple true-false questions on the Internet: feedback according to confidence about correct knowledge. *Medical Teacher, 23*, 158–163. doi:10.1080/01421590031075

Kilby, T. (2000). *What is Web-based training?* Retrieved July 5, 2003, from http://www .wbtic.com/primer_whatiswbt.aspx

Killian, C. (1997). F2F—Why teach online. *Educational Review, 32*(4), 31–34.

Kincannon, J. M. (2000, April). *From the classroom to the Web: A study of faculty change*. Paper presented at the annual meeting of the American Educational Research Association, New Orleans, LA. (ERIC Document Reproduction Service No. ED467096)

Kiplinger, N. (2003). Learner Support for Distance Learning. PRIME/IntraHealth.

Kirby, A. (2007). The production of private space and its implications for urban social relations. *Political Geography, 27*, 74–95. doi:10.1016/j.polgeo.2007.06.010

Kirkpatrick, D. L. (1996). Evaluating training programs. San Francisco: Berrett-Koehler.

Kirschner, P., Strijbos, J. W., Kreijns, K., & Beers, P. J. (2004). Designing Electronic Collaborative Learning Environments. *Educational Technology Research and Development, 52*(3), 47–66. doi:10.1007/BF02504675

Kitade, K. (2000). L2 Learners' Discourse and SLA Theories in CMC: Collaborative Interaction in Internet Chat. In Computer Assisted Language Learning. Oxford, UK: Intellect.

Klein, J., & Koroghlanian, C. (2004). The effect of audio and animation in multimedia instruction. [Norfolk, VA: AACE]. *Journal of Educational Multimedia and Hypermedia, 13*(1), 23–46.

Kluckhohn, C. (1962). Culture and Behavior. New York: The Free Press of Glencoe.

Knight, P., Tait, J., & Yorke, M. (2006). The professional learning of teachers in higher education. *Studies in Higher Education, 31*(3), 319–339. doi:10.1080/03075070600680786

Koda, T., Rehm, M., & André, E. (2008). Cross-cultural evaluations of avatar facial expressions designed by Western Designers. In *Intelligent Virtual Agents.* [Berlin: Springer.]. *Proceedings of IVA, 2008*, 245–252.

Kolb, D. A. (1984). Experimental learning: experience as the source of learning and development. Englewood Cliffs, NJ: Prentice Hall.

Kouku, B., Oyeyinka, E. & Rao (Eds.), (2000). *Information Technology opportunity and Higher Education in Africa.* New York: Macmillan.

Koutsojanis, C., Kontomina, I., Margari, G., Doulias, E., & Katsardi, M. (2007). Education in Computers Conquers Health Care Professionals Technophobia. *Social Applications of Technological Advances, 11th Panhellenic Conference on Informatics*, (pp. 406-413). Retrieved on December, 14, 2008 from http://pci2007.upatrs.gr.proceedings/PCI2007

Kramsch, C., A'Ness, F., & Lam, W. S. E. (2000). Authenticity and authorship in the computer-mediated acquisition of L2 literacy. *Language Learning & Technology*, *14*(2), 78–104.

Krashen, S. (1985). The Input Hypothesis: Issues and Implications. London: Longman.

Kreijns, C., Kirschner, P., & Jochems, W. (2002). The sociability of computer-supported collaborative learning environments. *Journal of Educational Technology & Society*, *5*(1), 8–22.

Kreijns, C., Kirschner, P., & Jochems, W. (2003). Identifying the pitfalls for social interaction in computer-supported collaborative learning environments: a review of the research. *Computers in Human Behavior*, *19*(3), 335–353. doi:10.1016/S0747-5632(02)00057-2

Kriegel, M., Lim, M. L., Nazir, A., Aylett, R., Cawsey, A., Enz, S., & Zoll, C. (2008). Culture-personality based affective model. Enculturating conversational interfaces by socio-cultural aspects of communication. In *Workshop on IUI 2008*, Canary Islands, Jan 13, 2008.

Kroeber, A., & Kluckhohn, C. (1952). Culture. New York: Meridian Books.

Kulski, M., & Groombridge. (2004). Aligning Teaching Quality Indicators with University Reward Mechanisms. *Tertiary Education and Management*, *10*, 45–59. doi:10.1023/B:TEAM.0000012236.63005.a2

Lan, J. (2001). WBI for education faculty: A needs assessment. *Journal of Research on Computing in Education*, *33*, 385–400.

Lankbeck, R., & Mugler, F. (2000). Distance learners of the South Pacific: Study strategies, learning conditions, and consequences for course design. *Journal of Distance Education*, *15*(1), 63-80. Retrieved June 19, 2009 from http://www.jofde.ca/index.php/jde/article/view/159/359

Larsen, L., Harlan, S. L., Bolin, B., Hackett, E. J., Hope, D., & Kirby, A. (2004). Bonding and Bridging. Understanding the Relationship between Social Capital and Civic Action. *Journal of Planning Education and Research*, *24*(1), 64–77. doi:10.1177/0739456X04267181

Laurillard, D. (2002). Rethinking University Teaching: A framework for effective use of learning technologies. London: Routledge.

Lave, J., & Wenger, E. (1991). Situated learning: Legitimate peripheral participation. Cambridge, UK: Cambridge University Press.

Lazarus, R. (1991). Emotion and adaptation. New York: Oxford University Press.

Lee, J. (2001). *Higher education on the Web,* (Report No. 034225). Washington, DC: National Education Association, Higher Education Research Center. ERIC Document Reproduction Service No. ED455751.

Leedy, P. D., & Ormrod, J. E. (2001). Practical research: Planning and design, (7th ed.) Upper Saddle River, N. J. Merrill/Prentice-Hall..

Leichtenstern, K., André, E., & Vogt, T. (2007). Role assignment via physical mobile interaction techniques in mobile multi-user applications for children. In *Ambient Intelligence.* [Berlin: Springer.]. *Proceedings of the AmI, 2007*, 38–54.

Lemke, J. L. (2000). Across the scales of time: Artifacts, activities, and meanings in ecosocial systems. *Mind, Culture, and Activity*, *7*(4), 273–290. doi:10.1207/S15327884MCA0704_03

Lenning, O. T. (1980). Needs as a Basis for Academic Programme Planning. *New Directions for Institutional Research*, *1980*(28), 9–25. doi:10.1002/ir.37019802803

Leslie, N. P. (1980). The history of television and radio in continuing education. *New Directions for Adult and Continuing Education, 5*, 15–29.

Lester, M. C., & Diekenhoff, G. M. (2002). A comparison of traditional and internet Cheaters. *Journal of College Student Development, 43*(6), 906–911.

Liang, X., & Kim, C. (2004). Classroom assessment in web-based instructional environment: instructors' experience. *Practical Assessment, Research & Evaluation, 9*(7). Retrieved March 23, 2009 from http://PAREonline.net/getvn.asp?v=9&n=7

Lim, D. H. (2002). Perceived Differences Between Classroom and Distance Education: Seeking Instructional Strategies for Learning Applications. *International Journal of Educational Technology, 3*(1), 20–32.

Lim, M. Y., Dias, J., Aylett, R., & Paiva, A. (2009) Intelligent NPCs for Educational Role Play Game. In Proceedings of Agents for Games and Simulation Workshop, AAMAS 09, Budapest, Hungary, May 10-15, 2009.

Lincoln, Y., & Guba, E. (2000). Paradigmatic controversies contradictions and emerging influences. In N. Denzin & Y. Lincoln (Eds.), Handbook of Qualitative Research, (pp.162-88) (2nd ed.). Thousand Oaks, CA: SAGE.

Linn, M. C., & Hyde, J. S. (1989). Gender, mathematics and science. *Educational Researcher, 18*, 17–19.

Linn, M. C., & Petersen, A. C. (1985). Emergence and characterization of sex differences in spatial ability: a meta-analysis. *Child Development, 56*, 1479–1498. doi:10.2307/1130467

Linn, R. (2000). Assessments and accountability. *Educational Researcher, 29*(2), 4–16.

Little, J., Page, C., Betts, K., Bonne, S., Faverty, P., & Joosten, T. (2009). Charting the Course and Tapping the Community: The EDUCAUSE Top Teaching and Learning Challenges 2009. *EDUCAUSE Review, 44*(3), 30–45.

Littlejohn, A., Falconer, I., & Mcgill, L. (2008). Characterising effective eLearning resources. *Computers & Education, 50*(3), 757–771. doi:10.1016/j.compedu.2006.08.004

Liu, J. (2007). Effective measures to Chinese general education. [Social Sciences]. *Journal of North China Electric Power University, 4*, 113–117.

Löfström, E., & Nevgi, A. (2007). From strategic planning to meaningful learning: diverse perspectives on the development of web-based teaching and learning in higher education. *British Journal of Educational Technology, 38*(2), 312–324. doi:10.1111/j.1467-8535.2006.00625.x

Lohaus, A., Jerusalem, M., & Klein-Heßling, J. (2006). Gesundheitsförderung im Kindes- und Jugendalter [Health promotion in education of children and adolescents]. Göttingen, Germany: Hogrefe.

Long, P., & Kiplinger, N. K. (1999). Making It Happen: Using Distance Learning to Improve Reproductive Health Provider Performance. PRIME/IntraHealth.

Lopez-Nores, M., Elexpuru-Eguia, A., Blanco-Fernandez, Y., Pazos-Arias, J., Gil-Solla, A., Garcia-Duque, J., et al. (2004). A Technological Framework for TV-supported Collaborative Learning. In *Proceedings of the IEEE Sixth International Symposium on Multimedia Software Engineering (ISMSE'04)*, Miami, USA.

Loughran, J. J. (2002). Effective reflective practice. *Journal of Teacher Education, 53*, 33–34. doi:10.1177/0022487102053001004

Love, R. K. (2004). Animations and learning: Value for money? In R. Atkinson, C. McBeath, D. Jnas-Dwyer, & R. Phillips (Eds.), *Beyond the comfort zone: Proceedings of the 21st ASCILITE Conference, Perth, Australia.* Retrieved on 11 June, 2006, from http:www.ascilite.org.au/conference/perth04/procs/lowe-r.html

Lu, M. (2002). Spark Notes Study Guide on ideal gases. In A. Davis, (2006), Developing an Infrastructure for Online Learning. Theory and Practice of Online Learning.

Lukes, (2000). *Preparing Your Campus for a Network Future: EDUCAUSE Leadership Strategies No. 1* San Francisco: Jossey Bass Publishers.

Lumbreras, M., & Sanchez, J. (1998). 3D aural interactive hyperstories for blind children. In *Proceedings of the 2nd European Conference on Disability, Virtual Reality and Associated Technologies*, Skovde, Sweden, 1998.

Lyon, E. (2001). Online education: An exploratory study into success factors. Journal of EducationalComputing Research, 24, 77-92.

Lytras, M., Lougos, C., Chozos, P., & Pouloudi, A. (2002). *Interactive Television and E-learning Convergence: Examining the Potential of T-learning.* Paper presented at the European Conference on e-learning, Brunel University, UK.

Ma, C. (2005). Some Ideas on System Reform and Innovation in China's Higher Education. *Science Education in Higher Education,* (Vol.2). Retrieved August 19, 2008 from http://scholar.ilib.cn/A-gdlkjy200502010.html

Ma, W. (2009). The prospects and dilemmas in Americanizing Chinese higher education. *Asia Pacific Education Review, 10,* 117–124. doi:10.1007/s12564-009-9006-3

Maccoby, E. E., & Jacklin, C. N. (1974). The psychology of sex differences. Stanford, CA: Stanford University Press.

Macdonald, J. (2004). Developing competent e-learners: the role of assessment. *Assessment & Evaluation in Higher Education, 29*(2), 215–226. doi:10.1080/0260293042000188483

MacGregor, S. (2002). New Perspectives for Distributed Design Support. *Journal of Desert Research, 2*(2).

Maclellan, E. (2004). How convincing is alternative assessment for use in higher education? *Assessment & Evaluation in Higher Education, 29*(3), 311–321. doi:10.1080/0260293042000188267

Malikowski, S. R. (2008). Factors related to breadth of use in course management systems. *The Internet and Higher Education, 11*(2), 81–86. doi:10.1016/j.iheduc.2008.03.003

Manar, A. (2009). Brunel University. *Wiki-pedia.* Retrieved from http://en.wikipedia.org/wiki/Brunel_University

Manogue, M., Kelly, M., Masaryk, S. B., Brown, G., Catalanotto, F., & Delap, E. (2002). Evolving methods of assessment. *European Journal of Dental Education, 6,* 53–66. doi:10.1034/j.1600-0579.6.s3.8.x

Mantovani, F. (2001). VR learning: Potential and challenges for the use of 3D environments in education and training. Towards CyberPsychology: Mind, Cognitions and Society in the Internet Age. Amsterdam: IOS Press.

Maor, D. (1999). Teacher and student reflections on interactions in an internet- based unit. In K. Martin, N. Stanley, & N. Davison (Ed.), *1999 Teaching* and Learning Forum: Teaching in the Disciplines/Learning in Context, The *Proceedings of the 8th Annual Teaching and Learning Forum,* (pp. 257–261). Perth, Australia: University of Western Australia.

Maor, D. (2003). Teacher's and students' perspectives on on-line learning in social constructivist learning environment. *Technology, Pedagogy and Education, 12*(2), 201–218. doi:10.1080/14759390300200154

Maor, D., & Hendriks, V. (2001, December). *Peer learning and reflective thinking in an on-line community of learners.* Paper presented at the Australian Association for research in Education (AARE), Fremantle, Australia. Retrieved from http://www.aare.edu.au/index.htm

Marquardt, M. J., & Kearsley, G. (1999). Technology-based learning: Maximizing human performance and corporate success. Boca Raton, FL: St. Lucie Press.

Marsh, G. E., II, Price, B. J., & McFadden, A. C. (2000, February). *An overview of online educational delivery applications.* Paper presented at the 11th Annual Society for Information and Teacher Education International Conference, San Diego, CA. ERIC Document Reproduction Service No. ED444476.

Martín-Blas, T., & Serrano-Fernández, S. (2009). The role of new technologies in the learning process: Moodle as a teaching tool in Physics. *Computers & Education, 52*, 35–44. doi:10.1016/j.compedu.2008.06.005

Mascarenhas, S., Dias, J., Afonso, N., Enz, S., & Paiva, A. (2009) Using Rituals to Express Cultural Differences in Synthetic Characters. In *Proceedings of AAMAS 2009*, Budapest, May 10-15, 2009.

Mashayekh, F. (2006). Reviewing the Meaning of Learning. In A. Khorsandi (Ed.) *Communication within the Educational System in Iran* (pp.59-71).Tehran: Institute for Cultural and Social Studies, Ministry of Science and Technology. Tehran, Iran (in Persian). Retrieved on May 22,2009, from http://pedagogy.ir/index.php?option=com_content&view=article&id=159&Itemid=99

Matteo, J. & Sangrà, A. (2007). Designing online learning assessment through alternative approaches: facing the concerns. *European Journal of open, distance and E-learning.*

Matthews, B. M. (2000). The Chinese Value Survey: An interpretation of value scales and consideration of some preliminary results. *International Education Journal, 1*(2), 2000.

Mayer, & Chandler. (2001). When learning is just a click away: does simple user interaction foster deeper understanding of multimedia messages. *Journal of educational Psychology, 93*, 390-397

Mayer, R. E. (1997). Multimedia learning: Are we asking the right questions? *Educational Psychologist, 32*, 1–19. doi:10.1207/s15326985ep3201_1

Mayer, R. E. (1999). The promise of educational psychology: Learning in the content areas. Upper Saddle River, NJ: PrenticeHall.

Mayer, R. E. (2001). Multimedia learning. New York: Cambridge University Press.

Mayer, R. E., & Anderson, R. B. (1992). The Instructive Animation: Helping students build connections between words and pictures in multimedia learning. *Journal of Educational Psychology, 84*, 444–452. doi:10.1037/0022-0663.84.4.444

Mayer, R. E., & Moreno, R. (1998). A split-attention effect in multimedia learning: evidence for dual processing systems in working memory. *Journal of Educational Psychology, 90*, 312–320. doi:10.1037/0022-0663.90.2.312

Mayer, R. E., & Moreno, R. (2000). A Learner-Centered Approach to Multimedia Explanations: Deriving Instructional Design Principles from Cognitive Theory. *Interactive Multimedia electronic of computer enhanced learning, 2*, 2.

Mayer, R. E., Dow, G. T., & Mayer, S. (2003). Multimedia learning in an interactive self-explaining environment: What works in the design of agent-based micro worlds? *Journal of Educational Psychology, 95*, 806–812. doi:10.1037/0022-0663.95.4.806

Mayer, R., & Gallini, J. K. (1990). When is an illustration worth ten thousand words? *Journal of Educational Psychology, 82*, 715–726. doi:10.1037/0022-0663.82.4.715

McAlpine, L., Weston, C., Beauchamp, J., Wiseman, C., & Beauchamp, C. (1999). Building a metacognitive model of reflection. *Higher Education, 37*(2), 105–131. doi:10.1023/A:1003548425626

McConnell, D. (2006). E-learning Groups and communities. Berkshire, UK: Open University Press.

McCormack, C., & Jones, D. (1998). Building a Web-based education system. New York: Wiley.

Mcgrath, I. (1995). Feeding, Leading, showing, throwing: Process Choices in Teacher training and Trainer Training, in Learning to Train: Perspectives on the Development of Language Teacher Trainers. (pp. 162-172). Upper Saddle River, NJ: Prentice Hall Europe in association with the British Council.

McGraw, K. L. (2001). *E-Learning strategy and infrastructure.* Retrieved from http://wwlearningcircuits.org/2001/mcgrawhtml

McKenzie, B. K., Mims, N., Bennett, E., & Waugh, M. (2000). Needs, concerns and practices of online instructors. *Online Journal of Distance Learning Administration, 3*(3). Retrieved July 15, 2003, from http://www.westga.edu/ ~distance/ojdla/fall33/mckenzie33.html

Mckeon, C. A. (2001). Email as a motivating literacy event for one struggling reader: Donna's case. *Reading Research and Instruction, 40*, 185–202.

McLaren, P. (1998). Life in schools: An introduction to critical pedagogy in the foundation of education, (3rd Ed.). New York: Longman.

McLoughlin, C., & Luca, J. (2002). A learner-centred approach to developing team skills through web-based learning and assessment. *British Journal of Educational Technology, 33*(5), 571–582. doi:10.1111/1467-8535.00292

McMahon, M. (1997, December). *Social Constructivism and the World Wide Web - A Paradigm for Learning.* Paper presented at the ASCILITE conference, Perth, Australia.

Mehraborz Institute of Higher Education (MAIHE). (2006). MAIHE Bylaws. Tehran, Iran: MIHE.

Merriam, S. B. (1998). Qualitative research and case study application in education. San Francisco, CA: Jossey-Bass.

Merryfield, M. (2000). Using electronic technologies to promote equity. *Education, 26*, 342–36.

Metiri, Group. (2006). *Technology in the schools: What the research says.* Cisco Systems. Retrieved from http://www.cisco/web/strategy/docs/education/technologyin-SchoolsReport.pdf

Meunier, F. (2002). The Pedagogical Value of Native and Learner Copora in EFL Grammar Teaching. In S. Granger, J. Hung, & S. Petch-Tyson, (Eds.), Computer Learner Corpora, Second Language Acquisition and Foreign Language Teaching. Philadelphia: John Benjamins Publishing Co.

Meyer, K.A. (2003). Face to face versus threaded discussions: the role of time and higher order thinking. *JALN, 7* (3).

Mezirow, J., & Associates. (2000). Learning as transformation: Critical perspective on a theory in progress. San Francisco: Jossey-Bass.

Middle Grade Mathematical Project. (1983). Spatial visualization test. Department of Mathematics, Michigan State University.

Miller, K. H. (2006). One course, two ways: Lessons learned from teaching the same graduate course online and face-to-face. *E-learn Magazine*. Retrieved from http://www.elearnmag.org/subpage

Mirza, S. (2008). *'Interactivity effect in E-learning systems'.* Unpublished Dissertation for the degree of Master of Science, Brunel University, UK.

Modarresi, S., Newman, D. L., & Abolafia, M. Y. (2001). Academic evaluators versus practitioners: alternative experiences of professionalism. *Evaluation and Program Planning, 24*, 1–11. doi:10.1016/S0149-7189(00)00041-0

Mohan, G., & Mohan, J. (2002). Placing social capital. *Progress in Human Geography, 26*(2), 191–210. doi:10.1191/0309132502ph364ra

Molla, A., & Licker, P. S. (2005). E-commerce adoption in developing countries; A model and instrument. *Information & Management, 42*, 877–899. doi:10.1016/j.im.2004.09.002

MoNE. (2007). National Education Statistics Formal Education 2006-2007. Ankara, Turkey: MoNE.

Montazer, Gh. A. (2007). Strategic Studies of Informational Development in Higher Education System in Iran (in Persian). *Quarterly Journal of Research and Planning in Higher Education (Special issue on e-learning), 13*(1), 1-26.

Montazer, Gh. A., & Bahreinejad, A. (2007). An Adaptive and Intelligent Framework for Virtual Higher Education in Iran. *Iranian Journal of Information Science and Technology, 5*(1), 11–26.

Monteiro, V., & Pereira, A. (2007). O blog como elemento agregador numa comunidade de aprendizagem. Actas do 2° Colóquio Luso-Brasileiro de Educação a distância e online, Lisbon, Portugal.

Moore, M. G. (1989). Three types of interaction. *The American Journal of Distance Education, 3*(2), 1-7. Retrieved May 17, 2003, from http://www.ajde.com/Contents/vol3-2.htm#editorial

Moore, M. G. (2002). Editorial: What Does Research Say About the Learners Using Computer-Mediated Communication in Distance Learning? *American Journal of Distance Education, 16*(2), 61–64. doi:10.1207/S15389286AJDE1602_1

Moore, M. G., & Kearsley, G. (1996). Distance Education: A systems View. Belmont, CA: Wadsworth Publishing Company.

Moreno, R., Mayer, R. E., Spires, H., & Lester, J. (2001). The case for social agency in computer-based teaching: Do students learn more deeply when they interact with animated pedagogical agents? *Cognition and Instruction, 19*, 177–213. doi:10.1207/S1532690XCI1902_02

Morgado, L., Pereira, A., Quintas-Mendes, A., & Aires, L. (2006). Towards a pedagogy of elearning: the contract as an instrument to mediate learning. In A.J. Mendes, (Eds.), Computers and education – towards educational change and innovation. Amsterdam: Springer Science.

Morgado, L., Quintas-Mendes, A., Oliveira, I., & Goulão, F. (2008). Empowering distance teachers – training teachers to teach online. In *European Distance E-Learning Annual Conference*, Lisbon, Portugal.

Morss, K., & Murray, R. (2005). Teaching at Universities: A guide for Postgraduates and Researchers. London: Sage Publications.

Motteram, G. (2001). The role of synchronous communication in fully distance education. *Australian Journal of Educational Technology, 17*(2), 131–149.

Moyer, P. S., Bolyard, J. J., & Spikell, M. A. (2001, August). *Virtual manipulatives in the K-12 classroom.* Paper presented at the International Conference on New Ideas in Mathematics Education, Palm Cove, Queensland, Australia.

Mukerji, S., & Tripathi, P. (2009). *Editorial: Cases on Technological Adaptability and Transnational Learning: Issues & Challenges, Riyadh.* Retrieved from http://www.igi-global.com/requests/details.asp?ID=588

Mukherjee, J. (2003). From corpus data to a theory of talk units in spoken English. In S. Granger & S. Petch-Tyson, (Eds.), Extending the scope of corpus-based research; new applications, new challenges. New York: Rodopi. Haughey, M., & Anderson, T. (1998). Networked Learning: The Pedagogy of the Internet. Montreal, Toronto: Cheneliere/McGraw-Hill.

Mullen, B., & Copper, C. (1994). The Relation between Group Cohesiveness and Performance: An Integration. *Psychological Bulletin, 115*, 210–227. doi:10.1037/0033-2909.115.2.210

Mungall, D., Green, C., & Skunza, B. (2001, October). *Challenges of creating an online doctoral program: Panel discussion of the trials and success of the Ohio State nontraditional Doctor of Pharmacy program.* Paper presented at WebNet 2001 World Conference on the WWW and Internet, Orlando, FL. (ERIC Document Reproduction Service No. ED466587).

Murphy, C., Harber, L., & Muhuhu, P. (2000). Innovations in Learning to Improve Performance: Learner Support Systems. PRIME/IntraHealth.

Murphy, K. L., & Cifuentes, L. (2001). Using Web Tools, collaborating and learning online. *Distance Education, 22*(2), 285–305. doi:10.1080/0158791010220207

Mwaura, C. W. (2003). An investigation of the innovation-decision process of faculty members with respect to Web-based instruction. *Dissertation Abstracts International, 65* (05), 1649.

Nasser, R., & Abouchedid, K. (2000). Attitudes and concerns towards distance education: The case of Lebanon. *Online Journal of Distance Learning Administration, 3*(4). Retrieved May 15, 2003, from http://www.westga.edu/~distance/ojdla/winter34/ nasser34.html

National Agency for Quality Assessment and Accreditation (ANECA). *Educational Programme Assessment and Institutional Assessment.* Retrieved May 7, 2009, from http://www.aneca.es/

National Center for Educational Statistics. (2009). *Numbers and types of public elementary and secondary education agencies from the common core of data: School year 2006-07* [Data file]. Retrieved from http://nces.ed.gov/pubs2009/pesagencies07/tables/table_06.asp

NCES, National Center for Education Statistics. (2003). *Distance Education at Degree-Granting Postsecondary Institutions: 2000-2001.* U.S. Department of Education, National Center for Education Statistics Report. Retrieved June 20, 2009 from http://nces.ed.gov/pubsearch/pubsinfo.asp

Neuhauser, C. (2002). Learning Style and Effectiveness of Online and Face-to- Face Instruction. *American Journal of Distance Education, 16*(2), 99–113. doi:10.1207/S15389286AJDE1602_4

Newcombe, N. S. (2006). A Plea for Spatial Literacy. *The Chronicle of Higher Education, 52*(26).

NGFL. (1998). *VTC-Virtual Teacher Centre (Reception).* Retrieved from http://www.scotland.gov.ulc/library/ict/appendmove3.html

Ngu, B. H. (2002). Online Instruction Versus Face-to-Face Instruction At UNIMAS. *International Journal of Educational Technology, 3*(1), 1–19.

Nightingale, P., & O'Neil, M. (1994). Achieving quality learning in higher education. London: Kogan Page.

Nijhuis, G. G., & Collis, B. (2003). Using a web-based course-management system. An evaluation of management tasks and time implications for the instructor. *Evaluation and Program Planning, 26*, 193–201. doi:10.1016/S0149-7189(03)00005-3

Novek, E. M. (1996, August). *Do professors dream of electronic sheep? Academic anxiety about the information age.* Paper presented at the 79th annual meeting of the Association for Education in Journalism and Mass Communication, Anaheim, CA. (ERIC Document Reproduction Service No. ED399594).

Nyerere, J. K. (1968). Freedom and Socialism. Dar es Salaam, Tanzania: Oxford University Press.

O'Quinn, L., & Corry, M. (2002). Factors that deter faculty from participating in distance education. *Online Journal of Distance Learning Administration, 5*(4). Retrieved from http://www.westga.edu/~distance/ojdla/winter54/Quinn54.htm

O'Sullivan, E. (2003). Bringing a perspective of transformative learning to globalized consumption. *International Journal of Consumer Studies, 27*(4), 326–330. doi:10.1046/j.1470-6431.2003.00327.x

Oakes, J. (1995). Keeping track: How schools structure inequality. New Haven, CT: Yale University Press.

Oakes, J., & Lipton, M. (2007). Teaching to change the world. Boston: McGraw- Hill.

Olakulein, F. K., & Olugbenga, D. (2006). Distance Education as a Women Empowerment Strategy in Africa. Turkish Online Journal of Distance Education – TOJDE January 2006, 7(1), Article 14.

Olgren, C. H. (2000). Distance learning in higher education. In K. Mantyla (Ed.), The 2000/2001 ASTD distance learning yearbook, (pp. 19-25). New York: McGraw-Hill.

Oliver, R. (2001). Assuring the Quality of Online Learning in Australian Higher Education. In M. Wallace, A. Ellis, & D. Newton (Eds.), *Proceedings of Moving Online II Conference,* (pp. 222-231). Limore, New Zealand: Southern Cross University. Retrieved on May 20, 2009 from http://elrond.scam.ecu.edu.au/oliver/2001/mocpaper.pdf

Olkun, S. (2003). Making connections: Improving spatial abilities with engineering drawing activities. *International Journal of Mathematics Teaching and Learning,* 1-10.

Ortony, A., Clore, G., & Collins, A. (1988). The cognitive structure of emotions. Cambridge: Cambridge University Press.

Orvis, K. L., & Lassiter, A. R. L. (2007). Computer-supported collaborative learning: best practices and principles for instructors. Hershey, PA: The Idea Group.

Orwig, G. (1999, October). *Academic support for Web course development: A successful top-down strategy.* Paper presented at WebNet 99: World Conference on the WWW and Internet, Honolulu, HI. (ERIC Document Reproduction Service No. ED448731).

Osborne, J. W. (2000). Prediction in multiple regression. *Practical Assessment, Research, and Evaluation, 7*(2). Retrieved June 15, 2005, from tp://pareonline.net/getvn.asp?v–7&n=2

Owston, R., Wideman, H., Murphy, J., & Lupshenyuk, D. (2008). Blended teacher professional development: A synthesis of three programme evaluations. *The Internet and Higher Education, 11*(3-4), 201–210. doi:10.1016/j.iheduc.2008.07.003

Ozkul, A. E. (2001). Anadolu University Distance Education System from Emergence to 21st Century. *The Turkish Online Journal of Distance Learning, 2*(1), Retrieved January 12, 2009, from http://tojde.anadolu.edu.tr/tojde3/2/ekremtxt.htm

Paiva, A., Dias, J., Aylett, R., Woods, S., Hall, L., & Zoll, C. (2005). Learning by feeling: Evoking empathy with synthetic characters. *Applied Artificial Intelligence, 19,* 235–266. doi:10.1080/08839510590910165

Paivio, A. (1986). Mental representation: A dual coding approach. Oxford, UK: Oxford University Press.

Palloff, R. M., & Pratt, K. (1999). Building learning communities in cyberspace: Effective strategies for the online classroom. San Francisco: Jossey-Bass Publishers.

Paragiotis, Z., & Angeliki, P. (2003). Identifying training needs for ICT skills Enhancement in South-Eastern Europe; Implications for designing web based learning courses. *Educational Technology and Society, 6*(1), 1–7.

Parrott, M. (1993). Tasks for Language Teachers. Cambridge, UK: CUP.

Patton, M. Q. (2007). Process use as usefulism. *New Directions for Evaluation, 2007*(116), 99–112. doi:10.1002/ev.246

Pedro, F. (2005). Comparing traditional and ICT-enriched university teaching methods: evidence from two empirical studies. *Higher Education in Europe, 30*(4), 339–411.

Pelgrum, W. J., & Anderson, R. E. (1999). "ICT and the Emerging Paradigm for Life Long Learning: A World wide Educational Assessment of Infrastructure, Goals and Practice." International Association for the Evaluation of Educational Achievement. The Hague, The Netherlands: IEA Publications Enschede.

Pennington, M. C. (1990). A professional development focus for the language teaching practicum. In Richards & Nunan (Eds.), pp.132 – 151.

Pereira, A., Mendes, A. Q., Morgado, L., Amante, L., & Bidarra, A. (2007). Universidade Aberta's Pedagogical Model for Distance Education: A University for the Future. Lisboa: Universidade Aberta.

Pereira, A., Oliveira, I., Tinoca, L. F., & Amante, L. Relvas, M.J., Pinto, M.C. & Moreira D. (2009). Evaluating continuous assessment quality in competence-based education online: the case of the e-folio. In *European Distance and Elearning Network annual conference.* Retrieved May 20, 2009, from http://sites.google.com/site/luistinoca/Home/papers-1/EDEN09.pdf?attredirects=0

Pereira, A., Tinoca, L., & Oliveira, I. (2008). Processes of Group Work Collaboration Online. In *European Distance and Elearning Network Annual Conference.* Lisbon: Portugal. Retrieved May 20, 2009, from http://sites.google.com/site/luistinoca/Home/papers-1/EDEN08.pdf?attredirects=0

Pereira, A., Tinoca, L., & Oliveira, I. (2009). Answering Bologna's challenge: How authentic assessment strategies can be used to promote competency based education in an online course. In *23rd ICDE/EADTU World Conference*, Maastricht, Netherlands.

Pereira, A., Tinoca, L., & Oliveira, I. (2009). The contribution of the Learning Contract for authentic assessment in online environments. Accepted for the *European Association for Research on Learning and Instruction 13th Biennial Conference*, Amsterdam, Netherlands.

Perkins, D. N. (1993). Person-plus: A distributed view of thinking and learning. In G. Salomon (Ed.), Distributed cognition: Psychological and educational considerations (pp.88-110). New York: Cambridge University Press.

Perlman, J. (2003). The megacity project. *Assessment Strategies for Global Learning*. Retrieved from http://megacitiesproject.org/default.asp

Perraton, H. (2000). Open and Distance Learning in the Developing World. London: Routledge.

Perry, B., & Edwards, M. (2005). Exemplary Online Educators; Creating a Community of Inquiry. *Turkish Online Journal of Distance education, 6*(2). Retrieved on May 20, 2009 from http://tojde.anadolu.edu.tr/tojde18/articles/article6.htm

Pettigrew, T. F., & Tropp, L. R. (2006). A meta-analytic test of intergroup contact theory. *Journal of Personality and Social Psychology, 90*, 751–783. doi:10.1037/0022-3514.90.5.751

Phipps, R., & Merisotis, J. (1999). What is the difference? A review of contemporary research on the effectiveness of distance learning in higher-education. Washington, DC: American Federation of Teachers, National Education Association, and The Institute for Higher-education Policy.

Phuong-Mai, N., Terlouw, C., & Pilot, A. (2005). Cooperative learning vs Confucian heritage culture's collectivism: confrontation to reveal some cultural conflicts and mismatch. *Asia Europe Journal, 3*, 403–419. doi:10.1007/s10308-005-0008-4

Picciano, A. G. (2002). Beyond student perceptions: issues of interaction, presence, and performance in an online course. *Journal of Asynchronous Learning Networks, 6*(1), 21–32.

Pinsonneault, A., & Kraemer, K. L. (1992). *Survey research methodology in management information systems: An assessment.* Retrieved May, 9, 2003, from http://www.crito.uci.edu/research-archives/pdf/urb-022.pdf

Pintrich, P. R., Smith, D. A. F., Garcia, T., & McKeachie, W. J. (1993). Reliability and predictive validity of the Motivated Strategies for Learning Questionnaire (MSLQ). *Educational and Psychological Measurement, 53*, 801–813. doi:10.1177/0013164493053003024

Pololi, L. H., Dennis, K., Winn, G. M., & Mitchell, J. (2003). A Needs Assessment of Medical School Faculty: Caring for the Caretakers. *The Journal of Continuing Education in the Health Professions, 23*, 21–29. doi:10.1002/chp.1340230105

Potter, C. S., & Van Der Merwe, E. (2003). Perception, imagery, visualization and engineering graphics. *European Journal of Engineering Education, 28*(1), 117–133. doi:10.1080/0304379031000065216

Pratt, D. D. (1991). Conceptions of self within China and the United States. *International Journal of Intercultural Relations, 15*(3), 285–310. doi:10.1016/0147-1767(91)90003-Y

Purcell, M. (2001). Neighborhood Activism among Homeowners as a Politics of Space. *The Professional Geographer, 53*(2), 178–194. doi:10.1111/0033-0124.00278

QAA (Quality Assurance Agency). (2006). *Section 6: Assessment of students. Code of practice for the assurance of academic quality and standards in higher education.* Retrieved February 2, 2009, from http://www.qaa.ac.uk

Qin, S. (2008, May 13). *The People's Daily.*

Rafi, A., & Khairulanuar, S. (2007). The relationship of spatial experience, previous mathematics achievement and gender with perceived ability in learning engineering drawing. *Journal of Technology Education, 18*(2), 52–66.

Rafi, A., & Khairulanuar, S. (2009). Practising mental rotation using interactive desktop mental rotation trainer (iDeMRT). *British Journal of Educational Technology, 40*(5), 889–900. doi:10.1111/j.1467-8535.2008.00874.x

Rafi, A., Khairulanuar, S., & Azniah, I. (2006). On improving spatial ability through computer-mediated engineering drawing instruction. *Educational Technology & Society, 9*(3), 149–159.

Rafi, A., Khairulanuar, S., & Said, C. S. (2008). Training in spatial visualization: The effects of training method and gender. *Educational Technology & Society, 11*(3), 127–140.

Ramsey, C. (2005). Narrative from learning in reflection to learning in performance. *Management Learning, 36*(2), 219–235. doi:10.1177/1350507605052558

Rashid, A.T., & Elder, Laurent. (2009). Mobile Phones and Development: An Analysis of IDRC-Supported Projects. *The Electronic Journal on Information Systems in Developing Countries, 36*(2), 1–16.

Razaie, M. (2008, December). *Identifying Necessary Policies for Expanding E-learning in Agricultural Higher Education* (in Persian). Paper Presented at the 3rd E-learning Conference, Tehran, December. Tehran: K.N.T. University of Technology.

Reeves, R., & Knell, J. (2009). The 80 Minute MBA. London: Headline.

Reeves, T. C. (2000). Alternative Assessment Approaches for Online Learning Environments in Higher Education. *Journal of Educational Computing Research, 23*(1), 101–111. doi:10.2190/GYMQ-78FA-WMTX-J06C

Rehm, M., André, E., Bee, N., Endrass, B., Wissner, M., Nakano, Y., et al. (2007). The CUBE-G approach – Coaching culture-specific nonverbal behavior by virtual agents. In I. Mayer, & H. Mastik (eds.), *Organizing and Learning through Gaming and Simulation. Proceedings of ISAGA 2007,* (pp. 313-321). Delft: Eburon.

Reid-Searle, K., & Moxham, L. (2005). Promoting the students' practicum, a CD-ROM for nursing preceptors. *Studies in learning, evaluation, innovation and development, 2*, 20-28. Retrieved on November, 20, 2007 from http://sleid.cqe.edu.au

Republic of South Africa. (2004). *White Paper on e-Education: transforming learning and teaching through information and communication technologies.* Pretoria, South Africa: Government Printers.

Resnick, L. B. (1987). Learning in school and out. *Educational Leadership, 16*(9), 13–20.

Rey-Lopez, M., Fernandez-Vilas, A., Diaz-Redondo, R. P., Pazos-Arias, J., & Bermejo-Munoz, J. (2006). *Adaptive Learning Objects for T-learning.* Paper presented at the 5th International Conference on Web-based Learning (ICWL), Penang, Malaysia.

Reynard, R. (2003). Internet-based ESL for Distance Adult Students – A Framework for Dynamic Language Learning. *Canadian Modern Language Review, 60*(2).

Rice, J., McBride, R., & Davis, J. (1998). *Defining a Web-based learning environment.* Retrieved August 28, 2003 from http://www.byu.edu/ipt/workshops/wbi/text.html

Richards, J. C. (2001). Curriculum Development in Language Teaching. Cambridge, UK: Cambridge University Press.

Richards, J. C., & Renandya, W. (2000). (Eds.). Methodology in Language Teaching: An Anthology of Current Practice. Cambridge: Cambridge University Press.

Richards, J., & Nunan, D. (Eds.). (1990). Second Language Teacher Education. Cambridge, UK: Cambridge University Press.

Rimor, R. (2001). Database as a cognitive tool. *Educational Researcher, 20*(3), 2–9.

Rimor, R., Reingold, R., & Heiman, T. (2008). Instructor's scaffolding in support of students' metacognition through an online course, In J. Zumbach, N. Schwartz, T. Seufert & L. Kester (Eds.), Beyond Knowledge: the Legacy of Competence- Meaningful Computer-based Learning Environments (pp. 43-53). Upper Saddle River, NJ: Springer.

Robert, J. E., & Bell, M. A. (2000). Sex differences on a mental rotation tesk: Variations in EGG hemispheric activation between children and college students. *Developmental Neuro-psychological, 17*, 199–224.

Robertson, I. (2004). *Teachers at the interface: A model of implementation.* Paper presented at the AARE conference, Melbourne. Retrieved August 3, 2008 from http://www.aare.edu.au/04pap/rob04192.pdf

Robinson, J. L. (2000). The new media, faculty, and Web-based instruction at the University of Florida: A study of implementation. Doctoral dissertation, University of Florida. *Dissertation Abstracts International, 61* (06), *2091.* (UMI No. 9976598).

Robinson, M. (1994). Improving science teaching with e-mail. *Computers in the Schools, 11*(1), 95–107.

Robinson, S. P. (2008). Settings for teacher education: Challenges in creating a stronger research base. In M. Cochran-Smith, S. Feiman-Nemser, & D. J. Mcintyre (Eds.), Handbook of research on teacher education: Enduring questions in changing contexts. New York: Routledge.

Rocio, V., Coelho, J., & Pereira, A. (2008). Implementation of a Learning Card in Moodle. In EADTU annual conference, Poitiers, France.

Rockwell, K., Schauer, J., Fritz, S. M., & Marx, D. B. (2000). Faculty education, assistance and support needed to deliver education via distance. *The Online* Journal of Distance Learning Administration, 3(2). Retrieved August 11, 2003, from http://www .westga.edu/~distance/rockwell32.html

Rogers, E. M. (2003). Diffusion of innovations, (5th Ed.). New York: The Free Press

Rogers, R. R. (2001). Reflection in Higher Education: A Concept Analysis. *Innovative Higher Education, 26*(1), 37–57. doi:10.1023/A:1010986404527

Rollett, H., Lux, M., Strohmaier, M., Dosinger, G., & Tochtermann, K. (2007). The Web 2.0 way of learning with technologies. *International Journal of Learning Technology, 3*(1), 87–107. doi:10.1504/IJLT.2007.012368

Roschelle, J., & Teasley, S. D. (1995). The construction of shared knowledge in collaborative problem solving. In C. E. O'Malley (Ed.), Computer-supported Collaborative Learning (pp. 69-197). Berlin: Springer.

Rosen, Y., & Rimor, R. (2009). Using collaborative database to enhance students' knowledge construction. *Interdisciplinary Journal of E-Learning and Learning Objects, 5*, 187–195.

Rosenberg, M. J. (2001). E-learning: Strategies for delivering knowledge in the digital age. New York: McGraw Hill.

Ross, J. A., & Ross, M. (2005). Student assessment in online courses: Research and practice, 1993-2004. *The Canadian Journal of University Continuing Education, 31*(2), 43–63.

Rossen, B., Lok, B., Johnsen, K., Lind, S., & Deladisma, A. (2008). Virtual Humans Elicit Skin-Tone Bias Consistent with Real-World Skin-Tone Biases. In *Intelligent Virtual Agents.* [Berlin: Springer.]. *Proceedings of IVA, 2008*, 237–244.

Rotter, J. B. (1954). Social learning and clinical psychology. New York: Prentice-Hall.

Rourke, L., Anderson, T., Garrison, D. R., & Archer, W. (2001). Assessing social presence in asynchronous, text-based computer conferencing. *Journal of Distance Education, 14*(3), 51–70.

Rovai, A. P. (2000). Online and traditional assessments: What's the difference? *The Internet and Higher Education, 3*(3), 141–151. doi:10.1016/S1096-7516(01)00028-8

Rovai, A. P. (2002). Building sense of community at a distance. *International Review of Research in Open and Distance Learning, 3*(1), 1–16.

Rovai, A. P. (2004). A constructivist approach to online college learning. *The Internet and Higher Education, 7*, 79–93. doi:10.1016/j.iheduc.2003.10.002

Rowe, J., McQuiggan, S., & Lester, J. (2007). Narrative Presence in Intelligent Learning Environments. In *Working Notes of the 2007 AAAI Fall Symposium on Intelligent Narrative Technologies* (pp. 126–133). Arlington, VA.

Ryan, R. C. (2000). Student assessment comparison of lecture and online construction equipment and methods classes. *T.H.E. Journal, 27*(6), 78–83.

Salmon, G. (1998). Developing learning through effective online moderation. *Active Learning, 9*.

Salmon, G. (2000). E-moderating: The key to teaching and learning online. London: Kogan Page.

Salomon, G. (2002). Technology and pedagogy: Why don't we see the promised revolution? *Educational Technology, 42*(2), 71–75.

Sanz de Acedo, M. L., & Garcia, J. M. (2003). Improvement of mental rotation in girls and boys. *Sex Roles, 49*(5-6), 277–286. doi:10.1023/A:1024656408294

Scales, A. Y. (2000). *The effect of learning style, major, and gender on learning computer-aided drawing in an introductory engineering/technical graphics course*. Unpublished doctoral dissertation, North Carolina State University.

Scardamalia, M., & Bereiter, C. (1993). Technologies for knowledge-building discourse. *Communications of the ACM, 36*(5). doi:10.1145/155049.155056

Scardamalia, M., & Bereiter, C. (1994). Computer support for knowledge-building communities. *Journal of the Learning Sciences, 3*, 265–283. doi:10.1207/s15327809jls0303_3

Schellens, T. (2004). *Studying in a blended learning environment: researching congruency between learning environment and student characteristics and the impact of CSCL on knowledge construction*. Ph.D dissertation, Ghent University, Belgium.

Schellens, T., & Valcke, M. (2000). Re-engineering conventional university education: Implications for students' learning styles. *Distance Education, 21*(2), 361–384. doi:10.1080/0158791000210210

Schifter, C. C. (2002). Faculty participation in asynchronous learning networks: A case study of motivating and inhibiting factors [Electronic version]. *Journal of Asynchronous Learning Networks, 4*(1), 15–22.

Schlager, M., Farooq, U., Fusco, J., Schank, P., & Dwyer, N. (2009). Analyzing online teacher networks: Cyber networks require cyber research tools. *Journal of Teacher Education, 60*(1), 86–100. doi:10.1177/0022487108328487

Schön, D. (1987). Educating the Reflective Practitioner. San Francisco: Jossey-Bass.

Schrum, L., & Berge, Z. (1997). Creating student interaction within the educational experience: a challenge for online educators. *Canadian Journal of Educational Communication, 26*(3), 133–144.

Schulz von Thun, F. (1001). *Miteinander reden 1: Störungen und Klärungen* [Talking to each other 1: interferences and clarifications]. Reinbek, Germany: Rowohlt.

Schunk, D. H., & Pajares, F. (2001). The Development of Academic Self-Efficacy. In A. Wigfield & J. Eccles (Eds.), *Development of achievement motivation*. San Diego: Academic Press. Retrieved July 3, 2009, from http://www.des.emory.edu/mfp/SchunkPajares2001.PDF

Schwan, S., & Buder, J. (2002). Lernen als Wissenserwerb in virtuellen Realitäten [Learning as knowledge acquisition in virtual realities]. In G. Bente, N. Krämer, A. Petersen (eds.), Virtuelle Realitäten (pp. 109-129). Göttingen, Germany: Hogrefe.

Schweber, C., Kelly, K., & Orr, G. J. (1998, August). Training, and retraining, faculty for online courses: Challenges and strategies. In *Proceedings of the 14th annual* conference on Distance Teaching & Learning, Madison, WI. (ERIC Document Reproduction Service No. ED422874).

Segall, M. H., Dasen, P. R., Berry, J. W., & Poortinga, Y. H. (1990). Human behavior in global perspective. New York: Pergamon.

Seligman, M. E. P. (1972). Learned helplessness. *Annual Review of Medicine*, *23*, 407–412. doi:10.1146/annurev.me.23.020172.002203

Shaeffer, J. M., & Farr, C. W. (1993). Evaluation: A key piece in the distance education puzzle. *T.H.E. Journal*, *20*(9), 79–82.

Shaw, R. (2001). *Information design and distance learning for international develoment*. Unpublished Master's thesis, Water, Engineering and Development Centre, Loughborough University, UK.

Shepard, R., & Cooper, L. (1982). Mental images and their transformations. Cambridge, MA: MIT Press.

Shephard, K. (2009). e is for exploration: Assessing hard-to-measure learning outcomes. *British Journal of Educational Technology*,*40*(2),386-398. doi:10.1111/j.1467-8535.2008.00927.x

Shroff, R. H., & Vogel, D. R. (2009). Assessing the Factors Deemed to Support Individual Student Intrinsic Motivation in Technology Supported Online and Face-to-Face Discussions. *Journal of Information Technology Education*, *8*, 59–85.

Shute, V. J. (2008). Focus on Formative Feedback. *Review of Educational Research*, *78*(1), 153–189. doi:10.3102/0034654307313795

Shute, V. J., & Psotka, J. (1996). Intelligent Tutoring Systems: Past, Present and Future. In D. Jonassen (ed.) Handbook of Research on Educational Communications and Technology. New York: Scholastic Publications.

Siemens, G. (n.d.). *Connectivism: a learning theory for the digital age*. Retrieved September 4, 2008, from http://www.elearnspace.org/articles/connectivism.htm

Silverman, D. (2005) Doing Qualitative Research. London: SAGE.

Simpson, M. (2006). Field experience in distance delivered initial teacher education programmes. *Journal of Technology and Teacher Education*, *14*(2), 241–254.

Sinkovics, R. R., Stottinger, B., Schlegelmilch, B. B., & Ram, S. (2002). Reluctance to use Technology Related Products: Development of Technophobia Scale. *Thunderbird International Business Review*, *44*(4), 477–494. doi:10.1002/tie.10033

Skinner, B. F. (1935). Two types of conditioned reflex and pseudo types. *The Journal of General Psychology*, *12*, 66–77.

Skylar, A. A., Higgins, K., Boone, R., & Jones, P. (2005). Distance education: An exploration of alternative methods and types of instructional media in teacher education. *Journal of Special Education Technology*, *20*(3), 25–33.

Slavin, R. E. (1995). Cooperative Learning: theory, research and practice. Boston: Allyn and Bacon.

Smith, G. G. (2001). Interaction evokes reflection: Learning efficiency in spatial visualization. *Interactive Multimedia Electronic Journal of Computer-Enhanced Learning, 3*. Retrieved March 17, 2006, from http://imej.wfu.edu/articles/2001/2/05/index.asp

Smith, G. G., Caris, M., & Ferguson, D. (2001, June). *Teaching over the Web versus face to face*. Paper presented at the ED-Media 2001 World Conference on Educational Multimedia, Hypermedia & Telecommunications, Tampere, Finland. (ERIC Document Reproduction Service No. ED466216).

Smith, G. G., Ferguson, D., & Caris, M. (2002). Teaching online versus face-to- face. *Journal of Educational Technology Systems*, *30*(4), 337–364. doi:10.2190/FFWX-TJJE-5AFQ-GMFT

Smith, P. J., & Smith, S. N. (1999). Differences between Chinese and Australian students: some implications for distance educators. *Distance Education*, *20*(1), 64–80. doi:10.1080/0158791990200106

Sofowora, O.A. (2009). Perceived effect of GSM on older adults in south-western Nigeria. *Ethiopian Journal of Education and Science.*

Soloway, E., & His, S. (1998, April). *Learner-Centre design.* Paper presented at the CHI 98 Conference, Los-Angeles, CA.

Sorby, S. A., & Baartmans, B. J. (2000). The development and assessment of a course for enhancing the 3D spatial visualization skills of first year engineering students. *Journal of Engineering Education, 89*(3), 301–307.

Spodick, E. F. (1996). *The evolution of distance learning.* Retrieved December 10, 2003, from http://sqzm14.ust.hk/distance/evolution-distance-learning.htm

Stahl, G., Koschmann, T., & Suthers, D. (2006). Computer-supported collaborative learning: An historical perspective. In Cambridge Handbook of the Learning Sciences. Cambridge, UK: Cambridge University Press.

Stake, R. E. (1995). The art of case study research. London: Sage Publication

Stalder, F. (2000). The Network Paradigm: Social Formations in the Age of Information. *The Information Society, 14*(1). Retrieved from http://www.indiana.edu:80/~tisj/readers/full-text/14-4%20Stalder.html

Stevahn, L., King, J. A., Ghere, G., & Minnema, J. (2005). Establishing Essential Competences for Programme Evaluators. *The American Journal of Evaluation, 26*(1), 43–59. doi:10.1177/1098214004273180

Stinehart, K. (1987). Factors affecting faculty attitudes toward distance teaching (Doctoral dissertation, Iowa State University, 1987). *Dissertation Abstracts International, 48* (7), 131B. (UMI No. 8721935).

Strauss, A., & Corbin, J. (1998). Basics of Qualitative Research: Techniques and Procedures for Developing Grounded Theory. London: SAGE Publications.

Strevens, P. (1974). Some basic principles of teacher training. *ELT Journal, 29*(1), 19–27.

Strobl, J. (2004). GIScience Education for Professionals – the UNIGIS Distance Learning Model. *Geospatial Today*, 6/2004.

Strobl, J. (2007). *Regional Models for Renewable Energy Potentials. Conference on "Eco-Energies for Future Generations.* Northwest Agricultural and Forestry University, Yangling, China.

Strobl, J. (2008). Digital Earth Brainware. A Framework for Education and Qualification Requirements. In J. Schiewe, & U. Michel (Eds.), Geoinformatics paves the Highway to Digital Earth. gi-reports@igf, Universität Osnabrück, S. 134-138.

Strong, S., & Smith, R. (2001). Spatial visualization: Fundamentals and trends in engineering graphics. *Journal of Information Technology, 18*(1), 1–13.

Sunal, W. D., Sunal, C. S., Odell, M. R., & Sundberg, C. L. (2003, Summer). Research-Supported Best Practices for Developing Online Learning. *Journal of Interactive Online learning, 2*(1), 1- 40.

Suskie, L. (2004). Assessing student learning. Bolton, MA: Anker Publishing Company, Inc.

Sweller, J. (1988). Cognitive load during problem solving: Effects on learning. *Cognitive Science, 12*, 257–285.

Sweller, J., & Chandler, P. (1994). Why some material is difficult to learn. *Cognition and Instruction, 12*, 185–233. doi:10.1207/s1532690xci1203_1

Sweller, J., Chandler, P., Tierney, P., & Cooper, M. (1990). Cognitive load and selective attention as factors in the structuring of technical material. *Journal of Experimental Psychology. General, 119*, 176–192. doi:10.1037/0096-3445.119.2.176

Tal, M. H., Tal, E. H., & Yair, Y. (2006). Wikis in Academic Courses: An Institutional Perspective. In Y. Eshet-Alkalai, A. Caspi, & N. Geri (Eds.) *Proceedings of the Chais conference on instructional technologies research 2008: Learning in the technological era,* (pp. 79 – 83). Raanana, Israel: The Open University of Israel.

Tallent-Runnels, M. K., Thomas, J. A., Lan, W. Y., Cooper, S., Ahern, T. C., Shaw, S. M., & Liu, X. (2006). Teaching Courses Online: A Review of the Research. *Review of Educational Research, 76*(1), 93–135. doi:10.3102/00346543076001093

Tan, W. (2004). Research Design 1: Case studies In Practical Research Methods, (2nd ed). Jurong, Singapore: Prentice Hall.

Taylor, C. (1995). *Cooperative Learning in an African Context.* Accessed via www.selu.edu/Academics/Faculty/dshwalb/files/Cooperative_Learning.pdf

Taylor, J. (1995). Distance Education Technologies: the fourth generation. *Australian Journal of Educational Technology, 11*(2), 1–7.

Taylor, J. C., & White, V. J. (1991). Faculty attitudes towards teaching in the distance education mode: An exploratory investigation. *Research in Dance Education, 3*(3), 7–11.

Taylor, P. J., Derudder, B., García, C. G., & Witlox, F. (2009). From North-South to 'Global' South An investigation of a changing 'South' using airline flows between cities, 1970-2005. *Geography Compass, 3*(2), 836–855. doi:10.1111/j.1749-8198.2009.00216.x

Taylor, P., & Maor, D. (2000). Assessing the efficacy of online teaching with the Constructivist On-Line Learning Environment Survey. In A. Herrmann & M. Kulski (Ed.) Flexible Futures in University Teaching, (pp. 207-218). Perth, Australia: University of Western Australia

Taylor-Powell, E., & Boyd, H. H. (2008). Evaluation capacity building in complex organizations. *New Directions for Evaluation, 2008*(120), 55–69. doi:10.1002/ev.276

Telematics Application Programme. (1998). *Project – t3, Telematics for teacher training.* Retrieved from http://www2.echo.lu/telematics/education/en/projects/files/ts.html

The Design-Based Research Collective (DBRC). (2003). Design-Based Research: An emerging paradigm for educational inquiry. *Educational Researcher, 32*(1), 5–8. doi:10.3102/0013189X032001005

Thomson, J. S., & Stringer, S. B. (1998, August). Evaluating for distance learning: Feedback from students and faculty. In Proceeding of the 14th Annual Conference *on Distance Teaching & Learning*, Madison, WI. (ERIC Document Reproduction Service No. ED422879).

Thorpe, M. (2002). Rethinking Learner Support: the Challenge of On-line Learning. *Open Learning, 17*(2), 105–120.

Tiffin, J., & Rajasinham, L. (1995). In search of the Virtual class: Education in an information society. London: Routledge.

Tinoca, L., Oliveira, I., & Pereira, A. (2007). Group work peer-assessment in an online environment. In *European Association of Distance Teaching Universities Conference.* Retrieved May 20, 2009, from http://www.eadtu.nl/conference-2007/files/SA A4.pdf

Tobin, K., Tippins, D., & Gallard, A. (1994). Research on instructional strategies for teaching science. In D. L. Gabel (Ed.), Handbook of research on science teaching and learning, (pp. 45-93). New York: Macmillan.

Tolbert, A., Mclean, G., & Myers, R. (2002). Creating the global learning organization. *International Journal of Intercultural Relations*, 1–15.

Triandis, H. C. (1989). The self and social behavior in differing cultural contexts. *Psychological Review, 96*(3), 506–520. doi:10.1037/0033-295X.96.3.506

Triandis, H. C., McCusker, C., & Hui, C. H. (1990). Multimethod probes of individualism and collectivism. *Journal of Personality and Social Psychology, 59*, 1006–1020. doi:10.1037/0022-3514.59.5.1006

Trompenaars, F., & Hampden-Turner, C. (1997). Riding the waves of culture: understanding cultural diversity in business. London: Nicholas Brealey.

Truman-Davis, B., & Hartman, J. (1998, November). *Online with the future: Web-based* program development at the University of Central Florida: Designing a university *for the 21st century.* Paper presented at Web-Net 98: World on the WWW and Internet Conference, Orlando, FL. (ERIC Document Reproduction Service No. ED427739).

Tuckman, B. (1965). Developmental sequence in small groups. *Psychological Bulletin, 63*, 384–399. doi:10.1037/h0022100

Turner, J. C. (1987). Rediscovering the social group. Oxford, UK: Blackwell.

Turos, J., & Ervin, A. (2000). Training and gender differences on a Web-based mental rotation task. *The Penn State Behrend Psychology Journal, 4*(2), 3-12. Retrieved from http://viz.bd.psu.edu/viz/conferences/Training-and-Gender

Turvey, K. (2005). Elearning, efacilitation, ecommunities, epedagogies: a professional standpoint based on evidence. *Reflecting Education, 1*(1-2), 24–40.

Tversky, B., Morrison, J., & Betrancourt, M. (2002). Animation: Can it facilitate? *International Journal of Human-Computer Studies, 57*, 247–262. doi:10.1006/ijhc.2002.1017

Twigg, C. (2003). *Change: Improving quality and reducing cost; design for effective learning.* Retrieved on November, 20, 2007 from http://proquest.umi.com/pdweb?did=592388111&sid=10&Fmt=3&clientld=21888&RQT=309&VName=PQD

U.S. Department of Education, Center for Education Statistics. (2003). Digest of education statistics, 2002 (NCES 20003-060). Washington, DC: Author.

Ukpokodu, O. N. (2002). Breaking through preservice teachers' defensive attitudes in a multicultural education course. *Multicultural Education Magazine, 9*(5), 25–33.

Ukpokodu, O. N. (2003). Teaching multicultural education from a critical perspective: Challenges and Dilemmas. *Multicultural Perspectives, 5*(4), 17–23. doi:10.1207/S15327892MCP0504_4

Ukpokodu, O. N. (2008, November). Teachers' reflections on pedagogies that enhance learning in an online course on teaching for equity and social justice. *Journal of Interactive Online Learning, 7*(3), 227–255.

UNESCO. (2009, July). *2009 World Conference on Higher Education: The New Dynamics of Higher Education and Research for Societal Change and Development.* UNESCO, Paris. Retrieved on August 05, 2009 from http://www.unesco.org/fileadmin/MULTIMEDIA/HQ/ED/ED/pdf/WCHE_2009/FINAL%20COMMUNIQUE%20WCHE%202009.pdf

University of Idaho, College of Engineering. (1999). *Distance education at a glance: Guide #1.* Retrieved August 15, 2003, from http://www.uidaho.edu/evo/dist1.html Valentine, D. (2002). Distance learning: Promises, problems, and possibilities. *Online* Journal of Distance Learning Administration, 5(3). Retrieved January 29, 2003, from http://www.westga.edu/%7Edistance/ojdla/fall53/valentine53.html

University of Arkansas at Little Rock. (2009). Retrieved May 28, 2009, from http://ualr.edu/www/

Valiathan, P. (2002). *Blended Learning Models.* Retrieved July 13, 2006 from http://www.learningcircuits.org/2002/aug2002/valiathan.html

Van Dam, N. (2004). The e-Learning Field book (Implementation lessons and case studies from companies that are making e-learning work). New York: McGraw-Hill.

Van Eekelen, I. M. (2005). *Teachers' will and way to learn: Studies on how teachers learn and their willingness to do so.* Unpublished doctoral dissertation, Maastricht University, The Netherlands.

Van Merriënboer, J. J. G., & Paas, F. (2003). Powerful learning and the many faces of instructional design: Toward a framework for the design of powerful learning environments. In E. de Corte, L.Verschaffel, N. Entwistle, & J. J. G. van Merriënboer (Eds.), Unravelling basic components and dimensions of powerful learning environments (pp. 3-20). Oxford: Elsevier Science.

Vavoula, G. N., Lefrere, P., O'Malley, C., & Sharples, M. (2003). Providing Guidelines for Learning, Teaching, and Tutoring in a Mobile Environment. In *Proceedings of the 2nd IEEE International Workshop.*

Vavoula, G., Meek, J., Sharples, M., Lonsdale, P., & Rudman, P. (2006). A lifecycle approach to evaluating MyArtSpace. In S. Hsi, Kinshuk, T. Chan, & D. Sampson (Eds.), *Proceedings of the 4th IEEE International Workshop on Wireless and Mobile Technologies in Education (WMUTE 2006)* (pp. 18-22). Athens, Greece: IEEE Computer Society.

Veerman, A., & Veldhuis-Diermanse, E. (2001). Collaborative learning through computer-mediated communication in academic education. In P. Dillenbourg, A. Eurelings & K. Hakkarainen (Eds.), *European Perspectives on Computer-Supported Collaborative Learning. Proceedings of the First European Conference on CSCL.* Maastricht: McLuhan Institute, University of Maastricht.

Velan, G. M., Kumar, R. K., Dziegielewski, M., & Wakefield, D. (2002). Web-based self-assessments in pathology with Questionmark Perception. *Pathology, 34*, 282–284. doi:10.1080/00313020220131372

Villar, L. M., & Alegre, O. M. (2004). Manual para la excelencia en la enseñanza superior, [Handbook for Excellence in Higher Education]. Madrid: McGraw-Hill.

Villar, L. M., & Alegre, O. M. (2006). Online Faculty Development in the Canary Islands: A Study of E-mentoring. *Higher Education in Europe, 31*(1), 65–81. doi:10.1080/03797720600861243

Villar, L. M., & Alegre, O. M. (2006). Competencias para la formación de evaluadores. [Competences for training evaluators]. Málaga, Spain: Aljibe.

Villar, L. M., & Alegre, O. M. (2007). Online Programme of Excellence Model (OPEM). *International Journal of Social Sciences (IJSS), 2* (2). Retrieved May 10, 2009, from http://www.waset.org/ijss/v2/v2-2-14.pdf

Villegas, A. M., & Lucas, T. (2002)... *Journal of Teacher Education, 53*(1), 20–32. doi:10.1177/0022487102053001003

Voithofer, R. (2005). Designing New Media Education Research: The Materiality of Data, Representation, and Dissemination. *Educational Researcher, 34*(9), 3–14. doi:10.3102/0013189X034009003

Vonderwell, S., Liang, X., & Alderman, K. (2007). Asynchronous discussions and assessment in online learning. *Journal of Research on Technology in Education, 39*(3), 309–328.

Vovides, Y., Sanchez-Alonso, S., Mitropoulou, V., & Nickmans, G. (2007). The use of e-learning course management systems to support learning strategies and to improve self-regulated learning. *Educational Research Review, 2*(1), 64–74. doi:10.1016/j.edurev.2007.02.004

Voyer, D., Voyer, S., & Bryden, P. (1995). Magnitude of sex differences in spatial abilities: A meta-analysis and consideration of critical variables. *Psychological Bulletin, 117*(2), 250–270. doi:10.1037/0033-2909.117.2.250

Vrasidas, C., & McIsaac, M. S. (2000). Principles of pedagogy and evaluation for web-based learning. *Educational Media International, 37*(2), 105–112. doi:10.1080/095239800410405

Vrba, V., Cvrk, L., & Sykora, M. (2006). Framework for digital TV applications. In *Proceedings of the International Conference on Networking, International Conference on Systems and International Conference on Mobile Communications and Learning Technologies,* (pp. 184-184).

Vygotsky, L. (1978). Mind in society: The development of higher psychological processes. Cambridge, MA: Harvard University Press.

Vygotsky, L. (1986). Thought and language. Cambridge, MA: MIT Press.

Wallace, M. (1991). Training Foreign Language Teachers: A Reflective Approach. Cambridge, UK: Cambridge University Press.

Wang, M. (2007). Designing online courses that effectively engage learners from diverse cultural backgrounds. *British Journal of Educational Technology, 38*(2), 294–311. doi:10.1111/j.1467-8535.2006.00626.x

Wang, M. J. (2004). Correlational analysis of student visibility and learning outcomes in an online setting. *Journal of Asynchronous Learning Networks, 8*(4), 71–82.

Warschauer, M. (1997). Computer-mediated collaborative learning: theory & practice. *Modern Language Journal, 81*(4), 470–481. doi:10.2307/328890

Warschauer, M. (2003). Technology and social inclusion: Rethinking the digital divide. Cambridge, MA: MIT Press.

Watkins, D., & Biggs, J. (1996). (Eds.). The Chinese learner: Cultural, psychological, and contextual influences. Victoria, Australia: Comparative Education Research Centre, University of Hong Kong and the Australian Council for Educational Research Ltd.

Watkins, D., & Biggs, J. (Eds.). (2001). Teaching the Chinese Learners: Psychological and Pedagogical Perspectives. Melbourne, Australia: Australian Council for Educational Research / Comparative Education Research Center.

Watkins, R. (2005). Developing Interactive E-Learning Activities. *Performance Improvement, 44*(5), 5–7. doi:10.1002/pfi.4140440504

Webb, N. M., Ender, P., & Lewis, S. (1986). Problem-solving strategies and group processes in small groups learning computer programming. *American Educational Research Journal, 23*(2), 243–261.

Web-Based Education Commission. (2000, December). *The power of the Internet for learning: Moving from promise to practice.* Retrieved June 2, 2009, from http://www.ed.gov/offices/AC/WBEC/FinalReport/

Weidner, M. (2006). Kooperatives Lernen im Unterricht [Cooperative learning in school]. Seelze, Germany: Erhard Friedrich Verlag.

Weinberger, A., & Fischer, F. (2006). A framework to analyze argumentative knowledge construction in computer-supported collaborative learning. *Computers & Education, 46*(1), 71–95. doi:10.1016/j.compedu.2005.04.003

Wenger, E. (1987). Artificial Intelligence and Tutoring Systems: Computational and Cognitive Approaches to the Communication of Knowledge. San Francisco: Morgan Kaufmann.

Wenger, E. (1998). Communities of Practice; learning, meaning, and identity. New York: Cambridge University Press.

White, C. (2003). Language learning in distance education. Cambridge, UK: Cambridge University Press.

Whittington, N. (1990). Characteristics of good state instructional telecommunications policy for higher education: Some research considerations. In M. G. Moore (Ed.), Contemporary issues in American distance education, (pp. 23-54). New York: Pergamon Press.

Widdowson, H. (1978). Teaching Language as Communication. Oxford, UK: Oxford University Press.

Wiebe, E. N. (1993). Visualization of three-dimensional form: A discussion of theoretical models of internal representation. *Engineering Design Graphics Journal, 57*(1), 18–28.

Wiesen, J. P. (2004, June). *An in-depth, content review of spatial ability tests.* Paper presented at the 28th Annual IPMAAC Conference on Personnel Assessment, Seattle.

Williams, A. E. (1996, June). *Integrating courses with the Internet: Preparing the teacher as well as the learner.* Paper presented at the Association of Small Computer Users in Education Summer Conference, North Myrtle Beach, SC. (ERIC Document Reproduction Service No. ED405839).

Williams, A. P., Sutton, K. J., & Allen, R. J. (2008). Spatial ability: Issues associated with engineering and gender. In *Proceedings of the 19th Annual Conference for the Australasian Association for Engineering Education*. Yeppoon, Queensland, 7- 10, December, 2008.

Williams, E., Duray, R., & Venkateshwar, R. (2006). Teamwork orientation, group cohesiveness, and student learning: A Study of the use of teams in online distance education. *Journal of Management Education, 30*, 592–616. doi:10.1177/1052562905276740

Willis, B. (1993). Distance education: A practical guide. Englewood, NJ: Education Technology.

Wilson, B., & Lowry, M. (2000). Constructivist Learning on the Web. *New Directions for Adult and Continuing Education, 2000*(88), 79–88. doi:10.1002/ace.8808

Winters, F., Greene, J., & Costich, C. (2008). Self-regulation of learning within computer-based learning environments. *Educational Psychology Review, 20*(4), 429–444. doi:10.1007/s10648-008-9080-9

Wolcott, L. L. (1997). *Tenure, promotion, and distance teaching: A study of faculty rewards and incentives.* Unpublished manuscript, Utah State University at Logan. (ERIC Document Reproduction Service No. ED413861).

Wolcott, L. L., & Haderlie, S. (1995, August). *The myth of dangling carrots: Incentives,* promotions, and rewards for teaching at distance. Paper presented at the 11th Annual Conference on Distance Teaching and Learning, Madison, WI.

Wood, K. (2006). Changing a person: the experience of learning to research in the social sciences. *Higher Education Research & Development, 25*(1), 53–66. doi:10.1080/13600800500453162

Wood, P. A. (2001). The U.S. Department of Education and student financial aid for distance education: An update. Washington, DC: ERIC Clearinghouse on Higher Education. (ERIC Document Reproduction Service No. ED457762).

Woodward, T. (1988). Loop Input. Exeter, CT: Pilgrim Publications.

World Bank. (2002). Constructing Knowledge Societies: New Challenges for Tertiary Education. Washington, DC: World Bank.

Wu, C. L. (2003). *Web-based training in Taiwan's fortune 500 corporations: Implementation factors.* Unpublished doctoral dissertation, The University of West Florida, Pensacola, FL.

Yadin, A., & Or-Bach, R. (2008). Fostering individual learning – when and how. *ACM's Inroads –. SIGCSE Bulletin, 40*(4), 83–86. doi:10.1145/1473195.1473227

Yan, Z. (2006). Different experiences, different effects: a longitudinal study of learning a computer program in a network environment. *Computers in Human Behavior, 22*(3), 364–380. doi:10.1016/j.chb.2004.09.005

Yates, C. (2004). *Teacher Education at a Distance: Lessons and Experience from Sub Saharan Africa.* Paper presented at the All-Africa Minister's Conference on Open Learning and Distance Education, 2004. http://moodle.org (n.d.). Retrieved 10th May 2009.

Yin Ho, N. (1999). Teaching and Learning via IT: Higher Order Thinking Skills in English Language, English Literature and Mathematics, (pp. 2-3).

Yin, R. K. (2003). Case study research design and methods, (3rd ed.) Thousand Oaks, CA: Sage Publications.

Yong, Y., & Wang, S. (1996). Faculty perceptions on a new approach to distance learning. *Journal of Instruction Delivery Systems, 10*(2), 3–5.

Yukawa, J. (2006). Co-reflection in online learning: Collaborative critical thinking as narrative. *International Journal of Computer-Supported Collaborative Learning, 1*(2), 203–228. doi:10.1007/s11412-006-8994-9

Zeichner, K. (2008). Settings for teacher education. In M. Cochran-Smith, S. Feiman-Nemser, & D. J. Mcintyre (Eds.), Handbook of research on teacher education: Enduring questions in changing contexts. New York: Routledge.

Zheng, J., & Niu, J. (2007). Computer and Computational SciencesUnified Mapping of Social Networks into 3D Space. In IMSCCS 2007, Second International Multi-Symposiums on Computer and Computational Sciences, 13.-15.8.2007, Iowa City.

Zhu, C., Valcke, M., & Schellens, T. (2008). The Relationship between epistemological beliefs, learning conceptions, and approaches to study: a cross-cultural structural model? *Asia Pacific Journal of Education*, *28*(4), 411–423. doi:10.1080/02188790802468823

Ziemek, T. R. (2006, March). *Two-D or not Two-D: Gender implications of visual cognition in electronic games.* Paper presented at the 2006 Symposium on Interactive 3D Graphics and Games, Redwood City, CA.

Zimmerman, B. J. (2000). Self-Efficacy: An Essential Motive to Learn. *Contemporary Educational Psychology*, *25*, 82–91. doi:10.1006/ceps.1999.1016

About the Contributors

Siran Mukerji is Jawahar Lal Nehru scholar for her doctorate in HRD and also has Masters in Distance Education and Public Administration. She has been International Research Fellow of Open University Business School (2009), Open University, UK. She was associated with Arab Open University Saudi Arabia Branch for three years as a faculty member in Business Administration and co edited teaching case books and contributed articles in standard national and international journals and also presented papers in national and international conferences. Her current research interests are Performance management and HRM in open and distance learning institutions. She is a member of review committees of a number of international conferences / journals. In her parent institution IGNOU, India, she is Assistant Director.

Purnendu Tripathi, an International Research Fellow of Open University Business School (2009), Open University, UK, is Ph.D. in Management, with Masters in Distance Education also. He was associated with Arab Open University Saudi Arabia Branch for three years as a faculty member in Business Administration. In his parent institution IGNOU, India, he is Assistant Director. He has co edited teaching case books and contributed articles in standard national and international journals and presented papers in national and international conferences. He is a member of review committees of a number of international conferences and journals. His current research interest is Academic Program Life Cycle (APLC) and Educational Marketing.

***

A. A. Adekomi is Senior Lecturer in the Department of Educational Technology at Obafemi Awolowo University in Nigeria. He is also a media consultant with specialisation in media production, ICT technical system assemblage and instructional design. He has PhD in Educational Technology.

Egbedokun Adeola is Assistant Lecturer in the Department of Educational Technology at Obafemi Awolowo University in Nigeria and has MA in Educational Technology. He is presently studying in the same department for his Doctoral degree.

J. O. Adeyanju is a Professor of Educational Technology and currently the Head of Department of Educational Technology in Obafemi Awolowo University in Nigeria. He is a media consultant with specialization in graphics, media design and production.

Gilbert Ahamer was born as a physicist (i.e. developer of original world views), later on Dr. Ahamer has collaborated with several institutions and on various projects in order to see as many sides of as many medals as possible: assessing environmental radioactivity in his home county after the Chernobyl disaster, evaluating the global biomass energy potential of his home planet, computing the air emissions for his city, developing climate protection measures his country's administration, supporting ex-communist countries of Europe to accede to the European Union by better mastering their environmental legislation, promoting a developmental curriculum at his university and e-teaching Technology Assessment to his flock, namely to future engineers who are subjectively convinced to act for a better future. Consequently, *creating suitable sustainable structures* that *enable dialogic learning* and *discursive consensus finding* became the final aim of his mixed experiences.

Mohammed Albalawi is Commander in the Saudi Arabian Navy. He has Master's degree in Educational Leadership with a specialization in Education and Training Management, Ed.D. in Curriculum and Instruction with a specialization in Instructional Technology and Distance Learning, from the University of West Florida (UWF). He has been director of three divisions in the training department: the Curriculum and Testing Division, the Training Aids Division, and the Naval Training Simulators Division. He is also Director of the E-learning Division and Director of eCurriculum at King Fahad Naval Academy (KFNA), where he is currently developing standards and guidelines for e-Learning and supervising an e-Book development project.

Olga M. Alegre is Professor of Didactics and School Organization at the University of La Laguna. Her specializations are inclusive education and University evaluation. She has 25 years of experience in the professional development of undergraduates. Her research focuses on the quantitative and qualitative analysis of inclusive teaching and learning and their impacts on multicultural education. Her general publications are related to effective diversity teaching practices and interventions for students with and at risk for emotional and behavioral disorders. Dr. Alegre has co-authored several books with Dr. Luis M. Villar and articles on e-mentoring, program assessment and staff development.

Ruth Aylett (www.macs.hw.ac.uk/~ruth) is a Professor of Computer Science at Heriot-Watt University in Edinburgh, UK, where she leads the research group VIS&GE – Vision, Interactive Systems and Graphical Environments. She researches the overlap between AI and interactive graphics and specifically affective agent architectures and interactive narrative. She coordinated the EU-funded project eCIRCUS in which the ORIENT system was developed and is now a partner in an EU project LIREC – Living with Robots and Interactive Characters. Dr. Aylett has more than 170 publications at refereed conferences, in journals and book chapters.

T. A. Bada is Senior Lecturer in the Department of Educational Technology at Obafemi Awolowo University in Nigeria. He has doctorate in Educational Technology and his area of specialization is graphics and media production.

Abbas Bazargan is Professor of Research Methodology and Statistics in the Faculty of Psychology and Education, University of Tehran. He is also Director of UNESCO Chair in Planning, Management and Quality Assurance in Higher Education at the Institute for Research and Planning in Higher Education (Tehran). Dr. Bazargan has previously served as Vice Chancellor of Bu-Ali Sina University (Hamadan,

Iran). He was formerly international consultant with UNDP, ILO and UNESCO in Asia and Africa. His current research interests address the role of pedagogy and assessment in e-learning.

Francesco Bellotti has M.Sc. (summa cum laude) and Ph.D. in Electronic Engineering from the University of Genoa. He is assistant professor at the University of Genova, where he teaches Object Oriented Programming and Databases. His research interests include Serious Gaming, interactive TV, Automotive Multimedia and Human-Computer Interaction. He has authored more than 80 papers on such themes. He participated in 11 EU-funded industrial research projects in the fields of new media and Human-Machine interaction in vehicles.

Giancarlo Bo is an Electronic Engineer from the University of Genoa. After collaborating as software developer with Advanced Engineering Technology S.r.l., in 1998 he joined the Signal Processing and Telecommunication Group, University of Genoa where in 2002, he attained the PhD in Space Science and Engineering. Since 1998, Dr. Bo worked on several national and international IT research programmes, both in the proposal preparation and management phases. In January 2001 he joined GIUNTI Labs S.r.l. as project manager of many research projects funded by the European Union. Dr. Bo is a member of both the Institute of Electrical and Electronics Engineers (IEEE) and the IEEE-Computer Society.

Bopelo Boitshwarelo, a PhD in Education (specializing in Instructional Technology and Flexible Learning) from Deakin University, Australia. He is presently in the Department of Distance Education, Centre for Continuing Education, University of Botswana. He is primarily involved with the development of an Online Master in Project Management. He is also academic staff trainer in the area of Instructional design for e-Learning. His research interests are in the area of online communities of practice, blended learning, course design and development, quality assurance issues in online learning and the use of activity theory in learning settings.

Paul Breen is an English Language lecturer, originally from Ireland, who has completed his post-graduate studies in Education in the University of Manchester, specializing in the field of educational technology, and has worked in a range of educational contexts in both the United Kingdom and overseas. He spent two years in South Korea working for Seoul National University of Technology and is presently based in London where he is teaching Business English and Communication Skills in the University of East London. His research interests are in the field of blended learning, educational technology, and English for Academic Purposes. His doctorate studies are related to the effectiveness of blended learning approaches.

Karina Clemmons is an Assistant Professor of Secondary Education at the University of Arkansas at Little Rock (UALR). Prior to joining the Teacher Education faculty at UALR, Dr. Clemmons had extensive experience in the U.S. and abroad teaching English Language Learners in diverse settings including middle school, high school, and adult programs. Some of Dr. Clemmons' research interests are second language acquisition, vocabulary in the content area, improving teacher quality in secondary education, and technology integration in education.

Merrilee Cunningham received her PhD. in Renaissance Studies at Vanderbilt University after having attained degrees from Northwestern University and Marshall University. An Associate Professor in the

Dept. of English at the University of Houston Downtown, she has published extensively in Renaissance Literature, Poetry, Film, Pedagogy, and Computer Theory. She was on the Board of Advisors of the Houston Teachers Institute, a participant in the 2009 Yale National Initiative to strengthen teaching in the public schools, and was designated as a 2008 Cultural Envoy from the US Dept. of State to Serbia and then again as a 2009 Cultural Envoy for the US Dept. of State in Macedonia, she continues working with teachers from the public schools through Houston's Writers in the Schools. Dr. Cunningham has published half a dozen articles on subjects relating to computer theory and pedagogy in numerous refereed journals with Dr. Robbins.

Orhan Curaoglu is a Ph.D. research scholar in Computer Education & Instructional Technologies. He has been working as a research assistant in the same department. His main areas of interest are school media and technology integration, distance education and instructional technology. He can be contacted by email: orhancuraoglu@gmail.com.

Sibylle Enz studied Psychology and Andragogy at the University of Bamberg. She has worked as a research fellow at the department for diagnostics and personality psychology at the University of Bamberg before she became a research fellow at the department for general psychology, also at the University of Bamberg. She was research associate in the EU FP 5 project VICTEC, in the FP 6 project eCIRCUS, and in the FP 7 project LIREC. In early 2009 she has finished a Ph.D. on the role of empathy in conflicts at the workplace. Her research interests focus on empathy, self-presentation, and social conflict.

Chris Evans is a Senior Lecturer at London's Brunel University and a Fellow of Brunel's Teaching Academy. He was nominated for a National Teaching Fellowship Award and received a commendation from the Higher Education Academy in e-Tutor of the Year. He has PhD from the Department of Computing at Imperial College, London. His research interests mainly include Human-computer interaction, the design of interactive multimedia systems for learning, the cognitive effects of interactivity in e-learning systems, usability engineering, the evaluation of interactivity in information systems, the adoption of technology and diffusion, and the use of collaborative and social networking tools for learning.

Alessandro De Gloria, an Electronic Engineer from the University of Genoa and with the specialization in Informatics Engineering, is Director of teaching of the Bachelor and the Master degree in Electronic Engineering at the University of Genoa, since 2000. He was one of the founders of SIIT, the Liguria District of the Integrated System Technologies and from 2007 he is member of the Administrative board and of the Executive Committee of the District. Prof. Alessandro De Gloria is currently teaching Electronics of Computers, Multimedia Electronic Systems, and Computer Graphics. His main research interests are in the field of Computer Graphics, Video Game, Mechatronics and Embedded Systems. He has been responsible of more than 30 research project in the last 10 years. He authored more than 100 papers in the subjects stated above.

Cheryl Grable, Assistant Professor, has been a member of the Teacher Education faculty at the University of Arkansas of Little Rock (UALR) since 1995. She currently serves as the science and mathematics advisor for the secondary education program at UALR. Dr. Grable's research interests include middle level and secondary science education, digital teaching and field supervision, classroom management in synchronous distance learning, and implementation of the ISTE standards.

Lynne Hall is a Principal Lecturer in the Faculty of Applied Sciences at the University of Sunderland and has had over 50 academic papers published. Lynne has special interests in emphatic engagements, technology enhanced learning. She also specialises in personal, social and emotional learning.

Wallace Hannum is a faculty member in the educational psychology program at the University of North Carolina and Associate Director for Technology of the National Research Center on Rural Education Support. Dr. Hannum teaches graduate level courses on learning theories, instructional design, and the use of technology in education. His research focuses on instructional uses of technology, especially distance education. He has participated in the design and implementation of numerous technology-based programs and projects. He has worked extensively on education projects in Africa, Asia and Latin America. Dr. Hannum is author of five books and numerous articles on topics related to technology and instructional design.

Andrew Hunt is the Department Chair of Teacher Education and an Associate Professor of Teacher Education at the University of Arkansas at Little Rock (UALR). Dr. Hunt is dedicated to the betterment of teacher education through best practices at UALR. This is evidenced by the systemic change brought about by the integration of technology into field assessment of pre-professionals and interns, as well as advancing the development of digital portfolios for candidate program defense. He is committed to increasing technology skills in others for utilizing technology in accessing and processing information into knowledge.

Lanre Idowu is Assistant Lecturer in the Department of Educational Technology at Obafemi Awolowo University in Nigeria and has MA in Educational Technology. He is currently a PhD scholar in the same Department.

Thomas Jekel is an educator and researcher at the Institute for Geographic Information Science at the Austrian Academy of Sciences as well as at the Department of Science Education and Teacher Training and the Department of Geography and Geoinformation, University of Salzburg. He is one of the pioneers in Austria's e-learning communities and has developed modes of teaching geography hands-on and feet-on by both using Geographic Information Science (GIS) to analyse virtual glaciers and alpinist school excursions on real-world glaciers. He co-developed the idea of PPGIS by combining the ethics of self-responsible civil society with the tools of spatial planning by GIS. Thomas Jekel's international activities comprise long-standing GIS contacts in South Asia where among others he has acted as guest lecturer at Jawarhalal Nehru University, New Delhi, India.

Stephanie Jones, Associate Professor of Organizational Behavior at Maastricht School of Management since January 2007, graduated from University College London and the London School of Economics. She managed consulting and training businesses in the UK, Hong Kong, PRC, India, Australia and Dubai. Moving to academe in 2002 she served in Kuwait and Dubai, and now teaches all over the world for the MSM MBA. She has also taught for the Universities of London, Exeter, Cranfield and Leicester in the UK. Dr Jones has authored over 25 full-length internationally-published books on business and management.

Nancy Kiplinger is an instructional designer and adult learning specialist who focuses on helping organizations develop and implement effective learning approaches. She has worked with a U.S.-based non-governmental agency (NGO), where she provided instructional design consultation to training projects in West, Central, and Northern Africa, as well as Europe/Eurasia and the Middle East. She has also held learning specialist positions with the University of North Carolina at Chapel Hill (Schools of Government, Medicine, and Nursing), SAS, Inc., and Battelle Pacific Northwest Laboratories. She has given workshops and presentations about designing effective learning experiences, distance learning, and blended learning in the U.S., Africa, and the Middle East. Dr. Kiplinger is the author of articles and reports and co-author of *Making it Happen: Using Distance Learning to Improve Reproductive Health Provider Performance* (1999).

Ioannis Kompatsiaris received the Diploma degree in electrical engineering and the Ph.D. degree in 3-D model based image sequence coding from Aristotle University of Thessaloniki in 1996 and 2001, respectively. He is a Senior Researcher with CERTH-ITI and director of its Multimedia Knowledge Laboratory. His research interests include multimedia content processing, multimodal techniques, multimedia and Semantic Web, multimedia ontologies, knowledge-based analysis, and context aware inference for semantic multimedia analysis, personalization and retrieval. He is the co-author of 10 book chapters, 30 papers in refereed journals and more than 100 papers in international conferences.

Pascal Lhoas owns a master of IT and Innovation from the University of Nancy in France. He has been working in international IT project management for a private company for more than 10 years. This experience is topped with a certification at the highest level (practitioner) in both Prince2 and HERMES methodologies. He joined the CRP Henri Tudor in 2004 to lead the QUAPITAL project(1). This project was aimed at enhancing the quality of the e-Government projects of the state of Luxembourg. Being responsible of the CRP-HT participation in the ELU(2) and PALETTE(3) European research projects, he also gained experience on European-wide research projects in the FP6 framework. He actually lead the e-Government strategic program of the Center for IT Innovation at the CRP-HT. More information: http://www.elu-project.com/.

Mei Yii Lim was born in Malaysia. She has Diploma and Advanced Diploma in Computer Science from Tunku Abdul Rahman College, Malaysia. She has also studied BSc in Computer Science from University of Campbell, USA and graduated in June 2002 with Summa Cum Laude. She completed her MSc with distinction in Virtual Environments from University of Salford, UK in July 2004. In 2007, she got her doctorate degree in Computing entitled Emotions, Behaviour and Belief Regulation in An Intelligent Guide with Attitude from Heriot-Watt University, Scotland. Currently, she is a research associate for the EU FP7 project LIREC. Her research is focused on Emotional Models, Emotional Memories, Intelligent Virtual Agents, Narrative, Mobile Technologies and Multimodal Interaction Interface.

Amin Mousavi is a Ph.D. student at the Department of Educational Measurement and Evaluation, Faculty of Psychology and Education. He is also a teaching assistant at Mehralborz University. He was involved in a research project on transnational education conducted at the national level in Iran. He has been co-author of papers on e-learning.

Amanda Nolen, Ph.D. is an Assistant Professor of Educational Foundations in the College of Education at the University of Arkansas at Little Rock (UALR). She teaches graduate level courses at the Master's and Doctoral levels including Qualitative Research Methods, Learning Theories and Instructional Design, and Educational Assessment. Her research interests include Qualitative Methodology and the Responsible Conduct of Researcher (RCR) Education in Higher Education. Prior to joining the College of Education at UALR, Dr. Nolen was the Chief Operating Officer for the Holmes Partnership, a national education reform organization while completing her doctoral studies in Educational Psychology at Baylor University.

Isolina Oliveira is an Assistant Professor at Universidade Aberta, in Portugal, in the Department of Education and Distance Teaching. She initiated her professional career as a high school teacher. During four years, she was a researcher focused on K-12 learning assessment at the Educational Innovation Institute, in Lisbon. She has developed and taught online, graduate and undergraduate, courses, as well as conducted research on online education, particularly on online assessment practices. She is a member of the Universidade Aberta Professional Development in E-learning team that has promoted the development of online distance education learning strategies, especially in the framework of the university's pedagogical model. She is also a member of the Education Research Center in the Education Institute in Lisbon.

F.M Oyeniran is Assistant Lecturer in the Department of Educational Technology at Obafemi Awolowo University in Nigeria. He has Masters in Educational Technology and is currently a PhD candidate in the same Department.

L. M. Oyewusi, PhD in Educational Technology, is Senior Lecturer in the Department of Educational Technology at Obafemi Awolowo University in Nigeria and her area of specialization is Curriculum and Instructional Design.

Ana Paiva is a research group leader at INESC-ID and a professor at Instituto Superior Técnico, Technical University of Lisbon. She is well known in the area of Intelligent Agents, User Modeling and Artificial Intelligence Applied to Education. Her research is focused on the affective elements in the interactions between users and computers and in particular in the interaction with synthetic characters. Her areas of application range from education, entertainment computing to virtual storytelling. She has (co)authored over 80 publications in refereed journals, conferences and books. Prof. Paiva coordinated the participation of INESC within several Portuguese and European projects, such as the Storyteller (Portuguese Science Foundation), IDEALS (funded under the Telematics program), NIMIS (an I3-ESE project), DiViLab, Safira, VICTEC and COLDEX (IST- 5th Framework), among others. Ana Paiva has been Chair of number of important international conferences and workshops.

Luis Palacios is a versatile researcher working in the areas of instructional technology and telecommunication. He is in Brunel University from July 2008, researching on interactive design of e-Learning systems. His previous experience includes working as a Learning Technologist in London School of Hygiene and Tropical Medicines and a project leader and as a researcher in the Open University, UK. In the Open University, he becomes part of the Institute of Educational Technology where he was participating in different projects as GUARDIANS, MOBILEARN, etc. He has a Master degree in

Education (M.Ed.) concentrated in instructional Technology and a Master in Telecommunication both from Pittsburgh University-USA.

Matteo Pellegrino received the M.Sc. degree in Computer Engineering from the University of Genoa. He is a PhD student at the ELIOS Lab, University of Genova, Dept. of Electronics and Biophysical Engineering (DIBE). His research interests include Serious Gaming, Virtual Reality and Interactive TV.

Alda Pereira is an Assistant Professor at Universidade Aberta – Portugal, in the Department of Education and Distance Teaching. She has a large experience in development and teaching of online undergraduate and graduate courses, and she is an active researcher in areas of online education and virtual learning communities. She was engaged in designing a new pedagogical model for the university. Presently, she is the director of the Distance Education Laboratory, a unit devoted to research in the field of the distance education, and conducts research on digital alternative assessment.

Shirley Pickle before becoming the Instructional Coordinator of the Arkansas Department of Education Distance Learning Center, taught business education, Spanish, and English in diverse settings including junior high, high school, Arkansas School for the Blind, and classes for distance-learning students in schools throughout Arkansas. Since 2003, she has trained and supervised distance-learning teachers and facilitators in Arkansas and has worked with legislators, educators, students, and parents to share the benefits of distance-learning courses to meet critical shortage content areas and address individual school and student needs throughout the state.

Ahmad Rafi is an architect and Associate Professor in the Faculty of Creative Multimedia. He is also the Director of Research and Development (R&D) Collaborations, Multimedia University. He has Bachelor Degree in Architecture (B Arch Hons.), Master of Science in Computer-Aided Building Design (MSc. in CABD) and Ph.D. in architectural animation and virtual reality from the University of Strathclyde. Dr. Rafi was the Dean, Faculty of Creative Multimedia and Chairman of Centre of Interpretation and Expression (CIE), Multimedia University from 2000-2006. His research includes 3D visualization, computer-aided learning, educational technology, virtual heritage and virtual reality. He has published more than 80 internationally multi-disciplinary refereed conference papers, journal articles and books.

Ruth Reynard has been involved in teaching and the teaching of teachers. Her graduate degrees were completed at the Ontario Institute for Studies in Education, University of Toronto (OISE/UT). She worked for the Center for Education and Training (CET), Peel Board of Education, Mississauga, Canada. As a program manager, Dr. Reynard designed and delivered the first Internet-based distance language learning course for adults in Canada and developed a process-based language curriculum for the workplace. She worked with the University of Toronto, Faculty of Pharmacy, the School of Pharmacy, HRDC Canada, and the CET to develop and pilot an Internet-based bridge course for foreign-trained pharmacists seeking professional accreditation in Ontario. In Tennessee, she was associate professor of education teaching and guiding students of M.Ed. and Ed.D. programs. Dr. Reynard has been published in various journals in the area of applied technology and faculty development. Currently, she is Dean of Faculty Services for Career Education Corporation, Illinois.

Rikki Rimor is currently a Faculty member and course designer at The Open University of Israel, Dept. of Education and Psychology, Graduate program of Learning Technologies. He has been an Academic Consultant at the Unit for advancement of learning and teaching. He was also the Head, Center for Pedagogy & Innovative Technologies, Teachers College of Technology at Tel-Aviv. He has Ph.D. on "From Search for Information to Construction of Knowledge" from University of the Negev. He was also at the Harvard Graduate School of Education for TAP program. His most recent publications include Rimor, R., Reingold, R., & Heiman, T. (2008). Instructor's scaffolding in support of student's metacognition through an online course: Why to promote and how to investigate. In: Zumbach, J., Schwartz, N., Seufert,. & Kester, L. (Eds.). Beyond Knowledge: the Legacy of Competence. Meaningful computer-based Learning environments. Springer. (pp. 43-53).

Ruth Robbins is a Professor of Computer Information Systems and the Coordinator of the Computer Information Systems program within the College of Business at the University of Houston Downtown and has more than 25 years of teaching experience. She has been on the board of Association of Computer Educators in Texas. She received her doctorate in Instructional Technology from University of Houston and has published several articles in numerous refereed journals. Many of these articles have been co-authored with Dr. Cunningham. Her most recent presentation was at John Moores University in Liverpool, England at the Bridging the Atlantic at the American Association of University Administrators Seventeenth Annual International Conference.

Yigal Rosen is currently a faculty member at The Open University of Israel, Dept. of Education and Psychology and at University of Haifa, Faculty of Education. He was earlier Evaluation Consultant at the Henrietta Szold Institute, The National Institute for Research in the Behavioural Sciences. In 2007-2008, he was Post-doctoral fellow at Graduate School of Education, Harvard University. He was also Post-doctoral fellow, School of Education, at the Tel Aviv University during 2006-2007. He completed his Ph.D. in Education from the Faculty of Education, University of Haifa in 2006. His most recent publication includes Rosen, Y. (in press). Effects of animation learning environment on knowledge transfer and motivation to learn science and technology. *Journal of Educational Computing Research, 40*(4).

Khairulanuar Samsudin, a Mechanical Engineering Graduate from the University of Leeds and has Master Degree in Advanced Manufacturing Technology from the UK. Currently, he is pursuing his Doctoral study focusing on multimedia application for human performance from Malaysia. He was at the General Instrument, Malaysia as a process engineer and later he joined Motorola Technology, Malaysia as a mechanical development engineer. He taught at Ungku Omar Polytechnic and Sultan Idris University of Education, Malaysia. His research interest includes educational technology, human performance in learning environment and engineering graphics. At present, he teaches Computer Aided Design and Technology in Education to the undergraduates at the same university. The author has also published a number of national and international journal papers and co-authored a technology book.

Tammy Schellens is Professor of Educational Technology at the Department of Educational Studies of Ghent University. Prof. Dr. Tammy Schellens can be contacted at tammy.schellens@ugent.be

Wolfgang Schneider is currently Professor of Psychology at the Department of Psychology, University of Würzburg, Germany. He received his PhD in Psychology from the University of Heidelberg.

His research interests include the development of memory and metacognition, giftedness and expertise, the development of reading and spelling, as well as the prevention of reading and math difficulties. He was Vice-president and President of the German Psychological Society (2000-2004), and has been Vice-president of the University of Würzburg since 2004. Dr. Schneider is author and (co-) editor of about 30 books, including the volume co-authored with Michael Pressley on "Memory Development between Two and Twenty", and (co-)authored about 350 journal articles and book chapters. He is currently President-Elect of the International Society for the Study of Behavioural Development (ISSBD).

Sibongile Simelane is an Instructional Designer at Tshwane University of Technology. She has obtained a Higher Diploma in Education (Computer Literacy) with distinction in 2000, then she completed B Ed (HONS) in Computer Based Education in 2002 at University of Johannesburg. She has also obtained a Blackboard Certified Trainer with distinction in 2007. Besides, she has also completed online facilitating course and obtained the e-Moderation certificate in 2006 and Efficient Online Tutoring @ e-Learning Africa Certificate in 2007. She has Masters in Educational Technology from Tshwane University of Technology. The study was on the implementation of a professional development programme in educational technology in higher education. She has presented international and national papers in various conferences that involve the integration of e-learning in higher education, besides, publishing articles in accredited journal and conference proceedings.

O. A. Sofowora is Senior Lecturer in the Department of Educational Technology at Obafemi Awolowo University in Nigeria. He has his Doctorate in Educational Technology and his area of specialization is photography, instructional media design and television production.

Luís Tinoca is an Assistant Professor at Universidade Aberta's Department of Education and Distance Teaching, with experience in the development of online, graduate and undergraduate courses, as well as an active researcher in the areas of competence-based learning assessment and group work collaboration in online environments. He is also involved in research projects from the European Association of Distance Teaching Universities, a member of the Education Research Center, and a collaborator of the Distance Education Laboratory. He earned his Ph.D. in Science Education from the University of Texas at Austin in 2004.

Sibitse Mirriam Tlhapane (nee Makgatho), M Phil (Applied Ethics), her career life started as a professional nurse at Ga-Rankuwa hospital in 1971, then moved over to the Nursing College, and finally came to Tshwane University of Technology. Her teaching experience is mainly in the field of community health. Her Interest in innovative teaching methodologies and philosophy was strengthened by participation in an academic staff development project funded by the Netherlands and the e-learning Parthers@ Work project by the Tshwane University of technology. This has led to her being to do research, present papers at conferences and publish.

Ioannis Tsampoulatidis is Associate Researcher at the Informatics and Telematics Institute, Center for Research and Technology Hellas. He has Bachelor (Hons.) in Computer Science from the University of Portsmouth, UK. During the last 9 years he has been involved in both European and National research projects. His main research interests include Internet technologies and protocols, design and development of interactive services for digital TV, Hypermedia and Semantic Web, Ontologies and metadata, System Analysis and Design and RDBMS. He has published more than 15 research papers, journals and book chapters.

Omiunota N. Ukpokodu is an associate professor of teacher education, social studies, multicultural education, diversity, urban education, global education, and social justice education in the Division of Curriculum and Instructional Leadership in the School of Education at the University of Missouri-Kansas City, Missouri.

Martin Valcke is Full Professor of Instructional Sciences at Ghent University, Belgium and head of the Department of Educational Studies. His research focuses on the innovation of Higher Education and the integrated use of Information and Communication Technologies (ICT) in higher education. Prof. Martin Valcke can be contacted at martin.valcke@ugent.be.

Natalie Vaninni has Dipl.-Psych. and she is a research fellow at the Institute of Educational Psychology at the University of Wuerzburg. She studied Psychology at the University of Amsterdam and the Humboldt-University of Berlin. Recently, she has worked for the eCircus project (http://www.e-circus.org) and is currently working on her PhD. Her scientific interests centre on social-emotional learning, virtual learning environments and evaluation.

Luis M. Villar is a professor of Didactics and School Organization, School of Education, University of Seville, Spain. He has over 20 years of experience as a professor at the universities of Granada and Seville. His research interests include assessing faculty learning and complex learning with computer-based learning environments. He has co-authored with Dr. Olga M. Alegre several books (*Manual para la excelencia en la enseñanza superior.* Madrid: McGraw-Hill, and *Evaluación de la formación en línea del profesorado universitario. Evaluation of online faculty development.* Madrid: VisionNet, among others), and articles on assessing continuing professional learning in higher education, mentoring as a mode for reflective teaching or e-learning.

Stefanos Vrochidis has Diploma degree in electrical and computer engineering from Aristotle University of Thessaloniki, Greece and the MSc degree in radio frequency communication systems from University of Southampton, UK. He is a Research Associate with the Multimedia Knowledge Lab at the Informatics and Telematics Institute - Centre for Research and Technology Hellas. His research interests include semantic multimedia analysis and retrieval, as well as patent search. He has successfully participated in many European and National projects related to image and video analysis, digital TV technologies and patent retrieval and he has been involved as a co-author in more than 15 related journal and conference publications.

Erman Yukselturk has a Ph.D. in Computer Education & Instructional Technologies with emphasis on factors affecting satisfaction with online learning. He has been working at the Internet Based Education Project (http://idea.metu.edu.tr) of Middle East Technical University for eight years. His main areas of interest are distance education, designing online learning environments, online collaboration, and instructional technology. He can be contacted by email: eyukselturk@gmail.com, or via post: Department of Computer Engineering, Middle East Technical University, 06531, Ankara, Turkey.

Chang Zhu holds a Ph.D. in Educational Sciences at Ghent University with a research focus on student and teacher characteristics in e-learning environments in different cultural contexts and computer supported collaborative learning. Previously she was a lecturer at Communication University of China in Beijing.

Carsten Zoll works as a research fellow at the department for general psychology at the University of Bamberg. He studied psychology and computer science. Before joining the department for general psychology, he worked at the professorship for economic and social psychology at the Technical University of Chemnitz. In his dissertation he investigated decision making processes among experts of the financial markets. His scientific work focuses on simulation of humanlike behaviour, modelling the human mind, empathy, evaluation, decision making and behavioural finance.

Index

C

D

E

F

G

H

I

M

N

O

P

T

U

V

W

Y